Lecture Notes in Computer Scienc

Commenced Publication in 1973
Founding and Former Series Editors:
Gerhard Goos, Juris Hartmanis, and Jan van Leeuwen

Carl Edward Rasmussen Heinrich H. Bülthoff
Martin A. Giese   Bernhard Schölkopf (Eds.)

Pattern
Recognition

26th DAGM Symposium
Tübingen, Germany, August 30 – September 1, 2004
Proceedings

 Springer

Volume Editors

Carl Edward Rasmussen
Heinrich H. Bülthoff
Bernhard Schölkopf
Max Planck Institute for Biological Cybernetics
Postfach 2169, 72076 Tübingen Germany
E-mail: {carl, heinrich.buelthoff, bernhard.schoelkopf}@tuebingen.mpg.de

Martin A. Giese
University Hospital Tübingen, Department for Cognitive Neurology
Schaffhausenstr. 113, 72072 Tübingen, Germany
E-mail: martin.giese@uni-tuebingen.de

Library of Congress Control Number: 2004110897

CR Subject Classification (1998): I.5, I.4, I.3.5, I.2.10, I.2.6, F.2.2

ISSN 0302-9743
ISBN 3-540-22945-0 Springer Berlin Heidelberg New York

Springer is a part of Springer Science+Business Media

springeronline.com

© Springer-Verlag Berlin Heidelberg 2004
Printed in Germany

Typesetting: Camera-ready by author, data conversion by PTP-Berlin, Protago-TeX-Production GmbH
Printed on acid-free paper   SPIN: 11310297   06/3142   5 4 3 2 1 0

Preface

We are delighted to present the proceedings of DAGM 2004, and wish to express our gratitude to the many people whose efforts made the success of the conference possible. We received 146 contributions of which we were able to accept 22 as oral presentations and 48 as posters. Each paper received 3 reviews, upon which decisions were based. We are grateful for the dedicated work of the 38 members of the program committee and the numerous referees. The careful review process led to the exciting program which we are able to present in this volume.

Among the highlights of the meeting were the talks of our four invited speakers, renowned experts in areas spanning learning in theory, in vision and in robotics:

- William T. Freeman, Artificial Intelligence Laboratory, MIT: *Sharing Features for Multi-class Object Detection*
- Pietro Perona, Caltech: *Towards Unsupervised Learning of Object Categories*
- Stefan Schaal, Department of Computer Science, University of Southern California: *Real-Time Statistical Learning for Humanoid Robotics*
- Vladimir Vapnik, NEC Research Institute: *Empirical Inference*

We are grateful for economic support from Honda Research Institute Europe, ABW GmbH, Transtec AG, DaimlerChrysler, and Stemmer Imaging GmbH, which enabled us to finance best paper prizes and a limited number of travel grants. Many thanks to our local support Sabrina Nielebock and Dagmar Maier, who dealt with the unimaginably diverse range of practical tasks involved in planning a DAGM symposium. Thanks to Richard van de Stadt for providing excellent software and support for handling the reviewing process. A special thanks goes to Jeremy Hill, who wrote and maintained the conference website. Without all of your dedicated contributions, the successful 26th DAGM Symposium in Tübingen would not have been possible.

June 2004   Carl Edward Rasmussen, Heinrich H. Bülthoff,
                             Martin A. Giese and Bernhard Schölkopf

Organization

DAGM e.V.: German Association for Pattern Recognition

Organizing Committee and Program Chairs

Carl Edward Rasmussen	Max Planck Institute for Biological Cybernetics
Heinrich H. Bülthoff	Max Planck Institute for Biological Cybernetics
Martin A. Giese	University Clinic Tübingen
Bernhard Schölkopf	Max Planck Institute for Biological Cybernetics

Since 1978 DAGM (German Association for Pattern Recognition) has organized annual scientific conferences at various venues. The goal of each DAGM symposium is to inspire conceptual thinking, support the dissemination of ideas and research results from different areas in the field of pattern recognition, stimulate discussions and the exchange of ideas among experts, and support and motivate the next generation of young researchers.

DAGM e.V. was founded as a registered research association in September 1999. Until that time, DAGM had been comprised of the following support organizations that have since become honorary members of DAGM e.V.:

DGaO	Deutsche Arbeitsgemeinschaft für angewandte Optik (German Society for Applied Optics)
GMDS	Deutsche Gesellschaft für Medizinische Informatik, Biometrie und Epidemiologie (German Society for Medical Informatics, Biometry, and Epidemiology)
GI	Gesellschaft für Informatik (German Informatics Society)
ITG	Informationstechnische Gesellschaft (Information Technology Society)
DGN	Deutsche Gesellschaft für Nuklearmedizin (German Society for Nuclear Medicine)
IEEE	Deutsche Sektion des IEEE (Institute of Electrical and Electronics Engineers, German Section)
DGPF	Deutsche Gesellschaft für Photogrammetrie und Fernerkundung (German Society for Photogrammetry, Remote Sensing and Geo-information)
VDMA	Fachabteilung industrielle Bildverarbeitung/Machine Vision im VDMA (Robotics + Automation Division within VDMA)
GNNS	German Chapter of the European Neural Network Society
DGR	Deutsche Gesellschaft für Robotik (German Robotics Society)

DAGM Prizes 2003

The main prize was awarded to

Ullrich Köthe
Universität Hamburg, Germany
Edge and Junction Detection with an Improved Structure Tensor

Further DAGM prizes for 2003 (sponsored by ABW) were awarded to

Christian Perwass, Vladimir Banarer, Gerald Sommer
Christian-Albrechts-Universität zu Kiel, Germany
Spherical Decision Surfaces Using Conformal Modelling

Martin Welk, Christian Feddern, Bernhard Burgeth, Joachim Weickert
Saarland Universität, Germany
Median Filtering of Tensor-Valued Images

Ivan Kovtun
Technische Universität Dresden, Germany
Partial Optimal Labelling Search for a NP-Hard Subclass of (max,+) Problems

Program Committee

Maximilian Buhmann	ETH Zürich
Hans Burkhardt	Universität Freiburg
Wolfgang Förstner	Universität Bonn
Matthias Franz	MPI Tübingen
Siegfried Fuchs	Technische Universität Dresden
Dariu Gavrila	DaimlerChrysler
Armin Grün	ETH Zürich
Gerd Hirzinger	DLR Oberpfaffenhofen
Thomas Hofmann	Brown University
Bernd Jähne	Universität Heidelberg
Reinhard Koch	Universität Kiel
Walter Kropatsch	TU Wien
Paul Levi	Universität Stuttgart
Claus-Eberhard Liedtke	Universität Hannover
Hanspeter Mallot	Universität Tübingen
Barbel Mertsching	Universität Hamburg
Rudolf Mester	Universität Frankfurt
Bernhard Nebel	Universität Freiburg
Heiko Neumann	Universität Ulm
Hermann Ney	RWTH Aachen
Heinrich Niemann	FORWISS Erlangen
Manfred Opper	Aston University
Bernd Radig	TU München
Gunnar Rätsch	MPI Tübingen
Helge Ritter	Universität Bielefeld
Gerhard Sagerer	Universität Bielefeld
Dietmar Saupe	Universität Konstanz
Bernt Schiele	ETH Zürich
Christoph Schnörr	Universität Mannheim
Hans-Peter Seidel	MPI Saarbrücken
Gerald Sommer	Universität Kiel
Gabor Székely	ETH Zürich
Luc Van Gool	ETH Zürich
Thomas Vetter	Universität Basel
Friedrich M. Wahl	Universität Braunschweig
Christian Wallraven	MPI Tübingen
Joachim Weickert	Universität des Saarlandes

Referees

Tim Bodenmüller
Gökhan Bakır
Klaus Arbter
Vladimir Banarer
Curzio Basso
Christian Bauckhage
Pierre Bayerl
Olivier Bousquet
Michael Brenner
Thomas Brox
Andres Bruhn
Gerd Brunner
Sven Buchholz
Bernhard Burgeth
Geert Caenen
Nikolaos Canterakis
Youssef Charfi
Dachuan Cheng
Kurt Cornelis
Cristobal Curio
Thomas Deselaers
Guido Dornhege
Christian Feddern
Bernd Fischer
Gernot A. Fink
Boris Flach
Jan-Michael Frahm
Rik Fransens
Jannik Fritsch
Indra Geys
Martin Giese
Toon Goedeme
Oliver Granert
Bernard Haasdonk
Alaa Halawani
Allan Hanbury
Stefan Harmeling
Sasa Hasan
Gunther Heidemann
Matthias Heiler
Malte Helmert
Jeremy Hill
Ulrich Hillenbrand
Heiko Hirschmüller

Frank Jäkel
Martin Kampel
Dimitris Katsoulas
Tanja Kämpfe
Jens Keuchel
Daniel Keysers
Wolf Kienzle
Alexander Kleiner
Istvan Kokai
Esther Koller-Meier
Ivan Kopilovic
Lars Krüger
Franz Kummert
Christian Köhler
Navin Lal
Christian Lange
Tilman Lange
Georg Langs
Pavel Laskov
Julian Laub
Bastian Leibe
Otto Löhlein
Wolfgang Macherey
Jocelyn Marchadier
Frank Meinecke
Sebastian Mika
Matthias Mühlich
Julia Neumann
Björn Ommer
Peter Orbanz
Mihai Osian
Nils Papenberg
Christian Perwass
Klaus-Dieter Peschke
Jean-Sebastian Pierrard
Martin Röder
Matthias Rätsch
Marco Ragni
Marco Reisert
Sami Romdhani
Olaf Ronneberger
Volker Roth
Mauro Ruggeri
Liu Rui

Axel Saalbach
Christin Schaefer
Helmut Schirmer
Friedhelm Schwenker
Edgar Seemann
Wolfgang Sepp
Nils T. Siebel
Martin Spengler
Harald Steck
Jochen Steil
Jürgen Toelke
Katharina Tluk v. Toschanowitz

Tinne Tuytelaars
Thorsten Twellmann
Maarten Vergauwen
Julia Vogel
Sven Wachsmuth
Jörg Walter
Quing Wang
Thilo Weigel
Olaf Weiss
Martin Welk
Alexey Zalesny
Andras Zolnay

Table of Contents

Learning

Predictive Discretization During Model Selection 1
  Harald Steck, Tommi S. Jaakkola

Adaptive Feature Selection in Image Segmentation 9
  Volker Roth, Tilman Lange

Semi-supervised Kernel Regression Using Whitened Function Classes 18
  Matthias O. Franz, Younghee Kwon, Carl Edward Rasmussen,
  Bernhard Schölkopf

Bayesian Approaches

Fast Monocular Bayesian Detection
of Independently Moving Objects by a Moving Observer 27
  Felix Woelk, Reinhard Koch

Kernel Density Estimation and Intrinsic Alignment
for Knowledge-Driven Segmentation: Teaching Level Sets to Walk 36
  Daniel Cremers, Stanley J. Osher, Stefano Soatto

Vision and Faces

3D Head Pose Estimation with Symmetry Based Illumination Model
in Low Resolution Video 45
  Martin Gruendig, Olaf Hellwich

Efficient Approximations for Support Vector Machines
in Object Detection 54
  Wolf Kienzle, Gökhan Bakır, Matthias Franz, Bernhard Schölkopf

Efficient Face Detection by a Cascaded Support Vector Machine
Using Haar-Like Features 62
  Matthias Rätsch, Sami Romdhani, Thomas Vetter

Vision / Motion

Differential Analysis of Two Model-Based
Vehicle Tracking Approaches 71
  Hendrik Dahlkamp, Arthur E.C. Pece, Artur Ottlik,
  Hans-Hellmut Nagel

Efficient Computation of Optical Flow Using the Census Transform 79
    Fridtjof Stein

Hybrid Model-Based Estimation of Multiple Non-dominant Motions 87
    Arne Jacobs, Thorsten Hermes, Otthein Herzog

Biologically Motivated Approaches

A Model of Motion, Stereo, and Monocular Depth Perception 95
    Pierre Bayerl, Heiko Neumann

POI Detection Using Channel Clustering and the 2D Energy Tensor 103
    Michael Felsberg, Gösta Granlund

Segmentation

3D Segmentation and Quantification of Human Vessels Based
on a New 3D Parametric Intensity Model 111
    Stefan Wörz, Karl Rohr

Hierarchical Image Segmentation
Based on Semidefinite Programming 120
    Jens Keuchel, Matthias Heiler, Christoph Schnörr

Fast Random Sample Matching of 3d Fragments 129
    *Simon Winkelbach, Markus Rilk, Christoph Schönfelder,
    Friedrich M. Wahl*

Object Recognition

Invariants for Discrete Structures – An Extension of Haar Integrals
over Transformation Groups to Dirac Delta Functions 137
    Hans Burkhardt, Marco Reisert, Hongdong Li

Scale-Invariant Object Categorization Using a Scale-Adaptive
Mean-Shift Search 145
    Bastian Leibe, Bernt Schiele

Pixel-to-Pixel Matching for Image Recognition
Using Hungarian Graph Matching 154
    Daniel Keysers, Thomas Deselaers, Hermann Ney

Object Recognition / Synthesis

Estimation of Multiple Orientations at Corners and Junctions 163
    Cicero Mota, Ingo Stuke, Til Aach, Erhardt Barth

Phase Based Image Reconstruction in the Monogenic Scale Space 171
    Di Zang, Gerald Sommer

Synthesizing Movements for Computer Game Characters............... 179
  Christian Thurau, Christian Bauckhage, Gerhard Sagerer

Poster Session

MinOver Revisited for Incremental Support-Vector-Classification........ 187
  Thomas Martinetz

A Semantic Typicality Measure for Natural Scene Categorization 195
  Julia Vogel, Bernt Schiele

Tunable Nearest Neighbor Classifier 204
  Yonglei Zhou, Changshui Zhang, Jingchun Wang

SVM-Based Feature Selection by Direct Objective Minimisation 212
  Julia Neumann, Christoph Schnörr, Gabriele Steidl

Learning with Distance Substitution Kernels 220
  Bernard Haasdonk, Claus Bahlmann

Features for Image Retrieval: A Quantitative Comparison 228
  Thomas Deselaers, Daniel Keysers, Hermann Ney

Learning from Labeled and Unlabeled Data Using Random Walks....... 237
  Dengyong Zhou, Bernhard Schölkopf

Learning Depth from Stereo 245
  Fabian H. Sinz, Joaquin Quiñonero Candela, Gökhan H. Bakır,
  Carl Edward Rasmussen, Matthias O. Franz

Learning to Find Graph Pre-images 253
  Gökhan H. Bakır, Alexander Zien, Koji Tsuda

Multivariate Regression via Stiefel Manifold Constraints 262
  Gökhan H. Bakır, Arthur Gretton, Matthias Franz,
  Bernhard Schölkopf

Hilbertian Metrics on Probability Measures
and Their Application in SVM's 270
  Matthias Hein, Thomas Navin Lal, Olivier Bousquet

Shape from Shading Under Coplanar Light Sources.................... 278
  Christian Wöhler

Pose Estimation for Multi-camera Systems 286
  Jan-Michael Frahm, Kevin Köser, Reinhard Koch

Silhouette Based Human Motion Estimation......................... 294
  Bodo Rosenhahn, Reinhard Klette, Gerald Sommer

Cooperative Optimization for Energy Minimization
in Computer Vision: A Case Study of Stereo Matching................. 302
     Xiaofei Huang

Building a Motion Resolution Pyramid
by Combining Velocity Distributions 310
     Julian Eggert, Volker Willert, Edgar Körner

A Stratified Self-Calibration Method for a Stereo Rig
in Planar Motion with Varying Intrinsic Parameters 318
     Yan Li, Yeung Sam Hung

Efficient Feature Tracking for Long Video Sequences.................. 326
     Timo Zinßer, Christoph Gräßl, Heinrich Niemann

Recognition of Deictic Gestures with Context....................... 334
     Nils Hofemann, Jannik Fritsch, Gerhard Sagerer

Mosaics from Arbitrary Stereo Video Sequences...................... 342
     Nicolas Gorges, Marc Hanheide, William Christmas,
     Christian Bauckhage, Gerhard Sagerer, Joseph Kittler

Accurate and Efficient Approximation
of the Continuous Gaussian Scale-Space............................ 350
     Ullrich Köthe

Multi-step Entropy Based Sensor Control for Visual Object Tracking 359
     Benjamin Deutsch, Matthias Zobel, Joachim Denzler,
     Heinrich Niemann

Spatio–temporal Segmentation
Using Laserscanner and Video Sequences............................ 367
     Nico Kaempchen, Markus Zocholl, Klaus C.J. Dietmayer

Fast Statistically Geometric Reasoning
About Uncertain Line Segments in 2D- and 3D-Space 375
     Christian Beder

A Statistical Measure for Evaluating Regions-of-Interest Based
Attention Algorithms.. 383
     Martin Clauss, Pierre Bayerl, Heiko Neumann

Modelling Spikes with Mixtures of Factor Analysers 391
     Dilan Görür, Carl Edward Rasmussen, Andreas S. Tolias,
     Fabian Sinz, Nikos K. Logothetis

An Algorithm for Fast Pattern Recognition with Random Spikes 399
     Udo A. Ernst, David Rotermund, Klaus R. Pawelzik

The Perceptual Influence of Spatiotemporal Noise
on the Reconstruction of Shape from Dynamic Occlusion 407
    Theresa Cooke, Douglas W. Cunningham, Heinrich H. Bülthoff

Level Set Based Image Segmentation with Multiple Regions 415
    Thomas Brox, Joachim Weickert

CVPIC Colour/Shape Histograms
for Compressed Domain Image Retrieval 424
    Gerald Schaefer

The Redundancy Pyramid and Its Application to Segmentation
on an Image Sequence 432
    Jocelyn Marchadier, Walter G. Kropatsch, Allan Hanbury

A Higher Order MRF-Model for Stereo-Reconstruction 440
    Dmitrij Schlesinger, Boris Flach, Alexander Shekhovtsov

Adaptive Computer Vision: Online Learning for Object Recognition 447
    Holger Bekel, Ingo Bax, Gunther Heidemann, Helge Ritter

Robust Pose Estimation for Arbitrary Objects in Complex Scenes 455
    Peter Dörfler, Clemens Schnurr

Vectorization-Free Reconstruction of 3D CAD Models
from Paper Drawings 463
    Frank Ditrich, Herbert Suesse, Klaus Voss

Globally Consistent 3-D Reconstruction by Utilizing Loops
in Camera Movement 471
    Ingo Scholz, Heinrich Niemann

A Probabilistic Framework for Robust and Accurate Matching
of Point Clouds 480
    Peter Biber, Sven Fleck, Wolfgang Strasser

Large Vocabulary Audio-Visual Speech Recognition
Using the Janus Speech Recognition Toolkit 488
    Jan Kratt, Florian Metze, Rainer Stiefelhagen, Alex Waibel

Lesion Preserving Image Registration
with Applications to Human Brains 496
    Stefan Henn, Lars Hömke, Kristian Witsch

Snake-Aided Automatic Organ Delineation 504
    *Weibing Xu, Saad A. Amin, Olivier C.L. Haas, Keith J. Burnham,
    John A. Mills*

Practical Gaze Point Detecting System 512
    Kang Ryoung Park, Juno Chang, Min Cheol Whang, Joa Sang Lim,
    Dae-Woong Rhee, Hung Kook Park, Yongjoo Cho

Using Pattern Recognition for Self-Localization
in Semiconductor Manufacturing Systems 520
    Michael Lifshits, Roman Goldenberg, Ehud Rivlin, Michael Rudzsky

Feature and Viewpoint Selection for Industrial Car Assembly 528
    Dirk Stößel, Marc Hanheide, Gerhard Sagerer, Lars Krüger,
    Marc Ellenrieder

Automating Microscope Colour Image Analysis
Using the Expectation Maximisation Algorithm 536
    Alexander Ihlow, Udo Seiffert

Camera Orientation of Mars Express Using DTM Information 544
    Christian Heipke, Heinrich Ebner, Ralph Schmidt, Michael Spiegel,
    Rüdiger Brand, Albert Baumgartner, Gerhard Neukum,
    the HRSC Co-Investigator Team

Detection and Classification of Gateways for the Acquisition
of Structured Robot Maps 553
    Derik Schröter, Thomas Weber, Michael Beetz, Bernd Radig

Real Time High Speed Measurement of Photogrammetric Targets 562
    Georg Wiora, Pavel Babrou, Reinhard Männer

A Simple New Method for Precise Lens Distortion Correction
of Low Cost Camera Systems 570
    Christian Bräuer-Burchardt

Author Index 579

Predictive Discretization During Model Selection

Harald Steck[1] and Tommi S. Jaakkola[2]

[1] Institute for Computational Science, ETH Zurich, 8092 Zurich, Switzerland
hsteck@inf.ethz.ch
[2] MIT CSAIL, Stata Center, Bldg. 32-Gates 498, Cambridge, MA 02139, USA
tommi@csail.mit.edu

Abstract. We present an approach to discretizing multivariate continuous data while learning the structure of a graphical model. We derive a
joint scoring function from the principle of predictive accuracy, which inherently ensures the optimal trade-off between goodness of fit and model
complexity including the number of discretization levels. Using the so-
called finest grid implied by the data, our scoring function depends only
on the number of data points in the various discretization levels (independent of the metric used in the continuous space). Our experiments
with artificial data as well as with gene expression data show that discretization plays a crucial role regarding the resulting network structure.

1 Introduction

Continuous data is often discretized as part of a more advanced approach to data
analysis such as learning graphical models. Discretization may be carried out
merely for computational efficiency, or because background knowledge suggests
that the underlying variables are indeed discrete. While it is computationally
efficient to discretize the data in a preprocessing step that is independent of the
subsequent analysis [6,10,7], the impact of the discretization policy on the subsequent analysis is often unclear in this approach. Existing methods that optimize
the discretization policy jointly with the graph structure [3,9] are computationally very involved and therefore not directly suitable for large domains.

We present a novel and more efficient scoring function for joint optimization of the discretization policy and the model structure. The objective relies
on predictive accuracy, where predictive accuracy is assessed sequentially as in
prequential validation [2] or stochastic complexity [12].

2 Sequential Approach

Let $Y = (Y_1, ..., Y_k, ..., Y_n)$ denote a vector of n continuous variables in the
domain of interest, and y any specific instantiation of these variables. The discretization of Y is determined by a *discretization policy* $\Lambda = (\Lambda_1, ..., \Lambda_n)$: for each
variable Y_k, let $\Lambda_k = (\lambda_{k,1}, ..., \lambda_{k,r_k-1})$ be ordered threshold values, and r_k be the

C.E. Rasmussen et al. (Eds.): DAGM 2004, LNCS 3175, pp. 1–8, 2004.

number of discretization levels. This determines the mapping $f_\Lambda : Y \mapsto X$, where $X = (X_1, ..., X_k, ..., X_n)$ is the corresponding discretized vector; for efficiency reasons we only consider *deterministic* discretizations, where each continuous value y is mapped to *exactly one* discretization level, $x_k = f_{\Lambda_k}(y_k)$.

We pretend that (continuous) *i.i.d.* data D arrive in a sequential manner, and then assess predictive accuracy regarding the data points along the sequence. This is similar to prequential validation or stochastic complexity [2,12]. We recast the joint marginal likelihood of the discretization policy Λ and the structure m of a graphical model in a sequential manner,

$$\rho(D|\Lambda, m) = \prod_{i=1}^{N} \rho(y^{(i)}|D^{(i-1)}, \Lambda, m),$$

where $D^{(i-1)} = (y^{(i-1)}, y^{(i-2)}, ..., y^{(1)})$ denotes the data points seen *prior to* step i along the sequence.

For deterministic discretization we can assume that at each step i the predicted density regarding data point $y^{(i)}$ factors according to $\rho(y^{(i)}|D^{(i-1)}, \Lambda, m) = \rho(y^{(i)}|x^{(i)}, \Lambda) \, p(x^{(i)}|D^{(i-1)}, m, \Lambda)$, where $x^{(i)} = f_\Lambda(y^{(i)})$. It is desirable that the structure m indeed captures *all* the relevant (conditional) dependences among the variables $Y_1, ..., Y_n$. Assuming that the dependences among continuous Y_k are described by the *discretized* distribution $p(X|m, \Lambda, D)$, then any two continuous variables Y_k and $Y_{k'}$ are independent conditional on X: $\rho(y^{(i)}|x^{(i)}, \Lambda) = \prod_{k=1}^{n} \rho(y_k^{(i)}|x^{(i)}, \Lambda_k)$.

The computational feasibility of this approach depends crucially on the efficiency of the mapping between the discrete and continuous spaces. A simple approach may use the *same* density to account for points y and y' that are mapped to the same discretized state x, cf. [9]. Assuming a *uniform* probability density is overly stringent and degrades the predictive accuracy; moreover, this might also give rise to "empty states", cf. [15]. In contrast, we require only *independence* of the variables Y_k.

3   Finest Grid Implied by the Data

The *finest grid implied by the data* is a simple mapping between Y and X that retains the desired independence properties with non-uniform densities, and can be computed efficiently.

This grid is obtained by discretizing each variable Y_k such that the corresponding (new) discrete variable Z_k has as many states as there are data points, and exactly one data point is assigned to each of those states (an extension to the case with identical data points is straightforward; also note that this grid is not unique, as any threshold value between neighboring data points can be chosen). Note that, in our predictive approach, this grid is based on data $D^{(i-1)}$ at each step i.

Based on this grid, we can now obtain an efficient mapping between Y and X as follows: we assume that two points y_k and y_k' in the continuous space get assigned the same density if they map to the same state of Z_k; and that two states z_k and z_k' of Z_k get assigned the same probability mass if they map to the same discretization level of X_k (we require that each state of Z_k is mapped to exactly one discretization level of X_k for computational efficiency). This immediately yields $\rho(y_k^{(i)}|x^{(i)}, \Lambda_k) = c/N_{x_k^{(i)}}^{(i)}$, where $N_{x_k^{(i)}}^{(i-1)}$ denotes the number of data points in discretization level $x_k^{(i)}$ of variable X_k before step i along the sequence $(N_{x_k^{(i)}}^{(i-1)} > 0)$. The constant c absorbs the mapping from Z to Y by means of the finest grid. Using the *same* grid for two models being compared, we have the important property that c is irrelevant for determining the optimal Λ and m. Unfortunately, details have to be skipped here due to lack of space, see also [15].

4   Predictive Discretization

In our sequential approach, the density at data point $y^{(i)}$ is predicted strictly without hindsight at each step i, i.e., only data $D^{(i-1)}$ is used. For this reason, this leads to a fair assessment of predictive accuracy. Since *i.i.d.* data lack an inherent sequential ordering, we may choose a *particular* ordering of the data points. This is similar in spirit to stochastic complexity [12], where also a *particular* sequential ordering is used. The basic idea is to choose an ordering such that, for all x_k, we have $N_{x_k}^{(i-1)} > 0$ for all $i \geq i_0$, where i_0 is minimal. The initial part of this sequence is thus negligible compared to the part where $i = i_0, ..., N$ when the number of data points is considerably larger than the number of discretization levels of any single variable, $N \gg \max_k |X_k|_\Lambda$. Combining the above equations, we obtain the following (approximate) predictive scoring function $\mathcal{L}(\Lambda, m)$:

$$\log \rho(D|\Lambda, m) \approx \mathcal{L}(\Lambda, m) + c' = \log p(D_\Lambda|m) - \log G(D, \Lambda) + c', \qquad (1)$$

where the approximation is due to ignoring the short initial part of the sequence; $p(D_\Lambda|m)$ is the marginal likelihood of the graph m in light of the data D_Λ discretized according to Λ. In a Bayesian approach, it can be calculated easily for various graphical models, e.g., see [1,8] concerning discrete Bayesian networks. The second term in Eq. 1 is given by

$$\log G(D, \Lambda) = \sum_{k=1}^{n} \sum_{x_k} \log \Gamma(N(x_k)),$$

where Γ denotes the Gamma function, $\Gamma(N(x_k)) = [N(x_k) - 1]!$, and $N(x_k)$ is the number of data points in discretization level x_k.[1] It is crucial that the constant c', which collects the constants c from above, is irrelevant for determining the optimal Λ and m. Obeying lack of space, the reader is referred to [15] for further details.

Our scoring function $\mathcal{L}(\Lambda, m)$ has several interesting properties: First, the difference between the two terms in Eq. 1 determines the trade-off dictating the optimal number of discretization levels, threshold values and graph structure. As both terms increase with a diminishing number of discretization levels,

---

[1] Note that $N(x_k) > 0$ is ensured in our approach, i.e., there are no "empty states" [15].

the second term can be viewed as a penalty for small numbers of discretization levels. Second, $\mathcal{L}(\Lambda, m)$ depends on the number of data points in the different discretization levels only. This is a consequence of the *finest grid implied by the data*. It has several interesting implications. First, and most important from a practical point of view, it renders efficient evaluation of the scoring function possible. Second, and more interesting from a conceptual perspective, $\mathcal{L}(\Lambda, m)$ is independent of the particular choice of the finest grid. Apart from that, $\mathcal{L}(\Lambda, m)$ is independent of the metric in the continuous space, and thus invariant under monotonic transformations of the continuous variables. Obviously, this can lead to considerable loss of information, particularly when the (Euclidean) *distances* among the various data points in the continuous space govern the discretization (cf. left graph in Fig. 1). On the other hand, the results of our scoring function are not degraded if the data is given w.r.t. an inappropriate metric. In fact, the optimal discretization w.r.t. our scoring function is based on *statistical dependence* of the variables, rather than on the *metric*. This is illustrated in our toy experiments with artificial data, cf. Section 5. Apart from that, our approach includes as a special case quantile discretization, namely when all the variables are independent of each other.

5   Experiments

In our first two experiments, we show that our approach discretizes the data based on statistical dependence rather than on the metric in the continuous space. Consider the left two panels in Fig. 1: when the variables are *independent*, our approach may not find the discretization suggested by the clusters; instead, our approach assigns the same number of data points to each discretization level (with one discretization level being optimal). Note that discretization of independent variables is, however, quite irrelevant when learning graphical models: the optimal discretization of each variable Y_k depends on the variables in its Markov blanket, and Y_k is (typically strongly) dependent on those variables. When the variables are *dependent* in Fig. 1, our scoring function favours the "correct" discretization (solid lines), as this entails best predictive accuracy (even when disregarding the metric). However, dependence of the variables itself does not necessarily ensure that our scoring function favours the "correct" discretization, as illustrated in the right two panels in Fig. 1 (as a constraint, we require two discretization levels): given low noise levels, our scoring function assigns the same number of data points to each discretization level; however, a sufficiently *high* noise level in the data can actually be beneficial, permitting our approach to find the "correct" discretization, cf. Fig. 1 (right).

Our third experiment demonstrates that our scoring function favours less complex models (i.e., sparser graphs and fewer discretization levels) when given smaller data sets. This is desirable in order to avoid overfitting when learning from small samples, leading to optimal predictive accuracy. We considered a pair of normally distributed random variables Y_0 and Y_1 with correlation coefficient $corr(Y_0, Y_1) = 1/\sqrt{2}$. Note that this distribution does not imply a 'natural' number of discretization levels; due to the dependence of Y_0 and Y_1 one may

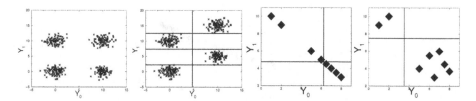

Fig. 1. Left two panels: each cluster comprises 100 points sampled from a Gaussian distribution; Y_0 and Y_1 are independent on the left, and dependent on the right. Right two panels: when Y_0 and Y_1 are dependent, *noise* may help in finding the 'correct' discretization.

hence expect the *learned* number of discretization levels to rise with growing sample size. Indeed, Fig. 2 shows exactly this behavior. Moreover, the learned graph structure implies independence of Y_0 and Y_1 when given very small samples (fewer than 30 data points in our experiment), while Y_0 and Y_1 are found to be dependent for all larger sample sizes.

In our fourth experiment, we were concerned with gene expression data. In computational biology, regulatory networks are often modeled by Bayesian networks, and their structures are learned from discretized gene-expression data, see, e.g., [6,11,7]. Obviously, one would like to recover the "true" network structure underlying the continuous data, rather than a degraded network structure due to a suboptimal discretization policy. Typically, the expression levels have been discretized in a preprocessing step, rather than jointly with the network structure, [6,11,7]. In our experiment, we employed our predictive scoring function (cf. Eq. 1) and re-analyzed the gene expression data concerning the pheromone response pathway in yeast [7], comprising 320 measurements concerning 32 continuous variables (genes) as well as the mating type (binary variable). Based on an error model concerning the micro-array measurements, a continuously differentiable, monotonic transformation is typically applied to the raw gene expression data in a preprocessing step. Since our predictive scoring function is invariant under this kind of transformation, this has no impact on our analysis, so that we are able to work directly with the raw data.

Instead of using a search strategy in the *joint* space of graphs and discretization policies — the theoretically best, but computationally most involved approach — we optimize the graph m and the discretization policy Λ alternately in a greedy way for simplicity: given the discretized data D_Λ, we use local search to optimize the graph m, like in [8]; given m, we optimize Λ iteratively by improving the discretization policy regarding a *single* variable given its Markov blanket at a time. The latter optimization is carried out in a hierarchical way over the number of discretization levels and over the threshold values of each variable. Local maxima are a major issue when optimizing the predictive scoring function due to the (strong) interdependence between m and Λ. As a simple heuristic, we alternately optimize Λ and m only slightly at each step.

The marginal likelihood $p(D_\Lambda|m)$, which is part of our scoring function, contains a free parameter, namely the so-called scale-parameter α regarding the

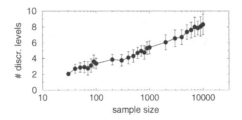

Fig. 2. The number of discretization levels (mean and standard deviation, averaged over 10 samples of each size) depends on the sample size (cf. text for details).

Dirichlet prior over the model parameters, e.g., cf. [8]. As outlined in [13], its value has a decisive impact on the resulting number of edges in the network, and must hence be chosen with great care. Assessing predictive accuracy by means of 5-fold cross validation, we determined $\alpha \approx 25$.

Fig. 3 shows the composite graph we learned from the used gene expression data, employing our predictive scoring function, cf. Eq. 1.[2] This graph is compiled by averaging over several Bayesian network structures in order to account for model uncertainty prevailing in the small data set. Instead of exploring model uncertainty by means of Markov Chain Monte Carlo in the model space, we used a non-parametric re-sampling method, as the latter is independent of any model assumptions. While the bootstrap has been used in [5,4,6,11], we prefer the jackknife when learning the graph structure, i.e., conditional independences. The reason is that the bootstrap procedure can easily induce spurious dependencies when given a small data set D; as a consequence, the resulting network structure can be considerably biased towards denser graphs [14]. The jackknife avoids this problem. We obtained very similar results using three different variants of the jackknife: delete-1, delete-30, and delete-64. Averaging over 320 delete-30 jackknife sub-samples, we found 65.7 ± 8 edges. Fig. 3 displays 65 edges: the solid ones are present with probability $> 50\%$, and the dashed ones with probability $> 34\%$. The orientation of an edge is indicated only if one direction is at least twice as likely as the contrary one. Apart from that, our predictive scoring function yielded that most of the variables have about 4 discretization levels (on average over the 320 jackknife samples), except for the genes MCM1, MFALPHA1, KSS1, STE5, STE11, STE20, STE50, SWI1, TUP1 with about 3 states, and the genes BAR1, MFA1, MFA2, STE2, STE6 with ca. 5 states.

In Fig. 3, it is apparent that the genes AGA2, BAR1, MFA1, MFA2, STE2, and STE6 (magenta) are densely interconnected, and so is the group of genes MFALPHA1, MFALPHA2, SAG1 and STE3 (red). Moreover, both of those groups are directly connected to the mating type, while the other genes in the network are (marginally) independent of the mating type. This makes sense

---

[2] We imposed no constraints on the network structure in Fig. 3. Unfortunately, the results we obtained when imposing constraints derived from location data have to be skipped due to lack of space.

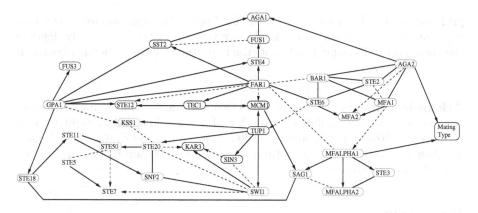

Fig. 3. This graph is compiled from 320 delete-30 jackknife samples (cf. [7] for the color-coding).

from a biological perspective, as the former genes (magenta) are only expressed in yeast cells of mating type A, while the latter ones (red) are only expressed in mating type ALPHA; the expression level of the other genes is rather unaffected by the mating type. Due to lack of space, a more detailed (biological) discussion has to be omitted here.

Indeed, this grouping of the genes is supported also when considering correlations as a measure of statistical dependence:[3] we find that the absolute value of the correlations between the mating type and each gene in either group from above is larger than 0.38, while any other gene is only weakly correlated with the mating type, namely less than 0.18 in absolute value.

The crucial impact of the used discretization policy Λ and scale-parameter α on the resulting network structure becomes apparent when our results are compared to the ones reported in [7]: their network structure resembles a naive Bayesian network, where the mating type is the root variable. Obviously, their network structure is notably different from ours in Fig. 3, and hence has very different (biological) implications. Unlike in [7], we have optimized the discretization policy Λ and the network structure m jointly, as well as the scale-parameter α. As the value of the scale-parameter α mainly affects the *number* of edges present in the learned graph [13], this suggests that the major differences in the obtained network structures are actually due to the discretization policy.

6   Conclusions

We have derived a principled yet efficient method for determining the resolution at which to represent continuous observations. Our discretization approach relies on predictive accuracy in the prequential sense and employs the so-called finest

---

[3] Note that correlations are applicable here, even though they measure only linear effects. This is because the mating type is a *binary* variable.

grid implied by the data as the basis for finding the appropriate levels. Our experiments show that a suboptimal discretization method can easily degrade the obtained results, which highlights the importance of the principled approach we have proposed.

Acknowledgements. We would like to thank Alexander Hartemink for making the pheromone data available to us. Harald Steck acknowledges support from the German Research Foundation (DFG) under grant STE 1045/1-2. Tommi Jaakkola acknowledges support from the Sloan Foundation in the form of the Sloan Research Fellowship.

References

1. G. Cooper and E. Herskovits. A Bayesian method for the induction of probabilistic networks from data. *Machine Learning*, 9:309–47, 1992.
2. A. P. Dawid. Statistical theory. The prequential approach. *Journal of the Royal Statistical Society, Series A*, 147:277–305, 1984.
3. N. Friedman and M. Goldszmidt. Discretization of continuous attributes while learning Bayesian networks. In *ICML*, pages 157–65, 1996.
4. N. Friedman, M. Goldszmidt, and A. Wyner. Data analysis with Bayesian networks: A bootstrap approach. In *UAI*, pages 196–205, 1999.
5. N. Friedman, M. Goldszmidt, and A. Wyner. On the application of the bootstrap for computing confidence measures on features of induced Bayesian networks. In *AI & STATS*, pages 197–202, 1999.
6. N. Friedman, M. Linial, I. Nachman, and D. Pe'er. Using Bayesian networks to analyze expression data. *Journal of Computational Biology*, 7:601–20, 2000.
7. A. J. Hartemink, D. K. Gifford, T. S. Jaakkola, and R. A. Young. Combining location and expression data for principled discovery of genetic regulatory networks. In *Pacific Symposium on Biocomputing*, 2002.
8. D. Heckerman, D. Geiger, and D. M. Chickering. Learning Bayesian networks: The combination of knowledge and statistical data. *Machine Learning*, 20:197–243, 1995.
9. S. Monti and G. F. Cooper. A multivariate discretization method for learning Bayesian networks from mixed data. 14th *UAI*, pages 404–13, 1998.
10. S. Monti and G. F. Cooper. A latent variable model for multivariate discretization. In *AI & STATS*, pages 249–54, 1999.
11. D. Pe'er, A. Regev, G. Elidan, and N. Friedman. Inferring subnetworks from perturbed expression profiles. *Bioinformatics*, 1:1–9, 2001.
12. J. Rissanen. Stochastic complexity and modeling. *The Annals of Statistics*, 14:1080–100, 1986.
13. H. Steck and T. S. Jaakkola. On the Dirichlet prior and Bayesian regularization. In *NIPS 15*, 2002.
14. H. Steck and T. S. Jaakkola. Bias-corrected bootstrap and model uncertainty. *NIPS 16*, 2003.
15. H. Steck and T. S. Jaakkola. (Semi-)predictive discretization during model selection. *AI Memo 2003-002, MIT*, 2003.

Adaptive Feature Selection in Image Segmentation

Volker Roth and Tilman Lange

ETH Zurich, Institut of Computational Science
Hirschengraben 84, CH-8092 Zurich
{vroth, langet}@inf.ethz.ch

Abstract. Most image segmentation algorithms optimize some mathematical similarity criterion derived from several low-level image features. One possible way of combining different types of features, e.g. color- and texture features on different scales and/or different orientations, is to simply stack all the individual measurements into one high-dimensional feature vector. Due to the nature of such stacked vectors, however, only very few components (e.g. those which are defined on a suitable scale) will carry information that is *relevant* for the actual segmentation task. We present an approach to combining *segmentation* and adaptive *feature selection* that overcomes this relevance determination problem. All free model parameters of this method are selected by a resampling-based stability analysis. Experiments demonstrate that the built-in feature selection mechanism leads to stable and meaningful partitions of the images.

1 Introduction

The goal of image segmentation is to divide an image into connected regions that are meant to be semantic equivalence classes. In most practical approaches, however, the semantic interpretation of segments is not modeled explicitly. It is, rather, modeled indirectly by assuming that semantic similarity corresponds with some mathematical similarity criterion derived from several low-level image features. Following this line of building segmentation algorithms, the question of how to combine different types of features naturally arises. One popular solution is to simply stack all different features into a high-dimensional vector, see e.g [1]. The individual components of such a feature vector may e.g. consist of color frequencies on different scales and also on texture features both on different scales and different orientations. The task of grouping such high-dimensional vectors, however, typically poses two different types of problems: on the technical side, most grouping algorithms become increasingly instable with growing input space dimension. Since for most relevant grouping criteria no efficient globally optimal optimization algorithms are known, this "curse of dimensionality" problem is usually related to the steep increase of local minima of the objective functions. Apart from this technical viewpoint, the special structure of feature vectors that arise from stacking several *types* of features poses another problem which is related to the *relevance* of features for solving the actual segmentation task. For instance, texture features on one particular scale and orientation might be highly relevant for segmenting a textile pattern from an unstructured background, while most other feature dimensions will basically contain useless "noise" with respect to this particular task. Treating all features

C.E. Rasmussen et al. (Eds.): DAGM 2004, LNCS 3175, pp. 9–17, 2004.
© Springer-Verlag Berlin Heidelberg 2004

equally, we cannot expect to find a reliable decomposition of the image into meaningful classes. Whereas the "'curse of dimensionality"-problem might be overcome by using a general regularization procedure which restricts the intrinsic complexity of the learning algorithm used for partitioning the image, the special nature of stacked feature vectors particularly emphasizes the need for an adaptive *feature selection* or *relevance determination* mechanism.

In *supervised* learning scenarios, feature selection has been studied widely in the literature. Selecting features in *unsupervised* partitioning scenarios, however, is a much harder problem, due to the absence of class labels that would guide the search for relevant information. Problems of this kind have been rarely studied in the literature, for exceptions see e.g. [2,9,15]. The common strategy of most approaches is the use of an iterated stepwise procedure: in the first step a set of hypothetical partitions is extracted (the *clustering* step), and in the second step features are scored for relevance (the *relevance determination* step). A possible shortcoming is the way of combining these two steps in an "ad hoc" manner: firstly, standard relevance determination mechanism do not take into account the properties of the clustering method used. Secondly, most scoring methods make an implicit independence assumption, ignoring feature correlations. It is thus of particular interest to combine feature selection and partitioning in a more principled way. We propose to achieve this goal by combining a Gaussian mixture model with a Bayesian relevance determination principle. Concerning computational problems involved with selecting "relevant" features, a Bayesian inference mechanism makes it possible to overcome the combinatorial explosion of the search space which consists of all subsets of features. As a consequence, we are able to derive an efficient optimization algorithm. The method presented here extends our previous work on combining clustering and feature selection by making it applicable to multi-segment problems, whereas the algorithms described in [13,12] were limited to the two-segment case.

Our segmentation approach involves two free parameters: the number of mixture components and a certain constraint value which determines the average number of selected features. In order to find reasonable settings for both parameters, we devise a resampling-based stability model selection strategy. Our method follows largely the ideas proposed in [8] where a general framework for estimating the number of clusters in unsupervised grouping scenarios is described. It extends this concept, however, in one important aspects: not only the model order (i.e. the number of segments) but also the model complexity for a fixed model order (measured in terms of the number of selected features) is selected by observing the stability of segmentations under resampling.

2   Image Segmentation by Mixture Models

As depicted in figure 1 we start with extracting a set of N image-sites, each of which is described by a stacked feature vector $x_i \in \mathbb{R}^d$ with d components. The stacked vector usually contains features from different cues, like color histograms and texture responses from Gabor filters, [10]. For assigning the sites to classes, we use a Gaussian mixture model with K mixture components sharing an identical covariance matrix Σ. Under this model, the data log-likelihood reads

$$l^{mix} = \sum_{i=1}^{N} \log \left(\sum_{\nu=1}^{K} \pi_\nu \phi(\boldsymbol{x}_i; \boldsymbol{\mu}_\nu, \Sigma) \right), \tag{1}$$

where the mixing proportions π_ν sum to one, and ϕ denotes a Gaussian density. It is well-known that the classical *expectation-maximization* (EM) algorithm, [3], provides a convenient method for finding both the component–membership probabilities and the model parameters (i.e. means and covariance) which maximize l^{mix}. Once we have trained the mixture model (which represents a parametric density on $\mathbb{R}^d$) we can easily predict the component–membership probabilities of sites different from those contained in the training set by computing Mahalonobis distances to the mean vectors.

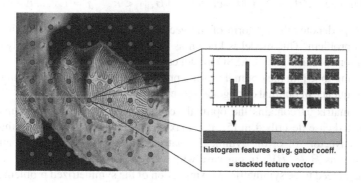

Fig. 1. Image-sites and stacked feature vectors (schematically).

2.1 Gaussian Mixtures and Bayesian Relevance Determination

In order to incorporate the feature selection mechanism into the Gaussian mixture model, the M-step of the EM-algorithm undergoes several reformulations. Following [5], the M-step can be carried out by linear discriminant analysis (LDA) which uses the "fuzzy labels" estimated in the preceding E-step. LDA is equivalent to an *optimal scoring* problem (cf. [6]), the basic ingredient of which is a linear regression procedure against the class-indicator variables. Since space here precludes a more detailed discussion of the equivalence of the classical M-step and indicator regression, we refer the interested reader to the above references and we will concentrate in the following on the aspect of incorporating the feature selection method into the regression formalism.

A central ingredient of optimal scoring is the "blurred" response matrix $\tilde{Z}$, whose rows consist of the current membership probabilities. Given an initial $(K \times K - 1)$ *scoring* matrix Θ, a sequence of $K - 1$ linear regression problems of the form

$$\text{find } \boldsymbol{\theta}_j, \boldsymbol{\beta}_j \text{ which minimize } \|\tilde{Z}\boldsymbol{\theta}_j - X\boldsymbol{\beta}_j\|_2^2, \quad j = 1, \ldots, K - 1 \tag{2}$$

is solved. X is the data matrix which contains the stacked feature vectors as rows. We incorporate the feature selection mechanism into the regression problems by specifying a prior distribution over the regression coefficients β. This distribution has the form of an *Automatic Relevance Determination* (ARD) prior: $p(\beta|\vartheta) \propto \exp[-\sum_{i=1}^{d} \vartheta_i \beta_i^2]$. For each regression coefficient, the ARD prior contains a free hyperparameter ϑ_i, which encodes the "relevance" of the i-th variable in the linear regression. Instead of explicitly selecting these relevance parameters, which would necessarily involve a search over of all possible subsets of features, we follow the Bayesian view of [4] which consists of "averaging" over all possible parameter settings: given exponential hyperpriors, $p(\vartheta_i) = \frac{\gamma}{2} \exp\{-\frac{\gamma\vartheta_i}{2}\}$, one can *analytically integrate out* the relevance-parameters from the prior distribution over the coefficients. Switching to the maximum a posteriori (MAP) solution in log-space, this Bayesian marginalization directly leads to the following ℓ_1-constrained regression problems:

$$\text{minimize } \|\tilde{Z}\theta_j - X\beta_j\|_2^2 \text{ subject to } \|\beta_j\|_1 < \kappa, \quad j = 1, \ldots, K - 1, \quad (3)$$

where $\|\beta_j\|_1$ denotes the ℓ_1 norm of the vector of regression coefficients in the j-th regression problem. This model is known as the LASSO, see [14]. A highly efficient algorithm for optimizing the LASSO model can be found in [11].

According to [5], in the optimal scoring problem the regression fits are followed by finding a sequence of optimal orthogonal scores $\widehat{\Theta}$ which maximize $trace\{\Theta^\top \tilde{Z}^\top X B\}$, where the matrix B contains the optimal vectors $\widehat{\beta}_1, \ldots, \widehat{\beta}_{K-1}$ as columns. In the unconstrained case described in [5], this maximization amounts to finding the $K - 1$ largest eigenvectors v_i of the symmetric matrix $M \equiv \Theta^\top \tilde{Z}^\top X B$. The matrix B is then updated as $B \leftarrow BV$. In our case with active ℓ_1 constraint, the matrix M is no longer guaranteed to be symmetric. Maximization of the symmetrized problem $M_{\text{sym}} \equiv 1/2 \cdot M^\top M$, however, may be viewed as a natural generalization. We thus propose to find the optimal scores by an eigen-decomposition of M_{sym}.

Summing up. For feature selection, we ideally would like to estimate the value of a *binary* selection variable: S_i equals one, if the i-th feature is considered relevant for the given task, and zero otherwise. Taking into account feature correlations, however, estimation of S involves searching the space of all possible subsets of features. In the Bayesian ARD formalism, this combinatorial explosion of the search space is overcome by relaxing the binary selection variable to a real-valued relevance parameter. Following a Bayesian inference principle, we introduce hyper-priors and integrate out these relevance parameters, and we finally arrive at a sequence of ℓ_1-constrained LASSO problems, followed by an eigen-decomposition to find the optimal scoring vectors. It is of particular importance that this method combines the issues of grouping and feature selection in a principled way: both goals are achieved simultaneously by optimizing the *same objective function*, which is simply the constrained data log-likelihood.

3   Model Selection and Experimental Evaluation

Our model has two free parameters, namely the number of mixture components and the value of the ℓ_1-constraint κ. Selecting the number of mixture components is referred to as the model order selection problem, whereas selecting the number of features can be viewed as the problem of choosing the complexity of the model. We now describe a method for selecting both parameters by observing the *stability* of segmentations.

Selecting the model complexity. We will usually find many potential splits of the data into clusters, depending on how many features are selected: if we select only one feature, it is likely to find many competing hypotheses for splits, since most of the feature vectors vote for a different partition. Taking into account the problem of noisy measurements, the finally chosen partition will probably tell us more about the exact noise realization than about meaningful splits. If, on the other hand, we select too many features, many of them will be irrelevant for the actual task, and with high probability, the EM-algorithm will find suboptimal solutions. Between these two extremes, we can hope to find relatively stable splits, which are robust against noise and also against inherent instabilities of the optimization method. For a fixed model order, we use the following algorithm for assessing the value of κ:

1. **Sampling:** draw randomly 100 datasets (i.e. sets of sites), each of which contains N sites. For each site extract the stacked feature vector.
2. **Stability analysis:** for different constraint values κ repeat:
   a) **Clustering:** For each set of sites, train a mixture model with K modes. Assign each of the the sites in the i-th set to one of K groups, based on the estimated membership probabilities. Store the labels l_i and the model parameters p_i.
   b) For each pair (i, j), $i \neq j$ of site sets do
      Prediction: use the i-th mixture model (we have stored all parameters in p_i) to predict the labels of the j-th sample. Denote these labels by l_i^j;
      Distance calculation: calculate the permutation–corrected Hamming distance between original and predicted labels by minimizing over all permutations π:

$$d_{i,j}^{\text{Hamming}} = \min_\pi \sum_{k=1}^N 1 - \delta\{l_j(k), \pi(l_i^j(k))\}, \qquad (4)$$

   (δ denotes the Kronecker symbol), and store it in the (100×100) matrix D. The minimization over all permutations can be done efficiently by using the Hungarian method for bipartite matching with time complexity $O(K^3)$, [7].
   c) **Partition clustering & prototype extraction:** use Wards agglomerative method to cluster the matrix D. Stop merging partition-clusters if the average within-cluster Hamming distance exceeds a threshold $\epsilon = \gamma \cdot (1 - 1/K)$ proportional to the expected distance in a random setting (for random labellings we expect an average distance of $(1-1/K)$). In the experiments we have chosen $\gamma = 0.05 = 5\%$. In each partition-cluster, select the partition which is nearest to the cluster centroid as the prototypical partition.

Selecting the model order. In order to select a suitable number K of mixture components, we repeat the whole complexity selection process for different values of K. We consider that K-value as the most plausible one, for which the percentage of partitions in the individual partition clusters attains a maximum. Since in most unsupervised grouping problems there is more than one "interesting" interpretation of the data, we might, however, gain further insights by also studying other K-values with high but not maximal stability, see figure 4 for an example.

Figures 2 and 3 show the results of the model selection process for an artificial image with five segments. Two of the segments are solely defined in terms of different grey value distributions without any texture information. Two other segments, on the other hand, contain the same texture pattern in different orientations which makes them indistinguishable in the terms of grey values. In order to capture both types of information, at each site we stacked 12 grey value histogram bins and 16 Gabor coefficients on different scales and orientations into a 28-dimensional feature vector. The features are normalized to zero mean and unit variance across the randomly chosen set of image-sites. The right panel of figure 2 depicts the outcome of the model-order selection process. The stability curve shows a distinct maximum for 5 mixture components. 83% of all partitions found in 100 resampling experiments are extremely similar: their average divergence is less than 5% of the expected divergence in a random setting.

Figure 3 gives more insight into the model-complexity selection process for this most stable number of mixture components. For small values of the ℓ_1 constraint κ only very few features are selected which leads to highly fluctuating segmentations. This observation is in accordance with our expectation that the selection of only a few single features would be highly sensitive to the sampling noise. The full model containing all features also turns out to be rather instable, probably due to the irrelevance of most feature dimensions. For the task of separating e.g. the two segments which contain the same texture in different orientations, all color features are basically uninformative noise dimensions. Between these two extremes, however, we find a highly stable segmentation result. On average, 13 features are automatically selected. More important than this average number, however, is the fact that in each of the 4 regression fits (we have $K = 5$ mixture components and thus $K - 1 = 4$ fits) the features are selected in an *adaptive* fashion: in one of the regression problems almost exclusively grey-value features are selected, whereas two other regression fits mainly extract texture information. By combining the 4 regression fits the model is able to extract both types of information while successfully suppressing the irrelevant noise content.

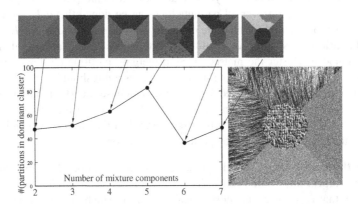

Fig. 2. Model-order selection by resampling: stability of segmentations (measured in terms of percentage of highly similar partitions) vs. number of mixture components. Right: input image.

Real word examples. We applied our method to several images from the corel database. Figure 4 shows the outcome of the whole model selection process for an

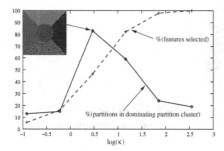

Fig. 3. Selecting the model-complexity for fixed number of mixture components $K = 5$. Solid curve: stability vs. ℓ_1 constraint κ. Dashed curve: number of selected features

image taken from the corel "shell-textures" category, see figure 5. The stability curve for assessing the correct model order favors the use of two mixture components. In this case, the most stable partitions are obtained for a highly constrained model which employs on average only 2 features (left panel). A closer look on the partition clusters show that there is a bimodal distribution of cluster populations: 44 partitions found in 100 resampling experiments form a cluster that segments out the textured shell from the unstructured environment (only texture features are selected in this case), whereas in 37 partitions only color features are extracted, leading to a bipartition of the image into shadow and foreground.

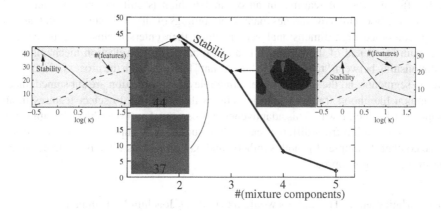

Fig. 4. A shell image from the corel database: model selection by resampling.

Both possible interpretations of the image are combined in the three-component model depicted in the right panel. The image is segmented into three classes that correspond to "shell", "coral" and "shadow". The most stable three-component model uses a combination of five texture and three color features. This example demonstrates that due to the unsupervised nature of the segmentation problem, sometimes there are more than one "plausible" solutions. Our feature selection process is capable of exploring such ambiguities, since it provides the user not only with a single optimal model but with a ranked list of possible segmentations. The reader should notice that also in this example the restriction of the model complexity enforced by the ℓ_1 constraint is crucial

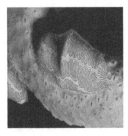 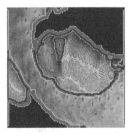

Fig. 5. The shell image and the three-component segmentation solution

for obtaining stable segmentations. We applied our method to several other images from the corel database, but due to space limitations we refer the interested reader to our web-page www.inf.ethz.ch/˜vroth/segments_dagm.html.

4   Discussion

In image segmentation, one often faces the problem that relevant information is spread over different cues like color and texture. And even within one cue, different scales might be relevant for segmenting out certain segments. The question of how to combine such different types of features in an optimal fashion is still an open problem. We present a method which overcomes many shortcomings of "naively" stacking all features into a combined high-dimensional vector which then enters a clustering procedure. The main ingredient of the approach is an automatic feature selection mechanism for distinguishing between "relevant" and "irrelevant" features. Both the process of grouping sites to segments and the process of selecting relevant information are subsumed under a common likelihood framework which allows the algorithm to select features in an adaptive task-specific way. This adaptiveness property makes it possible to combine the relevant information from different cues while successfully suppressing the irrelevant noise content. Examples for both synthetic and natural images effectively demonstrate the strength of this approach.

Acknowledgments. The authors would like to thank Joachim M. Buhmann for helpful discussions and suggestions.

References

1. S. Belongie, C. Carson, H. Greenspan, and J. Malik. Color- and texture-based image segmentation using the expectation-maximization algorithm and its application to content-based image retrieval. In *Int. Conf. Computer Vision*, 1998.
2. A. Ben-Dor, N. Friedman, and Z. Yakhini. Class discovery in gene expression data. In *Procs. RECOMB*, pages 31–38, 2001.
3. A.P. Dempster, N.M. Laird, and D.B. Rubin. Maximum likelihood from incomplete data via the EM algorithm. *J. R. Stat. Soc. B*, 39:1–38, 1977.
4. M. Figueiredo and A. K. Jain. Bayesian learning of sparse classifiers. In *CVPR2001*, 2001.

5. T. Hastie and R. Tibshirani. Discriminant analysis by gaussian mixtures. *J. R. Stat. Soc. B*, 58:158–176, 1996.
6. T. Hastie, R. Tibshirani, and A. Buja. Flexible discriminant analysis by optimal scoring. *J. Am. Stat. Assoc.*, 89:1255–1270, 1994.
7. H.W. Kuhn. The hungarian method for the assignment problem. *Naval Res. Logist. Quart.*, 2:83–97, 1955.
8. T. Lange, M. Braun, V. Roth, and J.M. Buhmann. Stability-based model selection. In *Advances in Neural Information Processing Systems*, volume 15, 2003.
9. M.H. Law, A.K. Jain, and M.A.T. Figueiredo. Feature selection in mixture-based clustering. In *Advances in Neural Information Processing Systems*, volume 15, 2003.
10. B. S. Manjunath and W. Y. Ma. Texture features for browsing and retrieval of image data. *IEEE Trans. Pattern Anal. Mach. Intell.*, 18(8):837–842, 1996.
11. M. Osborne, B. Presnell, and B. Turlach. On the lasso and its dual. *J. Comput. Graph. Stat.*, 9:319–337, 2000.
12. V. Roth and T. Lange. Feature selection in clustering problems. In *Advances in Neural Information Processing Systems 16*. MIT Press, 2004.
13. Volker Roth and Tilman Lange. Bayesian class discovery in microarray datasets. *IEEE Trans. on Biomedical Engineering*, 51(5), 2004.
14. R.J. Tibshirani. Regression shrinkage and selection via the lasso. *JRSS B*, 58:267–288, 1996.
15. A. v.Heydebreck, W. Huber, A. Poustka, and M. Vingron. Identifying splits with clear separation: a new class discovery method for gene expression data. *Bioinformatics*, 17, 2001.

Semi-supervised Kernel Regression Using Whitened Function Classes

Matthias O. Franz, Younghee Kwon, Carl Edward Rasmussen, and
Bernhard Schölkopf

Max-Planck-Institut für biologische Kybernetik
Spemannstr. 38, 72076 Tübingen
{mof;kwon;carl;bs}@tuebingen.mpg.de,
http://www.kyb.tuebingen.mpg.de/

Abstract. The use of non-orthonormal basis functions in ridge regression leads to an often undesired non-isotropic prior in function space. In this study, we investigate an alternative regularization technique that results in an implicit whitening of the basis functions by penalizing directions in function space with a large prior variance. The regularization term is computed from unlabelled input data that characterizes the input distribution. Tests on two datasets using polynomial basis functions showed an improved average performance compared to standard ridge regression.

1 Introduction

Consider the following situation: We are given a set of N input values $\mathbf{x}_i \in \mathbb{R}^m$ and the corresponding N measurements of the scalar output values t_i. Our task is to model the output by linear combinations from a dictionary of fixed functions φ_i of the input $\mathbf{x}$, i.e.,

$$\hat{y}_i = \sum_{j=1}^{M} \gamma_j \varphi_j(\mathbf{x}_i), \quad \text{or more conveniently,} \quad \hat{y}_i = \gamma^\top \phi(\mathbf{x}_i), \tag{1}$$

using $\phi(\mathbf{x}_i) = (\varphi_1(\mathbf{x}_i), \varphi_2(\mathbf{x}_i), \dots)^\top$. The number of functions M in the dictionary can be possibly infinite as for instance in a Fourier or wavelet expansion. Often, the functions contained in the dictionary are neither normalized nor orthogonal with respect to the input. This situation is common in kernel ridge regression with polynomial kernels. Unfortunately, the use of a non-orthonormal dictionary in conjunction with the ridge regularizer $\|\gamma\|^2$ often leads to an undesired behaviour of the regression solutions since the constraints imposed by this choice rarely happen to reflect the - usually unknown - prior probabilities of the regression problem at hand. This can result in a reduced generalization performance of the solutions found.

In this study, we propose an approach that can alleviate this problem either when unlabelled input data is available, or when reasonable assumptions can be

C.E. Rasmussen et al. (Eds.): DAGM 2004, LNCS 3175, pp. 18–26, 2004.

made about the input distribution. From this information, we compute a regularized solution of the regression problem that leads to an *implicit whitening* of the function dictionary. Using examples from polynomial regression, we investigate whether whitened regression results in an improved generalisation performance.

2 Non-orthonormal Functions and Priors in Function Space

The use of a non-orthonormal function dictionary in ridge regression leads to a non-isotropic prior in function space. This can be seen in a simple toy example where the function to be regressed is of the form $t_i = \sin(ax_i)/(ax_i) + n_i$ with the input x_i uniformly distributed in $[-1, 1]$ and an additive Gaussian noise signal $n_i \approx N(0, \sigma_\nu^2)$. Our function dictionary consists of the first six canonical polynomials $\phi_1(x) = 1, \phi_2(x) = x, \phi_3(x) = x^2, \ldots, \phi_6(x) = x^5$ which are neither orthogonal nor normalized with respect to the uniform input. The effects on the type of functions that can be generated by this choice of dictionary can be seen in a simple experiment: we assume that the weights in Eq. 1 are distributed according to an isotropic Gaussian, i.e., $\gamma \approx N(0, \sigma^2 I_6)$ such that no function in the dictionary receives a higher a priori weight. Together with Eq. 1, these assumptions define a prior distribution over the functions $\hat{y}(x)$ that can be generated by our dictionary. In our first experiment, we draw samples from this distribution (Fig. 1a) and compute the mean square of $\hat{y}(x)$ at all $x \in [-1, 1]$ for 1000 functions generated by the dictionary (Fig. 1b). It is immediately evident that, given a uniform input, our prior narrowly constrains the possible solutions around the origin while admitting a broad variety near the interval boundaries. If we do ridge regression with this dictionary (here we used a Gaussian Process regression scheme, for details see [5]), the solutions tend to have a similar behaviour as long as they are not enough constrained by the data points (see the diverging solution at the left interval boundary in Fig. 1c). This can lead to bad predictions in sparsely populated areas.

If we choose a dictionary of orthonormal polynomials instead (in our example these are the first six Legendre polynomials), we observe a different behaviour: the functions sampled from the prior show a richer structure (Fig. 1d) with a relatively flat mean square value over the interval $[-1, 1]$ (Fig. 1e). As a consequence, the ridge regression solution usually does not diverge in sparsely populated regions near the interval boundaries (Fig. 1f).

The reason for this behaviour can be seen if one thinks of the functions as points in a function space. The dictionary defines a basis in a subspace such that all possible solutions of the form Eq. 1 are linear combinations of these basis vectors. Assuming an isotropic distribution of the weights, a non-orthogonal basis results in a non-isotropic distribution of points in function space. As a result, any new function to be expressed (or regressed) in this basis will have a larger probability if its projection onto the basis happens to be along a larger principal component, i.e., we have a *non-isotropic prior* in function space. Conversely, an orthonormal basis in conjunction with an isotropic weight distribution results in

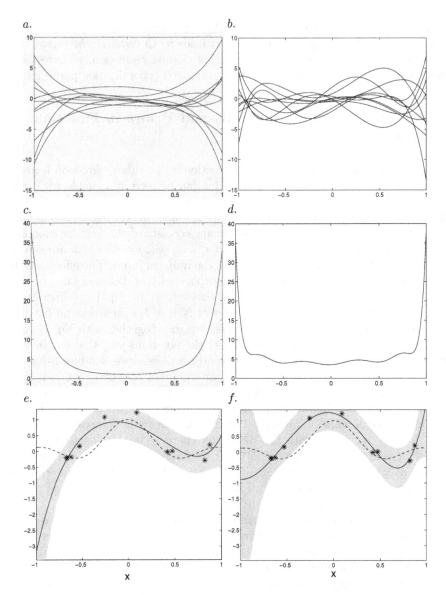

Fig. 1. Toy experiment using polynomial bases: *a.* 10 examples drawn from the prior in function space generated by the first 6 canonical polynomials and *b.* generated by the first 6 Legendre polynomials; *c.* Mean squared value in the interval $[-1, 1]$ of 1000 random linear combinations of the first 6 canonical polynomials and *d.*, of the first 6 Legendre polynomials; *e.* Regression on 10 training samples (stars) using the canonical polynomial basis and *f.*, the Legendre basis. The dashed line denotes the true function, the solid line the prediction from regression. The shaded areas show the 95%-confidence intervals.

an isotropic prior in function space such that no specific function is preferred over another. This situation may often be preferable if nothing is known in advance about the function to be regressed.

3 Whitened Regression

The standard solution to regression is to find the weight vector γ in Eq. 1 that minimizes the sum of the squared errors. If we put all $\phi(\mathbf{x}_i)$ into an $N \times M$ design matrix Φ with $\Phi = (\phi(\mathbf{x}_1)^\top, \phi(\mathbf{x}_2)^\top, \ldots \phi(\mathbf{x}_N)^\top)^\top$, the model (1) can be written as $\hat{\mathbf{y}} = \Phi\gamma$ such that the regression problem can be formulated as

$$\underset{\gamma}{\operatorname{argmin}}(\mathbf{t} - \Phi\gamma)^2. \tag{2}$$

The problem with this approach is that if the noises n_i are large, then forcing $\hat{\mathbf{y}}$ to fit as closely as possible to the data results in an estimate that models the noise as well as the function to be regressed. A standard approach to remedy such problems is known as the method of regularization in which the square error criterion is augmented with a penalizing functional

$$(\mathbf{t} - \Phi\gamma)^2 + \lambda J(\gamma), \quad \lambda > 0. \tag{3}$$

The penalizing functional J is chosen to reflect prior information that may be available regarding γ, λ controls the tradeoff between fidelity to the data and the penalty $J(\gamma)$. In many applications, the penalizing functional can be expressed as a quadratic form

$$J(\gamma) = \gamma^\top \Sigma_\gamma^{-1} \gamma \tag{4}$$

with a positive definite matrix Σ_γ^{-1}. The solution of the regression problem can be found analytically by setting the derivative of expression (3) with respect to γ to zero and solving for γ:

$$\gamma_{opt} = (\lambda \Sigma_\gamma^{-1} + \Phi^\top \Phi)^{-1} \Phi^\top \mathbf{t}. \tag{5}$$

Based on γ_{opt}, we can predict the output for the new input $\mathbf{x}_*$ using

$$\hat{y}_* = \gamma_{opt}^\top \phi(\mathbf{x}_*) = \mathbf{t}^\top \Phi (\lambda \Sigma_\gamma^{-1} + \Phi^\top \Phi)^{-1} \phi(\mathbf{x}_*) \tag{6}$$

Note that the solution depends only on products between basis functions evaluated at the training and test points. For certain function classes, these can be efficiently computed using *kernels* (see next section). In ridge regression, an isotropic penalty term on γ corresponding to $\Sigma_\gamma = \sigma^2 I_M$ is chosen. This can lead to a non-isotropic prior in function space as we have seen in the last section for non-orthonormal function dictionaries.

What happens if we transform our basis such that it becomes orthonormal? The proper transformation can be found if we know the covariance matrix C_ϕ of our basis with respect to the distribution of $\mathbf{x}$

$$C_\phi = E_\mathbf{x}[\phi(\mathbf{x})\phi(\mathbf{x})^\top] \tag{7}$$

where $E_{\mathbf{x}}$ denotes the expectation with respect to $\mathbf{x}$. The *whitening transform* is defined as

$$D = D^\top = C_\phi^{-\frac{1}{2}}. \tag{8}$$

The transformed basis $\tilde{\phi} = D\phi$ has an isotropic covariance as desired:

$$C_{\tilde{\phi}} = E_{\mathbf{x}}[\tilde{\phi}(\mathbf{x})\tilde{\phi}(\mathbf{x})^\top] = E_{\mathbf{x}}[D\phi(\mathbf{x})\phi(\mathbf{x})^\top D^\top] = DE_{\mathbf{x}}[\phi(\mathbf{x})\phi(\mathbf{x})^\top]D^\top = I_M. \tag{9}$$

Often, however, the matrix C_ϕ will not have full rank such that a true whitening transform cannot be found. In these cases, we propose to use a transform of the form

$$D = (C_\phi + I_M)^{-\frac{1}{2}}. \tag{10}$$

This choice prevents the amplification of possibly noise-contaminated eigenvectors of C_ϕ with small eigenvalues (since the minimal eigenvalue of $(C_\phi + I_M)$ is 1) while still leading to a whitening effect for eigenvectors with large enough eigenvalues.

When we substitute the transformed basis $\tilde{\phi} = D\phi$ into Eq. (5) using $\Sigma_\gamma = I_M$, we obtain

$$\gamma_{opt} = D^{-1}(\lambda(D^{-1})^2 + \Phi^\top\Phi)^{-1}\Phi^\top\mathbf{t}. \tag{11}$$

The prediction equation (6) is accordingly

$$\hat{y} = \mathbf{t}^\top\Phi(\lambda(D^{-1})^2 + \Phi^\top\Phi)^{-1}\phi(\mathbf{x}_*) \tag{12}$$

It follows that doing standard ridge regression with a withened, orthonormal basis is equivalent to doing regression in the original, non-orthonormal basis using the regularizer $J(\gamma) = \gamma^\top D^{-2}\gamma$. This allows us to use an implicitly whitened basis without the need to change the basis functions themselves. This is particularly useful when we do not have the freedom to choose our basis as, for instance, in kernel-based methods where the basis functions are determined by the kernel (see next section).

The proposed approach, however, suffers from a certain drawback because we need to know C_ϕ. In certain cases, the input distribution is known or can be approximated by reasonable assumptions such that C_ϕ can be computed beforehand. In other cases, *unlabelled data* is available which can be used to estimate C_ϕ. The training data itself, however, cannot be used to estimate C_ϕ since the estimate is proportional to $\Phi^\top\Phi$. When substituted into Eq. (12) this amounts to no regularization at all. As a consequence, for the proposed approach to work it is absolutely necessary to obtain C_ϕ from data independent of the training data.

4   Whitened Kernel Regression

When the number of basis functions is large, a direct solution to the regression problem as described in the previous section becomes infeasible. Fortunately, there is a work-around to this problem for many important function classes: We noted in the previous section that the regression solution depends only on products between basis functions evaluated at the training and test points. For certain function dictionaries, the product between the functions evaluated at two input values $\mathbf{x}_1$ and $\mathbf{x}_2$ can be expressed as

$$\phi(\mathbf{x}_1)^\top \phi(\mathbf{x}_2) = k(\mathbf{x}_1, \mathbf{x}_2). \tag{13}$$

The function $k(\mathbf{x}_1, \mathbf{x}_2)$ on $\mathbb{R}^m \times \mathbb{R}^m$ is a *positive definite kernel* (for a definition see [3]). As a consequence, the evaluation of a possibly infinite number of terms in $\phi(\mathbf{x}_1)^\top \phi(\mathbf{x}_2)$ reduces to the computation of the kernel k directly on the input. Equation (13) is only valid for *positive definite* kernels, i.e., functions k with the property that the *Gram matrix* $K_{ij} = k(\mathbf{x}_i, \mathbf{x}_j)$ is positive definite for all choices of the $\mathbf{x}_1, \dots, \mathbf{x}_N$. It can be shown that a number of kernels satisfies this condition including polynomial and Gaussian kernels [3].

A kernelized version of whitened regression is obtained by considering the set of n basis functions which is formed by the *Kernel PCA Map* [3]

$$\phi(\mathbf{x}) = K^{-\frac{1}{2}} (k(\mathbf{x}_1, \mathbf{x}), k(\mathbf{x}_2, \mathbf{x}), \dots k(\mathbf{x}_N, \mathbf{x}))^\top. \tag{14}$$

The subspace spanned by the $\phi(\mathbf{x}_i)$ has the structure of a *reproducing kernel Hilbert space (RKHS)*. By carrying out linear methods in a RKHS, one can obtain elegant solutions for various nonlinear estimation problems [3], examples being Support Vector Machines. When we substitute this basis in Eq. (5), we obtain

$$\gamma_{opt} = (\lambda \Sigma_\gamma^{-1} + K)^{-1} K^{\frac{1}{2}} \mathbf{t} \tag{15}$$

using the fact that $\Phi = K^{-\frac{1}{2}} K = K^{\frac{1}{2}} = \Phi^\top$. By setting $\mathbf{k}(\mathbf{x}) = (k(\mathbf{x}_1, \mathbf{x}), k(\mathbf{x}_2, \mathbf{x}), \dots k(\mathbf{x}_n, \mathbf{x}))^\top$, the prediction (6) becomes

$$\hat{y}_* = \mathbf{t}^\top (\lambda K^{\frac{1}{2}} \Sigma_\gamma^{-1} K^{-\frac{1}{2}} + K)^{-1} \mathbf{k}(\mathbf{x}_*). \tag{16}$$

It can be easily shown that this solution is exactly equivalent to Eq. 6 if Eq. 13 holds. When choosing $\Sigma_\gamma = I_N$, one obtaines the solution of standard kernel ridge regression [1]. Application of the whitening prior leads to

$$\hat{y}_* = \mathbf{t}^\top (\lambda R + K)^{-1} \mathbf{k}(\mathbf{x}_*) \tag{17}$$

Here, $C_\phi = K^{-\frac{1}{2}} C_\mathbf{k} K^{-\frac{1}{2}}$ and $C_\mathbf{k} = E_\mathbf{x} [\mathbf{k}(\mathbf{x}) \mathbf{k}(\mathbf{x})^\top]$. This results in $R = K^{-\frac{1}{2}} C_\mathbf{k}$ or $R = K^{-\frac{1}{2}} C_\mathbf{k} + I_N$, depending on the choice of D.

5   Experiments

We compare whitened regression to ridge regression [1] using the kernelized form of Eq. 17 with $R = K^{-\frac{1}{2}} C_\mathbf{k} + I_N$ and Eq. 16 with $\Sigma_\gamma = I_N$, respectively. We

Table 1. Average squared error for whitened and ridge regression. Significant p-values < 0.1 are marked by a star.

Kernel	Summed Polynomial	Adaptive Polynomial	Inhomogeneous Polynomial
Sinc dataset			
Ridge regression	1.126	1.578	0.863
Whitened regression	0.886	0.592	0.787
p-value (t-test)	0.471	0.202	0.064*
Boston house-price			
Ridge Regression	18.99	16.37	18.74
Whitened Regression	12.83	15.78	13.08
p-value (t-test)	0.022*	0.817	0.053*

consider three types of polynomial kernels that differ in the weights assigned to the different polynomial orders: the *summed polynomial kernel*

$$k_{sp}(\mathbf{x}_1, \mathbf{x}_2) = \sum_{i=0}^{d} (\mathbf{x}_1^\top \mathbf{x}_2)^i; \tag{18}$$

the *adaptive polynomial kernel*

$$k_{ap}(\mathbf{x}_1, \mathbf{x}_2) = \sum_{i=0}^{d} a_i (\mathbf{x}_1^\top \mathbf{x}_2)^i; \tag{19}$$

where the weights a_i are hyperparameters adapted during the learning process, and the *inhomogeneous polynomial kernel*

$$k_{ihp}(\mathbf{x}_1, \mathbf{x}_2) = (1 + \mathbf{x}_1^\top \mathbf{x}_2)^d = \sum_{i=0}^{d} \binom{d-i}{i} (\mathbf{x}_1^\top \mathbf{x}_2)^i. \tag{20}$$

In both experiments, we used a 10 fold cross-validation setup with disjoint test sets. For each of the 10 partitions and the different kernels, we computed the squared error loss. In addition to the average squared loss, we tested the significance of the performance difference between whitened and standard regression using a t-test on the squared loss values.

1. Sinc dataset. Our first experiment is the $\sin(ax)/(ax)$ toy example ($a = 8$, noise variance $\sigma_\nu^2 = 0.05$) of Sec. 2 with disjoint training sets of 10 examples and disjoint test sets of 80 examples. We estimated the covariance $C_\mathbf{k}$ for Eq. 17 from 4000 additional unlabelled cases. The hyperparameters λ, and a_i were estimated by conjugate gradient descent on the analytically computed leave-one-out error [4], the best degree d was also chosen according to the smallest leave-one-out error for all orders up to 10.

2. Boston Housing. For testing whitened regression on real data, we took disjoint test sets of 50/51 examples and training sets of 455/456 examples from the Boston house-price dataset [2]. Note that due to dependencies in the training sets, independence assumptions needed for the t-test could be compromised. Since the Boston house-price dataset does not provide additional unlabelled data, we had to generate 2000 artificial unlabelled datapoints for each of the 10 trials based on the assumption that the input is uniformly distributed between the minima and maxima of the respective training set. The artificial datapoints were used to estimate C_k. Instead of the leave-one-out error, we used conjugate gradient descent on a Bayesian criterion for selecting the hyperparameters, usually referred to as negative log evidence [5]. The maximal degree d tested was 5.

The results in Table 1 show that whitened regression performes on the average better than standard ridge regression. However the improvement appears to be relatively small in many cases such that we get a significant result with $p < 0.1$ only for the inhomogeneous polynomial kernel on both datasets and for the summed polynomial kernel on the Boston house-price set. The weaker significance of the results on the Sinc dataset can be attributed to the very small number of training samples which leads to a large variance in the results.

The assumption of a uniformly distributed input in the Boston housing data seems to be useful as it leads to a general improvement of the results. The significantly better performance for the summed and the inhomogeneous polynomial kernel is mainly caused by the fact that often the standard ridge regression found only the linear solution with a typical squared error around 25, whereas whitened regression always extracted additional structure from the data with squared errors between 10 and 16.

6   Conclusion

Using a non-orthonormal set of basis function for regression can result in an often unwanted prior on the solutions such that an orthonormal or whitened basis is preferable for this task. We have shown that doing standard regression in a whitened basis is equivalent to using a special whitening regularizer for the non-orthonormal function set that can be estimated from unlabelled data.

Our results indicate that whitened regression using polynomial bases leads only to small improvements in most cases. In some cases, however, the improvement is significant, particularly in cases where the standard polynomial regression could not find a non-trivial solution. As a consequence, whitened regression is always an option to try when unlabelled data is available, or when reasonable assumptions can be made about the input distribution.

Acknowledgements. C.E.R. was supported by the German Research Council (DFG) through grant RA 1030/1.

References

1. N. Cristianini and J. Shawe-Taylor. *Support vector machines.* Cambridge University Press, Cambridge, 2000.

2. D. Harrison and D. Rubinfeld. Hedonic prices and the demand for clean air. *J. Environ. Economics & Management*, 5:81–102, 1978. Data available from http://lib.stat.cmu.edu/datasets/boston.

3. B. Schölkopf and A. J. Smola. *Learning with kernels*. MIT Press, Cambridge, MA, 2002.

4. V. Vapnik. *Estimation of dependences based On empirical data*. Springer, New York, 1982.

5. C. K. I. Williams and C. E. Rasmussen. Gaussian processes for regression. In D. S. Touretzky, M. C. Mozer, and M. E. Hasselmo, editors, *Advances in Neural Processing Systems*, volume 8, pages 598–604, Cambridge, MA, 1996. MIT Press.

Fast Monocular Bayesian Detection of Independently Moving Objects by a Moving Observer[*]

Felix Woelk and Reinhard Koch

Christian-Albrechts-Universität zu Kiel,
Institute für Informatik und Praktische Mathematik,
Ohlshausenstr. 40, 24098 Kiel, Germany
{woelk, rk}@mip.informatik.uni-kiel.de

Abstract. A fast algorithm for the detection of independently moving objects by an also moving observer by means of investigating optical flow fields is presented. Since the measurement of optical flow is a computationally expensive operation, it is necessary to restrict the number of flow measurements. The proposed algorithm uses two different ways to determine the positions, where optical flow is calculated. A part of the positions is determined using a particle filter, while the other part of the positions is determined using a random variable, which is distributed according to an initialization distribution. This approach results in a restricted number of optical flow calculations leading to a robust real time detection of independently moving objects on standard consumer PCs.

1 Introduction

The detection of independently moving objects by an also moving observer is a vital ability for any animal. The early detection of an enemy while moving through visual clutter can be a matter of life and death. Also for modern humans it is useful, e.g. for collision prevention in traffic. Using the human head as an inspiration, a lightweight monocular camera mounted on a pan-tilt-unit (PTU) is chosen to investigate the environment in this application. The analysis of optical flow fields gathered from this camera system is a cheap and straight forward approach avoiding heavy and sensitive stereo rigs. Since determining highly accurate optical flow with subpixel precision is a computationally expensive operation, restrictions on the maximum number of optical flow computations have to be made in real time environments. The approach chosen in this work is inspired by [8] and determines the sample positions (i.e. points where optical flow will be calculated) partly by using a vector of random variables, which are distributed according to an initialization distribution function (IDF), and partly by propagating samples from the last time step using a particle filter approach. While a wide range of literature on the application of particle filters to tracking tasks [8,9,12] and lately on improvements on the particle filter to overcome the degeneracy problem [5,6,10,15] exist, only little work has been done in the field of using such probabilistic techniques for the investigation and interpretation of optical flow fields: In [2] motion discontinuities are tracked using optical flow and the CONDENSATION algorithm and in 2002 [16] used a particle filter to predict and therefore speedup a correlation based optical flow algorithm. In the

---

[*] This work was supported by BMBF Grant No. 1959156C.

following sections, the basic concept used for the detection of independent motion is explained first. The particle filter system used to speedup and stabilize the detection of independent motion is developed next. Finally experiments with synthetic and real data are shown.

2   Detection of Independently Moving Objects

The basic concepts used for the detection of independently moving objects by a moving observer through investigation of the optical flow are introduced in this section.

Computation of the Optical Flow: A large number of algorithms for the computation of optical flow exist [1]. Any of these algorithms calculating the full 2D optical flow can be used for the proposed algorithm. Algorithms calculating the normal flow only (i.e. the flow component component parallel to the image gradient) are, however, inappropriate. The optical flow in this work is calculated using an iterative gradient descend algorithm [11], applied to subsequent levels of a Gaussian image pyramid.

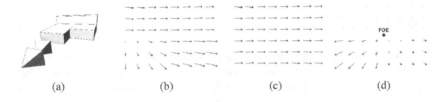

(a)   (b)   (c)   (d)

Fig. 1. Theoretical flow fields for a simple scene. The 3D scene is shown at (a). The scene consists of 3 blocks. The camera, displayed as small pyramids, translates towards the blocks while rotating around the y axis. The flow field F as induced by this movement is shown in (b). Its rotational component F_R (c) and translational component F_T (d) with the Focus of Expansion (FOE) are shown on the right.

Detection of Independent Motion: Optical flow fields consists of a rotational part and a translational part (Fig. 1). The rotational part is independent of the scene geometry and can be computed from the camera rotation. Subtraction of the rotational flow field from the overall flow field results in the translational flow field, where all flow vectors point away from the focus of expansion (FOE), which can be calculated from the camera motion. With known camera motion, only the direction of the translational part of the optical flow field can be predicted. The angle between the predicted direction and the (also rotation corrected) flow calculated from the two images serves as a measure for independent motion [14](Fig. 2). This detection method requires the exact knowledge of the camera motion. In our approach, the camera motion can be derived from rotation sensor and speed sensor data of the car, or it can alternatively be measured directly from the static scene [13].

3   Particle Filter

First the general concept of the CONDENSATION algorithm is summarized. Then the application of a particle filter for detection of independent motion is described.

3.1   CONDENSATION

The CONDENSATION algorithm is designed to handle the task of propagating any probability density function (pdf) over time. Due to the computational complexity of this task, pdfs are approximated by a set of weighted samples. The weight π_n is given by

$$\pi_n = \frac{p_z(s^{(n)})}{\sum_{j=1}^{N} p_z(s^{(j)})} \tag{1}$$

where $p_z(x) = p(z|x)$ is the conditional observation density representing the probability of a measurement z, given that the system is in the state x. $s^{(n)}$ represents the position of sample n in the state space.

Propagation: From the known a priori pdf, samples are randomly chosen with regard to their weight π_i. In doing so, a sample can be chosen several times. A motion model is applied to the sample positions and diffusion is done by adding Gaussian noise to each sample position. A sample that was chosen multiple times results in several spatial close samples after the diffusion step. Finally the weight is calculated by measuring the conditional observation $p(z|x)$ and using it in eq. 1. The a posteriori pdf represented by these samples is acting as a priori pdf in the next time step. This iterative evaluation scheme is closely related to Bayes' law

$$p(x|z) = \frac{p(z|x)p(x)}{p(z)} \tag{2}$$

where $p(z)$ can be interpreted as a normalization constant, independent of the system state x [8]. The sample representation of the posteriori pdf $p(x|z)$ is calculated by implicitly using the a priori pdf $p(x)$ as the sample base from which new samples are chosen and the probability of a measurement $p(z|x)$ given a certain state of the system x (eq. 1).

Initialization: In order to initialize without human interaction a fraction of the samples are chosen by using a random variable which is distributed according to an initialization distribution in every time step. In the first time step, all samples are chosen in this manner.

3.2   Bayesian Detection of Independent Motion

First an overview over the proposed algorithm is given, then the algorithm is explained in detail. Since optical flow (OF) is computationally expensive, the number of OF measurements have to be restricted. However, when computing OF at sparse locations, one would like to capture as much flow on independently moving objects as possible. An adapted particle filter is chosen for this task. In this application the probability for a position belonging to an independently moving object is chosen as the pdf for the CONDENSATION algorithm, resulting in a state dimension of 2. A fraction of the samples are chosen by using propagating samples from the last time step using the CONDENSATION approach. Hereby samples are chosen randomly with respect to their weight. Samples with a high weight (a high probability for an independently moving object) are chosen with a higher possibility. In general these high weight samples are chosen multiple times, resulting in more samples in the vicinity of the old sample after the diffusion in the next time step. The remaining part of the samples are generated by using a random variable with a distribution depending on the image gradient. OF is measured at each sample position.

Modifications of the standard CONDENSATION algorithm: A number of adaptations have been made to the CONDENSATION algorithm to ensure faster processing and optimization of the sample positions for the flow measurements:

- *Initialization Function:* The measurement of OF is only possible on regions with spatial structure. The lower eigenvalue of the structure tensor or "cornerness" [3] is chosen as initialization distribution density function (IDF). By placing samples randomly with respect to this IDF, the majority of the samples are located on positions with high "cornerness" and hence giving optimal conditions for the calculation of the OF. Due to the random nature of the sample placing, some samples are however placed in regions with lower spatial structure, giving less optimal conditions for OF calculation, but on the other hand allowing the detection of independently moving objects in these regions. Obviously, there has to be a lower bound on the minimum spatial structure necessary for OF calculation. To ensure a fast detection of moving objects, the fraction of samples positioned in this way is chosen to be as high as 0.7. This high initialization fraction obviously disturbs the posterior pdf, but on the other hand improves the response time of the detector. The high fraction of samples generated by using the IDF also reduces the degeneracy problem of particle filters.
- *Discretizing of the State Space:* The sample positions are discretized, i.e. a sample cannot lie between pixels. This leads to the fact that multiple samples are located on the same location in state space, i.e. on the same pixel. Obviously only one expensive measurement of OF is necessary for all those samples located on the same pixel. This leads not to a reduction of the sample numbers, but only to a reduction of the necessary measurements and probability calculations (typically by 25%) and therefore speeds up the process.
- *Motion Model:* In the special case of applying Bayesian sampling to locations of OF measurements, no motion model of the underlying process is needed, because every measurement (i.e. optical flow = apparent motion of a point between two consecutive frames) represents the motion of the according sample itself. The new sample position can be predicted by using the old position and adding the OF measured at this position.
- *Non-Isotropic Diffusion:* In typical traffic situations, large portions of the images are very low structured (e.g. the asphalt of the road), therefore a modified diffusion step

is used to increase the number of sample positions on structured image regions: A pointwise multiplication of the standard 2D Gaussian function with the cornerness in a window around the actual position is used as the diffusion density function. The window size is determined by the variances of the diffusion. Choosing randomly once with respect to this density results in the new sample position.

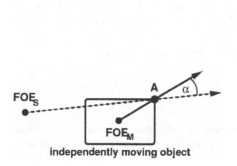

independently moving object

Fig. 2. Detection of moving object by the angle between the predicted flow direction (pointing away from FOE_S) and the measured flow direction (pointing away from FOE_M).

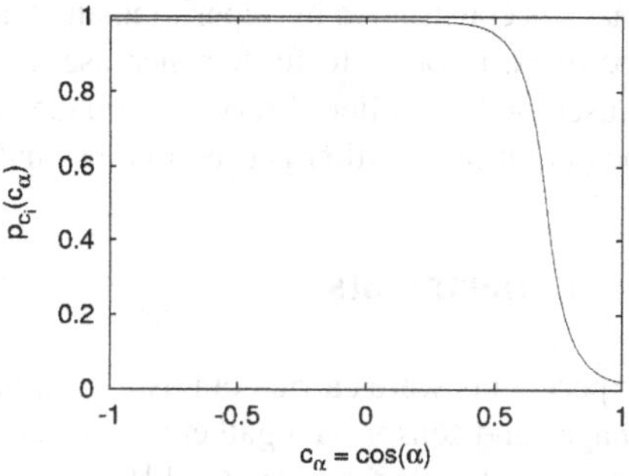

Fig. 3. The probability that a flow measurement is located on an independently moving object $p_{c_i}(c_\alpha)$ in dependence of $c_\alpha = \cos(\alpha)$ at a given inflection point $c_i = 0.7$.

Measurement. The measurement at each sample position should represent the probability $p(x)$ that this sample is located on an independently moving object. Let α denote the angle between the predicted translational optical flow pointing away from FOE_S and the rotation corrected OF vector pointing away from FOE_M (see Fig. 2). For speed reasons, $c_\alpha = \cos(\alpha)$ is used as a basis for the calculation of this probability [14].

The probability for an independently moving object $p_{c_i}(c_\alpha)$ in dependence of c_α is modeled as a rounded step function:

$$p_{c_i}(c_\alpha) = \begin{cases} e^{f(c_i) \cdot c_\alpha + \ln(0.5) - c_i \cdot f(c_i)} & \text{if } c_\alpha > c_i, \\ 1.0 - e^{-f(c_i) \cdot c_\alpha + \ln(0.5) + c_i \cdot f(c_i)} & \text{if } c_\alpha \leq c_i, \end{cases} \qquad (3)$$

where $f(c_i) = \frac{\ln(0.01) - \ln(0.5)}{1.0 - |c_i|}$ is a function of the inflection point c_i. Since it is not feasible to set probabilities to 1.0 or 0.0, $p_{c_i}(c_\alpha)$ is scaled and shifted to represent a minimum uncertainty. Fig. 3 shows $p_{c_i}(c_\alpha)$. In the proposed algorithm, the inflection point is chosen automatically to be $c_i = \tilde{c}_\alpha - \sigma_{c_\alpha}$, where $\tilde{c}_\alpha$ is the median of the all cosine angles not detected as "moving" in the last time step, and σ_{c_α} is the variance of the c_α. Choosing c_i automatically has the advantage, that erroneous camera positions do not disturb the measurement. This only holds under the assumption that more than half of the flow vectors are located on the static scene. Similar terms ensuring a minimum cornerness p_c (since OF can only be computed with spatial structure), a minimum flow length p_f (standing for the accuracy of the OF computation) and a minimum distance from the focus of expansion p_{FOE} (since errors in the FOE position influence the direction prediction for closer points more than for further points) are introduced. The overall probability $p(x) = p(z|x)$ is then given by:

$$p(x) = p_{c_i}(c_\alpha) \cdot p_c \cdot p_f \cdot p_{FOE} \tag{4}$$

Spatio Temporal Filtering. In order to detect whether independently moving objects are present, the sampled observation density is investigated. An outlier observation density image is constructed by superimposing Gaussian hills with a given sigma for all sample positions. In order to further increase the robustness a temporal digital low pass filter is used on the outlier observation image density sequence. A user selected threshold on the output of this filter is used to mark independently moving objects.

4   Experiments

Experiments were carried out using synthetic images and sensor information as well as images and sensor data gathered with the Urban Traffic Assistant (UTA) demonstrator from the DaimlerChrysler AG [4].

Fig. 4. Some images from the synthetic intersection sequence. The camera is moving on a straight line, while the car in the image is on a collision course. Points where the filter output is above a threshold of 0.35 are marked white.

Simulated Data. To test the algorithm a simulated intersection was realized in VRML. Simple block models of houses, textured with real image data, are located on the corners of the intersecting street (fig. 4). A model of a car was used as an independently moving object. Screenshots of a ride through this intersection provided the image data, while the sensor information was calculated from the known camera parameters at the time of the screenshots. Fig. 4 shows some images from the simulated image sequence. Points where the spatio-temporal filter output is above 0.35 are marked with white blobs. Only very few points are detected because the synthetic car color is uniform due to the simple texture model.

Real Data. The setup of UTA [4] includes a digital camera mounted on a pan-tilt-unit (PTU), GPS, map data, internal velocity and yawrate sensors, etc. The fusion of GPS and map data will be used to announce the geometry of an approaching intersection to the

Fig. 5. Some images from a real intersection sequence. Points where the spatio-temporal filter output is above 0.35 are marked white.

vision system. The camera then focuses on the intersection. Using the known egomotion of the camera, independently moving objects are detected and the driver's attention can be directed towards them. Fig. 5 shows the results on a real world image sequence.

Timing. The computation frequency is 18.2 ± 2.0 frames per second (fps) for the synthetic sequence and 20.0 ± 2.4 fps for the real world sequence. These timings were measured on a standard 2.4 GHz Pentium IV PC with an overall number of 1000 samples. The optical flow used a pyramid of size 3.

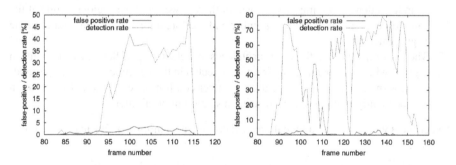

Fig. 6. False positive and detection rates for a synthetic (left) and real world (right) sequence. The ground truth image segmentation needed for obtaining these rates was known in the synthetic case and was generated by hand in the real world case. The moving object was approximated in the real world case by several rectangles. In the synthetic sequence (A) moving objects were visible between frame 72 and frame 117. In the real world image sequence (B), an image sequence of 80 images was evaluated. See text for further details.

Detection Rates. The detection rates and false positive rates were calculated on a pixel basis using a known image segmentation: For every pixel where the optical flow has been calculated, it is determined whether it is a false positive or a true detection, resulting in a detection rate of 100 % when every flow measurement on the moving object is detected as such by the algorithm. In the case of synthetic image data, the segmentation could be derived from the known 3D scene structure, in the case of the real world sequence, the image was segmented by hand. Several rectangles thereby approximated the moving object. Fig. 6 shows that a high detection rate combined with a low (nearly zero) false positive rate could be obtained with the chosen approach. The remaining false positive rate results from the spatio temporal filtering of the results. All false positives are located spatially very close to the moving object. Since the camera and the moving object were on collision course, independent motion was detected mainly at the object boundaries (car front). In the parts of the sequence where no moving object was visible the false positive rate stayed very low, causing no false object alarms. The evaluation of the real sequence showed essentially the same behavior and proves the robustness against noise.

5   Conclusions and Further Work

A fast and robust Bayesian based system for the detection of independently moving objects by a moving observer has been presented. The two advantages motivating the chosen approach lead to a very fast and robust algorithm:

1. By choosing the IDF to depend on the image gradient, most samples are positioned in high contrast regions resulting in optimal conditions for the calculation of optical flow. Because the IDF is however only the distribution function for the randomly chosen sample positions, their positions are not restricted to high contrast regions, but some of them are also positioned in lower contrast regions. This allows the detection of independently moving objects also in these lower contrast regions, while at the same time a maximum sample number and therfore a maximum computation time is guaranteed.
2. The use of the particle filter approach leads to a clustering of flow measurements in regions where independent motion was detected in the last time step. The surrounding flow measurements can be used to either confirm or reject the existence of an independently moving object by using a spatio-temporal filter.

Experiment with synthetic and real image data were accomplished. Further work should include:

- investigation of the trajectory extraction possibility of moving objects
- fast robust egomotion estimation refinement by fusing sensor information (speed, yawrate and steering angle) with image based measurements (optical flow from static scene)

References

1. J.L. Barron, D.J. Fleet, S.S. Beauchemin and T.A. Burkitt, "Performance Of Optical Flow Techniques", *Proc. CVPR*, Vol. 92, pp. 236-242, 1994.
2. M.J. Black and D.J. Fleet, "Probabilistic Detection and Tracking of Motion Discontinuities." *ICCV*, 1999.
3. W. Förstner,, "A feature based correspondence algorithm for image matching.", *International Archives of Photogrammetry and Remote Sensing*, 26-3/3. pp. 150-166, 1986.
4. S. Gehrig, S.Wagner and U. Franke, "System Architecture for an Intersection Assistant Fusing Image, Map and GPS Information" *Proc. IEEE Intelligent Vehicles*, 2003.

5. C. Hue, J.-P. Le Cardre and P. Perez, "Tracking Multiple Objects with Particle Filtering." *IEEE Transactions on Aerospace and Electronic Systems*, 38(3):791-812, 2002

6. Z.Khan, T. Balch and F. Dellaert "An MCMC-Based Particle Filter for Tracking Multiple Interacting Targets." *ECCV*, 2004

7. R. Hartley and A. Zisserman, *Multiple View Geometry*, Cambridge University Press, 2000.

8. M. Isard and A. Blake "Condensation – conditional density propagation for visual tracking." *IJCV*, 29(1), pp.5-28, 1998.

9. M. Isard and A. Blake "ICONDENSATION: Unifying low-level and high-level tracking in a stochastic framework." *ECCV*, vol. 1 893-908, 1998.

10. M. Isard, J. McCormick, "BraMBLe: A Bayesian Multiple-Blob Tracker." *ICCV*, 2001.

11. B. Lucas and T. Kanade, "An iterative image registration technique with an application to stereo vision" *Proc. DARPA IU Workshop*, pp. 121-130, 1981.

12. P. Perez et al., "Color-Based Probabilistic Tracking." *ECCV*, 2002.

13. M. Pollefeys, R. Koch and Luc J. Van Gool, "Self-Calibration and Metric Reconstruction in Spite of Varying and Unknown Internal Camera Parameters", *IJCV*, 32(1):7-25, 1999.

14. F. Woelk, S. Gehrig and R. Koch, "A Monocular Image Based Intersection Assistant." *IEEE Intelligent Vehicles*, Parma, Italy, 2004.

15. J. Vermaak et al., "Maintaining Multi-Modality through Mixture Tracking." *ICCV*, 2003.

16. J.S. Zelek, "Bayesian Real-time Optical Flow." *Proc VI*, 2002.

Kernel Density Estimation and Intrinsic Alignment for Knowledge-Driven Segmentation: Teaching Level Sets to Walk

Daniel Cremers[1], Stanley J. Osher[2], and Stefano Soatto[1]

[1] Department of Computer Science
University of California at Los Angeles, USA
[2] Department of Mathematics
University of California at Los Angeles, USA

Abstract. We address the problem of image segmentation with statistical shape priors in the context of the level set framework. Our paper makes two contributions: Firstly, we propose a novel multi-modal statistical shape prior which allows to encode multiple fairly distinct training shapes. This prior is based on an extension of classical kernel density estimators to the level set domain. Secondly, we propose an intrinsic registration of the evolving level set function which induces an invariance of the proposed shape energy with respect to translation. We demonstrate the advantages of this multi-modal shape prior applied to the segmentation and tracking of a partially occluded walking person.

1 Introduction

When interpreting a visual scene, human observers generally revert to higher-level knowledge about expected objects in order to disambiguate the low-level intensity or color information of the given input image. Much research effort has been devoted to imitating such an integration of prior knowledge into machine-vision problems, in particular in the context of image segmentation.

Among variational approaches, the level set method [16,10] has become a popular framework for image segmentation. The level set framework has been applied to segment images based on numerous low-level criteria such as edge consistency [13,2,11], intensity homogeneity [3,22], texture information [17,1] and motion information [6].

More recently, it was proposed to integrate prior knowledge about the shape of expected objects into the level set framework [12,21,5,20,8,9,4]. Building up on these developments, we propose in this paper two contributions. Firstly, we introduce a statistical shape prior which is based on the classical kernel density estimator [19,18] extended to the level set domain. In contrast to existing approaches of shape priors in level set segmentation, this prior allows to well approximate arbitrary distributions of shapes. Secondly, we propose a translation-invariant shape energy by an intrinsic registration of the evolving level set function. Such a closed-form solution removes the need to locally update explicit pose parameters. Moreover, we will argue that this approach is more accurate because the

C.E. Rasmussen et al. (Eds.): DAGM 2004, LNCS 3175, pp. 36–44, 2004.

resulting shape gradient contains an additional term which accounts for the effect of boundary variation on the location of the evolving shape. Numerical results demonstrate our method applied to the segmentation of a partially occluded walking person.

2   Level Set Segmentation

Originally introduced in the community of computational physics as a means of propagating interfaces [16][1], the level set method has become a popular framework for image segmentation [13,2,11]. The central idea is to implicitly represent a contour C in the image plane $\Omega \subset \mathbb{R}^2$ as the zero-level of an embedding function $\phi : \Omega \to \mathbb{R}$:

$$C = \{x \in \Omega \mid \phi(x) = 0\} \tag{1}$$

Rather than directly evolving the contour C, one evolves the level set function ϕ. The two main advantages are that firstly one does not need to deal with control or marker points (and respective regridding schemes to prevent overlapping). And secondly, the embedded contour is free to undergo topological changes such as splitting and merging which makes it well-suited for the segmentation of multiple or multiply-connected objects.

In the present paper, we use a level set formulation of the piecewise constant Mumford-Shah functional, c.f. [15,22,3]. In particular, a two-phase segmentation of an image $I : \Omega \to \mathbb{R}$ can be generated by minimizing the functional [3]:

$$E_{cv}(\phi) = \int_{\Omega} (I - u_+)^2 H\phi(x)dx + \int_{\Omega} (I - u_-)^2 (1 - H\phi(x))dx + \nu \int_{\Omega} |\nabla H\phi|dx, \tag{2}$$

with respect to the embedding function ϕ. Here $H\phi \equiv H(\phi)$ denotes the Heaviside step function and u_+ and u_- represent the mean intensity in the two regions where ϕ is positive or negative, respectively. While the first two terms in (2) aim at minimizing the gray value variance in the separated phases, the last term enforces a minimal length of the separating boundary. Gradient descent with respect to ϕ amounts to the evolution equation:

$$\frac{\partial \phi}{\partial t} = -\frac{\partial E_{cv}}{\partial \phi} = \delta_\epsilon(\phi) \left[\nu \, \mathrm{div} \left(\frac{\nabla \phi}{|\nabla \phi|} \right) - (I - u_+)^2 + (I - u_-)^2 \right]. \tag{3}$$

Chan and Vese [3] propose a smooth approximation δ_ϵ of the delta function which allows the detection of interior boundaries.

In the corresponding Bayesian interpretation, the length constraint given by the last term in (2) corresponds to a prior probability which induces the segmentation scheme to favor contours of minimal length. But what if we have more

---

[1] See [10] for a precursor containing some of the key ideas of level sets.

Fig. 1. Sample training shapes (binarized and centered).

informative prior knowledge about the shape of expected objects? Building up on recent advances [12,21,5,20,8,9,4] and on classical methods of non-parametric density estimation [19,18], we will in the following construct a shape prior which statistically approximates an arbitrary distribution of training shapes (without making the restrictive assumption of a Gaussian distribution).

3   Kernel Density Estimation in the Level Set Domain

Given two shapes encoded by level set functions ϕ_1 and ϕ_2, one can define their distance by the set symmetric difference (cf. [4]):

$$d^2(H\phi_1, H\phi_2) = \int_\Omega \left(H\phi_1(x) - H\phi_2(x)\right)^2 dx. \tag{4}$$

In contrast to the shape dissimilarity measures discussed in [20,8], the above measure corresponds to an L_2-distance, in particular it is non-negative, symmetric and fulfills the triangle inequality. Moreover it does not depend on the size of the image domain (as long as both shapes are entirely inside the image).

Given a set of training shapes $\{\phi_i\}_{i=1...N}$ – see for example Figure 1 – one can estimate a statistical distribution by reverting to the classical Parzen-Rosenblatt density estimator [19,18]:

$$\mathcal{P}(\phi) \propto \frac{1}{N} \sum_{i=1}^{N} \exp\left(-\frac{1}{2\sigma^2} d^2(H\phi, H\phi_i)\right). \tag{5}$$

This is probably the theoretically most studied density estimation method. It was shown to converge to the true distribution in the limit of infinite training samples (under fairly mild assumptions). There exist extensive studies as to how to optimally choose the kernel width σ. For this work, we simply fix σ to be the mean nearest-neighbor distance:

$$\sigma^2 = \frac{1}{N} \sum_{i=1}^{N} \min_{j \neq i} d^2(H\phi_i, H\phi_j). \tag{6}$$

The intuition behind this choice is that the width of the Gaussians is chosen such that on the average the next training shape is within one standard deviation.

In contrast to existing shape priors which are commonly based on the assumption of a Gaussian distribution (cf. [12]), the distribution in (5) is a multi-modal one (thereby allowing more complex training shapes). We refer to [7] for an alternative multi-modal prior for spline-based shape representations.

4 Translation Invariance by Intrinsic Alignment

By construction the shape prior (5) is not invariant with respect to certain transformations of the shape ϕ such as translation, rotation and scaling. In the following, we will demonstrate how such an invariance can be integrated analytically by an intrinsic registration process. We will detail this for the case of translation. But extensions to rotation and scaling are straight-forward.

Assume that all training shapes $\{\phi_i\}$ are aligned with respect to their center of gravity. Then we define the distance between a shape ϕ and a given training shape as:

$$d^2(H\phi, H\phi_i) = \int_\Omega \left(H\phi(x - x_\phi) - H\phi_i(x)\right)^2 dx, \tag{7}$$

where the function ϕ is evaluated in coordinates relative to its center of gravity x_ϕ given by:

$$x_\phi = \frac{\int x \, H\phi \, dx}{\int H\phi \, dx}. \tag{8}$$

This intrinsic alignment guarantees that in contrast to (4), the distance (7) is invariant to the location of the shape ϕ. The corresponding shape prior (5) is by construction invariant to translation of the shape ϕ. Analogous intrinsic alignments with respect to scale and rotation are conceivable but will not be considered here.

Invariance to certain group transformations by intrinsic alignment of the evolving shape as proposed in this work is different from numerically optimizing a set of explicit pose parameters [5,20,8]. The shape energy is by construction invariant to translation. This removes the necessity to intermittently iterate gradient descent equations for the pose. Moreover, as we will see in Section 6, this approach is conceptually more accurate in that it induces an additional term in the shape gradient which accounts for the effect of shape variation on the center of gravity x_ϕ. Current effort is focused on extending this approach to a larger class of invariance. For explicit contour representations, an analogous intrinsic alignment with respect to similarity transformation was proposed in [7].

5 Knowledge-Driven Segmentation

In the Bayesian framework, the level set segmentation can be seen as maximizing the conditional probability

$$\mathcal{P}(\phi \mid I) = \frac{\mathcal{P}(I \mid \phi) \, \mathcal{P}(\phi)}{\mathcal{P}(I)}, \tag{9}$$

with respect to the level set function ϕ, where $\mathcal{P}(I)$ is a constant. This is equivalent to minimizing the negative log-likelihood which is given by a sum of two energies:

$$E(\phi) = \frac{1}{\alpha} E_{cv}(\phi) + E_{shape}(\phi), \qquad (10)$$

with a positive weighting factor α and the shape energy

$$E_{shape}(\phi) = -\log \mathcal{P}(\phi), \qquad (11)$$

where $\mathcal{P}(\phi)$ is given in (5).

Minimizing the energy (10) generates a segmentation process which simultaneously aims at maximizing intensity homogeneity in the separated phases and a similarity of the evolving shape with respect to the training shapes encoded through the statistical estimator.

Gradient descent with respect to the embedding function amounts to the evolution:

$$\frac{\partial \phi}{\partial t} = -\frac{1}{\alpha} \frac{\partial E_{cv}}{\partial \phi} - \frac{\partial E_{shape}}{\partial \phi}, \qquad (12)$$

with the image-driven component of the flow given in (3) and the knowledge-driven component is given by:

$$\frac{\partial E_{shape}}{\partial \phi} = \frac{\sum \alpha_i \frac{\partial}{\partial \phi} d^2(H\phi, H\phi_i)}{2\sigma^2 \sum \alpha_i}, \qquad (13)$$

which simply induces a force in direction of each training shape ϕ weighted by the factor:

$$\alpha_i = \exp\left(-\frac{1}{2\sigma^2} d^2(H\phi, H\phi_i)\right), \qquad (14)$$

which decays exponentially with the distance from shape ϕ_i.

6   Euler-Lagrange Equations for Nested Functions

The remaining shape gradient in equation (13) is particularly interesting since the translation-invariant distance in (7) exhibits a two-fold (nested) dependence on ϕ. The computation of the corresponding Euler-Lagrange equations is fairly involved. For space limitations, we will only state the final result:

$$\frac{\partial}{\partial \phi} d^2(H\phi, H\phi_i) = 2\,\delta\left(\phi(x)\right) \left[\left(H\phi(x) - H\phi_i(x + x_\phi)\right)\right.$$
$$\left. -\frac{(x - x_\phi)^t}{\int H\phi \, dx} \int \left(H\phi(x) - H\phi_i(x + x_\phi)\right) \nabla H\phi(x)\, dx\right]. \qquad (15)$$

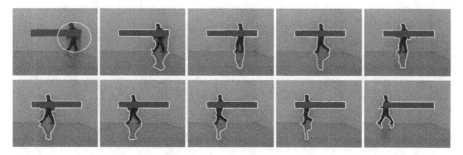

Fig. 2. Various frames showing the segmentation of a partially occluded walking person generated with the Chan-Vese model (2). Based on a pure intensity criterion, the walking person cannot be separated from the occlusion and darker areas of the background such as the person's shadow.

Note that as for the image-driven component of the flow in (3), the entire expression is weighted by the δ-function which stems from the fact that the function d only depends on $H\phi$. While the first term in (15) draws $H\phi$ to the template $H\phi_i$ in the local coordinate frame, the second term compensates for shape deformations which merely lead to a translation of the center of gravity x_ϕ. Not surprisingly, this second term contains an integral over the entire image domain because the change of the center of gravity through local deformation of ϕ depends on the entire function ϕ. In numerical experiments we found that this additional term increases the speed of convergence by a factor of 3 (in terms of the number of iterations necessary).

7   Tracking a Walking Person

In the following we apply the proposed shape prior to the segmentation of a partially occluded walking person. To this end, a sequence of a dark figure walking in a (fairly bright) squash court was recorded.[2] We subsequently introduced a partial occlusion into the sequence and ran an intensity segmentation by iterating the evolution (3) 100 times for each frame (using the previous result as initialization). For a similar application of the Chan-Vese functional (without statistical shape priors), we refer to [14]. The set of sample frames in Figure 2 clearly demonstrates that this purely image-driven segmentation scheme is not capable of separating the object of interest from the occluding bar and similarly shaded background regions such as the object's shadow on the floor.

In a second experiment, we manually binarized the images corresponding to the first half of the original sequence (frames 1 through 42) and aligned them to their respective center of gravity to obtain a set of training shape – see Figure 1. Then we ran the segmentation process (12) with the shape prior (5). Apart from adding the shape prior we kept the other parameters constant for comparability.

Figure 3 shows several frames from this knowledge-driven segmentation. A comparison to the corresponding frames in Figure 2 demonstrates several

---

[2] We thank Alessandro Bissacco and Payam Saisan for providing the image data.

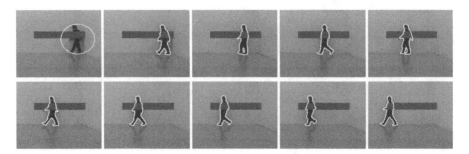

Fig. 3. Segmentation generated by minimizing energy (10) combining intensity information with the statistical shape prior (5). Comparison with the respective frames in Figure 2 shows that the multi-modal shape prior permits to separate the walking person from the occlusion and darker areas of the background such as the shadow. The shapes in the bottom row were not part of the training set.

properties of our contribution:

- The shape prior permits to accurately reconstruct an entire set of fairly different shapes. Since the shape prior is defined on the level set function ϕ – rather than on the boundary C (cf. [5]) – it can easily reproduce the topological changes present in the training set.
- The shape prior is invariant to translation such that the object silhouette can be reconstructed in arbitrary locations of the image. All training shapes are centered at the origin, and the shape energy depends merely on an intrinsically aligned version of the evolving level set function.
- The statistical nature of the prior allows to also reconstruct silhouettes which were not part of the training set (beyond frame 42).

8   Conclusion

We combined concepts of non-parametric density estimation with level set based shape representations in order to create a statistical shape prior for level set segmentation which can accurately represent arbitrary shape distributions. In contrast to existing approaches, we do not rely on the restrictive assumptions of a Gaussian distribution and can therefore encode fairly distinct shapes.

Moreover, we proposed an analytic solution to generate invariance of the shape prior to translation of the object of interest. By computing the shape prior in coordinates relative to the object's center of gravity, we remove the need to numerically update a pose estimate. Moreover, we argue that this intrinsic registration induces a more accurate shape gradient which comprises the effect of shape or boundary deformation on the pose of the evolving shape.

Finally, we demonstrate the effect of the proposed shape prior on the segmentation and tracking of a partially occluded human figure. In particular, these results demonstrate that the proposed shape prior permits to accurately reconstruct occluded silhouettes according to the prior in arbitrary locations (even silhouettes which were not in the training set).

Acknowledgments. DC and SS were supported by ONR N00014-02-1-0720/N00014-03-1-0850 and AFOSR F49620-03-1-0095/E-16-V91-G2. SO was supported by an NSF IIS-0326388-01, "ITR: Intelligent Deformable Models", Agreement # F5552-01.

References

1. T. Brox and J. Weickert. A TV flow based local scale measure for texture discrimination. In T. Pajdla and V. Hlavac, editors, *European Conf. on Computer Vision*, volume 3022 of *LNCS*, pages 578–590, Prague, 2004. Springer.
2. V. Caselles, R. Kimmel, and G. Sapiro. Geodesic active contours. In *Proc. IEEE Intl. Conf. on Comp. Vis.*, pages 694–699, Boston, USA, 1995.
3. T. Chan and L. Vese. Active contours without edges. *IEEE Trans. Image Processing*, 10(2):266–277, 2001.
4. T. Chan and W. Zhu. Level set based shape prior segmentation. Technical Report 03-66, Computational Applied Mathematics, UCLA, Los Angeles, 2003.
5. Y. Chen, H. Tagare, S. Thiruvenkadam, F. Huang, D. Wilson, K. S. Gopinath, R. W. Briggs, and E. Geiser. Using shape priors in geometric active contours in a variational framework. *Int. J. of Computer Vision*, 50(3):315–328, 2002.
6. D. Cremers. A variational framework for image segmentation combining motion estimation and shape regularization. In C. Dyer and P. Perona, editors, *IEEE Conf. on Comp. Vis. and Patt. Recog.*, volume 1, pages 53–58, June 2003.
7. D. Cremers, T. Kohlberger, and C. Schnörr. Shape statistics in kernel space for variational image segmentation. *Pattern Recognition*, 36(9):1929–1943, 2003.
8. D. Cremers and S. Soatto. A pseudo-distance for shape priors in level set segmentation. In N. Paragios, editor, *IEEE 2nd Int. Workshop on Variational, Geometric and Level Set Methods*, pages 169–176, Nice, 2003.
9. D. Cremers, N. Sochen, and C. Schnörr. Multiphase dynamic labeling for variational recognition-driven image segmentation. In T. Pajdla and V. Hlavac, editors, *European Conf. on Computer Vision*, volume 3024 of *LNCS*, pages 74–86, Prague, 2004. Springer.
10. A. Dervieux and F. Thomasset. A finite element method for the simulation of Raleigh-Taylor instability. *Springer Lecture Notes in Math.*, 771:145–158, 1979.
11. S. Kichenassamy, A. Kumar, P. J. Olver, A. Tannenbaum, and A. J. Yezzi. Gradient flows and geometric active contour models. In *Proc. IEEE Intl. Conf. on Comp. Vis.*, pages 810–815, Boston, USA, 1995.
12. M. E. Leventon, W. E. L. Grimson, and O. Faugeras. Statistical shape influence in geodesic active contours. In *Proc. Conf. Computer Vis. and Pattern Recog.*, volume 1, pages 316–323, Hilton Head Island, SC, June 13–15, 2000.
13. R. Malladi, J. A. Sethian, and B. C. Vemuri. Shape modeling with front propagation: A level set approach. *IEEE PAMI*, 17(2):158–175, 1995.
14. M. Moelich and T. Chan. Tracking objects with the chan-vese algorithm. Technical Report 03-14, Computational Applied Mathematics, UCLA, Los Angeles, 2003.

15. D. Mumford and J. Shah. Optimal approximations by piecewise smooth functions and associated variational problems. *Comm. Pure Appl. Math.*, 42:577–685, 1989.
16. S. J. Osher and J. A. Sethian. Fronts propagation with curvature dependent speed: Algorithms based on Hamilton–Jacobi formulations. *J. of Comp. Phys.*, 79:12–49, 1988.
17. N. Paragios and R. Deriche. Geodesic active regions and level set methods for supervised texture segmentation. *Int. J. of Computer Vision*, 46(3):223–247, 2002.
18. E. Parzen. On the estimation of a probability density function and the mode. *Annals of Mathematical Statistics*, 33:1065–1076, 1962.
19. F. Rosenblatt. Remarks on some nonparametric estimates of a density function. *Annals of Mathematical Statistics*, 27:832–837, 1956.
20. M. Rousson and N. Paragios. Shape priors for level set representations. In A. Heyden et al., editors, *Proc. of the Europ. Conf. on Comp. Vis.*, volume 2351 of *LNCS*, pages 78–92, Copenhagen, May 2002. Springer, Berlin.
21. A. Tsai, A. Yezzi, W. Wells, C. Tempany, D. Tucker, A. Fan, E. Grimson, and A. Willsky. Model–based curve evolution technique for image segmentation. In *Comp. Vision Patt. Recog.*, pages 463–468, Kauai, Hawaii, 2001.
22. A. Tsai, A. J. Yezzi, and A. S. Willsky. Curve evolution implementation of the Mumford-Shah functional for image segmentation, denoising, interpolation, and magnification. *IEEE Trans. on Image Processing*, 10(8):1169–1186, 2001.

3D Head Pose Estimation with Symmetry Based Illumination Model in Low Resolution Video

Martin Gruendig[1] and Olaf Hellwich[2]

[1] Robert Bosch GmbH, FV/SLH, P.O. Box 777 777, 31132 Hildesheim, Germany
[2] Computer Vision and Remote Sensing TU Berlin, 10623 Berlin, Germany

Abstract. A head pose estimation system is described, which uses low resolution video sequences to determine the orientation and position of a head with respect to a internally calibrated camera. The system employs a feature based approach to roughly estimate the head pose and an approach using a symmetry based illumination model to refine the head pose independent of the users albedo and illumination influences.

1 Introduction

3D head pose estimation and tracking from monocular video sequences is a very active field of research in computer vision. In this paper we want to introduce a 3D head pose estimation system which is designed to initialize a tracking framework to track arbitrary movements of a head. This paper concentrates on the initialization part of our system which has to work on low resolution video sequences. The head usually covers 60x40 pixels in the images, and it has to be robust with respect changes in illumination, facial gestures and different users. A number of different approaches have been proposed for the problem of 3D head pose estimation and tracking. Some using a 3D head model and tracking distinct image features through the sequence [2], [7], [4], [1]. The image features correspond to anchor points on the 3D head model which then can be aligned accordingly and the head pose is estimated. Another approach is to model 3D head movement as a linear combination of a set of bases, that are generated by changing the pose of the head and computing a difference image of the poses [14]. The coefficients of the linear combination that models the difference image best is used to determine the current head pose. A third popular approach is to employ optical flow constrained by the geometric structure of the head model [6], [5], [16]. Since optical flow is very sensitive with respect to illumination changes, [10] also included an illumination basis to model illumination influences in his optical flow approach. Except for [6] all approaches work on high resolution images. Except for [2] none of the mentioned approaches includes an automatic initialization of the tracking without the user to keep still and to look straight into the camera.

There are a number of 3D face pose estimation approaches. Systems which do not require high resolution images of the face, either lack the required accuracy which is needed to initialize a tracking system [8], or are not illumination and person invariant [13].

C.E. Rasmussen et al. (Eds.): DAGM 2004, LNCS 3175, pp. 45–53, 2004.

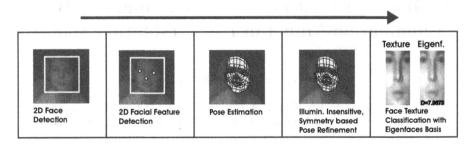

Fig. 1. Structure of head pose estimation system.

2   Motivation

A fully automatic head pose tracking system has to automatically initialize the tracking. This includes a reliable estimation of the 3D head pose without any customized model information. Some systems require the user to look straight into the camera to initialize [7], [14], [16], others only determine the relative change of pose with respect to the pose in the first frame [4], or the user is required to identify certain features like eyes and nose manually [5]. Since we intend to automatically initialize and track a head, in low resolution video sequences, all the above approaches are not an option. Our goal is to reliably estimate the head pose with respect to the camera if the deviation of the current orientation from a frontal view does not exceed 30 degrees. In case these conditions are not met by the current head pose, no initialization should occur until we reach a frame with a head pose that does meet the condition. One can think of it as a trap. The initialization process is divided into five parts, see Fig. 1

3   Implemented System

3.1   2D Face Detection

First we employ a face detection algorithm that is capable of detecting faces that meet our orientation condition. We use the OpenCV implementation [$http : //sourceforge.net/projects/opencvlibrary$] of the detection algorithm proposed by Viola and Jones [11] which works very fast and reliable. The face detection gives us a region of interest (ROI) in the image which is passed on to the next step of the initialization.

3.2   Facial Feature Detection and Rough Pose Estimation

In order to roughly estimate the current head pose we intend to detect the image positions of the eyes and the tip of the nose. A radial symmetry interest operator is employed [3] on the upper part of the ROI to detect possible eyes. Since in the low resolution images, each eye is usually a dark radial feature surrounded by a brighter area, eyes yield a large answer in the radial symmetry analysis. It is still difficult though to make an exact prediction for the eyes. Instead of taking the two largest local maximums from the radial symmetry analysis we rather allow 15 hypotheses of possible eye positions at this stage, to be sure to include the correct ones. The same strategy is used for the tip of the nose. Due to its prominent position, the tip of the nose reflects light very well and usually appears as a bright radial feature on a darker background. 3 hypotheses usually suffice for the nose to include the correct position.

For every combination of 2 eyes and a nose we can compute a resulting head pose using a weak geometry projection. We have the 3D object coordinates of the eyes and the nose on a 3D head model of an average person, and the 3 corresponding image positions of the combination. Having computed the pose of every combination, we can discard all the combinations which deviate more than 30 degrees from a frontal view. These heuristics usually do reduce the number of relevant combinations significantly. The remaining combinations are evaluated. For this evaluation we use a database of 3000 different eyes and noses in gabor wavelet space [15]. Each eye hypothesis and nose hypothesis is compared against the database and receives a final feature score. This feature score is the similarity value of the database entry that fits best. The sum of the feature-scores of the combination yields the combination-score. The associated pose of the combination that received the highest combination-score is an estimate of the current head pose.

3.3   Symmetry Considerations

For the refinement of the initialization a novel, illumination and albedo insensitive, symmetry based approach is employed. First we assume that the texture of the right half of the face is symmetric to the left. By projecting a 3D model of a face under the estimated pose into the image, we can extract the underlying texture of the face from the image. Now consider a point p on a lambertian surface. Ignoring attatched shadows, the irradiance value E_p of the surface point p is given by

$$E_p = k_p \left(\boldsymbol{N}_p \cdot \boldsymbol{L}_p \right) \tag{1}$$

where k_p is the nonnegative absorption coefficient (albedo) of the surface at point p, $\boldsymbol{N}_p$ is the surface normal at point p, and $\boldsymbol{L} \in \mathbb{R}^3$ characterizes the collimated light source, where $\|\boldsymbol{L}\|$ gives the intensity of the light source. The gray level intensity I_p measured by a camera is an observation of E_p. We can therefore write

$$I_p \sim k_p \left(\boldsymbol{N}_p \cdot \boldsymbol{L}_p \right) \tag{2}$$

We now assume that a face is symmetric with respect to a mirror axis along the nose. Therefore we can assume

$$k_{pr} = k_{pl} = \frac{I_{pr}}{(\boldsymbol{N}_{pr} \cdot \boldsymbol{L})} = \frac{I_{pl}}{(\boldsymbol{N}_{pl} \cdot \boldsymbol{L})} \Rightarrow \frac{I_{pr}}{I_{pl}} = \frac{(\boldsymbol{N}_{pr} \cdot \boldsymbol{L})}{(\boldsymbol{N}_{pl} \cdot \boldsymbol{L})} \tag{3}$$

where k_{pr} is the albedo of a point pr on the right side of the face and k_{pl} is the albedo of the symmetrically corresponding point pl on the left side of the face. Fig. 2 illustrates the computation.

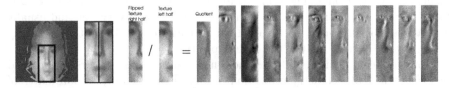

Fig. 2. *From left to right:* Extracted texture of the head under the current pose. Face texture divided into right and left half. Division of flipped right half of the face texture and the left half of the face texture. Quotient. *Right:* Illumination basis with 10 basis vectors that approximately span the space of albedo independent face texture quotients

3.4   Illumination Model

Following the symmetry considerations, we can now generate a parametric illumination model for human faces. The following is related to [14] and [10]. In contrast to [14] and [10] we do not generate the parametric illumination model based on the textures themselves. In order to achieve user independence we use the fraction $H(I) = \frac{I_r}{I_l}$. If we extract the face texture in form of a vector I_j from a set of images of a face illuminated from a different direction in each image j. We can then compute the fraction

$$H(I) = \frac{I_r}{I_l} \tag{4}$$

for each element of these textures $\boldsymbol{I}_j$. By performing a singular value decomposition on the texture fractions $\boldsymbol{H}_j$ we can generate a small set of 10 basis vectors b to form a illumination basis, so that every fraction $\boldsymbol{H}_j$ can be expressed as a linear combination of the columns of $\boldsymbol{B}$

$$\boldsymbol{B} = [\boldsymbol{b}_1 | \boldsymbol{b}_2 | \ldots | \boldsymbol{b}_{10}] \tag{5}$$

$$\boldsymbol{H}_j = \boldsymbol{Bw} \tag{6}$$

where $\boldsymbol{w}$ is the vector of linear coefficients. Fig. 2 illustrates the illumination basis. Note that the fraction $H = \frac{I_r}{I_l}$ is a value that is independent of the persons individual reflectance parameters (albedo). Therefore we do not need to know the persons albedo, in that aspect this new approach differs from [12] and [10]. Using this measure, it is therefore possible to get a albedo independent model of illumination influences of a face. In contrast to [14] where a normally illuminated face of the current person is subtracted from each illumination texture in order to build a user independent illumination basis, we strictly model illumination with the lambertian illumination model without the need to assume an additive nature of illumination influences. 10 basis vectors seem to suffice to account for the non lambertian influences and self shadowing.

3.5   Head Pose Refinement

In order to further refine the pose estimation we can now use the user independent illumination model and formulate the pose refinement as a least squares problem in the following way. Let $X_i \in \mathbb{R}^3$ be a point on the head in 3D space with respect to a head centered model coordinate system. $x_i \in \mathbb{R}^2$ is the corresponding 2D point in the image coordinate system.

X_i is projected onto x_i under the current head pose μ, which consists of the orientation $[\mu_1; \mu_2; \mu_3]$ and the 3D position $[\mu_4; \mu_5; \mu_6]$ of the head with respect to the camera.

$$\tilde{X}(X, \mu) = R(\mu_1, \mu_2, \mu_3)X + t(\mu_4, \mu_5, \mu_6) \tag{7}$$

The similarity transform in (7) aligns the model coordinate system with respect to the camera where R is a rotation about the angles μ_1, μ_2, μ_3 and t is the translation μ_4, μ_5, μ_6 that translates the origin of the model coordinate system to the origin of the camera coordinate system. The collinearity equation

$$x(\tilde{X}) = \left[\frac{k_1^T \cdot \tilde{X}}{k_3^T \cdot \tilde{X}}, \frac{k_2^T \cdot \tilde{X}}{k_3^T \cdot \tilde{X}} \right]^T ; \quad K = \begin{bmatrix} k_1^T \\ k_2^T \\ k_3^T \end{bmatrix} \tag{8}$$

formulates the central projection of the aligned model coordinates X_i into the image coordinates x_i, where K is a matrix containing the intrinsic camera calibration parameters. The gray value intensities I of the image can be formulated as a function of x (9). H can therefore be expressed as a function of μ (10).

$$I(x) = I \tag{9}$$
$$H(\mu) = H(I(x(\tilde{X}(\mu)))) \tag{10}$$

We can now formulate the objective function O that needs to be minimized. We want to find a head pose μ that can be confirmed by the illumination basis B as well as the roughly detected feature positions of the eyes and the nose in the image x_n in a least squares sense. We therefore set

$$O(\mu, w) = \sum_n P_n(x_n(\mu) - x_n)^2 + \sum_i P_i(H_i(\mu) - B_i(w))^2 \tag{11}$$

P_i and P_n are weights associated with every element i of the illumination basis and every feature point n of the detected feature positions. With these weights we can control how much influence the feature points have with respect to the illumination basis in the least squares adjustment. To equally weigh the feature points and the illumination basis and since we have 3 detected feature points we usually set $P_i = 1$ and $P_n = \frac{1}{3} \sum P_i$.

Since O is nonlinear, we need to expand the function into a taylor series in order to be able to iteratively solve the least squares adjustment in the fashion of a Gauss-Newton Optimization. As a starting point we can use the pose estimation from the feature based head pose estimation μ_0.

By setting

$$A = \begin{bmatrix} \nabla H & -\nabla B \\ \nabla x & 0 \end{bmatrix} ; \, \delta l = \begin{bmatrix} H(\mu_0) - B(w_0) \\ x(\mu_0) - x \end{bmatrix} ; \, P = \begin{bmatrix} diag(P_i) & 0 \\ 0 & diag(P_n) \end{bmatrix} \quad (12)$$

where A is a Matrix that includes the jacobians, δl is a vector and P is the diagonal matrix with the associated weights.

$$O(\delta\mu, \delta w) = \left\| P(A \, [\delta\mu, \delta w]^T + \delta l) \right\| \quad (13)$$

$$[\delta\mu, \delta w]^T = -(A^T P A)^{-1} A^T P \delta l \quad (14)$$

$$\mu_0 = \delta\mu + \mu_0 \; ; \; w_0 = \delta w + w_0 \quad (15)$$

Equation (13) formulates the linearized objective function in matrix notation. Solving the set of equations $\nabla O = 0$ gives the solution in (14). Equation (15) yields the update of the head pose μ and the illumination basis coefficients w for the next iteration step. Usually 10 iterations suffice for the adjustment to converge. After each iteration step a visibility analysis is performed to determine for which points on the face both symmetrically corresponding points on the left half and on the right half are visible under the current pose μ. If either of the two symmetrically corresponding points is not visible, the pair of points is excluded for the next iteration step. This way we can handle self occlusion.

3.6   Face Texture Verification

In order to evaluate the detected pose of the head and to discard gross orientation errors it is crucial to verify the detected pose. In our approach we use the face texture which was extracted from the image under the current head pose as a verification hint. By calculating the distance D from an eigenface basis of face textures [9], we can evaluate the current face texture. At this stage we assume that a correct head pose yields a face texture with a very low distance from the eigenface basis, hence these two measures are correlated. The eigenface basis was constructed from a database with 3000 high resolution images of 20 different people under varying lighting conditions and facial expressions.

After the head pose refinement the distance D of the current face texture from the eigenface basis can be used to classify the estimated head pose as correct or as incorrect. A key feature of the system design is therefore the threshold T_D for the classification $h(D)$

$$h(D) = \begin{cases} 1 & D < T_D \\ 0 & \text{otherwise} \end{cases} \quad (16)$$

If we set T_D to a very high value, we will get a relatively large number of false positives. If we set T_D to a very low value we will get a relatively small number of false positives but the fraction of true negatives will increase, which leads to a lower detection rate. Since the application we have in mind is to initialize a head pose tracking system, we are not explicitly interested in a very high detection rate. If the initialization fails in one frame, it is possible to simply try again in the next frame. The overall detection rate will significantly increase if several independent frames are evaluated instead of only one.

4   Experiments and Results

So far the system only works off line as a prototype in a Matlab implementation. We are confident though to achieve real time performance in a C implementation. The most time consuming part is the least squares head pose refinement, since it is a non linear adjustment with an iterative solution. Similar implementations of least squares approaches have achieved real time performance before though [6].

To test our system in real world conditions we recorded several sequences of 12 different people in low resolution, Fig. 3. The head usually covers 60x40 pixel. These images include all possible variations of face appearance. Arbitrary poses, facial expressions, different illumination conditions, and partial occlusions of the face are sampled by these images. In order to generate a ground truth, we manually determined the head pose in $j = 1500$ of these images by labeling the center of the eyes, the tip of the nose and the corners of the mouth and calculating the six parameters $[\bar{\mu}_1; \bar{\mu}_2; \bar{\mu}_3; \bar{\mu}_4; \bar{\mu}_5; \bar{\mu}_6]$ of the ground truth pose $\bar{\mu}$ from that. The mean errors of this ground truth is given in table 1. Table 1 also lists the mean errors of the rough pose estimate, the refined pose estimate and the refined pose estimate with a texture verification threshold set to $T_D = 11$. The mean errors decrease with each step of the system. It is also worth mentioning that the mean errors of our system with respect to the ground truth correspond to the accuracies of the ground truth itself, table 1. In other words, the real accuracies of our system might even be better. Fig. 3 shows the mean errors of the rotational and the translational pose parameters. The diagrams indicate a decreasing accuracy of the pose if the threshold T_D is set to high values in order to increase the detection rate and therefore the robustness. We can increase the robustness by performing the procedure on several subsequent frames and only taking the frame into account which received the lowest value in the distance from the eigenface basis D. This increases the detection rate and decreases the false positive rate. Fig. 3 shows a ROC diagram for setups with 1 frame, 2 frames and 6 frames. Fig. 3 also shows 3 samples of the test results.

5   Conclusion

We introduced a system to estimate the head pose in 6 degrees of freedom in low resolution images. The system is designed to automatically initialize a 3D head pose tracking system, e.g. as in [6]. The system is independent of illumination influences and requires no personalization training or user interaction. Since the

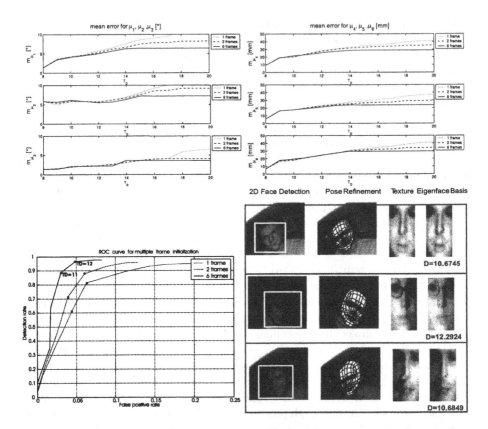

Fig. 3. *Top left and right:* Mean errors of parameters of the pose μ, with respect to the threshold T_D for setups with 1 frame, 2 frames and 6 frames. As the diagrams indicate, the accuracy of the system can not be improved by taking more frames into account. *Bottom left:* ROC diagram for setups with 1 frame, 2 frames and 6 frames. 2 discrete values for the thresholds T_D of the face Texture classification are plotted as a white dot for the value $T_D = 11$ and as a black dot for $T_D = 12$. The best results were achieved for a setup with 6 frames and a threshold $T_D = 11$. With fewer frames taken into account, the results gently decrease in quality. *Bottom right:* 3 samples of the test results. The results of the face detection the pose refinement and the face texture verification are displayed.

Table 1. Mean Errors

Mean Errors	m_{μ_1}	m_{μ_2}	m_{μ_3}	m_{μ_4}	m_{μ_5}	m_{μ_6}
Ground truth	6 deg.	6 deg.	3 deg.	27 mm	26 mm	25 mm
Rough Head Pose Estimate	10 deg.	13 deg.	5 deg.	38 mm	41 mm	40 mm
Refined Head Pose	8 deg.	7 deg.	3 deg.	30 mm	28 mm	29 mm
Refined with Texture verificat. $T_D = 11$	6 deg.	6 deg.	3 deg.	28 mm	22 mm	24 mm

system is based on global face symmetry only head poses in which both eyes are visible will be detected. In our experiments on low resolution images, we achieved a detection rate of 90% at a false positive rate of 3% if 6 subsequent frames are taken into account. Considering only one single frame we achieved a detection rate of 70% at a false positive rate of 6%. Our experiments indicated mean orientation errors of $m_{\mu_1} = m_{\mu_2} = 6$ degrees and of $m_{\mu_3} = 3$ degrees respectively. The mean positioning errors are about 25 mm in each dimension. This matches at least the accuracy of manual head pose estimation in low resolution images.

References

1. R. Cipolla A. Gee. Fast visual tracking by temporal consensus. *Image and Vision Computing*, 14:105–114, 1995.
2. T. Jebara A. Pentland. Parameterized structure from motion for 3d adaptive feedback tracking of faces. Technical Report,Media Laboratory, MIT, 1996.
3. G. Loy A. Zelinsky. Fast radial symmetry for detecting points of interest. *IEEE Transactions on Pattern analysis and Machine Intelligence*, 25(8):959–973, 2003.
4. Natsuko Matsuda Charles S. Wiles, Atsuto Maki. Hyperpatches for 3d model acquisition and tracking. *IEEE Transactions on Pattern Analysis and Machine Intelligence*, 23(12):1391–1403, 2001.
5. D. Metaxas D. DeCarlo. The integration of optical flow and deformable models with applications to human face shape and motion estimation. IEEE Conference on Computer Vision and Pattern Recognition, 1996.
6. T. Kanade J. F. Cohn, J. Xiao. Robust full motion recovery of head by dynamic templates and re-registration techniques. Automated Face and Gesture Recognition, 2002.
7. S. Basu A. Pentland J. Stroem, T. Jebara. Real time tracking and modelling of faces: An ekf-based analysis by synthesis approach. Proceedings of the Modelling People Workshop at ICCV'99, 1999.
8. Y. Wu K. Toyama. Wide-range, person and illumination insensitive head orientation estimation. Automated Face and Gesture Recognition, 2000.
9. A. P. Pentland M. A. Turk. Face recognition using eigenfaces. CVPR92, 1991.
10. G. D. Hager P. N. Belhumeur. Efficient region tracking with parametric models of geometry and illumination. *IEEE Transactions on Pattern analysis and Machine Intelligence*, 20(10):1025–1039, 1998.
11. M. Jones P. Viola. Robust real-time face detection. ICCV01, 2001.
12. D. W. Jacobs R. Basri. Lambertian reflectance and linear subspaces. *IEEE Transactions on Pattern analysis and Machine Intelligence*, 25(2):218–233, 2003.
13. J. Sherrah S. Gong. Fusion of 2d face alignment and 3d head pose estimation for robust and real-time performance. Recognition,analysis and tracking of faces and gestures in real-time systems 1999, 1999.
14. M. La Cascia S. Sclaroff. Fast reliable head tracking under varying illumination. CVPR99, 1999.
15. L. Wiskott. *Labeled Graphs and Dynamic Link Matching for Face Recognition and Scene Analysis*. Verlag Harri Deutsch, 1 edition, 1996.
16. C. Kambhamettu Y. Zhang. Robust 3d head tracking under partial occlusion. Automated Face and Gesture Recognition, 2000.

Efficient Approximations for Support Vector Machines in Object Detection

Wolf Kienzle, Gökhan Bakır, Matthias Franz, and Bernhard Schölkopf

Max Planck Institute for Biological Cybernetics
{kienzle,gb,mof,bs}@tuebingen.mpg.de
http://www.tuebingen.mpg.de
Dept. Schölkopf, Spemannstraße 38, 72076 Tübingen, Germany

Abstract. We present a new approximation scheme for support vector decision functions in object detection. In the present approach we are building on an existing algorithm where the set of support vectors is replaced by a smaller so-called reduced set of synthetic points. Instead of finding the reduced set via unconstrained optimization, we impose a structural constraint on the synthetic vectors such that the resulting approximation can be evaluated via separable filters. Applications that require scanning an entire image can benefit from this representation: when using separable filters, the average computational complexity for evaluating a reduced set vector on a test patch of size $h \times w$ drops from $O(h \cdot w)$ to $O(h+w)$. We show experimental results on handwritten digits and face detection.

1 Introduction

It has been shown that support vector machines (SVMs) provide state-of-the-art accuracies in object detection. In time-critical applications, however, they are of limited use due to their computationally expensive decision functions.

In SVMs the time complexity of a classification operation is characterized by the following two parameters. First, it is linear in the number of support vectors (SVs). Unfortunately, it is known that for noisy problems, the number of SVs can be rather large, essentially scaling linearly with the training set size [10]. Second, it scales with the number of operations needed for computing the similarity (or kernel function) between an SV and the input. When classifying $h \times w$ patches using plain gray value features, the decision function requires an $h \cdot w$ dimensional dot product for each SV. As the patch size increases, these computations become extremely expensive: the evaluation of a single 20×20 pattern on a 320×240 image at 25 frames per second already requires 660 million operations per second. For such systems to run in (or at least near) real-time, it is therefore necessary to lower the computational cost of the SV evaluations as well.

In the past, however, research towards speeding up kernel expansions has focused exclusively on the first issue, i.e., the number of expansion vectors. It has been pointed out that one can improve evaluation speed by using approximations

C.E. Rasmussen et al. (Eds.): DAGM 2004, LNCS 3175, pp. 54–61, 2004.
© Springer-Verlag Berlin Heidelberg 2004

with smaller expansion sets. In [2] Burges introduced a method that, for a given SVM, creates a set of so-called reduced set vectors (RSVs) which approximate the decision function. In the image classification domain, speedups of the order of 10 to 30 have been reported [2,3,5] while the full accuracy was retained.

In contrast, this work focuses on the second issue. To this end, we borrow an idea from image processing to compute fast approximations to SVM decision functions: by constraining the RSVs to be separable, they can be evaluated via separable convolutions. This works for most standard kernels (e.g. linear, polynomial, Gaussian and sigmoid) and decreases the computational complexity of the RSV evaluations from $O(h \cdot w)$ to $O(h + w)$. One of the primary target applications for this approach is face detection, an area that has seen significant progress of machine learning based systems over the last years [7,11,4,6,12,8].

2   Unconstrained Reduced Set Construction

The current section describes the reduced set method [2] on which our work is based. To simplify the notation in the following sections, image patches are written as matrices (denoted by capital letters).

Assume that an SVM has been successfully trained on the problem at hand. Let $\{\mathbf{X}_1, \dots \mathbf{X}_m\}$ denote the set of SVs, $\{\alpha_1, \dots \alpha_m\}$ the corresponding coefficients, $k(\cdot, \cdot)$ the kernel function and b the bias of the SVM solution. The decision rule for a test pattern $\mathbf{X}$ reads

$$f(\mathbf{X}) = \mathrm{sgn} \left(\sum_{i=1}^{m} y_i \alpha_i k(\mathbf{X}_i, \mathbf{X}) + b \right). \tag{1}$$

A central property of SVMs is that the decision surface induced by f corresponds to a hyperplane in the reproducing kernel Hilbert space (RKHS) associated with k [9]. The normal is given by

$$\Psi = \sum_{i=1}^{m} y_i \alpha_i k(\mathbf{X}_i, \cdot). \tag{2}$$

As the computational complexity of f scales with the number of SVs m, we can speed up its evaluation using a smaller reduced set (RS) $\{\mathbf{Z}_1, \dots \mathbf{Z}_{m'}\}$ of size $m' < m$, i.e. an approximation to Ψ of the form

$$\Psi' = \sum_{i=1}^{m'} \beta_i k(\mathbf{Z}_i, \cdot). \tag{3}$$

To find such Ψ', i.e. the $\mathbf{Z}_i$ and their corresponding expansion coefficients β_i, we fix a desired set size m' and solve

$$\min \|\Psi - \Psi'\|_{\mathrm{RKHS}}^2. \tag{4}$$

for β_i and $\mathbf{Z}_i$. Here, $\| \cdot \|_{\mathrm{RKHS}}$ denotes the Euclidian norm in the RKHS. The resulting RS decision function f' is then given by

$$f'(\mathbf{X}) = \mathrm{sgn} \left(\sum_{i=1}^{m'} \beta_i k(\mathbf{Z}_i, \mathbf{X}) + b \right).$$
(5)

In practice, $\beta_i, \mathbf{Z}_i$ are found using a gradient based optimization technique. Details are given in [2].

3   Constrained Reduced Set Construction

We now describe the concept of separable filters in image processing and show how this idea can be applied to a special class of nonlinear filters, namely those used by SVMs during classification.

3.1   Linear Separable Filters

Applying a linear filter to an image amounts to a two-dimensional convolution of the image with the impulse response of the filter. In particular, if $\mathbf{I}$ is the input image, $\mathbf{H}$ the impulse response, i.e. the filter mask, and $\mathbf{J}$ the output image, then

$$\mathbf{J} = \mathbf{I} * \mathbf{H}.$$
(6)

If $\mathbf{H}$ has size $h \times w$, the convolution requires $O(h \cdot w)$ operations for each output pixel. However, in special cases where $\mathbf{H}$ can be decomposed into two column vectors $\mathbf{a}$ and $\mathbf{b}$, such that

$$\mathbf{H} = \mathbf{a}\mathbf{b}^\top$$
(7)

holds, we can rewrite (6) as

$$\mathbf{J} = (\mathbf{I} * \mathbf{a}) * \mathbf{b}^\top,$$
(8)

since here, $\mathbf{a}\mathbf{b}^\top = \mathbf{a} * \mathbf{b}^\top$, and since the convolution is associative. This splits the original problem (6) into two convolution operations with masks of size $h \times 1$ and $1 \times w$, respectively. As a result, if a linear filter is separable in the sense of equation (7), the computational complexity of the filtering operation can be reduced from $O(w \cdot h)$ to $O(w + h)$ per pixel by computing (8) instead of (6). Note that for this to hold, the size of the image $\mathbf{I}$ is assumed to be considerably larger than h and w.

3.2   Nonlinear Separable Filters

Due to the fact that in 2D, correlation is identical with convolution if the filter mask is rotated by 180 degrees (and vice versa), we can apply the above idea to any image filter $f(\mathbf{X}) = g(c(\mathbf{H}, \mathbf{X}))$ where g is an arbitrary nonlinear function and $c(\mathbf{H}, \mathbf{X})$ denotes the correlation between images patches $\mathbf{X}$ and $\mathbf{H}$ (both of size $h \times w$). In SVMs this amounts to using a kernel of the form

$$k(\mathbf{H}, \mathbf{X}) = g(c(\mathbf{H}, \mathbf{X})). \tag{9}$$

If $\mathbf{H}$ is separable, we may split the kernel evaluation into two 1D correlations plus a scalar nonlinearity. As a result, if the RSVs in a kernel expansion such as (5) satisfy this constraint, the average computational complexity decreases from $O(m' \cdot h \cdot w)$ to $O(m' \cdot (h + w))$ per output pixel. This concept works for many off-the-shelf kernels used in SVMs. While linear, polynomial and sigmoid kernels are defined as functions of input space dot products and therefore immediately satisfy equation (9), the idea applies to kernels based on the Euclidian distance as well. For instance, the Gaussian kernel reads

$$k(\mathbf{H}, \mathbf{X}) = \exp(\gamma(c(\mathbf{X}, \mathbf{X}) - 2c(\mathbf{H}, \mathbf{X}) + c(\mathbf{H}, \mathbf{H}))). \tag{10}$$

Here, the middle term is the correlation which we are going to evaluate via separable filters. The first term is independent of the SVs. It can be efficiently pre-computed and stored in a separate image. The last term is merely a constant scalar independent of the image data. Once these quantities are known, their contribution to the computational complexity of the decision function becomes negligible.

3.3 The Proposed Method

In order to compute such separable SVM approximations, we use a constrained version of Burges' method. The idea is to restrict the RSV search space to the manifold spanned by all separable image patches, i.e. the one induced by equation (7). To this end, we replace the $\mathbf{Z}_i$ in equation (3) with $\mathbf{u}_i s_i \mathbf{v}_i^\top$. This yields

$$\Psi'' = \sum_{i=1}^{m'} \beta_i k(\mathbf{u}_i s_i \mathbf{v}_i^\top, \cdot) \tag{11}$$

where, for $h \times w$ patches, $\mathbf{u}_i$ and $\mathbf{v}_i$ are $h \times 1$ and $w \times 1$ vectors of unit length, while the scale of the RSV $\mathbf{u}_i s_i \mathbf{v}_i^\top$ is encoded in the scalar s_i. Analogously to the unconstrained case (4), we solve

$$\arg\min_{\beta, \mathbf{u}, s, \mathbf{v}} \|\Psi - \Psi''\|_{\text{RKHS}}^2 \tag{12}$$

via gradient decent. Note that during optimization, the unit length of $\mathbf{u}_i$ and $\mathbf{v}_i$ needs to be preserved. Instead of normalizing $\mathbf{u}_i$ and $\mathbf{v}_i$ after every step, we use an optimization technique for orthogonal matrices, where the $\mathbf{u}_i$ and $\mathbf{v}_i$ are updated using rotations rather than linear steps [1]. This allows us to perform relatively large steps, while $\mathbf{u}_i$ and $\mathbf{v}_i$ stay on the so-called Stiefel manifold which in our case is simply the unit sphere in $\mathbb{R}^h$ and $\mathbb{R}^w$, respectively. The derivation of the rotation matrix is somewhat technical. For detailed information about gradient decent on Stiefel manifolds, see [1].

4   Experiments

We have conducted two experiments: the first one shows the convergence of our approximations on the USPS database of handwritten digits [9]. Note that since this is usually considered a recognition task rather than a detection problem in the sense that we classify single patches as opposed to every patch within a larger image, this experiment can only illustrate effects on classification accuracy, not on speed. In contrast, the second part of this section describes how to speed up a cascade-based face detection system using the proposed method. Here, we illustrate the speedup effect which is achieved by using separable RSV approximations during early evaluation stages of the cascade.

4.1   Handwritten Digit Recognition

The USPS database contains gray level images of handwritten digits, 7291 for training and 2007 for testing. The patch size is 16×16. In this experiment we trained hard margin SVMs on three two-class problems, namely "0 vs. rest", "1 vs. rest" and "2 vs. rest", using a Gaussian kernel with $\sigma = 15$ (chosen according to [9], chapter 7). The resulting classifiers have 281, 80 and 454 SVs, respectively. Classification accuracies are measured via the area under the ROC curve (AUC), where the ROC curve plots the detection rate against the false positive rate for varying decision thresholds. Hence, an AUC equal to one amounts to perfect prediction, whereas an AUC of 0.5 is equivalent to random guessing.

Figure 1 shows the AUC of our approximations for RS sizes up to $m' = 32$. It further plots the performance of the unconstrained RS approximations as well as the full SVM classifier. We found that both unconstrained and constrained approximations converge to the full solution as m' grows. As expected, we need a larger number of separable RSVs than unconstrained RSVs to obtain the same classification accuracy. However, the next experiment will show that in a detection setting the accuracy is actually increased as soon as the number of required computations is taken into account.

4.2   Face Detection

We now give an example of how to speed up a cascade based face detection system using our method. The cascaded evaluation [6,12] of classifiers has become a popular technique for building fast object detection systems. For instance, Romdhani et al. presented an algorithm that on average uses only 2.8 RSV evaluations per scanned image position. The advantage of such systems stems from the fact that during early evaluation stages, fast detectors discard a large number of the false positives [6,12]. Hence, the overall computation time strongly depends on how much 'work' is done by these first classifiers. This suggests replacing the first stages with a separable RSV approximation that classifies equally well.

The full SVM was trained using our own face detection database. It consists of 19×19 gray value images, normalized to zero mean and unit variance. The

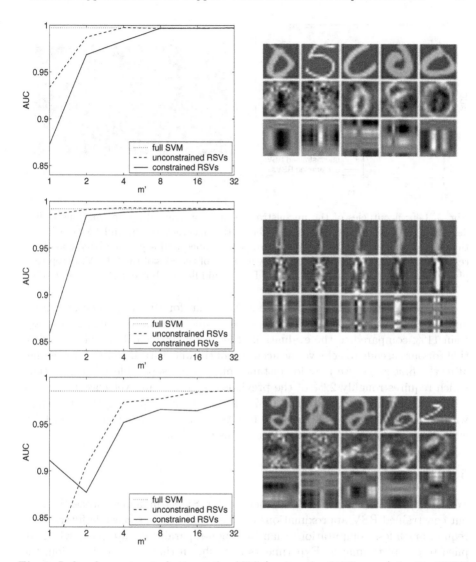

Fig. 1. Left column, top to bottom: the AUC (area under ROC curve) for the USPS classifiers "0 vs. rest", "1 vs. rest" and "2 vs. rest", respectively. For the approximations (dashed and solid lines), the size parameter m' was varied between 1 and 32. The right column shows subsets of the corresponding expansion vectors: In each figure, the top row illustrates five (randomly selected) SVs used in the full SVM, while the middle and bottom rows shows five of the unconstrained and separable RSVs, respectively.

training set contains 11204 faces and 22924 non-faces, the test set contains 1620 faces and 4541 non-faces. We used a Gaussian kernel with $\sigma = 10$, the regularization constant was set to $C = 1$. This yielded a classifier with 7190 SVs. Again, we computed RSV approximations up to size $m' = 32$, both separable and unconstrained.

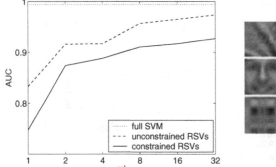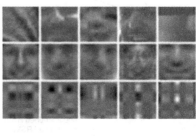

Fig. 2. Left: accuracies of the unconstrained and constrained approximations in face detection. As before, the dotted line shows the accuracy of the full SVM, whereas the dashed and solid line correspond to unconstrained and separable RSV classifiers, respectively. Right: additionally, we show a subset of the SVs of the full SVM (top row) plus five unconstrained and constrained RSVs (middle and bottom row, respectively).

The results are depicted in Figure 2. Note that for 19×19 patches, scanning an image with a separable RSV reduces the number of required operations to less than 11%, compared to the evaluation of an unconstrained RSV. This suggests that for our cascade to achieve the accuracy of the unconstrained $m' = 1$ classifier after the first stage, we may for instance plug in the separable $m' = 2$ version, which requires roughly 22% of the previous operations and yet classifies better (the AUC improves from 0.83 to 0.87). Alternatively, replacing the first stage with the separable $m' = 8$ classifier results in an AUC of 0.9 instead of 0.83, while the computational complexity remains the same.

5   Discussion

We have presented a reduced set method for SVMs in image processing. As our constrained RSV approximations can be evaluated as separable filters, they require much less computations than their non-separable counterparts when applied to complete images. Experiments have shown that for face detection, the degradation in accuracy caused by the separability constraint is more than compensated by the computational advantage. The approach is thus justified in terms of the expected speedup.

Another vital property of our approach is simplicity. By construction, it allows the use of off-the-shelf image processing libraries for separable convolutions. Since such operations are essential in image processing, there exist many — often highly optimized — implementations. Moreover, by directly working on gray values, separable RSVs can be mixed with unconstrained RSVs or SVs without affecting the homogeneity of the existing system. As a result, the required changes in existing code, such as for [6], are negligible.

We are currently integrating our method into a complete face detection system. Future work includes a comprehensive evaluation of the system as well as its extension to other detection problems such as component based object detection and interest operators. Furthermore, since SVMs are known to also yield good results in regression problems, the proposed method might provide a convenient tool for speeding up different types of image processing applications that require real-valued (as opposed to binary) outputs. As a final remark, note that separable filters can be applied to higher dimensional grid data as well (e.g. volumes or time sequences of images), providing further possible applications for our approach.

References

1. G .H. Bakir, A. Gretton, M.O. Franz, and B. Schölkopf. Multivariate regression via stiefel manifold constraints. *Proc. of the Pattern Recognition Symposium, DAGM*, 2004.
2. C. J. C. Burges. Simplified support vector decision rules. In L. Saitta, editor, *Proceedings of the 13th International Conference on Machine Learning*, pages 71–77, San Mateo, CA, 1996. Morgan Kaufmann.
3. C. J. C. Burges and B. Schölkopf. Improving the accuracy and speed of support vector learning machines. In M. Mozer, M. Jordan, and T. Petsche, editors, *Advances in Neural Information Processing Systems 9*, pages 375–381, Cambridge, MA, 1997. MIT Press.
4. B. Heisele, T. Poggio, and M. Pontil. Face detection in still gray images. Technical Report 1687, MIT A.I. Lab, 2000.
5. E. Osuna, R. Freund, and F. Girosi. Training support vector machines: An application to face detection. In *Proceedings IEEE Conference on Computer Vision and Pattern Recognition*, pages 130–136, 1997.
6. S. Romdhani, P. Torr, B. Schölkopf, and A. Blake. Fast face detection, using a sequential reduced support vector evaluation. In *Proceedings of the International Conference on Computer Vision*, 2001.
7. H. Rowley, S. Baluja, and T. Kanade. Neural network-based face detection. *IEEE Transactions on Pattern Analysis and Machine Intelligence*, 20:23–38, 1998.
8. H. Schneiderman. A statistical approach to 3d object detection applied to faces and cars. *Proceedings IEEE Conference on Computer Vision and Pattern Recognition*, 2000.
9. B. Schölkopf and A. J. Smola. *Learning with Kernels*. MIT Press, Cambridge, MA, 2002.
10. Ingo Steinwart. Sparseness of support vector machines—some asymptotically sharp bounds. In Sebastian Thrun, Lawrence Saul, and Bernhard Schölkopf, editors, *Advances in Neural Information Processing Systems 16*. MIT Press, Cambridge, MA, 2004.
11. K. Sung and T. Poggio. Example-based learning for view-based human face detection. *IEEE Transactions on Pattern Analysis and Machine Intelligence*, 20, 1998.
12. P. Viola and M. Jones. Rapid object detection using a boosted cascade of simple features. *Proceedings IEEE Conference on Computer Vision and Pattern Recognition*, 2001.

Efficient Face Detection by a Cascaded Support Vector Machine Using Haar-Like Features

Matthias Rätsch, Sami Romdhani, and Thomas Vetter

University of Basel, Computer Science Department, Bernoullistrasse 16,
CH - 4056 Basel, Switzerland
{matthias.raetsch,sami.romdhani,thomas.vetter}@unibas.ch

Abstract. In this paper, we present a novel method for reducing the computational complexity of a Support Vector Machine (SVM) classifier without significant loss of accuracy. We apply this algorithm to the problem of face detection in images. To achieve high run-time efficiency, the complexity of the classifier is made dependent on the input image patch by use of a Cascaded Reduced Set Vector expansion of the SVM. The novelty of the algorithm is that the Reduced Set Vectors have a Haar-like structure enabling a very fast SVM kernel evaluation by use of the Integral Image. It is shown in the experiments that this novel algorithm provides, for a comparable accuracy, a 200 fold speed-up over the SVM and an 6 fold speed-up over the Cascaded Reduced Set Vector Machine.

1 Introduction

Detecting a specific object in an image is a computationally expensive task, as all the pixels of the image are potential object centres. Hence all the pixels have to be classified. This is called the brute force approach and is used by all the object detection algorithms. Therefore, a method to increase the detection speed is based on a cascaded evaluation of hierarchical filters: pixels easy to discriminate are classified by simple and fast filters and pixels that resemble the object of interest are classified by more involved and slower filters. This is achieved by building a cascade of classifier of increasing complexity. In the case of face detection, if a pixel is classified as a non-face at any stage of the cascade, then the pixel is rejected and no further processing is spent on that pixel.

In the area of face detection, this method was independently introduced by Keren *et al.*[2], by Romdhani *et al.* [3] and by Viola and Jones [6]. These algorithms all use a 20×20 pixel patch around the pixel to be classified. The main difference between these approaches lies in the manner by which the hierarchical filters are obtained, and more specifically, the criterion optimised during training.

The detector from Keren *et al.* [2] assumes that the negative examples (i.e. the non-faces) are modeled by a Boltzmann distribution and that they are smooth. This assumption could increase the number of false positive in presence of a cluttered background. Here, we do not make this assumption: the negative example can be any image patch. Romdhani *et al.* [3] use a Cascaded Reduced Set Vectors expansion of a Support Vector Machine (SVM)[5]. The advantage of this detector is that it is based on an SVM classifier that is known to have optimal generalisation capabilities. Additionally, the learning stage is straightforward, automatic and does not require the manual selection of ad-hoc

C.E. Rasmussen et al. (Eds.): DAGM 2004, LNCS 3175, pp. 62–70, 2004.

parameters. At each stage of the cascade, one optimal 20×20 filter is added to the classifier. A drawback of these two methods is that the computational performances are not optimal, as at least one convolution of a 20×20 filter has to be carried out on the full image.

Viola & Jones [6] use Haar-like oriented edge filters having a block like structure enabling a very fast evaluation by use of an Integral Image. These filters are weak, in the sense that their discrimination power is low. They are selected, among a finite set, by the Ada-boost algorithm that yields the ones with the best discrimination. Then strong classifiers are produced by including several weak filters per stage using a voting mechanism. A drawback of their approach is that it is difficult to appreciate how many weak filters should be included at one stage of the cascade. Adding too many filters improves the accuracy but deteriorates the run-time performances and too few filters favours the run-time performances but decrease the accuracy. The number of filters per stage is usually set such as to reach a manually selected false positive rate. Hence it is not clear that the cascade achieves optimal performances. Practically, the training proceeds by trial and error, and often, the number of filters per stage must be manually selected so that the false positive rate decreases smoothly. Additionally, Ada-boost is a greedy algorithm that selects one filter at a time to minimise the current error. However, considering the training as an optimisation problem over both filters and thresholds, then, the greedy algorithm clearly does not result in the global optimum in general. Another drawback of the method is that the set of available filters is limited and manually selected (they have a binary block like structure), and, again, it is not clear that these filters provide the best discrimination for a given complexity. Additionally, the training of the classifier is very slow, as every filter (and there are about 10^5 of them) is evaluated on the whole set of training examples, and this is done every time a filter is added to a stage of the cascade.

In this paper, we present a novel face detection algorithm based on, and improving the run-time performance of the Cascaded Reduced Set Vector expansion of Romdhani et al. [3]. Both approaches benefit from the following features: (i) They both leverage on the guaranteed optimal generalisation performance of an SVM classifier. (ii) The SVM classifier is approximated by a Reduced Set Vector Machine (see Section 2) that provides a hierarchy of classifiers of increasing complexity. (iii) The training is fast, principled and automatic, as opposed to the Viola and Jones method. The speed bottleneck of [3] is that the Reduced Set Vectors (RSVs) are 20×20 image patches for which the pixels can take any value (see Section 2), resulting in a computationally expensive evaluation of the kernel with an image patch. Here we constraint the RSVs to have a Haar-like block structure. Then, similarly to Viola & Jones [6], we use the Integral Image to achieve very high speed-ups. So, this algorithm can be viewed as a combination of the good properties of the Romdhani et al. detector (guaranteed optimal generalisation, fast and automatic training, high accuracy) and of the Viola & Jones detector (high efficiency).

In this paper, we choose to start from an optimal detector and improve its run-time performance by making its complexity dependent on the input image patch. This is in contrast with the Viola & Jones approach that starts from a set of faster weak classi-fiers which are selected and combined to increase accuracy. This is a major conceptual distinction whose thorough theoretical comparison is still to be made.

Section 2 of this paper reviews the SVM and its Reduced Set Vector expansion. Section 3 details our novel training algorithm that constructs a Reduced Set Vectors expansion having a block-like structure. It is shown in Section 4 that the new expansion yields a comparable accuracy to the SVM while providing a significant speed-up.

2   Nonlinear Support Vector Machines and Reduced Set Expansion

Support Vector Machines (SVM), used as classifiers, are now well-known for their good generalisation capabilities. In this section, we briefly introduce them and outline the usage of an approximation of SVMs called Reduced Set Vector Machines (RVM)[4]. RVM provide a hierarchy of classifier of increasing complexity. Their use for fast face detection is demonstrated in [3].

Suppose that we have a labeled training set consisting of a series of 20×20 image patches $\mathbf{x}_i \in \mathcal{X}$ (arranged in a 400 dimensional vector) along with their class label $y_i \in \{\pm 1\}$. Support Vector classifiers implicitly map the data $\mathbf{x}_i$ into a dot product space F via a (usually nonlinear) map $\Phi : \mathcal{X} \to F$, $\mathbf{x} \mapsto \Phi(\mathbf{x})$. Often, F is referred to as the *feature space*. Although F can be high-dimensional, it is usually not necessary to explicitly work in that space [1]. There exists a class of kernels $k(\mathbf{x}, \mathbf{x}')$ which can be shown to compute the dot products in associated feature spaces, i.e. $k(\mathbf{x}, \mathbf{x}') = \langle \Phi(\mathbf{x}), \Phi(\mathbf{x}') \rangle$. It is shown in [5] that the training of a SVM classifier provides a classifier with the *largest* margin, i.e. with the *best* generalisation performances for the given training data and the given kernel. Thus, the classification of an image patch $\mathbf{x}$ by an SVM classification function, with N_s support vectors $\mathbf{x}_i$ with non-null coefficients α_i and with a threshold b, is expressed as follows:

$$y = \text{sgn}\left(\sum_i^{N_x} \alpha_i k(\mathbf{x}_i, \mathbf{x}) + b \right) \tag{1}$$

A kernel often used, and used here, is the Gaussian Radial Basis Function Kernel:

$$k(\mathbf{x}_i, \mathbf{x}) = \exp\left(\frac{-\|\mathbf{x}_i - \mathbf{x}\|^2}{2\,\sigma^2} \right) \tag{2}$$

The Support Vectors (SV) form a subset of the training vectors. The classification of one patch by an SVM is slow because there are many support vectors. The SVM can be approximated by a Reduced Set Vector (RVM) expansion [4]. We denote by $\Psi_1 \in F$, the vector normal to the separating hyperplane of the SVM, and by $\Psi'_{N_z} \in F$, the vector normal to the RVM with N_z vectors:

$$\Psi_1 = \sum_{i=1}^{N_x} \alpha_i \Phi(\mathbf{x}_i), \quad \Psi'_{N_z} = \sum_{i=1}^{N_z} \beta_i \Phi(\mathbf{z}_i), \quad \text{with } N_z \ll N_x \tag{3}$$

The $\mathbf{z}_i$ are the *Reduced Set Vectors* and are found by minimising $\|\Psi_1 - \Psi'_{N_z}\|^2$ with respect to $\mathbf{z}_i$ and to β_i. They have the particularity that they can take any values, they are not limited to be one of the training vectors, as for the support vectors. Hence, much less Reduced Set Vectors are needed to approximate the SVM. For instance, an

SVM with more than 8000 Support Vectors can be accurately approximated by an RVM with 100 Reduced Set Vectors. The second advantage of RVM is that they provide a hierarchy of classifiers. It was shown in [3] that the first Reduced Set Vector is the one that discriminates the data the most; and the second Reduced Set Vector is the one that discriminates most of the data that were mis-classified by the first Reduced Set Vector, etc. This hierarchy of classifiers is obtained by first finding β_1 and z_1 that minimises $\|\Psi_1 - \beta_1\Phi(z_1)\|^2$. Then the Reduced Set Vector k is obtained by minimising $\|\Psi_k - \beta_k\Phi(z_k)\|^2$, where $\Psi_k = \Psi_1 - \sum_{i=1}^{k-1}\beta_i\Phi(z_i)$.

Then, Romdhani $et\ al.$ used in [3] a $Cascaded\ Evaluation$y based on an early rejection principle, to that the number of Reduced Set Vectors necessary to classify a patch is, on average, much less than the number of Reduced Set Vectors, N_z. So, the classification of a patch $\mathbf{x}$ by an RVM with j Reduced Set Vector is:

$$y_j(\mathbf{x}) = \text{sgn}\left(\sum_{i=1}^{j}\beta_{j,i}k(\mathbf{x}, z_i) + b_j\right) \qquad (4)$$

This approach provides a significant speedup over the SVM (by a factor of 30), but is still not fast enough, as the image has to be convolved, at least by a 20×20 filter. The algorithm presented in this paper improves this method because it does not require to perform this convolution explicitly. Indeed, it approximates the Reduced Set Vectors by Haar-like filters and compute the evaluation of a patch using an Integral Image of the input image. An Integral Image [6] is used to compute the sum of the pixels in a rectangular area of the input image in constant time, by just four additions. They can be used to compute very efficiently the dot product of an image patch with an image that has a block-like structure, i.e. rectangles of constant values.

3 Reduced Set Vector with a Haar-Like Block Structure

As it is explained in Section 2, the speed bottleneck of the Cascaded Reduced Set Vector classifier is the computation of the kernel of a patch with a Reduced Set Vector (see Equation (4)). In the case of the Gaussian kernel, that we selected, the computational load is spent in evaluating the norm of the difference between a patch, $\mathbf{x}$ and a Reduced Set Vector, z_k (see Equation (2)). This norm can be expanded as follows:

$$\|\mathbf{x} - z_k\|^2 = \mathbf{x}'\mathbf{x} - 2\mathbf{x}'z_k + z_k'z_k \qquad (5)$$

As z_k is independent of the input image, it can be pre-computed. The sum of square of the pixels of a patch of the input image, $\mathbf{x}'\mathbf{x}$ is efficiently computed using the Integral Image of the squared pixel values of the input image. As a result, the computational load of this expression is determined by the term $\mathbf{x}'z_k$. We observe that if the Reduced Set Vector z_k has a block-like structure, similar to the Viola & Jones filters, then this operation can be evaluated very efficiently by use of the Integral Image: if z_k is an image patch with rectangles of constant (and different) grey levels then the dot product is evaluated by 4 additions per rectangle and one multiplication per grey level value (Note that many rectangles may have the same grey level). Hence we propose to approximate the SVM by a set of Reduced Vectors that do not have any values but have a block-like structure, as seen in Figure 1.

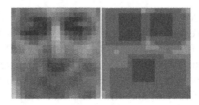

Fig. 1. First Reduced Set Vector of an SVM face classifier and its block-like approximation obtained by the learning algorithm presented in this section.

The block-like Reduced Set Vectors must (i) be a good approximation of the SVM, hence minimise $\|\Psi_1 - \Psi'_{N_z}\|$, and (ii) have a few rectangles with constant value to provide a fast evaluation. Hence, to obtain the kth Reduced Set Vector instead of minimising just $\|\Psi_k - \beta_k \Phi(\mathbf{z}_k)\|$ as in [3], we minimise the following energy with respect to β and to $\mathbf{z}_k$:

$$E_k = \|\Psi_k - \beta_k \Phi(\mathbf{z}_k)\|^2 + w(4n + v), \tag{6}$$

where n is the number of rectangles, v is the number of different grey levels in $\mathbf{z}_k$ and w is a weight that trades off the accuracy of the approximation with the run-time efficiency of the evaluation of z_k with an input patch.

To minimise the energy E_k, we use Simulated Annealing which is a global optimi-sation method. The starting value of this optimisation is the result of the minimisation of $\|\Psi_k - \beta_k \Phi(\mathbf{z}_k)\|^2$, i.e. the Reduced Vector as computed in [3]. To obtain a block-like structure the following two operations are performed, as shown in Figure 2:

1. **Quantisation:** The grey values of $\mathbf{z}_k$ are quantised into v bins. The threshold values of this quantisation are the $\frac{1}{v}$ percentiles of the grey values of $\mathbf{z}_k$. For instance if $v = 2$, then $\mathbf{z}_k$ will be approximated by 2 grey levels, and the 50% percentile is used as a threshold: the pixels of $\mathbf{z}_k$ for which the grey values are lower than the threshold are set to the mean of these pixels. The result of this quantisation on two Reduced Set Vectors is shown in the second column of Figure 2.
2. **Block structure generation:** The quantisation reduces the number of grey level values used to approximate a Reduced Set Vector $\mathbf{z}_k$, but it does not produce a block structure. To obtain a block structure two types of morphological operations are used: opening (a dilatation followed by an erosion) or closing (an erosion followed by a dilatation). The type of morphological operations applied is denoted by $M = \{\text{opening, closing}\}$, and the size of the structuring elements is denoted by S. The coordinates of the rectangles are obtained by looking for the maximum width and height of disjoined rectangular areas at the same grey level.

Simulated Annealing is used to obtain a minimum of the energy E_k by selecting the parameters v, M and S that minimises E_k. As these new Reduced Set Vectors have a Haar-like structure, we call them Haar-Reduced Set Vectors, or H-RVM.

Note that the thresholds b_i are chosen to minimise the False Rejection Rate (FRR), i.e. the number of face patches classified as non-face, using of the Receiver Operating Characteristic (ROC) (computed on the training set), as done in [3].

RSV	Quantised	After Morph. Op.	H-RSV

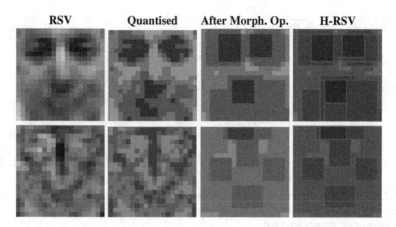

Fig. 2. Example of the Haar-like approximation of a face and an anti-face like RSV (1st *column*). 2nd *column*: discretized vectors by four gray levels, 3rd *column*: smoothed vector by morphological filters, 4th *column*: H-RSV's with computed rectangles.

3.1 Detection Process – Cascade Evaluation

Thanks to the Haar-like approximated RVM the kernel is computed very efficiently with the Integral Image. To classify an image patch, a cascaded evaluation based on an early rejection rule is used, similarly to [3]: We first approximate the hyperplane by a single H-RSV z_1, using the Equation (4). If y_1 is negative, then the patch is classified as a non-face and the evaluation stops. Otherwise the evaluation continues by incorporating the second H-RSV z_2. Then, again if it is negative, the patch is classified as a non-face and the evaluation stops. We keep on making the classifier more complex by incorporating more H-RSV's and rejecting as early as possible until a positive evaluation using the last H-RVM z_{N_z} is reached. Then the full SVM is used with (1).

4 Experimental Results

We used a training set that contains several thousand images downloaded from the World Wide Web. The training set includes 3500, 20×20, face patches and 20000 non-face patches and, the validation set, 1000 face patches, and 100,000 non-face patches. The SVM computed on the training set yielded about 8000 support vectors that we approximated by 90 Haar-like Reduced Set Vector by the method detailed in the previous section.

The first plot of Figure 3 shows the evolution of the approximation of the SVM by the RVM and by the H-RVM (in terms of the distance $\Psi - \Psi'$) as a function of the number of vectors used. It can be seen that for a given accuracy more Haar-like Reduced Set Vectors are needed to approximate the SVM than for the RVM. However, as is seen of the second plot, for a given computational load, the H-RVM rejects much more non-face patches than the RVM. This explains the improved run-time performances of the H-RVM. Additionally, it can be seen that the curve is more smooth for the H-RVM, hence a better trade-off between accuracy and speed can be obtained by the H-RVM. Figure 4 shows an example of face detection in an image using the H-RVM. As the stages in

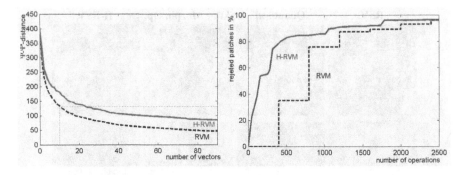

Fig. 3. Left: $\Psi_1 - \Psi'_{N_z}$ distance (*left*) as function of the number of vectors N_z for the RVM (*dashed line*, and the H-RVM (*solid line*). **Right:** Percentage of rejected non-face patches as a function of the number of operations required.

Fig. 4. Input image followed by images showing the amount of rejected pixels at the 1st, 3rd and 50th stages of the cascade. The white pixels are rejected and the darkness of a pixel is proportional to the output of the H-RVM evaluation. The penultimate image shows a box around the pixels alive at the end of the 90 H-RVM and the last image, after the full SVM is applied

the cascade increase fewer and fewer patches are evaluated. At the last H-RVM, only 5 pixels have to be classified using the full SVM.

Figure 5 shows the ROCs, computed on the validation set, of the SVM, the RVM (with 90 Reduced Set Vector) and the H-RVM (with 90 Haar-like Reduced Set Vectors). It can be seen that the accuracies of the three classifiers are similar without (left plot) and almost equal with (right plot) the final SVM classification for the remaining patches.

Table 1 compares the accuracy and the average time required to evaluate the patches of the validation set. As can be seen, the novel H-RVM approach provides a significant speed-up (200-fold over the SVM and almost 6-fold over the RVM), for no substantial loss of accuracy.

Table 1. Comparison of accuracy and speed improvement of the H-RVM to the RVM and SVM

method	FRR	FAR	time per patch in μs
SVM	1.4%	0.002%	787.34
RVM	1.5%	0.001%	22.51
H-RVM	1.4%	0.001%	3.85

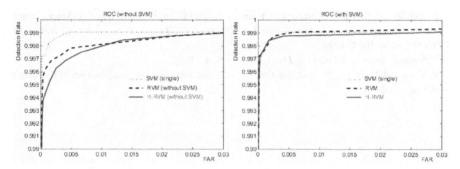

Fig. 5. ROCs for a set of the SVM, the RVM (with 90 Reduced Set Vectors) and the H-RVM (with 90 Haar-like Reduced Set Vectors) (*left*) without and (*right*) with the final SVM classification for the remaining patches. The FAR is related to non-face patches

Another source of speed-up in favour of the H-RVM over the SVM and the RVM is to detect faces, that is not shown in Table 1, so that no image pyramid is required to perform detection at several scales for the H-RVM. Indeed, thanks to the Integral Image implementation of the kernel, the classifier can be evaluated at different sizes in constant time, without having to rescale the input image.

5   Conclusion

In this paper we presented a novel efficient method for detecting faces in images. In our approach we separated the problem of finding an optimally classifying hyper-plane for separating faces from non-faces in image patches from the problem of implementing a computationally efficient representation of this optimal hyper-plane. This is in contrast to most methods where computational efficiency and classification performance are optimised simultaneously. Having obtained an hyper-plane with an optimal discrimination power but with a quite computational expensive SVM-classifier, we then concentrated on a reduction of the computational complexity for representing this hyper-plane. We developed a cascade of computationally efficient classifiers approximating the optimal hyper-plane. Computational efficiency is improved by transforming the feature vectors into block structured Haar-like vectors that can be evaluated extremely efficiently by exploiting the Integral Image method.

References

1. B. E. Boser, I. M. Guyon, and V. N. Vapnik. A training algorithm for optimal margin classifiers. In D. Haussler, editor, *Proc. of the 5th ACM Workshop on Computational Learning Theory*, pages 144–152, Pittsburgh, PA, 1992. ACM Press.
2. D. Keren, M. Osadchy, and C. Gotsman. Antifaces: a novel, fast method for image detection. *IEEE Transactions on Pattern Analysis and Machine Intelligence*, 23:747–761, July 2001.
3. S. Romdhani, P. Torr, B. Schölkopf, and A. Blake. Computationally efficient face detection. In *Proceedings of the 8th International Conference on Computer Vision*, July 2001.

4. B. Schölkopf, S. Mika, C. Burges, P. Knirsch, K.-R. Müller, G. Rätsch, and A. Smola. Input space vs. feature space in kernel-based methods. *IEEE Transactions on Neural Networks*, 10(5):1000 – 1017, 1999.
5. V. Vapnik. *Statistical Learning Theory*. Wiley, N.Y., 1998.
6. P. Viola and M. Jones. Robust real-time object detection. *International Journal of Computer Vision*, 2002.

Differential Analysis of Two Model-Based Vehicle Tracking Approaches

Hendrik Dahlkamp[1], Arthur E.C. Pece[2,3], Artur Ottlik[1], and
Hans-Hellmut Nagel[1]

[1] Institut für Algorithmen und Kognitive Systeme, Universität Karlsruhe (TH)
Postfach 6980, 76128 Karlsruhe, Germany
[2] Heimdall Vision, Bjørnsonsvej 29, DK-2500 Valby, Denmark
[3] Department of Computer Science, University of Copenhagen
Universitetsparken 1, DK-2100 Copenhagen, Denmark

Abstract. An experimental comparison of 'Edge-Element Association (EEA)' and 'Marginalized Contour (MCo)' approaches for 3D model-based vehicle tracking in traffic scenes is complicated by the different shape and motion models with which they have been implemented originally. It is shown that the steering-angle motion model originally associated with EEA allows more robust tracking than the angular-velocity motion model originally associated with MCo. Details of the shape models can also make a difference, depending on the resolution of the images. Performance differences due to the choice of motion and shape model can outweigh the differences due to the choice of the tracking algorithm. Tracking failures of the two approaches, however, usually do not happen at the same frames, which can lead to insights into the relative strengths and weaknesses of the two approaches.

1 Introduction

Detection and tracking of visible objects constitute standard challenges for the evaluation of image sequences. If the camera is stationary, then tracking by change detection (e.g. [11,7,5]) is feasible in real time, but can generate problems when the images of vehicles in a road traffic scene overlap significantly. Switching from 2D tracking in the image plane to 3D tracking in the scene domain often results in a substantially reduced failure rate, because more prior knowledge about the size and shape of objects to be tracked, their motion, and their environment, can be brought to bear.

Very few 3D model-based trackers have been developed for road vehicles. In order to understand the strengths and weaknesses of these trackers, they should be compared under a variety of driving conditions, camera geometry, illumination, and occlusion conditions. Such comparisons are complicated by the fact that differences in performance can be due to differences between initialisation methods, shape models, motion (dynamical) models, or pose-refinement methods. Pose-refinement methods can be further decomposed into the criterion used to evaluate the vehicle's pose and the method used to optimise the evaluation

C.E. Rasmussen et al. (Eds.): DAGM 2004, LNCS 3175, pp. 71–78, 2004.

criterion. Differences between pose-refinement methods are perhaps of greater scientific interest, yet differences between shape and/or motion models can be equally important for robust tracking. In the following, the term "approach" will be used as shorthand for pose-refinement method.

Here, two approaches to vehicle tracking with 3D shape and motion models are analysed: an approach based on optimising a marginalised likelihood ratio [8, 9] and an approach based on *edge-element association* [3]. A first comparison of these approaches has been reported in [1], but was carried out with two different implementations and different dynamical models. Experience with these initial experiments stimulated us to integrate modules corresponding to *each* approach *within the same system*. In this manner, the same shape and motion models can be used for both tracking approaches.

The next section outlines the test system (see also [2,10]) and the two tracking approaches. We then discuss the effects of different vehicle shape and motion models in Section 3, using the `rheinhafen` image sequence [12]. The insights gained thereby are exploited in Section 4 to compare the two approaches on a more complex image sequence (the 'dt_passat03' sequence, see [12]) with more vehicles being seen from a larger distance. Experiments have been carried out on the well-known `PETS-2000` [13] image sequence as well. Results are comparable to those obtained for the `rheinhafen` sequence and will be presented elsewhere.

2   The Approaches to Be Compared

The tracking experiments were performed within `MOTRIS` (**Mo**del-based **Tr**acking in **I**mage **S**equences), a framework implemented in Java (see, e. g., [10,2]), partially based on modules developed by other members of our laboratory and released under the GNU GPL [14]. In the experiments reported in this contribution, all vehicles were initialised interactively in order to avoid errors by automatic initialisation which might complicate the interpretation of the results.

2.1   Edge Element Association (EEA)

In the EEA approach, the boundaries between object and background in the image plane, as well as the internal boundaries of the object, are assumed to generate *edge elements* in the image. An edge element $\mathbf{e} = (u_e, v_e, \phi_e)^T$ represents a local maximum of the gradient norm in gradient direction ϕ at the position (u_e, v_e). As illustrated in Figure 1 (left), the distance measure $d_{\mathbf{m}}$ between an edge element $\mathbf{e}$ and a projected model segment $\mathbf{m}$ depends on (i) the Euclidean distance b between the edge element and the model segment and (ii) the difference Δ between the gradient direction of the edge element and the normal to the model segment:

$$d_{\mathbf{m}}(\mathbf{e}, \mathbf{x}) = \frac{b}{\cos \Delta} \quad . \tag{1}$$

It is assumed that $d_{\mathbf{m}}$ is normally distributed with zero mean and variance σ^2, implying a Mahalanobis distance which follows a $\chi^2(1)$ distribution. Edge elements which exceed the $(1 - \alpha)$ quantile of the Mahalanobis distance are rejected. Edge elements which can be assigned to several model segments are assigned to the segment associated with the smallest Mahalanobis distance. The object pose is refined by iteratively minimising the sum of squared distances between edge elements and projected model segments. Thus, the optimisation of the model pose is reduced to an iterated least-squares problem.

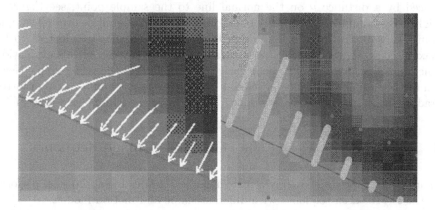

Fig. 1. Left: Edge elements and their distances from the closest model segment in the direction of the edge gradient. Right: Measurement points on the normals to the same model segment and estimated displacements for each normal, in the MCo approach.

2.2 Marginalised Contours (MCo)

The MCo approach is based on a statistical model of image generation and Maximum *a Posteriori* estimation of the vehicle pose. The principal assumptions underlying the MCo statistical model are

1. Grey value differences ΔI between adjacent pixels from the same region have a prior probability density $f_L(\Delta I)$ which is sharply peaked around zero, while grey value differences between pixels across an edge (object boundary) have a broad probability density $f_E(\Delta I)$ which may be considered to be uniform.
2. The visible object boundaries occur at distances, from the projection of the model into the image plane, which are randomly distributed with a Gaussian probability density f_D with zero mean and variance σ^2.

Assumption (1) implies that the likelihood ratio $f_E(\Delta I)/f_L(\Delta I)$ can be used as an estimator of whether a projected model edge falls between the pixels whose grey values are sampled. When assumption (2) is taken into account, it becomes necessary to integrate (marginalise) the likelihood ratios over all possible distances between projected model segments and object boundaries in the image plane. By approximating the integration with a discrete summation, we obtain an equation for the marginalised likelihood ratio r_k at a sample point k:

$$r_k = \sum_j \frac{f_E(\Delta I_{k,j})}{f_L(\Delta I_{k,j})} f_D(j\Delta\nu) \tag{2}$$

where the sum is over a number of measurement points indexed by j, equally spaced by a distance ν on the normal line to the sample point, see Figure 1 (right). By summing logarithms of marginalised likelihood ratios over all sample points k, we arrive at the evaluation function $E = \sum_k \log r_k$ which is to be maximised w.r.t. the vehicle's pose parameters. The Hessian of this evaluation function is not guaranteed to be negative definite and therefore the simple Newton method is not applicable for maximisation. However, a number of alternative gradient-based methods can be applied, for example the EM method used in [8].

3   Experiments Using the rheinhafen Image Sequence

In order to set the stage, we investigate how the two tracking approaches perform on the rheinhafen sequence with different shape and motion models.

In the original report [8], the MCo approach relied on an 'angular-velocity' motion model: the state of the vehicle to be tracked is described by position on the ground plane, orientation, tangential velocity, angular velocity, and tangential acceleration. An alternative 'steering-angle' motion model [4] was used in some of the experiments to be described in the following. This alternative includes the same state variables except for angular velocity and tangential acceleration, which are replaced by a steering angle and thus additional nonlinearities. Using the steering angle implies that the vehicle orientation change depends on the vehicle speed – this model does not allow an orientation change at zero tangential velocity. Since such a behaviour reflects driving physics more accurately, the steering angle model is expected to perform better on vehicles with changing speed.

3.1   Influence of Wheel Arches in the Vehicle Model

Initial tracking experiments indicated that the presence or absence of wheel arches constitutes an important feature of the shape model. This is confirmed by more systematic experiments.

Figure 2 illustrates the impact of the shape model for tracking of a notchback using different motion models and tracking approaches. The model has been manually optimised for this particular vehicle. Except in one case (using the EEA algorithm and the angular velocity motion model, discussed above and in Section 3.2), tracking results *improve* when using a model *with* wheel arches. The choice of the less accurate model without wheel arches leads to tracking failure for the combinations of EEA/steering angle and MCo/angular velocity.

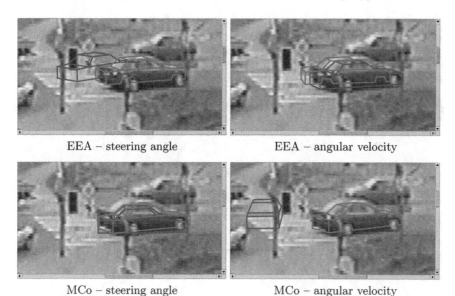

EEA – steering angle	EEA – angular velocity
MCo – steering angle	MCo – angular velocity

Fig. 2. Comparison of tracking results using vehicle model with (green) and without (red) wheel arches for a notchback at half-frame 2320 of the `rheinhafen` sequence for all combinations of tracking approaches and motion models.

3.2   Angular-Velocity Versus Steering-Angle Motion Model

Further experiments were carried out to compare the two motion models. Figure 3 shows tracking results on the same vehicle as in Figure 2 obtained for all possible combinations of tracking approaches and shape models.

As expected, introduction of the steering angle improves tracking performance. Only for the combination of the EEA tracking approach with a no-wheel-arch geometric model, the use of the steering-angle motion model leads to worse tracking results than the angular-velocity model.

Note that in all the experiments reported above, the same parameters were used for shape and motion models except, of course, for the shape parameters of the wheel arches and for the Kalman process noise associated with state variables present only in one of the two motion models.

Moreover, it can be seen that the choice of shape and motion model can outweigh the choice of the tracking approach (compare, e.g., top left panel (EEA / steering angle / wheel arches) and bottom right panel (MCo / angular velocity / no wheel arches) in Figure 2).

In conclusion, the experiments discussed so far suggest that the combination of a shape model with wheel arches and a motion model based on the steering angle - which has not been attempted before - is most efficient for model-based tracking in image sequences like those studied here.

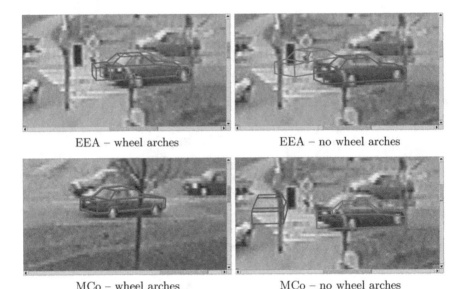

EEA – wheel arches	EEA – no wheel arches
MCo – wheel arches	MCo – no wheel arches

Fig. 3. Comparison of tracking results using steering angle (green) and angular velocity (red) motion model for a notchback at half-frame 2380 (lower left panel) and half-frame 2320 (other panels) of the `rheinhafen` sequence for all combinations of tracking approaches and shape models.

4   Experiments with a Traffic-Intersection Sequence

Figure 4 (left) shows a representative frame from the sequence 'dt_passat03' (see [12]). Here, vehicle images are smaller than in the `rheinhafen` sequence so that the presence or absence of wheel arches is no longer very important: in fact, in many cases the wheel arches can not be seen at all, due to the viewing distance and especially due to the viewing angles.

Figure 4 (right) summarises tracking results obtained by the 'optimal' combination of shape and motion models (wheel arches in the shape model and steering-angle motion model). The results obtained with either the EEA or the MCo approaches are not as good as those reported in [3]. However, this comparison is compromised by the fact that the latter results were obtained by a tracker including optical flow in addition to the EEA-approach: the integration of optical flow information reportedly leads to more robust tracking.

Vehicles 1, 6, 7, 13, and 15 are tracked successfully with the MCo approach while visible. Vehicles 1, 2, 6, 7, 9, 10, 12, 13, and 15 are tracked successfully with the EEA approach; vehicle 14 is tracked for much longer with the MCo approach, whereas vehicle 5, 9, and 10 can be tracked for much longer with the EEA approach. Tracking failures occur with both approaches for six other vehicles. Only five vehicles (1, 6, 7, 13, and 15) are tracked successfully by both approaches.

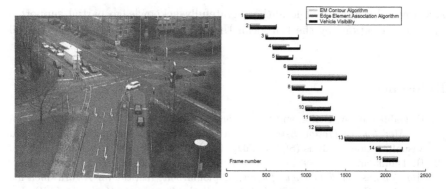

Fig. 4. Left: a typical frame of the dt_passat03 test sequence. Right: a graph illustrating the visibility of vehicles 1 to 15 as a function of frame number and the intervals during which the vehicles are successfully tracked by the EEA and MCo approaches, as determined by visual inspection.

5   Conclusions

Our experiments aim, first, at clarifying the effects of implementation alternatives and separate these effects from the effects of more fundamental assumptions underlying the two approaches under investigation; second, at gaining insight into the differential strengths and weaknesses of the two approaches when applied to challenging traffic sequences.

The experiments reported in this paper support the following conclusions:

1. Seemingly innocuous differences in the motion models used may, under certain circumstances (see Figures 2 and 3), be more important than the difference between the EEA and the MCo approaches.
2. Differences between the shape models can be more important than differences between motion models, again independently of the approach (EEA or MCo).
3. One must be careful, therefore, regarding tracking approaches carried out with different shape or motion models.
4. Similar to the results reported in [1], it is inconclusive which tracking approach performs best. The `rheinhafen` sequence seems to favor the MCo algorithm while the `dt_passat03` sequence gives an edge to the EEA approach.
5. Failures of the two approaches at different frames in the dt_passat03 sequence suggest that, even though the two approaches use the same information (grey value gradients in the image plane), a combination of their advantages might result in more robust tracking.

As a consequence, our experiments suggest to analyse the influence of other alternatives and parameter settings prior to the formulation of a 'final verdict' about a particular approach.

Acknowledgements. The authors gratefully acknowledge partial support of these investigations by the European Union FP5-project CogViSys (IST-2000-29404)

References

1. H. Dahlkamp, A. Ottlik, and H.-H. Nagel: *Comparison of Edge-driven Algorithms for Model-based Motion Estimation.* In Proc. Workshop on Spatial Coherence for Visual Motion Analysis (SCVMA'04), 15 May 2004, Prague, Czech Republic.
2. H. Dahlkamp: *Untersuchung eines Erwartungswert-Maximierung (EM)-Kontur-Algorithmus zur Fahrzeugverfolgung.* Diplomarbeit, Institut für Algorithmen und Kognitive Systeme, Fakultät für Informatik der Universität Karlsruhe (TH), Januar 2004.
3. M. Haag and H.-H. Nagel: *Combination of Edge Element and Optical Flow Estimates for 3D-Model-Based Vehicle Tracking in Traffic Image Sequences.* International Journal of Computer Vision **35**:3 (1999) 295-319.
4. H. Leuck, and H.-H. Nagel: *Automatic Differentiation Facilitates OF-Integration into Steering-Angle-Based Road Vehicle Tracking.* In: Proc. IEEE Computer Society Conference on Computer Vision and Pattern Recognition (CVPR'99), 23-25 June 1999, Fort Collins, Colorado/USA; IEEE Computer Society Press, Los Alamitos/CA, Vol. 2, pp. 360-365.
5. D.R. Magee: *Tracking Multiple Vehicles Using Foreground, Background and Motion Models.* Image and Vision Computing **22**:2 (2004) 143-155.
6. H.-H. Nagel, M. Middendorf, H. Leuck und M. Haag: *Quantitativer Vergleich zweier Kinematik-Modelle für die Verfolgung von Straßenfahrzeugen in Video-Sequenzen.* In S. Posch and H. Ritter (Hrsg.), *Dynamische Perzeption,* Proceedings in Artificial Intelligence Vol. 8, Sankt Augustin: infix 1998, pp. 71-88 (in German).
7. A. E. C. Pece: *Generative-model-based Tracking by Cluster Analysis of Image Differences.* Robotics and Autonomous Systems **39**:3-4 (2002) 181-194.
8. A.E.C. Pece and A.D. Worrall: *Tracking with the EM Contour Algorithm.* Proceedings of the 7th European Conference on Computer Vision 2002 (ECCV2002), 28-30 May 2002, Copenhagen, Denmark; A. Heyden, G. Sparr, M. Nielsen, P. Johansen (Eds.), LNCS 2350, Springer-Verlag, Berlin·Heidelberg·New York (2002), pp. 3-17.
9. A.E.C. Pece: *The Kalman-EM Contour Tracker.* Proceedings of the 3rd Workshop on Statistical and Computational Theories of Vision (SCTV 2003), 12 October 2003, Nice, France; http://www.stat.ucla.edu/~yuille/meetings/2003_workshop.php.
10. P. Reuter: *Nutzung des Optischen Flusses bei der modellgestützten Verfolgung von Fußgängern in Videobildfolgen.* Diplomarbeit, Institut für Algorithmen und Kognitive Systeme, Fakultät für Informatik der Universität Karlsruhe (TH), Oktober 2003.
11. C. Stauffer and W.E.L. Grimson: *Learning Patterns of Activity Using Real-Time Tracking.* IEEE Transactions on Pattern Analysis and Machine Intelligence (PAMI) **22**:8 (2000) 747-757.
12. http://i21www.ira.uka.de/image_sequences/
13. ftp://pets2001.cs.rdg.ac.uk/PETS2000/test_images/
14. http://kogs.iaks.uni-karlsruhe.de/motris/

Efficient Computation of Optical Flow
Using the Census Transform

Fridtjof Stein

DaimlerChrysler AG,
Research and Technology,
D-70546 Stuttgart, Germany
Fridtjof.Stein@DaimlerChrysler.com

Abstract. This paper presents an approach for the estimation of visual motion over an image sequence in real-time. A new algorithm is proposed which solves the correspondence problem between two images in a very efficient way. The method uses the Census Transform as the representation of small image patches. These primitives are matched using a table based indexing scheme. We demonstrate the robustness of this technique on real-world image sequences of a road scenario captured from a vehicle based on-board camera. We focus on the computation of the optical flow. Our method runs in real-time on general purpose platforms and handles large displacements.

1 Introduction

Recovering motion information from a visual input is a strong visual cue for understanding structure and three-dimensional motion. Visual motion allows us to compute properties of the observed three-dimensional world without the requirement of extensive knowledge about it.

In this paper we propose a strategy to efficiently determine the correspondences between consecutive image frames. The goal is to retrieve a set of promising image-to-image correspondence hypotheses. These correspondences are the basis for the computation of the optical flow. First we select a robust and descriptive primitive type. Then we match all primitives in one image with all the primitives in the consecutive image with a table based structural indexing scheme. Using structure as a means of correspondence search yields a matching method without search area limits.

This requires a computational complexity of $O(n)$ with n the number of pixels in the image. It is obvious that the number of matches has a complexity of $O(n^2)$ which is an intractable high number for a typical image with $n = \text{const} * 10^5$ pixels.

We describe a pruning technique based on *discriminative power* to reduce this complexity to $O(C * n)$. C is a small constant value. Discriminative power in this context is the descriptiveness of a primitive. The discriminative power of a primitive is inverse proportional to its occurrence frequency in an image. Temporal constraints further reduce the number of correspondence hypotheses to the resulting optical flow.

The structure of this paper is as follows: In the next section we give a brief overview of some previous work. In section 3 we discuss the feature type which we use: the Census Transform. The algorithm is presented in section 4. Section 5 explains the involved parameters. Some results illustrate the performance in section 6.

C.E. Rasmussen et al. (Eds.): DAGM 2004, LNCS 3175, pp. 79–86, 2004.
© Springer-Verlag Berlin Heidelberg 2004

2   Related Work

In recent years a large amount of different algorithms for the computation of optical flow was developed. A good overview was given by Barron et al. [1] and by Cédras et al. [2]. Barron et al. classify the optical flow techniques in four classes: differential methods, region-based matching, energy-based techniques, and phase-based approaches. All of these methods have to handle trade-offs between computational efficiency, the maximum length of the flow, the accuracy of the measurements, and the density of the flow. In order to tackle the real-time constraint (see e.g. [3,4,5,6]), several strategies were followed:

- Strong limitations on the maximum allowed translation between frames increases efficiency even for correlation based approaches.
- Image pyramids or coarse sampling lower the computational burden. E.g. using only selective features, and tracking them over an image sequence requires little computational power.
- Some methods were implemented on dedicated hardware to achieve real-time performance (see e.g. [3,6]).

Our method puts an emphasis on computational efficiency, and it allows a large span of displacement vector lengths. The accuracy is limited to pixel precision, and the density is texture driven. In areas with a lot of structural information the density is higher than in areas with little texture.

3   The Census Transformation

A very robust patch representation, the Census Operator, was introduced by Zabih and Woodfill [7]. It belongs to the class of non-parametric image transform-based matching approaches [8].

The Census Transform $R(P)$ is a non-linear transformation which maps a local neighborhood surrounding a pixel P to a binary string representing the set of neighboring pixels whose intensity is less than that of P. Each Census digit $\xi(P, P')$ is defined as

$$\xi(P, P') = \begin{matrix} 0 & P > P' \\ 1 & P \leq P' \end{matrix}$$

This is best demonstrated with an example. The left table shows the intensity values, the center table illustrates the Census values, and the right number is the corresponding clockwise unrolled *signature vector*.

124	74	32
124	64	18
157	116	84

$\rightarrow$

1	1	0
1	x	0
1	1	1

$\rightarrow$ 11001111

intensity values   Census digits   signature vector

We extended the Census Transform by introducing the parameter ε in order to represent "similar" pixel. This results in ternary signature vector digits.

$$\xi(P, P') = \begin{array}{ll} 0 & P - P' > \varepsilon \\ 1 & |P - P'| \le \varepsilon \\ 2 & P' - P > \varepsilon \end{array}$$

124	74	32
124	64	18
157	116	84

$\rightarrow$

2	1	0
2	x	0
2	2	2

$\rightarrow$ 21002222

We decided to use the Census Transform as the basic primitive due to its robustness with respect to outliers, and its simplicity to compute. In addition the Census primitive is highly discriminative. A signature vector of length c (its cardinality) represents 3^c different patches. This implicit discriminative power is the key to the proposed algorithm. The shape of the primitive, rectangular, circular, or star-like, is not significant.

While other approaches [7] use the Census Transform for correlation based matching we use it as an index into a table-based indexing scheme as described in the next section.

The correlation based approaches use the Hamming Distance for deciding whether two patches are similar. Our approach requires a Hamming Distance of zero. Therefore we lose a certain amount of "near matches" due to the binning effect. Beis and Lowe [9] discuss the issue of indexing in higher dimensions in their article. The exact analysis of this loss is part of our current research.

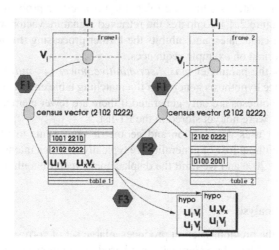

Fig. 1. The core algorithm with the resulting set of correspondence hypotheses.

4 The Algorithm

4.1 Finding Correspondences

All images are slightly low-pass filtered with a 3x3 mean filter before applying the algorithm below. All tables are implemented as hash-tables. The following steps are illustrated in Figure 1:

1. Scan image frame 1. Compute for every pixel $P_i^1 = (u_i^1, v_i^1)$ the signature $\xi(P_i^1)$.
2. The ternary $\xi(P_i^1)$ is interpreted as a decimal number and serves as the key to a table 1 in which the corresponding coordinate (u_i^1, v_i^1) is stored.

3. Scan image frame 2. Compute for every pixel $P_j^2 = (u_j^2, v_j^2)$ the signature $\xi(P_j^2)$.
4. Look for every $\xi(P_j^2)$ in table 1 whether there are one or more entries with the same signature vector.
5. All the resulting $(u_i^1, v_i^1) \leftrightarrow (u_j^2, v_j^2)$ pairs represent correspondence hypotheses.
6. If a consecutive image (e.g. in optical flow) has to be analyzed create a table 2 from all the $\xi(P_j^2)$.

It is obvious that this procedure leads to a huge amount of correspondence hypotheses. E.g. a patch with uniform intensity values and a center pixel U results in $\xi(U) = 1^c$. In our test images such uniform patches account for at least 10^4 such patches. Therefore we have to analyze at least 10^8 correspondence hypotheses.

The question is: How can we handle the explosion of the number of correspondence hypotheses?

In our work we use filters. They are labeled in Figure 1 with **F1** to **F3**.

F1 Some patch patterns do not contribute to any meaningful correspondence computation. They are filtered out early. Typical patches are the above mentioned uniform patch, or all the patches which are related to the aperture problem. An example is depicted in Figure 2. F1 compares the retrieved signature vector with a list (called the F1-list) of candidates, and inhibits the further processing if found in this table. This list is learned on example sequences.

F2 F2 introduces the parameter *max_discriminitive_power* (= mdp). F2 inhibits the correspondence hypothesis generation if a matching table entry has more than mdp elements. Hypotheses are only generated if there are fewer elements. F2 filters out patches which were not yet stored in the F1-list.

F3 The third filter uses illumination and geometric constraints to filter out unlikely hypotheses. Without loss of generality we typically allow an intensity change of the center pixel of 20% and we limit the displacement vector length to 70 pixel.

4.2   Temporal Analysis

The algorithm in the previous section produces a large set of correspondence hypotheses. They are created based on *similarity*, not based on any flow constraints. Using the correspondence hypotheses of the two previous frames (Figure 3), and attaching a certain inertia to every displacement vector, we get a geometrical continuation constraint, illustrated in Figure 4.

Such an inertia constraint filters out all flow hypotheses which have no predecessor among the correspondence matches. A valid predecessor has

- a similar direction angle,
- it is located close to the actual flow hypothesis (with respect to a moderate catch radius r as depicted in Figure 4),
- and its vector length has not changed too much.

Veenman et al. [10] address the temporal benefits extensively in their paper. It is important to note that our approach allows multiple associations as shown in Figure 5. We apply no heuristics to get a one-to-one correspondence. It is for the user to decide which interpretation serves him best.

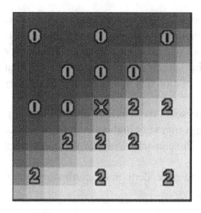

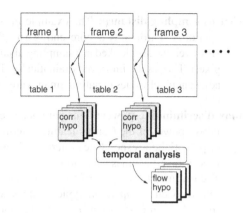

Fig. 2. Representation of an edge with the signature vector 0002 2220 0002 2220 and a frequency of occurrence of 1875 in Figure 6

Fig. 3. Using temporal constraints.

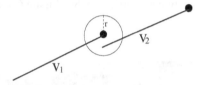

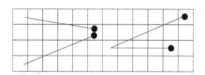

Fig. 4. Two consecutive correspondence vectors: v_1 originates from a correspondence between frame 1 and frame 2, v_2 originates from a match between frame 2 and frame 3.

Fig. 5. Multiple interpretations have to be resolved later.

5 Parameters

In the last sections several parameters were introduced. Their effect on the overall performance is as follows:

Census ε : This parameter was introduced in Section 3. ε represents the *similarity* between Census features. If $\varepsilon = 0$, the signature vector becomes more sensitive to noise. If $\varepsilon = \text{grey}_{\max}$, then $\xi(P_i) = 1^c$ for all pixel P_i. All patches have the same representation, and no discriminative power.

A typical value for 8 bit and 12 bit images is $\varepsilon = 16$.

Census cardinality c: The trade-off is discriminative power versus locality. Choosing a larger cardinality results in a patch representation with a higher discriminative power, but less locality. However, very local representation result in a high number of correspondence hypotheses.

For our road scenes we got the best results with large cardinalities (e.g. 20).

Census sampling distance: The example in Section 3 shows the design of a Census operator of cardinality 8 representing a neighborhood with a sampling distance of 1. However, we also looked at a sampling distance of 2 (skipping the adjacent neighbor pixel). The results improved dramatically. This supports an often ignored truth, that adjacent pixel values in natural images are not completely independent of each other [11].

max_discriminitive_power: This parameter represents the maximal allowed discriminitive power of the Census features. Setting it to a very high value results in a lot of potential correspondence interpretations. The constant C which was mentioned in Section 1 becomes very large.

The parameter $max\_discriminitive\_power$ is dependent on the cardinality of the selected Census Operator. Typical values are
$max\_discriminitive\_power_{c=8} = 12$, and
$max\_discriminitive\_power_{c=20} = 3$ or 2.

temporal analysis geometry constraints: Application driven we use a maximum direction angle change 10 deg, and we allow a vector length change of 30 %. The radius r is below 3 pixel.

min_age: The parameter min_age corresponds to the number of predecessors by which a flow vector is supported. We set this value typically to 1 or 2. See Figure 6 and 7 for an example.

Fig. 6. A typical road scene. The displacement vectors are color coded with respect to their length. Warmer colors denote longer vectors. The displacement vectors in the lower right corner along the reflection post have a length of 40 pixels. The parameter min_age is set to 1.

Fig. 7. The parameter min_age is set to 2. This results in fewer outliers, but also in a slightly reduced density.

6   Experimental Results

The following results on real images validate the approach. We applied to algorithm to a large set of image sequences recorded from a camera platform in a moving car. Figure 6 and Figure 7 show a frame from an image sequence of 12 bit images. in Figure 6 the parameter min_age is set to 1, in Figure 6 it is set to 2.

Notice, that even subtle distinctions on the road surface allow for the flow computation. The flow in the foreground is the flow on the hood of the car, functioning as a mirror of the scene.

Using a feature primitive type for matching always raises the question about its invariance properties. For the Census Transform the invariance with respect to translational motion is obvious. However, the signature vector is not implicitly invariant to rotational or scale transformations. We performed empirical tests on image sequences and observed the number of correspondences. We observe a graceful degradation with respect to rotation and scale. At an angle of 8 deg, or alternatively at a scale of 0.8 there are still half of the correspondences.

One of the contributions of our algorithm is its speed. The following times were measured on a 1.2 GHz Pentium III computer with our non-optimized program, implemented in C++. The scene in Figure 8 was processed. The image (frame) dimensions are 768 x 284. Every pixel was processed. The pixel depth is 8 bit.

parameter	value
cardinality	20
ε	12
min_age	2
max_discriminitive_power	2

function	time [ms]
smoothing	5
signature computation	45
table insertion	30
hypotheses generation	22

Altogether 6577 correlation hypotheses were found. The 2513 flow hypotheses are shown in Figure 8.

Fig. 8. An overtaking van. The original sequence consists of half frames. For aesthetical reasons the image is displayed vertically scaled. Notice that due to the filters **F1** and **F2** no displacements are computed along the shadow edge.

Fig. 9. Closeup from Figure 7: the aperture problem.

7 Future Research

As it can be seen in the closeup Figure 9, there are quite a few stable outliers along elongated edges. This is due to the imperfect nature of the filter F1. At the moment the adaption of the hard-coded F1-list is performed by collecting signature vectors with a high occurrence frequency. It is planned to automate this process.

At the moment we are investigating other "richer" representations of an image patch than the Census Transform. Here, richness is a synonym for discriminating power. We expect higher flow densities.

8 Summary and Conclusions

Though we present this paper in the context of optical flow, the approach serves as a general tool for pixel-precise image matching. It is applicable to other vision problems such as finding correspondences in stereo images. Due to the arithmetic-free nature of the algorithm, it has the potential of a straightforward implementation on an FPGA. For the Census operator itself this was already demonstrated in Woodfill et al. [12].

References

1. J. L. Barron, D. J. Fleet, and S. S. Beauchemin, "Performance of optical flow techniques," *International Journal of Computer Vision*, vol. 12, no. 1, pp. 43–47, 1994.
2. C. Cedras and M. Shah, "Motion-based recognition: A survey," *IVC*, vol. 13, no. 2, pp. 129–155, March 1995.
3. P. C. Arribas and F. M. H. Macia, "FPGA Implementation of Camus Correlation Optical Flow Algorithm for real-time Images," .
4. R. Cutler and M. Turk, "View-based interpretation of real-time optical flow for gesture recognition," in *Third IEEE International Conference on Automatic Face and Gesture Recognition*, Nara, Japan, April 1998.
5. T.A. Camus and H.H. Bülthoff, "Real-time optical flow extended in time," Tech. Rep. 13, Tübingen, Germany, Feb 1995.
6. W. Enkelmann, V. Gengenbach, W. Krüger, S. Rössle, and W. Tölle, "Hindernisdetektion durch Real-Zeit-Auswertung von optischen Fluß-Vektoren," in *Autonome Mobile Systeme 1994*, P. Levi and T. Bräunl, Eds., pp. 285–295. Springer, Berlin, Heidelberg, 1994.
7. R. Zabih and J. Woodfill, "Non-parametric local transforms for computing visual correspondence," in *Proceedings of the Third European Conference on Computer Vision*, Stockholm, May 1994.
8. D. Bhat and S. Nayar, "Ordinal measures for visual correspondence," 1996, pp. 351–357.
9. Jeffrey S. Beis and David G. Lowe, "Indexing without invariants in 3d object recognition," *PAMI*, vol. 21, no. 10, pp. 1000–1015, 1999.
10. C.J. Veenman, M.J.T. Reinders, and E. Backer, "Establishing motion correspondence using extended temporal scope," vol. 145, no. 1-2, pp. 227–243, April 2003.
11. E. Trucco and A. Verri, *Introductory Techniques for 3-D Computer Vision*, Prentice Hall, 1998.
12. J. Woodfill and B. Von Herzen, "Real-time stereo vision on the parts reconfigurable computer," in *Proceedings IEEE Symposium on Field-Programmable Custom Computing Machines*, Napa, April 1997.
13. J. Shi and C. Tomasi, "Good features to track," in *IEEE Conference on Computer Vision and Pattern Recognition*, Seattle, 1994, pp. 592–600.

Hybrid Model-Based Estimation of Multiple Non-dominant Motions

Arne Jacobs, Thorsten Hermes, and Otthein Herzog

University of Bremen
Center for Computing Technologies
Universitätsallee 21-23, 28359 Bremen, Germany

Abstract. The estimation of motion in videos yields information useful in the scope of video annotation, retrieval and compression. Current approaches use iterative minimization techniques based on intensity gradients in order to estimate the parameters of a 2D transform between successive frames. These approaches rely on good initial guesses of the motion parameters. For single or dominant motion there exist hybrid algorithms that estimate such initial parameters prior to the iterative minimization. We propose a technique for the generation of a set of *motion hypotheses* using blockmatching that also works in the presence of multiple non-dominant motions. These hypotheses are then refined using iterative techniques.

1 Introduction / Related Work

Motion is (besides audio) one of the major characteristics of video. Information about motion in a video can be useful in several applications, including video annotation, retrieval and compression. Mosaics built using the estimated motion can replace keyframes in video annotation and summarization [1]. The motion parameters themselves can be used as features in video retrieval or further content analysis [2]. Moreover, an efficient description of motion provides a straightforward method for compressing videos [3,4].

In this paper we will focus on the estimation of motion between two successive frames in a video. That is, given two frames, a transformation has to be found that maps points in one frame to corresponding points in the other frame. Current approaches use two-dimensional parametric motion models in order to constrain the possible number of transformations between successive frames [3, 4,5,6,7,8]. Iterative minimization techniques are applied in order to determine the motion parameters that yield the lowest intensity difference (these are also called direct techniques).

Thus, it is assumed that the intensity of a moving point remains constant over time. This assumption and the use of parametric models can cause problems in the following cases:

- The intensity of a moving point changes due to lighting changes, etc.
- Points that are visible in one frame get occluded or disappear in the other.

C.E. Rasmussen et al. (Eds.): DAGM 2004, LNCS 3175, pp. 87–94, 2004.

- The chosen model cannot sufficiently describe the given motion, e.g., if there are multiple independently moving objects.

In [4] and [5] these problems are addressed by using robust minimization techniques. Points that violate the brightness constancy assumption, occluded and differently moving points are treated as outliers and their influence on the estimation is reduced during the minimization process. Said robust methods can tolerate up to 50% of such outliers. A dominant motion component is needed for these methods to succeed.

If there are multiple moving objects in a scene (i.e., no dominant motion component can be found), other techniques have to be applied. Ayer et al. [3] propose a layered approach that explicitly models multiple motions. Using an EM-algorithm (*expectation-maximization*), their method alternately refines the layer support and the motion parameters for each layer. The number of motion layers is limited using an *minimum description length* criterion.

One general problem with the use of iterative minimization techniques is the need for good initial estimates of the motion parameters. Without such initial estimates, the algorithm may converge to local minima of the intensity error function, yielding incorrect results.

In their robust estimator, Smolic et al. [4] address this problem by using blockmatching to compute an initial translational motion estimate. This estimate is then refined to affine and parabolic motion models using direct techniques. They show that this hybrid technique produces good results in the presence of large translational motion. However, a dominant motion component is still needed for the algorithm to work. Szeliski [6] proposes a similar approach but uses phase correlation to get an initial translation estimate. The case of non-dominant multiple motions is not addressed.

Ayer et al. [3] initialize their layered algorithm with 16 layers. Each frame is divided into a 4 × 4 grid and the initial motion parameters for the 16 layers are computed by using direct robust estimation on each of the grid's subparts, starting with zero motion. Thus their approach still lacks the computation of real initial estimates without the use of iterative minimization techniques.

In the following section we propose a new technique for the generation of a set of initial translational motion estimates that is not based on iterative techniques and that does not need a dominant motion component. These initial parameters are then used as input to a direct layered approach based on [3]. Section 3 shows the results of our approach. We conclude our contribution with an outlook of our ongoing work in Sec. 4.

2   Proposed Algorithm

The proposed hybrid motion estimator is divided into two major stages. The first stage generates a set of initial translational motion estimates, called *motion hypotheses* according to [9]. These are then refined using a derivative of the layered iterative estimator described in [3]. The following sections describe the two stages in more detail. In Sec. 2.3 we will describe the computation of the *description length* that is used in both stages of the algorithm.

2.1   Generation of Motion Hypotheses

This stage is inspired by the work of Wiskott [9]. Wiskott took a dense motion field computed with a phase difference technique as input for the hypothesis generation and used the results for motion segmentation based on edge matching. He used a simple threshold to determine the number of motions. Instead, we will use a sparse motion vector field based on blockmatching and apply a *minimum description length* criterion to limit the number of motion hypotheses.

Input to this stage are two successive frames of one video shot. The central idea of the algorithm is the *motion histogram*. It measures the probability that any point moved under a certain translation between a given pair of frames. I.e., given a translation $\mathbf{t} = (t_x, t_y)^T$, the motion histogram at $\mathbf{t}$ determines the probability that any point $(x, y)^T$ in one frame moved to point $(x + t_x, y + t_y)^T$ in the other.

In our approach, we build up an approximated motion histogram using the results of a blockmatching algorithm on selected points. The use of blockmatching is motivated by the following advantages that are desirable in our case:

- It can identify arbitrary large displacements between two frames.
- It measures translation by comparing relatively small blocks, so its performance is mostly unaffected by the presence of multiple motions.
- It does not rely on good initial guesses and there are several efficient algorithms available.

The drawbacks of Blockmatching are:

- In principle, it can measure only translations.
- It is not as precise as direct iterative techniques.
- It measures translation by comparing relatively small blocks, so it suffers from the aperture and correspondence problem.

However, the first drawback does not matter in practice. This is due to the fact that in real videos, rotation and zoom between two frames are relatively small in general [10]. Furthermore, every transformation reduces to simple translations if the regarded blocks are small enough. The second drawback is acceptable as we only need rough initial motion estimates which are then refined using iterative techniques. The precision of blockmatching algorithms should generally be sufficient to get close to the desired global minimum of the error surface. For the case of dominant motion, this was shown in [4].

To cope with the third drawback, we perform blockmatching only at points where the aperture and correspondence problem reduce to an acceptable minimum. For the selection of these points we use the *Harris Detector* first introduced in [11], which was shown to be suitable for motion estimation purposes in [12]. The measure yields salient points that can be located well with blockmatching techniques.

As the similarity measure for our blockmatching we use the normalized correlation coefficient [13], with a block size of 16×16 pixels. Choosing the correlation coefficient instead of the typically used *mean squared difference* or *mean absolute difference* [14,15,16] has two reasons: The difference measures yield higher values in the case of low similarity, whereas a high correlation coefficient means greater similarity. The latter is what we need to use the results in the histogram generation. Furthermore, as pointed out in [13], the correlation coefficient can be used as a confidence measure for the match.

As the next step, the results of blockmatching on the selected points are written into the motion histogram, weighted by their similarity value. This decreases the influence of bad matches on the resulting histogram. A blockmatching vector $\mathbf{v} = (v_x, v_y)^T$ increases the value at $\mathbf{v}$ in the motion histogram by the corresponding similarity value. The spatial information of the motion vectors is totally discarded during the creation of the histogram. As a final step in the motion histogram creation, it is smoothed through convolution with a gaussian.

In practice, the blockmatching algorithm will always return some incorrect motion vectors. These errors may occur due to lighting changes or if a block lies on a motion border. Though, we expect these false vectors to be uncorrelated. In contrast, we expect the correct motion vectors to be highly correlated. This is based on the assumption that a frame contains to some extent homogenously moving regions that produce similar blockmatching results. Although we do not know which vectors are correct and which are not, the approximated motion histogram gives us an estimate of what translations really occured between two frames.

To generate our first motion hypothesis $\mathbf{h}_1$, i.e. the initial motion parameters of the first layer, we simply take the translation that corresponds to the maximum of the motion histogram. For the following hypotheses we generate new histograms, based on the previous histogram and all previous motion hypotheses. In each new histogram, the weights of the blockmatching vectors will be recalculated, depending on their contribution to the previous histogram maxima. This prevents a once found maximum to be selected again as a motion hypothesis.

The weights of the motion vectors are computed as follows: Let $\mathbf{v}_i$ be the motion vector resulting from the blockmatching with block i and be $s_i \in [0, 1]$ the corresponding similarity measure (higher values denote greater similarity). Then the weights w_{ij} used for the creation of the jth histogram are computed from $\mathbf{v}_i$, the similarity value s_i, the previous motion hypotheses $\mathbf{h}_1 \ldots \mathbf{h}_{j-1}$ and the variance σ^2 of the gaussian used for histogram smoothing:

$$
\begin{aligned}
w_{i1} &= s_i \\
w_{ij} &= s_i \cdot \left[1 - \max_{k=1\ldots j-1} e^{-\frac{(\mathbf{v}_i - \mathbf{h}_k)^2}{\sigma^2}} \right], j > 1
\end{aligned}
\tag{1}
$$

Given the vectors and the weights, the histograms are approximated by (including the gaussian smoothing):

$$
H_j(\mathbf{t}) = \sum_i w_{ij} \cdot e^{-\frac{(\mathbf{v}_i - \mathbf{t})^2}{\sigma^2}}
\tag{2}
$$

The hypothesis generation stops when the description length cannot be further decreased by adding the latest histogram maximum to the motion hypotheses. The description length is the number of bits needed to fully describe the second frame based on the first frame. The information that needs to be coded for that purpose consists of the estimated motion parameters, the layers of support for all motion components, and the residual error.

In general, the residual error will decrease with every motion hypothesis we add. In contrast, the number of bits needed to code the motion parameters and the layers of support will increase. For a motion hypothesis corresponding to real (and significant) motion, we expect the total description length to decrease [3]. Thus the later histograms, whose maxima are produced by erroneous motion vectors or correspond to insignificant motion, do not contribute any motion hypotheses. The underlying principle, called the *minimum description length* principle, is also used in the iterative refinement of the hypotheses. For its computation see Sec. 2.3.

Output of this stage is a set of translations that describe the motion between the two input frames.

2.2   Iterative Refinement

In general, the set of motion hypotheses will yield the optimal description of the motion between the two frames. For example, a simple rotation, that can be fully described by a single four-parameter-transform, is likely to produce multiple motion hypotheses. That is because the local translations caused by the rotation will vary between different parts of the frames.

We adapt the layered approach first described in [3] to refine our initial estimates and to then remove motion layers that became obsolete. Instead of the pyramidal approach described by Ayer et al., we use a complexity hierarchy like that used in [4]. Thus, instead of building gaussian pyramids of the input frames, we build up a complexity pyramid with the translational motion model on top, the four-parameter model and the affine model at intermediate levels, and the perspective model at the bottom. At each level of the pyramid, the model complexity is increased, the current motion parameters are refined and redundant motion layers are removed.

The following steps are performed at each level of the pyramid:

1. The complexity of the motion model is increased. For example, if the previous level used translations, the current level uses the four-parameter model.
2. The motion parameters and layer support are refined to minimize the intensity difference between the two input frames. This is done using an EM-algorithm that alternates the computation of the layers of support with fixed motion parameters and refines the motion parameters with fixed support layers using robust iterative minimization.
3. It is tested if the removal of a motion layer reduces the description length. If this is the case, the motion layer whose removal leads to the maximal decrease of the description length is removed. Refinement and removal are repeated until the description length cannot be further decreased.

2.3   Description Length

The description length L decomposes into three parts:

1. The number of bits L_p needed to code the motion parameters for each motion layer,
2. the number of bits L_l needed to code the layer support, i.e., the information concerning which points belong to which motion layer,
3. the number of bits L_r needed to code the residual error, i.e., the difference between the second frame and the first frame, transformed based on the motion layer information.

The motion parameters are $n \times m$ floating point values, where n is the motion model's number of parameters, e.g., $n = 6$ for the affine model, and m denotes the number of motion layers. According to [3] the number of bits needed to code these parameters with sufficient accuracy depends on the number of points p whose motion they describe. Thus, L_p is given as:

$$L_p = \frac{n \cdot m \cdot \mathrm{ld}(p)}{2} \tag{3}$$

To compute the description length of the layer support L_l, we create a membership image l such that $(l(\mathbf{x}) = j) \iff (\mathbf{x} \text{ belongs to layer } j)$. We then measure the information content of this image according to [17]. To account for spatial coherence in the motion layers, we separate all points into those who lie at the border of its motion layer (border points) and those whose neighbours all belong to the same layer (inner points). Let $p_l(j)$ be the probability of a border point belonging to the layer j. Accordingly, let p_{li} be the probability of a point being an inner point. Then the information content of the membership image and thus the description length L_l is given as:

$$L_l = p \cdot \left(-p_{li} \cdot \mathrm{ld}(p_{li}) + \sum_{j=1}^{m} -p_l(j) \cdot \mathrm{ld}(p_l(j)) \right) \tag{4}$$

The computation of the residual error description length is similar. However, spatial coherence is discounted. Let $p_r(i)$ be the probability of a point having the residual i. Assuming that the residual errors all lie in $[-255, 255]$, the description length L_r is given as:

$$L_r = \sum_{i=-255}^{255} -p_r(i) \cdot \mathrm{ld}(p_r(i)) \tag{5}$$

The total description length L is given by the sum of the three:

$$L = L_p + L_l + L_r \tag{6}$$

In the following section we will test our algorithm on real sequences and compare it to the non-hybrid direct layered approach.

3   Experimental Results

To show the benefits of the hybrid algorithm over the algorithm based only on iterative minimization, we apply it to sequences containing relatively large motion, the sequences *Horse* and *Basketball* (see Fig. 1). The first sequence

Fig. 1. From left to right: Frames one and 32 from the sequence *Horse*, Frames 7 and 50 from the sequence *Basketball*

shows a horseman galloping over a course from right to left, followed by a fast camera pan. Most frames do not contain a dominant motion component. The second sequence shows a basketball player walking on the field followed by the camera. Several frames do not contain a dominant motion component.

The results of the two approaches are compared in Fig. 2. The higher values for description length show the failure of the estimation without motion hypothesis generation. Note that in the cases where the non-hybrid algorithm converged correctly, the processing time was still approximately four times higher than with the hybrid algorithm. This is because the computation of initial parameter estimates permits the iterative minimization to start closer to the global optimum, thus leading to faster convergence.

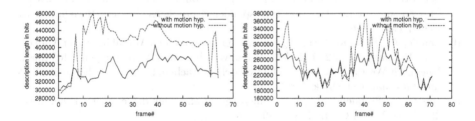

Fig. 2. Performance of the proposed algorithm on the sequences *Horse* (*left*) and *Basketball* (*right*). The results of the layered approach with (*solid line*) and without (*dashed line*) motion hypothesis generation are shown in bits needed for coding

4   Conclusions and Outlook

We have presented a hybrid algorithm for the estimation of multiple non-dominant motions. We showed that it yields superior performance compared to the non-hybrid algorithm if the need for good initial estimates is critical, e.g., in the presence of large translational motion. In other cases, our approach just reduces computation time. We are currently investigating the extension with so-called *mosaicing* techniques in order to create mosaics on scenes with multiple moving objects. This will be followed by an evaluation of the applicability of the resulting mosaics to video indexing and content retrieval.

References

1. Dammeyer, A., Jürgensen, W., Krüwel, C., Poliak, E., Ruttkowski, S., Schäfer, T., Sirava, M., Hermes, T.: Videoanalyse mit DIVA. In: Inhaltsbezogene Suche von Bildern und Videosequenzen in digitalen multimedialen Archiven; Beiträge zum Workshop auf der 22. Jahrestagung Künstliche Intelligenz (KI98), Bremen. (1998) 13–23
2. Irani, M., Anandan, P.: Video indexing based on mosaic representation. IEEE Transactions on PAMI **86** (1998) 905–921
3. Ayer, S., Sawhney, H.S.: Layered representation of motion video using robust maximum-likelihood estimation of mixture models and MDL encoding. In: ICCV. (1995) 777ff
4. Smolic, A., Sikora, T., Ohm, J.R.: Long-term global motion estimation and its application for sprite coding, content description, and segmentation. IEEE Transactions on Circuits and Systems for Video Technology **9** (1999) 1227–1242
5. Sawhney, H.S., Ayer, S., Gorkani, M.: Model-based 2D and 3D dominant motion estimation for mosaicing and video representation. In Grimson, E., ed.: International Conf. on Computer Vision, IEEE (1995) 583–590
6. Szeliski, R.: Image mosaicing for tele-reality applications. In: Proc. of the 2nd IEEE Workshop on Appplications of Computer Vision. (1994) 44–53
7. Szeliski, R.: Construction of panoramic image mosaics with global and local alignment. Internation Journal of Computer Vision **36** (2000) 101–130
8. Zelnik-Mano, L., Irani, M.: Multi-frame estimation of planar motion. IEEE Transactions on Pattern Analysis and Machine Intelligence **22** (2000) 1105–1116
9. Wiskott, L.: Segmentation from motion: Combining Gabor- and Mallat-wavelets to overcome the aperture and correspondence problems. Pattern Recognition **32** (1999) 1751–1766
10. Smolic, A.: Globale Bewegungsbeschreibung und Video Mosaiking unter Verwendung Parametrischer 2-D Modelle, Schätzverfahren und Anwendungen. PhD thesis, Rheinisch-Westfälische Technische Hochschule Aachen, Fakultät für Elektrotechnik und Informationstechnik (2000)
11. Harris, C., Stephens, M.: A combined corner and edge detector. In: Proc. of the 4th Alvey Vision Conf. (1988) 189–192
12. Shi, J., Tomasi, C.: Good features to track. In: Proc. of the Conf. on Computer Vision and Pattern Recognition, Los Alamitos, CA, USA, IEEE Computer Society Press (1994) 593–600
13. Brown, L.G.: A survey of image registration techniques. ACM Computing Surveys **24** (1992)
14. Chen, Y.S., Hung, Y.P., Fuh, C.S.: A fast block matching algorithm based on the winner-update strategy. In: Proc. of the 4th ACCV. Volume 2. (2000) 977–982
15. Cheng, K.W., Chan, S.C.: Fast block matching algorithms for motion estimation. In: Proc. of the IEEE International Conf. on Acoustics, Speech and Signal Processing. (1996) 2311–2314
16. Cheung, C.K., Po, L.M.: Normalized partial distortion search algorithm for block motion estimation. IEEE Transactions on Circuits and Systems for Video Technology **10** (2000) 417–422
17. Abmayr, W.: Einführung in die digitale Bildverarbeitung. B.G. Teubner Stuttgart (1994)

A Model of Motion, Stereo, and Monocular Depth Perception

Pierre Bayerl and Heiko Neumann

Abt. Neuroinformatik, Universität Ulm
{pierre,hneumann}@neuro.informatik.uni-ulm.de

Abstract. Visual cortical processing is segregated into pathways each consisting of several cortical areas. We identified key mechanisms of local competitive inter-action, feedforward integration and modulatory feedback as common principles of integration and segregation of ambiguous information to implement a princi-ple of evidence accumulation and feedback hypothesis testing and correction. In a previous work we demonstrated that a model of recurrent V1-MT interaction disambiguates motion estimates by filling-in. Here we show that identical mecha-nisms along the ventral V1-V2-V4 pathway are utilized for the interpretation of (1) stereoscopic disparity and (2) relative depth segregation of partially overlapping form. The results show that absolute and relative depth ambiguities are resolved by propagation of sparse depth cues. Lateral inhibition emerges at locations of unambiguous information and initiates the recurrent disambiguation process. Our simulations substantiate the proposed model with key mechanisms of integration and disambiguation in cortical form and motion processing.

1 Introduction

Feedback processing plays a crucial role in neural information processing. Many phys-iological studies substantiate the presence of feedback connections and its influence on neural activity in earlier areas [1,2]. Technically spoken, such a recurrent signal of in-formation can be interpreted as predictor from higher areas representing more reliable information due to a larger spatio-temporal context. In this work we present a general framework of bidirectional information processing, which is demonstrated to model parts of the dorsal and ventral pathway.

Model outline. We present a unified architecture to integrate visual information and resolve ambiguities for motion, stereo and monocular depth perception. The basic principles of our model have been developed in the context of shape processing and boundary completion [3,4]. The model consists of two bidirectional connected areas, each of which implements identical mechanisms, namely feedforward integration, lat-eral interaction and excitatory feedback modulation (see Fig. 1 and section "Methods"). Both model areas differ only in the size of receptive fields and the input layer. The input layer to the first model area consists of motion sensitive cells (for motion perception), of disparity sensitive cells (for binocular depth perception), or of cells sensitive to occlu-sions representing monocular cues of relative depth ordering or figure/ground separation. The activity distribution generated by the first model area projects to the second model area, which contains cells with larger receptive fields. Thus, neural activity in the latter

C.E. Rasmussen et al. (Eds.): DAGM 2004, LNCS 3175, pp. 95–102, 2004.
© Springer-Verlag Berlin Heidelberg 2004

area contains more context information and, as a consequence, is less ambiguous. In both model areas the summed output of all cells at each location (sensitive to different feature configurations) is utilized for normalization, which leads to flat tuning curves for ambiguous feature configurations, while sharp tuning curves occur for unambiguous signals [5]. Excitatory feedback modulation, in turn, acts as a predictor and serves to amplify neural activity in the previous model area, which matches the expectations of the higher model area [6]. The advantage of purely excitatory modulatory feedback is that the recurrent signal cannot generate activity in the absence of a feedforward signal and that feedforward information is not affected (inhibited) when no feedback signal is present [3,7,8]. The entire network realizes a mechanism of feedback hypothesis testing and correction in a biological plausible way, since purely excitatory back projections from higher areas to lower areas are applied [1] and only simple center-surround feedforward interaction schemes are utilized. The results demonstrate that our model is capable of processing different modalities, which substantiates our claim that we identified key mechanisms of integration and disambiguation in cortical form and motion processing.

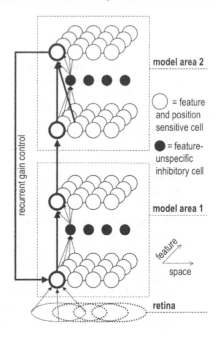

Fig. 1. Sketch of the model architecture with two bidirectionally interconnected model areas. The main difference between both model areas is the spatial size of RFs.

2   Results

Motion. We previously already presented our model for the perception of visual motion [7,9,10]. Here we only give a brief summary of computational results and the predictions arising from our simulations with motion sequences. An important detail is that feedback connections have to be shifted in order to follow the predicted signal (e.g. the target location of feedback from a cell indicating rightward motion has to be shifted to the right). Fig. 2a illustrates how initial unambiguous motion estimations are generated at line endings or junctions, while ambiguous motion is detected along elongated contrasts indicating normal flow (motion parallel to local contrast orientation; aperture problem). Consistent with physiological data [11], such ambiguities are resolved over time. Cells in the second model area (corresponding to cortical area MT) initially indicating normal flow gradually switch to finally signal the correct velocity. The spatial distance of ambiguous motion cues to unambiguous motion cues determines the time needed to propagate reliable information needed for disambiguation. Thus, the model

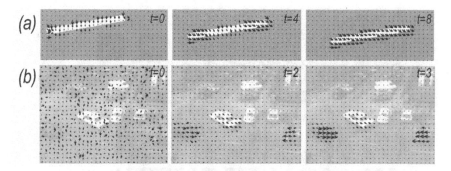

Fig. 2. Computational results processing motion sequences. (a) Example showing the solution of the aperture problem. Results obtained by processing an artificial sequence of a moving bar (220x85 pixel). Bold arrows illustrate the velocity indicated by cells in model V1 at different time steps of iterative bidirectional model V1-MT processing. Left. Initial velocity estimation is only accurate at line endings. Along elongated boundaries only normal flow, parallel to local gradient orientation can be detected (aperture problem). Center. After 4 steps of iterative feedback processing motion features at line endings have propagated inwardly to represent unambiguous motion along the boundary corresponding with the true image motion. Right. After 8 iterations motion is completely disambiguated and the correct motion is indicated for the entire object. (b) Example showing that the model also successfully processes real-world sequences (259x190 pixel).

solves the aperture problem through temporal integration in a scale invariant manner. As a consequence of feedback the motion signal in both model areas is disambiguated. We thus predict, that cells in area V1 (or at least a subset of cells in area V1) have similar temporal activity patterns as cells in MT.

We further demonstrate that our model is also capable of processing real-world images (Fig. 2b). One set of parameter settings was used for all simulations (see section "Methods").

Stereo. The perception of stereoscopic information is influenced by the correspondence of visual features in the left and right retinal images and by half-occlusions, which arise from features which are only visible from one eye [12]. Here we only consider the correspondence problem, which can be solved by applying the motion model on spatially displaced stereoscopic images instead of temporally delayed images (image sequences). To extract depth information from binocular images, the displacement of image features (disparity) from one eye to the other has to be detected. The only difference is that the detected displacements have to be interpreted as disparity instead of visual motion. Thus, the predictive feedback from the higher area has not to follow the motion signal, but instead to preserve its spatial location. We do not consider vertical disparities [13], therefore the range of detected vertical shifts was restricted to ± 1 pixel, which could arise from badly aligned stereo images. Fig. 3 shows a pair of stereo images and the detected horizontal disparities using the identical model as used for motion detection in Fig. 2 (except for minor changes mentioned above). The filling-in property, which disambiguates the motion signal in previous experiments, also disambiguates stereo cues and successfully integrates and segregates absolute depth information. Similar to results for motion processing (Fig. 2), the model is also capable of processing real-world images

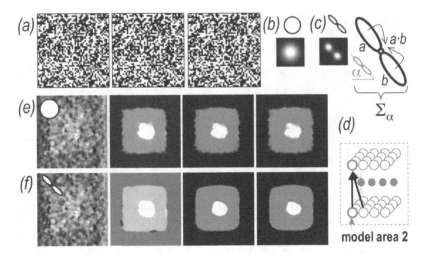

Fig. 3. Computational results processing a random dot stereogram. (a) input stimulus (100x100 pixel, left-right-left) showing a pyramidal object with three depth layers. (b) Cells with isotropic Gaussian RFs or (c) oriented bipole cells (sum over all orientations) are used to realize feedforward integration in model area 2 (d). (e-f) Results for different kinds of feedforwad information (superimposed RF icons are bigger than actual RFs). Depth indicated by cells in the first model area at different time steps of iterative bidirectional information processing (normalized gray-coded depth information, dark=far, light=near). Bipole cells (c) lead to a sharper segregation of objects lying in different depths (f) than cells with isotropic RFs (b,e).

(not shown). A modification of the model utilizes the sum of oriented bipole cells (8 orientations) [3] instead of isotropic kernels. Fig. 3f illustrate that bipole cells lead to a sharper segregation of objects lying in different depths.

Relative depth ordering. There are various monocular depth cues, such as occlusion, blurring, linear perspective, texture, shading, and size. Here we focus on relative depth from occlusions indicated by T-junctions (see Fig. 4a). Physiological studies [14] revealed that such overlay cues (combined with shape cues and binocular disparity) are utilized by cells of the ventral pathway (V1-V2-V4) to indicate border ownership. The input to our model is composed of features such as the absolute luminance gradient of the input image and T-junctions (illustrated in Fig. 4b), which were labeled manually, although this could be achieved automatically [15]. At each location there is a set of cells, sensitive to different relative depths. Initially all cells at each location with high contrast are stimulated in the same way (max. ambiguity) (see 4d, t=0). Propagation of relative depth is achieved in the same manner as for motion and stereo by isotropic Gaussian filters, except at locations with T-junctions. Here, the excitatory flow of information is restricted to follow the top of the T along object boundaries (indicated by connected white discs in Fig. 4c). Additionally, we included inhibitory connections between cells indicating the same depth located at the stem and the top of the T [16] (indicated by connected black discs in Fig. 4c, see section "Methods"). Computational results (Fig. 4d) illustrate how the model works. Remarkably, unresolvable ambiguities remain unresolved indicating multiple depths (see Fig 4d, t=150). Note, that if the number of represented depth layers is larger than the number of actual depth layers (in

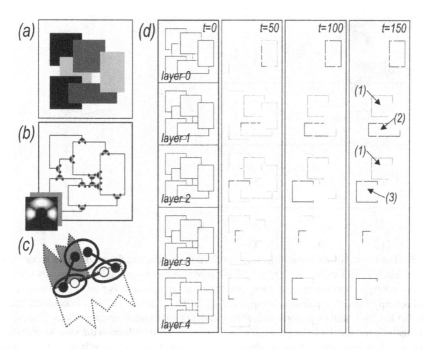

Fig. 4. Example illustrating the disambiguation of complicated depth ordering tasks. (a) input stimulus. (b) Normalized absolute luminance gradient and manually labeled occlusions (the spatial extent of receptive fields used for integration is overlaid). (c) Schematic interaction outline of subfields for cells at T-junctions. Information is guided along occluding boundaries (excitatory connection, white discs), while inhibitory connections (black discs) realize depth discontinuities (see section "Methods"). (d) Computational results at different time steps of feedback interaction. Activities of individual cells are illustrated on $n = 5$ different depth layers (light=low activitiy, dark=high activitiy). Note that unresolvable ambiguities remain unresolved, such as for the rectangle (1) for t=150, which could be located at the same depth as rectangle (2) and rectangle (3).

the stimulus), some objects are correctly represented on different contiguous depths. If the number of represented depth layers is insufficient to represent the scene, additional depth discontinuities appear along object boundaries. Our model predicts that contrast selective cells tuned to different depth layers (foreground/background) show a typical temporal development: cells located near occlusions are disambiguated earlier than cells far away from monocular depth cues. Fig. 5 shows the time course of neural activity sampled from six cell populations sensitive to figure/ground information at three different positions (1,2,3) for two different stimuli illustrating the model's temporal activity pattern.

3   Methods

The following equations describe the model dynamics of all model areas for iterative disambiguation of motion, stereo, and relative depth. We present the steady state versions

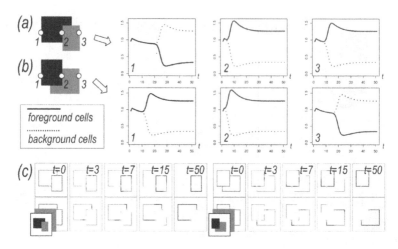

Fig. 5. Model simulations illustrating model predictions concerning figure/ground segregation of border-selective cells using $n = 2$ relative depth layers. (a,b) Two examples with locally identical contrast configurations. Activity of foreground and background cells is pooled in a small spatial neigborhood (9 pixel) at different locations (1-3). Different configurations of occlusion lead to different temporal activity patterns indicating different figure/ground segmentations. To generate more realistic temporal activity patterns, neural fatigue is realized through the same mechanisms, as for gated dipoles (see section "Methods"). (c) Activity of individual cells on different depth layers at different time steps for both examples.

of the equations used for all simulations. Differences for individual simulations or model areas are discussed below.

$v^{(1)}$ realizes the feedback modulation of the input to the model (net_{IN}) with the feedback signal from higher areas (net_{FB}). net_{EXT} is an additional external input (see below). C is a constant to control the strength of feedback and is set to $C = 100$ for model area 1 and $C = 0$ (no feedback) for model area 2 for all simulations.

$$v^{(1)} = net_{IN} \cdot (1 + C \cdot net_{FB}) + net_{EXT} \tag{1}$$

$$v^{(2)} = (v^{(1)})^2 * G_{\sigma_1}^{(\mathbf{x})} * G_{\sigma_2}^{(\mathbf{f})} \tag{2}$$

$$v^{(3)} = (v^{(2)} - B/2n \cdot \sum_{\mathbf{f}} v^{(2)}) / (0.01 + \sum_{\mathbf{f}} v^{(2)}) \tag{3}$$

$v^{(2)}$ is the result of feedforward integration. Except for stereo integration with oriented filters (see Fig. 3), feedforward integration is realized by isotropic Gaussian filters in the spatial and feature (motion or depth) domain: $\sigma_1 = 0$ (dirac) for model area 1 and $\sigma_1 \approx 7$ for model area 2; $\sigma_2 = 0.75$ for both model areas. $\mathbf{x}$ encodes the spatial location and $\mathbf{f}$ different feature configurations (e.g. velocities or depth). For stereoscopic integration with bipole cells we used the sum over all orientations $v^{(2)} = \sum_{\theta} F_{\theta}^{(\mathbf{x})} \{(v^{(1)})^2\} * G_{\sigma_1}^{(\mathbf{f})}$, where $F_{\theta}^{(\mathbf{x})}$ describes the multiplicative spatial interaction of subfields of bipole cells (see Fig. 3d).

$v^{(3)}$ describes the lateral competition, which is realized by shunting inhibition. $v^{(3)}$ is used for both, as feedback signal to earlier areas and as input to succeeding areas. n is the number of cells tuned to different features at one location. $B = 1$ for motion and stereo disambiguation and $B = 0$ for relative depth integration (B describes the subtractive part of inhibition).

For motion and stereo disambiguation the input signal net_{IN} to the first area is realized through correlation detectors [17] and $net_{EXT} = 0$. For relative depth disambiguation, the input signal net_{IN} is the normalized absolute luminance gradient (shunting inhibition), copied to n different depth layers. net_{EXT} is 0 except near T-junctions (occlusions). At T-junctions net_{EXT} is used to initiate the local disambiguation of relative depth. The possible depths indicated by neural activity patterns at the top (U) of T-junctions are used to interact with the activities in the different depth layers near the stem (L) of the T. $net_{EXT}^{U \to L}$ inhibits cells indicating impossible depths at the stem of the T according to the following formula: $net_{EXT}^{U \to L}(\mathbf{x}, n) = -f([depthlayer(\mathbf{x}, n) - depthlayer(\mathbf{x}, n - 1)]_+)$. f is a function which links the locations of the top of the T to locations of the stem of the T. Analogously, cells near the top of the T are inhibited using the following formula: $net_{EXT}^{L \to U}(\mathbf{x}, n) = -f^{-1}([depthlayer(\mathbf{x}, n) - depthlayer(\mathbf{x}, n + 1)]_+)$. The value of net_{EXT} is computed as the sum of $net_{EXT}^{U \to L}$ and $net_{EXT}^{L \to U}$. To generate the results in Fig. 5, we gated $v^{(3)}$ with an additional term, similar to those used for gated dipoles in order to simulate neural fatigue [18]. Finally a positive constant (0.4) is added to net_{EXT}.

4 Discussion and Conclusion

In this contribution we propose a general architecture for information integration and disambiguation. We demonstrate that models based on the proposed architecture are capable of processing different modalities, such as visual motion, binocular form information, and monocular depth ordering cues. We already presented and discussed our model for the integration of visual motion. Here we focused on binocular feature processing and monocular depth ordering. Compared to classical models of stereoscopic cue integration, our model could be classified as a cooperative-competitive model [19]. The feedback signal acts as ordering constraint and lateral interaction as uniqueness constraint [20]. In contrast to classical approaches we realized the spreading of information by feedback integration, while lateral interaction accounts for saliency estimations, which initiates the filling-in process. In contrast to motion and stereo stimuli, the least ambiguous relative depth ordering cues are still very ambiguous: in the presence of at least three objects a single occlusion does not yield enough information to judge if one object of interest is in the foreground or not. In contrast to motion and stereo, nearly no globally valid information can directly be extracted from initial input patterns. Thus, spreading of less ambiguous information is substantial to figure ground segmentation. Our model suggests that bidirectional processing in the ventral pathway is an indispensable process to relative depth perception. As a consequence, the model prediction of recurrent flow of information leads to impairment in figure ground segmentation tasks if feedback is suppressed. Our simulations further generate some predictions concerning the temporal development of cells selective to figure ground information or border ownership, which could be verified in cortical cells of the form path. Due to bidirectional processing, it should not matter, whether cells are observed in V1, V2 or V4. Our computational results illustrate that the same architecture is capable of processing different kinds of modalities, and thus substantiate the proposed model with key mechanisms of integration and disambiguation in cortical information processing.

References

1. Hupé, J.M., James, A.C., Girard, P., Lomber, S.G., Payne, B.R., & Bullier, J. Feedback connections act on the early part of the responses in monkey visual cortex. *J. of Neurophys.* **85** (2001) 134–145.
2. Friston, K.J., & Büchel, C. Attentional modulation of effective connectivity from V2 to V5/MT in humans. *PNAS* **97(13)** (2000) 7591–7596.
3. Neumann, H., & Sepp, W. Recurrent V1–V2 interaction in early visual boundary processing. *Biological Cybernetics* **81** (1999) 425–444.
4. Neumann, H. Completion phenomena in vision: A computational approach. In: *Filling-In – From perceptual completion to cortical reorganization*, L. Pessoa, P. De Weerd (eds.), Oxford Univ. Press, New York (2003) 151–173.
5. Simoncelli, E.P., & Heeger, D.J. A model of neuronal responses in visual area MT. *Vision Research* **38** (1998) 743–761.
6. Grossberg, S. How does a brain build a cognitive code? *Psych. Review* **87** (1980) 1–51.
7. Bayerl, P., & Neumann, H. complementary computations for motion binding, segregation and the neural solution to the aperture problem. *Perception Supplement* **32** (2003) 19-20.
8. Spratling, M.W., & Johnson, M.H. A feedback model of visual attention. *J. of Cognitive Neuroscience* **16(2)** (2004) 219-237.
9. Bayerl, P., & Neumann, H. . Disambiguating visual motion - a model of recurrent V1-MT interaction. *Eighth International Conference on Cognitive and Neural Systems (ICCNS '04)*, Boston, USA (2004) in press.
10. Bayerl, P., & Neumann, H. . Disambiguating visual motion by form-motion interaction - a computational model. *Early Cognitive Vision Workshop (ECOVISION '04)*, Isle of Skye, Scotland (2004) http://www.cn.stir.ac.uk/ecovision-ws/schedule.php.
11. Pack, C.C., & Born, R.T. Temporal dynamics of a neural solution to the aperture problem in cortical area MT. *Nature* **409** (2001) 1040–1042.
12. Egnal, G., & Wildes, R.P. Detecting binocular half-occlusions: experimental comparisons of five approaches. *Trans. on PAMI* **24(8)** (2002) 1127-1133.
13. Matthews, N., Meng, X., Xu, P., & Qian, N. A physiological theory of depth perception from vertical disparity. *Vision Research* **43** (2003) 85–99.
14. Zhou, H., Friedman, H.S., & von der Heydt, R. Coding of border ownership in monkey visual cortex. *J. of Neuroscience* **20(17)** (2000) 6594-6611.
15. Hansen, T., & Neumann, H. Neural mechanisms for the robust detection of junctions. *Neural Computation* **16(4)** (2004) in print.
16. Thielscher, A., & Neumann, H. Determining the depth of 2D surface patches using local relative depth cues in a model of local recurrent interactions. *7th Tübingen Perception Conference (TWK'04)*, Tübingen, Germany (2004) 166.
17. Adelson, E., & Bergen, J. Spatiotemporal energy models for the perception of motion. *Optical Society of America* **A 2(2)** (1985) 284-299.
18. Grossberg, S. A neural theory of punishment and avoidance, II: Quantitative theory. *Mathematical Biosciences* **15** (1972) 253–285.
19. Blake, R., & Wilson, H.R. Neural models of stereoscopic vision. *TINS* **14(10)** (1991) 445–452.
20. Marr, D., & Poggio, T. Cooperative computation of stereo disparity. *Science* **194** (1976) 283–287.

POI Detection Using Channel Clustering and the 2D Energy Tensor

Michael Felsberg[*] and Gösta Granlund

Linköping University, Computer Vision Laboratory,
SE-58183 Linköping, Sweden,
{mfe,gosta}@isy.liu.se, http://www.isy.liu.se/cvl/

Abstract. In this paper we address one of the standard problems of image processing and computer vision: The detection of points of interest (POI). We propose two new approaches for improving the detection results. First, we define an energy tensor which can be considered as a phase invariant extension of the structure tensor. Second, we use the channel representation for robustly clustering the POI information from the first step resulting in sub-pixel accuracy for the localisation of POI. We compare our method to several related approaches on a theoretical level and show a brief experimental comparison to the Harris detector.

1 Introduction

The detection of *points of interest* (POI) is a central image processing step for many computer vision systems. Object recognition systems and 3D reconstruction schemes are often based on the detection of distinct 2D features. Since the further processing often relies on the reliability of the detection and the accuracy of the localization, high requirements are put on the detection scheme. However, most systems simply use standard operators, e.g. the Harris detector [1], as a black-box without noticing some serious signal theoretic and statistical problems. The detection of POI mostly takes place in two steps:

1. The image is subject to a (mostly non-linear) operator which generates a continuous response (called *POI energy* in the sequel).

2. Relevant maxima of the POI energy are obtained by thresholds and non-maximum suppression.

In this paper we show up alternatives for both steps. The two proposed methods can be used in conjunction or separately:

1. For the generation of the POI energy we propose a new *2D energy tensor*, which can be considered as a combination of a quadrature filter and the structure tensor.

2. For the detection of relevant maxima, we propose a clustering method based on the *channel representation*, which allows to detect POI with sub-pixel accuracy and includes non-maxima suppression as a natural property of the decoding.

---

[*] This work has been supported by DFG Grant FE 583/1-2 and by EC Grant IST-2002-002013 MATRIS.

C.E. Rasmussen et al. (Eds.): DAGM 2004, LNCS 3175, pp. 103–110, 2004.
© Springer-Verlag Berlin Heidelberg 2004

The main advantages of the novel approaches are:
- phase invariance and suppression of aliasing in the POI energy,
- robustness of the detection (clustering), and
- sub-pixel accuracy.

The implementation of the proposed POI detector is straightforward and of low computational complexity. The (few) parameters have an intuitive meaning and are stable in a wide range. We describe both methods in detail in Sect. 2 and 3, respectively, and in Sect. 4 we summarise the results.

2   The Energy Tensor

In this section we introduce the 2D energy tensor. We start with briefly reviewing the 1D energy operator, which is a well known technique in the field of speech processing. We then propose a new 2D approach, the energy tensor, and relate it to several other approaches in the field of image processing.

2.1   The 1D Energy Operator

This brief review of the 1D energy operator is based on [2], but the operator was first published in [3]. The purpose of the energy operator is to compute directly the local energy of a signal, i.e., the squared magnitude of a quadrature or Gabor filter response, without computing the Hilbert transform. The shortcoming of all Hilbert transform based methods is the theoretically infinite extent of the Hilbert kernel whereas the energy operator is much more localised. Even if the quadrature filter is synthesized directly or optimized iteratively, there is a trade-off between large filter extent and phase distortions (which also imply amplitude distortions). This problem becomes even more severe in 2D.

For continuous signals $s(t)$, the energy operator is defined as

$$\Psi_c[s(t)] = [\dot{s}(t)]^2 - s(t)\ddot{s}(t) \; . \tag{1}$$

Switching to the Fourier domain, this equals

$$\int \Psi_c[s(t)] \exp(-i\omega t)\, dt = \frac{1}{2\pi}[(i\omega S(\omega)) * (i\omega S(\omega)) - S(\omega) * (-\omega^2 S(\omega))] \; , \tag{2}$$

where $S(\omega)$ is the Fourier transform of $s(t)$. If the signal is of small bandwidth, it can be approximated by an impulse spectrum $S(\omega) = A\delta(\omega - \omega_0) + \bar{A}\delta(\omega + \omega_0)$. Inserting this spectrum in the left part of (2) yields

$$\int [\dot{s}(t)]^2 \exp(-i\omega t)\, dt = \frac{-\omega_0^2}{2\pi}(A^2\delta(\omega - 2\omega_0) - 2A\bar{A}\delta(\omega) + \bar{A}^2\delta(\omega + 2\omega_0)) \; . \tag{3}$$

The right part of (2) gives the same expression, but with a positive sign for the second term $(+2A\bar{A}\delta(\omega))$, such that

$$\int \Psi_c[s(t)] \exp(-i\omega t)\, dt = \frac{2}{\pi}\omega_0^2|A|^2\delta(\omega) \; . \tag{4}$$

As it can be seen from this expression, the energy operator is phase invariant. It is important to notice that the square of the first derivative results in echo responses with frequency $2\omega_0$ which become alias components if ω_0 is larger than one fourth of the sampling frequency. For the 2D case, i.e., the structure tensor, this fact was pointed out in [4] where the author suggests to use an oversampling scheme. As it can be seen from (4), the product of signal and second derivative compensates the aliasing components which makes oversampling unnecessary.

2.2   The 2D Energy Tensor

In the literature a few attempts for definitions of a 2D energy operator can be found, see, e.g., [5]. Other related approaches are based on the idea of generalised quadrature filters using second order terms, i.e., product of filter responses, see [6,7]. All these approaches will be considered more in detail and compared to the 2D energy tensor. For continuous, 2D bandpass signals, i.e. bandpass filtered images, $b(\mathbf{x})$, $\mathbf{x} = (x, y)^T$, the 2D energy tensor is defined as

$$\Psi_c[b(\mathbf{x})] = [\nabla b(\mathbf{x})][\nabla b(\mathbf{x})]^T - b(\mathbf{x})[\mathbf{H}b(\mathbf{x})] \ , \tag{5}$$

where $\nabla = (\partial_x, \partial_y)^T$ indicates the gradient and $\mathbf{H} = \nabla\nabla^T$ indicates the Hessian. Switching to the Fourier domain, this equals

$$\int \Psi_c[b(\mathbf{x})] \exp(-i2\pi\mathbf{u}^T\mathbf{x}) \, d\mathbf{x} = 4\pi^2 \left\{ -[\mathbf{u}B(\mathbf{u})] * [\mathbf{u}B(\mathbf{u})]^T + B(\mathbf{u}) * [\mathbf{u}\mathbf{u}^T B(\mathbf{u})] \right\} \ , \tag{6}$$

where $B(\mathbf{u})$ $(\mathbf{u} = (u, v)^T)$ is the 2D Fourier transform of $b(\mathbf{x})$. If the signal is of small bandwidth, it can be approximated by an impulse spectrum $B(\mathbf{u}) = A\delta(\mathbf{u} - \mathbf{u}_0) + \bar{A}\delta(\mathbf{u} + \mathbf{u}_0)$. Inserting this spectrum in the left part of (6), i.e., the structure / orientation tensor according to [8,9], yields

$$-[\mathbf{u}B(\mathbf{u})] * [\mathbf{u}B(\mathbf{u})]^T = -\mathbf{u}_0\mathbf{u}_0^T(A^2\delta(\mathbf{u} - 2\mathbf{u}_0) - 2A\bar{A}\delta(\mathbf{u}) + \bar{A}^2\delta(\mathbf{u} + 2\mathbf{u}_0)) \ . \tag{7}$$

The right part of (6) gives the same expression, but with a positive sign for the second term $(+2A\bar{A}\delta(\mathbf{u}))$, such that

$$\int \Psi_c[b(\mathbf{x})] \exp(-i2\pi\mathbf{u}^T\mathbf{x}) \, d\mathbf{x} = 16\pi^2\mathbf{u}_0\mathbf{u}_0^T|A|^2\delta(\mathbf{u}) \ . \tag{8}$$

The energy tensor is a second order symmetric tensor like the structure tensor. The latter is included in the energy operator, but it is combined with a product of even filters, which assures the phase invariance as it can be seen in (8). The energy tensor can hence be classified as a phase invariant, orientation equivariant second order tensor [10]. Same as the 2D structure tensor, the energy operator can be converted into a complex double angle orientation descriptor [11]:

$$o(\mathbf{x}) = \Psi_c[b(\mathbf{x})]_{11} - \Psi_c[b(\mathbf{x})]_{22} + i2\Psi_c[b(\mathbf{x})]_{12} \tag{9}$$

which is equivalent to the 2D energy operator defined in [12]. As one can easily show, $|o(\mathbf{x})| = \lambda_1(\mathbf{x}) - \lambda_2(\mathbf{x})$, where $\lambda_1(\mathbf{x}) > \lambda_2(\mathbf{x})$ are the eigenvalues of the energy tensor. Since the trace of the tensor is given by the sum of eigenvalues, we obtain $2\lambda_{1,2} = \mathrm{tr}(\Psi_c[b(\mathbf{x})]) \pm |o(\mathbf{x})|$, which can be subject to the same analysis as suggested in [13,14] or for the Harris detector [1]. However, a minor problem might occur in the case of not well defined local frequencies: the second term in (5), i.e., the tensor based on even filters, can become positive, corresponding to reduced or negative eigenvalues of the energy tensor. In this case, the estimate is not reliable and should be neglected by setting the response to zero.

The operator (5) cannot be discretised directly since natural images are typically no bandpass signals. For this reason and in order to compute the derivatives for discrete data, the operator has to be regularized by a bandpass filter. For this purpose, we chose differences of Gaussian (DoG) filters since

1. Derivatives of DoG filters are easy to compute by using the Hermite polynomials.

2. Gaussian kernels are well approximated by truncation (rapid decay) or by binomial filters. They are much more localised than spherical harmonics.

Since the DoG filter is a comparably bad bandpass filter, multiple frequencies might occur. If these are not in phase, negative eigenvalues are possible. Further regions with potentially negative eigenvalues are intrinsically 2D neighborhoods. However, negative eigenvalues only occur sparsely and are easily compensated by setting the tensor to zero and by the in-filling of the subsequent processing.

Comparable to the 1D case, one could compute a 2D quadrature filter response and square its magnitude to obtain the energy (tensor). With the monogenic signal [16] a suitable approach exists which is compatible to the proposed 2D energy tensor concerning the phase model. In the monogenic signal, phase and orientation form a 3D rotation vector and invariance w.r.t. the phase results in a projection onto a circle representing the orientation. As in the 1D case, using the energy tensor instead of 2D quadrature filter is advantageous due to the better localization. The 2D pendant to the Hilbert transform is the Riesz transform, which also suffers from a polynomial decay, resulting in 2D quadrature filters with either large support or phase distortions.

2.3   Comparisons to Other Approaches

The advantage of the energy tensor compared to the structure tensor has already been mentioned above. The energy tensor avoids aliasing and is phase invariant, see also Fig. 1. A quite related approach to phase invariant operators was presented in [6]. The difference there is, however, that the Hessian of the signal is multiplied with the Laplacian of the image, which does not result in a phase invariant descriptor in a strict sense.

The approach of the boundary tensor in [7] proposes a similar combination of zero to second order terms in a tensor. However, the author proposes to use the square of the Hessian matrix for the even part of the tensor. Furthermore he makes use of spherical harmonics of even and odd orders (see also [17]) instead of Gaussian derivatives, which leads to less compact filter kernels.

Fig. 1. From left to right: detail from the image in Fig. 3, difference of the eigenvalues for the structure tensor, the second tensor in (5), and the energy tensor (divided by two). One can clearly see the echo responses for the first two tensors. The output from the energy tensor seems to be more blurred, but the applied regularisation (DoG filter with variances 1 and 2) of the derivatives was the same in all cases, which means in particular that all three responses show the same amount of rounding of corners.

The energy operator suggested in [12] is equivalent to the complex orientation descriptor of the energy tensor. By considering solely the complex descriptor, the rejection of negative eigenvalues becomes impossible. Furthermore, the authors use spherical harmonics with constant radial amplitude response, since they are interested in fringe analysis which implies small bandwidth signals. The comment on spherical harmonics above also applies in this case.

The energy operator suggested in [5] combines the 1D energy operators in x- and y-direction to compute the 2D response. Due to the missing cross-terms, this operator is not rotation invariant. It is compatible to extending quadrature filters to 2D by computing 1D filters in x- and y-direction and therefore, it corresponds to partial Hilbert transforms [18].

3   Channel Clustering of Orientation Information

As pointed out in Sect. 1, the second step for the POI detection is the clustering of the POI energy. In order to obtain robustness, we use channel smoothing (see [19] for details) of the complex orientation descriptor, modified by the test for positive eigenvalues. In the channel representation, the feature axis (here: the double angle orientation $\theta(\mathbf{x}) = \arg(o(\mathbf{x}))$) is sampled with a compact, smooth basis function (a quadratic B-spline $B_2(\cdot)$ in our case):

$$c_n(\mathbf{x}) = B_2(\theta(\mathbf{x}) - 2\pi n/N) \qquad n = 1 \ldots N \ . \tag{10}$$

The result is a pile of similarity maps, indicating the distance between the respective sampling points (channel centres) and the feature values. At every spatial position we therefore obtain an ND channel vector with non-negative entries which are large if the feature value is close to the corresponding channel centre and small (or zero) for large distances, see Fig. 2 for an example.

Channel smoothing means to average the channels along the spatial axes. Ergodicity of the channels (easier to assure than ergodicity of signals!) then implies that the channel vector at every spatial position approximates the probability density function of the feature at this position. Elementary task of the decoding process is to find the modes of this pdf in every point. In case of B-spline channels, an approximative decoding scheme is obtained by normalised convolution

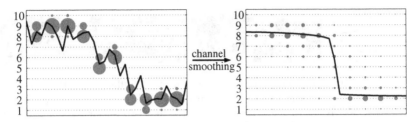

Fig. 2. Channel smoothing in 1D. Left: a noisy signal (solid line) is encoded in channels. The channel values are represented by the size of the circles. Right: after averaging the channels (along the rows), the channel vectors (column vectors) approximate the pdfs and channel decoding means to extract the modes of these pdfs. Taking the first mode in every point results in the smoothed signal (solid line).

[14] along the channel vector [19] (the spatial argument is omitted here):

$$\tilde{\theta} = \frac{2\pi}{N} \left(\frac{c_{m+1} - c_{m-1}}{c_{m-1} + c_m + c_{m+1}} + m \right) \qquad m = \mathrm{argmax}(c_{m-1} + c_m + c_{m+1}) \ . \tag{11}$$

In our particular case, we are interested in obtaining robust *orientation* estimates. Since orientation represents spatial relations, we can make use of the feature value, respective the channel centre, for choosing an anisotropic smoothing kernel, see [20]. These kernels can be learned from the autocorrelation functions of the channels by parametric or parameter-free methods. For the experiments below, we generated the kernels by optimising the parameters of a kernel which has a Gaussian function as radial amplitude response and a $\cos^2$ function as angular amplitude response (see also the 'hour-glass' filter in [4]).

Instead of extracting the first mode from the smoothed orientation channels corresponding to the main orientation, we extract the residual confidence $R = \sum_{n=1}^{N} c_n - c_{m-1} - c_m - c_{m+1}$ as POI energy. Since we use weighted channels, i.e., after the encoding the channel vectors are weighted by the difference of the eigenvalues, the confidences obtained after decoding correspond to the product of local energy and residual orientation error.

In order to get a POI list from the POI energy, we also make use of the channel representation. The orientation channels can be considered as 1D channel vectors over the spatial domain, but they can also be considered as a 3D channel representation of orientation, x-, and y-coordinate (similar to the channel representation of triplets in [21]). In this case, we consider a 3D (energy weighted) pdf, where each mode corresponds to a certain feature value at a certain spatial position. By extracting the residual confidences for the orientation, we project the (weighted) 3D pdf onto a (weighted) 2D pdf for POI. Knowing the radial shape of the averaging filters (Gaussian kernel), we can consider this instead of the quadratic B-spline to be the basis function for our 2D channel representation of the spatial position. From the basis function we obtain directly the corresponding decoding scheme to extract the modes – we can apply the same method as described above but with larger support for the normalized convolution since the Gaussian function corresponds to a B-spline of infinite degree.

Fig. 3. Left: first 75 corner features detected with the Harris detector and subsequent non-maximum suppression. Right: first 75 corner features detected with the proposed combination of energy tensor and channel clustering.

By extracting the modes, we get a sorted list of coordinates with corresponding confidences. This can be compared to performing a detection of local maxima and sorting these according to their absolute height. However, mode detection and maximum detection are not the same in general and channel decoding sorts the modes according to their robust error which is not necessarily related to the height of the maximum. Furthermore, the decoding of channels is a conceptional sound way with a statistical interpretation, i.e., it can be investigated in a statistical sense and probabilities can be calculated for the whole process. Finally, the decoding is not ad-hoc, but pre-determined by the averaging kernel which is subject to an optimisation process, i.e., the whole method is generic and adaptive.

To illustrate the results which can be achieved with the proposed method, we have run an experiment on one of the common test images for corner detection, see Fig. 3. Compared to the Harris detector, especially the higher localisation accuracy is striking. However, thorough experiments and comparisons according to [22] have to be done to verify the superior spatial localisation more in general.

4   Conclusion

We have proposed two new ingredients for POI detection algorithms: The energy tensor and the channel clustering. The energy tensor is a phase invariant and alias-free extension of the structure tensor which generalises the 1D energy operator. The channel clustering allows to detect spatially local energy concentrations by detecting them as modes of a 2D pdf, which is comparable to the detection of local maxima. Both methods have a consistent theoretic background and the performance of the implemented algorithm is superior to the Harris detector, especially concerning localisation.

References

1. Harris, C.G., Stephens, M.: A combined corner and edge detector. In: 4th Alvey Vision Conference. (1988) 147–151
2. Potamianos, A., Maragos, P.: A comparison of the energy operator and the Hilbert transform approach to signal and speech demodulation. Signal Processing **37** (1994) 95–120
3. Kaiser, J.F.: On a simple algorithm to calculate the 'energy' of a signal. In: Proc. IEEE Int'l. Conf. Acoust., Speech, Signal Processing (1990) 381–384
4. Köthe, U.: Edge and junction detection with an improved structure tensor. In 25. DAGM Symposium Mustererkennung. LNCS 2781, Springer (2003) 25–32
5. Maragos, P., Bovik, A.C., Quartieri, J.F.: A multi-dimensional energy operator for image processing. In: SPIE Conf. Visual Comm. and Image Proc. (1992) 177–186
6. Danielsson, P.E., Lin, Q.: Efficient detection of second-degree variations in 2D and 3D images. J. Visual Comm. and Image Representation **12** (2001) 255–305
7. Köthe, U.: Integrated edge and junction detection with the boundary tensor. In: Proc. of 9th Intl. Conf. on Computer Vision, Nice. Volume 1. (2003) 424–431
8. Förstner, W., Gülch, E.: A fast operator for detection and precise location of distinct points, corners and centres of circular features. In: ISPRS Intercommission Workshop, Interlaken. (1987) 149–155
9. Bigün, J., Granlund, G.H.: Optimal orientation detection of linear symmetry. In: Proc. IEEE First International Conference on Computer Vision (1987) 433–438
10. Nordberg, K.: Signal Representation and Processing using Operator Groups. PhD thesis, Linköping University, Sweden (1995) Dissertation No 366.
11. Bigün, J., Granlund, G.H., Wiklund, J.: Multidimensional orientation estimation with applications to texture analysis and optical flow. IEEE Transactions on Pattern Analysis and Machine Intelligence **13** (1991) 775–790
12. Larkin, K.G., Oldfield, M.A., Bone, D.J.: Demodulation and phase estimation of two-dimensional patterns. Australian patent AU 200110005 A1 (2001)
13. Jähne, B.: Digitale Bildverarbeitung. Springer, Berlin (1997)
14. Granlund, G.H., Knutsson, H.: Signal Processing for Computer Vision. Kluwer Academic Publishers, Dordrecht (1995)
15. Koenderink, J.J.: The structure of images. Biological Cybernetics **50** (1984) 363–370
16. Felsberg, M., Sommer, G.: The monogenic signal. IEEE Transactions on Signal Processing **49** (2001) 3136–3144
17. Felsberg, M., Sommer, G.: Image features based on a new approach to 2D rotation invariant quadrature filters. In Computer Vision - ECCV 2002. LNCS 2350, Springer (2002) 369–383
18. Hahn, S.L.: Hilbert Transforms in Signal Processing. Artech House (1996)
19. Felsberg, M., Forssén, P.E., Scharr, H.: B-spline channel smoothing for robust estimation. Tech. Rep. LiTH-ISY-R-2579, Dept. EE, Linköping University (2004)
20. Felsberg, M., Granlund, G.: Anisotropic channel filtering. In: Proc. 13th Scand. Conf. on Image Analysis. LNCS 2749, Springer (2003) 755–762
21. Granlund, G.H., Moe, A.: Unrestricted recognition of 3-d objects for robotics using multi-level triplet invariants. Artificial Intelligence Magazine (2004) to appear
22. Schmid, C., Mohr, R., Bauckhage, C.: Evaluation of interest point detectors. International Journal of Computer Vision **37** (2000) 151–172

3D Segmentation and Quantification of Human Vessels Based on a New 3D Parametric Intensity Model

Stefan Wörz and Karl Rohr

School of Information Technology, Computer Vision & Graphics Group
International University in Germany, 76646 Bruchsal
{woerz,rohr}@i-u.de

Abstract. We introduce an approach for 3D segmentation and quantification of vessels. The approach is based on a new 3D cylindrical parametric intensity model, which is directly fit to the image intensities through an incremental process based on a Kalman filter. The model has been successfully applied to segment vessels from 3D MRA images. Our experiments show that the model yields superior results in estimating the vessel radius compared to approaches based on a Gaussian model. Also, we point out general limitations in estimating the radius of thin vessels.

1 Introduction

Heart and vascular diseases are one of the main causes for the death of women and men in modern society. An abnormal narrowing of arteries (stenosis) caused by atherosclerosis is one of the main reasons for these diseases as the essential blood flow is hindered. Especially, the blocking of a coronary artery can lead to a heart attack. In clinical practice, images of the human vascular system are acquired using different imaging modalities, for example, ultrasound, magnetic resonance angiography (MRA), X-ray angiography, or ultra-fast CT. Segmentation and quantification of vessels (e.g., estimation of the radius) from these images is crucial for diagnosis, treatment, and surgical planning.

The segmentation of vessels from 3D medical images, however, is difficult and challenging. The main reasons are: 1) the thickness (radius) of vessels depends on the type of vessel (e.g., relatively small for coronary arteries and large for the aorta), 2) the thickness typically varies along the vessel, 3) the images are noisy and partially the boundaries between the vessels and surrounding tissues are difficult to recognize, and 4) in comparison to planar structures depicted in 2D images, the segmentation of curved 3D structures from 3D images is much more difficult. Previous work on vessel segmentation from 3D image data can be divided into two main classes of approaches, one based on differential measures (e.g., Koller *et al.* [6], Krissian *et al.* [7], Bullitt *et al.* [2]) and the other based on deformable models (e.g., Rueckert *et al.* [10], Noordmans and Smeulders [8], Frangi *et al.* [3], Gong *et al.* [5]). For a model-based 2D approach for measuring

C.E. Rasmussen et al. (Eds.): DAGM 2004, LNCS 3175, pp. 111–119, 2004.
© Springer-Verlag Berlin Heidelberg 2004

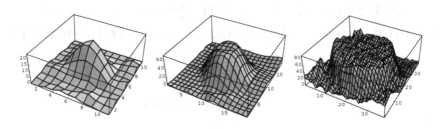

Fig. 1. Intensity plots of 2D slices of a thin vessel in the pelvis (left), the artery iliaca communis of the pelvis (middle), and the aorta (right) in 3D MR images.

intrathoracic airways see Reinhardt *et al.* [9]. The main disadvantage of differential measures is that only local image information is taken into account, and therefore these approaches are relatively sensitive to noise. On the other hand, approaches based on deformable models generally exploit contour information of the anatomical structures, often sections through vessel structures, i.e. circles or ellipses. While these approaches include more global information in comparison to differential approaches, only 2D or 3D contours are taken into account.

We have developed a new 3D parametric intensity model for the segmentation of vessels from 3D image data. This analytic model represents a cylindrical structure of variable radius and directly describes the image intensities of vessels and the surrounding tissue. In comparison to previous contour-based deformable models much more image information is taken into account which improves the robustness and accuracy of the segmentation result. In comparison to previously proposed Gaussian shaped models (e.g., [8],[5]), the new model represents a Gaussian smoothed cylinder and yields superior results for vessels of small, medium, and large sizes. Moreover, the new model has a well defined radius. In contrast, for Gaussian shaped models the radius is often heuristically defined, e.g., using the inflection point of the Gaussian function. We report experiments of successfully applying the new model to segment vessels from 3D MRA images.

2   3D Parametric Intensity Model for Tubular Structures

2.1   Analytic Description of the Intensity Structure

The intensities of vessels are often modeled by a 2D Gaussian function for a 2D cross-section or by a 3D Gaussian line (i.e. a 2D Gaussian swept along the third dimension) for a 3D volume (e.g., [8],[7],[5]). However, the intensity profile of 2D cross-sections of medium and large vessels is plateau-like (see Fig. 1), which cannot be well modeled with a 2D Gaussian function. Therefore, to more accurately model vessels of small, medium, and large sizes, we propose to use a Gaussian smoothed 3D cylinder, specified by the radius R (thickness) of the vessel segment and Gaussian smoothing σ. A 2D cross-section of this Gaussian smoothed 3D cylinder is defined as

$$g_{Disk}(x, y, R, \sigma) = \text{Disk}(x, y, R) \, * \, G_\sigma^{2D}(x, y) \tag{1}$$

where $*$ denotes the 2D convolution, Disk (x, y, R) is a two-valued function with value 1 if $r \leq R$ and 0 otherwise (for $r = \sqrt{x^2 + y^2}$), as well as the 2D Gaussian function $G_\sigma^{2D}(x, y) = G_\sigma(x)\, G_\sigma(y)$, where $G_\sigma(x) = (\sqrt{2\pi}\sigma)^{-1} e^{-\frac{x^2}{2\sigma^2}}$. By exploiting the symmetries of the disk and the 2D Gaussian function as well as the separability of the 2D convolution, we can rewrite (1) as

$$g_{Disk}(x, y, R, \sigma) = 2 \int_{-R}^{R} G_\sigma(r - \eta)\ \Phi_\sigma\left(\sqrt{R^2 - \eta^2}\right) d\eta$$
$$- (\Phi_\sigma(r + R) - \Phi_\sigma(r - R)) \tag{2}$$

using the Gaussian error function $\Phi(x) = \int_{-\infty}^{x} (2\pi)^{-1/2} e^{-\xi^2/2} d\xi$ and $\Phi_\sigma(x) = \Phi(x/\sigma)$. Unfortunately, a closed form of the integral in (2) is not known. Therefore, the exact solution of a Gaussian smoothed cylinder cannot be expressed analytically and thus is computationally expensive. Fortunately, in [1] two approximations $g_{Disk<}$ and $g_{Disk>}$ of g_{Disk} are given for the cases $R/\sigma < T_\Phi$ and $R/\sigma > T_\Phi$, respectively (using a threshold of $T_\Phi = 1$ to switch between the cases). Note that the two approximations are generally not continuous at the threshold value T_Φ. However, for our model fitting approach a continuous and smooth model function is required (see Sect. 3 for details). Therefore, based on these two approximations, we have developed a combined model using a Gaussian error function as a blending function such that for all ratios R/σ always the approximation with the lower approximation error is used. The blending function has two fixed parameters for controlling the blending effect, i.e. a threshold T_Φ which determines the ratio R/σ where the approximations are switched and a standard deviation σ_Φ which controls the smoothness of switching. We determined optimal values for both blending parameters (see Sect. 2.2 for details). The 3D cylindrical model can then be written as (using $\mathbf{x} = (x, y, z)^T$)

$$g_{Cylinder}(\mathbf{x}, R, \sigma) = g_{Disk<}(r, R, \sigma)\left(1 - \Phi_{\sigma_\Phi}\left(\frac{R}{\sigma} - T_\Phi\right)\right) +$$
$$g_{Disk>}(r, R, \sigma)\ \Phi_{\sigma_\Phi}\left(\frac{R}{\sigma} - T_\Phi\right) \tag{3}$$

where

$$g_{Disk<}(r, R, \sigma) = \frac{2R^2}{4\sigma^2 + R^2}\ e^{-\frac{2r^2}{4\sigma^2 + R^2}}\ , \tag{4}$$

$$g_{Disk>}(r, R, \sigma) = \Phi\left(\frac{c_2 - 1}{c_1} + c_1\right)\ , \tag{5}$$

$$c_1 = \frac{2}{3}\sigma\frac{\sqrt{\sigma^2 + x^2 + y^2}}{2\sigma^2 + x^2 + y^2}\ , \quad \text{and}\quad c_2 = \left(\frac{R^2}{2\sigma^2 + x^2 + y^2}\right)^{1/3}. \tag{6}$$

Fig. 2 shows 1D cross-sections (for different ratios R/σ) of the exact Gaussian smoothed cylinder g_{Disk} (numerically integrated), the two approximations $g_{Disk<}$ and $g_{Disk>}$, and our new model $g_{Cylinder}$. It can be seen that our model

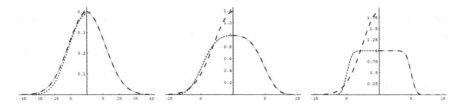

Fig. 2. For different ratios of $R/\sigma = 1.0; 3.0; 8.0$ (from left to right), the exact curve g_{Disk} of a 1D cross-section of a Gaussian smoothed disk is given (grey curve) as well as the approximations $g_{Disk<}$ and $g_{Disk>}$ (dashed resp. dotted curve for the *negative* axis) and the new model $g_{Cylinder}$ (dashed curve for the *positive* axis).

approximates the exact curve very well (see the *positive* axis). In addition, we include in our model the intensity levels a_0 (surrounding tissue) and a_1 (vessel) as well as a 3D rigid transform $\mathcal{R}$ with rotation parameters $\boldsymbol{\alpha} = (\alpha, \beta, \gamma)^T$ and translation parameters $\mathbf{t} = (x_0, y_0, z_0)^T$. This results in the parametric intensity model with a total of 10 parameters $\mathbf{p} = (R, a_0, a_1, \sigma, \alpha, \beta, \gamma, x_0, y_0, z_0)$:

$$g_{M,Cylinder}(\mathbf{x}, \mathbf{p}) = a_0 + (a_1 - a_0)\, g_{Cylinder}(\mathcal{R}(\mathbf{x}, \boldsymbol{\alpha}, \mathbf{t}), R, \sigma) \qquad (7)$$

2.2 Optimal Values T_Φ and σ_Φ for the Blending Function

In order to determine optimal values T_Φ and σ_Φ for the blending function used in (3), we computed the approximation errors of the approximations $g_{Disk<}$ and $g_{Disk>}$ for different values of $\sigma = 0.38, 0.385, \ldots, 0.8$ and fixed radius $R = 1$ (note, we can fix R as only the ratio R/σ is important). The approximation errors were numerically integrated in 2D over one quadrant of the smoothed disk (using Mathematica). From the results (see Fig. 3 left and middle) we found that the approximation errors intersect at $\sigma/R = 0.555 \pm 0.005$ in the L1-norm and at $\sigma/R = 0.605 \pm 0.005$ in the L2-norm. We here chose the mean of both intersection points as threshold, i.e. $T_\Phi = 1/0.58 \approx 1.72$. It is worth mentioning that this value for T_Φ is much better than $T_\Phi = 1$ originally proposed in [1]. For σ_Φ we chose a value of 0.1. From further experiments (not shown here) it turns out that these settings give relatively small approximation errors in both norms. It nicely turns out (see Fig. 3 left and middle) that our model not only combines the more accurate parts of both approximations but also has a lower error in the critical region close to T_Φ, where both approximations have their largest errors.

2.3 Analysis for Thin Structures

For thin cylinders, i.e. $R/\sigma < T_\Phi$, our model $g_{Cylinder}$ is basically the same as the approximation $g_{Disk<}$, which has the following remarkable property for some factor f with $0 < f \leq f_{max} = \sqrt{1 + 4\sigma^2/R^2}$:

$$a\, g_{Disk<}(r, R, \sigma) = \frac{a}{f^2}\, g_{Disk<}\left(r,\ R' = fR,\ \sigma' = \frac{1}{2}\sqrt{4\sigma^2 + R^2(1 - f^2)}\right) \qquad (8)$$

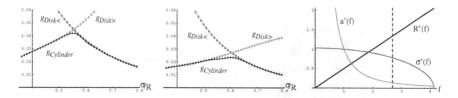

Fig. 3. For different values of $\sigma = 0.38, 0.385, \ldots, 0.8$ and radius $R = 1$, the errors of the approximations $g_{Disk<}$ and $g_{Disk>}$ (dark resp. light gray) as well as the error of the new model $g_{Cylinder}$ (black) are shown for the L1-norm (left) and L2-norm (middle). The right diagram shows $R'(f)$, $\sigma'(f)$, and $a'(f)$ for a varying factor f between 0 and f_{max} (for fixed $R = 0.5$, $\sigma = 1$, $a = 1$). The vertical dashed line indicates the ratio $f = R/\sigma = T_\Phi$, i.e. only the left part of the diagram is relevant for $g_{Disk<}$.

where a represents the contrast $a_1 - a_0$ of our model $g_{M,Cylinder}$ and $a' = a/f^2$. This means that this function is identical for different values of f, i.e. different settings of $R'(f)$, $\sigma'(f)$, and $a'(f)$ generate the same intensity structure. This relation is illustrated for one example in Fig. 3 (right). As a consequence, based on this approximation it is *not* possible to unambiguously estimate R, σ, and a from intensities representing a thin smoothed cylinder. In order to uniquely estimate the parameters we need additional information, i.e. a priori knowledge of one of the three parameters. With this information and the ambiguous estimates we are able to compute f and subsequently the remaining two parameters.

Obviously, it is unlikely that we have a priori knowledge about the radius of the vessel as the estimation of the radius is our primary task. On the other hand, even relatively accurate information about the smoothing parameter σ will not help us much as can be seen from (8) and also Fig. 3 (right): $\sigma'(f)$ is not changing much in the relevant range of f. Therefore, a small deviation in σ can result in a large deviation of f and thus gives an unreliable estimate for R. Fortunately, the opposite is the case for the contrast $a'(f)$. For given estimates $\hat{R}$ and $\hat{a}$ as well as a priori knowledge about a, we can compute $f = \sqrt{a/\hat{a}}$ and $R = \hat{R}/f = \hat{R}\sqrt{\hat{a}/a}$. For example, for an uncertainty of $\pm 10\%$ in the true contrast a the computed radius is only affected by ca. $\pm 5\%$, and for an uncertainty of -30% to $+56\%$ the computed radius is affected by less than 20%. Note, this consideration only affects thin vessels with a ratio $R/\sigma < T_\Phi = 1.72$, i.e. for typical values of $\sigma \approx 1$ voxel and thus a radius below 2 voxels, the error in estimating the radius is below 0.2 voxels even for a large uncertainty of -30% to $+56\%$.

We propose two strategies for determining a. In case we are segmenting a vessel with varying radius along the vessel, we can use the estimate of the contrast in parts of the vessel where $R/\sigma > T_\Phi$ (here the estimates of the parameters are unique) for the other parts as well. In case of a thin vessel without thicker parts we could additionally segment a larger close-by vessel for estimating the contrast, assuming that the contrast is similar in this region of the image.

Standard approaches for vessel segmentation based on a Gaussian function (e.g., [8],[7],[5]) only estimate two parameters: the image contrast a_g and a standard deviation σ_g. Assuming that the image intensities are generated by a Gaus-

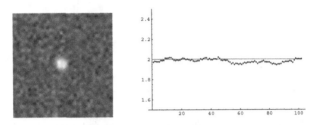

Fig. 4. Estimated radius R for 102 segments of a smoothed straight 3D cylinder with settings $R = 2$, $\sigma = 1$, $a_0 = 50$, and $a_1 = 150$ as well as added Gaussian noise ($\sigma_n = 10$). In addition, one 2D cross-section of the 3D synthetic data is shown.

sian smoothed cylinder based on $g_{Disk<}$, we can write $a_g = 2aR^2/(4\sigma^2 + R^2)$ and $\sigma_g = \sqrt{4\sigma^2 + R^2}/2$, see (4). Often, the radius of the vessel is defined by the estimated standard deviation σ_g, which implies that $\sigma = R\sqrt{3}/2$ holds. However, this is generally not the case and therefore leads to inaccurate estimates of R.

3   Incremental Vessel Segmentation and Quantification

To segment a vessel we utilize an incremental process which starts from a given point of the vessel and proceeds along the vessel. In each increment, the parameters of the cylinder segment are determined by fitting the cylindrical model in (7) to the image intensities $g(\mathbf{x})$ within a region-of-interest (ROI), thus minimizing

$$\sum_{\mathbf{x} \in \text{ROI}} \left(g_{M,Cylinder}\left(\mathbf{x}, \mathbf{p}\right) - g\left(\mathbf{x}\right) \right)^2 \tag{9}$$

For the minimization we apply the method of Levenberg-Marquardt, incorporating 1st order partial derivatives of the cylindrical model w.r.t. the model parameters. The partial derivatives can be derived analytically. The length of the cylinder segment is defined by the ROI size (in our case typically 9-21 voxels). Initial parameters for the fitting process are determined from the estimated parameters of the previous segment using a linear Kalman filter, thus the incremental scheme adjusts for varying thickness and changing direction.

4   Experimental Results

4.1   3D Synthetic Data

In total we have generated 388 synthetic 3D images of straight and curved tubular structures using Gaussian smoothed discrete cylinders and spirals (with different parameter settings, e.g., for the cylinders we used radii of $R = 1, \ldots, 9$ voxels, smoothing values of $\sigma = 0.5, 0.75, \ldots, 2$ voxels, and a contrast of 100 grey levels). We also added Gaussian noise ($\sigma_n = 0, 1, 3, 5, 10, 20$ grey levels). From the experiments we found that the approach is quite robust against noise and produces accurate results in estimating the radius as well as the other model

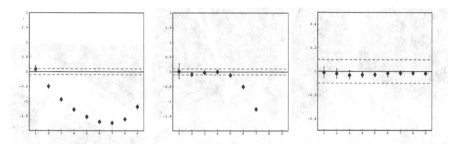

Fig. 5. Differences of the estimated radius (mean over ca. 99 segments) and the true radius for a synthetic straight cylinder with different radii $R = 1, \ldots, 9$ for the uncalibrated (left) and calibrated Gaussian line model (middle), as well as for the new cylindrical model (right). The dashed lines highlight the interval from -0.1 to 0.1 voxels.

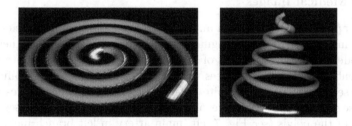

Fig. 6. Segmentation results of applying the cylindrical model to 3D synthetic data of a spiral (left) and a screw-like spiral (right). For visualization we used 3D Slicer [4].

parameters (i.e. contrast and image smoothing as well as 3D position and orientation). As an example, Fig. 4 shows the estimated radius for 102 segments of a relatively thin smoothed cylinder. The correct radius could be estimated quite accurately within ±0.06 voxels along the whole cylinder. Fig. 5 (right) shows the differences of the estimated radius to the true radius of smoothed cylinders for a range of different radii (for $\sigma = 1$ and $\sigma_n = 10$). It can be seen that the error in the estimated radius is in all cases well below 0.1 voxels. As a comparison we also applied a standard approach based on a 3D Gaussian line. To cope with the general limitations of the Gaussian line approach (see Sect. 2.3), we additionally calibrated the estimated radius (assuming an image smoothing of $\sigma = 1$, see [5] for details). It can be seen that the new approach yields a significantly more accurate result in comparison to both the uncalibrated and calibrated Gaussian line approach (Fig. 5 left and middle). Fig. 6 shows segmentation results of our new approach for a spiral and a screw-like spiral (for a radius of $R = 2$ voxels). It turns out that our new approach accurately segments curved structures of varying curvature, i.e. the estimated radius is within ±0.1 voxels to the true radius for nearly all parts of the spirals. Larger errors only occur for the last part of the innermost winding, where the curvature is relatively large.

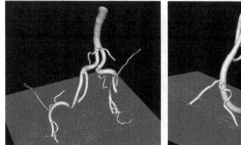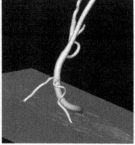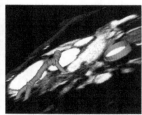

Fig. 7. Segmentation results of applying the new cylindrical model to arteries of the pelvis (left and middle) as well as to coronary arteries and the aorta (right).

4.2   3D Medical Images

With our approach both position and shape information (radius) are estimated from 3D images. Fig. 7 shows segmentation results of applying the new cylindrical model to 3D MRA images of the human pelvis and heart. Note that for the segmentation of the vessel trees we used starting points at each bifurcation. It can be seen that arteries of quite different sizes and high curvatures are successfully segmented. As a typical example, the computation time for segmenting an artery of the pelvis (see Fig. 7 left, main artery in left branch including the upper part) using a radius of the ROI of 10 voxels is just under 4min for a total of 760 segments (on a AMD Athlon PC with 1.7GHz, running Linux).

5   Discussion

The new 3D cylindrical intensity model yields accurate and robust segmentation results comprising both position and thickness information. The model allows to accurately segment 3D vessels of a large spectrum of sizes, i.e. from very thin vessels (e.g., a radius of only 1 voxel) up to relatively large arteries (e.g., a radius of 14 voxels for the aorta). Also, we pointed out general limitations in the case of thin structures and disadvantages of approaches based on a Gaussian function.

Acknowledgement. The MRA images are courtesy of Dr. med. T. Maier and Dr. C. Lienerth, Gemeinschaftspraxis Radiologie, Frankfurt/Main, Germany, as well as Prof. Dr. T. Berlage and R. Schwarz from the Fraunhofer Institute of Applied Information Technology (FIT), Sankt Augustin, Germany.

References

1. M. Abramowitz and I. Stegun, *Pocketbook of Mathematical Functions*, Verlag Harri Deutsch, 1984
2. E. Bullitt, S. Aylward, K. Smith, S. Mukherji, M.Jiroutek, K. Muller, "Symbolic Description of Intracerebral Vessels Segmented from MRA and Evaluation by Comparison with X-Ray Angiograms", *Medical Image Analysis*, 5, 2001, 157-169.
3. A. F. Frangi, W. J. Niessen, R. M. Hoogeveen, *et al.*, "Model-Based Quantitation of 3D Magnetic Resonance Angiographic Images", *T-MI*, 18:10, 1999, 946-956
4. D.T. Gering, A. Nabavi, R. Kikinis, *et al.*, "An integrated Visualization System for Surgical Planning and Guidance using Image Fusion and Interventional Imaging", *Proc. MICCAI'99*, 1999, 808-819
5. R.H. Gong, S. Wörz, and K. Rohr, "Segmentation of Coronary Arteries of the Human Heart from 3D Medical Images", *Proc. BVM'03*, 2003, 66-70
6. Th.M. Koller, G. Gerig, G. Székely, and D. Dettwiler, "Multiscale Detection of Curvilinear Structures in 2D and 3D Image Data", *Proc. ICCV'95*, 1995, 864-869
7. K. Krissian, G. Malandain, N. Ayache, R. Vaillant, and Y. Trousset, "Model Based Detection of Tubular Structures in 3D Images", *CVIU*, 80:2, 2000, 130-171
8. H.J. Noordmans, A.W.M. Smeulders, "High accuracy tracking of 2D/3D curved line structures by consecutive cross-section matching", *Pattern Recogn. Letters*, 19:1, 1998, 97-111
9. J.M. Reinhardt, N.D. D'Souza, and E.A. Hoffman, "Accurate Measurement of Intrathoracic Airways", *IEEE Trans. on Medical Imaging*, 16:6, 1997, 820-827
10. D. Rueckert, P. Burger, S.M. Forbat, R.D. Mohiaddin, G.Z. Yang, "Automatic Tracking of the Aorta in Cardiovascular MR Images Using Deformable Models", *IEEE Trans. on Medical Imaging*, 16:5, 1997, 581-590

Hierarchical Image Segmentation Based on Semidefinite Programming

Jens Keuchel, Matthias Heiler, and Christoph Schnörr

CVGPR-Group, Dept. Math. and Comp. Science
University of Mannheim, D-68131 Mannheim, Germany
{jkeuchel,heiler,schnoerr}@uni-mannheim.de
http://www.cvgpr.uni-mannheim.de

Abstract. Image segmentation based on graph representations has been a very active field of research recently. One major reason is that pairwise similarities (encoded by a graph) are also applicable in general situations where prototypical image descriptors as partitioning cues are no longer adequate. In this context, we recently proposed a novel convex programming approach for segmentation in terms of optimal graph cuts which compares favorably with alternative methods in several aspects.

In this paper we present a fully elaborated version of this approach along several directions: first, an image preprocessing method is proposed to reduce the problem size by several orders of magnitude. Furthermore, we argue that the hierarchical partition tree is a natural data structure as opposed to enforcing multiway cuts directly. In this context, we address various aspects regarding the fully automatic computation of the final segmentation. Experimental results illustrate the encouraging performance of our approach for unsupervised image segmentation.

1 Introduction

The segmentation of images into coherent parts is a key problem of computer vision. It is widely agreed that in order to properly solve this problem, both data-driven and model-driven approaches have to be taken into account [1].

Concerning the data-driven part, graph-theoretical approaches are more suited for *unsupervised* segmentation than approaches working in Euclidean spaces: as opposed to representations based on (dis-)similarity relations, class representations based on Euclidean distances (and variants) are too restrictive to capture signal variability in low-level vision [2]. This claim also appears to be supported by research on human perception [3].

The unsupervised partitioning of graphs constitutes a difficult combinatorial optimization problem. Suitable problem relaxations like the mean-field approximation [4,5] or spectral relaxation [6,7] are necessary to compromise about computational complexity and quality of approximate solutions.

Recently, a novel convex programming approach utilizing semidefinite relaxation has shown to be superior regarding optimization quality, the absence of heuristic tuning parameters, and the possibility to mathematically constrain

C.E. Rasmussen et al. (Eds.): DAGM 2004, LNCS 3175, pp. 120–128, 2004.
© Springer-Verlag Berlin Heidelberg 2004

Fig. 1. A color image from the Berkeley segmentation dataset [9] (left). Comparing the segmentation boundaries calculated with the semidefinite programming relaxation (right) to the human segmentations (middle), the high quality of the SDP relaxation result is reflected by a high F-measure (see Section 5) of 0.92.

segmentations, at the cost of an increased but still moderate polynomial computational complexity [8]. This motivates to elaborate this approach towards a fully automatic and efficient unsupervised segmentation scheme providing a hierarchical data structure of coherent image parts which, in combination with model-based processing, may be explored for the purpose of scene interpretation (see Fig. 1 for an example result).

To this end, we consider a hierarchical framework for the binary partitioning approach presented in [8] to obtain a segmentation into multiple clusters (Section 2). To reduce the problem size by several orders of magnitude (to less than 0.01% of the all-pixel-based graph), we discuss an over-segmentation technique [10] which forms coherent "superpixels" [11] in a preprocessing step (Section 3). Section 4 treats various aspects concerning the development of a fully automatic unsupervised segmentation scheme. Experimental results based on a benchmark dataset of real world scenes [9] and comparisons with the normalized cut criterion illustrate the encouraging performance of our approach (Section 5).

2   Image Segmentation via Graph Cuts

The problem of image segmentation based on pairwise affinities can be formulated as a graph partitioning problem in the following way: consider the weighted graph $G(V, E)$ with locally extracted image features as vertices V and pairwise similarity values $w_{ij} \in \mathbb{R}_0^+$ as edge-weights. Segmenting the image into two parts then corresponds to partitioning the nodes of the graph into disjoint groups S and $\overline{S} = V \setminus S$. Representing such a partition by an indicator vector $x \in \{-1, +1\}^n$ (where $n = |V|$), the quality of a binary segmentation can be measured by the weight of the corresponding cut in the graph: $\text{cut}(S, \overline{S}) = \sum_{i \in S, j \in \overline{S}} w_{ij} = \frac{1}{4} x^\top L x$, where $L = D - W$ denotes the graph Laplacian matrix, and D is the diagonal degree matrix with $D_{ii} = \sum_{j \in V} w_{ij}$.

As directly minimizing the cut favors unbalanced segmentations, several methods for defining more suitable measures have been suggested in the literature. One of the most popular is the normalized cut criterion [7], which tries to avoid unbalanced partitions by appropriately scaling the cut-value. Since the corresponding cost function yields an NP-hard minimization problem, a spectral relaxation method is used to compute an approximate solution which is based on calculating minimal eigenvectors of the normalized Laplacian $L' = D^{-\frac{1}{2}} L D^{-\frac{1}{2}}$.

To get a binary solution of the original problem, these eigenvectors are then thresholded appropriately.

SDP relaxation. In this paper, we employ an alternative technique to find balanced partitions which originates from spectral graph theory [6]. As a starting point consider the following combinatorial problem formulation:

$$\min_{x\in\{-1,+1\}^n} \quad x^\top L x$$
$$\text{s.t.} \quad c^\top x = b. \tag{1}$$

Thus, instead of *normalizing* the cut-value as in [7], in this case an *additional balancing constraint* $c^\top x = b$ is used to compute favorable partitions. A classical approach to find a balanced segmentation uses $c = (1,\dots,1)^\top$ and $b = 0$, which is reasonable for graphs where each vertex is equally important. However, this may not be the case for the preprocessed images considered here; we will therefore discuss alternative settings for c and b in Section 4.

In order to find an approximate solution for the NP-hard problem (1), an advanced method is proposed in [8] which in contrast to spectral relaxation is not only able to handle the general linear constraint, but also takes into account the integer constraint on x in a better way. Observing that the cut-weight can be rewritten as $x^\top L x = \text{tr}(Lxx^\top)$, the problem variables are lifted into a higher dimensional space by introducing the matrix variable $X = xx^\top$. Dropping the rank one constraint on X and using arbitrary positive semidefinite matrices $X \succeq 0$ instead, we obtain the following relaxation of (1):

$$\min_{X\succeq0} \quad \text{tr}(LX)$$
$$\text{s.t.} \quad \text{tr}(cc^\top X) = b^2 \tag{2}$$
$$\text{tr}(e_i e_i^\top X) = 1 \quad \text{for } i = 1,\dots,n,$$

where $e_i \in \mathbb{R}^n$ denotes the i-th unit vector (see [8] for details).

The important point is that (2) belongs to the class of *semidefinite programs* (SDP), which can be solved in polynomial time to arbitrary precision, without needing to adjust any additional tuning parameters (see, e.g., [12]). To finally recover an integer solution x from the computed solution matrix X of (2), we use a randomized approximation technique [13]. Since this method does not enforce the balancing constraint from (1), it rather serves as a strong bias to guide the search instead of a strict requirement (cf. [8]).

Hierarchical clustering. In order to find segmentations of the image into multiple parts, we employ a hierarchical framework (e.g. [14]). In contrast to direct multiclass techniques (cf. [15,16]), the original cost function is used throughout the segmentation process, but for different (and usually smaller) problems in each step. As a consequence, the number k of segments does not need to be defined in advance, but can be chosen during the computation (which is more feasible for *unsupervised* segmentation tasks). Moreover, the subsequent splitting of segments yields a hierarchy of segmentations, so that changing k leads to similar segmentations. However, as no global cost function is optimized, additional decision critera are needed concerning the selection of the next partitioning step

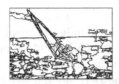

Fig. 2. 304 image patches are obtained for the image from Fig. 1 by over-segmenting it with mean shift. Note that in accordance with the homogeneous regions of the image, the patches differ in size. In this way, the splitting of such regions during the hierarchical graph cut segmentation is efficiently prevented.

and when to stop the hierarchical process. We will consider such criteria in Section 4.

3 Reducing the Problem Size

One important issue for segmentation methods based on graph representations is the size of the corresponding similarity matrix. If the vertex set V contains the pixels of an image, the size of the similarity matrix is equal to the squared number of pixels, and therefore generally too large to fit into computer memory completely (e.g. for an image of 481×321 pixels — the size of the images from the Berkeley segmentation dataset [9] — the similarity matrix contains $154401^2 \approx$ 23.8 billion entries). As reverting to sparse matrices (which works efficiently for spectral methods) is of no avail for the SDP relaxation approach, we suggest to reduce the problem size in a preprocessing step. While in this context, approaches based on probabilistic sampling have recently been applied successfully to image segmentation problems [17,18], we propose a different technique.

Over-segmentation with mean shift. Our method is based on the straightforward idea to abandon pixels as graph vertices and to use small image patches (or "superpixels" [11]) of coherent structure instead. In fact, it can be argued that this is even a more natural image representation than pixels as those are merely the result of the digital image discretization. The real world does not consist of pixels!

In principle, any unsupervised clustering technique could be used as a preprocessing step to obtain such image patches of coherent structure. We apply the mean shift procedure [10], as it does not smooth over clear edges and results in patches of varying size (see Fig. 2 for an example). In this way, the important structures of the image are maintained, while on the other hand the number of image features for the graph representation is greatly reduced.

In summary, the mean shift uses gradient estimation to iteratively seek modes of a density distribution in some Euclidean feature space. In our case, the feature vectors comprise the pixel positions along with their color in the perceptually uniform L*u*v* space. The number and size of the image patches is controlled by scaling the entries of the feature vectors with the spatial and the range bandwidth parameters h_s and h_r, respectively (see [10] for details).

In order to get an adequate problem size for the SDP relaxation approach, we determine these parameters semi-automatically: while the spatial bandwidth

h_s is set to a fixed fraction of the image size, we calculate the range bandwidth h_r by randomly picking a certain number of pixels from the image, computing their maximum distance $d_{\max}$ in the L*u*v* color space, and setting h_r to a fraction of $d_{\max}$. Moreover, we fix the minimum size of a region to $M = 50$ pixels. For the images from the Berkeley dataset [9], experiments showed that setting $h_s = 5.0$ and $h_r = \frac{d_{\max}}{15}$ results in an appropriate number of 100–700 image patches (corresponding to less than 0.01% of the number of pixels).

Constructing the graph. Using the image patches obtained with mean shift as graph vertices, the corresponding affinities are defined by representing each patch i with its mean color y_i in L*u*v* space, and calculating the similarity weights w_{ij} between neighboring patches as $w_{ij} = l_{ij} \exp\left(-\frac{\|y_i - y_j\|_2}{h_r}\right)$, where l_{ij} denotes the length of the edge in the image between the patches i and j. Hence, the problem is represented by a locally connected graph.

Assuming that each pixel originally is connected to its four neighbors, the multiplication with l_{ij} simulates a standard coarsening technique for graph partitioning [14]: the weight between two patches is calculated as the sum of the weights between the pixels contained within these patches. As each patch is of largely homogeneous color, using the mean color y_i instead of exact pixel colors does not change the resulting weights considerably.

Note that additional cues like texture or intervening contours can be incorporated into the classification process by computing corresponding similarity values based on the image patches, and combining them appropriately (see e.g. [14,19]). However, we do not consider modified similarities here.

4   Towards a Fully Automatic Segmentation

Based on the image patches obtained with mean shift the SDP relaxation approach is applied hierarchically to successively find binary segmentations. While solving the relaxation itself does not require tuning any parameters, the hierarchical application necessitates to discuss strategies for building up the segmentation tree, which is the subject of this section.

Segmentation constraints. Concerning the balancing constraint $c^\top x = b$ in (1), the graph vertices represented by the entries of c now correspond to image patches of varying size. For this reason, we calculate the number of pixels m_i contained in each patch i and set $c_i = m_i$ instead of $c_i = 1$, while retaining $b = 0$. In this way, the SDP relaxation seeks for two coherent parts with each containing approximately the same number of pixels.

However, if the part of the image under consideration in the current step contains a dominating patch k with $c_k = \max_i c_i \gg c_j$ for all $j \neq k$, segmentation into equally sized parts may not be possible. Nevertheless, we can still produce a feasible instance of the SDP relaxation in this case by adjusting the value of b in (1) appropriately, e.g. to $b = c_k - \frac{1}{2}\sum_{i \neq k} c_i$. Note that such an adjustment is not possible for spectral relaxation methods!

Which segment to split next? This question arises after each binary partitioning step. As the goal of unsupervised image segmentation mainly consists in capturing the global impression of the scene, large parts of coherent structure should always be preferred to finer details. For this reason, we generally select the largest existing segment as the next candidate to be split.

However, we allow for two exceptions to this general rule: (1) If the candidate segment contains less than a certain number of patches (which we set to 8 in our experiments), it is not split any further. This prevents dividing the image into too much detail. (2) If the cut-value obtained for the candidate segment is too large, this split is rejected, since this indicates that the structure of this segment is already quite coherent. To decide when a cut-value z is too large, we compare it against the sum of all edge-weights w' (which is an upper bound on z): only if z is smaller than 2% of w', the corresponding split is accepted.

Stopping criteria. The probably most difficult question in connection to unsupervised image segmentation concerns the number of parts the image consists of, or equivalently, when to stop the hierarchical segmentation process. As every human is likely to answer this question differently, one could even argue that without defining the desired granularity, image segmentation becomes an ill-posed problem. The hierarchical SDP relaxation approach offers two possible stopping criteria based on the desired granularity: the first one directly defines the maximum number of parts for the final segmentation. The second one is based on the fact that adding the cut-values results in an increasing function depending on the step number, which is bounded above by w'. Therefore, we can introduce the additional criterion to stop the hierarchical segmentation process when the complete cut value becomes larger than a certain percentage of w'.

5   Experimental Results

To evaluate the performance of our hierarchical segmentation algorithm, we apply it to images from the Berkeley segmentation dataset [9], which contains images of a wide variety of natural scenes. Moreover, this dataset also provides "ground-truth" data in the form of segmentations produced by humans (cf. Fig. 1), which allows to measure the performance of our algorithm quantitatively. Some exemplary results are depicted in Fig. 3. These encouraging segmentations are computed in less than 5 minutes on a Pentium 2 GHz processor.

As a quantitative measure of the segmentation quality, we use the precision-recall framework presented in [19]. In this context, the so-called F-measure is a valuable statistical performance indicator of a segmentation that captures the trade-off between accuracy and noise by giving values between 0 (bad segmentation) and 1 (good segmentation). For the results shown in Fig. 3, the corresponding F-measures confirm the positive visual impression.

For comparison, we also apply the normalized cut approach within the same hierarchical framework with identical parameter settings. While the results indicate the superiority of the SDP relaxation approach, this one-to-one comparison should be judged with care: as the normalized cut relaxation cannot appropriately take into account the varying patch sizes, the over-segmentation produced with mean shift may not be an adequate starting point for this method.

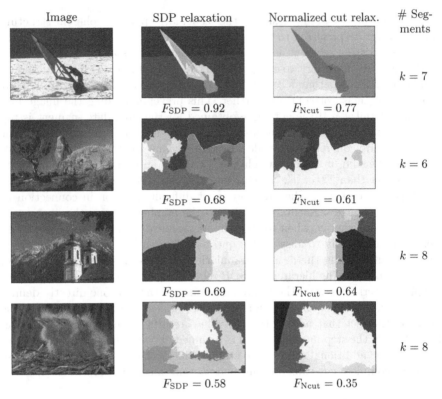

Fig. 3. Segmentation results for four color images (481×321 pixels) from the Berkeley segmentation dataset [9]. Note the superior quality of the segmentations obtained with the SDP relaxation approach in comparison to the normalized cut relaxation, which are approved by the higher F-measures.

Fig. 4. Evolution of the hierarchical segmentation for the image from Fig. 1. Note the coarse-to-fine nature of the evolution: First the broad parts of the image (water and sky) are segmented, while the finer details of the surfer arise later.

Finally, Fig. 4 gives an example of how the segmentation based on the SDP relaxation evolves hierarchically. In this context, note that although the water contains many patches (cf. Fig. 2), it is not split into more segments since the corresponding cut-values are too large.

6   Conclusion

We presented a hierarchical approach to unsupervised image segmentation which is based on a semidefinite relaxation of a constrained binary graph cut problem.

To prevent large homogeneous regions from being split (a common problem of balanced graph cut methods) we computed an over-segmentation of the image in a preprocessing step using the mean shift technique. Besides yielding better segmentations, this also reduced the problem size by several orders of magnitude.

The results illustrate an important advantage of the SDP relaxation in comparison to other segmentation methods based on graph cuts: As the balancing constraint can be adjusted to the current problem, we can appropriately take into account the different size of image patches. Moreover, it is easy to include additional constraints to model other conditions on the image patches, like connections to enforce the membership of certain patches to the same segment. We will investigate this aspect of semi-supervised segmentation in our future work.

References

1. S.-C. Zhu. Statistical modeling and conceptualization of visual patterns. *IEEE Trans. Patt. Anal. Mach. Intell.*, 25(6):691–712, 2003.
2. B. van Cutsem, editor. *Classification and Dissimilarity Analysis*, volume 93 of *Lecture Notes in Statistics*. Springer, 1994.
3. U. Hahn and M. Ramscar, editors. *Similarity and Categorization*. Oxford Univ. Press, 2001.
4. T. Hofmann and J. Buhmann. Pairwise data clustering by deterministic annealing. *IEEE Trans. Patt. Anal. Mach. Intell.*, 19(1):1–14, 1997.
5. J. Puzicha and J. M. Buhmann. Multiscale annealing for unsupervised image segmentation. *Comp. Vision and Image Underst.*, 76(3):213–230, 1999.
6. B. Mohar and S. Poljak. Eigenvalues in combinatorial optimization. In *Combinatorial and Graph-Theoretical Problems in Linear Algebra*, volume 50 of *IMA Vol. Math. Appl.*, pages 107–151. Springer, 1993.
7. J. Shi and J. Malik. Normalized cuts and image segmentation. *IEEE Trans. Patt. Anal. Mach. Intell.*, 22(8):888–905, 2000.
8. J. Keuchel, C. Schnörr, C. Schellewald, and D. Cremers. Binary partitioning, perceptual grouping, and restoration with semidefinite programming. *IEEE Trans. Patt. Anal. Mach. Intell.*, 25(11):1364–1379, 2003.
9. D. Martin, C. Fowlkes, D. Tal, and J. Malik. A database of human segmented natural images and its application to evaluating segmentation algorithms and measuring ecological statistics. In *Proc. 8th Int. Conf. Computer Vision (ICCV)*, volume 2, pages 416–423. IEEE Comp. Soc., 2001.
10. D. Comaniciu and P. Meer. Mean shift: A robust approach toward feature space analysis. *IEEE Trans. Patt. Anal. Mach. Intell.*, 24(5):603–619, 2002.
11. X. Ren and J. Malik. Learning a classification model for segmentation. In *Proc. 9th Int. Conf. Computer Vision (ICCV)*, pages 10–17. IEEE Comp. Soc., 2003.
12. H. Wolkowicz, R. Saigal, and L. Vandenberghe, editors. *Handbook of Semidefinite Programming*, volume 27 of *International series in operations research & management science*. Kluwer Acad. Publ., Boston, 2000.
13. M. X. Goemans and D. P. Williamson. Improved approximation algorithms for maximum cut and satisfiability problems using semidefinite programming. *Journal of the ACM*, 42(6):1115–1145, 1995.
14. J. Malik, S. Belongie, T. Leung, and J. Shi. Contour and texture analysis for image segmentation. *Int. J. Comp. Vision*, 43(1):7–27, 2001.

15. C. J. Alpert, A. B. Kahng, and S.-Z. Yao. Spectral partitioning with multiple eigenvectors. *Discrete Applied Math.*, 90:3–26, 1999.
16. S. X. Yu and J. Shi. Multiclass spectral clustering. In *Proc. 9th Int. Conf. Computer Vision (ICCV)*, pages 313–319. IEEE Comp. Soc., 2003.
17. Charless Fowlkes, Serge Belongie, Fan Chung, and Jitendra Malik. Spectral grouping using the Nyström method. *IEEE Trans. Pattern Anal. Mach. Intell.*, 26(2):214–225, 2004.
18. J. Keuchel and C. Schnörr. Efficient graph cuts for unsupervised image segmentation using probabilistic sampling and SVD-based approximation. In *3rd Internat. Workshop on Statist. and Comput. Theories of Vision*, Nice, France, 2003.
19. D. Martin, C. Fowlkes, and J. Malik. Learning to detect natural image boundaries using local brightness, color, and texture cues. *IEEE Trans. Patt. Anal. Mach. Intell.*, 26(5):530–549, 2004.

Fast Random Sample Matching
of 3d Fragments

Simon Winkelbach, Markus Rilk, Christoph Schönfelder, and
Friedrich M. Wahl

Institute for Robotics and Process Control, Technical University of Braunschweig,
Mühlenpfordtstr. 23, D-38106 Braunschweig, Germany
{S.Winkelbach, M.Rilk, C.Schoenfelder, F.Wahl}@tu-bs.de

Abstract. This paper proposes an efficient pairwise surface matching
approach for the automatic assembly of 3d fragments or industrial components. The method rapidly scans through the space of all possible solutions by a special kind of random sample consensus (RANSAC) scheme.
By using surface normals and optionally simple features like surface curvatures, we can highly constrain the initial 6 degrees of freedom search
space of all relative transformations between two fragments. The suggested approach is robust, very time and memory efficient, easy to implement and applicable to all kinds of surface data where surface normals
are available (e.g. range images, polygonal object representations, point
clouds with neighbor connectivity, etc.).

1 Introduction

The problem of surface matching is an important computer vision task with
many applications. The field of application comprises object recognition, pose
estimation, registration or fusion of partially overlapping range images or volumes, protein docking, reconstruction of broken objects like archaeologic artifacts and reduction of bone fractures in computer-aided surgery. The common
challenge is to find a rigid geometric transformation which aligns the surfaces
in an optimal way. This paper focuses on the reconstruction of broken arbitrary
objects by matching their fragments. Nevertheless, the proposed method is easy
adaptable to all other applications mentioned above. The problem of matching
complementary fragments of broken objects is largely similar to the problem of
matching partially overlapping surfaces (e.g. range images). The main common
difficulties are:

- The search space has six degrees of freedom (dof).
- Digitized surfaces often are inaccurate and noisy.
- Large data sets, i.e. a very high number of points in 3d.

In the case of broken objects there are some additional difficulties:

- A good initial guess, that can be used to iterate to the global minimum,
  generally is not available.

C.E. Rasmussen et al. (Eds.): DAGM 2004, LNCS 3175, pp. 129–136, 2004.

- Very large surface areas without correspondence at the complementary part.
- Object intersections must be avoided.
- Material deterioration.

1.1   Related Work

An outline of all publications dealing with registration techniques would go beyond the scope of this paper. Therefore we will only give an overview of the most relevant work. A very popular surface registration approach is the *iterative closest point* (ICP) algorithm [1]. The approach iteratively improves an initial solution by finding closest point pairs and subsequently calculating the relative transformation which aligns the two point sets in terms of least square error [2]. Although many enhancements to the original method have been suggested, they still require a good initial guess to find the global minimum. Many approaches are using local surface features to find corresponding point pairs. Features vary from simple properties like *surface normals* or *curvatures* to complex vectors like *point signatures* [3], *surface curves* e.g.[4], or *spin-images* [5]. However, their use cannot guarantee unique point correspondences; nevertheless they can highly constrain the search space.

A well-known category dealing with object recognition and localization are the *pose clustering* approaches (also known as *hypothesis accumulation* or *generalized Hough transform* e.g. [6],[7],[8]) The basic idea is to accumulate low level pose hypotheses in a voting table, followed by a maxima search which identifies the most frequented hypotheses. The drawback of voting tables is their relative high time and space complexity, particularly in case of large data sets.

A simple and robust approach for fitting models, like lines and circles in images, is the *RANSAC* algorithm introduced in [9]. The repeated procedure is simple but powerful: First, a likely hypothesis is generated by random (uniform distribution) from the input data set. Subsequently, the quality of the hypothesis (e.g. number of inliers) is evaluated. The method has been applied to a wide range of computer vision problems. The most related work [10] applies the RANSAC scheme to the registration of partially overlapping range images with a resolution of 64x64 pixels. The approach highly depends on the fact, that a range image can be treated as a projection of 3d points onto an index plane; this is why it is not applicable to the general case. Moreover, it does not take advantage of surface normals or any other features.

Many papers address matching of two-dimensional fragments like *jigsaw puzzles* or *thin-walled* fragments e.g. [11]. The problem of matching complementary three-dimensional object fragments (including the consideration of undesired fragment intersections) is rarely treated in the open literature. One of the recent approaches in this field of research is based on a pose error estimation using *z-buffers* of each fragment for each hypothesized pose [12]. The error minimization is performed by *simulated annealing* over a 7 dof search space of all possible poses of two fragments in relation to a separating reference plane. Although the approach makes use of the simulated annealing optimization, it degenerates to an exhaustive search if the optimal matching direction is limited to a small angular range, e.g. in case of matching a nut with a bolt. Another disadvantage is that the computation of each z-buffer has a time complexity of $O(n)$.

2   Method Overview

Our suggested approach rapidly finds the 'interesting regions' in the space of all possible relative rigid transformations of two fragments. Transformations where the parts do not get in contact are not considered at all. Moreover a desired surface contact is characterized by a preferably large touching area without a significant fragment penetration. Therefore the quality of a contact situation is determined by the size of the overlapping surface area and the absence of surface penetration, which is treated with a penalty. According to the RANSAC principle, the proposed method generates likely contact poses by random (see Sect. 2.1) and estimates the matching quality of each pose by an efficient combination of fast forecasting and by the use of a binary search tree (see Sect. 2.2). The basic procedure consists of the following steps:

1. Select a random surface point $p_i \in A$ and a random surface point $p_j \in B$. A surface contact at p_i and p_j constrains three degrees of freedom. Another two degrees of freedom are fixed by the respective vertex normals n_{p_i} and n_{p_j}, which are directed against each other. Only the rotation around these normals remains unknown.
   Optional: Select only pairs which satisfy $feature(p_i) \sim feature(p_j)$.
2. Select a random second point pair $(q_i \in A, q_j \in B)$ which forms a fully constrained two-point contact pose together with the first pair (p_i, p_j).
   Optional: Select only pairs which satisfy $feature(q_i) \sim feature(q_j)$.
3. Estimate the matching quality of the pose.
   Efficiency highly can be increased by using a fast forecasting technique combined with a dropout if the expected result is considerably worse than the last best match.
4. Repeat steps 1-3 and memorize the best match until the matching quality is good enough or a time limit is exceeded.

Here $A \subset \Re^3$ denotes the whole set of surface points of one fragment (B respectively). It is obvious, that the consideration of local surface properties or features can increase the likelihood that a pair corresponds to each other. In our experiments we compare the mean curvature of a point pair, which enables us to reject up to 90% as unsuitable. Curvatures can be obtained from all kinds of data sets which provide neighbor connectivity (see e.g. [13] for curvature computation on triangle meshes).

The strength of the algorithm is that it is independent of the fragment shapes. The efficiency is directly proportional to the size of compatible surface area (fracture interface) and independent of the tolerance of matching direction, etc.; thus the method is even applicable in case of components and assemblies with narrow mating directions (like nut and bolt or plug and socket) where approaches which iterate to a local minimum may fail.

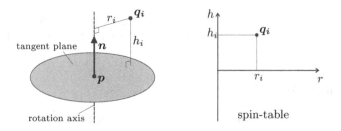

Fig. 1. Schematic illustration of the *spin-table coordinates*

2.1   Rapid Generation of Two-Point Contact Poses

a random pose where the fragments get in contact and the surfaces touch each other tangentially (contrariwise surface normals $\pm n$ at contact point p). Since this step only generates random surface point pairs, it is very fast and simple. The second step tries to find a second point pair (q_i, q_j) which can be brought into contact by rotating around an axis with origin p and direction n. A point pair which fulfills this condition must have an equal distance h to the tangent plane (see Fig. 1) and an equal distance r to the rotation axis. Referring to [5] we will call the parameter pair (r_i, h_i) the *spin-table coordinates* of a point q_i in relation to its rotation origin p. The following algorithm alternately adds point references of A and B into their respective spin-table M_a, M_b until a point pair with equal spin-table coordinates has been found, or until a counter exceeds the limit k, which is a strong indication for a contact situation with marginal surface overlap.

1.   Clear spin-tables $M_a := 0$, $M_b := 0$.
2.   Repeat k times
3.   Select a random point $q_i \in A$
4.   Calculate its spin-table coordinates (r_i, h_i) with respect to p
5.   Insert q_i into its respective spin-table $M_a(r_i, h_i) := q_i$
6.   Read out the opposite spin-table $q_j := M_b(r_i, h_i)$
7.   If $(q_j \neq 0)$ terminate loop; the new contact pair is (q_i, q_j)
8.   Repeat step 3-7 with reversed roles of A, B and M_a, M_b
9.   End-repeat

We achieve a good trade-off between accuracy and execution time with a table size of 64x64. The basic procedure can be improved by accepting only contact pairs (q_i, q_j) with compatible features and roughly contrariwise surface normals n_{qi}, n_{qj}. Furthermore, the efficiency can be increased by reusing one of both filled spin-table M_i of a point p_i for multiple assumed contact points p_j on the counterpart.

2.2   Fast Quality Estimation of a Given Pose

After generating a hypothesis we must measure its matching quality. For this we estimate the proportion of overlapping area Ω where surface A is in contact with the opposite surface B in the given pose. We assume that the surfaces are in contact at areas where the distances between surface points are smaller than ε. Ω can also be regarded as the probability that a random point $x \in A$ is in contact with the opposite surface B. Thus Ω can be forecasted by an efficient *Monte-Carlo* strategy using a sequence of random points, combined with a dropout if the expected result is considerably worse than the last best match. Suppose that $x_1, \ldots, x_n$ are independent random points with $x_i \in A$. Then Ω is given by

$$\Omega = \lim_{n \to \infty} \frac{\sum_{i=1}^{n} contact_B(x_i)}{n} \tag{1}$$

where $contact_B(x)$ is a function which determines whether point x is in contact with surface B

$$contact_B(x) = \begin{cases} 1 & \text{if } dist_B(x) < \varepsilon \\ 0 & \text{else} \end{cases} \tag{2}$$

and $dist_B(x)$ is a function which returns the minimal distance of a point x to surface B

$$dist_B(x) = \min_{y \in B} |x - y| \tag{3}$$

Our implementation of this function is based on a *kd-tree* data structure (see [15]) and therefore offers a logarithmical time complexity for the closest point search.

In contrast to Eq. (1) it is only possible to try a limited number n of random points; thus Ω only can be approximated up to an arbitrary level of confidence. (Notice that this restriction only holds if A and B contain an infinite number of points). Considering the margin of error, for every additional random point, the approximation of Ω can be recomputed as

$$\Omega \approx \frac{\sum_{i=1}^{n} contact_B(x_i)}{n} \pm \frac{1.96}{2\sqrt{n}} \tag{4}$$

with a 95% level of confidence. If the upper bound of this range is worse than the last best match, we abort the computation and try the next hypothesis.

Up to this point we have not considered surface penetrations at all. To ensure that the fragments do not penetrate each other we simply subtract a penalty for penetrating points (i.e. points which are more than ε 'below' the complementary fragment surface). This can be done by using an alternative contact rating

$$contact_B(x) = \begin{cases} 1 & \text{if } dist_B(x) < \varepsilon & \text{(at surface)} \\ -4 & \text{if } dist_B(x) \geq \varepsilon \ \wedge \ (x - y) \cdot n_y < 0 & \text{(inside)} \\ 0 & \text{else} & \text{(outside)} \end{cases} \tag{5}$$

Where $y \in B$ denotes the closest point to x, and n_y denotes the surface normal of y. Due to the fact that y can be determined simultaneous with the calculation of the minimal distance in Eq. (3), it is straightforward to test whether x lies inside or outside of fragment B. The execution time can be accelerated by an approximative early bound of the kd-tree search.

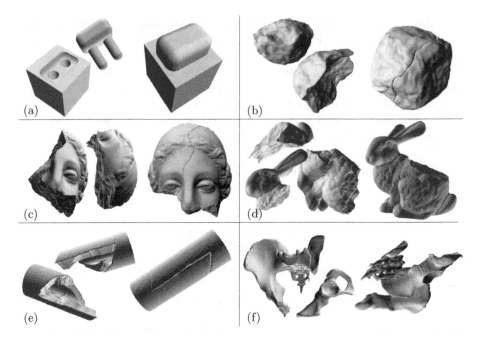

Fig. 2. Some matching results: (a) plug and socket; (b) broken boulder; (c) broken venus; (d) broken Stanford bunny; (e) broken bone model; (f) broken pelvis

2.3   Matching Constraints for Special Types of Fractures

Up to this point, we did not use any knowledge about the object. However, in many applications, additional information about the parts to be combined are available and can be used to constrain the search space. This includes information about the object shape (e.g. [16]), geometric features like a sharp curvature transition from an intact surface to a broken one (e.g. [4]), or knowledge of the roughness of the fracture. An integration of these constraints into our approach is straightforward and can drastically limit the search space and thus reduce the execution time. Particularly suitable for this matching procedure is the previous knowledge of surface points at the fracture interface which must be brought into contact with the counterpart. These 'contact constraints' can highly increase the efficiency of the contact pose generation of Sect. 2.1. A detailed discussion about these additional constraints is subject of further publications.

3   Experimental Results and Conclusion

The method has been evaluated on high-resolution triangle meshes of artificial and digitized objects with computer generated and real fractures. All computer generated fractures are distorted with some additive Gaussian noise and it is assured that the tesselation of one fragment is unrelated to its counterpart.

Table 1. Evaluation of 100 passes per experiment. The entries are: Total number of vertices; area of fracture interface (Overlap); added noise level in percent referring to the maximal object radius; lower limit (LRL), upper limit (URL), and mean execution time μ in seconds, and standard deviation of execution time σ

	Vertices	Overlap	Add.Noise	LRL	URL	μ	σ
plug(a)	41772	29%	0.0%	0.09	10.28	2.52	2.85
			1.0%	0.21	154.31	46.51	43.92
			1.5%	0.33	186.27	48.66	45.27
			2.0%	2.15	263.96	64.94	63.86
boulder(b)	21068	38%	0.1%	0.11	22.58	4.85	4.53
venus(c)	51837	28%	0.1%	0.31	27.42	6.39	5.79
bunny(d)	96170	30%	0.1%	0.41	64.31	11.61	10.68
bone(e)	35503	13%	0.0%	0.08	114.62	28.01	28.83
pelvis(f)	57755	1%	0.0%	-	-	-	-

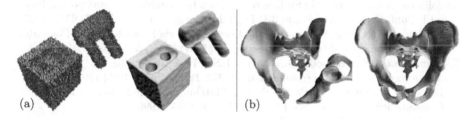

(a) | (b)

Fig. 3. (a) Example with 2% noise distortion and smoothing result; (b) broken pelvis and the 'constraint matching' result

Fig. 2 shows some representative test examples with different noise levels. To make the calculation of surface normals and curvatures robust against noise we apply a common mesh smoothing filter [13]. The left side of Fig. 3 visualizes the intensity of our maximal noise distortion, and the effect of smoothing. Some of our data sets are real human bone fractures (femurs and pelvis), which are extracted from computer tomographic scans. The medical relevance of a robust bone registration method is outlined in [16]. The required execution times for successful assembly of these fragments are listed in Table 1. The tests were performed on an AMD Athlon XP/1466MHz based PC. As can be seen, the method performs well with a variety of objects (3d fragments as well as industrial components). The desired matching accuracy is implicitly regulated by the input parameter ε (maximal contact distance of Eq. (2)) and the minimal matching quality Ω. In the unconstraint case the algorithm always finds the solution with the largest touching area, which is not always the desired one. This occurs if the portion of fracture interface is small in comparison to the total surface area, and if the intact object surface includes large smooth areas with similar regions on the counterpart (e.g. the pelvis in Fig. 2). In these cases additional constraints (which are discussed in Sect. 2.3) are indispensable to prevent the algorithm from finding "trivial solutions". The desired solution of the pelvis (see the right side of Fig. 3) can be achieved by constraining the matching direction, or by selecting some vertices at the fractured surface which must be brought into contact with the counterpart. In further publications we will discuss usage of these additional constraints.

References

1. Besl, P., McKay, N.: A method for registration of 3-D shapes. IEEE Trans. PAMI 14(2) (1992) 239–256
2. Horn, B.K.P.: Closed-form solution of absolute orientation using unit quaternions, J. Opt. Soc. Amer. A 4(4) (1987) 629–642
3. Chua, C.S., Jarvis, R.: Point Signatures: A New Representation for 3D Object Recognition, Int'l Journal of Computer Vision, 25(1) (1997) 63–85
4. Papaioannou, G., Theoharis, T.: Fast Fragment Assemblage Using Boundary Line and Surface Matching. IEEE Proc. ICPR/ACVA (2003)
5. Johnson, A.E., Hebert, M.: Surface registration by matching oriented points. Proc. Int'l. Conf. Recent Advances in 3-D Digital Imaging and Modeling (3DIM) (1997)
6. Stockman, G.: Object Recognition and Localization via Pose Clustering. Computer Vision, Graphics, and Image Processing, 40 (1987) 361–387
7. Linnainmaa, S.,Harwood, D., Davis, L.S.: Pose determination of a three-dimensional object using triangle pairs. IEEE Trans. PAMI 10(5) (1988) 634–647
8. Barequet, G., Sharir, M.: Partial Surface Matching by Using Directed Footprints. Computational Geometry'96, Philadelphia PA, USA (1996)
9. Fischler, M.A., Bolles, R.C.: Random sample consensus: A paradigm for model fitting with application to image analysis and automated cartography. Communication of the ACM, 24(6), (1981) 381–395
10. Chen, C.S., Hung, Y.P., Cheng, J.B.: RANSAC-Based DARCES: A New Approach to Fast Automatic Registration of Partially Overlapping Range Images. IEEE Trans. PAMI 21(11), (1999) 1229–1234
11. Leitão, H.C.G. , Stolfi, J.: A Multiscale Method for the Reassembly of Two-Dimensional Fragmented Objects. IEEE Trans. PAMI, 24(9) (2002) 1239–1251
12. Papaioannou, G., Karabassi E.A., Theoharis, T.: Reconstruction of Three-dimensional Objects through Matching of their Parts, IEEE Trans. PAMI, 24(1) (2002) 114-124
13. Desbrun, M., Meyer, M., Schröder, P., Barr, A.H.: Implicit Fairing of Irregular Meshes using Diffusion and Curvature Flow. Proc. SIGGRAPH 99, (1999) 317-324
14. Johnson, A.E., Hebert, M.: Control of Polygonal Mesh Resolution for 3-D Computer Vision. Tech. Report CMU-RI-TR-96-20, Robotics Institute, Carnegie Mellon University, April (1997)
15. Friedman, J.H., Bentley, J.L., Finkel, R.A.: An Algorithm for Finding Best Matches in Logarithmic Expected Time. ACM Trans. Mathematical Software 3(3), (1977) 209–226
16. Winkelbach, S., Westphal, R., Goesling, T.: Pose Estimation of Cylindrical Fragments for Semi-Automatic Bone Fracture Reduction. In: Michaelis, B., Krell, G. (Eds.): Pattern Recognition (DAGM 2003), Lecture Notes in Computer Science 2781, Springer (2003) 566–537

Invariants for Discrete Structures –
An Extension of Haar Integrals over
Transformation Groups to Dirac Delta Functions

Hans Burkhardt[1], Marco Reisert[1], and Hongdong Li[2]

[1] University of Freiburg, Computer Science Department,
79110 Freiburg i.Br., Germany
{burkhardt,reisert}@informatik.uni-freiburg.de
[2] National ICT Australia (NICTA), Dpt. of Sys. Eng., Australian National
University (ANU), Canberra ACT, Australia
hongdong.li@anu.edu.au

Abstract. Due to the increasing interest in 3D models in various applications there is a growing need to support e.g. the automatic search or the classification in such databases. As the description of 3D objects is not canonical it is attractive to use invariants for their representation. We recently published a methodology to calculate invariants for continuous 3D objects defined in the real domain $\mathbb{R}^3$ by integrating over the group of Euclidean motion with monomials of a local neighborhood of voxels as kernel functions and we applied it successfully for the classification of scanned pollen in 3D. In this paper we are going to extend this idea to derive invariants from discrete structures, like polygons or 3D-meshes by summing over monomials of discrete features of local support. This novel result for a space-invariant description of discrete structures can be derived by extending Haar integrals over the Euclidean transformation group to Dirac delta functions.

1 Introduction

Invariant features are an elegant way to solve the problem of e.g. space invariant recognition. The idea is to find a mapping T which is able to extract intrinsic features of an object, i.e., features that stay unchanged if the object's position and/or orientation changes. Such a transformation T necessarily maps all images of an equivalence class of objects under the transformations group G into one point of the feature space:

$$\mathbf{x}_1 \overset{G}{\sim} \mathbf{x}_2 \quad \Rightarrow \quad T(\mathbf{x}_1) = T(\mathbf{x}_2) \quad . \tag{1}$$

A mapping T which is invariant with respect to G is said to be *complete* if T is a bijective mapping between the invariants and the equivalence classes, i.e. if we additionally ask

$$T(\mathbf{x}_1) = T(\mathbf{x}_2) \quad \Rightarrow \quad \mathbf{x}_1 \overset{G}{\sim} \mathbf{x}_2 \quad . \tag{2}$$

C.E. Rasmussen et al. (Eds.): DAGM 2004, LNCS 3175, pp. 137–144, 2004.

For a given gray scale image $\mathbf{X}$ and a kernel function $f(\mathbf{X})$ it is possible to construct an invariant feature $T[f](\mathbf{X})$ by integrating $f(g\mathbf{X})$ over the transformation group G:

$$T[f](\mathbf{X}) := \int_G f(g\mathbf{X})dg. \qquad (3)$$

As kernel functions f we typically use monomials from a local pixel- or voxel-neighborhood (FLSs $\underline{F}$unctions of $\underline{L}$ocal $\underline{S}$upport). These Haar integrals are defined for continuous objects in $\mathbb{R}^2$ or $\mathbb{R}^3$ ([4,5,6,2,3]). This integral can in practice only be evaluated for compact groups, which means that the parameters describing the group lie in a finite region. In the sequel we will call these invariants HIs ($\underline{H}$aar $\underline{I}$nvariants).

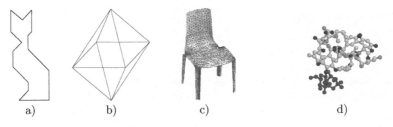

Fig. 1. Discrete structures in 2D and 3D: (a) closed contour described by a polygon (b) wireframe object (c) 3D triangulated surface mesh (d) molecule.

For discrete objects $\mathbf{\Delta}$ (see Fig. 1) which vanish almost everywhere this integral delivers, however, trivial or zero results (depending on the kernel function). Discrete structures can be described by Dirac delta functions (examples of distributions or generalized functions), which are different from zero on a set of measure zero of the domain. However, properly chosen integrals of these delta functions exist and deliver finite values. We will use this concept to define proper Haar invariants from discrete structures (DHIs $\underline{D}$iscrete $\underline{H}$aar $\underline{I}$nvariants).

There exist a vast literature on invariant-based shape representations and object recognition problems; space limitations do not allow here a thorough review. However, to the best of the authors' knowledge there exist no similar approaches to the DHIs.

2   Invariants for Discrete Objects

For a discrete object $\mathbf{\Delta}$ and a kernel function $f(\mathbf{\Delta})$ it is possible to construct an invariant feature $T[f](\mathbf{\Delta})$ by integrating $f(g\mathbf{\Delta})$ over the transformation group $g \in G$. Let us assume that our discrete object is different from zero only at its vertices. A rotation and translation invariant local discrete kernel function h takes care for the algebraic relations to the neighboring vertices and we can write

$$f(\mathbf{\Delta}) = \sum_{i \in \mathbb{V}} h(\mathbf{\Delta}, \mathbf{x}_i) \delta(\mathbf{x} - \mathbf{x}_i) \quad , \tag{4}$$

where $\mathbb{V}$ is the set of vertices and $\mathbf{x}_i$ the vector representing vertex i.

In order to get finite values from the distributions it is necessary to introduce under the Haar integral another integration over the spatial domain $\mathbf{X}$. By choosing an arbitrary integration path in the continuous group G we can visit each vertex in an arbitrary order the integral is transformed into a sum over all local discrete functions allowing all possible permutations of the contributions of the vertices. As the discrete neighborhood functions are attached to the vertices they are already invariant to G, i.e. $h(g\mathbf{\Delta}, g\mathbf{x}_i) = h(\mathbf{\Delta}, \mathbf{x}_i)$ and hence we get

$$T[f](\mathbf{\Delta}) := \int_G \int_X f(g\mathbf{\Delta}) dx dg = \int_G \left[\int_X \sum_{i \in \mathbb{V}} h(g\mathbf{\Delta}, g\mathbf{x}_i) \delta(g\mathbf{x} - g\mathbf{x}_i) dx \right] dg$$

$$= \int_G \left[\sum_{i \in \mathbb{V}} h(\mathbf{\Delta}, \mathbf{x}_i) \right] dg = \sum_{i \in \mathbb{V}} h(\mathbf{\Delta}, \mathbf{x}_i) \quad . \tag{5}$$

Therefore we get invariants by simply adding local Euclidean-invariant (rotation and translation) DFLS $h(\mathbf{\Delta}, \mathbf{x}_i)$ (DFLSs Discrete Functions of Local Support) over all vertices. The interpretation of the result is very obvious: summing over locally Euclidean-invariants provides also global Euclidean invariants.

2.1   Invariants for Polygons

Let us apply the general principles for DHIs for polygons. As discrete functions of local support (DFLS) we choose monomials of the distances between neighboring vertices (which are obvious invariant to rotation) up to degree $k = 4$ in the following example:

$$\tilde{x}_{n_1, n_2, n_3, n_4} = \sum_{i \in \mathbb{V}} h(\mathbf{\Delta}, \mathbf{x}_i) = \sum_{i \in \mathbb{V}} d_{i,1}^{n_1} d_{i,2}^{n_2} d_{i,3}^{n_3} d_{i,4}^{n_4} \tag{6}$$

and the $d_{i,k}$ denote the Euclidean distance of vertex i and its k-th righthand neighbor:

$$d_{i,k} = ||\mathbf{x}_i - \mathbf{x}_{<i+k>}|| \quad . \tag{7}$$

The brackets $<>$ denote a reduction modulo the number of vertices of a contour.

By varying the exponents we can build up a feature space. The nonlinear nature of this monomial-based kernel functions endow themselves with rich behaviors in the sense of discriminative ability. In general, the discrimination performance of this feature space will increase with the number of used features.

Principle of rigidity It can easily be shown that the features $\{d_{i,1}, d_{i,2}, d_{i,3}\}$ (see Fig. 2) uniquely define a complete polygon (up to a mirror-polygon) because we can iteratively construct the polygon by rigidly piecing together rigid triangles

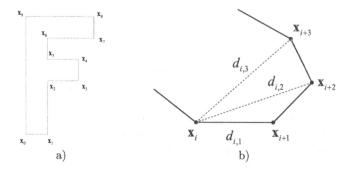

Fig. 2. (a) Example of a polygon (b) basic features $\{d_{i,1}, d_{i,2}, d_{i,3}\}$

(hereby we do not allow consecutive collinear edges in a polygon). Therefore we call these elements a basis. We expect to get a more and more complete feature space by integrating over more and more monomials from these basic features.

Looking at a triangle as the most simplest polygon one can show that the following three features derived from the three sides $\{a, b, c\}$ form a complete set of invariants:

$$\tilde{x}_0 = a + b + c, \qquad \tilde{x}_1 = a^2 + b^2 + c^2, \qquad \tilde{x}_2 = a^3 + b^3 + c^3 \qquad . \qquad (8)$$

These features are equivalent to the elementary symmetrical polynomials in 3 variables which are a complete set of invariants with respect to all permutations.

It is not our intention to compare the results here with Fourier Descriptors (see e.g. [1]). First the approaches are rather different (integration over the transformation group versus normalization technique) and second the proposed method is much easier to extend from 2D to 3D.

2.2 3D-Meshes

Although we will not elaborate a rigorous concept for 3D discrete objects we want to outline that it is straightforward to extend the concept e.g to a 3D-Surface mesh or a real 3D wireframe model. Again we derive DFLS of a certain neighborhood and sum over all vertices. It is appropriate to use here also basic features which meet the requirement that they constitute rigid local polyhedra which can rigidly pieced together to a solid surface or polyhedral object (see Fig. 3). *Similar to the triangle as a basic building block for a planar polygon we can use a tetrahedron as a basic building block for a polyhedron.* And as we can find three invariants for a triangle we similarly can find invariants for a tetrahedron derived from its edge lengths.

2.3 Discrimination Performance and the Question of Completeness

A crucial question is how many features we need to get a good discrimination performance and avoid ambiguities up to the point to use a complete set of

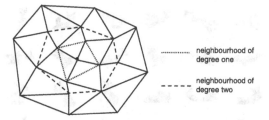

Fig. 3. Part of a surface mesh with neighborhood of degree one and two.

features. Asking for completeness is a very strong demand because it guarantees that no ambiguities between two different objects exist. For a practical pattern recognition problem we have to solve the much easier problem of *separability* to discriminate between a finite number of representatives of object classes (like the 26 classes in character recognition). Therefore we are typically content with a finite number of invariants which is typically much less than the number of features needed for completeness.

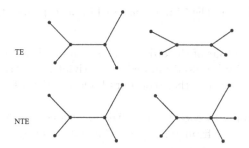

Fig. 4. Topologically equivalent (TE) and non topologically equivalent discrete structures (NTE).

As we use discrete features the methodology is sensitive to topological changes in the structure (see Fig. 4). So if we introduce another vertex on a polygon in the middle of an edge for example the invariants will clearly change. Discrete similarities are not necessarily visual similarities. Introducing an atom into a molecule also has a high impact on the function.

3   Experiments: Object Classification in a Tangram Database

We will demonstrate the construction of DHIs for the simplest case of closed polygons. As an example we have chosen a subset of 74 samples from the Tangram-Man-Database[1]. Fig. 5 shows a selection of objects. As characteristic feature we

---

[1] see "Tangram Man" at http://www.reijnhoudt.nl/tangram

Fig. 5. The 74 tangrams used in the experiment.

extract the outer contour of the objects. This example is interesting because the objects can not easily be discriminated with trivial geometric features, as they all have the same area and their contours build clusters of rather few possible numbers.

As noise we added to each vertex a vector of a certain length with an uniformly distributed angle from $[0 : 2\pi]$. The amount of noise was measured against the standard deviation of all edges of the polygon $\sigma = \sqrt{(\frac{1}{|V|}||\mathbf{x}_i - \bar{\mathbf{x}}||^2}$. Fig. 6 shows an example with 10% noise added which leads already to remarkable distortions.

As the calculation of the monomials is a continuous function of the coordinates of the vertices we henceforth get a continuous propagation of the additive noise through the invariants. Therefore: little distortions will also cause little changes in the magnitude of the invariants.

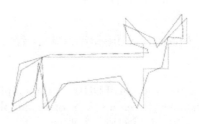

Fig. 6. Exact Contour and with 10% noise added.

Table 1. Exponent table for monomials built from $\{d_{i,1}^{n_1} d_{i,2}^{n_2} d_{i,3}^{n_3} d_{i,4}^{n_4}\}$ for calculating 14 invariants

i	$\tilde{x}_0$	$\tilde{x}_1$	$\tilde{x}_2$	$\tilde{x}_3$	$\tilde{x}_4$	$\tilde{x}_5$	$\tilde{x}_6$	$\tilde{x}_7$	$\tilde{x}_8$	$\tilde{x}_9$	$\tilde{x}_{10}$	$\tilde{x}_{11}$	$\tilde{x}_{12}$	$\tilde{x}_{13}$
n_1	1	0	0	1	1	0	0	1	0	0	2	0	0	0
n_2	0	1	0	1	0	1	0	0	1	0	0	2	0	0
n_3	0	0	1	0	1	1	0	0	0	1	0	0	2	0
n_4	0	0	0	0	0	0	1	1	1	1	0	0	0	2

Table 2. Classification result for 5%, 10% and 20% noise for 74 tangrams with an Euclidean (E) and a Mahalanobis (M) Classifier

noise (in percent)	5	5	5	10	10	10	20	20	20
# of invariants	6	10	14	6	10	14	6	10	14
metric	E	E	E	M	M	M	M	M	M
class. error (in percent)	30	10	6	1.5	0	0	25	7	3

The experiments were conducted with three sets of 6, 10 and 14 invariants respectively according to eq. (6) (see Table 1) (the subset of 6 and 10 are just the first 6 and 10 of the 14 invariants. The classification performance was measured against additive noise of 5%, 10% and 20%.

Table 2 shows the result of our experiments averaged over 50 samples. Choosing for the sake of simplicity an Euclidean classifier measuring the distance to the expectation of the class centers leads to rather bad classification results. Adding only 5% noise results in a misclassification of 30% of the tangrams using 6 invariants. This number can be reduced to 10% false classifications adding further 4 invariants and to 6% using 14 invariants. This result is not surprising. Looking at the invariants we can observe a large variance of their magnitudes due to the differences in the degree of the monomials. We can, however, drastically improve the result by using a Mahalanobis-Classifier. This is due to the fact that the noise covariance matrices of all objects are very similar. Therefore we made experiments with a Mahalanobis-Classifier based on an averaged covariance matrix over all object classes. Now even an increase of noise by a factor two to 10% leads only to 1.5% errors with 6 invariants and 0% errors for 10 and 14 invariants which demonstrates the very good performance of the invariants. Even with 20% noise and 14 invariants we get a rather low error rate of only 3%.

If we constrain our calculation to a finite number of invariants we end up with a simple linear complexity in the number of vertices. This holds if the local neighborhood of vertices is resolved already by the given data structure; otherwise the cost for resolving local neighborhoods must be added. In contrast to graph matching algorithms we apply here algebraic techniques to solve the problem. This has the advantage that we can apply hierarchical searches for retrieval tasks, namely, to start only with one feature and hopefully eliminate already a large number of objects and then continue with an increasing number of features etc.

4   Conclusions

In this paper we have introduced a novel set of invariants for discrete structures in 2D and 3D. The construction is a rigorous extension of Haar integrals over transformation groups to Dirac Delta Functions. The resulting invariants can easily be calculated with linear complexity in the number of vertices. The proposed approach has the potential to be extended to other discrete structures and even to the more general case of weighted graphs.

Acknowledgement. This paper has been worked out while the first author was on a sabbatical leave at the National ICT Australia (NICTA), Department of Systems Engineering, The Australian National University (ANU), Canberra ACT, Australia.

We are very thankful to Mr. Frans Reijnhoudt who allowed us to use his Tangram-Database. We also thank Bernard Haasdonk and the anonymous reviewers for their helpful comments and suggestions.

References

1. K. Arbter, W. Snyder, H. Burkhardt, and G. Hirzinger. Application of Affine-Invariant Fourier Descriptors to 3-D Objects. *IEEE Trans. on Pattern Analysis and Machine Intelligence*, PAMI-12(7):640–647, July 1990.
2. H. Burkhardt and S. Siggelkow. Invariant features in pattern recognition – fundamentals and applications. In C. Kotropoulos and I. Pitas, editors, *Nonlinear Model-Based Image/Video Processing and Analysis*, pages 269–307. John Wiley & Sons, 2001.
3. O. Ronneberger, H. Burkhardt, and E. Schultz. General-purpose Object Recognition in 3D Volume Data Sets using Gray-Scale Invariants – Classification of Airborne Pollen-Grains Recorded with a Confocal Laser Scanning Microscope. In *Proceedings of the International Conference on Pattern Recognition*, Quebec, Canada, September 2002.
4. H. Schulz-Mirbach. On the Existence of Complete Invariant Feature Spaces in Pattern Recognition. In *Proc. of the 11th International Conference on Pattern Recognition, Conference B: Pattern Recognition Methodology and Systems*, volume II, pages 178–182, Den Haag, 1992.
5. H. Schulz-Mirbach. *Anwendung von Invarianzprinzipien zur Merkmalgewinnung in der Mustererkennung*. PhD thesis, Technische Universität Hamburg-Harburg, February 1995. Reihe 10, Nr. 372, VDI-Verlag.
6. H. Schulz-Mirbach. Invariant features for gray scale images. In G. Sagerer, S. Posch, and F. Kummert, editors, *17. DAGM - Symposium "Mustererkennung"*, pages 1–14, Bielefeld, 1995. Reihe Informatik aktuell, Springer. DAGM-Preis.

Scale-Invariant Object Categorization Using a Scale-Adaptive Mean-Shift Search

Bastian Leibe[1] and Bernt Schiele[1,2]

[1] Perceptual Computing and Computer Vision Group, ETH Zurich, Switzerland
leibe@inf.ethz.ch, http://www.vision.ethz.ch/leibe

[2] Multimodal Interactive Systems, TU Darmstadt, Germany
schiele@informatik.tu-darmstadt.de

Abstract. The goal of our work is object categorization in real-world scenes. That is, given a novel image we want to recognize and localize unseen-before objects based on their similarity to a learned object category. For use in a real-world system, it is important that this includes the ability to recognize objects at multiple scales.

In this paper, we present an approach to multi-scale object categorization using scale-invariant interest points and a scale-adaptive Mean-Shift search. The approach builds on the method from [12], which has been demonstrated to achieve excellent results for the single-scale case, and extends it to multiple scales. We present an experimental comparison of the influence of different interest point operators and quantitatively show the method's robustness to large scale changes.

1 Introduction

Many current object detection methods deal with the scale problem by performing an exhaustive search over all possible object positions and scales [17,18,19]. This exhaustive search imposes severe constraints, both on the detector's computational complexity and on its discriminance, since a large number of potential false positives need to be excluded. An opposite approach is to let the search be guided by image structures that give cues about the object scale. In such a system, an initial interest point detector tries to find structures whose extend can be reliably estimated under scale changes. These structures are then combined to derive a comparatively small number of hypotheses for object locations and scales. Only those hypotheses that pass an initial plausibility test need to be examined in detail. In recent years, a range of scale-invariant interest point detectors have become available which can be used for this purpose [13,14,15,10].

In this paper, we apply this idea to extend the method from [12,11]. This method has recently been demonstrated to yield excellent object detection results and high robustness to occlusions [11]. However, it has so far only been defined for categorizing objects at a known scale. In practical applications, this is almost never the case. Even in scenarios where the camera location is relatively fixed, objects of interest may still exhibit scale changes of at least a factor of two simply because they occur at different distances to the camera. Scale invariance is thus one of the most important properties for any system that shall be applied to real-world scenarios without human intervention.

This paper contains four main contributions: (1) We extend our approach from [12, 11] to multi-scale object categorization, making it thus usable in practice. Our extension

C.E. Rasmussen et al. (Eds.): DAGM 2004, LNCS 3175, pp. 145–153, 2004.
© Springer-Verlag Berlin Heidelberg 2004

Table 1. Comparison of results on the UIUC car database reported in the literature.

Method	Agarwal et al [1]	Garg et al [9]	Leibe et al [11]	Fergus et al [8]	Our approach
Equal Error Rate	~79%	~88%	97.5%	88.5%	91.0%
Scale Inv.	no	no	no	yes	yes

is based on the use of scale-invariant interest point detectors, as motivated above. (2) We formulate the multi-scale object detection problem in a Mean-Shift framework, which allows to draw parallels to Parzen window probability density estimation. We show that the introduction of a scale dimension in this scheme requires the Mean-Shift approach to be extended by a scale adaption mechanism that is different from the variable-bandwidth methods proposed so far [6,4]. (3) We experimentally evaluate the suitability of different scale-invariant interest point detectors and analyze their influence on the recognition results. Interest point detectors have so far mainly been evaluated in terms of repeatability and the ability to find exact correspondences [15,16]. As our task requires the generalization to unseen objects, we are more interested in finding similar and typical structures, which imposes different constraints on the detectors. (4) Last but not least, we experimentally evaluate the robustness of the proposed approach to large scale changes. While other approaches have used multi-scale interest points also for object class recognition [7,8], no quantitative analysis of their robustness to scale changes has been reported. Our results show that the proposed approach outperforms state-of-the-art methods while being robust to scale changes of more than a factor of two. In addition, our quantitative results allow to draw some interesting conclusions for the design of suitable interest point detectors.

The paper is structured as follows. The next section discusses related work. After that, we briefly review the original single-scale approach. Section 3 then describes our extension to multiple scales. In Section 4, we examine the influence of different interest point detectors on the recognition result. Finally, Section 5 evaluates the robustness to scale changes.

2   Related Work

Many current methods for detection and recognition of object classes learn global or local features in fixed configurations or using configuration classifiers [17,18,19]. They recognize objects of different sizes by performing an exhaustive search over scales. Other approaches represent objects by more flexible models involving hand-defined or learned object parts. [20] models the joint spatial probability distribution of such parts, but does not explicitly deal with scale changes. [8] extends this approach to learn scale-invariant object parts and estimates their joint spatial and appearance distribution. However, the complexity of this combined estimation step restricts the method to a small number of parts. [7] also describes a method for selecting scale-invariant object parts, but this method is currently defined only for part detection, not yet on an object level. Most directly related to our approach, [1] learns a vocabulary of object parts for recognition and applies a SNoW classifier on top of them (which is later combined with the output of a more global classifier in [9]). [3] learns a similar vocabulary for generating class-specific segmentations. Both approaches only consider objects at a single scale. Our approach combines both ideas and integrates the two processes of recognition and figure-ground segmentation into a common probabilistic framework [12,11], which will also be the basis for our scale-invariant system. The following section briefly reviews this approach. As space does not permit to give a complete description, we only highlight the most important points and refer to [12,11] for details.

2.1 Basic Approach

The variability of a given object category is represented by learning, in a first step, a class-specific codebook of local appearances. For this, fixed-size image patches are extracted around Harris interest points from a set of training images and are clustered with an agglomerative clustering scheme. We then learn the spatial distribution of codebook entries for the given category by storing all locations the codebook entries were matched to on the training objects. During recognition, this information is used in a probabilistic extension of the Generalized Hough Transform [2,14]. Each patch $\mathbf{e}$ observed at location ℓ casts probabilistic votes for different object identities o_n and positions x according to the following equation:

$$p(o_n, x | \mathbf{e}, \ell) = \sum_i p(o_n, x | I_i, \ell) p(I_i | \mathbf{e}). \tag{1}$$

where $p(I_i | \mathbf{e})$ denotes the probability that patch $\mathbf{e}$ matches to codebook entry I_i, and $p(o_n, x | I_i, \ell)$ describes the stored spatial probability distribution for the object center relative to an occurrence of that codebook entry. In [12], object hypotheses are found as maxima in the voting space using a fixed-size search window W:

$$score(o_n, x) = \sum_k \sum_{x_j \in W(x)} p(o_n, x_j | \mathbf{e}_k, \ell_k). \tag{2}$$

For each such hypothesis, we then obtain the per-pixel probabilities of each pixel being *figure* or *ground* by the following double marginalization, thus effectively segmenting the object from the background (again see [12,11] for details):

$$p(\mathbf{p} = figure | o_n, x) = \sum_{\mathbf{p} \in (\mathbf{e}, \ell)} \sum_I p(\mathbf{p} = fig. | o_n, x, I, \ell) \frac{p(o_n, x | I, \ell) p(I | \mathbf{e}) p(\mathbf{e}, \ell)}{p(o_n, x)} \tag{3}$$

The per-pixel probabilities are then used in an MDL-based hypothesis verification stage in order to integrate only information about the object and discard misleading influences from the background [11]. The resulting approach achieves impressive results (as a comparison with other methods in Tab. 1 shows), but it has the inherent limitation that it can only recognize objects at a known scale. In practical applications, however, the exact scale of objects is typically not known beforehand, and there may even be several objects with different scales in the same scene. In order to make the approach applicable in practice, it is thus necessary to achieve scale-invariant recognition.

3 Extension to Multiple Scales

A major point of this paper is to extend recognition to multiple scales using scale-invariant interest points. The basic idea behind this is to replace the single-scale Harris codebook used up to now by a codebook derived from a scale-invariant detector. Given an input image, the system applies the detector and obtains a vector of point locations, together with their associated scales. Patches are extracted around the detected locations with a radius relative to the scale σ of the interest point (here: $r = 3\sigma$). In order to match image structures at different scales, the patches are then rescaled to the codebook size (in our case 25×25 pixels).

The probabilistic framework can be readily extended to multiple scales by treating scale as a third dimension in the voting space. If an image patch found at location $(x_{img}, y_{img}, s_{img})$ matches to a codebook entry that has been observed at position $(x_{occ}, y_{occ}, s_{occ})$ on a training image, it votes for the following coordinates:

$$x_{vote} = x_{img} - x_{occ}(s_{img}/s_{occ}) \tag{4}$$

$$y_{vote} = y_{img} - y_{occ}(s_{img}/s_{occ}) \tag{5}$$

$$s_{vote} = (s_{img}/s_{occ}) \tag{6}$$

However, the increased dimension of the voting space makes the maxima search computationally more expensive. For this reason, we employ a two-stage search strategy. In a first stage, votes are collected in a binned 3D Hough accumulator array in order to quickly find local maxima. Candidate maxima from this first stage are then refined in the second stage using the original (continuous) 3D votes. Instead of a simple but expensive sliding-window technique, we formulate the search in a Mean-Shift framework. For this, we replace the simple search window W from equation (2) by the following kernel density estimate:

$$\hat{p}(o_n, x) = \frac{1}{nh^d} \sum_k \sum_j p(o_n, x_j | \mathbf{e}_k, \ell_k) K\left(\frac{x - x_j}{h}\right) \tag{7}$$

where the kernel K is a radially symmetric, nonnegative function, centered at zero and integrating to one. From [5], we know that a Mean-Shift search using this formulation will quickly converge to local modes of the underlying distribution. Moreover, the search procedure can be interpreted as a Parzen window probability density estimation for the position of the object center.

From the literature, it is also known that the performance of the Mean-Shift procedure depends critically on a good selection for the kernel bandwidth h. Various approaches have been proposed to estimate the optimal bandwidth directly from the data, e.g. [6,4]. In our case, however, we have an intuitive interpretation for the bandwidth as a search window for the position of the object center. As the object scale increases, the *relative errors* introduced by equations (4)-(6) cause votes to be spread over a larger area around the hypothesized object center and thus reduce their density in the voting space. As a consequence, the kernel bandwidth should also increase in order to compensate for this effect. We can thus make the bandwidth dependent on the scale coordinate and obtain the following *balloon density estimator* [6]:

$$\hat{p}(o_n, x) = \frac{1}{nh(x)^d} \sum_k \sum_j p(o_n, x_j | \mathbf{e}_k, \ell_k) K\left(\frac{x - x_j}{h(x)}\right) \tag{8}$$

For K we use a uniform spherical kernel with a radius corresponding to 5% of the hypothesized object size. Since a certain minimum bandwidth needs to be maintained for small scales, though, we only adapt it for scales greater than 1.0.

We have thus formulated the multi-scale object detection problem as a scale-adaptive Mean-Shift search procedure. Our experimental results in Section 5 will show that this

Fig. 1. Scale-invariant interest points found by (from left to right) the exact DoG, the fast DoG, the regular Harris-Laplace, and the fast Harris-Laplace detector on two example images (The smallest scales are omitted in order to reduce clutter).

scale adaptation step is indeed needed in order to provide stable results over large scale changes. The performance of the resulting approach depends on the capability of the underlying patch extractor to find image structures that are both typical for the object category and that can be accurately localized in position and scale. As different detectors are optimized for finding different types of structures, the next section evaluates the suitability of various scale-invariant interest point detectors for categorization

4   Influence of Interest Point Detectors

Typically, interest point detectors are only evaluated in terms of their repeatability. Consequently, significant effort has been spent on making the detectors discriminant enough that they find exactly the same structures again under different viewing conditions. However, we strongly believe that the evaluation should be in the context of a task. In our case, the task is to recognize and localize previously unseen objects of a given category. This means that we cannot assume to find exactly the same structures again; instead the system needs to generalize and find structures that are similar enough to known object parts while still allowing enough flexibility to cope with variations. Also, because of the large intra-class variability, more potential matching candidates are needed to compensate for inevitable mismatches. Last but not least, the interest points should provide a sufficient cover of the object, so that it can be recognized even if some important parts are occluded. Altogether, this imposes a rather different set of constraints on the interest point detector. As a first step we therefore have to compare the performance of different interest point operators for the categorization task.

In this work, we evaluate two different types of scale-invariant interest point operators: the Harris-Laplace detector [15], and the DoG (Difference of Gaussian) detector [14]. Both operators have been shown to yield high repeatability [16], but they differ in the type of structures they respond to. The Harris-Laplace prefers corner-like structures by searching for multi-scale Harris points that are simultaneously extrema of a scale-space Laplacian, while the DoG detector selects blob-like structures by searching for scale-space maxima of a Difference-of-Gaussian. For both detectors, we additionally examine two variants: a regular and a speed-optimized implementation (operating on a Gaussian pyramid). Figure 1 shows the kind of structures that are captured by the different detectors. As can already be observed from these examples, all detectors manage to

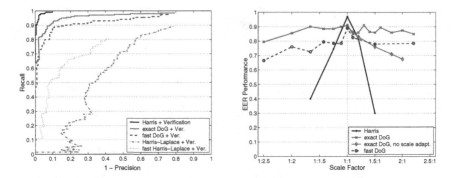

Fig. 2. Performance comparison on the UIUC database. (left) Precision-Recall curves of different interest point detectors for the single-scale case. (right) EER performance over scale changes relative to the size of the training examples.

capture some characteristic object parts, such as the car's wheels, but the range of scales and the distribution of points over the object varies considerably between them.

In order to obtain a more quantitative assessment of their capabilities, we compare the different interest point operators on a car detection task using our extended approach. As a test set, we use the UIUC database [1], which consists of 170 images containing a total of 200 sideviews of cars. For all experiments reported below, training is done on a set of 50 hand-segmented images (mirrored to represent both car directions). In a first stage, we compare the recognition performance if the test images are of the same size as the training images. Since our detectors are learned at a higher resolution than the cars in the test set, we rescale all test images by the same factor prior to recognition. (Note that this step does not increase the images' information content.)

Figure 2(left) shows a comparison of the detectors' performances. It can be seen that the single-scale Harris codebook from [11] achieves the best results with 97.5% equal error rate (EER). Compared to its performance, all scale-invariant detectors result in codebooks that are less discriminant. This could be expected, since invariance always comes at the price of reduced discriminance. However, the exact DoG detector reaches an EER performance of 91%, which still compares favorably to state-of-the-art methods (see Tab. 1). The fast DoG detector performs only slightly worse with 89% EER. In contrast, both Harris-Laplace variants are notably inferior with 59.5% for the regular and 70% for the speed-optimized version.

The main reason for the poorer performance of the Harris-Laplace detectors is that they return a smaller absolute number of interest points on the object, so that a sufficient cover is not always guaranteed. Although previous studies have shown that the Harris-Laplace points are more discriminant individually [7], their smaller number is a strong disadvantage. The DoG detectors, on the other hand, both find enough points on the objects and are discriminant enough to allow reliable matches to the codebook. They are thus better suited for our categorization task. For this reason, we only consider DoG detectors in the following experiments.

Fig. 3. (top) Visualization of the range of scales tested in the experiments, and the corresponding car detections. Training has been performed at scale 1.0.; (bottom) Segmentations automatically obtained for these examples. (white: *figure*, black: *ground*, gray: *not sampled*)

5   Robustness to Scale Changes

We now analyze the robustness to scale changes. In particular, we are interested in the limit to the detectors' performance when the scale of the test images is altered by a large factor and the fraction of familiar image structures is thus decreased. Rather than to test individual thresholds, we therefore compare the maximally achievable performance by looking at how the equal error rates are affected by scale changes.

In the following experiment, the UIUC database images are rescaled to different sizes and the performance is measured as a function of the scaling factor relative to the size of the training examples. Figure 2(right) shows the EER performances that can be achieved for scale changes between factor 0.4 (corresponding to a scale reduction of 1:2.5) and factor 2.2. When the training and test images are approximately of the same size, the single-scale Harris codebook is highly discriminant and provides the superior performance described in the previous section. However, the evaluation shows that it is only robust to scale changes up to about 20%, after which its performance quickly drops. The exact-DoG codebook, on the other hand, is not as discriminative and only achieves an EER of 91% for test images of the same scale. However, it is far more robust to scale changes and can compensate for both enlargements and size reductions of more than a factor of 2. Up to a scale factor of 0.6, its performance stays above 89%. Even when the target object is only half the size of those seen during training, it still provides an EER of 85%. For the larger scales, the performance gradation is similar. The fast DoG detector performs about 10% worse, mainly because its implementation with a Gaussian pyramid restricts the number and precision of points found at higher scales. Figure 2(right) also shows that the system's performance quickly degrades without the scale adaptation step from Section 3, confirming that this step is indeed important.

An artifact of the interest point detectors can be observed when looking at the performance gradation over scale. Our implementation of the exact DoG detector estimates characteristic scale by computing three discrete levels per scale octave [14] and interpolates between them using a second-order polynomial. Correspondingly, recognition performance is highest at scale levels where structure sizes can be exactly computed (namely $\{0.6, 1.0, 1.3, 1.6, 2.0\}$, which correspond to powers of ($\sqrt[3]{2}$)). In-between those levels, the performance slightly dips. Although this effect can easily be alleviated by using more levels per scale octave, it shows the importance of this design decision.

Figure 3 shows a visualization of the range of scales tested in this experiment. Our approach's capability to provide robust performance over this large range of image variations marks a significant improvement over [11]. In the bottom part of the figure, the automatically generated segmentations are displayed for the different scales. Compared to the single-scale segmentations from [11], the segmentation quality is only slightly inferior, while being stable over a wide range of scales.

6   Conclusion and Future Work

In this paper, we have presented a scale invariant extension of the approach from [12,11] that makes the method applicable in practice. By reformulating the multi-scale object detection problem in a Mean-Shift framework, we have obtained a theoretically founded interpretation of the hypothesis search procedure which allows to use a principled scale adaptation mechanism. Our quantitative evaluation over a large range of scales shows that the resulting method is robust to scale changes of more than a factor of 2. In addition, the method retains the capability to provide an automatically derived object segmentation as part of the recognition process.

As part of our study, we have also evaluated the suitability of different scale-invariant interest point detectors for the categorization task. One interesting result is that, while found to be more discriminant in previous studies [15,7], the Harris-Laplacian detector on its own does not detect enough points on the object to enable reliable recognition. The DoG detector, on the other hand, both finds enough points on the object and is discriminant enough to yield good recognition performance. This emphasizes the different characteristics the object categorization task brings with it, compared to the identification of known objects, and the consequent need to reevaluate design decisions. An obvious extension would be to combine both Harris-type and DoG-type interest points in a common system. Since both detectors respond to different image structures, they can complement each other and compensate for missing detections. Consequently, we expect such a combination to be more robust than the individual detectors.

Acknowledgments. This work is part of the CogVis project, funded by the Comission of the EU (IST-2000-29375) and the Swiss Federal Office for Education and Science (BBW 00.0617).

References

1. S. Agarwal and D. Roth. Learning a sparse representation for object detection. In *ECCV'02*, 2002.
2. D.H. Ballard. Generalizing the hough transform to detect arbitrary shapes. *Pattern Recognition*, 13(2):111–122, 1981.
3. E. Borenstein and S. Ullman. Class-specific, top-down segmentation. In *ECCV'02*, 2002.
4. R. Collins. Mean-shift blob tracking through scale space. In *CVPR'03*, 2003.
5. D. Comaniciu and P. Meer. Mean shift: A robust approach toward feature space analysis. *Trans. PAMI*, 24(5):603–619, 2002.

6. D. Comaniciu, V. Ramesh, and P. Meer. The variable bandwidth mean shift and data-driven scale selection. In *ICCV'01*, 2001.
7. G. Dorko and C. Schmid. Selection of scale invariant parts for object class recognition. In *ICCV'03*, 2003.
8. R. Fergus, A. Zisserman, and P. Perona. Object class recognition by unsupervised scale-invariant learning. In *CVPR'03*, 2003.
9. A. Garg, S. Agarwal, and T. Huang. Fusion of global and local information for object detection. In *ICPR'02*, 2002.
10. T. Kadir and M. Brady. Scale, saliency, and image description. *IJCV*, 45(2):83–105, 2001.
11. B. Leibe, A. Leonardis, and B. Schiele. Combined object categorization and segmentation with an implicit shape model. In *ECCV'04 Workshop on Stat. Learn. in Comp. Vis.*, 2004.
12. B. Leibe and B. Schiele. Interleaved object categorization and segmentation. In *BMVC'03*, 2003.
13. T. Lindeberg. Feature detection with automatic scale selection. *IJCV*, 30(2):79–116, 1998.
14. D. Lowe. Object recognition from local scale invariant features. In *ICCV'99*, 1999.
15. K. Mikolajczyk and C. Schmid. Indexing based on scale invariant interest points. In *ICCV'01*, pages 525–531, 2001.
16. K. Mikolajczyk and C. Schmid. A performance evaluation of local descriptors. In *CVPR'03*, 2003.
17. C. Papageorgiou and T. Poggio. A trainable system for object detection. *IJCV*, 38(1), 2000.
18. H. Schneiderman and T. Kanade. A statistical method of 3d object detection applied to faces and cars. In *CVPR'00*, 2000.
19. P. Viola and M. Jones. Rapid object detection using a boosted cascade of simple features. In *CVPR'01*, pages 511–518, 2001.
20. M. Weber, M. Welling, and P. Perona. Unsupervised learning of object models for recognition. In *ECCV'00*, 2000.

Pixel-to-Pixel Matching for Image Recognition Using Hungarian Graph Matching

Daniel Keysers, Thomas Deselaers, and Hermann Ney

Lehrstuhl für Informatik VI, Computer Science Department
RWTH Aachen University, D-52056 Aachen, Germany
{keysers, deselaers, ney}@informatik.rwth-aachen.de

Abstract. A fundamental problem in image recognition is to evaluate the similarity of two images. This can be done by searching for the best pixel-to-pixel matching taking into account suitable constraints. In this paper, we present an extension of a zero-order matching model called the image distortion model that yields state-of-the-art classification results for different tasks. We include the constraint that in the matching process each pixel of both compared images must be matched at least once. The optimal matching under this constraint can be determined using the Hungarian algorithm. The additional constraint leads to more homogeneous displacement fields in the matching. The method reduces the error rate of a nearest neighbor classifier on the well known USPS handwritten digit recognition task from 2.4% to 2.2%.

1   Introduction

In image recognition, a common problem is to match two given images, e.g. when comparing an observed image to given references. In that process, different methods can be used. For this purpose we can define cost functions depending on the distortion introduced in the matching and search for the best matching with respect to a given cost function [6]. One successful and conceptually simple method for determining the image matching is to use a zero-order model that completely disregards dependencies between the pixel mappings. This model has been described in the literature several times independently and is called image distortion model (IDM) here. The IDM yields especially good results if the local image context for each pixel is considered in the matching process by using gradient information and local sub windows [5,6].

In this paper, we introduce an extension of the IDM that affects the pixel mapping not by incorporating explicit restrictions on the displacements (which can also lead to improvements [5,6]), but by adding the global constraint that each pixel in both of the compared images must be matched at least once. To find the best matching under this constraint, we construct an appropriate graph representing the images to be compared and then solve the 'minimum weight edge cover' problem that can be reduced to the 'minimum weight matching' problem. The latter can then be solved using the Hungarian algorithm [7]. The resulting model leads to more homogeneous displacement fields and improves

C.E. Rasmussen et al. (Eds.): DAGM 2004, LNCS 3175, pp. 154–162, 2004.

the error rate for the recognition of handwritten digits. We refer to this model as the Hungarian distortion model (HDM).

The HDM is evaluated on the well known US Postal Service database (USPS), which contains segmented handwritten digits from US zip codes. There are many results for different classifiers available on this database and the HDM approach presented here achieves an error rate of 2.2% which is – though not being the best known result – state-of-the-art and an improvement over the 2.4% error rate achieved using the IDM alone.

Related work. There is a large amount of literature dealing with the application of graph matching to computer vision and pattern recognition tasks. For example, graph matching procedures can be used for labeling of segmented scenes. Other examples, more related to the discussed method include the following: In [9] the authors represent face images by elastic graphs which have node labels representing the local texture information as computed by a set of Gabor filters and are used in the face localization and recognition process. In [1] a method for image matching using the Hungarian algorithm is described that is based on representations of the local image context called 'shape contexts' which are only extracted at edge points. An assignment between these points is determined using the Hungarian algorithm and the image is matched using thin-plate splines, which is iterated until convergence. Yet, all applications of graph matching to comparable tasks that are known to the authors operate on a level higher than the pixel level. The novelty of the presented approach therefore consists in applying the matching at the pixel level.

2   Decision Rule and Image Matching

In this work, we focus on the invariant distance resulting from the image matching process and therefore only use a simple classification approach. We briefly give a formal description of the decision process: To classify a test image A with a given training set of references $B_{1k}, \ldots, B_{N_k k}$ for each class $k \in \{1, \ldots, K\}$ we use the nearest neighbor (NN) decision rule

$$r(A) = \arg \min_k \left\{ \min_{n=1,\ldots,N_k} D(A, B_{nk}) \right\},$$

i.e. the test image is assigned to the class of the nearest reference image. For the distance calculation the test image $A = \{a_{ij}\}, i = 1, \ldots, I, j = 1, \ldots, J$ must be explained by a suitable deformation of the reference image $B = \{b_{xy}\}, x = 1, \ldots, X, y = 1, \ldots, Y$. Here, the image pixels take U-dimensional values $a_{ij}, b_{xy} \in \mathbb{R}^U$, where the vector components are denoted by a superscript u. It has been observed in previous experiments that the performance of deformation models is significantly improved by using local context at the level of the pixels [5,6]. For example, we can use the horizontal and vertical image gradient as computed by a Sobel filter and/or local sub images that represent the image context of a pixel. Furthermore, we can use appropriately weighted position features (e.g. $\frac{i-1}{I-1}, \frac{j-1}{J-1}, \ldots$) that describe the relative pixel position in order to assign higher costs to mappings that deviate much from a linear matching.

We now want to determine an image deformation mapping $(x_{11}^{IJ}, y_{11}^{IJ})$: $(i, j) \mapsto (x_{ij}, y_{ij})$ that results in the distorted reference image $B_{(x_{11}^{IJ}, y_{11}^{IJ})} = \{b_{x_{ij} y_{ij}}\}$. The resulting cost given the two images and the deformation mapping is defined as

$$C(A, B, (x_{11}^{IJ}, y_{11}^{IJ})) = \sum_{i,j} \sum_{u} ||a_{ij}^u - b_{x_{ij} y_{ij}}^u||^2,$$

i.e. by summing up the local pixel-wise distances, which are squared Euclidean distances here. Now, the distance measure between images A and B is determined by minimizing the cost over the possible deformation mappings:

$$D(A, B) = \min_{(x_{11}^{IJ}, y_{11}^{IJ}) \in \mathcal{M}} \left\{ C(A, B, (x_{11}^{IJ}, y_{11}^{IJ})) \right\}$$

The set of possible deformation mappings $\mathcal{M}$ determines the type of model used. For the IDM these restrictions are $x_{ij} \in \{1, \ldots, X\} \cap \{i' - w, \ldots, i' + w\}$, $i' = \left[i\frac{X}{I} \right]$, $y_{ij} \in \{1, \ldots, Y\} \cap \{j' - w, \ldots, j' + w\}$, $j' = \left[j\frac{Y}{J} \right]$, with warp range w, e.g. $w = 2$. For different models, the minimization process can be computationally very complex. A preselection of the e.g. 100 nearest neighbors with a different distance measures like the Euclidean distance can then significantly improve the computation time at the expense of a slightly higher error rate.

2.1   Image Distortion Model

The IDM is a conceptually very simple matching procedure. It neglects all dependencies between the pixel displacements and is therefore a zero-order model of distortion. Although higher order models have advantages in some cases, the IDM is chosen here for comparison to the HDM since the Hungarian algorithm does not easily support the inclusion of dependencies between pixel displacements. The formal restrictions of the IDM are given in the previous section, a more informal description is as follows: for each pixel in the test image, determine the best matching pixel within a region of size $w \times w$ at the corresponding position in the reference image and use this match. Due to its simplicity and efficiency this model has been introduced several times in the literature with differing names. When used with the appropriate pixel-level context description it produces very good classification results for object recognition tasks like handwritten digit recognition [6] and radiograph classification [5].

2.2   Hungarian Matching

The term 'matching' is a well-known expression in graph theory, where it refers to a selection of edges in a (bipartite) graph. We can also view the concept of pixel-to-pixel image matchings in this context. To do so, we construct an appropriate graph from the two images to be compared and apply the suitable algorithms known from graph theory. In this section we explore this application and use the so called Hungarian algorithm to solve different pixel-to-pixel assignment problems for images. The Hungarian algorithm has been used before to assign image region descriptors of two images to each other [1].

Construction of the bipartite graph. The construction of the bipartite graph in the case discussed here is straight forward: Each pixel position of one of the two images to be compared is mapped to a node in the graph. Two nodes are connected by an edge if and only if they represent pixels from different images. This means that the two components of the bipartite graph represent the two images. The weight of an edge is chosen to be the Euclidean distance between the respective pixel representations, possibly enlarged by penalties for too large absolute distortions.

Outline of the Hungarian algorithm. This outline of the Hungarian algorithm is included for the interested reader but it is not essential for the understanding of the proposed method. The outline follows [7, pp. 74–89], which was also the basis for the used implementation. The name 'Hungarian' algorithm is due to a constructive result published by two Hungarian mathematicians in 1931 that is used in the algorithm [7, p. 78].

To explain the basic idea, we assume that the weights of the edges are given by the entries of a matrix W and we assume that both components of the graph have N vertices and thus $W \in \mathbb{R}^{N \times N}$ is square. The goal of the algorithm is to find a permutation $\pi : \{1, \ldots, N\} \mapsto \{1, \ldots, N\}$ minimizing $\sum_{n=1}^{N} W_{n\pi(n)}$. Now, we can make the following observations:

(a) Adding a constant to any row or column of the matrix does not change the solution, because exactly one term in the sum is changed by that amount independent of the permutation.

(b) If W is nonnegative and $\sum_n W_{n\pi(n)} = 0$ then π is a solution.

Let two zeroes in W be called independent if they appear in different rows and columns. The algorithm now uses the following 'Hungarian' theorem: The maximum number of mutually independent zeroes in W is equal to the minimum number of lines (rows or columns) that are needed to cover all zeroes in W. Given an algorithm that finds such a maximum set of mutually independent zeroes and the corresponding minimum set of lines (as summarized below) the complete algorithm can be formulated as follows:

1. from each line (row or column) subtract its minimum element
2. find a maximum set of N' mutually independent zeroes
3. *if* $N' = N$ such zeroes have been found: output their indices and stop
   otherwise: cover all zeroes in W with N' lines and find the minimum uncovered value; subtract it from all uncovered elements, and add it to all doubly covered elements; go to 2

To show that the algorithm always terminates and yields the correct result, it is necessary to illustrate how step 2 works. The detailed discussion of the termination is beyond the scope of this overview. We try to give a short idea and otherwise refer to [7]:

1. Choose an initial set of independent zeroes (e.g. greedily constructed) and call these 'special'. *2.* Cover rows containing one of the special zeroes and mark all other rows. *3.* While there are marked rows, choose the next marked row: for each zero in the row that is not in a covered column, two cases are possible: a) the column already contains a special zero in another row 'ρ': cover the column and uncover and mark ρ. b) a new special zero is found and processed. When the row is processed completely, unmark it.

Termination of the algorithm is guaranteed, because in step 3 either the number of mutually independent zeroes or the number of covered columns is increased by the newly introduced zero and this can happen at most N times. The total running time of this algorithm is $O(N^3)$, where the average case can be much lower if good initial assignments can be determined. This implies that the application of the HDM to large images is only possible at a high computational cost. Note that there are other algorithms to solve the assignment problem, but most of these algorithms are developed for special cases of the structure of the graph (which is always a complete bipartite graph here).

Application of the Hungarian algorithm. The Hungarian algorithm is a tool to solve an assignment problem. For image matching, we can determine the best matching of pixels onto each other, where each pixel is matched exactly once. It is possible to directly use the Hungarian algorithm, but in many cases it is more appropriate to match the pixels onto each other such that each pixel is matched at least once or such that each pixel of the test image is matched exactly once. This last case corresponds to the most frequently used setting. We then require that the reference image *explains* all the pixels in the test image. We thus have three applications of the Hungarian algorithm for image matching:

Each pixel matched exactly once. This case is trivial. Construct the weight matrix as discussed above and apply the Hungarian algorithm to obtain a minimum weight matching.

Each pixel matched at least once. For this case, we need to solve the 'minimum weight edge cover' problem. A reduction to the exact match case can be done following an idea presented in [3]:
   1. construct the weight matrix as discussed above *2.* for each node find one of the incident edges with minimum weight *3.* subtract from each edge weight the minimum weight of both connected nodes as determined in the previous step *4.* make the edge weight matrix nonnegative (by subtracting the minimum weight) and apply the Hungarian algorithm *5.* from the resulting matching, remove all edges with a nonzero weight (their nodes are covered better by using the minimum weight incident edges) *6.* for each uncovered node add an edge with minimum weight to the cover

Each pixel of the test image matched exactly once. This task is solved by the image distortion model, we only need to choose the best matching pixel for each pixel in the test image.
   Another method to obtain such a matching evolves from the previous algorithm if it is followed by the step: *7.* for each pixel of the test image delete all edges in the cover except one with minimum weight.
   The resulting matching then does not have the overall minimum weight (as determined by the IDM) but respects larger parts of the reference image due

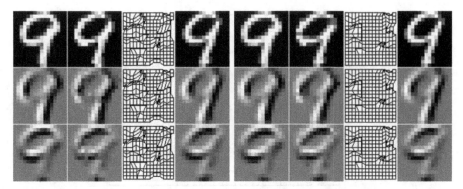

Fig. 1. Examples of pixel displacements; left: image distortion model; right: Hungarian distortion model. Top to bottom: grey values, horizontal, and vertical gradient; left to right: test image, distorted reference image, displacement field, and original reference image. The matching is based on the gradient values alone, using 3×3 local sub images and an absolute warp range of 2 pixels.

to the construction of the matching. Therefore, the resulting matching is more homogeneous. In informal experiments this last choice showed the best performance and was used for the experiments presented in the following.

3   Experiments and Results

The software used in the experiments is available for download at http://www-i6.informatik.rwth-aachen.de/~gollan/w2d.html. We performed experiments on the well known US Postal Service handwritten digit recognition task (USPS). It contains normalized greyscale images of size 16×16 pixels of handwritten digits from US zip codes. The corpus is divided into 7,291 training and 2,007 test images. A human error rate estimated to be 1.5-2.5% shows that it is a hard recognition task. A large variety of classification algorithms

Table 1. Best reported recognition results for the USPS corpus (top: general results for comparison; bottom: results related to the discussed method)

method		ER[%]
invariant support vector machine	[8]	3.0
extended tangent distance	[6]	2.4
extended support vector machine	[2]	2.2
local features + tangent distance	[4]	2.0
ext. pseudo-2D HMM, local image context, 3-NN	[6]	1.9
no matching, 1-NN		5.6
IDM, local image context, 1-NN	[6]	2.4
HDM, local image context, 1-NN	this work	**2.2**

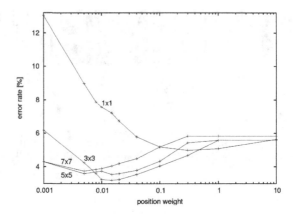

Fig. 2. Error rates on USPS vs. position weight and sub image size using HDM with greyvalues (preselection: 100 nearest neighbors, Euclidean distance).

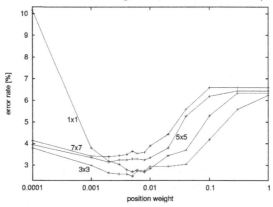

Fig. 3. Error rates on USPS vs. position weight and sub image size using HDM with gradients (preselection: 100 nearest neighbors, Euclidean distance).

have been tried on this database and some of the best results are summarized in Table 1.

Figure 1 shows two typical examples of pixel displacements resulting from IDM and HDM in the comparison of two images showing the digit '9'. It can be observed that the HDM leads to a significantly more homogeneous displacement field due to the additional restriction imposed in the calculation of the mapping.

Figure 2 shows the error rate of the HDM with respect to the weight of the position feature in the matching process. The pixel features used are the grayvalue contexts of sizes 1×1, 3×3, 5×5, and 7×7, respectively. Interestingly, already using only pixel greyvalues (1×1), the error rate can be somewhat improved from 5.6% to 5.0% with the appropriate position weight. Best results are obtained using sub images of size 3×3 leading to 3.2% error rate.

Figure 3 shows the error rate of the HDM with respect to the weight of the position feature using the vertical and horizontal gradient as the image features with different local contexts. Interestingly, the 1×1 error rate is very competitive when using the image gradient as features and reaches an error rate of 2.7%. Again, best results are obtained using sub images of size 3×3 and position weights around 0.005 relative to the other features, with an error rate of 2.4%.

All previously described experiments used a preselection of the 100 nearest neighbors with the Euclidean distance to speed up the classification process. (One image comparison takes about 0.1s on a 1.8GHz processor for 3×3 gradient contexts.) Using the full reference set in the classifier finally reduces the error rate from 2.4% to 2.2% for this setting. Note that this improvement is not statistically significant on a test corpus of size 2,007 but is still remarkable in combination with the resulting more homogeneous displacement fields.

4   Conclusion

In this paper, we extended the image distortion model which leads to state-of-the-art results in different classification tasks when using an appropriate representation of the local image context. The extension uses the Hungarian algorithm to find the best pixel-to-pixel mapping with the additional constraint that each pixel in both compared images must be matched at least once. This constraint leads to more homogeneous displacement fields in the matching process. The error rate on the USPS handwritten digit recognition task could be reduced from 2.4% to 2.2% using a nearest neighbor classifier and the IDM and HDM as distance measures, respectively.

Acknowledgments. This work was partially funded by the DFG (Deutsche Forschungsgemeinschaft) under contract NE-572/6. The authors would like to thank Christian Gollan for implementing the software framework the experiments benefited from.

References

1. S. Belongie, J. Malik, J. Puzicha: Shape Matching and Object Recognition Using Shape Contexts. *IEEE Trans. Pattern Analysis and Machine Intelligence*, 24(4):509–522, April 2002.
2. J.X. Dong, A. Krzyzak, C.Y. Suen: A Practical SMO Algorithm. In *Proc. Int. Conf. on Pattern Recognition*, Quebec City, Canada, August 2002.
3. J. Keijsper, R. Pendavingh: An Efficient Algorithm for Minimum-Weight Bibranching. Technical Report 96-12, Amsterdam Univ., Amsterdam, The Netherlands, 1996.
4. D. Keysers, R. Paredes, H. Ney, E. Vidal: Combination of Tangent Vectors and Local Representations for Handwritten Digit Recognition. In *SPR 2002, Statistical Pattern Recognition*, Windsor, Ontario, Canada, pp. 538–547, August 2002.
5. D. Keysers, C. Gollan, H. Ney: Classification of Medical Images using Non-linear Distortion Models. In *Proc. BVM 2004, Bildverarbeitung für die Medizin*, Berlin, Germany, pp. 366–370, March 2004.

6. D. Keysers, C. Gollan, H. Ney: Local Context in Non-linear Deformation Models for Handwritten Character Recognition. In *ICPR 2004, 17th Int. Conf. on Pattern Recognition*, Cambridge, UK, August 2004. In press.
7. D.E. Knuth: *The Stanford GraphBase: A Platform for Combinatorial Computing.* Addison-Wesley, Reading, MA, 1994.
8. B. Schölkopf, P. Simard, A. Smola, V. Vapnik: Prior Knowledge in Support Vector Kernels. In *Advances in Neural Information Processing Systems 10.* MIT Press, pp. 640–646, 1998.
9. L. Wiskott, J. Fellous, N. Krüger, C. v.d. Malsburg: Face Recognition by Elastic Bunch Graph Matching. *IEEE Trans. Pattern Analysis and Machine Intelligence*, 19(7):775–779, July 1997.

Estimation of Multiple Orientations at Corners and Junctions

Cicero Mota[1], Ingo Stuke[2], Til Aach[2], and Erhardt Barth[1]

[1] Institute for Neuro- and Bioinformatics, University of Luebeck, Germany
{mota, barth}@inb.uni-luebeck.de
[2] Institute for Signal Processing, University of Luebeck, Germany
{aach, stuke}@isip.uni-luebeck.de

Abstract. Features like junctions and corners are a rich source of information for image understanding. We present a novel theoretical framework for the analysis of such 2D features in scalar and multispectral images. We model the features as occluding superpositions of two different orientations and derive a new constraint equation based on the tensor product of two directional derivatives. The eigensystem analysis of a 3×3-tensor then provides the so-called mixed-orientation parameters (MOP) vector that encodes the two orientations uniquely, but only implicitly. We then show how to separate the MOP vector into the two orientations by finding the roots of a second-order polynomial. Based on the orientations, the occluding boundary and the center of the junction are easily determined. The results confirm the validity, robustness, and accuracy of the approach.

1 Introduction

It is well known that corners and junctions are a rich source of information for image understanding: T-junctions are associated to object occlusions; L- and Y-junctions to object corners; X-junctions to the occurrence of transparencies; and Ψ-junctions to the presence of bending surfaces of objects [2, 12]. Accordingly different approaches for junction localization have been reported [9, 11, 13, 14, 17, 19, 22].

In addition to the above semantic importance of junctions and corners, their significance is determined by basic properties of the image function itself: flat regions in images are the most frequent but also redundant; one-dimensional features like straight edges are still redundant since two-dimensional regions have been shown to fully specify an image [4, 15]; corners and junctions are the least frequent but most significant image features [23].

In this paper we model an image junction as a superposition of oriented structures and show how to estimate the multiple orientations occurring at such positions. Our approach differs from previous attempts [10, 18, 19] in that we provide a closed-form solution. Moreover, our results are an extension of earlier results that have dealt with the problems of estimating transparent motions [16, 21], occluded motions [6, 5], and multiple orientations in images based on an additive model [20, 1].

C.E. Rasmussen et al. (Eds.): DAGM 2004, LNCS 3175, pp. 163–170, 2004.

2   Theoretical Results

Let $\mathbf{f}(\mathbf{x})$ be an image that is ideally oriented in a region Ω, i.e., there is a direction (subspace) E of the plane such that $\mathbf{f}(\mathbf{x}+\mathbf{v}) = \mathbf{f}(\mathbf{x})$ for all $\mathbf{x}, \mathbf{v}$ such that $\mathbf{x}, \mathbf{x}+\mathbf{v} \in \Omega$, $\mathbf{v} \in E$. This is equivalent to

$$\frac{\partial \mathbf{f}(\mathbf{x})}{\partial \mathbf{v}} = \mathbf{0} \quad \text{for all } \mathbf{x} \in \Omega \text{ and } \mathbf{v} \in E , \tag{1}$$

which is a system of q equations for $\mathbf{f}(\mathbf{x}) \in \mathbb{R}^q$. For intensity images $q = 1$ and for RGB images $q = 3$. The direction E can be estimated as the set of vectors that minimize the energy functional

$$\mathcal{E}(\mathbf{v}) = \int_\Omega \left| \frac{\partial \mathbf{f}}{\partial \mathbf{v}} \right|^2 d\Omega = \mathbf{v}^T \mathbf{J} \mathbf{v} , \tag{2}$$

where $\mathbf{J}$ is given by

$$\mathbf{J} = \int_\Omega \begin{bmatrix} |\mathbf{f}_x|^2 & \mathbf{f}_x \cdot \mathbf{f}_y \\ \mathbf{f}_x \cdot \mathbf{f}_y & |\mathbf{f}_y|^2 \end{bmatrix} d\Omega . \tag{3}$$

In the above equation, $\mathbf{f}_x$, $\mathbf{f}_y$ are short notations for $\partial \mathbf{f}/\partial x$, $\partial \mathbf{f}/\partial y$.

The tensor $\mathbf{J}$ is the natural generalization of the structure tensor [7–9, 11] for multi-spectral images. Since $\mathbf{J}$ is symmetric and non-negative, Eq. (1) is equivalent to $\mathbf{J}\mathbf{v} = \lambda\mathbf{v}, \mathbf{v} \neq \mathbf{0}$, where ideally $\lambda = 0$. This implies that E is the null-eigenspace of $\mathbf{J}$ and in practice estimated as the eigenspace associated to the smallest eigenvalues of $\mathbf{J}$. Confidence for the estimation can thus be derived from the eigenvalues (or, equivalently, scalar invariants) of $\mathbf{J}$ (see [16]): two small eigenvalues correspond to flat regions of the image; only one small eigenvalue to the presence of oriented structures; and two significant eigenvalues to the presence of junctions or other 2D structures. Below we show how to estimate the orientations at junctions where two oriented structures predominate.

2.1   Multiple Orientations

Let Ω be a region of high confidence for a junction. We model junctions by the following constraint on $\mathbf{f}(\mathbf{x})$ that is the occluded superposition

$$\mathbf{f}(\mathbf{x}) = \chi(\mathbf{x})\mathbf{g}_1(\mathbf{x}) + (1 - \chi(\mathbf{x}))\mathbf{g}_2(\mathbf{x}) , \tag{4}$$

where $\mathbf{g}_1(\mathbf{x}), \mathbf{g}_2(\mathbf{x})$ are ideally oriented with directions $\mathbf{u} = (u_x, u_y)^T$ and $\mathbf{v} = (v_x, v_y)^T$ respectively; and where $\chi(\mathbf{x})$ is the characteristic function of some half-plane P through the 'center' (to be defined later) of the junction. This model is appropriate for the local description of junction types T, L and Ψ. X-junctions better fit a transparent model and have been treated in [1, 20].

The Constraint Equation. To estimate two orientations in Ω, we observe that Eq. (4) is equivalent to

$$\mathbf{f}(\mathbf{x}) = \begin{cases} \mathbf{g}_1(\mathbf{x}) \text{ if } \mathbf{x} \in P \\ \mathbf{g}_2(\mathbf{x}) \text{ otherwise.} \end{cases} \tag{5}$$

Therefore, $\partial\mathbf{f}(\mathbf{x})/\partial\mathbf{u} = \mathbf{0}$ if $\mathbf{x}$ is inside of P and $\partial\mathbf{f}(\mathbf{x})/\partial\mathbf{v} = \mathbf{0}$ if $\mathbf{x}$ is outside of P. From the above we can draw the important and, as we shall see, very useful conclusion that the expression

$$\frac{\partial\mathbf{f}(\mathbf{x})}{\partial\mathbf{u}} \otimes \frac{\partial\mathbf{f}(\mathbf{x})}{\partial\mathbf{v}} = \mathbf{0} \tag{6}$$

is valid everywhere except for the border of P where it may differ from zero. The symbol $\otimes$ denotes the tensor product of two vectors. Eq. (6) may not hold at the border of P because there the derivatives of the characteristic function $\chi(\mathbf{x})$ are not defined. This is not the case if $\mathbf{u}$ and the border of P have the same direction, e.g., in case of a T-junction. Given Eq. (6), the tensor product should be symmetric in $\mathbf{u}$ and $\mathbf{v}$. Since in practice symmetry might be violated, we expand the symmetric part of the above tensor product to obtain

$$c_{xx}\mathbf{f}_x \otimes \mathbf{f}_x + \frac{c_{xy}}{2}(\mathbf{f}_x \otimes \mathbf{f}_y + \mathbf{f}_y \otimes \mathbf{f}_x) + c_{yy}\mathbf{f}_y \otimes \mathbf{f}_y = \mathbf{0} \tag{7}$$

where

$$c_{xx} = u_x v_x, \quad c_{yy} = u_y v_y, \quad c_{xy} = u_x v_y + u_y v_x . \tag{8}$$

Note that for an image with q spectral components, the system in Eq. (7) has $q(q+1)/2$ equations, which makes the system over-constrained if $q > 2$. The vector $\mathbf{c} = (c_{xx}, c_{xy}, c_{yy})^T$ is the so-called *mixed orientation parameters vector* and is an implicit representation of the two orientations.

Estimation of the Mixed Orientation Parameters. An estimator of the mixed orientation parameters is obtained by a least-squares procedure that finds the minimal points of the energy functional

$$E(\mathbf{c}) = \int_\Omega \left\| c_{xx}\mathbf{f}_x \otimes \mathbf{f}_x + \frac{c_{xy}}{2}(\mathbf{f}_x \otimes \mathbf{f}_y + \mathbf{f}_y \otimes \mathbf{f}_x) + c_{yy}\mathbf{f}_y \otimes \mathbf{f}_y \right\|^2 d\Omega, \tag{9}$$

i.e., $\mathbf{c}$ is estimated as an eigenvector $\hat{\mathbf{c}}$ associated to the smallest eigenvalue of

$$\mathbf{J}_2 = \int_\Omega \begin{bmatrix} |\mathbf{f}_x|^4 & |\mathbf{f}_x|^2\mathbf{f}_x \cdot \mathbf{f}_y & |\mathbf{f}_x \cdot \mathbf{f}_y|^2 \\ |\mathbf{f}_x|^2\mathbf{f}_x \cdot \mathbf{f}_y & \frac{1}{2}(|\mathbf{f}_x|^2|\mathbf{f}_y|^2 + |\mathbf{f}_x \cdot \mathbf{f}_y|^2) & |\mathbf{f}_y|^2\mathbf{f}_x \cdot \mathbf{f}_y \\ |\mathbf{f}_x \cdot \mathbf{f}_y|^2 & |\mathbf{f}_y|^2\mathbf{f}_x \cdot \mathbf{f}_y & |\mathbf{f}_y|^4 \end{bmatrix} d\Omega . \tag{10}$$

The actual region of integration can be kept smaller for multi-spectral images since the system in Eq. (7) is over-constrained in this case. However, the estimator $\hat{\mathbf{c}}$ represents two orientations only if it is consistent with Eq. (8). This is the case if and only if $c_{xy}^2 - 4c_{xx}c_{yy} > 0$.

Separation of the Orientations. To separate the orientations it suffices to know the matrix

$$C = \begin{bmatrix} u_x v_x & u_x v_y \\ u_y v_x & u_y v_y \end{bmatrix} \tag{11}$$

because its rows represent one orientation and its columns the other, cf. [1] for the case of transparency. Since we already know that $c_{xx} = u_x v_x$ and $c_{yy} = u_y v_y$, we need only to obtain $z_1 = u_x v_y$ and $z_2 = u_y v_x$. To this end, observe that $z_1 + z_2 = c_{xy}$ and $z_1 z_2 = c_{xx} c_{yy}$. Therefore, z_1, z_2 are the roots of

$$Q_2(z) = z^2 - c_{xy}z + c_{xx}c_{yy} . \tag{12}$$

Pruning of the Orientation Fields. After the separation, each point of a junction neighborhood has two directions assigned to it, see Fig. 1 (b,e) and Fig. 2 (b,e). Since only one of these is correct, we need to prune the other. For this, we observe that at each position only one of the equations

$$\partial \mathbf{f}(\mathbf{x})/\partial \mathbf{u} = \mathbf{0}, \quad \partial \mathbf{f}(\mathbf{x})/\partial \mathbf{v} = \mathbf{0} \tag{13}$$

is valid. To prune the wrong vector at a given position $\mathbf{p}$, we first compute the local histogram of the orientations in a small neighborhood (3×3 pixels) of $\mathbf{p}$ and separate the two orientations by the median. We then assign to $\mathbf{p}$ the correct direction depending on which equation in (13) is better satisfied in the sense that the sum of squares is lowest. This is equivalent to a procedure that would choose the direction of smallest variation of the image $\mathbf{f}(\mathbf{x})$.

Junction Localization. Since measures of confidence only give us a region where multiple orientations can occur, it is useful to have a method for deciding which point in this region is actually the center of the junction. We follow the approach in [9] for the localization of the junction. Let Ω represent a region of high confidence for a junction. For an ideal junction located at $\mathbf{p}$ we have

$$d\mathbf{f_x}(\mathbf{x} - \mathbf{p}) = \mathbf{0} \tag{14}$$

where $d\mathbf{f_x}$ is the Jacobian matrix of $\mathbf{f}(\mathbf{x})$. The center of the junction is therefore defined and estimated as the minimal point of

$$\int_\Omega | d\mathbf{f_x}(\mathbf{x} - \mathbf{p})|^2 \, d\Omega \tag{15}$$

which gives

$$\hat{\mathbf{p}} = \mathbf{J}^{-1}\mathbf{b}, \text{ where } \mathbf{b} = \int_\Omega d\mathbf{f_x}^T \, d\mathbf{f_x}\mathbf{x} \, d\Omega . \tag{16}$$

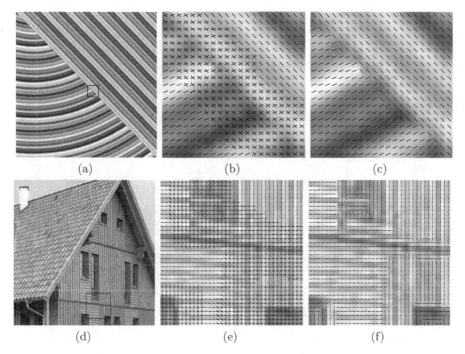

Fig. 1. Synthetic example: panel (a) depicts a sinusoidal pattern (b) the estimated orientations for the marked region and (c) the orientations after pruning. Real example: panel (d) shows a picture of a house; (e) and (f) are analogous to (b) and (c) above.

3   Results

Fig. 1 depicts the results of the estimation of single and double orientations in a synthetic and a natural image. In panel (a) two oriented sinusoidal patterns were combined to form T-junctions along the main diagonal of the image to which Gaussian white noise was added (SNR of 25 dB). The estimated orientations for the selected region in (a) are shown in panel (b). Note that in a region around the T-junction two orientations are estimated at each pixel. Panel (c) shows the result obtained after the pruning process. Note that the occluding boundary and the orientations on both sides of the boundary are well estimated. Panel (d) depicts a natural image with many oriented regions and junctions. The estimated orientations for the selected region in (d) are shown in panel (e). The orientations after the pruning process are depicted in panel (f).

Fig. 2 presents results for L-junctions of different angles. Panel (a) depicts the letter 'A' (image with additive Gaussian noise, SNR of 25 dB). In panel (d) a segmentation of the 'A' in terms of the number of estimated orientations is shown: white for no orientation, black for one, and gray for two orientations. Note that, around all corners of the letter, two orientations are found. The estimated orientations for the upper-left corner of the 'A' are shown in panels (b) (before pruning) and (c) (after pruning). Panel (e) depicts the estimated orientations

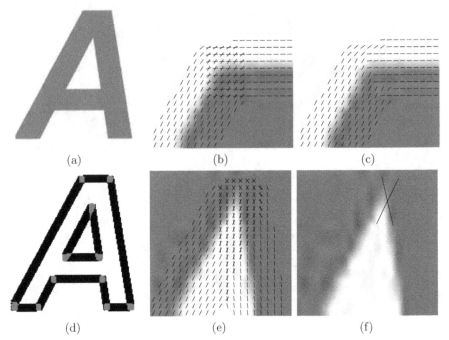

(a)   (b)   (c)

(d)   (e)   (f)

Fig. 2. Panel (a) shows the 'A'-letter input image. The estimated orientations before and after pruning are shown in (b) and (c) respectively for the upper left corner of the 'A'. Panel (d) depicts the segmentation in terms of the number of observed orientations (see text), (e) the estimated orientations for the corner with the smallest angle, and (f) indicates the corner location estimated according to Eq. (16) and the two orientations at that location.

for the corner of the 'A' with the smallest angle. Pixels with two orientations are then used according Eq. (16) to locate the corner position. The result is indicated by the cross in panel (f) which also shows the corresponding orientations at that corner location.

In all examples, we first search for at least one single orientation. If confidence for at least one orientation is low, we search for double orientations. Confidence is based on the invariants of $\mathbf{J}_N$ according to [16]. Thus, for $\mathbf{J}_1$, the confidence criteria are $H > \epsilon$ and $\sqrt{K} < c_1 H$. For $\mathbf{J}_2$, the confidence criterion for two orientations is $\sqrt[3]{K} < c_2 \sqrt[2]{S}$. The numbers H, K, and S are the invariants, i.e., the trace, the determinant, and the sum of the diagonal minors of $\mathbf{J}_{1,2}$. For the examples in Fig. 1, we used an integration window size of 11×11 pixels, $c_1 = 0.5$, $c_2 = 0.6$., and $\epsilon = 0.001$. For the example in Fig. 2, we used an integration window size of 7×7 pixels, $c_1 = 0.4$, $c_2 = 0.6$, and $\epsilon = 0.01$. The above parameter settings have been found experimentally. Derivatives were taken with a $[-1, 0, 1]^T[1, 1, 1]$ kernel in $x-$ and analogously in y direction.

4   Conclusions

We have presented a new and accurate method for the estimation of two orientations at image features that satisfy an occlusion model. Typical features are corners and various kinds of junctions that occur frequently in natural images. The method only involves first-order derivatives and has closed-form solutions. Iterative procedures are not involved, unless one chooses to estimate the eigenvectors of a 3×3 tensor iteratively. This can be avoided as shown in [3]. Experiments on synthetic and real images show that junctions and corners are well described by the proposed model and confirm the accuracy of the method. Nevertheless, our results can be further improved. An obvious improvement is the use of optimized derivative kernels. Derivatives could also be replaced by more general filters as a consequence of results obtained in [16]. A straightforward extension of our approach may allow for the estimation of more than two orientations.

We have formulated our results such as to include multi-spectral images in a natural but non-trivial way. If q is the number of colors, the constraint that we use consists of $q(q + 1)/2$ equations. This implies that for only two colors we already have a well conditioned system and can use even smaller neighborhoods for the estimation of two orientations. Forthcoming results will show the additional advantages when applying our method to multi-spectral images.

The benefits of using corners and junctions for image analysis, registration, tracking etc. have often been highlighted. The estimation of the orientations that form these features may add further robustness and new kinds of invariant features. It might, for example, be easier to register a junction in terms of its orientations since the orientations will change less than the appearance and other features of the junction. The orientations seem especially useful as they can now be well estimated with low computational effort.

Acknowledgment. Work is supported by the *Deutsche Forschungsgemeinschaft* under Ba 1176/7-2.

References

1. T. Aach, I. Stuke, C. Mota, and E. Barth. Estimation of multiple local orientations in image signals. In *Proc. IEEE Int. Conf. Acoustics, Speech and Signal Processing*, volume III, pages 553–6, Montreal, Canada, May 17–21, 2004.
2. E. H. Adelson. Lightness perception and lightness illusions. In M. Gazzaniga, editor, *The New Cognitive Neurosciences*, pages 339–51. MIT Press, 2000.
3. E. Barth. The minors of the structure tensor. In G. Sommer, editor, *Mustererkennung 2000*, pages 221–228. Springer, Berlin, 2000.
4. E. Barth, T. Caelli, and C. Zetzsche. Image encoding, labeling, and reconstruction from differential geometry. *CVGIP: Graphical Model and Image Processing*, 55(6):428–46, Nov. 1993.
5. E. Barth, I. Stuke, T. Aach, and C. Mota. Spatio-temporal motion estimation for transparency and occlusion. In *Proc. IEEE Int. Conf. Image Processing*, volume III, pages 69–72, Barcelona, Spain, Sept. 14–17, 2003. IEEE Signal Processing Soc.

6. E. Barth, I. Stuke, and C. Mota. Analysis of motion and curvature in image sequences. In *Proc. IEEE Southwest Symp. Image Analysis and Interpretation*, pages 206–10, Santa Fe, NM, Apr. 7–9, 2002. IEEE Computer Press.

7. J. Bigün, G. H. Granlund, and J. Wiklund. Multidimensional orientation estimation with application to texture analysis and optical flow. *IEEE Trans. Pattern Analysis and Machine Intelligence*, 13(8):775–90, 1991.

8. S. Di Zenzo. A note on the gradient of a multi-image. *Computer Vision, Graphics, and Image Processing*, 33:116–25, Jan. 1986.

9. W. Förstner and E. Gülch. A fast operator for detection and precise locations of distinct points, corners, and centres of circular features. In *Intercommission Conference on Fast Processing of Photogrammetric Data*, pages 281–305, 1987.

10. W. T. Freeman and E. H. Adelson. The design and use of steerable filters. *IEEE Trans. Pattern Analysis and Machine Intelligence*, 13(9):891–906, 1991.

11. C. Harris and M. Stephens. A combined corner and edge detector. In *Proc. The Fourth Alvey Vision Conference*, pages 147–152, 1988.

12. D. A. Huffman. Impossible objects as non-sense sentences. *Machine Intelligence*, VI:295–323, 1971.

13. L. Kitchen and A. Rosenfeld. Gray level corner detection. *Pattern Recognition Letters*, pages 95–102, 1982.

14. U. Köthe. Edge and junction detection with an improved structure tensor. In B. Michaelis and G. Krell, editors, *Pattern Recognition, 25th DAGM Symposium*, volume 2781 of *LNCS*, pages 25–32, 2003.

15. C. Mota and E. Barth. On the uniqueness of curvature features. In G. Baratoff and H. Neumann, editors, *Dynamische Perzeption*, volume 9 of *Proceedings in Artificial Intelligence*, pages 175–8, Köln, 2000. Infix Verlag.

16. C. Mota, I. Stuke, and E. Barth. Analytic solutions for multiple motions. In *Proc. IEEE Int. Conf. Image Processing*, volume II, pages 917–20, Thessaloniki, Greece, Oct. 7–10, 2001. IEEE Signal Processing Soc.

17. H. H. Nagel and W. Enkelmann. Investigation of second order greyvalue variations to estimate corner point displacements. In *International Conference on Pattern Recognition*, pages 768–773, 1982.

18. L. Parida, D. Geiger, and R. Hummel. Kona: A multi-junction detector using minimum description length principle. In M. Pelillo and E. R. Hancock, editors, *Energy Minimization Methods in Computer Vision and Pattern Recognition*, volume 1223 of *LNCS*, pages 51–65, 1997.

19. K. Rohr. Recognizing corners by fitting parametric models. *International Journal of Computer Vision*, 9:213–230, 1992.

20. I. Stuke, T. Aach, E. Barth, and C. Mota. Analysing superimposed oriented patterns. In *Proc. IEEE Southwest Symp. Image Analysis and Interpretation*, pages 133–7, Lake Tahoe, NV, Mar. 28–30, 2004.

21. I. Stuke, T. Aach, C. Mota, and E. Barth. Estimation of multiple motions: regularization and performance evaluation. In B. Vasudev, T. R. Hsing, A. G. Tescher, and T. Ebrahimi, editors, *Image and Video Communications and Processing 2003*, volume 5022 of *Proceedings of SPIE*, pages 75–86, May 2003.

22. C. Tomasi and T. Kanade. Detection and tracking of point features. Technical report, Carnegie Mellon University Technical, april 1991. Report CMU-CS-91-132.

23. C. Zetzsche, E. Barth, and B. Wegmann. The importance of intrinsically two-dimensional image features in biological vision and picture coding. In A. B. Watson, editor, *Digital Images and Human Vision*, pages 109–38. MIT Press, Oct. 1993.

Phase Based Image Reconstruction
in the Monogenic Scale Space

Di Zang* and Gerald Sommer

Cognitive Systems Group,
Institute of Computer Science and Applied Mathematics,
Christian Albrechts University of Kiel,
24118 Kiel, Germany
{zd,gs}@ks.informatik.uni-kiel.de

Abstract. In this paper, we present an approach for image reconstruction from local phase vectors in the monogenic scale space. The local phase vector contains not only the local phase but also the local orientation of the original signal, which enables the simultaneous estimation of the structural and geometric information. Consequently, the local phase vector preserves a lot of important information of the original signal. Image reconstruction from the local phase vectors can be easily and quickly implemented in the monogenic scale space by a coarse to fine way. Experimental results illustrate that an image can be accurately reconstructed based on the local phase vector. In contrast to the reconstruction from zero crossings, our approach is proved to be stable. Due to the local orientation adaptivity of the local phase vector, the presented approach gives a better result when compared with that of the Gabor phase based reconstruction.

1 Introduction

In the past decades, signal reconstruction from partial information has been an active area of research. Partial information such as zero crossing, Fourier magnitude and localized phase are considered to represent important features of the original signal. Therefore, we are able to reconstruct the original signal based on only the partial information. The variety of results on signal reconstruction has a major impact on the research fields like image processing, communication and geophysics.

Reconstruction from zero crossings in the scale space is investigated by Hummel [1]. He has demonstrated that reconstruction based on zero crossings is possible but can be unstable, unless gradient values along the zero crossings are added. In [2], it is proved that many features of the original image are clearly identifiable in the phase only image but not in the magnitude only image, and reconstruction from Fourier phase is visually satisfying. However, the application of this approach is rather limited in practice due to the computational complexity. Behar et al. have stated in [3] that image reconstruction from localized phase

---

* This work has been supported by DFG Graduiertenkolleg No. 357

C.E. Rasmussen et al. (Eds.): DAGM 2004, LNCS 3175, pp. 171–178, 2004.
© Springer-Verlag Berlin Heidelberg 2004

only information is more efficient and faster than that from the global phase. The reconstruction errors produced by this method can be very small. However, compared with this approach, the way of image reconstruction presented in this paper is more easier and faster.

In this paper, we present an approach of image reconstruction from the local phase vector in the monogenic scale space. Image reconstruction is easy, fast, accurate and stable when compared with the above mentioned approaches. In [4], Felsberg and Sommer proposed the first rotationally invariant 2D analytical signal. As one of its features, the monogenic phase vector preserves most of the important information of the original signal. The local phase vector contains not only the local phase but also the orientation information of the original signal, which enables the evaluation of structure and geometric information at the same time. The embedding of local phase and local orientation into monogenic scale space improves the stability and robustness. However, in the Gaussian scale space, there is no common filter set which could evaluate the local orientation and local phase simultaneously. To show the advantage of our approach, we replace the Gaussian kernel with the Gabor filter for phase evaluation, the reconstruction results of these two approaches are compared in this paper.

2   The Monogenic Scale Space

The structure of the monogenic scale space [5] is illustrated in Fig.1. The Riesz transform of an image yields the corresponding figure flow, a vector field representing the Riesz transformed results. If we define $\mathbf{u} = (u_1, u_2)^T$ and $\mathbf{x} = (x_1, x_2)^T$, then the Riesz kernel in the frequency domain reads $H(\mathbf{u}) = -i\frac{\mathbf{u}}{|\mathbf{u}|}$ and the convolution mask of the Riesz transform is given by $\mathbf{h}(\mathbf{x}) = \frac{\mathbf{x}}{2\pi|\mathbf{x}|^3}$. The combination of the signal and its Riesz transformed result is defined as the monogenic signal. Let $f(\mathbf{x})$ represent the input signal, the corresponding monogenic signal thus takes the form: $\mathbf{f}_M(\mathbf{x}) = f(\mathbf{x}) + (\mathbf{h} * f)(\mathbf{x})$. The monogenic signal is a vector valued extension of the analytical signal, it is rotation invariant. The monogenic scale space is built by the monogenic signals at all scales, it can alternatively be regarded as the combination of the Poisson scale space and its harmonic conjugate. The Poisson scale space and its harmonic conjugate form the monogenic scale space, they are obtained as follows, respectively.

$$p(\mathbf{x}; s) = (f * P)(\mathbf{x}) \quad \text{where} \quad P(\mathbf{x}) = \frac{s}{2\pi(|\mathbf{x}|^2 + s^2)^{3/2}} \tag{1}$$

$$q(\mathbf{x}; s) = (f * Q)(\mathbf{x}) \quad \text{where} \quad Q(\mathbf{x}) = \frac{\mathbf{x}}{2\pi(|\mathbf{x}|^2 + s^2)^{3/2}} \tag{2}$$

In the above formulas, P and Q indicate the Poisson kernel and the conjugate Poisson kernel, respectively. At scale zero, the conjugate Poisson kernel is exactly the Riesz kernel. The Poisson scale space $p(\mathbf{x}; s)$ is obtained from the original image by Poisson filtering, its harmonic conjugate is the conjugate Poisson scale

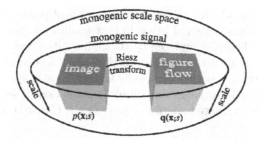

Fig. 1. The structure of the Monogenic Scale Space [5]

space $\mathbf{q}(\mathbf{x}; s)$, which can be formed by the figure flows at all scales. The unique advantage of the monogenic scale space, compared with the Gaussian scale space, is the figure flow being in quadrature phase relation to the image at each scale. Therefore, the monogenic scale space is superior to the Gaussian scale space if a quadrature relation concept is required.

3   Important Features of the Monogenic Scale Space

As an analytical scale space, the monogenic scale space provides very useable signal features including local amplitude and local phase vector. The local phase vector contains both the local phase and local orientation information, which enables the simultaneous estimation of structural and geometric information. The local amplitude represents the local intensity or dynamics, the local phase indicates the local symmetry and the local orientation describes the direction of highest signal variance. Let $p(\mathbf{x}; s)$ and $\mathbf{q}(\mathbf{x}; s)$ represent the Poisson scale space and its harmonic conjugate, the logarithm of the local amplitude, namely the local attenuation in the monogenic scale space reads:

$$A(\mathbf{x}; s) = \log(\sqrt{|\mathbf{q}(\mathbf{x}; s)|^2 + (p(\mathbf{x}; s))^2}) = \frac{1}{2}\log(|\mathbf{q}(\mathbf{x}; s)|^2 + (p(\mathbf{x}; s))^2) \qquad (3)$$

The local orientation and the local phase are best represented in a combined form, namely, the local phase vector $\mathbf{r}(\mathbf{x}; s)$. It is defined as the following form:

$$\mathbf{r}(\mathbf{x}; s) = \frac{\mathbf{q}(\mathbf{x}; s)}{|\mathbf{q}(\mathbf{x}; s)|} \arctan(\frac{|\mathbf{q}(\mathbf{x}; s)|}{p(\mathbf{x}; s)}) \qquad (4)$$

Whenever an explicit representation of phase or orientation is needed, the local orientation can be extracted from $\mathbf{r}$ as the orientation of the latter, and the local phase is obtained by projecting $\mathbf{r}$ onto the local orientation. The local phase vector thus denotes a rotation by the phase angle around an axis perpendicular to the local orientation. In the monogenic scale space, the local phase and orientation information are scale dependent, which means the local phase and orientation information can be correctly estimated at an arbitrary scale simultaneously. Unlike the monogenic scale space, there is no common filter set in the

Gaussian scale space which enables the estimation of phase and orientation at the same time. The evaluation of phase in that traditional framework is possible when the Gaussian kernel is replaced by the Gabor filter, and by using Gaussian derivatives, orientation can be evaluated. However, the Gabor filter and Gaussian derivatives are not compatible in the Gaussian scale space, the phase and orientation obtained from them are simply a collection of features, these two features can not be evaluated simultaneously in the Gaussian framework.

4   Image Reconstruction in the Monogenic Scale Space

It is reported in [6] that the local attenuation and the phase response of a minimum phase filter form a Hilbert pair. Under certain conditions, this could also be generalized to 2D. For a 2D signal with an intrinsic dimension of one, if the scale space representation has no zeros in the half space with $s \geq 0$, then the local attenuation and the local phase vector form a Riesz triplet [5]

$$\mathbf{r}(\mathbf{x}; s) \approx (\mathbf{h} * A)(\mathbf{x}; s) \tag{5}$$

where $\mathbf{h}$ refers to the Riesz kernel. In practice, images are in general not globally intrinsical 1D signal. However, they commonly have lots of intrinsically 1D neighborhoods which makes the reconstruction from the local phase vector available. In most practical applications zeros occur in the positive half-space, but as we can see from [5], the influence of the zeros can mostly be neglected. To recover the amplitude information from only the phase vector information, we take the inverse Riesz transform of the local phase vector. By definition, the Riesz transform of the local phase vector is DC free. This means that the transformed output has no DC component. Consequently, the DC-free local attenuation in the scale space is approximated by the following form

$$A(\mathbf{x}; s) - \overline{A}(\mathbf{x}; s) \approx -(\mathbf{h} * \mathbf{r})(\mathbf{x}; s) \tag{6}$$

where $\overline{A}(\mathbf{x}; s)$ indicates the DC component of the local attenuation that should be calculated beforehand. Hence, the original image reconstruction based on the local phase vector reads

$$f(\mathbf{x}) = \exp(\overline{A}(\mathbf{x}; 0))\exp(-(\mathbf{h} * \mathbf{r})(\mathbf{x}; 0))\cos(|\mathbf{r}(\mathbf{x}; 0)|) + C_{DC} \tag{7}$$

where C_{DC} denotes a further DC correction term corresponding to a gray value shift. To reconstruct a real image, we use only the real part of the local phase vector $\cos(|\mathbf{r}(\mathbf{x}; 0)|)$. The above introduction indicates that image reconstruction from the local phase vector can be easily and quickly implemented, no iterative procedure is needed.

To investigate the image reconstruction in the monogenic scale space, a scale pyramid structure is employed. The differences of monogenic signals at adjacent scales are first computed as the bandpass decomposition at different frequencies in the monogenic scale space. The information of different bandpasses forms a

Laplacian pyramid. Local phase vectors of the corresponding bandpass information are considered as the partial information. Signals can thus be reconstructed
in the scale space by a coarse to fine way. Let $g^{(s)}$ denote the representation of
the image in the pyramid at scale s, then the one scale higher representation
reads $g^{(s+1)}$. By interpolation, $g^{(s+1)}$ is expanded as $\widehat{g}^{(s+1)} = T_I g^{(s+1)}$, where
T_I refers to the operation of interpolation and $\widehat{g}^{(s+1)}$ has the same size of $g^{(s)}$.
The difference of adjacent scales can then be computed as

$$l^{(s)} = g^{(s)} - \widehat{g}^{(s+1)} = g^{(s)} - T_I g^{(s+1)} \tag{8}$$

where $l^{(s)}$ can be regarded as a bandpass decomposition of the original image.
Based on only the local phase vector of the intermediate representation, the
reconstruction at different scales can be implemented as follows

$$\widetilde{l}^{(s)} = \exp(\overline{A}(\mathbf{x}; s))\exp(-(\mathbf{h} * \mathbf{r})(\mathbf{x}; s))\cos(|\mathbf{r}(\mathbf{x}; s)|) + C_{DC} \tag{9}$$

where $\widetilde{l}^{(s)}$ describes the reconstructed result at a certain scale. By means of a
coarse to fine approach, all the scale space images can be combined together
to make the final reconstruction of the original image. Starting from the most
coarse level, the recovery of one scale lower image takes the following form

$$\widetilde{g}^{(s)} = \widetilde{l}^{(s)} + T_I \widetilde{g}^{(s+1)} \tag{10}$$

This is an iterative procedure. It will end until s goes to zero, hence, $\widetilde{g}^{(0)}$ indicates
the final reconstruction.

Fig. 2. Test images, from left to right, are *lena*, *bird*, and *circles (synthetic image)*

5   Experimental Results

In this section, we present some experiments to check the performance of image
reconstruction based on the local phase vector in the monogenic scale space.
Three images used for the experiment are shown in Fig. 2. Image reconstruction
in the monogenic scale space is illustrated in Fig.3. Although we use pyramid
structures for scale space reconstruction, the results shown in Fig.3 at different
scales are scaled to the same size as the original one. The top row shows the
original image and the corresponding absolute error multiplied by 8. Bottom
row demonstrates the reconstructed results in the monogenic scale space. The

left image in the bottom row is the final result, which is reconstructed by a coarse to fine way. The final reconstruction has a normalized mean square error (NMSE) of 0.0018 when compared with the original one. This demonstrates that image reconstruction can be implemented accurately from the local phase vector.

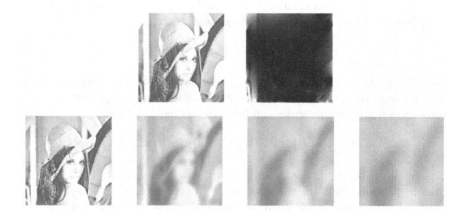

Fig. 3. Image reconstruction in the monogenic scale space. The original image and the absolute error image multiplied by 8 are shown in the top row. Bottom row: right three images demonstrate the intermediate reconstruction in the monogenic scale space, the left image indicates the final result.

A successful reconstruction from partial information requires a stable output. To investigate the performance of reconstruction from the local phase vector, we conduct another experiment by adding noise to contaminate the input images and checking the outputs. In this experiment, the *bird* image and the *lena* image are used as the noise contaminated inputs, outcomes are shown in Fig.4. The NMSEs increase when the signal noise ratio (SNR) is reduced. However, for both cases, our approach results in limited reconstruction errors even the SNR is set to zero. The results indicate that reconstruction based on the local phase vector is a stable process, hence, the local phase vector can be regarded as stable representation of the original signal. In contrast to this, reconstruction from only zero crossings is proved to produce unstable results [1] unless the gradient data along the zero crossings are combined for reconstruction.

There is no common filter set in the Gaussian framework to evaluate the phase and orientation simultaneously. However, phase information can be estimated when the Gaussian kernel is replaced by the Gabor filter. To show the advantage of our approach, we compare the results of our method with that of the Gabor phase based case. A certain orientation must be assigned to the Gabor filter beforehand. In this case, the orientation is independent with the scale space, local orientation estimation does not change when the scale is changed. Superior to the Gabor phase, the monogenic phase vector enables the estimation of structural and geometric information simultaneously at each scale space.

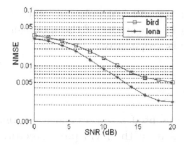

Fig. 4. Normalized mean square error with respect to signal noise ratio

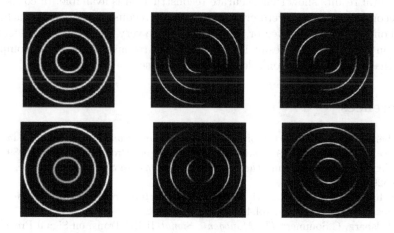

Fig. 5. Upper row: images from left to right are the original image and the reconstructed results based on Gabor phases with orientations of 45^0 and 135^0, the corresponding NMSEs are 0.0833 and 0.0836. Bottom row: the Left one shows the reconstruction based on the monogenic phase, it has a NMSE of 0.0014. The middle and the right images are the results from Gabor phases with orientations of 0^0 and 90^0, the NMSEs are 0.0812 and 0.0815, respectively.

In the monogenic scale space, local phase vector and local attenuation form a Riesz triplet, which means that the amplitude can be easily recovered from the local phase vector simply by using inverse Riesz transform. Unfortunately, the Gabor phase and the local amplitude do not have the property of orthogonality. Hereby, we have to employ an iterative algorithm to reconstruct the image based on local Gabor phases. The iterative reconstruction procedure is similar to the Gerchberg Saxton algorithm [7]. By alternatively imposing constrains in the spatial and frequency domains, an image could be reconstructed in an iterative way. The comparison results are illustrated in Fig.5, four channels with orientations of 0^0, 45^0, 90^0 and 135^0 are considered, the corresponding normalized mean square errors are 0.0812, 0.0833, 0.0815, 0.0836. It is obvious that Gabor phase only preserves the information at the given orientation, however, the monogenic phase results in an accurate and isotropic outcome with an NMSE of 0.0014. Due to the rotation invariant property of the monogenic signal, signals can be well reconstructed in the isotropic way.

6   Conclusions

In this paper, we have presented an approach to reconstruct an image in the monogenic scale space based on the local phase vector. According to the estimated local structural and geometric information, an image can be easily and quickly reconstructed in the monogenic scale space by a coarse to fine way. Experimental results show that accurate reconstruction is available. In contrast to the reconstruction from zero crossings, a stable reconstruction can be achieved based on the local phase vector. Furthermore, the very nice property of local orientation adaptivity can result in a much better reconstruction when compared with that of the orientation selective Gabor phase.

References

1. Robert Hummel, Robert Moniot: *Reconstructions from Zero Crossings in Scale Space.* IEEE Trans. on Acoustic, Speech, and Signal Processing, vol.37, 1989
2. A.V.Oppenheim, J.S. Lim: *The Importance of Phase in Signals.* Proc. IEEE, vol.69, pp.529-541, 1981
3. J.Behar, M.Porat, Y.Y.Zeevi: *Image Reconstruction from Localized Phase.* IEEE Trans. Signal Processing, vol.40, pp.736-743, 1992
4. M.Felsberg, G.Sommer: *The Monogenic Signal.* IEEE Trans. on Signal Processing, vol.49, pp.3136-3144, 2001
5. M.Felsberg, G.Sommer: *The Monogenic Scale Space: A Unifying Approach to Phase-based Image Processing in Scale Space.* Journal of Mathematical Imaging and Vision, vol.21, 2004
6. Papoulis, A.:*The Fourier Integral and its Applications.* McGraw-Hill, New York, 1962
7. Norman E.Hurt: *Phase Retrieval and Zero Crossings Mathematical Methods in Image Reconstruction.* Kluwer Academic Publishers, 1989

Synthesizing Movements for Computer Game Characters

Christian Thurau, Christian Bauckhage, and Gerhard Sagerer

Faculty of Technology, Applied Computer Science
Bielefeld University, P.O. Box 100131, 33501 Bielefeld, Germany
{cthurau,cbauckha,sagerer}@techfak.uni-bielefeld.de

Abstract. Recent findings in biological neuroscience suggest that the brain learns body movements as sequences of motor primitives. Simultaneously, this principle is gaining popularity in robotics, computer graphics and computer vision: movement primitives were successfully applied to robotic control tasks as well as to render or to recognize human behavior. In this paper, we demonstrate that movement primitives can also be applied to the problem of implementing lifelike computer game characters. We present an approach to behavior modeling and learning that integrates several pattern recognition and machine learning techniques: trained with data from recorded multiplayer computer games, neural gas networks learn topological representation of virtual worlds; PCA is used to identify elementary movements the human players repeatedly executed during a match and complex behaviors are represented as probability functions mapping movement primitives to locations in the game environment. Experimental results underline that this framework produces game characters with humanlike skills.

1 Motivation and Overview

Computer games have become an enormous business; just recently, its annual sales figures even surpassed those of the global film industry [3]. While it seems fair to say that this success boosted developments in fields like computer graphics and networking, commercial game programming and modern artificial intelligence or pattern recognition hardly influenced each other. However, this situation is about to change. On the one hand, the game industry is beginning to fathom the potential of pattern recognition and machine learning to produce life-like artificial characters. On the other hand, the AI and pattern recognition communities and even roboticists discover computer games as a testbed in behavior learning and action recognition (cf. e.g. [1,2,10,13]).

This paper belongs to the latter category. Following an idea discussed in [2], we report on analyzing the network traffic of multiplayer games in order to realize game agents that show human-like movement skills. From a computer game perspective, this is an interesting problem because many games require the player to navigate through virtual worlds (also called *maps*). Practical experience shows that skilled human players do this more efficiently than their computer controlled counterparts. They make use of

C.E. Rasmussen et al. (Eds.): DAGM 2004, LNCS 3175, pp. 179–186, 2004.
© Springer-Verlag Berlin Heidelberg 2004

shortcuts or perform movements which artificial agents cannot perform simply because their programmers did not think of it[1].

An intuitive idea to address this problem is to identify elementary building blocks of movements and to learn how they have to be sequenced in order to produce the desired complex movement behavior. In fact, as recent results from biological neuroscience suggest, this seems to be the way the human brain constructs body movements [7,16]. This observation is substantiated by psychological experiments on imitation learning which suggest that infants devote much of their time to the learning of elementary limb movements and of how to combine them to reach a certain goal [14]. Not surprisingly, movement primitives are thus becoming popular in robotics and computer vision, too. Schaal et al. [15] describe how nonlinear differential equations may be used as dynamic movement primitives in skill learning for humanoid robots. Given motion sensor data, Mataric et al. [4] apply PCA and linearly superimpose resulting elementary movements to reproduce arm movements demonstrated by human subjects. Using spatio-temporal morphable models, Ilg and Giese [9] and Giese et al. [8] linearly combine primitive movements extracted from data recorded with motion capture systems to produce high quality renderings of karate moves and facial expressions, respectively. Galata et al. [6] apply variable length Markov models trained with vectors describing elementary 2D or 3D motions to synthesize or recognize complex activities of humans.

However, the preconditions for moving a character through a virtual world differ from the ones in the cited contributions. While these focus on movements of limbs or facial muscles and neglect the environment, a game character moves as a whole and appropriate movement sequences will depend on its current location and surroundings. For instance, movements leading the agent into a virtual perils like abysses or seas of lava would be fatal and must be avoided. We are thus in need of a methodology that except for elementary moves also learns a representation of the environment and generates movement sequences with respect to the current spatial context. As the next section will show, neural gases are well suited to learn topological representations of game environments. In section 3, we shall discuss the extraction of movement primitives from network traffic of multiplayer games and how to relate them to the neural gas representation of the environment. Section 4 will present experiments carried out within this framework and a conclusion will close this contribution.

2 Neural Gas for Learning Topological Representations

For a representation of the virtual world we are learning a topology using a Neural Gas [12] algorithm, which is a cluster algorithm showing good performance when it comes to topology learning [11]. The training data used for Neural Gas learning consists of all locations $p = \{x, y, z\}$ a human player visited during various plan executions, thus staying very close to the actual human movement paths. Application of a Neural Gas algorithm to the player's positions results in a number of prototypical positions,

---

[1] An example is the *rocket jump* in ID Software's (in)famous game Quake II. Shortly after the game was released, players discovered that they can jump higher if they make use of the recoil of a fired rocket. I.e. if they fired a rocket to the ground immediately after they jumped, their avatar was able to reach heights never planned by the programmers.

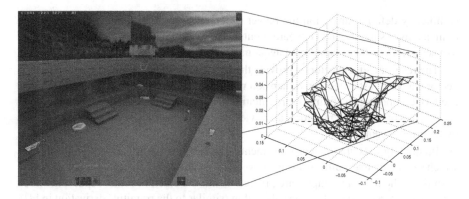

Fig. 1. A simple map and its corresponding topological representation

which are interconnected only by the player's actions. Thereby non-reachable (or at times unimportant) world positions are excluded in advance (in theory any point in the gaming world could be reached by using game exploits such as the rocket jump, therefore topology learning reveals a more accurate discretization of the 3D gaming world).

Since a sufficient number of cluster centres varies among maps, we were also using the Growing Neural Gas [5] to determine the number of cluster centres to reach a given error value. Thereby we can choose proportional number of cluster centres for each map, once a suitable error value is found. The experiments were carried out using an mean squared error value of 0.006 and resulted in 800 to 1400 cluster centres for larger maps, and about 100 to 200 centres for smaller maps.

For our approach the interconnections between nodes are not needed, therefore we can safely skip the edge learning. Figure 1 shows a small map and its corresponding topological representation, edges were drawn for clarification reasons, they are of no further use in the presented approach.

By assigning training samples of recorded player actions to cluster centres in the topological map, small sets of localized training samples are generated. Each separated training set defines the legal actions for a specific region, not only in the topological map, but also in the simulated 3D world. However, for a further investigation of the player's behavior we first have to introduce movement and action primitives.

3   Movement Primitive Extraction

Evidence form neuroscience indicates that complex movements in humans/animals are built up by combinations of simpler motor or movement primitives [7]. For a more life-like appearance of computer game character motions, a biological approach utilizing movement primitives seems promising. To identify the underlying set of basic movements, PCA is applied to the training samples. A training sample set consists of a number of eight dimensional motion vectors

$$t = [yaw\ angle, pitch\ angle, ..., veclocity\ forward, player\ fire]$$

completely defining an action the player executed (a motion vector corresponds to a human player's mouse and keyboard inputs). These motion vectors can be directly send to a server, no further mapping on agent motor commands is needed.

The resulting eigenvectors e provide the elementary movements, of which a motion vector can be constructed. No dimension reduction is applied at this stage, PCA is just used for computing an optimal representation. Thereby a projection of the observed motion vectors onto the eigenvectors can be viewed as a reconstruction of player movements by their movement primitives.

Frequently executed player movements can be grouped to gain *action primitives*, which are of course built up using movement primitives. To acquire a set of action primitives, the training samples are projected onto the eigenmovement space, in which they are clustered using a k-means algorithm (similar to the primitive derivation in [4]). This results in a set of cluster centers, each of which representing a single action primitive. The number of action primitives does have an influence on the overall smoothness of the later motion sequences, we achieved good results by choosing 500 to 700 cluster centers. The right number of cluster centres depends on the number of training samples and on the variety of observed motions. However, even the representation of a large number of training samples could not be further improved by choosing a higher number of cluster centres. This indicates, that there might be a fixed number of action primitives, which guarantee a smooth execution of motion sequences.

Sequentially executed action primitives lead to complex behaviors (in fact all human behaviors can be interpreted as sequences of action primitives). In order to generate human-like motions, the action primitives need to be executed in a convincing manner, based on the training set motion vectors.

Since the actual player's movement depends on the surrounding and his position on the map, the probability of executing a specific action primitive v_i can be denoted as

$$P_{v_i} = P(v_i|w_k) \tag{1}$$

where w_k denotes a certain node in the topological map. The acquisition of the conditional probabilities is fairly easy, each movement vector can be assigned to a node in the topological representation and it can be assigned to an action primitive. Counting the evidences of action primitives in all nodes results in a $m \times n$ matrix, where m denotes the number of nodes in the topological map and n denotes the number of action primitives. A matrix entry at position k, i denotes the probability $P(v_i|w_k)$ of executing an action primitive v_i for node number k.

However, in a sequence of action primitives, not every primitive can be executed as a successor of any primitive. On the one hand humans tend to move in a smooth way, at least compared to what would be possible for an artificial player, on the other hand humans are bound to physical limitations of their hand motion, besides, some player's might have certain *habits*, they tend to jump for no reason or make other kinds of useless, yet very human movements. To reflect those aspects, the probability of executing a primitive v_i as a successor of a primitive v_l should be incorporated. It can be denoted as

$$P_{v_i} = P(v_i|v_l) \tag{2}$$

Fig. 2. The artificial game character, observed while executing one of the experiment movements - a jump to an otherwise not reachable item

The probabilities can be extracted from the training samples by inspecting the observed action primitive sequence, resulting in a $n \times n$ transition matrix, where n denotes the number of action primitives.

Assuming the conditional probabilities $P(v_i|v_l)$ and $P(v_i|w_k)$ are independent, the overall probability for the execution of a primitive v_i can now be denoted as

$$P_{v_i} = \frac{P(v_i|v_l, w_k)}{\sum_{u=1}^{n} P(v_u|v_l, w_k)} = \frac{P(v_i|v_l)P(v_i|w_k)}{\sum_{u=1}^{n} P(v_u|v_l)P(v_u|w_k)} \qquad (3)$$

More conditional probabilities, expressing a greater variety of dependencies, could be incorporated at this point. For example, action primitive selection based on an enemy player's relative position or based on the current internal state of the player. In the presented approach we wanted to concentrate on movements for handling environmental difficulties, while still creating the impression of a human player, therefore ignoring further possibilities of the presented approach.

When placed in the game world, the next action for the artifical game character is chosen randomly using a roulette wheel selection according to the P_v.

4 Experiments

To test the presented approach, we carried out a set of eight smaller experiments. Each experiment consisted of a separate training sample set, in which (at times) complicated movement sequences were executed several times by a human player. The observable motions varied from simple ground movements to more complex jump or shooting maneuvers (or combinations of both). In addition, a larger training sample set, this time a real match between two human players, was used.

In all but one experiments the observed movement could be reproduced in a convincing manner. In one experiment the artifical player usually ended in front of wall and stopped moving. More training samples, containing hints for mastering the described situation, could have led to a smarter impression and a better recreation of the observed motion.

Although staying very close to the training set movements, an exact reproduction almost never occurred because of the randomness in sequence generation. While this

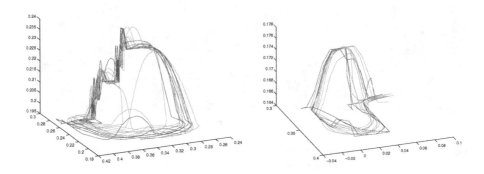

Fig. 3. Comparison of the artificial player's (blue) movement trajectories in 3D and the trajectories of a human player (red). The left picture shows a combination of different jumps to get to reach an item located on a platform. The right image shows a repeated jump through a window.

might seem like a disadvantage, it definitely adds to a more human-like impression. Figure 3 and Figure 4 show the trajectories of the artificial player compared to a human test player in 3D.

Besides the basic reconstruction of certain motions, the artificial player's motions themselves, his way of turning, jumping and running, were naturally looking - creating the illusion of a human player (this applies to it's motion, not the tactical/strategic decisions). Even complicated actions, for example the famous *rocket jump* (an impossible maneuver for an inexperienced human player) could be learned and executed.

The more realistic training set, two human players competing on a smaller map, finally resulted in a very good imitation of a broader repertoire of a human player's motion, indicating, that our approach is suitable for larger scale problems. The strong coupling between the game characters position in the topological representation and the selection of motion primitives made the character appear smart, by acting in an appropriate way to the architecture of the 3D game world - jumping over cliffs or standing still when using an elevator. In addition the approach preserved certain player habits by (in one case) executing senseless jumps from time to time. Since no information about the enemy player was introduced during live play, some kind of shadow fighting could be observed, as if an enemy would be present.

A further incorporation in already developed approaches [17] for strategic movement should be established. The human motion generation does not hinder the agent to occasionally walk in circles or do other kinds of human looking but nevertheless stupid movements, after all the approach pays attention to realistic motions, goal oriented movements were not intended.

5   Conclusion and Future Work

In order to create life-like motion for computer game characters, we decided for a biologically inspired approach by using movement primitives as the basic building blocks

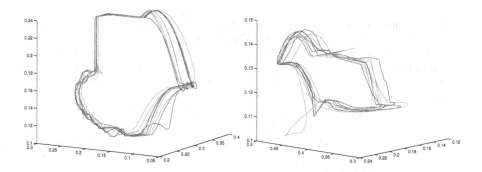

Fig. 4. Comparison of the artificial player's (blue) movement trajectories in 3D and the trajectories of a human player (red). The experiment underlying the left image contained an elevator usage and a long jump to a platform. While the right image displays the trajectories extracted from the experimental results illustrated in Figure 2

of motion. PCA applied to observed human motions revealed the eigenmoves, or in our case movement primitives. Prototypical motion vectors were extracted using k-means clustering in the eigenspace of the used training samples. Finally conditional probabilities of the execution of a specific motion primitive were computed, dependent on the position in a topological map and on the last executed action primitive. When playing, the artificial player selects its next action based on the conditional probabilities, thus favoring more common sequences of action. And indeed, our experiments show a good performance by reproducing -even complicated- training movement sequences. The artificial player's motion appears surprisingly realistic and preserves certain human habits, which of course adds to a life-like impression.

Besides the topological map position, there might be other features on which motion primitive selection may depend. For example, an enemy player's movement might be of importance. Integration of such conditional probabilities should be possible and could provide improvements. Besides a further development of the described approach, an integration in available approaches for strategical and reactive imitation of human players would be desirable. After all life-like motion for computer game characters is only one aspect for the imitation of a human player, though of great importance. It also is of interest, if our approach could be applied to other domains in the field of action recognition/simulation for humans as well as for animals. First ideas have already been discussed with biologists, who are investigating sequences in the courtship behavior of zebra finches.

Acknowledgments. This work was supported by the German Research Foundation (DFG) within the graduate program "Strategies & Optimization of Behavior".

References

1. E. Amir and P. Doyle. Adventure games: A challenge for cognitive robotics. In *Proc. Int. Cognitive Robotics Workshop*, Edmonton, Canada, 2002.
2. C. Bauckhage, C. Thurau, and G. Sagerer. Learning Human-like Opponent Behavior for Interactive Computer Games. In B. Michaelis and G. Krell, editors, *Pattern Recognition*, Lecturenotes in Computer Science 2781, pages 148–155. Springer-Verlag, 2003.
3. S. Cass. Mind games. *IEEE Spectrum*, pages 40–44, December 2002.
4. A. Fod, M.J. Mataric, and O.C. Jenkins. Automated Derivation of Primitives for Movement Classification. *Autonomous Robots*, 12(1):39–54, 2002.
5. B. Fritzke. A growing neural gas network learns topologies. In G. Tesauro, D. S. Touretzky, and T. K. Leen, editors, *Advances in Neural Information Processing Systems 7*, pages 625–632. MIT Press, Cambridge MA, 1995.
6. A. Galata, N. Johnson, and D. Hogg. Learning Variable-Length Markov Models of Behaviour. *Computer Visiosn and Image Understanding*, 81(3):398–413, 2001.
7. Z. Gharamani. Building blocks of movement. *Nature*, 407:682–683, October 2000.
8. M.A. Giese, B. Knappmeyer, and H.H. Bülthoff. Automatic synthesis of sequences of human movements by linear combination of learned example patterns. In H.H. Bülthoff, S.W. Lee, T. Poggio, and C. Walraven, editors, *Biologically Motivated Computer Vision*, volume 2525 of *LNCS*, pages 538–547. Springer, 2002.
9. W. Ilg and M.A. Giese. Modeling of movement sequences based on hierarchical spatio-temporal correspondences of movement primitives. In H.H. Bülthoff, S.W. Lee, T. Poggio, and C. Walraven, editors, *Biologically Motivated Computer Vision*, volume 2525 of *LNCS*, pages 528–537. Springer, 2002.
10. J. E. Laird and M. v. Lent. Interactice Computer Games: Human-Level AI's Killer Application. In *Proc. AAAI*, pages 1171–1178, 2000.
11. T. Martinez and K. Schulten. A neural gas network learns topologies. In *Artificial Neural Networks*. Elseviers Science Publishers B.V, 1991.
12. T.M. Martinez, S.G. Berkovich, and K.J. Schulten. Neural gas network for vector quantization and its application to time-series prediction. *IEEE Trans. on Neural Networks*, 4(4):558–569, 1993.
13. A. Naraeyek. Computer Games – Boon or Bane for AI Research. *Künstliche Intelligenz*, pages 43–44, February 2004.
14. R.P.N. Rao and A.N. Meltzoff. Imitation learning in infoants and robots: Towards probabilistic computational models. In *Proc. AISB 2003 Convention: Cognition in Machines and Animals*, Aberystwyth, UK, 2003.
15. S. Schaal, J. Peters, J. Nakanishi, and A. Ijspeert. Learning movement primitives. In *Proc. Int. Symposium on Robotics Research*, Siena, Italy, 2003.
16. K.A. Thoroughman and R. Shadmehr. Learning of action through adaptive combination of motor primitives. *Nature*, 407:742–747, October 2000.
17. C. Thurau, C. Bauckhage, and G. Sagerer. Learning Human-Like Movement Behavior for Computer Games. In *Proc. 8th Int. Conf. on the Simulation of Adaptive Behavior (SAB'04)*, 2004. to appear.

MinOver Revisited for Incremental Support-Vector-Classification

Thomas Martinetz

Institute for Neuro- and Bioinformatics
University of Lübeck
D-23538 Lübeck, Germany
martinetz@informatik.uni-luebeck.de
http://www.inb.uni-luebeck.de

Abstract. The well-known and very simple MinOver algorithm is reformulated for incremental support vector classification with and without kernels. A modified proof for its $\mathcal{O}(t^{-1/2})$ convergence is presented, with t as the number of training steps. Based on this modified proof it is shown that even a convergence of at least $\mathcal{O}(t^{-1})$ is given. This new convergence bound for MinOver is confirmed by computer experiments on artificial data sets. The computational effort per training step scales as $\mathcal{O}(N)$ with the number N of training patterns.

1 Introduction

The Support-Vector-Machine (SVM) [1], [12] is an extremely successful concept for pattern classification and regression and has found widespread applications (see, e.g. [6], [9], [11]). It became a standard tool like Neural Networks or classical approaches. A major drawback, particularly for industrial applications where easy and robust implementation is an issue, is its complicated training procedure. A large Quadratic-Programming problem has to be solved, which requires numerical optimization routines which many users do not want or cannot implement by themselves. They have to rely on existing software packages which are hardly comprehensive and, in many cases at least, error-free. This is in contrast to most Neural Network approaches where learning has to be simple and incremental almost by definition.

For this reason a number of different approaches to obtain more or less simple and incremental SVM training procedures have been introduced [2], [3], [10], [4], [7]. We will revisit the MinOver algorithm which was introduced by Krauth and Mézard [5] for spin-glass models of Neural Networks. As a slight modification of the perceptron algorithm, it is well-known that MinOver can be used for maximum margin classification. In spite of the fact that a training procedure can hardly be more simple, and in spite of the fact that advantageous learning behaviour has been reported [8], so far it has not become a standard training algorithm for maximum margin classification. To make MinOver more attractive we give a simplified formulation of this algorithm and show that, in contrast to the $\mathcal{O}(t^{-1/2})$ convergence bound given in [5], in fact one can expect a $\mathcal{O}(t^{-1})$ convergence, with t as the number of learning steps.

C.E. Rasmussen et al. (Eds.): DAGM 2004, LNCS 3175, pp. 187–194, 2004.

1.1   The Problem

Given a linearly separable set of patterns $\mathbf{x}_\nu \in \mathbb{R}^D$, $\nu = 1, \ldots, N$ with corresponding class labels $y_\nu \in \{ \ 1, 1\}$. We want to find the hyperplane which separates the patterns of these two classes with maximum margin. The hyperplane for classification is determined by its normal vector $\mathbf{w} \in \mathbb{R}^D$ and its offset $b \in \mathbb{R}$. It achieves a separation of the two classes, if

$$y_\nu(\mathbf{w}^T \mathbf{x}_\nu \quad b) > 0 \qquad \text{for all} \qquad \nu = 1, \ldots, N$$

is valid. The margin Δ of this separation is given by

$$\Delta = \min_\nu [y_\nu(\mathbf{w}^T \mathbf{x}_\nu \quad b)/||\mathbf{w}||].$$

For convenience we introduce $\mathbf{z}_\nu = y_\nu(\mathbf{x}_\nu, \quad 1) \in \mathbb{R}^{D+1}$ and $\mathbf{v} = (\mathbf{w}, b) \in \mathbb{R}^{D+1}$. We look for the $\mathbf{v}$ which maximizes $\Delta(\mathbf{v}) = \min_\nu [\mathbf{v}^T \mathbf{z}_\nu / ||\mathbf{w}||]$. With

$$d(\mathbf{v}) = \min_\nu [\mathbf{v}^T \mathbf{z}_\nu / ||\mathbf{v}||]$$

we introduce the margin of separation of the augmented patterns $(\mathbf{x}_\nu, \quad 1)$ in the $(D + 1)$-space. The $\mathbf{v}$ which provides the maximum margin d_* in the $(D+1)$-space also provides the maximum margin Δ^* in the D-dimensional subspace of the original patterns $\mathbf{x}_\nu \in \mathbb{R}^D$. This is the case since (i) the $\mathbf{v}_*$ which provides Δ^* also provides at least a local maximum of $d(\mathbf{v})$ and (ii) $d(\mathbf{v})$ and $\Delta(\mathbf{v})$ are convex and both have only one global maximum. Therefore,

$$\mathbf{v}_* = (\mathbf{w}_*, b_*) = \arg \max_{||\mathbf{v}||=1} [\min_\nu (\mathbf{v}^T \mathbf{z}_\nu) / ||\mathbf{w}||]$$

$$= \arg \max_{||\mathbf{v}||=1} [\min_\nu (\mathbf{v}^T \mathbf{z}_\nu)]$$

is valid. Instead of looking for the $\mathbf{v}_*$ which provides the maximum Δ, we look for the $\mathbf{v}_*$ which provides the maximum d. Both $\mathbf{v}_*$ are identical. Since $||\mathbf{v}_*||^2 = ||\mathbf{w}_*||^2 + b_*^2 = 1$, we obtain Δ^* from d_* and $\mathbf{v}_* = (\mathbf{w}_*, b_*)$ through

$$\Delta^* = \frac{d_*}{||\mathbf{w}_*||} = \frac{d_*}{\sqrt{1 \quad b_*^2}}.$$

2   The MinOver Algorithm Reformulated

The well-known MinOver algorithm is a simple and iterative procedure which provides the maximum margin classification in linearly separable classification problems. It was introduced in [5] for spin-glass models of Neural Networks. The MinOver algorithm yields a vector $\mathbf{v}_t$ the direction of which converges against $\mathbf{v}_*$ with increasing number of iterations t. This is valid as long as a full separation, i.e. a $\mathbf{v}_*$ with $\Delta^* > 0$ exists.

The MinOver algorithm works like the perceptron algorithm, with the slight modification that for training always the pattern $\mathbf{z}_\alpha(t)$ out of the training set $\mathcal{T} = \{\mathbf{z}_\nu | \nu = $

$1, \ldots, N\}$ with the worst, i.e. the minimum residual margin (overlap) $\mathbf{v}^T \mathbf{z}_\nu$ is chosen. Hence, the name MinOver.

Compared to [5] we present a simplified formulation of the MinOver algorithm, with the number of desired iterations t_{max} prespecified:

0. Set $t = 0$, choose a t_{max}, and set $\mathbf{v}_{t=0} = 0$.
1. Determine the $\mathbf{z}_\alpha(t)$ out of the training set $\mathcal{T}$ for which $\mathbf{v}_t^T \mathbf{z}$ is minimal.
2. Set $\mathbf{v}_{t+1} = \mathbf{v}_t + \mathbf{z}_\alpha(t)$.
3. Set $t = t + 1$ and go to 1.) if $t < t_{max}$.

2.1 MinOver in Its Dual Formulation and with Kernels

The vector $\mathbf{v}_t$ which determines the dividing hyperplane is given by

$$
\mathbf{v}_t = \sum_{\tau=0}^{t-1} \mathbf{z}_\alpha(\tau)
$$

$$
= \sum_{\mathbf{z}_\nu \in \mathcal{V}_t} n_\nu(t) \mathbf{z}_\nu
$$

with $\mathcal{V}_t \subseteq \mathcal{T}$ as the set of all patterns which have been used for training so far. The coefficient $n_\nu(t) \in \mathbb{N}$ denotes the number of times $\mathbf{z}_\nu \in \mathcal{V}_t$ has been used for training up to time step t. $\sum_{\mathcal{V}_t} n_\nu(t) = t$ is valid. With $V_t = |\mathcal{V}_t| \leq t$ we denote the number of training patterns which determine the normal vector $\mathbf{v}_t$.

In the dual representation the expression which decides the class assignment by being smaller or larger than zero can be written as

$$
\mathbf{v}^T \mathbf{z} = \sum_{\mathbf{x}_\nu \in \mathcal{V}} n_\nu y_\nu (\mathbf{x}_\nu^T \mathbf{x}) \quad b \tag{1}
$$

with

$$
b = \sum_{y_\nu \in \mathcal{V}} n_\nu y_\nu. \tag{2}
$$

In the dual formulation the training of the MinOver algorithm consists of either adding the training pattern $\mathbf{z}_\alpha$ to $\mathcal{V}$ as a further data point or, if $\mathbf{z}_\alpha$ is already element of $\mathcal{V}$, to increase the corresponding n_α by one.

If the input patterns $\mathbf{x} \in \mathbb{R}^D$ are transformed into another (usually higher dimensional) feature space $\mathbf{\Phi}(\mathbf{x}) \in \mathbb{R}^{D'}$ before classification, MinOver has to work with $\mathbf{z}_\nu = y_\nu (\mathbf{\Phi}(\mathbf{x}_\nu), \quad 1)^T$. Due to Equation (1) it does not have to do it explicitly. With $K(\mathbf{x}_\nu, \mathbf{x}) = \mathbf{\Phi}^T(\mathbf{x}_\nu) \mathbf{\Phi}(\mathbf{x})$ as the kernel which corresponds to the transformation $\mathbf{\Phi}(\mathbf{x})$, we obtain

$$
\mathbf{v}^T \mathbf{z} = y \left(\sum_{\mathbf{x}_\nu \in \mathcal{V}} n_\nu y_\nu K(\mathbf{x}_\nu, \mathbf{x}) \quad b \right), \tag{3}
$$

with the b of Equation (2).

In its dual formulation the MinOver algorithm is simply an easy procedure of selecting data points out of the training set:

0. Set $t = 0$, choose a t_{max}, and set $\mathcal{V} = \emptyset$.
1. Determine the $\mathbf{z}_\alpha(t)$ out of the training set $\mathcal{T}$ for which $\mathbf{v}_t^T \mathbf{z}$ according to Equation (3) is minimal.
2. If $\mathbf{z}_\alpha(t) \notin \mathcal{V}$, add $\mathbf{z}_\alpha(t)$ to $\mathcal{V}$ and assign to it an $n_\alpha = 1$. If $\mathbf{z}_\alpha(t) \in \mathcal{V}$ already, increase its n_α by one.
3. Set $t = t + 1$ and go to 1.) if $t < t_{max}$.

3   Convergence Bounds for MinOver

Krauth and Mézard gave a convergence proof for MinOver [5]. Within the context of spin-glass Neural Networks they showed that the smallest margin $d_t = \mathbf{v}_t^T \mathbf{z}_\alpha(t)$ provided by $\mathbf{v}_t$ converges against the maximum margin d_* at least as $\mathcal{O}(t^{-1/2})$. We give a modified proof of this $\mathcal{O}(t^{-1/2})$ convergence. Based on this proof we show that the margin converges even at least as $\mathcal{O}(t^{-1})$ against the maximum margin.

3.1 $\mathcal{O}(t^{-1/2})$ Bound

We look at the convergence of the angle γ_t between $\mathbf{v}_t$ and $\mathbf{v}_*$. We decompose the learning vector $\mathbf{v}_t$ into

$$\mathbf{v}_t = \cos\gamma_t \|\mathbf{v}_t\| \|\mathbf{v}_* + \mathbf{u}_t \qquad \mathbf{u}_t \mathbf{v}_* = 0. \qquad (4)$$

$\|\mathbf{u}_t\| \le R\sqrt{t}$ is valid, with R as the norm of the augmented pattern with maximum length, i.e., $R = \max_\nu \|\mathbf{z}_\nu\|$. This can be seen from

$$\mathbf{u}_{t+1}^2 \quad \mathbf{u}_t^2 = (\mathbf{u}_t + \mathbf{z}_\alpha(t) \quad [\mathbf{z}_\alpha(t)\mathbf{v}_*]\mathbf{v}_*)^2 \quad \mathbf{u}_t^2 \qquad (5)$$
$$= 2\mathbf{u}_t^T \mathbf{z}_\alpha(t) + \mathbf{z}_\alpha(t)^2 \quad [\mathbf{z}_\alpha(t)^T \mathbf{v}_*]^2$$
$$\le R^2.$$

We have used $\mathbf{u}_t^T \mathbf{z}_\alpha(t) \le 0$. Otherwise the condition

$$\min_\nu \frac{(\lambda\mathbf{v}_* + \mathbf{u}_t)^T \mathbf{z}_\mu}{\|\lambda\mathbf{v}_* + \mathbf{u}_t\|} \le \Delta^* \qquad \forall \lambda \in \mathbb{R}$$

would be violated. Since also

$$\mathbf{v}_*^T \mathbf{v}_t = \mathbf{v}_*^T \sum_{\tau=0}^{t\ 1} \mathbf{z}_\alpha(\tau) \ge d_* t$$

is valid, we obtain the bounds

$$\sin\gamma_t \le \gamma_t \le \tan\gamma_t = \frac{\|\mathbf{u}_t\|}{\mathbf{v}_*^T \mathbf{v}_t} \le \frac{R\sqrt{t}}{d_* t} = \frac{R/d_*}{\sqrt{t}}. \qquad (6)$$

The angle γ between the hyperplane provided by MinOver and the maximum margin hyperplane converges to zero at least as $\mathcal{O}(t^{-1/2})$.

After a finite number of training steps the $\mathbf{z}_\alpha(t)$ selected for learning will always be support vectors with $d_* = \mathbf{v}_*^T \mathbf{z}_\alpha(t)$. This can be seen from the following arguments: with Equation (4) we obtain

$$d_* \geq \frac{\mathbf{v}_t^T \mathbf{z}_\alpha(t)}{\|\mathbf{v}_t\|} = \mathbf{v}_*^T \mathbf{z}_\alpha(t) \cos \gamma_t + \frac{\mathbf{u}_t^T \mathbf{z}_\alpha(t)}{\|\mathbf{u}_t\|} \sin \gamma_t. \tag{7}$$

If $\mathbf{z}_\alpha(t)$ is not a support vector, $\mathbf{v}_*^T \mathbf{z}_\alpha(t) > d_*$ is valid. Since the prefactor of the sinus is bounded, after a finite number of training steps the right hand side would be larger than d_*. Hence, after a finite number of learning steps the $\mathbf{z}_\alpha(t)$ can only be support vectors.

Equation (7) yields the convergence of d_t. We obtain

$$d_* \geq d_t \geq d_* \cos \gamma_t \quad R \sin \gamma_t \geq d_*(1 \quad \gamma_t^2/2) \quad R\gamma_t \ .$$

With the term leading in γ_t and with our upper bound for γ_t, the convergence of the margin with increasing t is bounded by

$$0 \leq \frac{d_*}{d_*} \frac{d_t}{d_*} \leq \frac{R}{d_*} \gamma_t \leq \frac{R^2/d_*^2}{\sqrt{t}} \ .$$

3.2 $\mathcal{O}(t^{-1})$ Bound

From Equation (6) we can discern that we obtain a $\mathcal{O}(t^{-1})$ bound for the angle γ_t and, hence, a $\mathcal{O}(t^{-1})$ convergence of the margin d_t to the maximum margin d_*, if $\|\mathbf{u}_t\|$ remains bounded. This is indeed the case:

We introduced $\mathbf{u}_t$ as the projection of $\mathbf{v}_t$ onto the maximum margin hyperplane given by the normal vector $\mathbf{v}_*$. In addition we introduce $\mathbf{s}_\nu = \mathbf{z}_\nu \quad (\mathbf{v}_*^T \mathbf{z}_\nu) \mathbf{v}_*$ as the projection of the training patterns $\mathbf{z}_\nu$ onto the maximum margin hyperplane given by $\mathbf{v}_*$. As we have seen above, after a finite $t = t_{start}$ each $\mathbf{s}_\alpha(t)$ corresponds to one of the N_S support vectors. Then looking for the $\mathbf{z}_\alpha(t)$ out of the training set T for which $\mathbf{v}_t^T \mathbf{z}$ is minimal becomes equivalent to looking for the $\mathbf{s}_\alpha(t)$ out of the set S' of projected support vectors for which $\mathbf{u}_t^T \mathbf{z} = \mathbf{u}_t^T \mathbf{s}$ is minimal.

We now go one step further and introduce $\mathbf{u}'_t$ as the projection of $\mathbf{u}_t$ onto the subspace spanned by the $\mathbf{s}_\nu \in S'$. This subspace is at most N_S-dimensional. Since $\mathbf{u}_t^T \mathbf{s}_\nu = \mathbf{u}_t'^T \mathbf{s}_\nu$ for the $\mathbf{s}_\nu \in S'$, we now look for the $\mathbf{s}_\alpha(t) \in S'$ for which $\mathbf{u}_t'^T \mathbf{s}$ is minimal. Note that for $t \geq t_{start}$ always $\mathbf{u}_t^T \mathbf{z}_\alpha(t) = \mathbf{u}_t^T \mathbf{s}_\alpha(t) = \mathbf{u}_t'^T \mathbf{s}_\alpha(t) \leq 0$ is valid.

The following analysis of the development of $\mathbf{u}$ over time starts with $\mathbf{u}_{t_{start}}$. We have

$$\mathbf{u}_t = \mathbf{u}_{t_{start}} + \sum_{\tau=t_{start}}^{t \ 1} \mathbf{s}_\alpha(\tau).$$

$\mathbf{u}_t$ remains bounded, if $\mathbf{u}'_t$ remains bounded. We discriminate the following three cases:

i) $\max_{\|\mathbf{u}'\|=1} \min_{\mathbf{s}_\nu \in S'} (\mathbf{u}'^T \mathbf{s}_\nu) < 0$

ii) $\max_{\|\mathbf{u}'\|=1} \min_{\mathbf{s}_\nu \in S', \|\mathbf{s}_\nu\|>0} (\mathbf{u}'^T \mathbf{s}_\nu) > 0$

iii) $\max_{\|\mathbf{u}'\|=1} \min_{\mathbf{s}_\nu \in S', \|\mathbf{s}_\nu\|>0} (\mathbf{u}'^T \mathbf{s}_\nu) = 0$

Note that the vector $\mathbf{u}'$ with $||\mathbf{u}'|| = 1$ varies only within the subspace spanned by the $\mathbf{s}_\nu \in \mathcal{S}'$. If this subspace is of dimension one, only i) or ii) can occur. For i) and ii) it can quickly be proven that $\mathbf{u}'_t$ remains bounded. Case iii) can be redirected to i) or ii), which is a little bit more tedious.

i) There is an $\epsilon > 0$ such that for each training step $\mathbf{u}'^T_t \mathbf{s}_\alpha(t) \leq \epsilon||\mathbf{u}'_t||$. Analog to Equation (5) we obtain

$$\Delta \mathbf{u}'^2_t = 2\mathbf{u}'^T_t \mathbf{s}_\alpha(t) + \mathbf{s}_\alpha(t)^2$$
$$\leq 2\epsilon||\mathbf{u}'_t|| + R^2.$$

The negative contribution to the change of $||\mathbf{u}'_t||$ with each training step increases with $||\mathbf{u}'_t||$ and keeps it bounded.

ii) There is a $\mathbf{u}'$ such that $\mathbf{u}'^T \mathbf{s}_\nu > 0$ for each $||\mathbf{s}_\nu|| > 0$. In this case there is a $\mathbf{s}_\nu \in \mathcal{S}'$ with $||\mathbf{s}_\nu|| = 0$, since always $\mathbf{u}'^T \mathbf{s}_\alpha(t) \leq 0$ has to be valid. If $\mathbf{s}_\alpha(t) = 0$, the change of the vector $\mathbf{u}'_t$ terminates, since also $\mathbf{s}_\alpha(t + 1)$ will be zero. Will $\mathbf{s}_\alpha(t)$ be zero after a finite number of training steps? It will since there is a $\mathbf{u}'$ which separates the $||\mathbf{s}_\nu|| > 0$ from $\mathbf{s}_\nu = 0$ with a positive margin. We know from perceptron learning that in this case also $\mathbf{u}'_t$ will separate these $||\mathbf{s}_\nu|| > 0$ after a finite number of learning steps. At the latest when this is the case $\mathbf{s}_\alpha(t)$ will be zero and $||\mathbf{u}'_t||$ will stay bounded.

iii) We will redirect this case to i) or ii). With $\mathbf{u}'_*$ we denote the $\mathbf{u}'$, $||\mathbf{u}'|| = 1$ which maximizes $\min_{\mathbf{s}_\nu \in \mathcal{S}', ||\mathbf{s}_\nu||>0}(\mathbf{u}'^T \mathbf{s}_\nu)$. The set of those $\mathbf{s}_\nu \in \mathcal{S}'$ with $\mathbf{u}'^T_* \mathbf{s}_\nu = 0$ we denote by $\mathcal{S}''$. The $\mathbf{s}_\nu \in \mathcal{S}'/\mathcal{S}''$ are separated from the origin by a positive margin. After a finite number of learning steps $\mathbf{s}_\alpha(t)$ will always be an element of $\mathcal{S}''$. Then looking for the $\mathbf{s}_\alpha(t)$ out of $\mathcal{S}'$ for which $\mathbf{u}'^T_t \mathbf{s}$ is minimal becomes equivalent to looking for the $\mathbf{s}_\alpha(t)$ out of the set $\mathcal{S}''$ for which $\mathbf{u}''^T_t \mathbf{s}$ is minimal, with $\mathbf{u}''_t$ as the projection of $\mathbf{u}'_t$ onto the subspace spanned by the $\mathbf{s}_\nu \in \mathcal{S}''$. Note that the dimension of this subspace is reduced by at least one compared to the subspace spanned by the $\mathbf{s}_\nu \in \mathcal{S}'$. For $\mathbf{s}_\nu \in \mathcal{S}''$ again $\mathbf{u}^T_t \mathbf{z}_\alpha(t) = \mathbf{u}^T_t \mathbf{s}_\alpha(t) = \mathbf{u}'^T_t \mathbf{s}_\alpha(t) = \mathbf{u}''^T_t \mathbf{s}_\alpha(t) \leq 0$ is valid. $\mathbf{u}'$ remains bounded, if $\mathbf{u}''$ remains bounded. We have the same problem as in the beginning, but within a reduced subspace. Either case i), ii), or iii) applies. If again case iii) applies, it will again lead to the same problem, but within a subspace reduced even further. After a finite number of these iterations the dimension of the respective subspace will be one. Then only case i) or ii) can apply and, hence, $||\mathbf{u}||$ will stay bounded.

It is possible to show that the $\mathcal{O}(t^{-1})$ convergence bound for $\tan \gamma_t$ is a tight bound. Due to the limited space we have to present the proof in a follow-up paper.

4   Computer Experiments

To illustrate these bounds with computer experiments, we measured the convergence of $\tan \gamma_t$ on two artificial data sets. Both data sets consisted of $N = 1000$ patterns $\mathbf{x}_\nu \in \mathbb{R}^D$, half of them belonging to class $+1$ and -1, respectively. The pattern space was two-dimensional ($D = 2$) for the first data set, and 100-dimensional ($D = 100$) for the second one.

Each data set was generated as follows: a random normal vector for the maximum margin hyperplane was chosen. On a hypersquare on this hyperplane with a sidelength of 2 the $N = 1000$ random input patterns were generated. Then half of them were shifted to one halfspace (class $+1$) by a random amount uniformly chosen from the interval $[0.1, 1]$, and the other half was shifted to the other halfspace (class -1) by a random amount uniformly chosen from $[-0.1, -1]$. To make sure that the chosen normal vector indeed defines the maximum margin hyperplane, for 30% of the patterns a margin of exactly 0.1 was chosen.

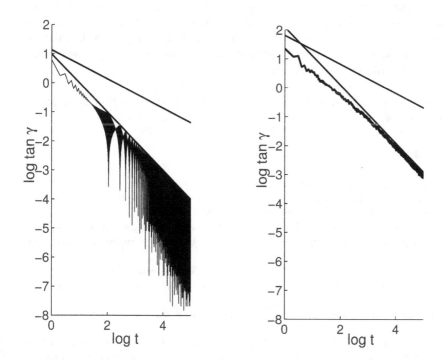

Fig. 1. Double-logarithmic plot of the angle γ_t between the maximum margin hyperplane and the hyperplane provided by MinOver against the number of learning steps t. After a finite number of learning steps the plot follows a line of slope -1, which demonstrates the $\mathcal{O}(t^{-1})$ convergence. For comparison the old $\mathcal{O}(t^{-1/2})$ convergence bound is shown. At the end of the learning procedure $\tan \gamma_t$ is about three orders of magnitude smaller than predicted by the old $\mathcal{O}(t^{-1/2})$-bound.

After each training step we calculated $\tan \gamma_t$ of the angle γ_t between the known maximum margin hyperplane and the hyperplane defined by $\mathbf{v}_t$. The result for both data sets is shown in Fig. 1. To visualize the convergence rate we chose a double logarithmic plot. As expected, in this double logarithmic plot convergence is bounded by a line with a slope of -1, which corresponds to the $\mathcal{O}(t^{-1})$ convergence we have proven. For comparison we also plotted the $\mathcal{O}(t^{-1/2})$-bound given by Equation (6), which corresponds to a line of slope $-1/2$. After 100.000 training steps $\tan \gamma_t$ is about three orders of magnitude smaller than predicted by the old $\mathcal{O}(t^{-1/2})$-bound.

5   Conclusions

The well-known MinOver algorithm as a simple and iterative procedure for obtaining maximum margin hyperplanes has been reformulated for the purpose of support vector classification with and without kernels. We have given an alternative proof for its well-known $\mathcal{O}(t^{-1/2})$ convergence. Based on this proof we have shown that the Min-Over algorithm converges even at least as $\mathcal{O}(t^{-1})$ with increasing number of learning steps. We illustrated this result on two artificial data sets. With such a guarantee in convergence speed, with its simplicity, and with a computational effort which scales like $\mathcal{O}(N)$ with the number of training patterns the MinOver algorithm deserves a more widespread consideration in applications.

Acknowledgment. The author would like to thank Kai Labusch for his help preparing the manuscript.

References

1. C. Cortes and V. Vapnik. Support-vector-networks. *Machine Learning*, 20(3):273–297, 1995.
2. Y. Freund and R.E. Schapire. Large margin classification using the perceptron algorithm. In *Computational Learing Theory*, pages 209–217, 1998.
3. T.T. Friess, N. Cristianini, and C. Campbell. The kernel adatron algorithm: a fast and simple learning procedure for support vector machine. *Proc. 15th International Conference on Machine Learning*, 1998.
4. S. S. Keerthi, S. K. Shevade, C. Bhattacharyya, and K. R. K. Murthy. A fast iterative nearest point algorithm for support vector machine classifier design. *IEEE-NN*, 11(1):124–136, January 2000.
5. W. Krauth and M. Mezard. Learning algorithms with optimal stability in neural networks. *J.Phys.A*, 20:745–752, 1987.
6. Y. LeCun, L. Jackel, L. Bottou, A. Brunot, C. Cortes, J. Denker, H. Drucker, I. Guyon, U. Muller, E. Sackinger, P. Simard, and V. Vapnik. Comparison of learning algorithms for handwritten digit recognition. *Int.Conf.on Artificial Neural Networks*, pages 53–60, 1995.
7. Y. Li and P.M. Long. The relaxed online maximum margin algorithm. *Machine Learning*, 46(1-3):361–387, 2002.
8. H.D. Navone and T. Downs. Variations on a kernel-adatron theme. *VII Internacional Congress on Information Engineering, Buenos Aires*, 2001.
9. E. Osuna, R. Freund, and F. Girosi. Training support vector machines:an application to face detection. *CVPR'97*, pages 130–136, 1997.
10. J.C. Platt. *Advances in Kernel Methods - Support Vector Learning*, chapter Fast Training of Support Vector Machines using Sequential Minimal Optimization, pages 185–208. MIT Press, 1999.
11. B. Schölkopf. Support vector learning, 1997.
12. V. Vapnik. *The Nature of Statistical Learning Theory*. Springer-Verlag, New York, 1995.

A Semantic Typicality Measure
for Natural Scene Categorization

Julia Vogel[1] and Bernt Schiele[1,2]

[1] Perceptual Computing and Computer Vision Group, ETH Zurich, Switzerland
vogel@inf.ethz.ch
http://www.vision.ethz.ch/vogel
[2] Multimodal Interactive Systems, TU Darmstadt, Germany
schiele@informatik.tu-darmstadt.de

Abstract. We propose an approach to categorize real-world natural scenes based on a semantic typicality measure. The proposed typicality measure allows to grade the similarity of an image with respect to a scene category. We argue that such a graded decision is appropriate and justified both from a human's perspective as well as from the image-content point of view. The method combines bottom-up information of local semantic concepts with the typical semantic content of an image category. Using this learned category representation the proposed typicality measure also quantifies the semantic transitions between image categories such as coasts, rivers/lakes, forest, plains, mountains or sky/clouds. The method is evaluated quantitatively and qualitatively on a database of natural scenes. The experiments show that the typicality measure well represents the diversity of the given image categories as well as the ambiguity in human judgment of image categorization.

1 Introduction

Scene categorization or scene classification is still a challenge on the way to reduce the semantic gap between "the information that one can extract from visual data and the users' interpretation for the same data in a given situation" [1]. In the context of this paper, scene categorization refers to the task of grouping images into semantically meaningful categories. But what are "semantically meaningful" categories? In image retrieval, meaningful categories correspond to those basic-level image categories that act as as a starting point when users describe verbally the particular image they are searching for. In general however, any natural scene category will be characterized by a high degree of diversity and potential ambiguities. The reason is that those categories depend strongly on the subjective perception of the viewer.

We argue that high categorization accuracies should not be the primary evaluation criterion for categorization. Since many natural scenes are in fact ambiguous, the categorization accuracy only reflects the accuracy with respect to the opinion of the particular person that performed the annotation. Therefore, the attention should also be directed at modeling the typicality of a particular scene. Here, typicality can be seen as a measure for the uncertainty of annotation judgment. Research in psychophysics especially addresses the concept of typicality in categorization. In each category, typical and less typical items can be found with typicality differences being the most reliable effect in categorization research [2].

C.E. Rasmussen et al. (Eds.): DAGM 2004, LNCS 3175, pp. 195–203, 2004.
© Springer-Verlag Berlin Heidelberg 2004

coasts   rivers/lakes   forests   plains   mountains   sky/clouds

Fig. 1. Images of each category. Top three rows: typical images. Bottom row: less typical image.

We propose a semantic typicality measure that grades the similarity of natural real-world image with respect to six scene categories. Furthermore, the typicality measure allows to categorize the images into one of those categories. Images are represented through the frequency of occurrence of nine local semantic concepts. Based on this information, a prototypical category representation is learned for each scene category. The proposed typicality measure is evaluated both qualitatively and quantitatively using cross-validation on an image database of 700 natural scenes.

Previous research in scene classification usually aims for high classification accuracies by using very "clean" databases. Early research covers city/landscape- [3], indoor/outdoor- [4] and indoor/outdoor-, city/landscape-, sunset/mountain/forest-classification [5]. These approaches employ only global image information rather than localized information. The goal of more recent work is to automatically annotate local image regions [6]-[9], but the majority does not try to globally describe the retrieved images. Oliva and Torralba [10] attach global labels to images based on local and global features, but do not use any intermediate semantic annotation.

In the next section, we discuss the selection of image categories. The image and category representations are introduced in Section 3 and 4. We present our typicality measure and the categorization based on it in Section 5. Section 6 summarizes the categorization results using automatically classified image subregions as input. Finally, Section 7 shows the categorization performance visually on new, unseen images.

2   Basic Level Image Categories

Our selection of scene categories has been inspired by work in psychophysics. In search of a taxonomy of environmental scenes, Tversky and Hemenway [11] found indoors and outdoors to be superordinate-level categories, with the outdoors category being composed of the basic-level categories city, park, beach and mountains. The experiments of Rogowitz et al. [12] revealed two main axes in which humans sort photographic images: human vs. non-human and natural vs. artificial. For our experiments, we selected the non-human/natural coordinate as superordinate and extended the natural, basic-level categories of [11] to coasts, rivers/lakes, forests, plains, mountains and sky/clouds. The diversity of those categories is illustrated in Figure 1. It displays a sample of images for each category. The top three lines correspond to typical examples for each category. The bottom line shows images which are far less typical but which are – arguably – still part of the respective category. Obviously, those examples are more difficult to classify and literally correspond to borderline cases. In the following, we aim for a semantic typicality measure based on the global composition of local semantic concepts which reflects that those less typical images in the bottom part of Figure 1 are less similar to the semantic category than those, more typical images in the upper part of the figure.

3   Image Representation

Many studies have shown that in categorization, members and non-members form a continuum with no obvious break in people's membership judgment. Quite importantly, typicality differences are probably the strongest and most reliable effect in the categorization literature [2]. For example it has been found that typical items were more likely to serve as cognitive reference points [13] and that learning of category representations is faster if subjects are taught on mostly typical items than if they are taught on less typical items [14]. In our opinion, any successful category representation has to take these findings into account and should be consistent with them.

A representation which is predictive of typicality is the so-called "attribute score" [15]. That is, items that are most typical have attributes that are very common in the category. In this approach each attribute is weighted in order to take into account their respective importance for the category. In our case, it is the local semantic concepts that act as scene category attributes. By analyzing the semantic similarities and dissimilarities of the aforementioned categories, the following set of nine local semantic concepts emerged as being most discriminant: *sky, water, grass, trunks, foliage, field, rocks, flowers* and *sand*. In our current implementation, the local semantic concepts are extracted on an arbitrary regular 10x10 grid of image subregions. For each local semantic concept, its frequency of occurrence in a particular image is determined and each image is represented by a so-called concept occurrence vector. Figure 2 shows an exemplary image with its local semantic concepts and its concept occurrence vector. Since the statistics of the local semantic concepts vary significantly when analyzing certain image areas separately (e.g. top/middle/bottom), we evaluate the concept occurrence vector for at least three image areas.

Database. The database consists of 700 images in the categories coasts, forests, rivers/lakes, plains, mountains and sky/clouds. All image subregions have been manually annotated with the above mentioned nine local semantic concepts.

4   Prototypical Representation of Scene Categories

The representation of the scene categories should take into account the typicality effect and the prototype phenomenon. A category prototype is an example which is most

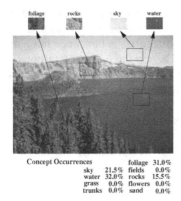

Concept Occurrences

		foliage	31.0%
sky	21.5%	fields	0.0%
water	32.0%	rocks	15.5%
grass	0.0%	flowers	0.0%
trunks	0.0%	sand	0.0%

Fig. 2. Image representation

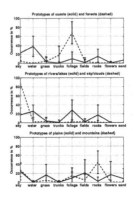

Fig. 3. Prototypes and standard deviations of the scene categories

typical for the category, even though the prototype is not necessarily an existing category member. Given the image representation presented in the previous section, a prototypical representation for the six scene categories can be learned. This prototypical representation allows to grade the different members of the category by an appropriate semantic typicality measure. The measure takes into account the occurrence statistics of the semantic concepts and weights them according to their variance within the category. The prototypical representation corresponds to the means over the concept occurrence vectors of all category members. Figure 3 displays those prototypes and the standard deviations for all categories. From this figure, it becomes apparent which local semantic concepts are especially discriminant. For example, forests are characterized through a large amount of *foliage* and *trunks*, whereas mountains can be differentiated when a large amount of *rocks* is detected.

5   Typicality and Categorization

The proposed category representation has the advantage of not representing binary decisions about the semantic concepts being present in the image or not ("Yes, there are *rocks*." vs. "No, there are no *rocks*."). Instead it represents soft decisions about the degree to which a particular semantic concept is present. The distances of the category members to the prototypical representation thus allow to assess the typicality of these images without excluding them from the category. There might be mountains scenes that hardly contain any *rocks*, but quite some *foliage*. They do belong to the mountains category, but they are much less typical than mountains scenes that contain a larger amount of *rocks*. In fact, they might be quite close to the borderline of being forest scenes.

The image typicality is measured by computing the Mahalanobis distance between the images' concept occurrence vector and the prototypical representation. All experiments have been 10-fold cross-validated. Hence, the category prototypes are computed on 90% of the database. All following depicted images belong to the respective test sets. Figures 4, 5, and 6 show the transitions between two categories with the typicality distance measure printed below the images, normalized to the range [0, 1]. A value close to

| D = 0.06 | D = 0.29 | D = 0.34 | D = 0.81 | D = 0.83 | D = 0.95 |

Fig. 4. Transition from `rivers/lakes` to `forests` with normalized typicality value

| D = 0.05 | D = 0.11 | D = 0.39 | D = 0.48 | D = 0.62 | D = 0.87 |

Fig. 5. Transition from `forests` to `mountains` with normalized typicality value

| D = 0.11 | D = 0.40 | D = 0.49 | D = 0.67 | D = 0.77 | D = 0.82 |

Fig. 6. Transition from `mountains` to `rivers/lakes` with normalized typicality value

0 corresponds to a close similarity of the particular image to the first of the two categories and vice versa. For example Figure 4 shows clearly the increase in "`forest`-ness" from left to right. Figure 5 depicts the transition from `forests` to `mountains` and Figure 6 the transition from `mountains` back to `rivers/lakes`.

With the typicality measure, also the categorization of unseen images can be carried out. For a new image, the similarity to the prototypical representation of each category is computed and the image is assigned to the category with the smallest distance. Table 2(a) shows the confusion matrix for the categorization of the annotated database images (10-fold cross-validated) resulting in an overall categorization rate of 89.3%. The analysis of the mis-categorized images shows that most of the confusions can be explained due to similarities of the different categories. Another way to evaluate the performance is to use the rank statistics of the categorization shown in Table 2(a). Using both the best and the second best match the categorization rate raises to 98.0%. This proves that images which are incorrectly categorized as first match are on the borderline between two similar categories and therefore most often correctly categorized with the second best match. It is also true, that the typicality values of those two matches are often very close to each other.

6   Categorization of Classified Images

The categorization experiment of the previous section was carried out using the manually annotated images of our database. In this section, we discuss the categorization results when the 70'000 image subregions have automatically been classified into one of the

Table 1. Categorization Confusion Matrix and Rank Statistics - Annotated Image Regions

							1	2	3	4	5	6
coasts	**86.0**	14.0	0.0	0.0	0.0	0.0	**86.0**	100.0	100.0	100.0	100.0	100.0
rivers/lakes	7.9	**92.1**	0.0	0.0	0.0	0.0	**92.1**	100.0	100.0	100.0	100.0	100.0
forests	0.0	6.8	**91.3**	1.9	0.0	0.0	**91.3**	98.1	98.1	100.0	100.0	100.0
plains	1.6	0.0	0.0	**95.3**	3.1	0.0	**95.3**	98.4	100.0	100.0	100.0	100.0
mountains	1.1	7.9	0.0	8.4	**82.6**	0.0	**82.6**	94.4	98.9	100.0	100.0	100.0
sky/clouds	0.0	0.0	0.0	0.0	0.0	**100**	**100.0**	100.0	100.0	100.0	100.0	100.0
OVERALL							**89.3**	98.0	99.4	100.0	100.0	100.0

(a) Confusion Matrix   (b) Rank Statistics

Table 2. Categorization Confusion Matrix and Rank Statistics - Classified Image Regions

							1	2	3	4	5	6
coasts	**59.9**	12.0	3.5	6.3	10.6	7.7	**59.9**	83.8	95.1	99.3	100.0	100.0
rivers/lakes	15.9	**41.6**	13.3	2.7	23.0	3.5	**41.6**	80.5	96.5	98.2	100.0	100.0
forests	0.0	2.0	**94.1**	0.0	2.9	1.0	**94.1**	95.1	97.1	97.1	100.0	100.0
plains	9.2	2.3	14.6	**43.8**	20.0	10.0	**43.8**	59.2	78.5	99.2	100.0	100.0
mountains	4.5	3.4	1.1	5.1	**84.3**	1.7	**84.3**	91.6	96.1	99.4	100.0	100.0
sky/clouds	0.0	0.0	0.0	0.0	0.0	**100**	**100.0**	100.0	100.0	100.0	100.0	100.0
OVERALL							**67.2**	83.1	93.0	98.8	99.9	100.0

(a) Confusion Matrix   (b) Rank Statistics

semantic concept classes. The subregions are represented by a combined 84-bin linear HSI color histogram and a 72-bin edge direction histogram, and classified by a k-Nearest Neighbor classifier. Features and classifier have been selected through an extensive series of experiments. These pre-tests also showed that the use of neighborhood information in face decreases the overall classification accuracy since it penalizes concepts that appear as "singularities" in the image instead of as contiguous regions (e.g. *trunks* or *grass*). The classification accuracy of the concept classification is 68.9%.

The prototypical representation of the categories is computed on ten image areas (ten rows from top to bottom, see Section 3). Both concept classification and categorization are 10-fold cross-validated on the same test and training set. That is, a particular training set is used to train the concept classifier and to learn the prototypes. The images of the corresponding test set are classified locally with the learned concept classifier and subsequently categorized.

The overall categorization rate of the classified images is 67.2%. The corresponding confusion matrix is displayed in Table 3(a). A closer analysis of the confusions leads to the following insights. Good and less good categorization is strongly correlated with the performance of the concept classifier that is most discriminant for the particular category. Three of the six categories have been categorized with high accuracy: forest, mountains and sky/clouds. The reason is that the important local concepts for those categories, that is *sky*, *foliage* and *rocks* have been classified with high accuracy and thus lead to a better categorization. Critical for the categorization especially of the category plains is the classification of *fields*. Since *fields* is frequently confused with either *foliage* or *rocks*, plains is sometimes mis-categorized as forests or mountains.

mountains   rivers/lakes   plains

Fig. 7. Examples for "correctly" categorized images.

forest (instead of rivers/lakes)   mountains (instead of forest)   coasts (instead of rivers/lakes)

Fig. 8. Examples for "incorrectly" categorized images.

Another semantic concept that is critical for the categorization is *water*. If not enough *water* is classified correctly, rivers/lakes images are confused with forests or mountains depending on the amount of *foliage* and *rocks* in the image. If too much *water* has incorrectly been detected in rivers/lakes images, they are confused with coasts.

Table 3(b) displays the rank statistics for the categorization problem. When using both the best and the second best match, the categorization rate is 83.1%. As before with the labeled data, there is a large jump in categorization accuracy from the first to the second rank. This leads to the conclusion that the wrong classifications on subregion level move many images closer to the borderline between two categories and thus cause mis-categorizations.

7   More Categorization Results

In order to verify the results of Section 6, both concept classification and scene categorization were tested on new images that do not belong to the cross-validated data sets. Exemplary categorization results are displayed in Figure 7 and Figure 8. "Correctly" and "incorrectly" are quoted on purpose since especially Figure 8 exemplifies how difficult it is to label the respective images. When does a forest-scene become a rivers/lakes-scene or a mountains-scene a forest-scene? The reason for the "mis-categorization" of the first image in Figure 8 is that a large amount of *water* has been classified as *foliage* thus moving the scene closer to the forest-prototype. The reason for the other two "mis-categorizations" is the ambiguity of the scenes. The typicality measure returned for all three images in Figure 8 low confidence values for either of the two relevant categories whereas the typicality value for the scenes in Figure 7 is higher. This shows that we are able to detect difficult or ambiguous scenes using our image representation in combination with the typicality measure.

8   Discussion and Conclusion

In this paper, we have presented a novel way to categorize natural scenes based on a semantic typicality measure. We have shown that it is indispensable both from a human's perspective and from a system's point of view to model the local content and thus the diversity of scene categories. With our typicality measure ambiguous images can be marked as being less typical for a particular image category, or the transition between two categories can be determined. This behavior is of interest for image retrieval systems since humans are often interested in searching for images that are somewhere "between mountains and rivers/lakes, but have no flowers".

Considering the diversity of the images and scene categories used, classification rates of 89.3% with annotated concept regions and 67.2% using semantic concept classifiers are convincing. By also including the second best match in the categorization, an increase to 98.0% and 83.1%, respectively, could be reached. In particular this latter result reveals that many of the images misclassified with the first match are indeed at the borderline between two semantically related categories. This supports the claim that we are able to model the typicality and ambiguity of unseen images. The results also show that the categorization performance is strongly dependent on the performance of the individual concept classifiers which will be the topic of further research.

Acknowledgments. This work is part of the CogVis project, funded by the Comission of the European Union (IST-2000-29375) and the Swiss Federal Office for Education and Science (BBW 00.0617).

References

1. Smeulders, A., Worring, M., Santini, S., Gupta, A., Jain, R.: Content-based image retrieval at the end of the early years. IEEE Trans. on PAMI **22** (2000)
2. Murphy, G.L.: The Big Book of Concepts. MIT Press (2002)
3. Gorkani, M., Picard, R.: Texture orientation for sorting photos at a glance. In: Int. Conf. on Pattern Recognition ICPR, Jerusalem, Israel (1994)
4. Szummer, M., Picard, R.: Indoor-outdoor image classification. In: IEEE Int. Workshop on Content-based Access of Image and Video Databases, Bombay, India (1998)
5. Vailaya, A., Figueiredo, M., Jain, A., Zhang, H.: Image classification for content-based indexing. IEEE Trans. on Image Processing **10** (2001)
6. Maron, O., Ratan, A.L.: Multiple-instance learning for natural scene classification. In: Int. Conf. on Machine Learning, Morgan Kaufmann, San Francisco, CA (1998)
7. Town, C., Sinclair, D.: Content based image retrieval using semantic visual categories. Technical Report 2000.14, AT&T Laboratories Cambridge (2000)
8. Naphade, M., Huang, T.: A probabilistic framework for semantic video indexing, filtering, and retrieval. IEEE Trans. on Multimedia **3** (2001)
9. Barnard, K., Duygulu, P., de Freitas, N., Forsyth, D.: Object recognition as machine translation - part 2: Exploiting image data-base clustering models. In: European Conf. on Computer Vision, Copenhagen, Denmark (2002)

10. Oliva, A., Torralba, A.: Modeling the shape of the scene: A holistic representation of the spatial envelope. Int. Journal of Computer Vision **42** (2001)
11. Tversky, B., Hemenway, K.: Categories of environmental scenes. Cognitive Psychology **15** (1983)
12. Rogowitz, B., Frese, T., Smith, J., Bouman, C., Kalin, E.: Perceptual image similarity experiments. In: SPIE Conf. Human Vision and Electronic Imaging, San Jose, California (1998)
13. Rosch, E.: Cognitive representations of semantic categories. J. Exp. Psychology 104 (1975)
14. Posner, M., Keele, S.: On the genesis of abstract ideas. J. Exp. Psychology **77** (1968)
15. Rosch, E., Mervis, C.: Family resemblance: Studies in the internal structure of categories. Cognitive Psychology **7** (1975)

Tunable Nearest Neighbor Classifier

Yonglei Zhou, Changshui Zhang, and Jingchun Wang

Department of Automation, Tsinghua University,
Beijing 100084, P.R. China,
zhouyonglei98@mails.tsinghua.edu.cn

Abstract. A tunable nearest neighbor (TNN) classifier is proposed to handle the discrimination problems. The TNN borrows the concept of feature line spaces from the nearest feature line (NFL) classifier, to make use of the information implied by the interaction between each pair of points in the same class. Instead of the NFL distance, a tunable distance metric is proposed in the TNN. The experimental evaluation shows that in the given feature space, the TNN consistently achieves better performance than NFL and conventional nearest neighbor methods, especially for the tasks with small training sets.

1 Introduction

We address a discrimination problem with N labeled training samples originated from C categories. Denote the training set as $X = \left\{ \{x_i^c\}_{i=1}^{N_c} \right\}_{c=1}^{C}$, where $\{x_i^c\}_{i=1}^{N_c}$ represents the sample subset for the c-th class and N_c is the subset's size which satisfy $N = \sum_{c=1}^{C} N_c$. The task is to predict the class membership of an unlabeled sample x.

The k-nearest-neighbor (k-NN) method[4] is a simple and efficient approach to this task. We find the k nearest neighbors of x in the training set and classify x as the majority class among the k nearest neighbors. In a given feature space, it's very important to select an appropriate distance metric for k-NN.

There have been various distance metrics used in k-NN, which can be divided into two categories. The distance metrics in the first category are defined between an unlabeled point and a labeled point in the feature space, e.g. Euclidean distance, Hamming distance, Cosine distance, Kullback-Leibler (KL) distance[8], etc. Using these distance metrics, the training points are regarded as some isolated ones in the feature space. Hence, some useful information implied by the interaction of samples is ignored. Different from the first category, the distance metrics in the second category make use of some prior knowledge for the whole training set, such as Mahalanobis distance, Quadratic distance. Especially, a discriminant adaptive nearest neighbor (DANN) classification method is proposed in [5], where a local linear discriminant analysis (LDA) is adopted to estimate an effective local quadratic distance metric to find neighbors. However, these distance metrics are effective only if the training set is large enough.

In this paper, we consider the discrimination problem with multiple but very limit samples for each class, e.g. face recognition task. In these problems,

C.E. Rasmussen et al. (Eds.): DAGM 2004, LNCS 3175, pp. 204–211, 2004.

1-NN (also called as NN for simplicity) is frequently adopted because of the small training set. And the mentioned distance metrics in the second category are inappropriate. In [1][2], a nearest feature line (NFL) method is proposed to make use of the information implied by each pair of points in the same class by constituting some feature line (FL) spaces. The NFL distance is defined as the Euclidean distance between an unlabeled point and its projection onto the FL. The experimental results have shown the NFL can consistently produce superior results over the NN methods based on conventional distances[1][2]. However, the NFL distance will bring some problems, which weaken the NFL's performance in some cases such as the example in Fig. 1. A tunable nearest neighbor (TNN) method is proposed to strengthen the original NFL by using a new distance metric which can be tuned through a parameter. The parameter selection process is robust using cross-validation. Our experimental results substantiate the efficiency of the TNN , especially in the cases when only a small training set is available and the data distribution in the feature space is nonlinear.

2 Related Work

A discriminant adaptive nearest neighbor (DANN) method is proposed in [5], where a local LDA metric Σ_0 for the test point x_0 is learned using its nearest neighbor points through an iterative process. At completion, use the distance $d(x, x_0) = (x - x_0)^T \Sigma_0^{-1}(x - x_0)$ to obtain x_0's k-nearest neighbors for classification. Obviously, some prior knowledge has been introduced to the DANN. The DANN classifier can be expected to achieve better performance than the conventional NN classifiers. However, a large sample set is needed for good estimations of the local Quadratic metrics.

The nearest feature line (NFL) method[1][2] constructs some feature line spaces to make use of the information implied by the interaction between each pair of points in the same class. A feature line (FL) is defined as a straight line $\overline{x_i^c x_j^c}$ passing through two points x_i^c and x_j^c which belong to the same class in the feature space (see Fig. 2). All FLs in the same class constitute a FL Space of that class, $S_c = \{\overline{x_i^c x_j^c} | 1 \leq i, j \leq N_c, i \neq j\}$, and there are C FL spaces.

In the NFL classifier, the distance between an unlabeled point and its projection onto the FL is calculated and used as the metric. Let $x_p^{c,ij}$ represent the projection of the test point x to the FL $\overline{x_i^c x_j^c}$, as shown in Fig. 2. Then the NFL distance is described as $d_{NFL}(x, \overline{x_i^c x_j^c}) = \| x - x_p^{c,ij} \|$. According to the NN rule, x is classified into the class c^o , which satisfies $d_{NFL}(x, \overline{x_{i^o}^{c^o} x_{j^o}^{c^o}}) = \min_{1 \leq c \leq C} \min_{1 \leq i,j \leq N_c, i \neq j} d_{NFL}(x, \overline{x_i^c x_j^c})$.

Using the NFL distance d_{NFL} in the FL spaces is equivalent to extending each pair of training points in the same class to an infinite number of points lying on the corresponding FL, using interpolation and extrapolation. And this infinite extension of the original training set will bring some problems [3]. That is, the extension part of one class has a possibility to cross other classes, especially in the nonlinear cases such as the example illustrated in Fig. 1. In practice, this problem can be partly handled by using only close neighbors in the same

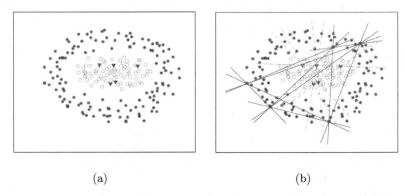

(a)   (b)

Fig. 1. The points come from two categories: class 1 denoted by circles and class 2 denoted by asterisks. (a) Five training points are randomly selected from each class, denoted by solid triangles and squares respectively. (b) The feature line spaces. As we can see, the extended parts of class 1 and class 2 are interwoven.

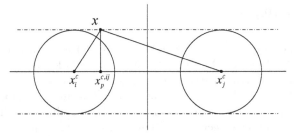

Fig. 2. The contours for an FL $\overline{x_i^c x_j^c}$ with different distance metrics. Two real-line circles are for Euclidean distance. Two parallel dashdotted lines are for the NFL distance.

class to create FL spaces. For the example illustrated in Fig. 1, if only the FLs constituted by each sample and its nearest neighbor in the same class are used, the FL space of class 2 will not cross that of class 1. However, the FL space of class 1 will still cross that of class 2. In addition, if the training set is too small, the usable FLs will be very limit. Hence, in the next section, we will handle this problem by designing a new distance metric in the original FL spaces.

3   Tunable Nearest Neighbor Method (TNN)

Similar to the NFL, the NN based on Euclidean distance can also be reformulated in the FL space by setting the distance metric as $d_{NN}(x, \overline{x_i^c x_j^c}) = \min\{d(x, x_i^c), d(x, x_j^c)\}$. However, it does not make use of the virtue of the FL spaces. The reason is that while calculating the distance $d_{NN}(x, \overline{x_i^c x_j^c})$, the pair of points, x_i^c and x_j^c, are treated as isolated ones.

Let us discuss the effects of various distance metrics in the FL spaces using a concept of equal-distance surface (also called a contour in 2-dimensional cases).

An equal-distance surface for an FL is defined as a surface in the feature space on which the points have the same distances to the FL. For a 2-dimensional case illustrated in Fig. 2, the contour for an FL with Euclidean distance consists of two circles or a close curve formed by the intersection of two circles, and the contour for an FL with the NFL distance is two parallel lines. Obviously, the equal-distance surfaces for an FL, which reflect the form of the interaction between the corresponding pair of points, should be adapted to the given data set. Hence, though the NFL achieves appealing results in many cases, it may perform poorly in some cases such as the example illustrated in Fig. 1.

Here, we propose a new distance metric which can be tuned through a parameter. The new distance from x to the FL $\overline{x_i^c x_j^c}$ is calculated as follow:

- Calculate two ratios: $r_1 = ||x - x_i^c||/||x_j^c - x_i^c||$, and $r_2 = ||x - x_j^c||/||x_j^c - x_i^c||$;
- Set $\mu_m = (r_m)^\alpha$ ($m = 1, 2$ and $\alpha \geq 0$). Get two points $x_m^{c,ij}$ ($m = 1, 2$) on the FL $\overline{x_i^c x_j^c}$ as $x_1^{c,ij} = x_i^c + \mu_1(x_j^c - x_i^c)$ and $x_2^{c,ij} = x_j^c + \mu_2(x_i^c - x_j^c)$;
- Let $d_{TNN}(x, \overline{x_i^c x_j^c}) = \min\{d(x, x_1^{c,ij}), d(x, x_2^{c,ij})\}$.

Tuning α is equivalent to adjusting the equal-distance surface forms for the FL lines. The contours for an FL using the TNN distance d_{TNN} with different values for α, are illustrated in Fig. 3. If α equals to zero, d_{TNN} is equivalent to d_{NN}. When α is near unit, the equal-distance surfaces for the FL using d_{TNN} are similar to that using d_{NFL}. As α gets larger, the equal-distance surfaces will become fatter, which indicates that the interaction between each pair is gradually eased up. And when α is large enough, d_{TNN} will approximate d_{NN}. The change of the equal-distance surface form is continuous.

Specially, when $\alpha = 2$, the TNN distance turns into

$$d_{TNN}(x, \overline{x_i^c x_j^c}) = || x - x_i^c || \cdot || x - x_j^c || / || x_i^c - x_j^c || \tag{1}$$

Using d_{TNN} with $\alpha = 2$, the interaction between each pair of points is moderate. In many cases, 2 is a recommendable value for α in d_{TNN}, though it may not be the optimum value.

According to the NN rule, x is classified into the class c^o, which satisfies $d_{TNN}(x, \overline{x_{i^o}^{c^o} x_{j^o}^{c^o}}) = \min_{1 \leq c \leq C} \min_{1 \leq i,j \leq N_c, i \neq j} d_{TNN}(x, \overline{x_i^c x_j^c})$. We call the NN classifier based on d_{TNN} as the tunable nearest neighbor (TNN) classifier.

The classification results for the example in Fig. 1 with 3 distance metrics are shown in Fig. 4, which show that the TNN has better adaptability to this specific data set than the NFL and the NN based on Euclidean distance.

4   Experimental Evaluation

To substantiate the efficiency of the TNN, we apply it to real data classification tasks. Here, we evaluate TNN's performance over some UCI datasets and the AR face database, versus NFL, NN and k-NN based on Euclidean distance.

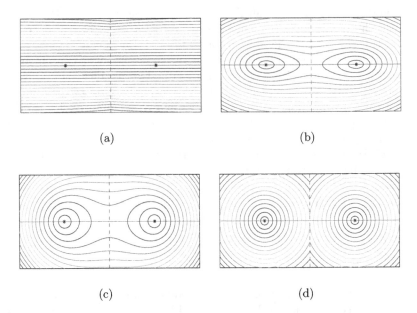

Fig. 3. The contours for an FL using d_{TNN} with α equaling to (a) 1.0, (b) 1.5, (c) 2.0, and (d) 10.0. Two points denoted by asterisks are the pair used to construct the FL.

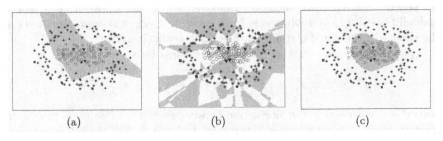

Fig. 4. The classification results for the example illustrated in Fig. 1 with five training samples per class, using the NN classifiers based on (a)Euclidean distance, (b)the NFL distance, and (c) the TNN distance with $\alpha = 2$.

4.1   UCI Datasets

We select some datasets from the UCI data repository which satisfy the following requirements: (1)There are no missing features in the data; (2)The sample number for each class is not large. Many people's results on each dataset have been reported to evaluate the performance of various algorithms. However, the experimental settings are not always the same. Hence, we don't compare our results with those results reported elsewhere. In our experiment, each dataset is randomly divided into 5 disjoint subsets of equal size. For each time, we select three subsets to constitute the training set and treat the rest as the testing set.

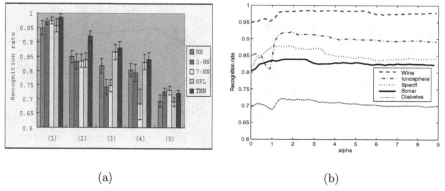

(a)   (b)

Fig. 5. Experimental results over five UCI datasets. (a)Recognition rate of TNN over (1)Wine, (2)Ionosphere, (3)Spectf, (4)Sonar and (5)Diabetes, versus NFL, NN and k-NN ($k = 3, 7$) based on Euclidean distance. (b)The TNN's average recognition rate curves against the parameter α.

There are totally 10 different trials over each dataset. Using the results of these trials, we can calculate the mean and standard deviation of the recognition rates.

Nearly over all selected datasets, TNN performs better than NFL, NN and k-NN ($k = 3, 7$) based on Euclidean distance. For limited space, we only list the results on the following five datasets in Fig. 5: 'Wine', 'Ionosphere', 'Spectf', 'Sonar' and 'Diabetes'. The optimum parameters α_o for TNN obtained through cross-validation are near 2.0 over all these five datasets. The average recognition rate curves for TNN against the parameter α over these datasets are shown in Fig. 5(b). From these curves, we can observe 3 remarkable facts: 1) The recognition rates of TNN with $\alpha = 1$ is comparable to that of NFL; 2) As α becomes large enough, the recognition rate of TNN will be stable; 3) The recognition rate curve against the parameter α varies smoothly around the optimum value.

4.2 Face Recognition

Face recognition task is carried out over AR face database. In the experiments, 50 persons are randomly selected from the total 126 persons and 7 frontal view faces with no occlusions are selected from the first session for each person. We have manually carried out the localization step, followed by a morphing step so that each face occupies a fixed 27×16 array of pixels. And they are converted to gray-level images by adding all three color channels, i.e., $I = (R + G + B)/3$. The principle component analysis (PCA)[7] is adopted here for dimensionality reduction. Hence, the data set is transformed into d-dimensional PCA space. Different from [7], the PCA features are normalized using the corresponding eigenvalues here. (Note that in the un-normalized PCA feature space, TNN can also achieve a similar increase in recognition rate compared with NN and NFL. However, the normalized PCA features are more suitable for this face database.) Three samples per subject are randomly selected as the training samples and the rest as the testing ones. The procedure is repeated for 10 times.

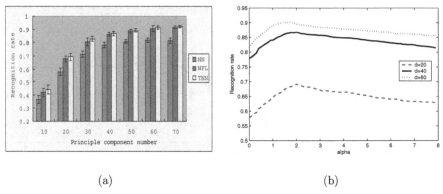

(a)   (b)

Fig. 6. Experimental results over AR face data with various PC numbers d. (a)Recognition rate of TNN, versus NFL and NN based on Euclidean distance. (b)The TNN's average recognition rate curves against the parameter α with $d = 20, 40, 60$.

We evaluate the performance of TNN, NFL and NN based on Euclidean distance with various principle component (PC) numbers. The optimum values for α are all close to 2.0. As shown in Fig. 6(a), in this experiment, TNN is comparable to NFL, and both of them are superior to NN based on Euclidean distance, nearly with an 8 percent increase in recognition rate. The TNN's average recognition rate curves against the parameter α are shown in Fig. 6(b), with $d = 20, 40, 60$. From these curves, we can observe the similar facts as have been referred to in the first experiment.

4.3   Discussions on the Parameter Selection and Computational Load

Besides the two experiments in this paper, the discrimination results over many other data sets, which are not presented here for limited space, exhibit some common facts. These facts accord well with the characteristics of the equal-distance surfaces for an FL using d_{TNN} with different α, e.g.

– The recognition rates of TNN with $\alpha = 1$ is comparable to that of NFL. The underlying reason is that when α is near unit, equal-distance surfaces for an FL using d_{TNN} are similar to that using d_{NFL}.
– The recognition rate curve against the parameter α is smooth. It may be because of the continuous change of the equal-distance surface form against α, as illustrated in Fig. 3.
– TNN with $\alpha = 2$ consistently achieves better performance than NN based on Euclidean distance. Hence, 2 is a recommendable value for α. As has been referred to in section 3, the interaction between each pair of points in the same class is moderate when using d_{TNN} with $\alpha = 2$.
– As α becomes large enough ($\alpha > 10$), the recognition rate of the TNN will be stable, which also accords with the trend of the equal-distance surfaces' evolution against α.

Through these facts and analysis, we can expect that TNN will perform better than NFL and NN based on Euclidean distance. And because of TNN's gradual change of recognition rates against α, we can adopt a large step size to search for the optimum value for α in a limited interval (generally set as $[0, 5]$).

Similar to NFL, TNN has to calculate the TNN distance for M times to classify a sample, where $M = \sum_{c=1}^{C} N_c(N_c - 1)/2$. Hence, TNN's computational load is obviously heavier than that of NN. However, in the task with small training set, the increase of the computational load is tolerable. On the other hand, cross validation is used to determine the optimal value for α, which also adds complexity to TNN in the training process. This problem exists in nearly all the methods which need to select optimal parameters for the algorithms.

5 Conclusions

A tunable nearest neighbor (TNN) method is proposed to make use of the information implied by the interaction between each pair of points in the same class. The TNN borrows the concept of feature line (FL) from the nearest feature line (NFL) method. Instead of the NFL distance in the NFL, a tunable distance metric is defined in the TNN. Hence, the effect caused by the interaction between each pair of points can be adjusted to adapt well to the given data set. The parameter selection process is predictable and robust using cross-validation. Moreover, there is a recommendable value, 2, for the parameter. The experimental results show that in the given feature space, the TNN consistently achieves better performance than the NFL and the NN based on Euclidean distance.

References

1. S.Z. Li and J. Lu. Face recognition using the nearest feature line method. IEEE Trans. Neural Networks, vol. 10, no.2, pp. 439-443, Mar. 1999.
2. S.Z. Li, K.L. Chan and C.L. Wang. Performance evaluation of the nearest feature line method in image classification and retrieval. IEEE Trans. Pattern Analysis and Machine Intelligence, vol. 22, No.11, November 2000.
3. L. Zhao, W.Qi, S.Z. Li, S.Q. Yang, H.J. Zhang. A new content-based shot retrieval approach: key-frame extraction based earest feature line (NFL) classification. ACM Multimedia Information Retrieval 2000, Oct 2000, Los Angeles, USA.
4. T.M. Cover and P. Hart. Nearest neighbor pattern classification. Annals of Statistics, 1967.
5. T. Hastie and R. Tibshirani. Discriminant adaptive nearest neighbor classfication. IEEE Trans. Pattern Analysis and Machine Intelligence, vol. 18, No.6, June 1996.
6. A.M. Martinez and R. Benavente. The AR-face database. CVC Technical Report 24, June 1998.
7. A.M. Martinez and A.C. Kak. PCA versus LDA. IEEE Trans. On Pattern Analysis and Machine Intelligence, vol. 23, No.2, February 2001.
8. J. Goldberger, S. Gordon and H. Greenspan. An efficient image similarity measure based on approximations of KL-Divergence between two gaussian mixtures. Proceedings of the 9th IEEE International Conference on Computer Vision.

SVM-Based Feature Selection
by Direct Objective Minimisation

Julia Neumann, Christoph Schnörr, and Gabriele Steidl

Dept. of Mathematics and Computer Science
University of Mannheim, 68131 Mannheim, Germany
http://www.cvgpr.uni-mannheim.de, http://kiwi.math.uni-mannheim.de
{jneumann,schnoerr,steidl}@uni-mannheim.de

Abstract. We propose various novel embedded approaches for (simultaneous) feature selection and classification within a general optimisation framework. In particular, we include linear and nonlinear SVMs. We apply difference of convex functions programming to solve our problems and present results for artificial and real-world data.

1 Introduction

Overview and related work. Given a pattern recognition problem as a training set of labelled feature vectors, our goal is to find a mapping that classifies the data correctly. In this context, *feature selection* aims at picking out some of the original input dimensions (*features*) (i) for performance issues by facilitating data collection and reducing storage space and classification time, (ii) to perform semantics analysis helping to understand the problem, and (iii) to improve prediction accuracy by avoiding the "curse of dimensionality" (cf. [6]).

Feature selection approaches divide into *filters* that act as a preprocessing step independently of the classifier, *wrappers* that take the classifier into account as a black box, and *embedded approaches* that simultaneously determine features and classifier during the training process (cf. [6]). In this paper, we deal with the latter method and focus on *direct objective minimisation*. Our linear classification framework is based on [4], but takes into account that the *Support Vector Machine* (SVM) provides good generalisation ability by its ℓ_2-regulariser. There exist only few papers on nonlinear classification with embedded feature selection. An approach for the quadratic 1-norm SVM was suggested in [12]. An example for a wrapper method employing a Gaussian kernel SVM error bound is [11].

Contribution. We propose a range of new embedded methods for feature selection regularising linear embedded approaches and construct feature selection methods for nonlinear SVMs. To solve the non-convex problems, we apply the general difference of convex functions (d.c.) optimisation algorithm.

Structure. In the next section, we present various extensions of the linear embedded approach proposed in [4] and consider feature selection methods in conjunction with nonlinear classification. The d.c. optimisation approach and its application to our problems is described in Sect. 3. Numerical results illustrating and evaluating various approaches are given in Sect. 4.

C.E. Rasmussen et al. (Eds.): DAGM 2004, LNCS 3175, pp. 212–219, 2004.

2   Feature Selection by Direct Objective Minimisation

Given a training set $\{(\mathbf{x}_i, y_i) \in \mathcal{X} \times \{-1, 1\} : i = 1, \ldots, n\}$ with $\mathcal{X} \subset \mathbb{R}^d$, our goal is both to find a classifier $F : \mathcal{X} \to \{-1, 1\}$ and to select features.

2.1   Linear Classification

The linear classification approaches construct two parallel bounding planes in $\mathbb{R}^d$ such that the differently labelled sets are to some extent in the two opposite half spaces determined by these planes. More precisely, one solves the minimisation problem

$$\min_{\mathbf{w} \in \mathbb{R}^d, b \in \mathbb{R}} (1 - \lambda) \sum_{i=1}^{n} (1 - y_i(\mathbf{w}^T \mathbf{x}_i + b))_+ + \lambda \rho(\mathbf{w}) \tag{1}$$

with $\lambda \in [0, 1)$, regulariser ρ and $x_+ := \max(x, 0)$. Then the classifier is $F(\mathbf{x}) = \text{sgn}(\mathbf{w}^T \mathbf{x} + b)$. For $\rho = 0$, the linear method (1) was proposed as *Robust Linear Programming* (RLP) by Bennett and Mangasarian [2]. Note that these authors weighted the training errors by $1/n_{\pm 1}$, where $n_{\pm 1} = |\{i : y_i = \pm 1\}|$.

In order to maximise the margin between the two parallel planes, the original SVM penalises the ℓ_2-norm $\rho(\mathbf{w}) = \frac{1}{2} \|\mathbf{w}\|_2^2$. Then (1) can be solved by a convex Quadratic Program (QP).

In order to suppress features, ℓ_p-norms with $p < 2$ are used. In [4], the ℓ_1-norm (lasso penalty) $\rho(\mathbf{w}) = \|\mathbf{w}\|_1$ leads to good feature selection and classification results. Moreover, for the ℓ_1-norm, (1) can be solved by a linear program.

The feature selection can be further improved by using the so-called ℓ_0-"norm" $\|\mathbf{w}\|_0 = |\{i : w_i \neq 0\}|$ [4,10]. Since the ℓ_0-norm is non-smooth, it was approximated in [4] by the concave functional

$$\rho(\mathbf{w}) = \mathbf{e}^T \left(\mathbf{e} - \left(e^{-\alpha |w_i|} \right)_{i=1}^{d} \right) \approx \|\mathbf{w}\|_0 \tag{2}$$

with approximation parameter $\alpha \in \mathbb{R}_+$ and $\mathbf{e} = (1, \ldots, 1)^T$. Problem (1) with penalty (2) is known as *Feature Selection concaVe* (FSV). Now the solution of (1) becomes more sophisticated and can be obtained, e.g., by the *Successive Linearization Algorithm* (SLA) as proposed in [4].

New feature selection approaches. Since the ℓ_2 penalty term leads to very good classification results while the ℓ_1 and ℓ_0 penalty terms focus on feature selection, we suggest using combinations of these terms. As common, to eliminate the absolute values in the ℓ_1-norm or in the approximate ℓ_0-norm, we introduce additional variables $v_i \geq |w_i|$ $(i = 1, \ldots, d)$ and consider $\nu \rho(\mathbf{v}) + \chi_{[-\mathbf{v}, \mathbf{v}]}(\mathbf{w})$ instead of $\lambda \rho(\mathbf{w})$, where χ_C denotes the indicator function $\chi_C(x) = 0$ if $x \in C$ and $\chi_C(x) = \infty$ otherwise (cf. [7,8]). As a result, for $\mu, \nu \in \mathbb{R}_+$, we minimise

$$f(\mathbf{w}, b, \mathbf{v}) := \frac{\mu}{n} \sum_{i=1}^{n} (1 - y_i(\mathbf{w}^T \mathbf{x}_i + b))_+ + \frac{1}{2} \|\mathbf{w}\|_2^2 + \nu \rho(\mathbf{v}) + \chi_{[-\mathbf{v}, \mathbf{v}]}(\mathbf{w}) . \tag{3}$$

In case of the ℓ_1-norm, problem (3) can be solved by a convex QP. For the approximate ℓ_0-norm an appropriate method is presented in Sect. 3.

2.2 Nonlinear Classification

For problems which are not linearly separable a so-called *feature map* ϕ which usually maps the set $\mathcal{X} \subset \mathbb{R}^d$ onto a higher dimensional space $\phi(\mathcal{X}) \subset \mathbb{R}^{d'}$ ($d' \geq d$) is used. Then the linear approach (1) is applied in the new feature space $\phi(\mathcal{X})$. This results in a nonlinear classification in the original space $\mathbb{R}^d$, i.e., in nonlinear separating surfaces.

Quadratic feature map. We start with the simple quadratic feature map

$$\phi : \mathcal{X} \to \mathbb{R}^{d'} , \quad \mathbf{x} \mapsto (\mathbf{x}^{\boldsymbol{\alpha}} : \boldsymbol{\alpha} \in \mathbb{N}_0^d , 0 < \|\boldsymbol{\alpha}\|_1 \leq 2) ,$$

where $d' = \frac{d(d+3)}{2}$, and apply (1) in $\mathbb{R}^{d'}$ with the approximate ℓ_0-penalty (2):

$$
\begin{aligned}
f(\mathbf{w}, b, \mathbf{v}) :=& (1 - \lambda) \sum_{i=1}^{n} (1 - y_i(\mathbf{w}^T \phi(\mathbf{x}_i) + b))_+ + \lambda \mathbf{e}^T(\mathbf{e} - e^{-\alpha \mathbf{v}}) \\
&+ \sum_{i=1}^{d'} \sum_{\phi_i(\mathbf{e}_j) \neq 0} \chi_{[-v_j, v_j]}(w_i) \quad \longrightarrow \quad \min_{\mathbf{w} \in \mathbb{R}^{d'}, b \in \mathbb{R}, \mathbf{v} \in \mathbb{R}^d} ,
\end{aligned}
\tag{4}
$$

where $\mathbf{e}_j \in \mathbb{R}^d$ denotes the j-th unit vector. We want to select features in the *original* space $\mathbb{R}^d$ due to (i)-(ii) in Sect. 1. Thus we include the appropriate indicator functions. A similar approach in [12] does not involve this idea and achieves only a feature selection in the *transformed* feature space $\mathbb{R}^{d'}$. We will refer to (4) as *quadratic FSV*. In principle, the approach can be extended to other feature maps ϕ, especially to other polynomial degrees.

Gaussian kernel feature map. Next we consider SVMs with the feature map related to the Gaussian kernel

$$K(\mathbf{x}, \mathbf{z}) = K_{\boldsymbol{\theta}}(\mathbf{x}, \mathbf{z}) = e^{-\|\mathbf{x} - \mathbf{z}\|_{2,\boldsymbol{\theta}}^2 / 2\sigma^2} \tag{5}$$

with weighted ℓ_2-norm $\|\mathbf{x}\|_{2,\boldsymbol{\theta}}^2 = \sum_{k=1}^{d} \theta_k |x_k|^2$ by $K(\mathbf{x}, \mathbf{z}) = \langle \phi(\mathbf{x}), \phi(\mathbf{z}) \rangle$ for all $\mathbf{x}, \mathbf{z} \in \mathcal{X}$. We apply the usual SVM classifier. For further information on nonlinear SVMs see, e.g., [9]. Direct feature selection, i.e., the setting of as many θ_k to zero as possible while retaining or improving the classification ability, is a difficult problem. One possible approach is to use a wrapper as in [11]. In [5], the alignment $\hat{A}(\mathbf{K}, \mathbf{y}\mathbf{y}^T) = \mathbf{y}^T \mathbf{K} \mathbf{y} / (n \|\mathbf{K}\|_F)$ was proposed as a measure of conformance of a kernel with a learning task. Therefore, we suggest to maximise in a modified form $\mathbf{y}_n^T \mathbf{K} \mathbf{y}_n$ where $\mathbf{y}_n = (y_i / n_{y_i})_{i=1}^n$. Then, with penalty (2), we define our *kernel-target alignment approach* for feature selection as

$$f(\boldsymbol{\theta}) := -(1 - \lambda) \frac{1}{2} \mathbf{y}_n^T \mathbf{K}_{\boldsymbol{\theta}} \mathbf{y}_n + \lambda \frac{1}{d} \mathbf{e}^T(\mathbf{e} - e^{-\alpha \boldsymbol{\theta}}) + \chi_{[0, \mathbf{e}]}(\boldsymbol{\theta}) \longrightarrow \min_{\boldsymbol{\theta} \in \mathbb{R}^d} . \tag{6}$$

The scaling factors $\frac{1}{2}$, $\frac{1}{d}$ ensure that both objective terms take values in $[0, 1]$.

3   D.C. Programming and Optimisation

A robust algorithm for minimising non-convex problems is the *Difference of Convex functions Algorithm* (DCA) proposed in [7]. Its goal is to minimise a function $f : \mathbb{R}^d \to \mathbb{R} \cup \{\infty\}$ which reads

$$f(\mathbf{x}) = g(\mathbf{x}) - h(\mathbf{x}) \longrightarrow \min_{\mathbf{x} \in \mathbb{R}^d} \, , \tag{7}$$

where $g, h : \mathbb{R}^d \to \mathbb{R} \cup \{\infty\}$ are lower semi-continuous, proper convex functions cf. [8]. In the next subsections, we first introduce the DCA and then apply it to our non-convex feature selection problems.

3.1   D.C. Programming

For g as assumed above, we introduce the *domain* of g, its *conjugate function* at $\tilde{\mathbf{x}} \in \mathbb{R}^d$ and its *subdifferential* at $\mathbf{z} \in \mathbb{R}^d$ by $\operatorname{dom} g := \{\mathbf{x} \in \mathbb{R}^d : g(\mathbf{x}) < \infty\}$, $g^*(\tilde{\mathbf{x}}) := \sup_{\mathbf{x} \in \mathbb{R}^d} \{\langle \mathbf{x}, \tilde{\mathbf{x}} \rangle - g(\mathbf{x})\}$ and $\partial g(\mathbf{z}) := \{\tilde{\mathbf{x}} \in \mathbb{R}^d : g(\mathbf{x}) \geq g(\mathbf{z}) + \langle \mathbf{x} - \mathbf{z}, \tilde{\mathbf{x}} \rangle \; \forall \mathbf{x} \in \mathbb{R}^d\}$, respectively. For differentiable functions we have that $\partial g(\mathbf{z}) = \{\nabla g(\mathbf{z})\}$. According to [8, Theorem 23.5], it holds

$$\partial g(\mathbf{x}) = \arg \max_{\tilde{\mathbf{x}} \in \mathbb{R}^d} \{\mathbf{x}^T \tilde{\mathbf{x}} - g^*(\tilde{\mathbf{x}})\} \, , \quad \partial g^*(\tilde{\mathbf{x}}) = \arg \max_{\mathbf{x} \in \mathbb{R}^d} \{\tilde{\mathbf{x}}^T \mathbf{x} - g(\mathbf{x})\} \, . \tag{8}$$

Further assume that $\operatorname{dom} g \subset \operatorname{dom} h$ and $\operatorname{dom} h^* \subset \operatorname{dom} g^*$. It was proved in [7] that then every limit point of the sequence $(\mathbf{x}^k)_{k \in \mathbb{N}_0}$ produced by the following algorithm is a critical point of f in (7):

Algorithm 3.1: D.C.minimisation Algorithm (DCA)(g, h, tol)

choose $\mathbf{x}^0 \in \operatorname{dom} g$ arbitrarily
for $k \in \mathbb{N}_0$
do $\begin{cases} \text{select } \tilde{\mathbf{x}}^k \in \partial h(\mathbf{x}^k) \text{ arbitrarily} \\ \text{select } \mathbf{x}^{k+1} \in \partial g^*(\tilde{\mathbf{x}}^k) \text{ arbitrarily} \\ \textbf{if } \min \left(|x_i^{k+1} - x_i^k|, \left| \frac{x_i^{k+1} - x_i^k}{x_i^k} \right| \right) \leq tol \quad \forall i = 1, \ldots, d \\ \quad \textbf{then return } (\mathbf{x}^{k+1}) \end{cases}$

We can show – but omit this point due to lack of space – that the DCA applied to a *particular* d.c. decomposition (7) of FSV coincides with the SLA.

3.2   Application to Our Feature Selection Problems

The crucial point in applying the DCA is to define a suitable d.c. decomposition (7) of the objective function. The aim of this section is to propose such decompositions for our different approaches.

ℓ_2-ℓ_0-**SVM.** A viable d.c. decomposition for (3) with (2) reads

$$g(\mathbf{w}, b, \mathbf{v}) = \frac{\mu}{n} \sum_{i=1}^{n} (1 - y_i(\mathbf{w}^T \mathbf{x}_i + b))_+ + \frac{1}{2} \|\mathbf{w}\|_2^2 + \chi_{[-\mathbf{v}, \mathbf{v}]}(\mathbf{w}) \, ,$$

$$h(\mathbf{v}) = -\nu \mathbf{e}^T (\mathbf{e} - e^{-\alpha \mathbf{v}})$$

which gives rise to a convex QP in each DCA step.

Quadratic FSV. To solve (4) we use the d.c. decomposition

$$g(\mathbf{w}, b, \mathbf{v}) = (1 - \lambda) \sum_{i=1}^{n} (1 - y_i(\mathbf{w}^T \phi(\mathbf{x}_i) + b))_+ + \sum_{i=1}^{d'} \sum_{\phi_i(\mathbf{e}_j) \neq 0} \chi_{[-v_j, v_j]}(w_i) ,$$

$$h(\mathbf{v}) = -\lambda \mathbf{e}^T(\mathbf{e} - e^{-\alpha \mathbf{v}}) ,$$

which leads to a linear problem in each DCA step.

Kernel-target alignment approach. For the function defined in (6), as the kernel (5) is convex in $\boldsymbol{\theta}$, we split f as

$$g(\boldsymbol{\theta}) = \frac{1 - \lambda}{2n_{+1}n_{-1}} \sum_{\substack{i,j=1 \\ y_i \neq y_j}}^{n} e^{-\|\mathbf{x}_i - \mathbf{x}_j\|_{2,\boldsymbol{\theta}}^2/2\sigma^2} + \chi_{[0,\mathbf{e}]}(\boldsymbol{\theta}) ,$$

$$h(\boldsymbol{\theta}) = \frac{1 - \lambda}{2} \sum_{\substack{i,j=1 \\ y_i = y_j}}^{n} \frac{1}{n_{y_i}^2} e^{-\|\mathbf{x}_i - \mathbf{x}_j\|_{2,\boldsymbol{\theta}}^2/2\sigma^2} - \frac{\lambda}{d} \mathbf{e}^T(\mathbf{e} - e^{-\alpha \boldsymbol{\theta}}) .$$

Now h is differentiable, so applying the DCA we find the solution in the first step of iteration k as $\tilde{\boldsymbol{\theta}}^k = \nabla h(\boldsymbol{\theta}^k)$. In the second step, we are looking for $\boldsymbol{\theta}^{k+1} \in \partial g^*(\tilde{\boldsymbol{\theta}}^k) \overset{(8)}{=} \arg\max_{\boldsymbol{\theta}} \{\boldsymbol{\theta}^T \tilde{\boldsymbol{\theta}}^k - g(\boldsymbol{\theta})\}$ which leads to solving the *convex non-quadratic* problem

$$\min_{\boldsymbol{\theta} \in \mathbb{R}^d} \frac{1 - \lambda}{2n_{+1}n_{-1}} \sum_{\substack{i,j=1 \\ y_i \neq y_j}}^{n} e^{-\|\mathbf{x}_i - \mathbf{x}_j\|_{2,\boldsymbol{\theta}}^2/2\sigma^2} - \boldsymbol{\theta}^T \tilde{\boldsymbol{\theta}}^k \quad \text{subject to } \mathbf{0} \leq \boldsymbol{\theta} \leq \mathbf{e}$$

with a valid initial point $\mathbf{0} \leq \boldsymbol{\theta}^0 \leq \mathbf{e}$. We efficiently solve this problem by a penalty/barrier multiplier method with logarithmic-quadratic penalty function as proposed in [1].

4   Evaluation

4.1   Ground Truth Experiments

In this section, we consider artificial training sets in $\mathbb{R}^2$ and $\mathbb{R}^4$ where y is a function of the first two features x_1 and x_2. The examples in Fig. 1 show that our quadratic FSV approach indeed performs feature selection and finds classification rules for quadratic, not linearly separable problems. For the non-quadratic chess board classification problems in Fig. 2, our kernel-target alignment approach performs very well, in contrast to all other feature selection approaches presented. Remarkably, the alignment functional incorporates implicit feature selection for $\lambda = 0$. In both cases, only relevant feature sets are selected as can be seen in the bottom plots.

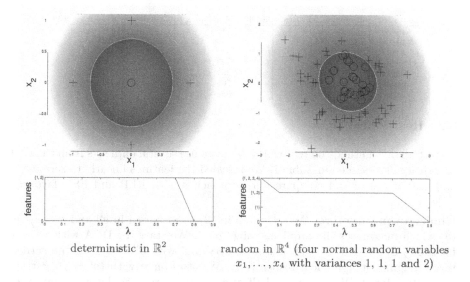

deterministic in $\mathbb{R}^2$ random in $\mathbb{R}^4$ (four normal random variables
$x_1, \ldots, x_4$ with variances 1, 1, 1 and 2)

Fig. 1. Quadratic classification problems with $y = \operatorname{sgn}(x_1^2 + x_2^2 - 1)$. *Top:* Training points and decision boundaries (*white lines*) computed by (4) for $\lambda = 0.1$, *left:* in $\mathbb{R}^2$, *right:* projection onto selected features. *Bottom:* Features determined by (4)

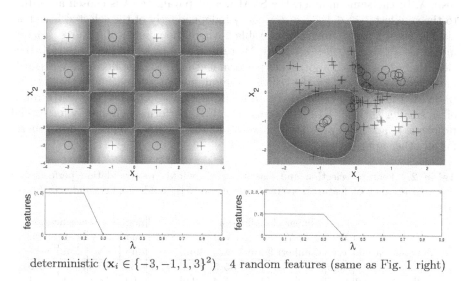

deterministic ($\mathbf{x}_i \in \{-3, -1, 1, 3\}^2$)   4 random features (same as Fig. 1 right)

Fig. 2. Chess board classification problems with $\frac{y+1}{2} = (\lfloor \frac{x_1}{2} \rfloor \bmod 2) \oplus (\lfloor \frac{x_2}{2} \rfloor \bmod 2)$. *Top:* Training points and Gaussian SVM decision boundaries (*white lines*) for $\sigma = 1$, $\lambda = 0.1$, *left:* in $\mathbb{R}^2$, *right:* projection onto selected features. *Bottom:* Features determined by (6)

Table 1. Statistics for data sets used

data set	number of features d	number of samples n	class distribution n_{+1}/n_{-1}
wpbc60	32	110	41/ 69
wpbc24	32	155	28/127
liver	6	345	145/200
cleveland	13	297	160/137
ionosphere	34	351	225/126
pima	8	768	500/268
bcw	9	683	444/239

4.2 Real-World Data

To test all our methods on real-world data, we use several data sets from the UCI repository [3] resumed in Table 1. We rescaled the features linearly to zero mean and unit variance and compare our approaches with RLP and FSV favoured in [4].

Choice of parameters. We set $\alpha = 5$ in (2) as proposed in [4] and $\sigma = \frac{\sqrt{d}}{2}$ in (5) which maximises the problems' alignment. We start the DCA with $\mathbf{v}^0 = \mathbf{1}$ for the ℓ_2-ℓ_0-SVM, FSV and quadratic FSV and with $\boldsymbol{\theta}^0 = \mathbf{e}/2$ for the kernel-target alignment approach, respectively. We stop on $\mathbf{v}$ with $tol = 10^{-5}$ resp. $tol = 10^{-3}$ for $\boldsymbol{\theta}$. We retain one half of each run's cross-validation training set for parameter selection. The parameters are chosen to minimise the validation error from $\ln \mu \in \{0, \ldots, 10\}, \ln \nu \in \{-5, \ldots, 5\}, \lambda \in \{0.05, 0.1, 0.2, \ldots, 0.9, 0.95\}$ for (quadratic) FSV and $\lambda \in \{0, 0.1, \ldots, 0.9\}$ for the kernel-target alignment approach. In case of equal validation error, we choose the larger values for (ν, μ) resp. λ. In the same manner, the SVM weight parameter λ is chosen according to the smallest $\frac{1-\lambda}{\lambda} \in \{e^{-5}, e^{-4}, \ldots, e^5\}$ independently of the selected features.

The results are summarised in Table 2 where the number of features is determined as $|\{j = 1, \ldots, d : |v_j| > 10^{-8}\}|$ resp. $|\{j = 1, \ldots, d : |\theta_j| > 10^{-2}\}|$. It is clear that all proposed approaches perform feature selection: linear FSV discards most features followed by the kernel-target alignment approach and then the ℓ_2-ℓ_0-SVM, then the ℓ_2-ℓ_1-SVM. In addition, for all approaches the test error is often smaller than for RLP. The quadratic FSV performs well mainly for special problems (e.g., 'liver' and 'ionosphere'), but the classification is good in general for all other approaches.

Table 2. Feature selection and classification tenfold cross-validation performance (average number of features, average test error [%]); bold numbers indicate lowest errors

			linear classification								nonlinear classification			
	RLP		FSV		ℓ_2-ℓ_1-SVM		ℓ_2-ℓ_0-SVM		quad. FSV		k.-t. align.	
data set	dim.	err	dim.	err	dim.	err	dim.	err	dim.	err	dim.	err
wpbc60	32.0	40.9	0.4	36.4	12.4	**35.5**	13.4	37.3	3.2	37.3	3.9	**35.5**
wpbc24	32.0	27.7	0.0	18.1	12.6	**17.4**	2.9	18.1	0.0	18.1	1.9	18.1
liver	6.0	**31.9**	2.1	36.2	6.0	35.1	5.0	34.2	3.2	**32.5**	2.5	35.4
cleveland	13.0	**16.2**	1.8	23.2	9.9	**16.5**	8.2	**16.5**	9.2	30.3	3.2	23.6
ionosphere	33.0	13.4	2.3	21.7	24.8	13.4	14.0	15.7	32.9	10.8	6.6	**7.7**
pima	8.0	**22.5**	0.7	28.9	6.6	25.1	6.1	24.7	4.7	29.9	1.6	25.7
bcw	9.0	3.4	2.4	4.8	8.7	**3.2**	7.9	**3.1**	5.4	9.4	2.8	4.2

5 Summary and Conclusion

We proposed several novel methods that extend existing linear embedded feature selection approaches towards better generalisation ability by improved regularisation and constructed feature selection methods in connection with nonlinear classifiers. In order to apply the DCA, we found appropriate splittings of our non-convex objective functions. In the experiments with real data, effective feature selection was always carried out in conjunction with a small classification error. So direct objective minimisation feature selection is profitable and viable for different types of classifiers. In higher dimensions, the curse of dimensionality affects the classification error even more such that our methods will become more important here. A further evaluation of high-dimensional problems as well as the incorporation of other feature maps is future work.

Acknowledgements. This work was funded by the DFG, Grant Schn 457/5.

References

1. A. Ben-Tal and M. Zibulevsky. Penalty/barrier multiplier methods for convex programming problems. *SIAM Journal on Optimization*, 7(2):347–366, May 1997.
2. K. P. Bennett and O. L. Mangasarian. Robust linear programming discrimination of two linearly inseparable sets. *Optimization Methods and Software*, 1:23–34, 1992.
3. C. L. Blake and C. J. Merz. UCI repository of machine learning databases, 1998.
4. P. S. Bradley and O. L. Mangasarian. Feature selection via concave minimization and support vector machines. In *Proceedings of the 15th International Conference on Machine Learning*, pages 82–90, San Francisco, CA, USA, 1998. Morgan Kaufmann.
5. N. Cristianini, J. Shawe-Taylor, A. Elisseeff, and J. Kandola. On kernel-target alignment. In T. G. Dietterich, S. Becker, and Z. Ghahramani, editors, *Advances in Neural Information Processing Systems 14*, pages 367–373. MIT Press, Cambridge, MA, USA, 2002.
6. I. Guyon and A. Elisseeff. An introduction to variable and feature selection. *Journal of Machine Learning Research*, 3:1157–1182, Mar. 2003.
7. T. Pham Dinh and L. T. Hoai An. A d.c. optimization algorithm for solving the trust-region subproblem. *SIAM Journal on Optimization*, 8(2):476–505, May 1998.
8. R. T. Rockafellar. *Convex Analysis*. Princeton University press, Princeton, NJ, USA, 1970.
9. B. Schölkopf and A. J. Smola. *Learning with Kernels*. MIT Press, Cambridge, MA, USA, 2002.
10. J. Weston, A. Elisseeff, B. Schölkopf, and M. Tipping. Use of the zero-norm with linear models and kernel methods. *Journal of Machine Learning Research*, 3:1439–1461, Mar. 2003.
11. J. Weston, S. Mukherjee, O. Chapelle, M. Pontil, T. Poggio, and V. Vapnik. Feature selection for SVMs. In T. K. Leen, T. G. Dietterich, and V. Tresp, editors, *Advances in Neural Information Processing Systems 13*, pages 668–674. MIT Press, Cambridge, MA, USA, 2001.
12. J. Zhu, S. Rosset, T. Hastie, and R. Tibshirani. 1-norm support vector machines. In S. Thrun, L. Saul, and B. Schölkopf, editors, *Advances in Neural Information Processing Systems 16*. MIT Press, Cambridge, MA, USA, 2004.

Learning with Distance Substitution Kernels

Bernard Haasdonk[1] and Claus Bahlmann[2]

[1] Computer Science Department
Albert-Ludwigs-University Freiburg
79110 Freiburg, Germany
haasdonk@informatik.uni-freiburg.de
[2] Siemens Corporate Research, Inc.
755 College Road East
Princeton, NJ 08540, USA
claus.bahlmann@scr.siemens.com

Abstract. During recent years much effort has been spent in incorporating problem specific a-priori knowledge into kernel methods for machine learning. A common example is a-priori knowledge given by a distance measure between objects. A simple but effective approach for kernel construction consists of substituting the Euclidean distance in ordinary kernel functions by the problem specific distance measure. We formalize this *distance substitution* procedure and investigate theoretical and empirical effects. In particular we state criteria for definiteness of the resulting kernels. We demonstrate the wide applicability by solving several classification tasks with SVMs. Regularization of the kernel matrices can additionally increase the recognition accuracy.

1 Introduction

In machine learning so called kernel methods have developed to state-of-the-art for a variety of different problem types like regression, classification, clustering, etc. [14]. Main ingredient in these methods is the problem specific choice of a kernel function. This choice should ideally incorporate as much a-priori knowledge as possible. One example is the incorporation of knowledge about pairwise proximities. In this setting, the objects are not given explicitly but only implicitly by a distance measure.

This paper focusses on the incorporation of such distance measures in kernel functions and investigates the application in support vector machines (SVMs) as the most widespread kernel method. Up to now mainly three approaches have been proposed for using distance data in SVMs. One approach consists of representing each training object as vector of its distances to all training objects and using standard SVMs on this data [5,12]. The second method is embedding the distance data in a vector space, regularizing the possibly indefinite space and performing ordinary linear SVM classification [5, 12]. These approaches have the disadvantage of losing the sparsity in the sense that all training objects have to be retained for classification. This makes them inconvenient for large scale data.

The third method circumvents this problem by using the Gaussian rbf-kernel and plugging in problem specific distance measures [1,4,8,11]. The aim of this paper is to formalize and extend this approach to more kernel types including polynomial kernels.

C.E. Rasmussen et al. (Eds.): DAGM 2004, LNCS 3175, pp. 220–227, 2004.
© Springer-Verlag Berlin Heidelberg 2004

The paper is structured as follows: We formalize distance substitution in the next section. Statements on theoretical properties of the kernels follow in Section 3 and comments on consequences for use in SVMs are given in Section 4. In Section 5 we continue with SVM experiments by distance substitution and investigate regularization methods for the resulting kernel matrices. We conclude with Section 6.

2 Distance Substitution Kernels

The term *kernel* refers to a real valued symmetric function $k(x, x)$ of objects x in a set $\mathcal{X}$. A kernel function is *positive definite* (pd), if for any n, any objects $x_1, \ldots, x_n \in \mathcal{X}$ and any vector $\mathbf{c} \in I\!R^n$ the induced *kernel matrix* $\mathbf{K} := (k(x_i, x_j))_{i,j=1}^n$ satisfies $\mathbf{c}^T \mathbf{K} \mathbf{c} \geq 0$. The larger set of *conditionally positive definite* (cpd) kernels consists of those which satisfy this inequality for all $\mathbf{c}$ with $\mathbf{c}^T \mathbf{1} = 0$. These pd/cpd kernel functions got much attention as they have nice properties, in particular they can be interpreted/related to inner products in Hilbert spaces.

In distance based learning the data samples x are not given explicitly but only by a *distance* function $d(x, x')$. We do not impose strict assumptions on this distance measure, but require it to be symmetric, have zero diagonal, i.e. $d(x, x) = 0$, and be nonnegative. If a given distance measure does not satisfy these requirements, it can easily be symmetrized by $\bar{d}(x, x') := \frac{1}{2}(d(x, x') + d(x', x))$, given zero diagonal by $\bar{d}(x, x') := d(x, x') - \frac{1}{2}(d(x, x) + d(x', x'))$ or made positive by $\bar{d}(x, x') := |d(x, x')|$. We call such a distance *isometric to an L^2-norm* if the data can be embedded in a Hilbert space $\mathcal{H}$ by $\Phi : \mathcal{X} \to \mathcal{H}$ such that $d(x, x') = \|\Phi(x) - \Phi(x')\|$. After choice of an origin $O \in \mathcal{X}$ every distance d induces a function

$$\langle x, x' \rangle_d^O := -\frac{1}{2}(d(x, x')^2 - d(x, O)^2 - d(x', O)^2). \tag{1}$$

This notation reflects the idea that in case of d being the L^2-norm in a Hilbert space $\mathcal{X}$, $\langle x, x' \rangle_d^O$ corresponds to the inner product in this space with respect to the origin O.

For any kernel $k(\|\mathbf{x} - \mathbf{x}'\|)$ and distance measure d we call $k_d(x, x') := k(d(x, x'))$ its *distance substitution kernel* (DS-kernel). Similarly, for a kernel $k(\langle \mathbf{x}, \mathbf{x}' \rangle)$ we call $k_d(x, x') := k(\langle x, x' \rangle_d^O)$ its DS-kernel. This notion is reasonable as in terms of (1) indeed distances are substituted. In particular for the simple linear, negative-distance, polynomial, and Gaussian kernels, we denote their DS-kernels by

$$k_d^{\text{lin}}(x, x') := \langle x, x' \rangle_d^O \qquad\qquad k_d^{\text{nd}}(x, x') := -d(x, x')^\beta, \beta \in [0, 2] \tag{2}$$
$$k_d^{\text{pol}}(x, x') := \left(1 + \gamma \langle x, x' \rangle_d^O\right)^p \qquad k_d^{\text{rbf}}(x, x') := e^{-\gamma d(x, x')^2}, p \in I\!N, \gamma \in I\!R^+.$$

Of course, more general distance- or dot-product based kernels exist and corresponding DS-kernels can be defined, e.g. sigmoid, multiquadric, B_n-spline [14], etc.

3 Definiteness of DS-Kernels

The most interesting question posed on new kernels is whether they are (c)pd. In fact, for DS-kernels given by (2) the definiteness can be summed up quite easily. The necessary tools and references can be found in [14].

Proposition 1 (Definiteness of Simple DS-Kernels). *The following statements are equivalent for a (nonnegative, symmetric, zero-diagonal) distance d:*

    i) d is isometric to an L^2-norm

    ii) k_d^{nd} is cpd for all $\beta \in [0,2]$ *iii) k_d^{lin} is pd*

    iv) k_d^{rbf} is pd for all $\gamma \in \mathbb{R}^+$ *v) k_d^{pol} is pd for all $p \in \mathbb{N}, \gamma \in \mathbb{R}^+$.*

Proof. *i*) implies *ii*): [14, Prop. 2.22] covers the case $\beta = 2$ and [14, Prop. 2.23] settles the statement for arbitrary $\beta \in [0,2]$. The reverse implication *ii*) $\Rightarrow$ *i*) follows by [14, Prop. 2.24]. Equivalence of *ii*) and *iii*) also is a consequence of [14, Prop. 2.22]. [14, Prop. 2.28] implies the equivalence of *ii*) and *iv*). Statement *v*) follows from *iii*) as the set of pd functions is closed under products and linear combinations with positive coefficients. The reverse can be obtained from the pd functions $\frac{1}{\gamma} k_d^{\text{pol}}$. With $p = 1$ and $\gamma \to \infty$ these functions converge to $\langle x, x' \rangle_d^O$. Hence the latter also is pd. $\qquad\blacksquare$

Further statements for definiteness of more general dot-product or distance-based kernels are possible, e.g. by Taylor series argumentation.

For some distance measures, the relation to an L^2-norm is apparent. An example is the *Hellinger distance* $H(p, p')$ between probability distributions which is defined by $(H(p, p'))^2 := \int \left(\sqrt{p} - \sqrt{p'} \right)^2 dx$. However, the class of distances which are isometric to L^2-norms is much wider than the obvious forms $d = \|x - x'\|$. For instance, [2] proves very nicely that $k_{\sqrt{\chi^2}}^{\text{rbf}}$ is pd, where

$$\chi^2(\mathbf{x}, \mathbf{y}) := \frac{1}{2} \sum_i \frac{(x_i - y_i)^2}{x_i + y_i}$$

denotes the χ^2-distance between histograms. Thus, according to Proposition 1, $\sqrt{\chi^2}$ is isometric to an L^2-norm. Only looking at the χ^2-distance, the corresponding Hilbert space is not apparent. In summary we can conclude that not only k_H^{lin} (Bhattacharyya's affinity) and $k_{\sqrt{\chi^2}}^{\text{rbf}}$, but all DS-kernels given by (2) are pd/cpd when using $\sqrt{\chi^2}$ or H.

In practice however, problem specific distance measures often lead to DS-kernels which are not pd. A criterion for disproving pd-ness is the following corollary, which is a simple consequence of Proposition 1 as L^2-norms are in particular metrics. It allows to conclude missing pd-ness of DS-kernels that arise from distances which are non-metric, e.g. violate the triangle inequality. It can immediately be applied to kernels based on tangent-distance [8], dynamic-time-warping (DTW) distance [1] or Kullback-Leibler (KL) divergence [11].

Corollary 1 (Non-Metricity Prevents Definiteness). *If d is not metric then the resulting DS-kernel k_d^{nd} is not cpd and $k_d^{\text{lin}}, k_d^{\text{rbf}}, k_d^{\text{pol}}$ are not pd.*

Note, that for certain values β, γ, p, the resulting DS-kernels are possibly (c)pd. Remind also that the reverse of the corollary is not true. In particular, the L^p-metrics for $p \neq 2$ can be shown to produce non-pd DS-kernels.

4   SVMs with Indefinite Kernels

In the following we apply DS-kernels on learning problems. For this we focus on the very successful SVM for classification. This method can traditionally be applied if the kernel functions are pd or cpd. If a given distance produces DS-kernels which are pd, these can be applied in SVMs as usual. But also in the non-pd case they can be useful, as non-cpd kernels have shown convincing results in SVMs [1,4,8,11]. This empirical success is additionally supported by several theoretical statements:

1. *Feature space:* Indefinite kernels can be interpreted as inner products in indefinite vector spaces, enabling geometric argumentation [10].
2. *Optimal hyperplane classifier:* SVMs with indefinite kernels can be interpreted as optimal hyperplane classifiers in these indefinite spaces [7].
3. *Numerics:* Convergence of SVM implementations to a (possibly local) stationary point can be guaranteed [9].
4. *Uniqueness:* Even with extreme non-cpd kernel matrices unique solutions are possible [7].

5   Experiments

We performed experiments using various distance measures. Most of them were used in literature before. We do not explicitly state the definitions but refer to the corresponding publications. For each distance measure we used several labeled datasets or several labelings of a single dataset.

The dataset *kimia* (2 sets, each 72 samples, 6 classes) is based on binary images of shapes. The dissimilarity is measured by the modified Hausdorff distance. Details and results from other classification methods can be found in [12]. We applied a multiclass-SVM. The dataset *proteins* (226 samples) consists of evolutionary distances between amino acid sequences of proteins [6]. We used 4 different binary labelings corresponding to one-versus-rest problems. The dataset *cat-cortex* (65 samples) is based on a matrix of connectivity strengths between cortical areas of a cat. Other experiments with this data have been presented in [5,6]. Here we symmetrized the similarity matrix and produced a zero diagonal distance matrix. Again we used 4 binary labelings corresponding to one-versus-rest classification problems. The datasets *music-EMD* and *music-PTD* are based on sets of 50 and 57 music pieces represented as weighted point sets. The earth-mover's distance (EMD) and the proportional transportation distance (PTD) were chosen as distance measures, see [16]. As class labels we used the corresponding composers resulting in 2 binary classification problems per distance measure. The dataset *USPS-TD* (4 sets, 250 samples per set, 2 classes) uses a fraction of the well known USPS handwritten digits data. As distance measure we use the two-sided tangent distance [15], which incorporates certain problem specific transformation knowledge. The set *UNIPEN-DTW* (2 sets, 250 samples per set, 5 classes) is based on a fraction of the the huge UNIPEN online handwriting sequence dataset. Dissimilarities were defined by the DTW-distance [1], again we applied a multiclass-SVM.

These different datasets represent a wide spectrum from easily to difficultly separable data. None of these distances are isometric to an L^2-norm. The restricted number of samples is consequence of the size of the small original datasets or due to the fact, that regularization experiments presented in Section 5.2 are only feasible for reasonably sized datasets.

5.1 Pure Distance Substitution

In this section we present results with pure distance substitution and compare them with the 1-nearest-neighbour and best k-nearest-neighbour classifier. These are natural classifiers when dealing with distance data.

We computed the leave-one-out (LOO) error of an SVM while logarithmically varying the parameter C along a line, respectively C, γ in a suitable grid. For the k_d^{pol} kernel a fixed polynomial degree p among $\{2, 4, 6, 8\}$ was chosen after simple initial experiments. The origin O was chosen to be the point with minimum squared distance sum to the other training objects. As $\frac{1}{2} k_d^{\text{nd}}$ with $\beta = 2$ and k_d^{lin} are equivalent in SVMs (which follows by plugging (1) in the SVM optimization problem and making use of the equality constraint), we confine ourselves to using the former. We report the best LOO-error for all datasets in Table 1. Note that these errors might be biased compared to the true generalization error, as we did not use training/validation partitions for parameter optimization.

Table 1. Base LOO-errors [%] of classification experiments

dataset	k_d^{nd}	k_d^{pol}	k_d^{rbf}	1-nn	k-nn	dataset	k_d^{nd}	k_d^{pol}	k_d^{rbf}	1-nn	k-nn
kimia-1	15.28	11.11	4.17	5.56	5.56	music-EMD-1	40.00	22.00	20.00	42.00	42.00
kimia-2	12.50	9.72	9.72	12.50	12.50	music-EMD-2	42.11	43.86	10.53	21.05	21.05
proteins-H-α	0.89	0.89	0.89	1.33	1.33	music-PTD-1	34.00	30.00	32.00	46.00	34.00
proteins-H-β	3.54	2.21	2.65	3.54	3.54	music-PTD-2	31.58	33.33	28.07	38.60	38.60
proteins-M	0.00	0.00	0.00	0.00	0.00	USPS-TD-1	10.40	5.20	3.20	3.60	3.60
proteins-GH	0.00	0.44	0.00	1.77	1.77	USPS-TD-2	14.40	7.60	2.40	3.20	3.20
cat-cortex-V	3.08	1.54	0.00	3.08	3.08	USPS-TD-3	12.80	6.80	4.00	5.20	5.20
cat-cortex-A	6.15	3.08	4.62	6.15	6.15	USPS-TD-4	10.80	6.40	3.20	4.40	4.00
cat-cortex-S	6.15	3.08	3.08	6.15	3.08	UNIPEN-DTW-1	14.40	6.00	5.20	5.60	5.60
cat-cortex-F	7.69	6.15	4.62	4.62	3.08	UNIPEN-DTW-2	10.80	7.60	6.00	7.20	6.40

The identical low errors of the 1-nn and k-nn in the datasets *kimia, proteins, cat-cortex, USPS-TD,* and *UNIPEN-DTW* demonstrate that the data clusters well with the given labeling. For the music data sets the labels obviously not define proper clusters.

As SVMs with kernels $k_d^{\text{nd}}, \beta = 2$ can be interpreted as linear classifiers [7], the good performance of these on proteins and cat-cortex data is a hint on their linear separability. Simultaneously, the sets with higher error indicate that a nonlinear classifier in the dissimilarity space has to be applied. Indeed, the polynomial and Gaussian DS-kernel improve the results of the linear kernel for most datasets. The Gaussian DS-kernel even slightly outperforms the polynomial in most cases.

Compared to the nearest neighbour results, the nonlinear distance substitutions compare very favorable. The polynomial kernel can compete with or outperform the best k-nn for the majority of datasets, The Gaussian DS-kernel competes with or outperforms the best k-nn for all but one dataset.

For the last two distance measures, large scale experiments with certain distance substitution kernels have already been successfully presented in [1,8]. In this respect, scalability of the results to large datasets is expected. To summarize, the experiments demonstrate the effectiveness of distance substitution kernels despite producing indefinite kernel matrices. The result is a sparse representation of the solution by training examples, that is, only a small subset of training objects has to be retained. Thus, it is particularly suited for large training sets.

5.2 Regularization of Kernel Matrices

In this section we investigate different regularization methods to eliminate the negative eigenvalues of the kernel matrices. Similar regularizations have been performed in literature, e.g. regularizing linear SVMs [5,12] or embedding of non-metric data [13]. The method denoted off-diagonal addition (ODA) simply adds a suitable constant on the off-diagonal elements of the squared distance matrix, which results in a Euclidean distance matrix and therefore can be used for distance substitution resulting in pd kernels. Two other methods center the kernel matrix [12] and perform an eigenvalue decomposition. The approach (CNE) cuts off contributions corresponding to negative eigenvalues and (RNE) reflects the negative eigenvalues by taking their absolute values.

These operations particularly imply that the same operations have to be performed for the testing data. If the testing data is known beforehand, this can be used during training for computing and regularizing the kernel matrix. Note that this is *not* training on the testing data, as only the data points but not the labels are used for the kernel computations. Such training is commonly called *transductive* learning. If a test sample is not known at the training stage, the vector of kernel evaluations has to undergo the same regularization transformation as the kernel matrix before. Hence the diagonalizing vectors and eigenvalues have to be maintained and involved in this remapping of each testing vector. Both methods have the consequence that the computational complexity is increased during training and testing and the sparsity is lost, i.e. the solution depends on all training instances. So these regularization methods only apply, where computational demands are not so strict and sparsity is not necessary. For the experiments we used the transductive approach for determining the LOO errors.

If one can do without sparsity, another simple method is used for comparisons: Representing each training instance by a vector of squared distances to all training points makes a simple linear or Gaussian SVM applicable. We denoted these approaches as lin-SVM resp. rbf-SVM in Table 2, which lists the classification results.

The experiments demonstrate that regularization of kernel matrices can remarkably improve recognition accuracies and compete with or outperform SVMs on distance-vectors. The ODA regularization can increase accuracies, but it is clearly outperformed by the CNE and RNE methods which maintain or increase accuracy in 52 resp. 50 of the 60 experiments. Regularization seems to be advantageous for linear and polynomial kernels. For the Gaussian DS-kernels only few improvements can be observed. A comparison to the last columns indicates that the (non-ODA) regularized k_d^{nd} classifiers can compete with the linear SVM. The latter however is clearly inferior to the regularized

Table 2. LOO-errors [%] of classification experiments with regularized kernel matrices

dataset	k_d^{nd} ODA	CNE	RNE	k_d^{pol} CNE	RNE	k_d^{rbf} CNE	RNE	lin-SVM	rbf-SVM
kimia-1	13.89	8.33	4.17	8.33	4.17	4.17	4.17	8.33	6.94
kimia-2	16.67	9.72	8.33	9.72	8.33	9.72	8.33	8.33	8.33
proteins-H-α	0.44	0.89	0.89	0.89	0.89	0.89	0.89	1.33	0.44
proteins-H-β	3.10	3.54	3.98	2.21	2.21	2.65	2.65	5.75	2.65
proteins-M	0.00	0.00	0.00	0.00	0.00	0.00	0.00	0.00	0.00
proteins-GH	0.00	0.00	0.00	0.44	0.44	0.00	0.00	0.00	0.00
cat-cortex-V	6.15	3.08	3.08	3.08	3.08	1.54	3.08	4.62	3.08
cat-cortex-A	6.15	4.62	6.15	4.62	6.15	4.62	6.15	1.54	1.54
cat-cortex-S	6.15	3.08	4.62	3.08	3.08	3.08	3.08	3.08	3.08
cat-cortex-F	6.15	4.62	4.62	4.62	4.62	4.62	4.62	1.54	1.54
music-EMD-1	44.00	38.00	40.00	30.00	40.00	30.00	30.00	44.00	20.00
music-EMD-2	42.11	15.79	21.05	12.28	12.28	14.04	10.53	21.05	15.79
music-PTD-1	38.00	44.00	40.00	40.00	38.00	32.00	32.00	40.00	28.00
music-PTD-2	47.37	29.82	38.60	26.32	22.81	28.07	17.54	29.82	21.05
USPS-TD-1	9.60	4.00	6.00	4.80	4.00	3.20	3.20	6.80	4.80
USPS-TD-2	14.40	9.60	7.20	5.60	4.00	2.40	2.40	6.00	4.40
USPS-TD-3	12.00	6.80	8.00	4.00	4.40	4.00	4.40	6.80	4.40
USPS-TD-4	11.20	7.60	6.40	5.20	5.60	3.20	3.20	7.20	1.60
UNIPEN-DTW-1	13.20	8.40	8.40	5.20	5.60	4.40	4.80	8.00	6.80
UNIPEN-DTW-2	11.20	7.60	9.60	6.80	6.40	6.00	5.60	9.60	8.40

nonlinear DS-kernels k_d^{pol} and k_d^{rbf}. In comparison to the rbf-SVM the k_d^{nd} experiments can not compete. The k_d^{pol}-CNE experiments also perform worse than the rbf-SVM in 12 cases. But the k_d^{pol}-RNE, k_d^{rbf}-CNE resp. k_d^{nd}-RNE settings obtain identical or better results than the rbf-SVM in the majority of classification problems.

6   Conclusion and Perspectives

We have characterized a class of kernels by formalizing distance substitution. This has so far been performed for the Gaussian kernel. By the equivalence of inner product and L^2-norm after fixing an origin, distances can also be used in inner-product kernels like the linear or polynomial kernel. We have given conditions for proving/disproving (c)pd-ness of the resulting kernels. We have concluded that DS-kernels involving e.g. the χ^2-distance are (c)pd, and others, e.g. resulting from KL-divergence, are not.

We have investigated the applicability of the DS-kernels by solving various SVM-classification problems with different data sets and different distance measures, which are not isometric to L^2-norms. The conclusion of the experiments was, that good classification is possible despite indefinite kernel matrices. Disadvantages of other methods are circumvented, e.g. test-data involved in training, approximate embeddings, non-sparse solutions or explicit working in feature space. This indicates that distance substitution kernels in particular are promising for large datasets. In particular the Gaussian and polynomial DS-kernels are good choices for general datasets due to their nonlinearity. If sparsity of the solution is not necessary and computational demands during classification are not so strict, then regularizations of the kernel matrices and the test-kernel evaluations can be recommended. It has been shown that this procedure can substantially improve recognition accuracy for e.g. the linear and polynomial DS-kernels.

Perspectives are to apply distance substitution on further types of kernels, further distance measures and in other kernel methods. This would in particular support recent promising efforts to establish non-cpd kernels for machine learning [3].

Acknowledgements. The authors want to thank Rainer Typke and Elzbieta Pekalska for making their distance data available and Harald Stepputtis for initial experiments.

References

1. C. Bahlmann, B. Haasdonk, and H. Burkhardt. On-line Handwriting Recognition with Support Vector Machines—A Kernel Approach. In *Proc. of the 8th IWFHR*, pages 49–54, 2002.
2. S. Belongie, C. Fowlkes, F. Chung, and J. Malik. Spectral partitioning with indefinite kernels using the Nyström extension. In *ECCV*, volume 2, pages 21–31, 2002.
3. S. Canu. Learning with non-positive kernels. Submitted to ICML, 2004.
4. O. Chapelle, P. Haffner, and V. Vapnik. Support vector machines for histogram-based image classification. *IEEE-NN*, 10(5):1055–1064, September 1999.
5. T. Graepel, R. Herbrich, P. Bollmann-Sdorra, and K. Obermayer. Classification on pairwise proximity data. In *NIPS 12*, pages 438–444. MIT Press, 1999.
6. T. Graepel, R. Herbrich, B. Schölkopf, A. Smola, P. Bartlett, K.-R. Müller, K. Obermayer, and B. Williamson. Classification on proximity data with LP–machines. In *Proc. of the 9th ICANN*, pages 304–309, 1999.
7. B. Haasdonk. Feature space interpretation of SVMs with non positive definite kernels. Internal report 1/03, IIF-LMB, University Freiburg, October 2003. Submitted to IEEE TPAMI.
8. B. Haasdonk and D. Keysers. Tangent distance kernels for support vector machines. In *Proc. of the 16th ICPR*, volume 2, pages 864–868, 2002.
9. H.-T. Lin and C.-J. Lin. A study on sigmoid kernels for SVM and the training of non-PSD kernels by SMO-type methods. Technical report, National Taiwan University, March 2003.
10. X. Mary. *Hilbertian subspaces, subdualities and applications.* PhD thesis, INSA Rouen, 2003.
11. P.J. Moreno, P. Ho, and N. Vasconcelos. A Kullback-Leibler divergence based kernel for SVM classification in multimedia applications. In *NIPS 17*, 2003.
12. E. Pekalska, P. Paclik, and R. Duin. A generalized kernel approach to dissimilarity based classification. *J. of Mach. Learn. Research*, 2:175–211, 2001.
13. V. Roth, J. Laub, M. Kawanabe, and J.M. Buhmann. Optimal cluster preserving embedding of nonmetric proximity data. *IEEE TPAMI*, 25(12):1540–1551, 2003.
14. B. Schölkopf and A.J. Smola. *Learning with Kernels.* MIT Press, 2002.
15. P.Y. Simard, Y.A. LeCun, and J.S. Denker. Efficient pattern recognition using a new transformation distance. In *NIPS 5*, pages 50–58. Morgan Kaufmann, 1993.
16. R. Typke, P. Giannopoulos, R.C. Veltkamp, F. Wiering, and R. van Oostrum. Using transportation distances for measuring melodic similarity. In *ISMIR*, pages 107–114, 2003.

Features for Image Retrieval:
A Quantitative Comparison

Thomas Deselaers, Daniel Keysers, and Hermann Ney

Lehrstuhl für Informatik VI – Computer Science Department,
RWTH Aachen University – D-52056 Aachen, Germany
{deselaers, keysers, ney}@informatik.rwth-aachen.de

Abstract. In this paper, different well-known features for image retrieval are quantitatively compared and their correlation is analyzed. We compare the features for two different image retrieval tasks (color photographs and medical radiographs) and a clear difference in performance is observed, which can be used as a basis for an appropriate choice of features. In the past a systematic analysis of image retrieval systems or features was often difficult because different studies usually used different data sets and no common performance measures were established.

1 Introduction

For content-based image retrieval (CBIR), i.e. searching in image databases based on image content, several image retrieval systems have been developed. One of the first systems was the QBIC system [4]. Other popular research systems are BlobWorld [1], VIPER/GIFT [16], SIMBA [15], and SIMPLIcity [18].

All these systems compare images based on specific features in one way or another and therefore a large variety of features for image retrieval exists. Usually, CBIR systems do not use all known features as this would involve large amounts of data and increase the necessary computing time. Instead, a set of features appropriate to the given task is ususally selected, but it is difficult to judge beforehand which features are appropriate for which tasks. The difficulty to assess the performance of a feature described in a publication is increased further by the fact that often the systems are evaluated on different datasets and few if any quantitative results are reported.

In this work, a short overview of common features used for image retrieval is given and the correlation of different features for different tasks is analyzed. Furthermore, quantitative results for two databases representing different image retrieval tasks are given to compare the performance of the features. To our knowledge no such comparison exists yet, whereas [13] presents a quantitative comparison of different dissimilarity measures.

C.E. Rasmussen et al. (Eds.): DAGM 2004, LNCS 3175, pp. 228–236, 2004.
© Springer-Verlag Berlin Heidelberg 2004

In the system[1] used, images are represented by features and compared using specific distance measures. These distances are combined in a weighted sum

$$D(Q, X) := \sum_{m=1}^{M} w_m \cdot d_m(Q_m, X_m)$$

where Q is the query image, $X \in \mathcal{B}$ is an image from the database $\mathcal{B}$, Q_m and X_m are the mth features of the images, respectively, d_m is the corresponding distance measure, and w_m is a weighting coefficient. For each d_m, $\sum_{X \in \mathcal{B}} d_m(Q_m, X_m) = 1$ is enforced by normalization. A set $\mathcal{R}(Q)$ of K database images is returned with

$$\mathcal{R}(Q) = \{X \in \mathcal{B} : D(Q, X) \leq D(Q, X') \ \forall X' \in \mathcal{B} \backslash \mathcal{R}(Q)\} \text{ with } |\mathcal{R}(Q)| = K$$

Using only one feature at a time, this architecture allows us to compare the impact of different features on the retrieval results directly. The issue of choosing appropriate weightings of features is addressed in [2,3]. For the quantification of retrieval results two problems arise:

1. Only very few datasets with hand-labelled relevances are available to compare different retrieval systems and these datasets are not commonly used. A set of 15 queries with manually determined relevant results is presented in [15], and experiments on these data can be used for a first comparison [2]. Nevertheless, due to the small number of images it is difficult to use these data for a thorough analysis. Therefore we use databases containing general images which are partitioned into separate classes of images.
2. No standard performance measure is established in image retrieval. It has been proposed to adopt some of the performance measures used in textual information retrieval for image retrieval [8]. The precision-recall-graph is a common performance measure which can be summarized in one number by the area under the graph. In previous experiments it was observed that the error rate (ER) of the best match is strongly correlated (with a correlation coefficient of -0.93) to this area [3] and therefore we use the ER as retrieval performance measure in the following. This allows us to compare the results to published results of classification experiments on the same data.

2   Features for Image Retrieval

In this section we present different types of features for image retrieval and the method of multidimensional scaling to visualize similarities between different features. We restrict the presentation to a brief overview of each feature and refer to references for further details. In this work, the goal is not to introduce new features but to give quantitative results for a comparison of existing features for image retrieval tasks.

Table 1 gives an overview of the features and comparison measures used.

---
[1] http://www-i6.informatik.rwth-aachen.de/~deselaers/fire.html

Image Features. The most straight forward approach is to directly use the pixel values as features. For example, the images might be scaled to a common size and compared using the Euclidean distance. In optical character recognition and for medical data improved methods based on image features usually obtain excellent results. In this work we use the Euclidean distance and the image distortion model (IDM) [6] to directly compare images.

Color Histograms. Color histograms are widely used in image retrieval, e.g. [4]. It is one of the most basic approaches and to show performance improvement image retrieval systems are often compared to a system using only color histograms. Color histograms give an estimation of the distribution of the colors in the image. The color space is partitioned and for each partition the pixels within its range are counted, resulting in a representation of the relative frequencies of the occurring colors. In accordance with [13], we use the Jeffrey divergence to compare histograms.

Invariant Features. A feature is called invariant with respect to certain transformations, if it does not change when these transformations are applied to the image. The transformations considered here are mainly translation, rotation, and scaling. In this work, invariant feature histograms as presented in [15] are used. These features are based on the idea of constructing features invariant with respect to certain transformations by integration over all considered transformations. The resulting histograms are compared using the Jeffrey divergence [13].

Invariant Fourier Mellin Features. It is well known that the amplitude spectrum of the Fourier transformation is invariant against translation. Using this knowledge and log-polar coordinates it is possible to create a feature invariant with respect to rotation, scaling, and translation [14]. These features are compared using the Euclidean distance.

Gabor Features. In texture analysis Gabor filters are frequently used [5]. In this work we apply the method presented in [10] where the HSV color space is used and hue and saturation are represented as one complex value. From these features we create histograms which are compared using the Jeffrey divergence [13].

Tamura Texture Features. In [17] the authors propose six texture features corresponding to human visual perception: *coarseness, contrast, directionality, line-likeness, regularity*, and *roughness*. From experiments testing the significance of these features with respect to human perception, it was concluded that the

Table 1. Used features along with associated distance measures.

Feature X_m	distance measure d_m
image features	Euclidean distance, Image Distortion Model [6]
color histograms	Jeffrey divergence [13]
invariant feature histograms	Jeffrey divergence [13]
Gabor feature histograms	Jeffrey divergence [13]
Tamura texture feature histograms	Jeffrey divergence [13]
local features	direct transfer, LFIDM, Jeffrey divergence [2]
region based features	integrated region matching [18]

first three features are very important. Thus in our experiments we use coarseness, contrast, and directionality to create a histogram describing the texture [2] and compare these histograms using the Jeffrey divergence [13]. In the QBIC system [4] histograms of these features are used as well.

Local Features. Local features are small (square) sub-images extracted from the original image. It is known that local features can yield good results in various classification tasks [11]. Local features have some interesting properties for image recognition, e.g. they are inherently robust against translation. These properties are also interesting for image retrieval. To use local features for image retrieval, three different methods are available [2]:

1. direct transfer: The local features are extracted from each database image and from the query image. Then, the nearest neighbors for each of the local features of the query are searched and the database images containing most of these neighbors are returned. *2. local feature image distortion model (LFIDM)*: The local features from the query image are compared to the local features of each image of the database and the distances between them are summed up. The images with the lowest total distances are returned. *3. histograms of local features*: A reasonably large amount of local features from the database is clustered and then each database image is represented by a histogram of indices of these clusters. These histograms are then compared using the Jeffrey divergence.

Region-based Features. Another approach to representing images is based on the idea to find image regions which roughly correspond to objects in the images. To achieve this objective the image is segmented into regions. The task of segmentation has been thoroughly studied [9] but most of the algorithms are limited to special tasks because image segmentation is closely connected to understanding arbitrary images, a yet unsolved problem. Nevertheless, some image retrieval systems successfully use image segmentation techniques [1,18]. We use the approach presented in [18] to compare region descriptions of images.

2.1 Correlation of Features

Since we have a large variety of features at our disposal, we may want to select an appropriate set of features for a given image retrieval task. Obviously, there are some correlations between different features. To detect these correlations, we propose to create a distance matrix for a database using all available features. Using a leaving-one-out approach, the distances between all pairs of images from a database are determined for each available feature. For a database of N images with M features this results in an $N' \times M$ distance matrix D obtained from $N' = N \cdot (N - 1)/2$ image pairs. From this matrix, the covariances $\Sigma_{mm'}$ and correlations $R_{mm'}$ are determined as

$$\Sigma_{mm'} = \frac{1}{N'} \sum_{n=1}^{N'} D_{nm} D_{nm'} - \left(\frac{1}{N'} \sum_{n=1}^{N'} D_{nm}\right)\left(\frac{1}{N'} \sum_{n=1}^{N'} D_{nm'}\right), \quad R_{mm'} = \frac{\Sigma_{mm'}}{\sqrt{\Sigma_{mm} \Sigma_{m'm'}}}$$

Fig. 1. Example images from the WANG database.

where D_{nm} and $D_{nm'}$ denote the distances of the nth image comparison using the m-th and m'-th feature, respectively. The entries of the correlation matrix R are interpreted as similarities of different features. A high value $R_{mm'}$ denotes a high similarity in the distances calculated based on the features m and m', respectively. This similarity matrix R is easily converted into a dissimilarity matrix W by setting $W_{mm'} := 1 - |R_{mm'}|$. This dissimilarity matrix W is then visualized using multi-dimensional scaling.

Multi-dimensional scaling seeks a representation of data points in a low dimensional space while preserving the distances between data points as much as possible. Here, the data is presented in a two-dimensional space for visualization. A freely available MatLab library[2] was used for multi-dimensional scaling.

3   Databases

Due to the lack of a common database for evaluation in CBIR with known relevances we use two databases where relevances are implicitly given by classifications. These databases are chosen as representatives for two different types of CBIR tasks: The WANG database represents an CBIR task with arbitrary photographs. In contrast, the IRMA database represents a CBIR task in which the images involved depict more clearly defined objects, i.e. the domain is considerably narrower.

WANG. The WANG database is a subset of 1000 images of the Corel database which were selected manually to form 10 classes of 100 images each. The images are subdivided into 10 sufficiently distinct classes (e.g. 'Africa', 'beach', 'monuments', 'food') such that it can be assumed that a user wants to find the other images from the class if the query is from one of these ten classes. This database was created at the Pennsylvania State University and is publicly available[3]. The images are of size 384×256 and some examples are depicted in Figure 1.

IRMA. The IRMA database is a database of 1617 medical radiographs collected in a collaboration project of the RWTH Aachen University [7]. The complete data are labelled using a multi-axial code describing several properties of the images. For the experiments presented here, the data were divided into the six classes 'abdomen', 'skull', 'limbs', 'chest', 'breast' and 'spine', describing different body regions. The images are of varying sizes. Some examples are depicted in Figure 2.

---

[2] http://www.biol.ttu.edu/Strauss/Matlab/matlab.htm
[3] http://wang.ist.psu.edu/

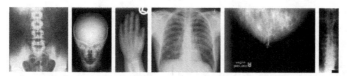

Fig. 2. Examples images from the IRMA database.

4 Results

To obtain systematic results for different features used in CBIR, we first analyze the characteristics of the features using their correlation. Then the performance of the retrieval system is determined for the IRMA and the WANG task. That is, we give leaving-one-out error rates for these two databases. Obviously one can expect to obtain better results using a combination of more than one feature but here we limit the investigation to the impact of single features on the retrieval result. Details about combinations of features are presented in [2,3].

4.1 Correlation of Features

For improved performance, the advantages of different features can be combined. However, it is not clear how to choose the appropriate combination. To analyze which features have similar properties, we perform a correlation analysis as described in Section 2.1 for the WANG and IRMA database in a leaving-one-out manner. The results from multi-dimensional scaling are shown in Figure 3. The points in these graphs denote the different features. Several points of the same type represent different settings for the feature. The distances between the points indicate the correlations of the features. That is, points that are close together stand for features that are highly correlated and points farther away denote features with different characteristics.

The graphs show that there are clear clusters of features. Both graphs have a large cluster of invariant feature histograms with monomial kernel functions. Also, the graphs show clusters of local features, local feature histograms, and Gabor feature histograms. The texture features do not form a cluster. This suggests that they describe different textural properties of the images and that it may be useful to combine them. In contrast, the cluster of invariant features shows that it is not suitable to use different invariant features at the same time. From Figure 3 it can be observed that region features, image features, invariant feature histograms, and Gabor histograms appear to have low correlation for the WANG data and therefore a combination of these features may be useful for photograph-like images. For the radiograph data the interpretation of Figure 3 suggests to use texture features, image features, invariant feature histograms, and Gabor histograms. The combination of these features is addressed in [2,3].

4.2 Different Features for Different Tasks

As motivated above we use the error rate (ER) to compare the performance of different features. In [3] it has been observed that the commonly used measures

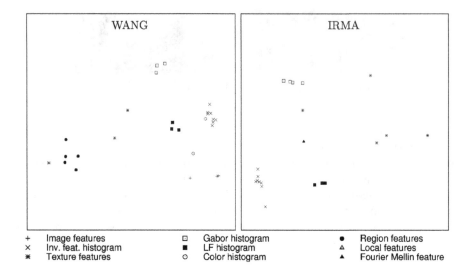

+	Image features	□	Gabor histogram	● Region features
×	Inv. feat. histogram	■	LF histogram	▲ Local features
✳	Texture features	○	Color histogram	▲ Fourier Mellin feature

Fig. 3. Two-dimensional representation from multi-dimensional scaling for features on the WANG and IRMA database.

precision and recall are strongly correlated to the error rate. Furthermore, the error rate is one number that is easy to interpret and widely used in the context of image classification.

Table 2 shows error rates for different features for the WANG and IRMA databases. From this table it can be observed that these different tasks require different features. For the WANG database, consisting of very general photographs, invariant feature histograms and color histograms perform very well but for the IRMA database, consisting of images with mainly one clearly defined object per image, these features perform badly. In contrast to this, the pixel values as features perform very well for the IRMA task and badly for the WANG task. Also, the strong correlation of invariant feature histograms with

Table 2. Error rates [%] different features for the WANG and IRMA databases.

WANG

Feature	ER [%]
inv. feat. histogram	15.9
color histogram	17.9
pixel values (IDM)	22.3
Tamura histogram	31.0
local feature histogram	32.5
Gabor histogram	48.2
regions	54.3
pixel values (Euclidean)	55.1
local features	62.5

IRMA

Feature	ER [%]
pixel values (IDM)	6.7
local feature histogram	9.3
local features	13.0
pixel values (Euclidean)	17.7
Tamura histogram	19.3
Gabor histogram	24.4
inv. feat. histogram	29.2
Fourier Mellin feature	53.1
extended tangent distance [6]	8.0
pseudo 2D HMM [6]	5.3

color histograms is visible: for the WANG database the invariant feature histograms yield only small improvement. In both cases, the Tamura histograms obtain good results taken into account that they represent the textures of the images only. It is interesting to observe that for the IRMA database the top four methods are different representations and comparison methods based on the pixel values, i.e. appearance-based representations.

5 Conclusion

In this work, we quantitatively compared different features for CBIR tasks. The results show clearly that the performance of features is task dependent. For databases of arbitrary color photographs features like color histograms and invariant feature histograms are essential to obtain good results. For databases from a narrower domain, i.e. with clearly defined objects as content, the pixel values of the images in combination with a suitable distance measure are most important for good retrieval performance. Furthermore, a method to visualize the correlation between features was introduced, which allows us to choose features of different characteristics for feature combination. In the future, the observations regarding the suitability of features for different tasks have to be experimentally validated on further databases.

References

1. C. Carson, M. Thomas, S. Belongie, J.M. Hellerstein, and J. Malik. Blobworld: A system for region-based image indexing and retrieval. In *Int. Conf. Visual Information Systems*, pp. 509–516, Amsterdam, The Netherlands, June 1999.
2. T. Deselaers. Features for image retrieval. Diploma thesis, Lehrstuhl für Informatik VI, RWTH Aachen University, Aachen, Germany, Dec. 2003.
3. T. Deselaers, D. Keysers, and H. Ney. Classification error rate for quantitative evaluation of content-based image retrieval systems. In *Int. Conf. on Pattern Recognition*, Cambridge, UK, Aug. 2004. In press.
4. C. Faloutsos, R. Barber, M. Flickner, J. Hafner, W. Niblack, D. Petkovic, and W. Equitz. Efficient and effective querying by image content. *Journal of Intelligent Information Systems*, 3(3/4):231–262, July 1994.
5. Q. Iqbal and J. Aggarwal. Using structure in content-based image retrieval. In *Int. Conf. Signal and Image Processing*, pp. 129–133, Nassau, Bahamas, Oct. 1999.
6. D. Keysers, C. Gollan, and H. Ney. Classification of medical images using nonlinear distortion models. In *Bildverarbeitung für die Medizin*, pp. 366–370, Berlin, Germany, Mar. 2004.
7. T. Lehmann, M. Güld, C. Thies, B. Fischer, K. Spitzer, D. Keysers, H. Ney, M. Kohnen, H. Schubert, and B. Wein. The IRMA project – A state of the art report on content-based image retrieval in medical applications. In *Korea-Germany Workshop on Advanced Medical Image*, pp. 161–171, Seoul, Korea, Oct. 2003.
8. H. Müller, W. Müller, D. M. Squire, S. Marchand-Maillet, and T. Pun. Performance Evaluation in Content-based Image Retrieval: Overview and Proposals. *Pattern Recognition Letters*, 22(5):593–601, 2001.

9. N.R. Pal and S.K. Pal. A review on image segmentation techniques. *Pattern Recognition*, 26(9):1277–1294, Nov. 1993.

10. C. Palm, D. Keysers, T. Lehmann, and K. Spitzer. Gabor filtering of complex hue/saturation images for color texture classification. In *Int. Conf. on Computer Vision*, volume 2, pp. 45–49, Atlantic City, NJ, Feb. 2000.

11. R. Paredes, J. Perez-Cortes, A. Juan, and E. Vidal. Local representations and a direct voting scheme for face recognition. In *Workshop on Pattern Recognition in Information Systems*, pp. 71–79, Setúbal, Portugal, July 2001.

12. M. Park, J.S. Jin, and L.S. Wilson. Fast content-based image retrieval using quasi-Gabor filter and reduction of image feature. In *Southwest Symposium on Image Analysis and Interpretation*, pp. 178–182, Santa Fe, NM, Apr. 2002.

13. J. Puzicha, Y. Rubner, C. Tomasi, and J. Buhmann. Empirical evaluation of dissimilarity measures for color and texture. In *Int. Conf. on Computer Vision*, volume 2, pp. 1165–1173, Corfu, Greece, Sept. 1999.

14. B.S. Reddy and B. Chatterji. An FFT-based technique for translation, rotation and scale invariant image registration. *IEEE Trans. Image Proc.*, 5(8):1266–1271, Aug 1996

15. S. Siggelkow. *Feature Histograms for Content-Based Image Retrieval*. Ph.D. thesis, University of Freiburg, Institute for Computer Science, Freiburg, Germany, 2002.

16. D.M. Squire, W. Müller, H. Müller, and J. Raki. Content-based query of image databases, inspirations from text retrieval: Inverted files, frequency-based weights and relevance feedback. In *Scandinavian Conference on Image Analysis*, pp. 143–149, Kangerlussuaq, Greenland, June 1999.

17. H. Tamura, S. Mori, and T. Yamawaki. Textural features corresponding to visual perception. *IEEE Trans. Systems, Man, and Cybernetics*, 8(6):460–472, June 1978.

18. J.Z. Wang, J. Li, and G. Wiederhold. SIMPLIcity: Semantics-sensitive Integrated Matching for Picture LIbraries. *IEEE Trans. Pattern Analysis and Machine Intelligence*, 23(9):947–963, Sept. 2001.

Learning from Labeled and Unlabeled Data
Using Random Walks

Dengyong Zhou and Bernhard Schölkopf

Max Planck Institute for Biological Cybernetics
Spemannstr. 38, 72076 Tuebingen, Germany
{dengyong.zhou, bernhard.schoelkopf}@tuebingen.mpg.de

Abstract. We consider the general problem of learning from labeled and unlabeled data. Given a set of points, some of them are labeled, and the remaining points are unlabeled. The goal is to predict the labels of the unlabeled points. Any supervised learning algorithm can be applied to this problem, for instance, Support Vector Machines (SVMs). The problem of our interest is if we can implement a classifier which uses the unlabeled data information in some way and has higher accuracy than the classifiers which use the labeled data only. Recently we proposed a simple algorithm, which can substantially benefit from large amounts of unlabeled data and demonstrates clear superiority to supervised learning methods. Here we further investigate the algorithm using random walks and spectral graph theory, which shed light on the key steps in this algorithm.

1 Introduction

We consider the general problem of learning from labeled and unlabeled data. Given a set of points, some of them are labeled, and the remaining points are unlabeled. The task is to predict the labels of the unlabeled points. This is a setting which is applicable to many real-world problems. We generally need to also predict the labels of the testing points which are unseen before. However, in practice, we almost always can add the new points into the set of the unlabeled data.

Any learning algorithm can be applied to this problem, especially supervised learning methods, which train the classifiers with the labeled data and then use the trained classifiers to predict the labels of the unlabeled data. At present, one of the most popular supervised learning methods is the Support Vector Machine (SVM) [9]. The problem of interest here is if we can implement a classifier which uses the unlabeled data in some way and has higher accuracy than the classifiers which use the labeled data only [10].

Such a learning problem is often called semi-supervised. Since labeling often requires expensive human labor, whereas unlabeled data is far easier to obtain, semi-supervised learning is very useful in many real-world problems and has recently attracted a considerable amount of research. A typical application is web categorization, in which manually classified web pages are always a very

C.E. Rasmussen et al. (Eds.): DAGM 2004, LNCS 3175, pp. 237–244, 2004.
© Springer-Verlag Berlin Heidelberg 2004

small part of the entire web, but the number of unlabeled examples can be almost as large as you want.

Recently we proposed a simple algorithm, which can substantially benefit from large amounts of unlabeled data and works much better than the supervised learning methods [11]. Here we further investigate the algorithm using random walks and spectral graph theory, which shed light on some key steps in this algorithm, especially normalization.

The paper is organized as follows. In Section 2 we describe our semi-supervised learning algorithm in details. In Section 3 the method is interpreted in the framework of lazy random walks. In Section 4 we define calculus on discrete objects and then build the regularization framework of the method upon the discrete calculus. In Section 5 we use a toy problem to highlight the key steps in the method, and also validate the method on a large-scale real-world dataset.

2   Algorithm

Given a point set $\mathcal{X} = \{x_1, \ldots, x_l, x_{l+1}, \ldots, x_n\} \subset \mathbb{R}^m$ and a label set $\mathcal{L} = \{-1, 1\}$, the first l points $x_i (i \leq l)$ are labeled as $y_i \in \mathcal{L}$ and the remaining points $x_u (l + 1 \leq u \leq n)$ are unlabeled. Define a $n \times 1$ vector y with $y_i = 1$ or -1 if x_i is labeled as positive or negative, and 0 if x_i is unlabeled. We can view y as a real-valued function defined on $\mathcal{X}$, which assigns a value y_i to point x_i. The data is classified as follows:

1. Define a $n \times n$ affinity matrix W in which the elements are nonnegative, symmetric, and furthermore the diagonal elements are zeros.
2. Construct the matrix $S = D^{-1/2} W D^{-1/2}$ in which D is a diagonal matrix with its (i, i)-element equal to the sum of the i-th row of W.
3. Compute $f = (I - \alpha S)^{-1} y$, where I denotes the identity matrix and α is a parameter in $(0, 1)$, and assign a label $\text{sgn}(f_i)$ to point x_i.

The affinity matrix can typically be defined by a Gaussian $W_{ij} = \exp(-\|x_i - x_j\|^2 / 2\sigma^2)$ except that $W_{ii} = 0$, where $\|\cdot\|$ represents Euclidean norm. We would like to emphasize the affinity matrix have not to be derived from a kernel [8]. For instance, construct a k-NN or ϵ-ball graph on data, and then define $W_{ij} = 1$ if points x_i and x_j are connected by an edge, and 0 otherwise. Note that in this case the requirement $W_{ii} = 0$ is satisfied automatically since there is no self-loop edge.

3   Lazy Random Walks

In this section we interpret the algorithm in terms of random walks inspired by [6]. We will see that this method simply classifies the points by comparing a specific distance measure between them and the labeled points of different classes.

Let $\Gamma = (V, E)$ denote a graph with a set V of n vertices indexed by number from 1 to n and an edge collection E. Assume the graph is undirected and connected, and has no self-loops or multiple edges. A weight function $w : V \times V \rightarrow \mathbb{R}$ associated to the graph satisfies $w(i, j) = w(j, i)$, and $w(i, j) \geq 0$. Moreover, define $w(i, j) = 0$ if there is no edge between i and j. The degree d_i of vertex i is defined to be

$$d_i = \sum_{j \sim i} w(i, j), \qquad (3.1)$$

where $j \sim i$ denotes the set of the points which are linked to point i.

Let D denote the diagonal matrix with the (i, i)-th entry having value d_i. Let W denote the matrix with the entries $W_{ij} = w(i, j)$. A lazy random walk on the graph is decided by the transition probability matrix $P = (1 - \alpha)I + \alpha D^{-1}W$. Here α is a parameter in $(0, 1)$ as before. This means, with the probability α, following one link which connects the vertex of the current position and is chosen with the probability proportional to the weight of the link, and with the probability $1 - \alpha$, just staying at the current position.

There exists a unique stationary distribution $\pi = [\pi_1, \dots, \pi_n]$ for the lazy random walk, i.e. a unique probability distribution satisfying the balance equation

$$\pi = \pi P. \qquad (3.2)$$

Let $\mathbf{1}$ denote the $1 \times n$ vector with all entries equal to 1. Let vol Γ denote the volume of the graph, which is defined by the sum of vertex degrees. It is not hard to see that the stationary distribution of the random walk is

$$\pi = \mathbf{1}D/\text{vol } \Gamma. \qquad (3.3)$$

Note that π does not depend on α.

Let X_t denote the position of the random walk at time t. Write $T_{ij} = \min\{t \geq 0 | X_t = x_j, X_0 = x_i, x_i \neq x_j\}$ for the *first hitting time* to x_j with the initial position x_i, and write $T_{ii} = \min\{t > 0 | X_t = x_i, X_0 = x_i\}$, which is called the *first return time* to x_i [1]. Let H_{ij} denote the expected number of steps required for a random walk to reach x_j with an initial position x_i, i.e. H_{ij} is the expectation of T_{ij}. H_{ij} is often called the *hitting time*. Let C_{ij} denote the expected number of steps for a random walk starting at x_i to reach x_j and then return, i.e. $C_{ij} = H_{ij} + H_{ji}$, which is often called the *commute time* between x_i and x_j. Clearly, C_{ij} is symmetrical, but H_{ij} may be not.

Let G denote the inverse of the matrix $D - \alpha W$. Then the commute time satisfies [6]:

$$C_{ij} \propto G_{ii} + G_{jj} - G_{ij} - G_{ji}, \text{ if } x_i \neq x_j, \qquad (3.4)$$

and [1]

$$C_{ii} = 1/\pi_i. \qquad (3.5)$$

The relation between G and C is similar to the inner product and the norm in Euclidean space. Let $\langle x_i, x_j \rangle$ denote the Euclidean inner product between x_i and x_j. Then the Euclidean norm of the vector $x_i - x_j$ satisfies

$$\|x_i - x_j\|^2 = \langle x_i - x_j, x_i - x_j \rangle = \langle x_i, x_i \rangle + \langle x_j, x_j \rangle - \langle x_i, x_j \rangle - \langle x_j, x_i \rangle.$$

In other words, we can think of G as a Gram matrix which specifies a kind of inner product on the dataset. The commute time is the corresponding norm derived from this inner product.

Note that H_{ij} is quite small whenever x_j is a node with a large stationary probability π_j. Thus we naturally consider to normalize H_{ij} by

$$\bar{H}_{ij} = \sqrt{\pi_i \pi_j} H_{ij}. \tag{3.6}$$

Accordingly the normalized commute time is

$$\bar{C}_{ij} = \bar{H}_{ji} + \bar{H}_{ij}. \tag{3.7}$$

Let $\bar{G}$ denote the inverse of the matrix $I - \alpha S$. Then the normalized commute time satisfies

$$\bar{C}_{ij} \propto \bar{G}_{ii} + \bar{G}_{jj} - \bar{G}_{ij} - \bar{G}_{ji}. \tag{3.8}$$

Noting the equality (3.5), we have

$$\bar{G}_{ij} = \frac{G_{ij}}{\sqrt{C_{ii}C_{jj}}}, \tag{3.9}$$

which is parallel to the normalized Euclidean product $\langle x_i, x_j \rangle / \|x_i\|\|x_i\|$ or cosine.

Let

$$p_+(x_i) = \sum_{\{j|y_j=1\}} \bar{G}_{ij}, \text{ and } p_-(x_i) = \sum_{\{j|y_j=-1\}} \bar{G}_{ij}. \tag{3.10}$$

Then the classification given by $f = (I - \alpha S)^{-1} y$ is simply checking which of the two values $p_+(x_i)$ or $p_-(x_i)$ is larger, which is in turn comparing the normalized commute times to the labeled points of different classes.

If we just want to compare the non-normalized commute times to the different class labeled points, then the classification is given by $f = (D - \alpha W)^{-1} y$. Although the normalized commute time seems to be a more reasonable choice, there is still lack of the statistical evidence showing the superiority of the normalized commute time to the non-normalized one. However, we can construct a subtle toy problem (see Section 5) to essentially expose the necessity of normalization.

4   Regularization Framework

In this section we define *calculus* on graphs inspired by spectral graph theory [4] and [3]. A regularization framework for classification problems on graphs then can be naturally built upon the discrete calculus, and the algorithm derived from the framework is exactly the method presented in Section 2.

Let $\mathcal{F}$ denote the space of functions defined on the vertices of graph Γ, which assigns a value f_i to vertex i. We can view f as a $n \times 1$ vector. The *edge derivative* of f along the edge $e(i, j)$ at the vertex i is defined to be

$$\frac{\partial f}{\partial e}\bigg|_i = \sqrt{w(i, j)} \left(\frac{1}{\sqrt{d_i}} f_i - \frac{1}{\sqrt{d_j}} f_j \right). \tag{4.1}$$

Clearly

$$\left.\frac{\partial f}{\partial e}\right|_i = -\left.\frac{\partial f}{\partial e}\right|_j. \tag{4.2}$$

The definition (4.1) in fact splits the function value at each point among the edges incident with it before computing the local changes of the function, and the value assigned to each edge is proportional to its weight. This statement can be clearer if we rewrite (4.1) as

$$\left.\frac{\partial f}{\partial e}\right|_i = \sqrt{\frac{w(i,j)}{d_i}} f_i - \sqrt{\frac{w(i,j)}{d_j}} f_j.$$

The *local variation* of function f at each vertex i is then defined by:

$$\|\nabla_i f\| = \sqrt{\sum_{e \vdash i} \left(\left.\frac{\partial f}{\partial e}\right|_i\right)^2}, \tag{4.3}$$

where $e \vdash i$ means the set of the edges incident with vertex i. The *smoothness* of function f is then naturally measured by the sum of the local variations at each point:

$$S(f) = \frac{1}{2} \sum_i \|\nabla_i f\|^2. \tag{4.4}$$

The graph *Laplacian* is defined to be [4]

$$\Delta = D^{-1/2}(D - W)D^{-1/2} = I - D^{-1/2}WD^{-1/2} = I - S, \tag{4.5}$$

where S is defined to be $S = D^{-1/2}WD^{-1/2}$. The Laplacian can be thought of as an operator defined on the function space:

$$\left.\Delta f\right|_i = \frac{1}{\sqrt{d_i}} \sum_{i \sim j} w(i,j) \left(\frac{1}{\sqrt{d_i}} f_i - \frac{1}{\sqrt{d_j}} f_j\right). \tag{4.6}$$

The smallest eigenvalue of the Laplacian is zero because the largest eigenvalue of S is 1. Hence the Laplacian is symmetric and positive semi-definite. Let $\mathbf{1}$ denote the constant function which assumes the value 1 on each vertex. We can view $\mathbf{1}$ as a column vector. Then $D^{-1/2}\mathbf{1}$ is the eigenvector corresponding to the smallest eigenvalue of Δ. Most importantly, we have the following equality

$$f^T \Delta f = S(f), \tag{4.7}$$

which exposes the essential relation between the Laplacian and the gradient.

For the classification problem on graphs, it is natural to define the cost function associated to a classification function f to be

$$\arg \min_{f \in \mathcal{F}} \left\{ S(f) + \frac{\mu}{2} \|f - y\|^2 \right\}. \tag{4.8}$$

The first term in the bracket is called the *smoothness term* or *regularizer*, which requires the function to be as smooth as possible. The second term is called the *fitting term*, which requires the function to be as close to the initial label assignment as possible. The trade-off between these two competitive terms are captured by a positive parameter μ. It is not hard to show that the solution of (4.8) is

$$f = (1 - \alpha)(I - \alpha S)^{-1}y, \qquad (4.9)$$

where $\alpha = 1/(1 + \mu)$. Clearly, it is equivalent to $f = (I - \alpha S)^{-1}y$.

Finally, we discuss the non-normalized variant of the definition of edge derivative:

$$\left. \frac{\partial f}{\partial e} \right|_i = \sqrt{w(i,j)}(f_i - f_j).$$

If we further define the graph Laplacian to be $L = D - W$, then the equality (4.7) still holds. Substituting the local variation based on the non-normalized edge derivative into the optimization problem (4.8), we then can obtain a different closed form solution $f = \mu(\mu I + L)^{-1}y$, which is quite close to the algorithm proposed by [2]. In Section 5, we will provide the experimental evidence to demonstrate the superiority of the algorithm based on the normalized edge derivative (4.1).

5   Experiments

5.1   Toy Problem

Shown in Figure 1(a) is the doll toy data, in which the density of the data varies substantially across different clusters. A similar toy dataset was used by [7] for clustering problems. The affinity matrix is defined by a Gaussian. The result given by the algorithm of $f = (D - \alpha W)^{-1}y$ derived from non-normalized commute time is shown in Figure 1(b). The result given by the algorithm $f = (\mu I + L)^{-1}y$ derived from non-normalized edge derivative is shown in Figure 1(c). Obviously, both methods fail to capture the coherent clusters aggregated by the data. The result given by the algorithm $f = (I - \alpha S)^{-1}y$, presented in Section 2, which can be derived from both normalized commute time and edge derivative is shown in Figure 1(d). This method sensibly classifies the dataset according with the global data distribution.

In addition, we use the toy problem to demonstrate the importance of zero diagonal in the first step of the standard algorithm. If we define the affinity matrix using a RBF kernel without removing the diagonal elements, the result is shown in Figure 1(e). The intuition behind setting the diagonal elements to zero is to avoid self-reinforcement.

Finally, we investigate the fitting term of the regularization framework using the toy problem. Note that we assign *a prior* label 0 to the unlabeled points in the fitting term. This is different from the regularization frameworks of supervised learning methods, in which the fitting term is only for the labeled points. If

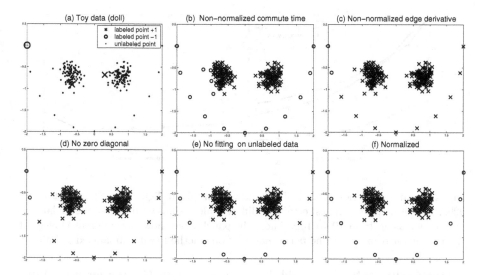

Fig. 1. Classification on the doll toy data. Both methods in (b) and (c) without normalization fail to classify the points according with the coherent clusters. The importance of zero diagonal and the fitting on the unlabeled data are demonstrated respectively in (d) and (e). The result from the standard algorithm is shown in (f).

we remove the fitting on the unlabeled points, the result is given in Figure 1(f). The intuition behind the fitting on the unlabeled points is to make the algorithm more stable.

5.2   Digit Recognition

we addressed a classification task using the USPS dataset containing 9298 handwritten digits. Each digit is a 16x16 image, represented as a 256 dimensional vector with entries in the range from -1 to 1.

We used k-NN [5] and one-vs-rest SVMs [8] as baselines. Since there is no reliable approach for model selection if only very few labeled points are available, we chose the respective optimal parameters of these methods. The k in k-NN was set to 1. The width of the RBF kernel for the SVM was set to 5. The affinity matrix used in our method was derived from a RBF kernel with its width equal to 1.25. In addition, the parameter α was set to 0.95.

The test errors for different methods with the number of labeled points increasing from 10 to 100 are summarized in the left panel of Figure 2, in which each error point is averaged over 100 random trials, and samples are chosen so that they contain at least one labeled point for each class. The results shows clear superiority of our algorithm (marked as *random walk*) over the supervised learning methods k-NN and SVMs. The right panel of Figure 2 shows how the parameter α influences the performances of the method, in which the number of labeled points is fixed at 50. Obviously, this method is not sensitive to the value of α.

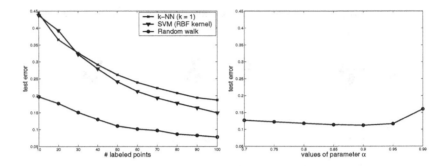

Fig. 2. Digit recognition with USPS handwritten 16x16 digits dataset for a total of 9298. The left panel shows test errors for different algorithms with the number of labeled points increasing from 10 to 100. The right panel shows how the different choices of the parameter α influence the performance of our method (with 50 labeled points).

Acknowledgments. We would like to thank Arthur Gretton for helpful discussions on normalized commute time in random walks.

References

1. D. Aldous and J. Fill. *Reversible Markov Chains and Random Walks on Graphs.* In Preparation, http://stat-www.berkeley.edu/users/aldous/RWG/book.html.
2. M. Belkin, I. Matveeva, and P. Niyogi. Regression and regularization on large graphs. Technical report, University of Chicago, 2003.
3. T. Chan and J. Shen. Variational restoration of non-flat image features: Models and algorithms. *SIAM Journal of Applied Mathematics*, 61(4):1338–1361, 2000.
4. F. Chung. *Spectral Graph Theory.* Number 92 in Regional Conference Series in Mathematics. American Mathematical Society, 1997.
5. P. A. Devijver and J. Kittier. *Pattern Recognition: A Statistical Approach.* Prentice-Hall, London, 1982.
6. J. Ham, D. D. Lee, S. Mika, and B. Schölkopf. A kernel view of the dimensionality reduction of manifolds. In *Proceedings of the 21st International Conference on Machine Learning*, 2004.
7. A. Y. Ng, M. I. Jordan, and Y. Weiss. On spectral clustering: analysis and an algorithm. In *Advances in Neural Information Processing Systems 14*. MIT Press, Cambridge, MA, 2002.
8. B. Schölkopf and A. J. Smola. *Learning with kernels.* MIT Press, Cambridge, MA, 2002.
9. V. N. Vapnik. *Statistical learning theory.* Wiley, NY, 1998.
10. T. Zhang and F. Oles. A probability analysis on the value of unlabeled data for classification problems. In *Proceedings of the 17th International Conference on Machine Learning*, 2000.
11. D. Zhou, O. Bousquet, T. N. Lal, J. Weston, and B. Schölkopf. Learning with local and global consistency. In *Advances in Neural Information Processing Systems 16*. MIT Press, Cambridge, MA, 2004.

Learning Depth from Stereo

Fabian H. Sinz[1], Joaquin Quiñonero Candela[2], Gökhan H. Bakır[1],
Carl Edward Rasmussen[1], and Matthias O. Franz[1]

[1] Max Planck Institute for Biological Cybernetics
Spemannstraße 38, 72076 Tübingen
{fabee;jqc;gb;carl;mof}@tuebingen.mpg.de
[2] Informatics and Mathematical Modelling, Technical University of Denmark,
Richard Petersens Plads, B321, 2800 Kongens Lyngby, Denmark
jqc@imm.dtu.dk

Abstract. We compare two approaches to the problem of estimating
the depth of a point in space from observing its image position in two
different cameras: 1. The classical photogrammetric approach explicitly
models the two cameras and estimates their intrinsic and extrinsic parameters using a tedious calibration procedure; 2. A generic machine
learning approach where the mapping from image to spatial coordinates
is directly approximated by a *Gaussian Process* regression. Our results
show that the generic learning approach, in addition to simplifying the
procedure of calibration, can lead to higher depth accuracies than classical calibration although no specific domain knowledge is used.

1 Introduction

Inferring the three-dimensional structure of a scene from a pair of stereo images
is one of the principal problems in computer vision. The position $\mathbf{X} = (X, Y, Z)$
of a point in space is related to its image at $\mathbf{x} = (x, y)$ by the equations of
perspective projection

$$x = x_0 - s_{xy}c \cdot \frac{r_{11}(X - X_0) + r_{21}(Y - Y_0) + r_{31}(Z - Z_0)}{r_{13}(X - X_0) + r_{23}(Y - Y_0) + r_{33}(Z - Z_0)} + \Xi_x(\mathbf{x}) \quad (1)$$

$$y = y_0 - c \cdot \frac{r_{12}(X - X_0) + r_{22}(Y - Y_0) + r_{32}(Z - Z_0)}{r_{13}(X - X_0) + r_{23}(Y - Y_0) + r_{33}(Z - Z_0)} + \Xi_y(\mathbf{x}) \quad (2)$$

where $\mathbf{x}_0 = (x_0, y_0)$ denotes the image coordinates of the principal point of the
camera, c the focal length, $\mathbf{X}_0 = (X_0, Y_0, Z_0)$ the 3D-position of the camera's
optical center with respect to the reference frame, and r_{ij} the coefficients of a
3×3 rotation matrix R describing the orientation of the camera. The factor s_{xy}
accounts for the difference in pixel width and height of the images, the 2-D-vector
field $\Xi(\mathbf{x})$ for the lens distortions.

The classical approach to stereo vision requires a *calibration procedure* before
the projection equations can be inverted to obtain spatial position, i.e., estimat-
ing the *extrinsic* ($\mathbf{X}_0$ and R) and *intrinsic* ($\mathbf{x}_0$, c, s_{xy} and Ξ) parameters of each
camera from a set of points with known spatial position and their corresponding

C.E. Rasmussen et al. (Eds.): DAGM 2004, LNCS 3175, pp. 245–252, 2004.
© Springer-Verlag Berlin Heidelberg 2004

image positions. This is normally done by repeatedly linearizing the projection equations and applying a standard least square estimator to obtain an iteratively refined estimate of the camera parameters [1]. This approach neglects the nonlinear nature of the problem, which causes that its convergence critically depends on the choice of the initial values for the parameters. Moreover, the right choice of the initial values and the proper setup of the models can be a tedious procedure.

The presence of observations and desired target values on the other hand, makes depth estimation suitable for the application of nonlinear supervised learning algorithms such as *Gaussian Process Regression*. This algorithm does not require any specific domain knowledge and provides a direct solution to nonlinear estimation problems. Here, we investigate whether such a machine learning approach can reach a comparable performance to classical camera calibration. This can lead to a considerable simplification in practical depth estimation problems as off-the-shelf algorithms can be used without specific adaptations to the setup of the stereo problem at hand.

2   Classical Camera Calibration

As described above, the image coordinates of a point are related to the cameras parameters and its spatial position by a nonlinear function $\mathbf{F}$ (see Eqs. 1 and 2)

$$\mathbf{x} = \mathbf{F}(\mathbf{x}_0, c, s_{xy}, R, \mathbf{X}_0, \Xi, \mathbf{X}) \tag{3}$$

The estimation of parameters is done by a procedure called *bundle adjustment* which consists of iteratively linearizing the camera model in parameter space and estimating an improvement for the parameter from the error on a set of m known pairs of image coordinates $\mathbf{x}_i = (x_i, y_i)$ and spatial coordinates $\mathbf{X}_i = (X_i, Y_i, Z_i)$. These can be obtained from an object with a distinct number of points whose coordinates with respect to some reference frame are known with high precision such as, for instance, a calibration rig.

Before this can be done, we need to choose a low-dimensional parameterization of the lens distortion field Ξ because otherwise the equation system 3 for the points $1 \ldots m$ would be underdetermined. Here, we model the x- and y-component of Ξ as a weighted sum over products of one-dimensional Chebychev polynomials T_i in x and y, where i indicates the degree of the polynomial

$$\Xi_x(\mathbf{x}) = \sum_{i,j=0}^{t} a_{ij} T_i(s_x x) T_j(s_y y), \quad \Xi_y(\mathbf{x}) = \sum_{i,j=0}^{t} b_{ij} T_i(s_x x) T_j(s_y y), \tag{4}$$

The factors s_x, s_y scale the image coordinates to the Chebychev polynomials' domain $[-1, 1]$. In the following, we denote the vector of the complete set of camera parameters by $\theta = (\mathbf{x}_0, c, s_{xy}, R, \mathbf{X}_0, a_{11}, \ldots, a_{tt}, b_{11}, \ldots, b_{tt})$.

In the iterative bundle adjustment procedure, we assume we have a parameter estimate θ_{n-1} from the previous iteration. The residual $\mathbf{l}_i$ of point i for the camera model from the previous iteration is then given by

$$\mathbf{l}_i = \mathbf{x}_i - \mathbf{F}(\theta_{n-1}, \mathbf{X}_i). \tag{5}$$

This equation system is linearized by computing the Jacobian $\mathcal{J}(\theta_{n-1})$ of $\mathbf{F}$ at θ_{n-1} such that we obtain

$$\mathbf{l} \approx \mathcal{J}(\theta_{n-1})\Delta\theta \qquad (6)$$

where $\mathbf{l}$ is the concatenation of all $\mathbf{l}_i$ and $\Delta\theta$ is the estimation error in θ that causes the residuals. Usually, one assumes a prior covariance Σ_{ll} on $\mathbf{l}$ describing the inaccuracies in the image position measurements. $\Delta\theta$ is then obtained from a standard linear estimator [3]

$$\Delta\theta = (\mathcal{J}^\top \Sigma_{ll}^{-1} \mathcal{J})^{-1} \mathcal{J} \Sigma_{ll}^{-1} \mathbf{l} . \qquad (7)$$

Finally, the new parameter estimate θ_n for iteration n is improved according to $\theta_n = \theta_{n-1} + \Delta\theta$. Bundle adjustment needs a good initial estimate θ_0 for the camera parameters in order to ensure that the iterations converge to the correct solution. There exists a great variety of procedures for obtaining initial estimates which have to be specifically chosen for the application (e.g. aerial or near-range photogrammetry).

The quality of the estimation can still be improved by modelling uncertainties in the spatial observations $\mathbf{X}_i$. This can be done by including all spatial observations in the parameter set and updating them in the same manner which requires the additional choice of the covariance Σ_{XX} of the measurements of spatial position [1]. Σ_{XX} regulates the tradeoff between the trust in the accuracy of the image observations on the one hand and the spatial observations on the other hand. For more detailed information on bundle adjustment please refer to [1].

Once the parameter sets $\theta^{(1)}$ and $\theta^{(2)}$ of the two camera models are known, the spatial position $\mathbf{X}^*$ of a newly observed image point ($\mathbf{x}_1^*$ in the first and $\mathbf{x}_2^*$ in the second camera) can be estimated using the same technique. Again, $\mathbf{F}$ describes the stereo camera's mapping from spatial to image coordinates according to Eqns. 1 and 2

$$\mathbf{x}_k^* = \mathbf{F}(\theta^{(k)}, \mathbf{X}^*), \quad k = 1, 2 \qquad (8)$$

but this time the θ are kept fixed and the bundle adjustment is computed for estimates of $\mathbf{X}^*$ [1].

3   Gaussian Process Regression

The machine learning algorithm used in our study assumes that the data are generated by a Gaussian Process (GP). Let us call $f(\mathbf{x})$ the non-linear function that maps the D-dimensional input $\mathbf{x}$ to a 1-dimensional output. Given an arbitrary set of inputs $\{\mathbf{x}_i | i = 1, \ldots, m\}$, the joint prior distribution of the corresponding function evaluations $\mathbf{f} = [f(\mathbf{x}_1), \ldots, f(\mathbf{x}_m)]^\top$ is jointly Gaussian:

$$p(\mathbf{f}|\mathbf{x}_1, \ldots, \mathbf{x}_m, \theta) \sim \mathcal{N}(0, K) , \qquad (9)$$

with zero mean (a common and arbitrary choice) and covariance matrix K. The elements of K are computed from a parameterized covariance function, $K_{ij} = k(\mathbf{x}_i, \mathbf{x}_j, \theta)$, where θ now represents the GP parameters. In Sect. 4 we present the two covariance functions we used in our experiments.

We assume that the output observations y_i differ from the corresponding function evaluations $f(\mathbf{x}_i)$ by Gaussian additive i.i.d. noise of mean zero and variance σ^2. For simplicity in the notation, we absorb σ^2 in the set of parameters θ. Consider now that we have observed the targets $\mathbf{y} = [y_1, \dots, y_m]$ associated to our arbitrary set of m inputs, and would like to infer the predictive distribution of the unknown target y_* associated to a new input $\mathbf{x}_*$. First we write the joint distribution of all targets considered, easily obtained from the definition of the prior and of the noise model:

$$p\left(\begin{bmatrix} \mathbf{y} \\ y_* \end{bmatrix} \middle| \mathbf{x}_1, \dots, \mathbf{x}_m, \theta \right) \sim \mathcal{N}\left(0, \begin{bmatrix} K + \sigma^2 \mathcal{I} & \mathbf{k}_* \\ \mathbf{k}_*^\top & k(\mathbf{x}_*, \mathbf{x}_*) + \sigma^2 \end{bmatrix} \right) , \qquad (10)$$

where $\mathbf{k}_* = [k(\mathbf{x}_*, \mathbf{x}_1), \dots, k(\mathbf{x}_*, \mathbf{x}_m)]^\top$ is the covariance between y_* and $\mathbf{y}$, and $\mathcal{I}$ is the identity matrix. The predictive distribution is then obtained by conditioning on the observed outputs $\mathbf{y}$. It is Gaussian:

$$p(y_* | \mathbf{y}, \mathbf{x}_1, \dots, \mathbf{x}_m, \theta) \sim \mathcal{N}(m(\mathbf{x}_*), v(\mathbf{x}_*)) , \qquad (11)$$

with mean and variance given respectively by:

$$m(\mathbf{x}_*) = \mathbf{k}_*^\top [K + \sigma^2 \mathcal{I}]^{-1} \mathbf{y} ,$$
$$v(\mathbf{x}_*) = \sigma^2 + k(\mathbf{x}_*, \mathbf{x}_*) - \mathbf{k}_*^\top [K + \sigma^2 \mathcal{I}]^{-1} \mathbf{k}_* . \qquad (12)$$

Given our assumptions about the noise, the mean of the predictive distribution of $f(\mathbf{x}_*)$ is also equal to $m(\mathbf{x}_*)$, and it is the optimal point estimate of $f(\mathbf{x}_*)$. It is interesting to notice that the prediction equation given by $m(\mathbf{x}_*)$ is identical to the one used in Kernel Ridge Regression (KRR) [2]. However, GPs differ from KRR in that they provide full predictive distributions.

One way of learning the parameters θ of the GP is by maximizing the evidence of the observed targets $\mathbf{y}$ (or marginal likelihood of the parameters θ). In practice, we equivalently minimize the negative log evidence, given by:

$$-\log p(\mathbf{y} | \mathbf{x}_1, \dots, \mathbf{x}_1, \theta) = \frac{1}{2} \log |K + \sigma^2 \mathcal{I}| + \frac{1}{2} \mathbf{y}^\top [K + \sigma^2 \mathcal{I}]^{-1} \mathbf{y} . \qquad (13)$$

Minimization is achieved by taking derivatives and using conjugate gradients. An alternative way of inferring θ is to use a Bayesian variant of the leave-one-out error (GPP, Geisser's surrogate predictive probability, [4]). In our study we will use both methods, choosing the most appropriate one for each of our two covariance functions. More details are provided in Sect. 4.

4   Experiments

Dataset. We used a robot manipulator holding a calibration target with a flattened LED to record the data items. The target was moved in planes of different

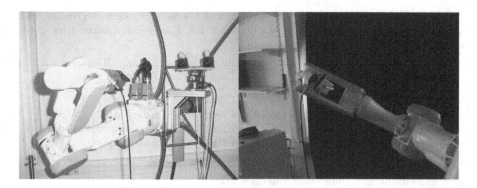

Fig. 1. Robot arm and calibration target, which were used to record the data items.

depths, perpendicular to the axis of the stereo setup. The spatial position of the LED was determined from the position encoders of the robot arm with a nominal positioning accuracy of $0.01mm$. The center of the LED was detected using several image processing steps. First, a threshold operation using the upper 0.01 percentile of the image's gray-scale values predetected the LED. Then a two-dimensional spline was fitted through a window around the image of the LED with an approximate size of $20px$. A *Sobel* operator was used as edge detector on the spline and a *Zhou* operator located the LED center with high accuracy (see [1]). We recorded 992 pairs of spatial and image positions, 200 of which were randomly selected as training set. The remaining 792 were used as test set.

Classical calibration. During bundle adjustment, several camera parameters were highly correlated with others. Small variations of these parameters produced nearly the same variation of the function values of $\mathbf{F}$, which lead to a linear dependency of the columns of $\mathcal{J}$ and thus to a rank deficiency of $\mathcal{J}^{\top} \Sigma_{ll}^{-1} \mathcal{J}$. Therefore, the parameters of a correlating pair could not be determined properly. To avoid such high correlations we excluded $\mathbf{x}_0, a_{00}, b_{00}, a_{10}, b_{01}, a_{12}, b_{21}, a_{01}, a_{20}$ and a_{02} from estimation and set a_{01}, a_{20}, a_{02} to the values of b_{01}, b_{02}, b_{20} (see [7] for more detailed information on the parameterization of the camera model and [6] for the exact procedure in our setting).

We used a ten-fold crossvalidation scheme to determine whether the corresponding coefficients should be included in the model or not. The error in the image coordinates was assumed to be conditionally independent with $\sigma^2 = 0.25px$, so the covariance matrix Σ_{ll} became diagonal with $\Sigma_{ll} = 0.25 \cdot \mathcal{I}$. The same assumption was made for Σ_{XX}, though the value of the diagonal elements was chosen by a ten fold cross validation.

Gaussian Process Regression. For the machine learning approach we used both the *inhomogeneous polynomial kernel*

$$k(x, x') = \sigma_\nu^2 \langle x, x' + 1 \rangle^g \tag{14}$$

Table 1. Test error for bundle adjustment and Gaussian Process Regression with various kernels, computed on a set of 792 data items. Root mean squared error of the spatial residua was used as error measure.

METHOD	TEST ERROR	PREPROCESSING
Bundle adjustment	0.38mm	-
Inhomogeneous polynomial $(g = 4)$	0.29mm	scaled input
Inhomogeneous polynomial $(g = 4)$	0.28mm	transformed, scaled input
Squared exponential	0.31mm	scaled input
Squared exponential	0.27mm	transformed, scaled input

of degree g and the *squared exponential kernel*

$$k(x, x') = \sigma_\nu^2 \exp\left(-\frac{1}{2} \sum_{d=1}^{D} \frac{1}{\lambda_d^2}(x_d - x'_d)^2\right) . \tag{15}$$

with automatic relevance determination (ARD). Indeed, the lengthscales λ_d can grow to eliminate the contribution of any irrelevant input dimension.

The parameters σ_ν^2, σ^2 and g of the polynomial covariance function were estimated by maximizing the GPP criterion [4]. The parameters σ_ν^2, σ^2 and the λ_d of the squared exponential kernel were estimated by maximizing their marginal log likelihood [5]. In both cases, we used the conjugate gradient algorithm as optimization method.

We used two different types of preprocessing in the experiments: 1. Scaling each dimension of the input data to the interval $[-1, 1]$; 2. Transforming the input data according to

$$(x_1, y_1, x_2, y_2) \mapsto (0.5(x_1 - x_2), 0.5(x_1 + x_2), 0.5(y_1 - y_2), 0.5(y_1 + y_2)) .$$

The output data was centered for training.

5 Results

The cross validation for the camera model yielded $\sigma_X = 2mm$ as best a priori estimation for the standard deviation of the spatial coordinates. In the same way, a maximal degree of $t = 3$ for the Chebychev polynomials was found to be optimal for the estimation of the lens distortion. Table 1 shows the test errors of the different algorithms and preprocessing methods.

All algorithms achieved error values under one millimeter. Gaussian Process regression with both kernels showed a superior performance to the classical approach. Fig. 2 shows the position error according to the test points actual depth and according to the image coordinates distance to the lens center, the so called *excentricity*. One can see that the depth error increases nonlinearly with increasing spatial distance to the camera. Calculation of errors shows that the depth error grows quadratically with the image position error, so this behaviour is expected and indicates the sanity of the learned model. Another hint that all of the used algorithms are able to model the lens distortions is the absence of a trend in the right figure. Again, the learning algorithms do better and show a smaller error for almost all excentricities.

The superiority of the squared exponential kernel to the polynomial can be explained by its ability to assign different length scales to different dimensions of the data and therefore set higher weights on more important dimensions. In our experiments $\frac{1}{\lambda_1^2}$ and $\frac{1}{\lambda_3^2}$ were always approximately five times larger than $\frac{1}{\lambda_2^2}$ and $\frac{1}{\lambda_4^2}$, which is consistent with the underlying physical process, where the depth of a point is computed by the disparity in the x-direction of the image coordinates. The same phenomenon could be observed for the transformed inputs, where higher weights where assigned to the x_1 and x_2.

6   Discussion

We applied Gaussian Process Regression to the problem of estimating the spatial position of a point from its coordinates in two different images and compared its performance to the classical camera calibration. Our results show that the generic learning algorithms performed better although maximal physical knowledge was used in the explicit stereo camera modelling.

As both approaches are able to model the depth estimation very precisely, the different error rates can be explained by their different abilities to account for lens distortions. The flexible parameterization of Gaussian Processes allows for a spatially detailed modeling of lens distortion. In contrast, a significant estimation of the higher-order Chebychev polynomials capable of modeling strongly space-variant distortion fields turned out to be impossible. A further reason might lie in the sensitivity of bundle adjustment to parameter initialization since there is no obvious a priori choice for the initial values of the Chebychev coefficients in most cases.

An additional advantage of our approach is the mechanical and therefore simple way of model selection, while the correct parametrization of a camera

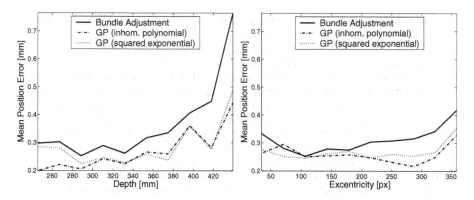

Fig. 2. Position error depending on the actual depth of the test point (left figure) and on the distance to the lens center, the so called *excentricity* (right figure).

model and elimination of correlating terms is a painful and tedious procedure. Moreover the convergence of the regression process does not depend on good starting values like the estimation of the camera model's parameters does.

A disadvantage of the machine learning approach is that it does not give meaningful parameters such as position and orientation in space or the camera's focal length. Moreover, it does not take into account situations where the exact spatial positions of the training examples are unknown, whereas classical camera calibration allows for an improvement of the spatial position in the training process.

The time complexity for all algorithms is $\mathcal{O}(m^3)$ for training and $\mathcal{O}(n)$ for the computation of the predictions, where m denotes the number of training examples and n the number of test examples. In both training procedures, matrices with a size in the order of the number of training examples have to be inverted at each iteration step. So the actual time needed also depends on the number of iteration steps, which scale with the number of parameters and can be assumed constant for this application. Without improving the spatial coordinates, the time complexity for the training of the camera model would be $\mathcal{O}(p^3)$, where p denotes the number of parameters. But since were are also updating the spatial observations, the number of parameters is upper bounded by a multiple of the number of training examples such that the matrix inversion in (7) is in $\mathcal{O}(m^3)$. An additional advantage of GP is the amount of time actually needed for computing the predictions. Although predicting new spatial points is in $\mathcal{O}(n)$ for GP and the camera model, predictions with the camera model always consume more time. This is due to the improvements of the initial prediction with a linear estimator which again is an iterative procedure involving an inversion of a matrix of constant size at each step (cf. end of section 2).

Acknowledgements. CER was supported by the German Research Council (DFG) through grant RA 1030/1.

References

1. Thomas Luhmann: Nahbereichsphotogrammetrie - Grundlagen, Methoden und Anwendungen. Wichmann (2000) [in German]
2. Nello Cristianini and John Shawe-Taylor: Support Vector Machines - and other kernel-based methods. Cambridge University Press (2000)
3. Steven M. Kay: Statistical Signal Processing Vol. I. Prentice Hall (1993)
4. S. Sundararajan, S.S. Keerthi: Predictive Approaches for Choosing Hyperparameters in Gaussian Processes. Neural Computation 13, 1103-1118 (2001). MIT
5. C. K. I. Williams and C. E. Rasmussen: Gaussian processes for regression. Advances in Neural Information Processing Systems 8 pp. 514-520 MIT Press (1996)
6. Fabian Sinz: Kamerakalibrierung und Tiefenschätzung - Ein Vergleich von klassischer Bündelblockausgleichung und statistischen Lernalgorithmen.
   http://www.kyb.tuebingen.mpg.de/~fabee (2004) [in German]
7. Steffen Abraham, Wolfgang Förstner: Zur automatischen Modellwahl bei der Kalibrierung von CCD-Kameras. 19. DAGM-Symposium Mustererkennung 1997. Springer Verlag pp. 147-155

Learning to Find Graph Pre-images

Gökhan H. Bakır[1], Alexander Zien[1], and Koji Tsuda[1,2]

[1] Max Planck Institute for Biological Cybernetics
Dept. Schölkopf, Spemannstraße 38, 72076 Tübingen, Germany
[2] AIST Computational Biology Research Center
2-43, Aomi, Koto-ku, Tokyo, 135-0064, Japan
{goekhan.bakir, alexander.zien, koji.tsuda}@tuebingen.mpg.de
http://www.tuebingen.mpg.de/index.html

Abstract. The recent development of graph kernel functions has made it possible to apply well-established machine learning methods to graphs. However, to allow for analyses that yield a graph as a result, it is necessary to solve the so-called pre-image problem: to reconstruct a graph from its feature space representation induced by the kernel. Here, we suggest a practical solution to this problem.

1 Introduction

Many successful classical machine learning methods are originally linear and operate on vectorial data, e.g. PCA, k-means clustering and SVM. As these algorithms can be expressed in terms of dot products only, their scope is extended by kernelization [8]: the dot products are replaced by a kernel function, which implicitly maps input data into a vectorial space (the feature space). Kernelization not only makes the algorithms effectively non-linear (in input space), but also allows them to work on structured data. For example, kernels on strings and graphs were proposed in [3], leading to text classification systems [5] or a chemical compound classification system [7], where every chemical compound is considered as an undirected graph.

Once a suitable kernel function is developed, the kernel approach works fine for algorithms with numerical output (like regression, classification or clustering). If the output shall be a point in the space of the original (structured) data, additionally the pre-image problem has to be solved: a point in the featuer space must be mapped back to the input space. For example, outputs in input space are desired when averages of input data are computed or elements optimizing some criteria are sought for; other applications are described in [1].

The pre-image problem can be formalized as follows. We are given a positive definite kernel function k which computes dot products of pairs of members $\mathbf{g}, \mathbf{g}'$ of an input space $\mathcal{G}$. The kernel induces some Reproducing Kernel Hilbert Space (RKHS) $\mathcal{F}$, called the feature space, and a mapping $\phi : \mathcal{G} \to \mathcal{F}$, such that $k(\mathbf{g}, \mathbf{g}') = \langle \phi(\mathbf{g}), \phi(\mathbf{g}') \rangle$ [8]. Finally, we are given the feature space representation $\psi = \phi(\mathbf{g}^*)$ of a desired output $\mathbf{g}^*$. Then the pre-image problem consists of finding $\mathbf{g}^*$. Note that this is often not possible, since $\mathcal{F}$ is usually a far larger space than

C.E. Rasmussen et al. (Eds.): DAGM 2004, LNCS 3175, pp. 253–261, 2004.

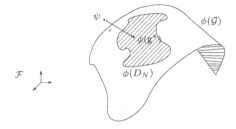

Fig. 1. Searching for pre-images $\mathbf{g}^*$ of a point ψ given in feature space $\mathcal{F}$, corresponds to finding the nearest point $\phi(\mathbf{g}^*)$ on a nonlinear manifold.

$\mathcal{G}$ (see Figure 1). In these cases, the (approximate) pre-image $\mathbf{g}^*$ is chosen such that the squared distance of ψ and $\phi(\mathbf{g}^*)$ is minimized,

$$\mathbf{g}^* = \arg\min_{\mathbf{g}} \|\psi - \phi(\mathbf{g})\|^2. \tag{1}$$

A general learning-based framework for finding pre-images is described in [1]. The pre-image problem is particularly challenging with input spaces of discrete structures like strings or graphs, because it is difficult to apply gradient-based optimization to combinatorial problems. For strings, it is often possible to take advantage of their linear structure, for example by dynamic programming; a different, but also incremental approach is presented in [1].

In this paper we consider the pre-image problem for graphs. More precisely, we take the input space $\mathcal{G}$ to be the set of node-labeled graphs, and assume the kernel k to be the graph kernel described in [7]. For this setting, we propose an algorithm to approximate the pre-image of a graph $\mathbf{g}^* \in \mathcal{G}$ of a point $\psi \in \mathcal{F}$. To our knowledge, no such algorithm has been published before. In contrast to the computation of intermediate graphs [4], our approach also allows for extrapolation. Furthermore, it can be directly used with a large number of established machine learning algorithms.

There are many potential applications of pre-images of graphs. One example would be the reconstruction of finite automata or the regular languages represented by them. Probably the most intriguing scenario is the synthesis of molecules, the 2D representations of which are essentially labeled, undirected graphs. Since molecules with appropriate properties serve for examples as chemical materials or as drugs, their directed design is very attractive. Correspondingly, some work on the *de novo* design of drugs has been done. One strategy, persued in [6], is to focus on linear chain molecules (like RNA and peptides). This makes the problem much easier, but restricts applicability. A rather general genetic algorithm for molecular design is presented in [9]. While it could, in principle, also be used to optimize our criterion (1), it does not take advantage of the structure of the RKHS implied by the kernel function. Thus, our approach is probably better suited for use in combination with kernel methods that rely on this kernel.

In the following section, we briefly review the used kernel for labeled graphs, and its induced feature space geometry. Thereafter, we present the main contribution: a proposed method to approximate pre-images for undirected graphs. In the experimental section, we demonstrate its feasibility with a linear interpolatation between two molecules represented as graphs. We conclude by discussing weaknesses and further directions.

2   Comparing Graphs: The Marginalized Graph Kernel

In the following we consider node-labeled, undirected graphs $\mathbf{g} = (v, E)$, where the nodes are identified with the set $V = \{1, \ldots, |\mathbf{g}|\}$, $|\mathbf{g}|$ is the order of the graph, the function $v : V \rightarrow \Sigma$ supplies the labels of the nodes which are taken from some finite set Σ, and $E \in \{0, 1\}^{|\mathbf{g}| \times |\mathbf{g}|}$ is the adjacency matrix, i.e. $e(i, j) = 1$ iff there is an edge between nodes i and j. $\mathcal{G}$ denotes the set of all possible graphs.

We briefly review the marginalized graph kernel introduced in [7], basically following the notation used there while omitting edge labels. Let $\Omega(\mathbf{g})$ denote the set of all possible node paths $\mathbf{h}$ on a graph $\mathbf{g} = (V, E)$, i.e. $\mathbf{h} \in V^n$ satisfies $E(\mathbf{h}_i, \mathbf{h}_{i+1}) = 1$ for every $i < n$; $|\mathbf{h}| := n$ is the path length. We define a probability distribution $p(\mathbf{h}|\mathbf{g})$ over $\Omega(\mathbf{g})$ by considering random walks with start probability $p_s(i)$ at node i, a constant termination probability $p_q(i) = \lambda$ and a transition probability $p_t(i, j)$ which is positive only for edges, i.e. if $E(i, j) = 1$. Therefore the posterior probability for a path $\mathbf{h}$ is described as

$$p(\mathbf{h}|\mathbf{g}) = p_s(\mathbf{h}_1) \prod_{i=2}^{|\mathbf{h}|} p(\mathbf{h}_i|\mathbf{h}_{i-1}) p_e(\mathbf{h}_i). \tag{2}$$

Now any kernel k_h on node paths induces a kernel on graphs via

$$k(\mathbf{g}, \mathbf{g}') = \mathbb{E}_{\mathbf{h}, \mathbf{h}'}[k_h(\mathbf{h}, \mathbf{h}')] = \sum_{\mathbf{h} \in \Omega(\mathbf{g})} \sum_{\mathbf{h}' \in \Omega(\mathbf{g}')} k_h(\mathbf{h}, \mathbf{h}') p(\mathbf{h}|\mathbf{g}) p(\mathbf{h}'|\mathbf{g}'). \tag{3}$$

In the following, we will only consider the matching kernel (or δ-kernel) on the *labels* of the nodes visited by the pathes:

$$k_h(\mathbf{h}, \mathbf{h}') = \begin{cases} 1 \text{ if } |\mathbf{h}| = |\mathbf{h}'| \wedge \bigwedge_{i=1}^{|\mathbf{h}|} v_{\mathbf{h}_i} = v'_{\mathbf{h}'_i} \\ 0 \text{ otherwise} \end{cases} \tag{4}$$

For the efficient computation of the graph kernel, it is convenient to define the following matrices:

$$s(\mathbf{h}_1, \mathbf{h}'_1) = \delta(v_{\mathbf{h}_1}, v_{\mathbf{h}'_1}) p_s(\mathbf{h}_1) p_s(\mathbf{h}'_1),$$
$$T(\mathbf{h}_k, \mathbf{h}_{k-1}, \mathbf{h}'_k, \mathbf{h}'_{k-1}) = \delta(v_{\mathbf{h}_k}, v_{\mathbf{h}'_k}) p(\mathbf{h}_k|\mathbf{h}_{k-1}) p(\mathbf{h}'_k|\mathbf{h}'_{k-1}), \tag{5}$$
$$q(\mathbf{h}_i, \mathbf{h}'_j) = p_e(\mathbf{h}_i) p_e(\mathbf{h}'_j).$$

Substituting (2), (4) and (5) into (3), one can derive a compact form of the graph kernel (see [7] for details):

$$k(\mathbf{g}, \mathbf{g}') = \mathbf{s}(\mathbf{g}, \mathbf{g}')^\top (\mathbf{I} - T(\mathbf{g}, \mathbf{g}'))^{-1} \mathbf{q}(\mathbf{g}, \mathbf{g}'). \tag{6}$$

3   Pre-images for Undirected Graphs

In the following we discuss an approximative solution to the problem stated in equation (1), that is we reconstruct the graph $\mathbf{g}^*$ given its representation ψ in feature space $\mathcal{F}$, such that $\phi(\mathbf{g}^*)$ is as close as possible to ψ. Note that solving problem (1) requires to determine the vertex label set $\Sigma_v^* \in \mathbf{g}^*$ and the adjacency matrix $E^* \in \mathbf{g}^*$. Since joint optimization over the discrete set Σ_v and the adjacency matrix A is not feasible, we introduce a sequential approach to solve (1) approximately. This is quite natural, since the structure of the adjacency matrix depends on the size and the labels of the label set Σ_v.

We assume in the following that the point ψ is expressed as a linear combination of some given points $\{\phi(\mathbf{g}_1), \ldots, \phi(\mathbf{g}_N)\} \in D_N$, that is

$$\sum_{i=1}^{N} \alpha_i \phi(\mathbf{g}_i) = \psi. \tag{7}$$

This assumption is always satisfied in the case of kernel methods. In the following we will use relation (7) of the given data D_N to ψ and properties of the marginalized graph kernel to infer Σ^* and E^*.

3.1   Determining the Order of the Graph

It may come as a surprise that the kernel values do not contain information about the graph sizes. To see why this is the case, consider an easy example. Fix an arbitrary graph $\mathbf{g}$ and its kernel values with other graphs. Now consider the graph $2\mathbf{g}$ which is defined by duplicating $\mathbf{g}$, i.e. it consists of two unconnected copies of $\mathbf{g}$. Thus, the start probabilities (for each copy of each node) are divided by two, while the transition and termination probabilities remain unchanged. Thus, for each of the two copies, the feature space representation (the histogram of label pathes) is also divided by two. Adding the histograms of the two copies (which corresponds to using the combined graph) recovers the original feature space representation. Therefore, all kernel values have to be the same.

Since the kernel does not help in determining the size, we have to make use of heuristics. Below, we consider three simple ideas to fix $m^* := |\mathbf{g}^*|$, the size of $\mathbf{g}^*$: (i) linear combination of the input graph sizes; (ii) exhaustive search in a range; and (iii) learning (regression).

An intuitive idea is to determine m^* as a linear combination of the input graph sizes. It is natural to give each input graph the same amount (α_i) of influence on the size of $\mathbf{g}$ as it has on $\mathbf{g}$. Thus we have the weighted average

$$m^* = \frac{\sum_{i=1}^{N} \alpha_i m_i}{\sum_{i=1}^{N} \alpha_i},$$

where m_i is the size of graph $\mathbf{g}_i$.

For exhaustive search we need to restrict ourselves to a finite range of plausible sizes, for example between minimum and maximum size of the input graphs.

Then a tentative graph is reconstructed for each size in the range, and the one best approximating ψ is chosen afterwards.

The most sophisticated approach is to *learn* the graph size. Since we have example graphs given in D_N, we can state the order estimation as a regression problem: Using the kernel map, we explicitly construct features x_i, $1 \leq i \leq N$ by $x_i = (k(\mathbf{g}_i, \mathbf{g}_1), \ldots, k(\mathbf{g}_i, \mathbf{g}_N)) \in \mathbb{R}^N$. Letting $y_i = |\mathbf{g}_i|$, we can apply any regression method to estimate their dependence on the x. Learning the graph order has the advantage that it does not use any knowledge of the graph kernel itself, but has the disadvantage to be the computationally most expensive approach. Once the order $|\mathbf{g}^*|$ is estimated, we are able to determine the vertices in $\Sigma_v^* \in \mathbf{g}^*$.

3.2   Determining the Vertex Set

The vertex set Σ_v^* contains the labels of vertices in the graph $\mathbf{g}^*$. Determining Σ_v^* requires to decide if a label v_i is a member of Σ_v^*, and if so, how many times it appears in the graph. To answer these two questions, we will use special properties of the marginalized graph kernel. We introduce the *trivial* graph, $\mathbf{g}_{v_i}$, which consists just of one vertex $v_i \in \Sigma$ and zero edges. A random walk on the trivial graph $\mathbf{g}_{v_i}$ creates a single path of length 1 consisting of the single vertex label v_i itself. Reconsidering the terms appearing in the graph kernel, one sees that the only nonzero terms are

$$s(\mathbf{h}_1 = v_i, \mathbf{h}_1' = v_i) = p_s(\mathbf{h}_1' = v_i),$$
$$q(\mathbf{h}_1 = v_i, \mathbf{h}_1' = v_i) = p_e(\mathbf{h}_1 = v_i)p_e(\mathbf{h}_1' = v_i),$$

while $T \in \mathbb{R}^{|\mathbf{g}| \times |\mathbf{g}|}$ becomes a zero matrix. Assuming a constant termination probability $p_e(v_k) = \lambda$ and uniform start probabilities $p_s(\mathbf{h}_1 = v_k) = 1/m_i$, the evaluation of the graph kernel yields

$$k(\mathbf{g}_{v_k}, \mathbf{g}_i) = m_{ik} \cdot p_s(\mathbf{h}_i = v_k) \cdot p_e^2(v_k) = m_{ik} \cdot \lambda^2/m_i,$$
$$k(\mathbf{g}_{v_k}, \mathbf{g}_*) = m_{*k} \cdot p_s(\mathbf{h}_* = v_k) \cdot p_e^2(v_k) = m_{*k} \cdot \lambda^2/m_*,$$

where m_{ik} and m_{*k} denote the numbers of occurrence of the label v_k in the graph $\mathbf{g}_i$ and $\mathbf{g}_*$, respectively.

We are now able to find the vertex set by solving for m_{*k}:

$$m_{*k} = k(\mathbf{g}_{v_k}, \mathbf{g}_*) \cdot m_*/\lambda^2 = \frac{m_*}{\lambda^2} \sum_{i=1}^{N} \alpha_i \lambda^2 \frac{m_{ik}}{m_i} = m_* \sum_{i=1}^{N} \alpha_i \frac{m_{ik}}{m_i}. \tag{8}$$

The last equality shows that the fractions m_{*k}/M_* of labels in $\mathbf{g}_*$ are just the linear combinations of the fractions in the input graphs. This can be combined with any preset order m_* of $\mathbf{g}_*$.

3.3   Estimating the Adjacency Matrix

As a final step, we have to determine the adjacency matrix E. Since the adjacency matrix consists of boolean variables, and our objective function is not linear, the optimal solution would require to solve a non-convex non-linear combinatorial optimization problem. We therefore propose a stochastic search approach.

We define the distance of a graph $\mathbf{g}$ to the point ψ as the distance of the image $\phi(\mathbf{g})$ to ψ, the square of which can be calculated by

$$d^2(\mathbf{g}, \mathbf{g}^*) = \|\phi(\mathbf{g}) - \psi\|^2 = k(\mathbf{g}, \mathbf{g}) - 2\sum_{i=1}^{N} \alpha_i k(\mathbf{g}, \mathbf{g}_i) + \sum_{i,j=1}^{N} \alpha_i \alpha_j k(\mathbf{g}_i, \mathbf{g}_j).$$

Let $D_k = \{\mathbf{g}_1, \ldots, \mathbf{g}_k\} \subset D_N$ be the set of k nearest neighbors to ψ. Starting from that set, we construct a Markov chain $\hat{\mathbf{g}}_0, \hat{\mathbf{g}}_1, \ldots$, that is $P(\hat{\mathbf{g}}_{i+1}|\hat{\mathbf{g}}_0, \hat{\mathbf{g}}_1, \ldots, D_k) = P(\hat{\mathbf{g}}_{i+1}|\hat{\mathbf{g}}_i, D_k)$, with the property that

$$d(\hat{\mathbf{g}}_{i+1}, \mathbf{g}^*) \leq d(\hat{\mathbf{g}}_i, \mathbf{g}^*)$$

and $\hat{\mathbf{g}}_i$ being the actual state of the Markov chain. New proposal states are created by sampling from the vicinity of graphs in $D_k \cup \{\hat{\mathbf{g}}_i\}$ and are rejected if the distance to ψ is larger than the actual state.

Before we describe the sampling strategy in detail, we define the *spread* $\chi(D_s)$ of an arbitrary set $D_s = \{\mathbf{g}_1, \ldots, \mathbf{g}_s\}$ as the sample variance of the feature coordinates $\{k_{D_s}(\mathbf{g}_1), \ldots, k_{D_N}(\mathbf{g}_s)\}$ with $k_{D_N}(\mathbf{g}) = (k(\mathbf{g}, \mathbf{g}_1), \ldots, k(\mathbf{g}, \mathbf{g}_N))^{\top}$ and $\mathbf{g}_1, \ldots, \mathbf{g}_N \in D_N$.

Now that we have defined spread, we can propose a sampling strategy. For each graph $\mathbf{g}_s \in D_k \cup \{\hat{\mathbf{g}}_i\}$, we generate a set $\mathsf{G}_{\mathbf{g}_s}$ of l new graphs $\mathbf{g}_s^{(t)} \in \mathsf{G}_{\mathbf{g}_s}$, $1 \leq t \leq l$ by randomly inserting and deleting edges to $\mathbf{g}_s$. Since the spread $\chi(\mathsf{G}_{\mathbf{g}_s})$ corresponds to the size of the sampled area in $\mathcal{G}$, we require the distance $d(\mathbf{g}_s, \mathbf{g}^*)$ to be proportional to $\chi(\mathsf{G}_{\mathbf{g}_s})$. That is, the further the graph $\mathbf{g}_s$ is from $\mathbf{g}^*$, the more diverse will the generated set $\mathsf{G}_{\mathbf{g}_s}$ be. This can be achieved by using a monotone function $f : \mathbb{R} \to \mathbb{N}$, which maps the distance $d(\mathbf{g}_s, \mathbf{g}^*)$ to the number of random modifications. For example the natural logarithm with a proper scaling of the distance can be used: $f(d(\mathbf{g}_s, \mathbf{g}^*)) = \lceil \log(\alpha \cdot d(\mathbf{g}_s, \mathbf{g}^*)) \rceil$. We are now ready to formulate the stochastic search for the adjacency matrix E^* of $\mathbf{g}^*$.

Algorithm 1   *Let $\hat{\mathbf{g}}_0 = \arg\min_{\mathbf{g}} D_N$ be the nearest neighbor of ψ in D_N.*
  Let D_k be the set consisting of k nearest neighbors of ψ in D_N.
  Let $i = 1$.
  While $r < r_{max}$
- *Generate l new proposal graphs $\{\mathbf{g}_s^{(t)}\}_{t=1}^{l} =: G_{\mathbf{g}_s}$ for each $\mathbf{g}_s \in D_k \cup \{\hat{\mathbf{g}}_i\}$ by adding and deleting $f(d(\mathbf{g}_s, \mathbf{g}^*))$ edges.*
- *$\hat{\mathbf{g}}_{new} = \arg\min_{\mathbf{g} \in \bigcup_{s=1}^{k} G_{\mathbf{g}_s}} \|\phi(\mathbf{g}) - \psi\|$.*
- *If $d(\hat{\mathbf{g}}_{new}, \mathbf{g}^*) \leq d(\hat{\mathbf{g}}_i, \mathbf{g}^*)$*
      $\hat{\mathbf{g}}_{i+1} = \hat{\mathbf{g}}_{new}$, $i = i + 1$, $r = 0$
    else
      $r = r + 1$

The stochastic search is stopped if it could not find k_{max} times a better $\mathbf{g}^*$.

4   Experiment: Graph Interpolation

In this section, we will demonstrate the introduced technique to interpolate between two randomly selected graphs of the Mutag dataset [2] consisting of 230 molecules (aromatic and heteroaromatic nitro compounds). The vertex labels identify the atom types and edge labels indicate the bonding type. For our experiment we ignore the edge label information and just set the adjacency entries to 1 if there exists any type of bond between two atoms (0 otherwise).

For the graph kernel, we use the same parameter $\lambda = 0.03$ as in [7]. We select randomly two molecules which we denote by $\mathbf{g}_1$, $\mathbf{g}_2$ and set $\psi = \alpha\phi(\mathbf{g}_1) + (1 - \alpha)\phi(\mathbf{g}_2)$. We perform algorithm 1 for every $\alpha \in [0, 0.1, \ldots, 1]$, where we use $k = 5$ nearest neighbors. We used $r_{max} = 10$ and $l = 500$ in our simulation. A series of resulting graphs is shown in Figure 2. The quality of the computed pre-images is compared to the nearest neighbor approach in Figure 3. The pre-images have much smaller distances to ψ than the nearest neighbor in the database.

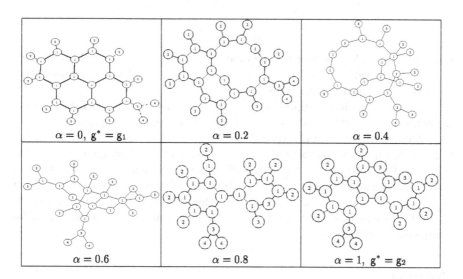

Fig. 2. Pre-images for interpolated graphs (using the marginalized graph kernel) found by stochastic search by Algorithm 1.

5   Discussion and Outlook

We presented a pre-image technique for graphs. The stochastic search approach is able to synthesize graph pre-images, if there are examples in the vicinity of the pre-image. However, where no examples are provided in the region of the pre-image, the quality of the found pre-image also decreases (i.e., its distance increases). This phenomenon is illustrated as the correlation between the two measures shown in Figure 3. A likely explanation is that the generation of graphs (the proposal states in Section 3.3) fails to sample the space in the direction

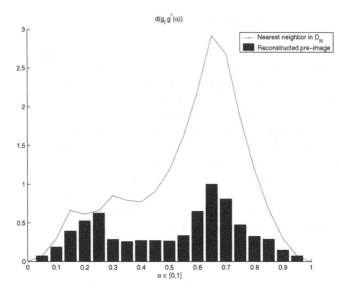

Fig. 3. The distance of the reconstructed graph $\phi(\hat{g}_i)$ to $\alpha\phi(g_1) + (1 - \alpha)\phi(g_1)$ vs. the distance of the nearest neighbor in D_N. The maximum reconstruction error was used for normalization.

towards ψ. We plan to improve the quality of the stochastic search method by using *a priori* knowledge of the pre-image to be found, and also to explore other stochastic optimization techniques.

Although chemical engineering provides a strong motivation for our work, we point out that this paper deals with pre-images of general graphs, and that almost no use is made of the special properties of molecular graphs. As an important example, the numbers of incident bonds (edges) must agree to the atom types (node labels). Such properties will have to be taken into account for serious applications to chemical problems. However, this paper takes an important first step towards molecular engineering within the powerful RKHS framework, which allows to utilize many established algorithms, and may provide a basis for many other applications.

References

1. G. H. Bakır, J. Weston, and B. Schölkopf. Learning to find pre-images. In S. Thrun, L. Saul, and B. Schölkopf, editors, *Advances in Neural Information Processing Systems (NIPS 2003)*, Cambridge, MA, 2004. MIT Press. to appear.
2. A.K. Debnath, R.L. Lopez de Compadre, G. Debnath, A.J. Shustermann, and C. Hansch. Structure-Activity Relationship of Mutagenic Aromatic and Heteroaromatic Nitro Compounds. Correlation with Molecular Orbital Energies and Hydrophobicity. *J Med Chem*, 34:786–797, 1991.
3. D. Haussler. Convolutional kernels on discrete structures. Technical Report UCSC-CRL-99-10, Computer Science Department, U. of California at Santa Cruz, 1999.
4. X. Jiang, A. Münger, and H. Bunke. On Median Graphs: Properties, Algorithms, and Applications. *IEEE Transactions on Pattern Analysis and Machine Intelligence*, 23(10):1144–1151, October 2001.

5. T. Joachims. Text categorization with support vector machines: Learning with many relevant features. In Claire Nédellec and Céline Rouveirol, editors, *Proceedings of the European Conference on Machine Learning*, pages 137–142, Berlin, 1998. Springer.
6. S. Kamphausen, N. Holtge, F. Wirsching, C. Morys-Wortmann, D. Riester, R. Goetz, M. Thurk, and A. Schwienhorst. Genetic algorithm for the design of molecules with desired properties. *J Comput Aided Mol Des*, 16(8-9):551–567, 2002.
7. H. Kashima, K. Tsuda, and A. Inokuchi. Marginalized kernels between labeled graphs. In *Proceedings of the 20th International Conference on Machine Learning*, pages 321–328, Menlo Park, CA, 2003. AAAI Press.
8. B. Schölkopf and A. J. Smola. *Learning with Kernels*. MIT Press, Cambridge, MA, 2002.
9. H. M. Vinkers, M. R. de Jonge, F. F. Daeyaert, J. Heeres, L. M. Koymans, J. H. van Lenthe, P. J. Lewi, H. Timmerman, K. Van Aken, and P. A. Janssen. SYNOPSIS: SYNthesize and OPtimize System in Silico. *J Med Chem*, 46(13):2765–2773, 2003.

Multivariate Regression via Stiefel Manifold Constraints

Gökhan H. Bakır, Arthur Gretton, Matthias Franz, and Bernhard Schölkopf

Max Planck Institute for Biological Cybernetics
{gb,ag,mof,bs}@tuebingen.mpg.de
http://www.tuebingen.mpg.de/index.html
Dept. Schölkopf, Spemannstraße 38, 72076 Tübingen, Germany

Abstract. We introduce a learning technique for regression between high-dimensional spaces. Standard methods typically reduce this task to many one-dimensional problems, with each output dimension considered independently. By contrast, in our approach the feature construction and the regression estimation are performed jointly, directly minimizing a loss function that we specify, subject to a rank constraint. A major advantage of this approach is that the loss is no longer chosen according to the algorithmic requirements, but can be tailored to the characteristics of the task at hand; the features will then be optimal with respect to this objective, and dependence between the outputs can be exploited.

1 Introduction

The problem of regressing between a high dimensional input space and a *continuous, univariate* output has been studied in considerable detail: classical methods are described in [5], and methods applicable when the input is in a reproducing kernel Hilbert space are discussed in [8]. When the output dimension is high (or even infinite), however, is becomes inefficient or impractical to apply univariate methods separately to each of the outputs, and specialized multivariate techniques must be used.

We propose a novel method for regression between two spaces $\mathcal{F}_x$ and $\mathcal{F}_y$, where both spaces can have arbitrarily large dimension. Our algorithm works by choosing low dimensional subspaces in both $\mathcal{F}_x$ and $\mathcal{F}_y$ for each new set of observations made, and finding the mapping between these subspaces for which a particular loss is small.[1] There are several reasons for learning a mapping between low dimensional subspaces, rather than between $\mathcal{F}_x$ and $\mathcal{F}_y$ in their entirety. First, $\mathcal{F}_x$ and $\mathcal{F}_y$ may have high dimension, yet our data are generally confined to smaller subspaces. Second, the outputs may be statistically dependent, and learning all of them at once allows us to exploit this dependence. Third, it is common practice (for instance in principal component regression (PCR)) to ignore certain directions in the input and/or output spaces, which decreases the variance in the regression coefficients (at the expense of additional bias): this is a form of regularization.

Given a particular subspace dimension, classical multivariate regression methods use a variety of heuristics for subspace choice.[2] The mapping between subspaces is then

---

[1] The loss is specified by the user.

[2] For instance, PCR generally retains the input directions with highest *variance*, whereas partial least squares (PLS) approximates the input directions along which *covariance* with the outputs is high.

C.E. Rasmussen et al. (Eds.): DAGM 2004, LNCS 3175, pp. 262–269, 2004.

achieved as a second, independent step. By contrast, our method, Multivariate Regression via Stiefel Constraints (MRS), jointly optimises over the subspaces *and* the mapping; its goal is to find the subspace/mapping *combination* with the smallest possible loss. Drawing on results from differential geometry [3], we represent each subspace projection operator as an element on a Stiefel manifold. Our method then conducts gradient descent over these projections.

We begin our discussion in Section 2 with some basic definitions, and give a formal description of the multivariate regression setting. In Section 3, we introduce the MRS procedure for the L_2 loss. Finally, in Section 4, we apply our method in estimating a high dimensional image denoising transformation.

2   Problem Setting and Motivation

We first describe our regression setting in more detail, and introduce the variables we will use. We are given m pairs of input and output variables, $z := ((\mathbf{x}_1, \mathbf{y}_1), \dots, (\mathbf{x}_m, \mathbf{y}_m))$, where $\mathbf{x}_i \in \mathcal{F}_x$, $\mathbf{y}_i \in \mathcal{F}_y$, and $\mathcal{F}_x$ and $\mathcal{F}_y$ are reproducing kernel Hilbert spaces[3] with respective dimension l_x and l_y. We write the matrices of *centered* observations as

$$\mathbf{X} := \begin{bmatrix} \mathbf{x}_1 \dots \mathbf{x}_m \end{bmatrix} \mathbf{H}, \quad \mathbf{Y} := \begin{bmatrix} \mathbf{y}_1 \dots \mathbf{y}_m \end{bmatrix} \mathbf{H},$$

where $\mathbf{H} := \mathbf{I} - \frac{1}{m} \mathbf{1}\mathbf{1}^\top$, and $\mathbf{1}$ is the $m \times 1$ matrix of ones.

We now specify our learning problem: given observations $\mathbf{X}$ and $\mathbf{Y}$, and a loss function $L(\mathbf{Y}, \mathbf{X}, \mathbf{F}_{(r)})$, we want to find the best predictor $\mathbf{F}_{(r)}$, defined as

$$\mathbf{F}_{(r)} = \min_{\mathbf{G} \in \mathcal{H}_{(r)}} L(\mathbf{Y}, \mathbf{X}, \mathbf{G}), \tag{1}$$

where

$$\mathcal{H}_{(r)} := \left\{ \mathbf{F} \in \mathcal{F}_y^{\mathcal{F}_x} \mid \operatorname{rank} \mathbf{F} = r \right\} \tag{2}$$

and $\mathcal{F}_y^{\mathcal{F}_x}$ denotes the set of linear mappings from $\mathcal{F}_x$ to $\mathcal{F}_y$. This rank constraint is crucial to our approach: it allows us to restrict ourselves to subspaces *smaller* than those spanned by the input and/or output observations, which can reduce the variance in our estimate of the mapping $\mathbf{F}_{(r)}$ while increasing the bias. We select the rank that optimises over this bias/variance tradeoff using cross validation.

As we shall see in Section 3, our approach is not confined to any particular loss function. That said, in this study we address only the *least squares* loss function,

$$L_2(\mathbf{Y}, \mathbf{X}, \mathbf{F}_{(r)}) = \| \mathbf{Y} - \mathbf{F}_{(r)} \mathbf{X} \|_F^2, \tag{3}$$

where the F subscript denotes the Frobenius norm.

---

[3] A reproducing kernel Hilbert space is a Hilbert space $\mathcal{F}_x$ for which at each $x \in \mathcal{X}$, the point evaluation functional, $\delta_x : \mathcal{F}_x \to \mathbb{R}$, which maps $f \in \mathcal{F}_x$ to $f(x) \in \mathbb{R}$, is continuous. To each reproducing kernel Hilbert space, there corresponds a unique positive definite kernel $k : \mathcal{X} \times \mathcal{X} \to \mathbb{R}$ (the reproducing kernel), which constitutes the inner product on this space; this is guaranteed by the Moore-Aronszajn theorem. See [7] for details.

We now transform the rank constraint in (1) and (2) into a form more amenable to optimisation. By diagonalizing the predictor $\mathbf{F}_{(r)}$ via its singular basis, we obtain

$$\mathbf{F}_{(r)} = \mathbf{V}_{(r)} S_{(r)} \mathbf{W}_{(r)}{}^{\top}, \tag{4}$$

where

$$\mathbf{V}_{(r)}{}^{\top}\mathbf{V}_{(r)} = \mathbf{I}_{r,r}, \tag{5}$$

$$\mathbf{W}_{(r)}{}^{\top}\mathbf{W}_{(r)} = \mathbf{I}_{r,r}, \tag{6}$$

$$S \in \text{diagonal } \mathbb{R}^{r \times r}. \tag{7}$$

In other words, $\mathbf{W}_{(r)} \in \mathbb{S}(l_y, r)$ and $\mathbf{V}_{(r)} \in \mathbb{S}(l_x, r)$, where $\mathbb{S}(n, r)$ is called the *Stiefel* manifold, and comprises the matrices with n rows and r orthonormal columns. In the L_2 case, finding a rank constrained predictor (4) is thus equivalent to finding the triplet $\theta = (\mathbf{V}_{(r)}, S_{(r)}, \mathbf{W}_{(r)})$ for which

$$\theta = \underset{\mathbf{V}_{(r)}, S_{(r)}, \mathbf{W}_{(r)}}{\arg\min} \|\mathbf{Y} - \mathbf{V}_{(r)} S_{(r)} \mathbf{W}_{(r)}{}^{\top}\mathbf{X}\|_F^2, \tag{8}$$

subject to constraints (5)-(7).[4] We will refer to $\mathbf{W}_{(r)}$ and $\mathbf{V}_{(r)}$ as *feature matrices*.

It is clear from (8) that the columns of $\mathbf{W}_{(r)}$ and $\mathbf{V}_{(r)}$ form a basis for particular subspaces in $\mathcal{F}_x$ and $\mathcal{F}_y$ respectively, and that the regression procedure is a mapping between these subspaces. A number of classical multivariate regression methods, such as multivariate PCR and PLS, also have this property; although the associated subspaces are not chosen to optimise a user specified loss function. In the next section, we introduce an optimization technique – based on concepts borrowed from differential geometry – to solve (8) *directly*.

3   Multivariate Regression via Stiefel Constraints

In this section, we present a direct solution of the optimisation problem defined in (1) and (2). We begin by noting that the alternative statement of the rank constraint (2), which consists in writing the mapping $\mathbf{F}_{(r)}$ in the form (4), still leaves us with a non-trivial optimisation problem (8). To see this, let us consider an iterative approach to obtain an approximate solution to (8), by constructing a sequence of predictors $\mathbf{F}_{(r)_1}, \ldots, \mathbf{F}_{(r)_i}$ such that

$$\mathsf{L}(\mathbf{X}, \mathbf{Y}, \mathbf{F}_{(r)_i}) \geq \mathsf{L}(\mathbf{X}, \mathbf{Y}, \mathbf{F}_{(r)_{i+1}}). \tag{9}$$

We might think to obtain this sequence by updating $\mathbf{V}_{i+1}$, S_{i+1} and $\mathbf{W}_{i+1}$ according to their *free* matrix gradients $\frac{\partial \mathsf{L}}{\partial \mathbf{V}}|_{\theta_i}$, $\frac{\partial \mathsf{L}}{\partial S}|_{\theta_i}$, and $\frac{\partial \mathsf{L}}{\partial \mathbf{W}}|_{\theta_i}$ respectively, where θ_i denotes the solution $(\mathbf{V}_i, \mathbf{W}_i, S_i)$ at the ith iteration (*i.e.*, the point at which the gradients are evaluated). This is unsatisfactory, however, in that updating $\mathbf{V}$ and $\mathbf{W}$ linearly along their free gradients does *not* result in matrices with orthogonal columns.

---

[4] This is a more general form of the *Procrustes* problem [1] for which $\mathbf{F}_{(r)}$ is orthogonal rather than being rank constrained.

Thus, to define a sequence along the lines of (9), we must first show how to optimise over $\mathbf{V}$ and $\mathbf{W}$ in such a way as to retain orthogonal columns. As we saw in Section 2, the feature matrices are elements on the Stiefel manifold; thus any optimisation procedure must take into account the geometrical structure of this manifold. The resulting optimisation problem is *non-convex*, since the Stiefel manifold $\mathbb{S}(n, r)$ is not a convex set.

In the next subsection, we describe how to update $\mathbf{V}$ and $\mathbf{W}$ as we move along geodesics on the Stiefel manifold $\mathbb{S}(n, r)$. In the subsection that follows it, we use these updates to conduct the minimisation of the L_2 loss.

3.1 Dynamics on Stiefel Manifolds

We begin with a description of the geodesics for the simpler case of $\mathbb{S}(n, n)$, followed by a generalisation to $\mathbb{S}(n, r)$ when $n > r$. Let $O(n)$ denote the group of orthogonal matrices. Suppose we are given a matrix $\mathbf{V}(t) \in O(n)$ that depends on a parameter t, such that for t in some interval $[t_a, t_b]$, $\mathbf{V}(t)$ describes a geodesic on the manifold $O(n)$. Our goal in this subsection is to describe how $\mathbf{V}(t)$ changes as we move along the geodesic. Since $O(n)$ is not only a manifold but also a *Lie group* (a special manifold whose elements form a group), there is an elegant way of moving along geodesics which involves an exponential map. We will give an informal but intuitive derivation of this map; for a formal treatment, see [3, 2]. We begin by describing a useful property of the derivative of $\mathbf{V}(t)$;

$$\mathbf{I} = \mathbf{V}(t)^\top \mathbf{V}(t),$$

$$\mathbf{0} = \frac{d}{dt}\left(\mathbf{V}(t)^\top \mathbf{V}(t)\right),$$

$$\mathbf{0} = \left(\frac{d}{dt}\mathbf{V}(t)\right)^\top \mathbf{V}(t) + \mathbf{V}(t)^\top \left(\frac{d}{dt}\mathbf{V}(t)\right),$$

$$\mathbf{0} = \mathbf{Z}(t)^\top + \mathbf{Z}(t),$$

with

$$\mathbf{Z}(t) := \mathbf{V}(t)^\top \left(\frac{d}{dt}\mathbf{V}(t)\right). \tag{10}$$

It follows that $\mathbf{Z}(t)$ is skew symmetric, which we write as $\mathbf{Z}(t) \in \sim(n, n)$, where $\sim$ consists of the set of all skew symmetric matrices of size $n \times n$. For particular curves corresponding to 1-parameter subgroups of $O(n)$, we can show that $\mathbf{Z}(t)$ is constant. Thus (10) becomes an ordinary differential equation of the form

$$\frac{d}{dt}\mathbf{V}(t) = \mathbf{V}(t)\mathbf{Z} \tag{11}$$
$$\text{with } \mathbf{V}(0) = \mathbf{V},$$

which has solution

$$\mathbf{V}(t) = \mathbf{V}(0)e^{t\mathbf{Z}}, \tag{12}$$

where $e^{\mathbf{Z}}$ denotes the matrix exponential [4].[5] We can see from (11) that the skew-symmetric matrix $\mathbf{Z}$ specifies a tangent at point $\mathbf{V}(0)$ on the Stiefel manifold $\mathbb{S}(n,n)$.

We now generalize to the case where $\mathbf{V}$ does not have full rank, *i.e.* $\mathbf{V} \in \mathbb{S}(n,r)$ and $r < n$. We can embed $\mathbb{S}(n,r)$ into $O(n)$ by extending any $\mathbf{V} \in \mathbb{S}(n,r)$ with an $n - r$ matrix $\mathbf{V}_\perp \in \mathbb{S}(n, n-r)$ such that $\mathbb{R}^n = \mathbf{V}_\perp \oplus \mathbf{V}$. Therefore $\mathbf{V}_\perp$ spans the orthogonal complement to the space spanned by the columns of $\mathbf{V}$. Two orthogonal matrices $\mathbf{A}, \mathbf{B}$ in $O(n)$ are considered to be the same from the viewpoint of $\mathbb{S}(n,r)$ if they relate as

$$\mathbf{B} = [\mathbf{I}_{n,r}, \mathbf{P}] \, \mathbf{A} \tag{13}$$

for any matrix $\mathbf{P} \in \mathbb{S}(n, n - r)$, where $\mathbf{I}_{n,r}$ contains the first r columns of the $n \times n$ unit matrix. We can thus replace $\mathbf{V}(t)$ by $[\mathbf{V}(t), \mathbf{V}_\perp(t)]$ in (11) (with a small abuse of notation), to get

$$\frac{d}{dt} [\mathbf{V}(t), \mathbf{V}_\perp(t)] \bigg|_{t=0} = [\mathbf{V}(0), \mathbf{V}_\perp(0)] \, \hat{\mathbf{Z}} \tag{14}$$

and

$$\mathbf{V}(t) = [\mathbf{V}(0), \mathbf{V}_\perp(0)] \, e^{t\hat{\mathbf{Z}}} [\mathbf{I}_{n,r}, \mathbf{0}]. \tag{15}$$

For the gradient descent, we need to find the tangent direction $\hat{\mathbf{G}}$ (which replaces the tangent direction $\mathbf{Z}$ in (12)) that is as close as possible to the free gradient $\mathbf{G}$, since $\mathbf{G}$ does not generally have the factorization (11). The constrained gradient $\hat{\mathbf{G}}$ can be calculated directly by projecting the free gradient onto the tangent space of $\mathbf{V}$; see [3]. Intuitively speaking, we do this by removing the symmetric part of $\mathbf{G}^\top \mathbf{V}$, leaving the skew symmetric remainder.[6] The constrained gradient is thus

$$\hat{\mathbf{G}} = \mathbf{G} - \mathbf{V}\mathbf{G}^\top \mathbf{V}. \tag{16}$$

Finally, the skew symmetric matrix $\hat{\mathbf{Z}} \in \mathbb{R}^{n \times n}$ is given by (10) as

$$\hat{\mathbf{Z}} = \begin{pmatrix} \hat{\mathbf{G}}^\top \mathbf{V} & -(\hat{\mathbf{G}}^\top \mathbf{V}_\perp)^\top \\ \hat{\mathbf{G}}^\top \mathbf{V}_\perp & \mathbf{0} \end{pmatrix}. \tag{17}$$

We can now describe the nonlinear update operator π_{Stiefel}.

Algorithm 1 ($\pi_{\text{Stiefel}}(\mathbf{V}, \mathbf{G}, t)$) *Given a free gradient* $\mathbf{G} \in \mathbb{R}^{n,r}$, *a matrix* $\mathbf{V} \in \mathbb{S}(n,r)$ *with orthogonal columns, and a scalar step parameter* γ, *the update of* $\mathbf{V}$ *specified by* $\mathbf{G}$ *and* γ *can be calculated as follows:*

1) Calculate constrained gradient in (16).
2) Calculate basis $\mathbf{V}_\perp$ *for the orthogonal complement of* $\mathbf{V}$.
3) Calculate the tangent coordinates $\mathbf{Z}$ *in (17).*
4) $\mathbf{V}(\gamma) = [\mathbf{V}, \mathbf{V}_\perp] e^{\gamma \mathbf{Z}} [\mathbf{I}_{n,r}, \mathbf{0}].$

---

[5] When verifying that (12) is indeed a solution for (11), note that the skew-symmetric matrix $\mathbf{Z}$ is *normal, i.e.* $\mathbf{Z}\mathbf{Z}^\top = \mathbf{Z}^\top \mathbf{Z}$.

[6] Note that any square matrix can be expressed as a unique sum of a symmetric and a skew-symmetric matrix.

3.2 Multivariate Regression with L_2 Loss

Now that we have defined π_{Stiefel}, we can apply a gradient descent approach to (8). We first calculate the free gradients,

$$\frac{\partial L_2}{\partial \mathbf{V}}|_{\theta_i} = -\mathbf{Y}\mathbf{X}^\top \mathbf{W}_i S_i, \tag{18}$$

$$\frac{\partial L_2}{\partial \mathbf{W}}|_{\theta_i} = -\mathbf{X}\mathbf{Y}^\top \mathbf{V}_i S_i + \mathbf{X}\mathbf{X}^\top \mathbf{W}_i S_i^2, \tag{19}$$

$$\frac{\partial L_2}{\partial S}|_{\theta_i} = -\mathbf{I}_{r,r} \odot \mathbf{W}_i^\top \mathbf{X}\mathbf{Y}^\top \mathbf{V}_i$$
$$+ \mathbf{I}_{r,r} \odot \mathbf{W}_i^\top \mathbf{X}\mathbf{X}^\top \mathbf{W}_i S_i, \tag{20}$$

where $\odot$ denotes the Hadamard (element-wise) product. The multivariate regression algorithm for the L_2 loss is then:

Algorithm 2 *MRS for L_2 loss function.*

Initialization
$\quad \mathbf{V}_0 = \mathbf{I}_{l_x,r} \quad S_0 = \mathbf{I}_{r,r} \quad \mathbf{W}_0 = \mathbf{I}_{l_y,r}$
$\quad \theta_0 = (\mathbf{V}_0, S_0, \mathbf{W}_0) \quad \mathbf{F}_{(r)_0} = \mathbf{W}_0 S_0 \mathbf{V}_0 \quad i = 0$
Repeat until convergence:
$\quad$ *1) Calculate free gradients, equations (18)-(20)*
$\quad$ *2)* $t_\mathbf{V}^*, t_S^*, t_\mathbf{W}^* = \arg\min_{t_\mathbf{V}, t_S, t_\mathbf{W}} L_2(\mathbf{V}(t_\mathbf{V}), S(t), \mathbf{W}(t_\mathbf{W}))$
$\qquad$ *with* $\mathbf{W}(t_\mathbf{W}) = \pi_{stiefel}(\mathbf{W}_i, \frac{\partial \mathcal{L}}{\partial \mathbf{W}}|_{\theta_i}, t_\mathbf{W})$,
$\qquad \quad \mathbf{V}(t_\mathbf{V}) = \pi_{stiefel}(\mathbf{V}_i, \frac{\partial \mathcal{L}}{\partial \mathbf{V}}|_{\theta_i}, t_\mathbf{V})$,
$\qquad$ *and* $S(t) = S_i + t_S \frac{\partial \mathcal{L}}{\partial S}|_{\theta_i}$
$\quad$ *3)* $\mathbf{V}_{i+1} = \mathbf{V}(t_\mathbf{V}^*), \mathbf{W}_{i+1} = \mathbf{W}(t_\mathbf{W}^*), S_{i+1} = S(t_S^*)$
$\quad$ *4)* $\mathbf{F}_{(r)_{i+1}} = \mathbf{V}_{i+1} S_{i+1} \mathbf{W}_{i+1}$
$\quad$ *5)* $\theta_{i+1} = (\mathbf{V}_{i+1}, S_{i+1}, \mathbf{W}_{i+1})$
$\quad$ *6)* $i = i + 1$
After convergence : $\mathbf{F}_{(r)} = \mathbf{F}_{(r)_i}$

4 Application Example: Image Restoration

We demonstrate the application of MRS to an artificial image restoration task. The goal is to restore the corrupted part of an image, given examples of corrupted images and the corresponding clean images. The images are taken from the USPS postal database, which consists of 16×16 grayscale patches representing handwritten digits. We independently perturbed the gray values of each pixel in the lower half of each image with Gaussian noise having standard deviation 0.1. Our data consisted of 2000 digits chosen at random, with 1000 reserved for training.

To perform restoration, we first applied kernel PCA to extract 500 nonlinear features from the noisy digits,[7] using a Gaussian kernel of width 10. Thus the restoration task

---

[7] For more detail on this feature extraction method, see [8]

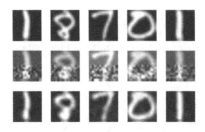

Fig. 1. Example of image denoising using MRS. Each column contains a hand-written digit chosen at random from the 1000 images in our test set. The first row displays the original images, the second row contains the noisy images, and the third row shows the images as reconstructed using MRS.

is a regression problem with a 500 dimensional input space $\mathcal{F}_x$, where we predict the *entire* clean digits in a 256 dimensional output space $\mathcal{F}_y$.

In our experiments, we compared ridge regression (RR), PLS, and MRS. We used the ridge parameter $1e - 6$, which we optimised using 5-fold cross validation. For our PLS solution, we used a rank 123 mapping, again finding this optimal rank with 5-fold cross validation. We initialised MRS using a low rank approximation to the predictor $\mathbf{F}_{(r)_{RR}}$ found by ridge regression. To do this, we decomposed $\mathbf{F}_{(r)_{RR}}$ as $\mathbf{U}S\mathbf{V}^{\top}$ via the singular value decomposition, and set $\mathbf{U}_0$ and $\mathbf{V}_0$ to be the first 110 components (determined by cross validation on the MRS solution) of $\mathbf{U}$ and $\mathbf{V}$ respectively, while initialising $S_0 = \mathbf{I}$. We give sample outcomes in Figure 1, and a summary of the results in Table 1. We also give the result obtained by simply using the first 110 components of the SVD of $\mathbf{F}_{(r)_{RR}}$: the performance is worse than both ridge regression and MRS.

In this image restoration task, it appears that MRS performs substantially better than PLS while using a lower dimensional mapping, which validates our method for optimising over input and output subspaces. In addition, MRS has a small advantage over ridge regression in eliminating irrelevant features from the subspaces used in prediction (whereas RR shrinks the weights assigned to *all* the features).

Table 1. Test error (using squared loss) of MRS, PLS, and RR for the digit restoration problem, with results averaged over 1000 digits. The first column gives the performance of RR alone. The second column uses a low rank (*i.e.* rank 110) approximation to the RR solution. The third and fourth columns respectively show the PLS and MRS results with the rank in parentheses, where MRS was initialised using the low rank RR solution.

	RR	RR(110)	PLS(123)	MRS(110)
RMSE	552.5 ± 0.1	554.9 ± 0.1	648.5 ± 0.1	$\mathbf{550.53 \pm 0.1}$

5   Conclusions

We have introduced a novel method, MRS, for performing regression on multivariate problems of high dimension, and demonstrated its performance in removing noise from images. We anticipate that this method will readily generalise to additional settings with high dimensional outputs: examples include regression to a reproducing kernel Hilbert space (of high or even infinite dimension), which can be used to recover images from incomplete or corrupted data; or as a means of classification, through mapping to a suitable output space [10]; and regression between discrete spaces, such as graphs [9,6], on which similarity measures may be defined via kernels.

References

1. A. W. Bojanczyk and A. Lutoborski. The Procrustes problem for orthogonal Stiefel matrices. *SIAM Journal on Scientific Computing*, 21(4):1291–1304, 2000.
2. M. Crampin and F. A. E. Pirani. *Applicable Differential Geometry*. Cambridge University Press, Cambridge, U. K., 1986.
3. A. Edelman, T. A. Arias, and S. T. Smith. The geometry of algorithms with orthogonality constraints. *SIAM Journal on Matrix Analysis and Applications*, 20(2):303–353, 1999.
4. G. H. Golub and C. F. Van Loan. *Matrix Computations*. John Hopkins University Press, Baltimore, MD, 3rd edition, 1996.
5. T. Hastie, R. Tibshirani, and J. Friedman. *The Elements of Statistical Learning*. Springer, New York, 2001.
6. H. Kashima, K. Tsuda, and A. Inokuchi. Marginalized kernels between labeled graphs. In *ICML 2003*, pages 321–328, 2003.
7. S. Saitoh. *Theory of Reproducing Kernels and its Applications*. Longman Scientific & Technical, Harlow, England, 1988.
8. B. Schölkopf and A. J. Smola. *Learning with Kernels*. MIT Press, Cambridge, MA, 2002.
9. A.J. Smola and R. Kondor. Kernels and regularization on graphs. In *Proceedings of the Annual Conference on Computational Learning Theory and Kernel Workshop*. Springer, 2003.
10. J. Weston, O. Chapelle, A. Elisseeff, B. Schölkopf, and V. Vapnik. Kernel dependency estimation. In *Advances in Neural Information Processing Systems*, volume 15, Cambridge, MA, USA, 2003. MIT Press.

Hilbertian Metrics on Probability Measures and Their Application in SVM's

Matthias Hein, Thomas Navin Lal, and Olivier Bousquet

Max Planck Institute for Biological Cybernetics
Spemannstr. 38
72076 Tuebingen, Germany
{matthias.hein, navin.lal, olivier.bousquet}@tuebingen.mpg.de

Abstract. In this article we investigate the field of Hilbertian metrics on probability measures. Since they are very versatile and can therefore be applied in various problems they are of great interest in kernel methods. Quit recently Topsøe and Fuglede introduced a family of Hilbertian metrics on probability measures. We give basic properties of the Hilbertian metrics of this family and other used metrics in the literature. Then we propose an extension of the considered metrics which incorporates structural information of the probability space into the Hilbertian metric. Finally we compare all proposed metrics in an image and text classification problem using histogram data.

1   Introduction

Recently the need for specific design of kernels for a given data structure has been recognized by the kernel community. One type of structured data are probability measures $\mathcal{M}_+^1(\mathcal{X})^1$ on a probability space $\mathcal{X}$. The following examples show the wide range of applications of this class of kernels:

- Direct application on probability measures e.g. histogram data [1].
- Having a statistical model for the data one can first fit the model to the data and then use the kernel to compare two fits, see [5,4].
- Given a bounded probabiliy space $\mathcal{X}$ one can use the kernel to compare sets in that space, by putting e.g. the uniform measure on each set.

In this article we study instead of positive definite (PD) kernels the more general class of conditionally positive definite (CPD) kernels. Or to be more precise we concentrate on Hilbertian metrics, that are metrics d which can be isometrically embedded into a Hilbert space, that is $-d^2$ is CPD. This choice can be justified by the fact that the support vector machine (SVM) only uses the metric information of the CPD[2] kernel, see [3], and that every CPD kernel is generated by a Hilbertian metric.

We propose a general method to build Hilbertian metrics on $\mathcal{M}_+^1(\mathcal{X})$ from

---

[1] $\mathcal{M}_+^1(\mathcal{X})$ denotes the set of positive measures μ on $\mathcal{X}$ with $\mu(\mathcal{X}) = 1$
[2] Note that every PD kernel is a CPD kernel.

C.E. Rasmussen et al. (Eds.): DAGM 2004, LNCS 3175, pp. 270–277, 2004.
© Springer-Verlag Berlin Heidelberg 2004

Hilbertian metrics on $\mathbb{R}_+$. Then we completely characterize the Hilbertian metrics on $\mathcal{M}^1_+(\mathcal{X})$ which are invariant under the change of the dominating measure using results of Fuglede. As a next step we introduce a new family of Hilbertian metrics which incorporates similarity information of the probability space. Finally we support the theoretical analysis by two experiments. First we compare the performance of the basic metrics on probability measures in an image and text classification problem. Second we do the image classification problem again but now using similarity information of the color space.

2   Hilbertian Metrics

An interesting subclass of metrics is the class of Hilbertian metrics, that are metrics which can be isometrically embedded into a Hilbert space. In order to characterize this subclass of metrics, we first introduce the following function class:

Definition 1. *A real valued function k on $\mathcal{X} \times \mathcal{X}$ is positive definite (PD) (resp. conditionally positive definite (CPD)) if and only if k is symmetric and $\sum_{i,j}^n c_i c_j k(x_i, x_j) \geq 0$, for all $n \in \mathbb{N}$, $x_i \in \mathcal{X}, i = 1, ..., n$, and for all $c_i \in \mathbb{R}, i = 1, ..., n$, (resp. for all $c_i \in \mathbb{R}, i = 1, ..., n$, with $\sum_i^n c_i = 0$).*

The following theorem describes the class of Hilbertian metrics:

Theorem 1 (Schoenberg [6]). *A metric space $(\mathcal{X}, d)$ can be embedded isometrically into a Hilbert space if and only if $-d^2(x, y)$ is CPD.*

What is the relevance of this notion for the SVM? Schölkopf showed that the class of CPD kernels can be used in SVM's due to the translation invariance of the maximal margin problem in the RKHS, see [7]. Furthermore it is well known that the maximal margin problem is equivalent to the optimal separation of the convex hulls of the two classes. This was used in [3] to show that the properties of the SVM only depend on the Hilbertian metric. That is all CPD kernels are generated by a Hilbertian metric $d(x, y)$ through $k(x, y) = -d^2(x, y) + g(x) + g(y)$ where $g : \mathcal{X} \to \mathbb{R}$ and the solution of the SVM only depends on the Hilbertian metric $d(x, y)$.

3   Hilbertian Metrics on Probability Measures

It would be very ambitious to address the question of all possible Hilbertian metrics on probability measures. Instead we restrict ourselves to a special family. Nevertheless this special case encompasses almost all measures previously used in the machine learning community. In the first section we use recent results of Fuglede and Topsøe, which describe all α-homogeneous[3], continuous Hilbertian (semi)-metrics on $\mathbb{R}_+$[4]. Using these results it is straightforward to characterize all Hilbertian metrics on $\mathcal{M}^1_+(\mathcal{X})$ of a certain from. In the second part we extend the framework and incorporate similarity information of $\mathcal{X}$.

---

[3] That means $d^2(c\,p, c\,q) = c^\alpha d^2(p, q)$ for all $c \in \mathbb{R}_+$

[4] $\mathbb{R}_+$ is the positive part of the real line with 0 included

3.1 Hilbertian Metrics on Probability Measures Derived from Hilbertian Metrics on $\mathbb{R}_+$

For simplicity we will first only treat the case of discrete probability measures on $D = \{1, 2, \ldots, N\}$, where $1 \leq N \leq \infty$. Given a Hilbertian metric d on $\mathbb{R}_+$ it is easy to see that the metric $d_{\mathcal{M}_+^1}$ given by $d_{\mathcal{M}_+^1}^2(P, Q) = \sum_{i=1}^{N} d_{\mathbb{R}_+}^2(p_i, q_i)$ is a Hilbertian metric on $\mathcal{M}_+^1(D)$. The following proposition extends the simple discrete case to the general case of a Hilbertian metric on a probability space $\mathcal{X}$. In order to simplify the notation we define $p(x)$ to be the Radon-Nikodym derivative $(dP/d\mu)(x)$ [5] of P with respect to the dominating measure μ.

Proposition 1. *Let P and Q be two probability measures on $\mathcal{X}$, μ an arbitrary dominating measure[6] of P and Q and $d_{\mathbb{R}_+}$ a 1/2-homogeneous Hilbertian metric on $\mathbb{R}_+$. Then $d_{\mathcal{M}_+^1(\mathcal{X})}$ defined as*

$$d_{\mathcal{M}_+^1(\mathcal{X})}^2(P, Q) := \int_{\mathcal{X}} d_{\mathbb{R}_+}^2(p(x), q(x)) d\mu(x), \tag{1}$$

is a Hilbertian metric on $\mathcal{M}_+^1(\mathcal{X})$. $d_{\mathcal{M}_+^1(\mathcal{X})}$ is independent of the dominating measure μ.

Proof. First we show by using the 1/2-homogeneity of $d_{\mathbb{R}_+}$ that $d_{\mathcal{M}_+^1(\mathcal{X})}$ is independent of the dominating measure μ. We have

$$\int_{\mathcal{X}} d_{\mathbb{R}_+}^2 \left(\frac{dP}{d\mu}, \frac{dQ}{d\mu} \right) d\mu = \int_{\mathcal{X}} d_{\mathbb{R}_+}^2 \left(\frac{dP}{d\nu} \frac{d\nu}{d\mu}, \frac{dQ}{d\nu} \frac{d\nu}{d\mu} \right) \frac{d\mu}{d\nu} d\nu = \int_{\mathcal{X}} d_{\mathbb{R}_+}^2 \left(\frac{dP}{d\nu}, \frac{dQ}{d\nu} \right) d\nu$$

where we use that $d_{\mathbb{R}_+}^2$ is 1-homogeneous. It is easy to show that $-d_{\mathcal{M}_+^1(\mathcal{X})}^2$ is conditionally positive definite, simply take for every $n \in \mathbb{N}$, $P_1, \ldots, P_n$ the dominating measure $\frac{\sum_{i=1}^{n} P_i}{n}$ and use that $-d_{\mathbb{R}_+}^2$ is conditionally positive definite.

It is in principle very easy to construct Hilbertian metrics on $\mathcal{M}_+^1(\mathcal{X})$ using an arbitrary Hilbertian metric on $\mathbb{R}_+$ and plugging it into the definition (1). But the key property of the method we propose is the independence of the metric d on $\mathcal{M}_+^1(\mathcal{X})$ of the dominating measure. That is we have generated a metric which is invariant with respect to general coordinate transformations on $\mathcal{X}$, therefore we call it a covariant metric. For example the euclidean norm on $\mathbb{R}_+$ will yield a metric on $\mathcal{M}_+^1(\mathcal{X})$ but it is not invariant with respect to arbitrary coordinate transformations. We think that this could be the reason why the naive application of the linear or the Gaussian kernel yields worse results than Hilbertian metrics resp. kernels which are invariant, see [1,5].

Quite recently Fuglede completely characterized the class of homogeneous Hilbertian metrics on $\mathbb{R}_+$. The set of all 1/2-homogeneous Hilbertian metrics on $\mathbb{R}_+$ characterizes then all invariant Hilbertian metrics on $\mathcal{M}_+^1(\mathcal{X})$ of the form (1).

---

[5] In $\mathbb{R}^n$ the dominating measure μ is usually the Lebesgue measure. In this case we can think of $p(x)$ as the normal density function.

[6] Such a dominating measure always exists take, e.g. $M = (P + Q)/2$.

Theorem 2 (Fuglede [2]). *A symmetric function* $d : \mathbb{R}_+ \times \mathbb{R}_+ \to \mathbb{R}_+$ *with* $d(x, y) = 0 \iff x = y$ *is a γ-homogeneous, continuous Hilbertian metric d on $\mathbb{R}_+$ if and only if there exists a (necessarily unique) non-zero bounded measure $\mu \geq 0$ on $\mathbb{R}_+$ such that d^2 can be written as*

$$d^2(x, y) = \int_{\mathbb{R}_+} \left| x^{(\gamma+i\lambda)} - y^{(\gamma+i\lambda)} \right|^2 d\mu(\lambda)$$

Topsøe proposed the following family of 1/2-homogeneous Hilbertian metrics.

Theorem 3 (Topsøe, Fuglede). *The function* $d : \mathbb{R}_+ \times \mathbb{R}_+ \to \mathbb{R}$ *defined as:*

$$d^2_{\alpha|\beta}(x, y) = \frac{\alpha\beta}{\beta - \alpha} \left[\left(\frac{x^\alpha + y^\alpha}{2} \right)^{1/\alpha} - \left(\frac{x^\beta + y^\beta}{2} \right)^{1/\beta} \right] \tag{2}$$

is a 1/2-homogeneous Hilbertian metric on $\mathbb{R}_+$, if $1 \leq \alpha \leq \infty$, $1/2 \leq \beta \leq \alpha$. Moreover $-d^2$ is strictly CPD except when $\alpha = \beta$ or $(\alpha, \beta) = (1, 1/2)$.

Obviously one has $d^2_{\alpha|\beta} = d^2_{\beta|\alpha}$. Abusing notation we denote in the following the final metric on $\mathcal{M}^1_+(\mathcal{X})$ generated using (1) by the same name $d^2_{\alpha|\beta}$. The following special cases are interesting:

$$d^2_{\infty|1}(P, Q) = \frac{1}{2} \int_{\mathcal{X}} |p(x) - q(x)| d\mu(x), \quad d^2_{\frac{1}{2}|1}(P, Q) = \frac{1}{4} \int_{\mathcal{X}} (\sqrt{p(x)} - \sqrt{q(x)})^2 d\mu(x)$$

$$d^2_{1|1}(P, Q) = \frac{1}{2} \int_{\mathcal{X}} p(x) \log \left(\frac{2p(x)}{p(x) + q(x)} \right) + q(x) \log \left(\frac{2q(x)}{p(x) + q(x)} \right) d\mu(x)$$

$d^2_{\infty|1}$ is the total variation[7]. $d^2_{\frac{1}{2}|1}$ is the square of the Hellinger distance. It is induced by the positive definite Bhattacharyya kernel, see [4]. $d^2_{1|1}$ can be derived by a limit process, see [2]. It was not used in the machine learning literature before. Since it is the proper version of a Hilbertian metric which corresponds to the Kullback-Leibler divergence $D(P||Q)$, it is especially interesting. In fact it can be written with $M = (P + Q)/2$ as $d^2_{1|1}(P, Q) = \frac{1}{2} (D(P||M) + D(Q||M))$. For an interpretation from information theory, see [9]. We did not consider other metrics from this family since they all have similar properties as we show later. Another 1/2-homogeneous Hilbertian metric previously used in the machine learning literature is the modified χ^2-distance : $d^2_{\chi^2}(P, Q) = \sum_{i=1}^n \frac{(p_i - q_i)^2}{p_i + q_i}$. $d^2_{\chi^2}$ is not PD, as often wrongly assumed in the literature, but CPD. See [8] for a proof and also for the interesting upper and lower bounds on the considered metrics:

$$d^2_{\frac{1}{2}|1} \leq d^2_{\alpha|\beta} \leq d^2_{\infty|1} \leq \frac{1}{2} d_{\frac{1}{2}|1}, \quad 4d^2_{\frac{1}{2}|1} \leq d^2_{\chi^2} \leq 8d^2_{\frac{1}{2}|1}, \quad 2d^4_{\infty|1} \leq d^2_{\chi^2} \leq 2d^2_{\infty|1}$$

In order to compare all different kinds of metrics resp. kernels on $\mathcal{M}^1_+(\mathcal{X})$ which were used in the kernel community, we also considered the geodesic distance of the multinomial statistical manifold used in [5]: $d_{geo}(P, Q) =$

---

[7] This metric was implicitly used before, since it is induced by the positive definite kernel $k(P, Q) = \sum_{i=1}^n \min(p_i, q_i)$.

$\arccos(\sum_{i=1}^{N} \sqrt{p_i q_i})$. We could not prove that it is Hilbertian. In [5] they actually use the kernel $\exp(-\lambda d^2(P,Q))$ as an approximation to the first order parametrix of the heat kernel of the multinomial statistical manifold. Despite the mathematical beauty of this approach, there remains the problem that one can only show that this kernel is PD for $\lambda < \epsilon^8$. In practice ϵ is not known which makes it hard to judge when this approach may be applied.

It is worth mentioning that all the Hilbertian metrics explicitly mentioned in this section can be written as f-divergences. It is a classical result in information geometry that all f-divergences induce up to scaling the Fisher metric. In this sense all considered metrics are locally equivalent. Globally we have the upper and lower bounds introduced earlier. Therefore we expect in our experiments relatively small deviations in the results of the different metrics.

3.2   Hilbertian Metrics on Probability Measures Incorporating Structural Properties of the Probability Space

If the probability space $\mathcal{X}$ is a metric space $(\mathcal{X}, d_{\mathcal{X}})$ one can use $d_{\mathcal{X}}$ to derive a metric on $\mathcal{M}_+^1(\mathcal{X})$. One example of this kind is the Kantovorich metric:

$$d_K(P,Q) = \inf_{\mu} \left\{ \int_{\mathcal{X} \times \mathcal{X}} d(x,y) d\mu(x,y) \middle| \mu \in \mathcal{M}_+^1(\mathcal{X} \times \mathcal{X}), \pi_1(\mu) = P, \pi_2(\mu) = Q \right\}$$

where π_i denotes the marginal with respect to i-th coordinate. When $\mathcal{X}$ is finite, the Kantovorich metric gives the solution to the mass transportation problem. In a similar spirit we extend the generation of Hilbertian metrics on $\mathcal{M}_+^1(\mathcal{X})$ based on (1) by using similarity information of the probability space $\mathcal{X}$. That means we do not only compare the densities pointwise but also the densities of distinct points weighted by a similarity measure $k(x,y)$ on $\mathcal{X}$. The only requirement we need is that we are given a similarity measure on $\mathcal{X}$, namely a positive definite kernel $k(x,y)$[9]. The disadvantage of our approach is that we are not anymore invariant with respect to the dominating measure. On the other hand if one can define a kernel on $\mathcal{X}$, then one can build e.g. by the induced semi-metric a uniform measure μ on $\mathcal{X}$ and use this as a dominating measure. We denote in the following by $\mathcal{M}_+^1(\mathcal{X}, \mu)$ all probability measure which are dominated by μ.

Theorem 4. *Let k be a PD kernel on $\mathcal{X}$ and $\hat{k}$ a PD kernel on $\mathbb{R}_+$ such that*
$\int_{\mathcal{X}} \sqrt{k(x,x) \, \hat{k}(q(x), q(x))} \, d\mu(x) < \infty$, $\forall q \in \mathcal{M}_+^1(\mathcal{X}, \mu)$. *Then*

$$K(P,Q) = \int_{\mathcal{X}} \int_{\mathcal{X}} k(x,y) \, \hat{k}(p(x), q(y)) \, d\mu(x) \, d\mu(y) \tag{3}$$

is a positive definite kernel on $\mathcal{M}_+^1(\mathcal{X}, \mu) \times \mathcal{M}_+^1(\mathcal{X}, \mu)$.

Proof. Note first that the product $k(x,y)\hat{k}(r,s)$ $(x, y \in \mathcal{X}, r, s \in \mathbb{R}_+)$ is a positive definite kernel on $\mathcal{X} \times \mathbb{R}_+$. The corresponding RKHS $\mathcal{H}$ is the tensor product

---

[8] which does not imply that $-d_{geo}^2$ is CPD.

[9] Note that a positive definite kernel k on $\mathcal{X}$ always induces a semi-metric on $\mathcal{X}$ by $d_{\mathcal{X}}^2(x,y) = k(x,x) + k(y,y) - 2k(x,y)$.

of the RKHS $\mathcal{H}_k$ and $\mathcal{H}_{\hat{k}}$, that is $\mathcal{H} = \mathcal{H}_k \otimes \mathcal{H}_{\hat{k}}$. We denote the corresponding feature map by $(x, r) \to \phi_x \otimes \psi_r$. Now let us define a linear map $L_q : \mathcal{H} \to \mathbb{R}$ by

$$L_q : \phi_x \otimes \psi_r \longrightarrow \int_{\mathcal{X}} k(x, y) \hat{k}(r, q(y)) d\mu(y) = \int_{\mathcal{X}} \langle \phi_x, \phi_y \rangle_{\mathcal{H}_k} \langle \psi_r, \psi_{q(y)} \rangle_{\mathcal{H}_{\hat{k}}} d\mu(y)$$

$$\leq \|\phi_x \otimes \psi_r\|_{\mathcal{H}} \int_{\mathcal{X}} \|\phi_y \otimes \psi_{q(y)}\|_{\mathcal{H}} d\mu(y)$$

Therefore by the assumption L_q is continuous. By the Riesz lemma, there exists a vector u_q such that $\forall v \in \mathcal{H}, \langle u_q, v \rangle_{\mathcal{H}} = L_q(v)$. It is obvious from

$$\langle u_p, u_q \rangle_{\mathcal{H}} = \int_{\mathcal{X}} \langle u_p, \phi_y \otimes \psi_{q(y)} \rangle_{\mathcal{H}} d\mu(y) = \int_{\mathcal{X}^2} \langle \phi_x \otimes \psi_{p(x)}, \phi_y \otimes \psi_{q(y)} \rangle_{\mathcal{H}} d\mu(y) d\mu(x)$$

$$= \int_{\mathcal{X}^2} k(x, y) \, \hat{k}(p(x), q(y)) \, d\mu(x) \, d\mu(y)$$

that K is positive definite.

The induced Hilbertian metric D of K is given by

$$D^2(P, Q) = \int_{\mathcal{X}^2} k(x, y) \left[\hat{k}(p(x), p(y)) + \hat{k}(q(x), q(y)) - 2\hat{k}(p(x), q(y)) \right] d\mu(x) d\mu(y)$$

$$= \int_{\mathcal{X}} \int_{\mathcal{X}} k(x, y) \left\langle \psi_{p(x)} - \psi_{q(x)}, \psi_{p(y)} - \psi_{q(y)} \right\rangle d\mu(x) d\mu(y). \tag{4}$$

4   Experiments

The performance of the following Hilbertian metrics on probability distributions

$$d^2_{geo}(P, Q) = \arccos^2 \left(\sum_{i=1}^{N} \sqrt{p_i} \sqrt{q_i} \right), \qquad d^2_{\chi^2}(P, Q) = \sum_{i=1}^{N} \frac{(p_i - q_i)^2}{p_i + q_i}$$

$$d^2_H(P, Q) = \frac{1}{4} \sum_{i=1}^{N} (\sqrt{p_i} - \sqrt{q_i})^2, \qquad d^2_{TV}(P, Q) = \frac{1}{2} \sum_{i=1}^{N} |p_i - q_i|$$

$$d^2_{JS}(P, Q) = \frac{1}{2} \sum_{i=1}^{N} p_i \log \left(\frac{2p_i}{p_i + q_i} \right) + q_i \log \left(\frac{2q_i}{p_i + q_i} \right) \tag{5}$$

respectively of the transformed "Gaussian" metrics

$$d^2_{exp}(P, Q) = 1 - \exp(-\lambda d^2(P, Q)) \tag{6}$$

was evaluated in three multi-class classification tasks:
The *Reuters* data set. The documents are represented as term histograms. Following [5] we used the five most frequent classes *earn, acq, moneyFx, grain* and *crude*. We excluded documents that belong to more than one of theses classes. This resulted in a data set with 8085 examples of dimension 18635. The *WebKB* web pages data set. The documents are also represented as histograms. We

used the four most frequent classes *student, faculty, course* and *project*. 4198 documents remained each of dimension 24212 (see [5]). The *Corel* image data base. We chose the data set Corel14 as in [1], which has 14 classes. Two different features were used. First the histogram was computed directly from the RGB data second from the CIE Lab color space, which has the advantage that the euclidean metric in that space locally discriminates colors according to the human vision uniformly over the whole space. Therefore the quantization process is more meaningful in CIE Lab than in RGB space[10]. In both spaces we used 16 bins per dimension, yielding a 4096-dimensional histogram. All the data sets were split into a training (80%) and a test (20%) set . The multi-class problem was solved by one-vs-all with SVM's using the CPD kernels $K = -d^2$. For each metric d from (5) we either used the metric directly with varying penalty constants C in the SVM, or we used the transformed metric d_{exp} defined in (6) again with different penalty constants C and λ. The best parameters were found using 10-folds cross-validation from the set $C \in \{10^k \mid k = -2, -1, ..., 4\} =: R_C$ respectively $(C, \lambda) \in R_C \times \frac{1}{\sigma}\{2, 1, \frac{2}{3}, \frac{1}{2}, \frac{2}{5}, \frac{1}{3}, \frac{1}{4}, \frac{1}{5}, \frac{1}{7}, \frac{1}{10}\}$, where σ was set to $\{\frac{\pi}{4}, \frac{\sqrt{2}}{2}, \frac{\sqrt{2}}{2}, \frac{\sqrt{\log 2}}{2}, \frac{\sqrt{2}}{2}\}$ to compensate for the different maximal distances of $d_{geo}, d_{\chi^2}, d_H, d_{JS}, d_{TV}$ respectively. For the best parameters the classifier was trained then on the whole training set and its error evaluated on the test set. The results are shown in Table 1. In a second experiment we used (4) for the Corel data[11]. We employ the euclidean CIE 94 distance on the color space since it models the color perception of humans together with the compactly supported RBF $k(x, y) = (1 - \|x - y\|)^2_+$, see e.g. [10], to generate a similarity kernel for the color space. Then the same experiments are done again for the RGB histograms and the CIE histograms with all the distances except the geodesic one, since it is not of the form (1). The results are shown in rows CIE CIE94 and RGB CIE94The results show that

Table 1. The table shows the test errors with the optimal values of the parameters of C resp. C, λ found from 10-fold cross-validation. The first row of each data set is obtained using the metric directly, the second row shows the errors of the transformed metric (6).

	Geodesic			χ^2			Hellinger			JS			Total Var.		
	error	C	σ	error	C	σ	error	C	σ	error	C	σ	error	C	σ
Reuters	0.015	1		0.016	1		0.016	10^2		0.014	10		0.018	10^2	
	0.015	10	1/10	0.015	10	1/7	0.016	10	1/10	0.015	10	1/5	0.019	10^3	1/13
WebKB	0.052	1		0.046	1		0.046	1		0.045	10		0.052	1	
	0.045	10	1/2	0.048	10^3	2/5	0.044	10	1/2	0.049	10^4	2/3	0.050	10	1/10
Corel RGB	0.254	1		0.171	1		0.225	10		0.171	10		0.161	10	
	0.171	10^2	1/2	0.157	10^2	1	0.154	10^2	1	0.161	10^2	1/2	0.161	10^2	1/5
Corel CIE	0.282	1		0.179	10		0.200	10		0.196	10^3		0.186	10^2	
	0.154	10	1	0.146	10	2/5	0.139	10	2/3	0.146	10^2	2/3	0.171	10	2/3
RGB CIE94				0.161	1		0.214	10		0.168	10		0.168	10	
				0.157	10	1/4	0.164	100	1/2	0.161	100	2/3	0.157	100	1/5
CIE CIE94				0.161	10		0.182	10		0.150	10^2		0.193	10	
				0.154	10	2/5	0.143	10^2	2/5	0.146	10^2	2/3	0.179	10	2/5

---

[10] In principle we expect no difference in the results of RGB and CIE Lab when we use invariant metrics. The differences in practice come from the different discretizations.

[11] The geodesic distance cannot be used since it cannot be written in appropriate form.

there is not a "best" metric. It is quite interesting that the result of the direct application of the metric are comparable to that of the transformed "Gaussian" metric. Since the "Gaussian" metric requires an additional search for the optimal width parameter, in the case of limited computational resources the direct application of the metric seems to yield a good trade-off.

5   Conclusion

We presented a general method to build Hilbertian metrics on probability measures from Hilbertian metrics on $\mathbb{R}_+$. Using results of Fuglede we characterized the class of Hilbertian metrics on probability measures generated from Hilbertian metrics on $\mathbb{R}_+$ which are invariant under the change of the dominating measure. We then generalized this framework by incorporating a similarity measure on the probability space into the Hilbertian metric. Thus adding structural information of the probability space into the distance. Finally we compared all studied Hilbertian metrics in two text and one image classification tasks.

Acknowledgements. We would like to thank Guy Lebanon for kindly providing us with the WebKB and Reuters dataset in preprocessed from. Furthermore we are thankful to Flemming Topsøe and Bent Fuglede for providing us with preprints of their papers [9,2], to Olivier Chapelle for his help with the experiments in the early stages of this article and finally to Jeremy Hill, Frank Jäkel and Felix Wichmann for helpful suggestions on color spaces and color distances.

References

1. O. Chapelle, P. Haffner, and V. Vapnik. SVMs for histogram-based image classification. *IEEE Transactions on Neural Networks*, 10:1055–1064, 1999.
2. B. Fuglede. Spirals in Hilbert space. With an application in information theory. To appear in Expositiones Mathematicae, 2004.
3. M. Hein and O. Bousquet. Maximal margin classification for metric spaces. In *16th Annual Conference on Learning Theory (COLT)*, 2003.
4. T. Jebara and R. Kondor. Bhattacharyya and expected likelihood kernels. In *16th Annual Conference on Learning Theory (COLT)*, 2003.
5. J. Lafferty and G. Lebanon. Diffusion kernels on statistical manifolds. Technical Report CMU-CS-04-101, School of Computer Science, Carnegie Mellon University, Pittsburgh, 2004.
6. I. J. Schoenberg. Metric spaces and positive definite functions. *Trans. Amer. Math. Soc.*, 44:522–536, 1938.
7. B. Schölkopf. The kernel trick for distances. NIPS, 13, 2000.
8. F. Topsøe. Some inequalities for information divergence and related measures of discrimination. *IEEE Trans. Inform. Th.*, 46:1602–1609, 2000.
9. F. Topsøe. Jenson-shannon divergence and norm-based measures of discrimination and variation. Preprint, 2003.
10. H. Wendland. Piecewise polynomial, positive definite and compactly supported radial basis functions of minimal degree. *Adv. Comp. Math.*, 4:389–396, 1995.

Shape from Shading Under Coplanar Light Sources

Christian Wöhler

DaimlerChrysler Research and Technology, Machine Perception
P. O. Box 2360, D-89013 Ulm, Germany
christian.woehler@daimlerchrysler.com

Abstract. In this paper image-based techniques for 3D surface reconstruction are presented which are especially suitable for (but not limited to) coplanar light sources. The first approach is based on a single-image shape from shading scheme, combined with the evaluation of at least two further images of the scene that display shadow areas. The second approach allows the reconstruction of surfaces by an evaluation of quotients of images of the scene acquired under different illumination conditions and is capable of separating brightness changes due to surface shape from those caused by variable albedo. A combination of both techniques is suggested. The proposed approaches are applied to the astrogeological task of three-dimensional reconstruction of regions on the lunar surface using ground-based CCD images. Beyond the planetary science scenario, they are applicable to classical machine vision tasks such as surface inspection in the context of industrial quality control.

1 Introduction

A well-known method for image-based 3D reconstruction of surfaces is *shape from shading* (SFS). This technique aims at deriving the orientation of the surface at each pixel by using a model of the reflectance properties of the surface and knowledge about the illumination conditions.

1.1 Related Work

Traditional applications of such techniques in planetary science, mostly referred to as *photoclinometry*, rely on single images of the scene and use line-based, integrative methods designed to reveal a set of profiles along one-dimensional lines rather than a 3D reconstruction of the complete surface [1, 5]. In contrast to these approaches, *shape from shading* and *photometric stereo* techniques based on the minimization of a global error term for multiple images of the scene have been developed in the field of computer vision – for detailed surveys on the SFS and photometric stereo methodology see [1, 3]. For a non-uniform surface albedo, however, these approaches require that the directions of illumination are not coplanar [3]. Recent work in this field [6] deals with the reconstruction of planetary surfaces based on shape from shading by means of multiple images acquired from precisely known locations at different illumination conditions, provided that the reflectance properties of the surface are thoroughly modelled. In

C.E. Rasmussen et al. (Eds.): DAGM 2004, LNCS 3175, pp. 278–285, 2004.

[7] shadows are used in the context of photometric stereo with multiple non-coplanar light sources to recover locally unique surface normals from two image intensities and a zero intensity caused by shadow.

1.2   Shape from Shading: An Overview

For a single image of the scene, parallel incident light and an infinite distance between camera and object the intensity $I(u, v)$ of image pixel (u, v) amounts to

$$I(u, v) = \kappa I_i \Phi \left(\boldsymbol{n}(x, y, z), \boldsymbol{s}, \boldsymbol{v} \right). \tag{1}$$

Here, κ is a camera constant, $\boldsymbol{v}$ the direction to the camera, I_i the intensity of incident light and $\boldsymbol{s}$ its direction, and Φ the so-called *reflectance function*. A well-known example is the Lambertian reflectance function $\Phi(\boldsymbol{n}, \boldsymbol{s}) = \alpha \cos \theta$ with $\theta = \angle(\boldsymbol{n}, \boldsymbol{s})$ and α as a surface-specific constant. The product $\kappa I_i \alpha = \rho(u, v)$ is called *surface albedo*. In the following, the surface normal $\boldsymbol{n}$ will be represented by the directional derivatives $p = z_x$ and $q = z_y$ of the surface function $z(u, v)$ with $\boldsymbol{n} = (-p, -q, 1)$. The term $R(p, q) = \kappa I_i \Phi$ is called *reflectance map*. Solving the SFS problem requires to determine the surface $z(u, v)$ with gradients $p(u, v)$ and $q(u, v)$ that minimizes the average deviation between the measured pixel intensity $I(u, v)$ and the modelled reflectance $R(p(u, v), q(u, v))$. This corresponds to minimizing the *intensity error term*

$$e_i = \sum_{u,v} \left[I(u, v) - R\left((p(u, v), q(u, v)) \right) \right]^2. \tag{2}$$

Surface reconstruction based on a single monocular image with no constraints is an ill-posed problem as for a given image $I(u, v)$ there exists an infinite number of minima of e_i for the unknown values of $p(u, v)$, $q(u, v)$, and $\rho(u, v)$. A well-known method to alleviate this ambiguity consists of imposing regularization constraints on the shape of the surface. A commonly used constraint is smoothness of the surface, implying small absolute values of the directional derivatives p_x and q_x of the surface gradients p and q (cf. [1, 3]). This leads to an additional error term

$$e_s = \sum_{u,v} \left[p_x^2 + p_y^2 + q_x^2 + q_y^2 \right]. \tag{3}$$

Solving the problem of surface reconstruction then consists of globally minimizing the overall error function $e = e_s + \lambda e_i$, where the Lagrangian multiplier λ denotes the relative weight of the error terms. As explained in detail in [1–3], setting the derivatives of e with respect to the surface gradients p and q to zero leads to an iterative update rule to be repeatedly applied pixelwise until convergence of $p(u, v)$ and $q(u, v)$ is achieved. Once the surface gradients are determined, the surface profile $z(u, v)$ is obtained by numerical integration of the surface gradients as described in [3]. According to [2], constraint (3) can be replaced by or combined with the physically intuitive assumption of an integrable surface gradient vector field within the same variational framework.

The ambiguity of the solution of the shape from shading problem can only be completely removed, however, by means of *photometric stereo* techniques, i. e. by making use of several light sources. A traditional approach is to acquire $L = 3$ images of the scene (or an even larger number) at different illumination conditions represented by s_l, $l = 1, \ldots, L$. As long as these vectors are not coplanar and a Lambertian reflectance map can be assumed, a unique solution for both the surface gradients $p(u, v)$ and $q(u, v)$ and the non-uniform surface albedo $\rho(u, v)$ can be obtained analytically in a straightforward manner [3].

In many application scenarios, however, it is difficult or impossible to obtain $L \geq 3$ images acquired with non-coplanar illumination vectors s_l, $l = 1, \ldots, L$. For example, the equatorial regions of the Moon (only these appear nearly undistorted for ground-based telescopes) are always illuminated either exactly from the east or exactly from the west, such that all possible illumination vectors s are coplanar. The illumination vectors are thus given by $s_l = (-\cot \mu_l, 0, 1)$ with μ_l denoting the solar elevation angle for image l. Identical conditions occur e. g. for the planet Mercury and the major satellites of Jupiter. In scenarios beyond planetary science applications, such as visual quality inspection systems, there is often not enough space available to sufficiently distribute the light sources.

Hence, this paper proposes shape from shading techniques based on multiple images of the scene, including the evaluation of shadows, which are especially suitable for (but not limited to) the practically very relevant case of coplanar light sources, and which do not require a Lambertian reflectance map.

2   Shadow-Based Initialization of the SFS Algorithm

A uniform albedo $\rho(u, v) = \rho_0$ and oblique illumination (which is necessary to reveal subtle surface details) will be assumed throughout this section. Despite this simplification the outcome of the previously described SFS scheme is highly ambigous if only one image is used for reconstruction, and no additional information is introduced by further shading images due to the coplanarity of the illumination vectors. Without loss of generality it is assumed that the scene is illuminated exactly from the left or the right hand side. Consequently, the surface gradients $q(u, v)$ perpendicular to the direction of incident light cannot be determined accurately for small illumination angles by SFS alone unless further constraints, e. g. boundary values of $z(u, v)$ [1], are imposed.

Hence, a novel concept is introduced, consisting of a shadow analysis step performed by means of at least two further images (in the following called "shadow images") of the scene acquired under different illumination conditions (Fig. 1a). All images have to be pixel-synchronous such that image registration techniques (for a survey cf. [4]) have to be applied. After image registration is performed, shadow regions can be extracted either by a binarization of the shadow image or by a binarization of the quotient of the shading and the shadow image. The latter technique prevents surface parts with a low albedo from being erroneously classified as shadows; it will therefore be used throughout this paper. A suitable binary threshold is derived by means of histogram analysis in a straightforward

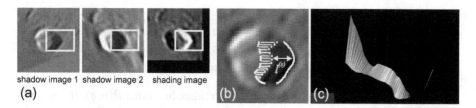

shadow image 1 shadow image 2   shading image

(a)   (b)   (c)

Fig. 1. Shadow-based initialization of the SFS algorithm. (a) Shadow and shading images. The region inside the rectangular box is reconstructed. (b) Surface part between the shadows. (c) Initial 3D profile $\tilde{z}_0(u, v)$ of the surface patch between the shadows.

manner. The extracted shadow area is regarded as being composed of S *shadow lines*. As shown in Fig. 1b, shadow line s has a length of $l^{(s)}$ pixels. This corresponds to an altitude difference $(\Delta z)_{\text{shadow}}^{(s)} = l^{(s)} \tan \mu_{\text{shadow}}$, where the angle μ_{shadow} denotes the elevation angle of the light source that produces the shadow.

Altitude difference $(\Delta z)_{\text{shadow}}^{(s)}$ can be determined at high accuracy as it is independent of a reflectance model. It is used to introduce an additional shadow-based error term e_z into the variational SFS scheme according to

$$e_z = \sum_{s=1}^{S} \left[\frac{(\Delta z)_{\text{sfs}}^{(s)} - (\Delta z)_{\text{shadow}}^{(s)}}{l^{(s)}} \right]^2. \tag{4}$$

This leads to a minimization of the overall error term $e = e_s + \lambda e_i + \eta e_z$ with η as an additional Lagrangian multiplier, aiming at an adjustment of the altitude difference $(\Delta z)_{\text{sfs}}^{(s)}$ measured on the surface profile along the shadow line to the altitude difference obtained by shadow analysis. For details cf. [8].

This concept of shading and shadow based 3D surface reconstruction is extended by initializing the SFS algorithm based on two or more shadow images, employing the following iterative scheme:

1. Initially, it is assumed that the altitudes of the ridges casting the shadows (solid line in Fig. 1b) are constant, respectively, and identical. The iteration index m is set to $m = 0$. The 3D profile $\tilde{z}_m(u, v)$ of the small surface patch between the two shadow lines (hatched area in Fig. 1b) is derived from the measured shadow lengths (Fig. 1c).
2. The surface profile $\tilde{z}_m(u, v)$ directly yields the surface gradients $p_0(u, v)$ and $q_0(u, v)$ for all pixels belonging to the surface patch between the shadow lines. They are used to compute the albedo ρ_0, serve as initial values for the SFS algorithm, and will be kept constant throughout the following steps of the algorithm. Outside the region between the shadow lines, $p_0(u, v)$ and $q_0(u, v)$ are set to zero.
3. Using the single-image SFS algorithm with the initialization applied in step 2, the complete surface profile $z_m(u, v)$ is reconstructed based on the shading image. The resulting altitudes of the ridges casting the shadows are extracted from the reconstructed surface profile $z_m(u, v)$. This yields a new profile $\tilde{z}_{m+1}(u, v)$ for the surface patch between the shadow lines.

4. The iteration index m is incremented ($m := m + 1$). The algorithm cycles through steps 2, 3, and 4 until it terminates once convergence is achieved, i. e. $\langle (z_m(u, v) - z_{m-1}(u, v))^2 \rangle_{u,v}^{1/2} < \Theta_z$. A threshold value of $\Theta_z = 0.01$ pixels is applied for termination of the iteration process.

This approach is applicable to arbitrary reflectance functions $R(p, q)$. It mutually adjusts in a self-consistent manner the altitude profiles of the floor and of the ridges that cast the shadows. It allows to determine not only surface gradients $p(u, v)$ in the direction of incident light, as it can be achieved by SFS without additional constraints, but to estimate surface gradients $q(u, v)$ in the perpendicular direction as well. Furthermore, it can be extended in a straightforward manner to more than two shadows and to shape from shading algorithms based on multiple light sources or regularization constraints beyond those described by eq. (3) and (4).

3   Quotient-Based Photometric Stereo

The second approach to SFS under coplanar light sources copes with a non-uniform albedo $\rho(u, v)$ and the very general class of reflectance maps given by $R(\rho, p, q) = \rho(u, v)\tilde{R}(p, q)$. At least two pixel-synchronous images of the scene acquired under different illumination conditions and containing no shadow areas are required. For each pixel position (u, v), the quotient $I_1(u, v)/I_2(u, v)$ of pixel intensities is desired to be identical to the quotient $R_1(u, v)/R_2(u, v)$ of reflectances. This suggests a quotient-based intensity error term

$$\tilde{e}_i = \sum_{u,v} \left(\frac{I_1(u, v)\tilde{R}_2(u, v)}{I_2(u, v)\tilde{R}_1(u, v)} - 1 \right)^2 \tag{5}$$

which is independent of the albedo (cf. [5] for a quotient-based approach for merely one-dimensional profiles). This error term can easily be extended to $L > 2$ images by computing the $L(L - 1)/2$ quotient images from all available image pairs and summing up the corresponding errors. This method allows to separate brightness changes due to surface shape from those caused by variable albedo. Similar to SFS with a single image and constant albedo, however, the values for $q(u, v)$ obtained with this approach are quite uncertain as long as the illumination vectors are coplanar, so error term (5) should be combined with the shadow-based approach of Section 2 provided that corresponding shadow information is available.

4   Experimental Results

Fig. 2 illustrates the performance of the proposed algorithms on a synthetically generated object (Fig. 2a). The shadow-based technique outlined in Section 2 and utilizing intensity error term (2) reveals the surface gradients in image v direction

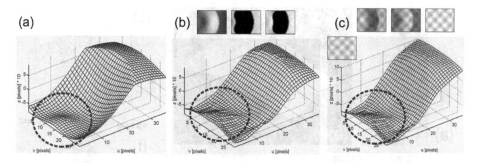

Fig. 2. Surface reconstruction of synthetic images. (a) Ground truth surface profile.
(b) One shading and two shadow images (top, $\mu_{SFS} = 175°$, $\mu_{shadow}^{(1)} = 4.0°$, $\mu_{shadow}^{(2)} = 5.0°$) along with surface profile (bottom) obtained according to Section 2. (c) Two
shading images and true albedo map (top, $\mu_{SFS}^{(1)} = 15°$, $\mu_{SFS}^{(2)} = 170°$) along with the
reconstructed surface profile and albedo map (bottom) obtained by using the quotient-
based error term (5) instead of single-image error term (2).

(dashed circles). Traditional single-image SFS as outlined in Section 1.2 is not
able to extract these surface gradients. As suggested in Section 3, the single-
image error term (2) was then replaced by the quotient-based error term (5) for
a reconstruction of the same synthetic object but now with a non-uniform albedo
(Fig. 2c). Consequently, two shading images are used in combination with the
shadow information. As a result, a similar surface profile is obtained, and the
albedo is extracted at an accuracy (root mean square error) of 1.1 percent.

For 3D reconstruction of regions on the lunar surface it is possible to use
a Lambertian reflectance map because for small parts of the lunar surface, the
relative Lambertian reflectance (an absolute calibration of the images is not
necessary) differs by only a few percent from those values derived from more
sophisticated models such as the Lunar-Lambert function [6] – the presented
framework, however, can also be applied to non-Lambertian reflectance models.
The CCD images were acquired with ground-based telescopes of 125 mm and
200 mm aperture. Image scale is 800 m per pixel.

Fig. 3 shows the reconstructed surface profile of the floor of lunar crater
Theaetetus, generated by the technique outlined in Section 2. Both the simulated
shading image and the shapes of the simulated shadows correspond well with
their real counterparts. Even the ridge crossing the crater floor, which is visible in
the upper left corner of the region of interest in Fig. 1a and in the Lunar Orbiter
photograph in Fig. 3d shown for comparison, is apparent in the reconstructed
surface profile (arrow). Furthermore, it turns out that the crater floor is inclined
from the north to the south, and a very shallow central elevation rising to about
250 m above floor level becomes apparent. This central elevation does not appear
in the images in Fig. 1a used for reconstruction, but is clearly visible in the
ground-based image acquired at higher solar elevation shown in Fig. 3e (left,
lower arrow). The simulated image (right half of Fig. 3e) is very similar to the
corresponding part of the real image although that image has not been used for

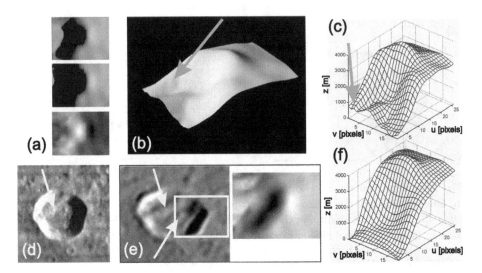

Fig. 3. Reconstruction result for the western part of lunar crater Theaetetus (see Fig. 1 for original images). (a) Simulated regions of interest. (b) Reconstructed surface profile. The z axis is two-fold exaggerated. (c) Reconstructed surface profile with absolute z values. (d) Lunar Orbiter image IV-110-H2 (not used for reconstruction). (e) Ground-based image, solar elevation $\mu = 28.7°$, real image (left) and simulated image (right). This image has not been used for reconstruction. (f) Reconstruction result obtained with traditional SFS, selecting the solution consistent with the first shadow image.

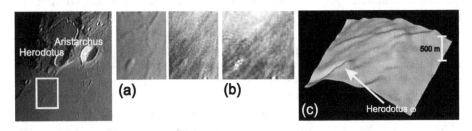

Fig. 4. Reconstruction result for the region around lunar dome Herodotus ω. (a) Original images. Solar elevation angles are $\mu_1 = 5.0°$ and $\mu_2 = 15.5°$. (b) Albedo map. (c) Reconstructed surface profile. The slight overall bending of the surface profile reflects the Moon's spherical shape.

reconstruction. This kind of comparison is suggested in [2] as an independent test of reconstruction quality. For comparison, traditional SFS as outlined in Section 1.2 yields an essentially flat crater floor and no ridge (Fig. 3f). Here, the uniform surface albedo was adjusted to yield an SFS solution consistent with the first shadow image (for details cf. [8]).

Fig. 4 shows the region around lunar dome Herodotus ω, obtained with the quotient-based approach outlined in Section 3. The images are rectified due to the proximity of this region to the moon's apparent limb. The reconstructed surface profile contains several shallow ridges with altitudes of roughly 50 m along with the lunar dome, whose altitude was determined to 160 m. The resulting albedo map displays a gradient in surface brightness from the lower right to the upper left corner along with several ray structures running radially with respect to the crater Aristarchus.

5 Summary and Conclusion

In this paper, shape from shading techniques for 3D reconstruction of surfaces under coplanar light sources are proposed. The first presented method relies on an initialization of the surface gradients by means of the evaluation of a pixel-synchronous set of at least one shading image and two shadow images and yields reliable values also for the surface gradients perpendicular to the direction of illumination. The second approach is based on at least two pixel-synchronous, shadow-free images of the scene acquired under different illumination conditions. A shape from shading scheme relying on an error term based on the quotient of pixel intensities is introduced which is capable of separating brightness changes due to surface shape from those caused by variable albedo. A combination of both approaches has been demonstrated.

In contrast to traditional photometric stereo approaches, both presented methods can cope with coplanar illumination vectors. They are successfully applied to synthetically generated data and to the 3D reconstruction of regions on the lunar surface using ground-based CCD images. The described techniques should be as well suitable for space-based exploration of planetary surfaces. Beyond the planetary science scenario, they are applicable to classical machine vision tasks such as surface inspection in the context of industrial quality control.

References

1. B. K. P. Horn. Shape from Shading. MIT Press, Cambridge, Massachusetts, 1989.
2. B. K. P. Horn. Height and Gradient from Shading. MIT technical report, 1989. http://www.ai.mit.edu/people/bkph/papers/newsfs.pdf
3. X. Jiang, H. Bunke. Dreidimensionales Computersehen. Springer-Verlag, Berlin, 1997.
4. L. Gottesfeld Brown. A Survey of Image Registration Techniques. ACM Computing Surveys, vol. 24, no. 4, pp. 325-376, 1992.
5. A. S. McEwen. Albedo and Topography of Ius Chasma, Mars. *Lunar and Planetary Science XVI*, pp. 528-529, 1985.
6. C. Piechullek. Oberflächenrekonstruktion mit Hilfe einer Mehrbild-Shape-from-Shading-Methode. Ph. D. thesis, Technical University of Munich, Munich, 2000.
7. K. Schlüns. Shading Based 3D Shape Recovery in the Presence of Shadows. *Proc. First Joint Australia & New Zealand Biennial Conference on Digital Image & Vision Computing*, Albany, Auckland, New Zealand, pp. 195-200, 1997.
8. C. Wöhler. 3D surface reconstruction by self-consistent fusion of shading and shadow features. Accepted for publication at *International Conference on Pattern Recognition*, Cambridge, UK, 2004.

Pose Estimation for Multi-camera Systems

Jan-Michael Frahm, Kevin Köser, and Reinhard Koch

Institute of Computer Science and Applied Mathematics
Hermann-Rodewald-Str. 3,
24098 Kiel, Germany
{jmf,koeser,rk}@mip.informatik.uni-kiel.de

Abstract. We propose an approach for pose estimation based on a multi-camera system with known internal camera parameters. We only assume for the multi-camera system that the cameras of the system have fixed orientations and translations between each other. In contrast to existing approaches for reconstruction from multi-camera systems we introduce a rigid motion estimation for the multi-camera system itself using all information of all cameras simultaneously even in the case of non-overlapping views of the cameras. Furthermore we introduce a technique to estimate the pose parameters of the multi-camera system automatically.

1 Introduction

Robust scene reconstruction and camera pose estimation is still an active research topic. During the last twelve years many algorithms have been developed, initially for scene reconstruction from a freely moving camera with fixed calibration [2] and later even for scene reconstruction from freely moving uncalibrated cameras [3]. All these approaches are using different self-calibration methods, which have been developed in the last decade, to estimate the internal calibration of the camera. This self-calibration can be used to estimate the internal parameters of multi-camera systems (MCS). However, all these methods still suffer from ill-conditioned pose estimation problems which cause flat minima in translation and rotation error functions [4]. Furthermore the relatively small viewing angle is also a problem which influences the accuracy of the estimation [4]. Due to these problems we introduce a new pose estimation technique which combines the information of several rigidly coupled cameras to avoid the ambiguities which occur in the single camera case. In our novel approach we estimate a rigid body motion for the MCS as a whole. Our technique combines the observations of all cameras to estimate the six degrees of freedom (translation and orientation in 3D-space) for the pose of the MCS. It exploits the fixed rotations and translations between the cameras of the MCS. These fixed rotations and translations are denoted as a *configuration* in the following. We also give a technique to determine these parameters automatically from an image sequence of the MCS.

The paper is organized as follows. At first we discuss the previous work in pose estimation from a single camera or a MCS. Afterwards we introduce our novel

C.E. Rasmussen et al. (Eds.): DAGM 2004, LNCS 3175, pp. 286–293, 2004.

pose estimation approach. In section 4 we provide a technique to automatically estimate the configuration of the MCS. Furthermore in section 5 we show some experimental results to measure the robustness of our approach.

1.1   Notation

In this subsection we introduce some notations. The projection of scene points onto an image by a calibrated camera may be modeled by the equation $x = PX$. The image point in projective coordinates is $x = [x^x, x^y, x^w]^T$, while $X = [X^x, X^y, X^z, X^w]^T$ is the 3D-world point $[\frac{X^x}{X^w}, \frac{X^y}{X^w}, \frac{X^z}{X^w}]^T$ in homogeneous coordinates and P is the 3×4 camera projection matrix. The matrix P is a rank-3 matrix. If it can be decomposed as $P = [R^T | - R^T C]$, the P-matrix is called metric, where the rotation matrix R (orientation of the camera) and the translation vector C (position of the camera) represent the Euclidian transformation between the camera coordinate system and the world coordinate system.

2   Previous Work

For a single moving camera, Fermüller et. al. discussed in [4] the ambiguities for motion estimation in the three dimensional space. They proved that there were ambiguities in estimation of translation and rotation for one camera for all types of given estimation algorithms. These ambiguities result in flat minima of the cost functions. Baker et. al. introduced in [5] a technique to avoid these ambiguities when using a MCS. For each camera the pose is estimated separately and the ambiguities are calculated before the fusion of the ambiguous subspaces is used to compute a more robust pose of the cameras. In contrast to our approach the technique of [5] does not use one pose estimation for all information from all cameras simultaneously. There is some work in the area of polydioptric cameras [7] which are in fact MCSs with usually very small translations between the camera centers. In [8] a hierarchy of cameras and their properties for 3D motion estimation is discussed. It can be seen that the pose estimation problem is well-conditioned for an MCS in contrast to the ill-conditioned problem for a single camera.

The calibration of a MCS is proposed in [5]. The line-based calibration approach is used to estimate the internal and external parameters of the MCS. For a MCS with zooming cameras a calibration approach is introduced in [9,10]. An approach for an auto-calibration of a stereo camera system is given in [1]. Nevertheless, all standard calibration, pose-estimation and structure from motion approaches for stereo camera systems exploit the overlapping views of the cameras, what is in contrast to our pose estimation approach, which does not depend on this.

3   Pose Estimation for Multi-camera Systems

In this section we introduce our novel approach for rigid motion estimation of the MCS. The only assumptions are that we have a MCS with an internal calibration K_i for each of the cameras and a fixed configuration. That assumption is valid for most of the currently used MCSs because all these systems are mounted on some type of carrier with fixed mount points. The computation of the configuration from the image sequence itself is introduced in section 4. The internal camera calibration K_i can be determined using the techniques of [10,3]. For convenience we will always talk about K-normalized image coordinates and P-matrices, therefore K_i can be omitted for pose estimation.

3.1   Relation Between World and Multi-camera System

The general structure from motion approach uses an arbitrary coordinate system $\mathcal{C}_{world}$ to describe the camera position by the rotation R of the camera, the position C of the camera center and the reconstructed scene. Normally the coordinate system $\mathcal{C}_{world}$ is equivalent with the coordinate system of the first camera. In this case the projection matrix of camera i with orientation R_i and translation C_i is given by

$$P_i = \left[R_i^T \mid - R_i^T C_i \right].$$ (1)

For a multi camera-system we use two coordinate systems during the pose estimation. The absolute coordinate system $\mathcal{C}_{world}$ is used to describe the positions of 3D-points and the pose of the MCS in the world. The second coordinate system used, $\mathcal{C}_{rig}$, is the relative coordinate system of the MCS describing the relations between the cameras (configuration). It has its origin at C_v and it is rotated by R_v and scaled isotropically by λ_v with respect to $\mathcal{C}_{world}$.

Now we discuss the transformations between the different cameras of the MCS and the transformation into the world coordinate system $\mathcal{C}_{world}$. Without loss of generality we assume all the translations ΔC_i and rotations ΔR_i of the cameras are given in the coordinate system $\mathcal{C}_{rig}$. Then with (1) the camera projection matrix of each camera in $\mathcal{C}_{rig}$ is given by

$$P_i^{\mathcal{C}_{rig}} = \left[\Delta R_i^T \mid - \Delta R_i^T \Delta C_i \right].$$ (2)

The position C_i of camera i and the orientation R_i in $\mathcal{C}_{world}$ is given by

$$C_i = C_v + \frac{1}{\lambda_v} R_v \Delta C_i, \qquad\qquad R_i = R_v \Delta R_i,$$ (3)

where translation C_v, orientation R_v and scale λ_v are the above described relations between the MCS coordinate system $\mathcal{C}_{rig}$ and the world coordinate system $\mathcal{C}_{world}$. Then the projection matrix of the camera i in $\mathcal{C}_{world}$ is given by

$$P_i = \left[\Delta R_i^T R_v^T \mid - \Delta R_i^T R_v^T (C_v + \frac{1}{\lambda_v} R_v \Delta C_i) \right].$$ (4)

With (3) we are able to describe each camera's position in dependence of the position and orientation of camera i in the coordinate system of the multi-camera system $\mathcal{C}_{rig}$ and the pose of the MCS in the world $\mathcal{C}_{world}$. Furthermore with (4) we have the transformation of world points X into the image plane of camera i in dependence of the position and orientation of the MCS and the configuration of the MCS.

3.2   Virtual Camera as a Representation of a Multi-camera System

We now introduce a *virtual camera* as a representation of the MCS, which is used to determine the position of the MCS in C_{world} independent of its configuration.

The virtual camera v which represents our MCS is at the origin of the coordinate system C_{rig} and is not rotated within this system. It follows immediately that it has position C_v and orientation R_v in C_{world} because it is rotated and translated in the same manner as the MCS. With (1) the projection matrix P_v of the virtual camera v is

$$P_v = \left[R_v^T | - R_v^T C_v \right],$$ (5)

where rotation R_v and position C_v are the above given rotation and position of the MCS. From (4) and (5) it follows that the projection matrix P_i of camera i depends on the virtual camera's projection matrix P_v :

$$P_i = \Delta R_i^T \left(P_v + \left[0_{3x3} | - \frac{1}{\lambda_v} \Delta C_i \right] \right).$$ (6)

3.3   Pose Estimation of the Virtual Camera

Now we propose a pose estimation technique for the virtual camera using the observations of all cameras simultaneously. The image point x_i in camera i of a given 3D-point X is given as $x_i \cong P_i X$, where $x_i \in \mathbb{P}^2$, $X \in \mathbb{P}^3$ and $\cong$ is the equality up to scale. With equation (6) the image point x_i depends on the virtual camera's pose by

$$x_i \cong P_i X = \Delta R_i^T \left(P_v + \left[0_{3x3} | - \frac{1}{\lambda_v} \Delta C_i \right] \right) X,$$ (7)

For a MCS with known configuration, namely camera translations ΔC_i, camera orientations ΔR_i and scale λ_v, this can be used to estimate the virtual camera's position C_v and orientation R_v in dependence of the image point x_i in camera i as a projection of 3D-point X.

Now we deduce a formulation for the estimation of the virtual camera's position C_v and orientation R_v given the translations ΔC_i, orientations ΔR_i, and scale λ_v of the cameras of the MCS. From (7) we get

$$\underbrace{\Delta R_i x_i}_{\tilde{x}_i} \cong \underbrace{P_v X - \frac{X_w}{\lambda_v} \Delta C_i}_{\hat{x}},$$

where $X = [X^x, X^y, X^z, X^w]^T \in \mathbb{P}^3$ is the 3D-point in the 3D projective space. Using the same affine space for $\tilde{x}_i$ and $\hat{x}$ leads to the following linear equations

$$X^x \tilde{x}_i^x (P_v)_{3,1} + X^y \tilde{x}_i^x (P_v)_{3,2} + X^z \tilde{x}_i^x (P_v)_{3,3} + X^w \tilde{x}_i^x (P_v)_{3,4}$$
$$- (X^x \tilde{x}_i^w (P_v)_{1,1} + X^y \tilde{x}_i^w (P_v)_{1,2} + X^z \tilde{x}_i^w (P_v)_{1,3} + X^w \tilde{x}_i^w (P_v)_{1,4}$$

$$= (\Delta \tilde{C}_i)_3 X^w \tilde{x}_i^x - (\Delta \tilde{C}_i)_1 X^w \tilde{x}_i^w, \tag{8}$$

$$X^x \tilde{x}_i^y (P_v)_{3,1} + X^y \tilde{x}_i^y (P_v)_{3,2} + X^z \tilde{x}_i^y (P_v)_{3,3} + X^w \tilde{x}_i^y (P_v)_{3,4}$$
$$- (X^x \tilde{x}_i^w (P_v)_{2,1} + X^y \tilde{x}_i^w (P_v)_{2,2} + X^z \tilde{x}_i^w (P_v)_{2,3} + X^w \tilde{x}_i^w (P_v)_{2,4})$$
$$= (\Delta \tilde{C}_i)_3 X^w \tilde{x}_i^y - (\Delta \tilde{C}_i)_2 X^w \tilde{x}_i^w \tag{9}$$

in the entries of P_v with $\tilde{x}_i = [\tilde{x}_i^x, \tilde{x}_i^y, \tilde{x}_i^w]^T$ and $\Delta \tilde{C}_i = \frac{1}{\lambda_v} \Delta C_i$.

Note that the above equations are a generalization of the case of a single camera which can be found in [1] and analogous methods to those given in [1] can be used to estimate P_v from these equations and to finally extract the unknown orientation R_v and the unknown position C_v. The extension for the MCS is that the rotation compensated image points $\tilde{x}_i$ are used and terms for the translation ΔC_i of camera i in the multi-camera coordinate system $\mathcal{C}_{rig}$ are added. In the case of pose estimation for a single camera using our approach it is assumed without loss of generality that the coordinate system $\mathcal{C}_{rig}$ is equivalent to the camera's coordinate system. Then ΔC_i vanishes and the rotation ΔR_i is the identity. In this case (8) and (9) are the standard (homogeneous) pose estimation equations from [1].

4   Calibration of the Multi-camera System

In the previous section we always assumed that we know the orientation ΔR_i and translation ΔC_i of each camera in the coordinate system $\mathcal{C}_{rig}$ and the scale λ_v between $\mathcal{C}_{rig}$ and $\mathcal{C}_{world}$. In this section we present a technique to estimate these parameters from the image sequence of a MCS with overlapping views. However, note that the simultaneous pose estimation of the MCS itself does not depend on overlapping views, once the configuration is known. Suppose we are given n cameras in the MCS and grab images at time t_0. After a motion of the MCS (time t_1), we capture the next image of each camera. We now have $2n$ frames with overlapping views, for which a standard structure-from-motion approach (for example as described in [6]) for single cameras can be applied to obtain their positions and orientations.

For each of the two groups of n cameras (the MCS at t_0 and t_1) the virtual camera is set to the first camera of the system. Then the rigid transformations for the other cameras are computed and averaged, which yields an initial approximate configuration of the system. In order to obtain a mean rotation we use the axis-angle representation, where axes and angles are averaged arithmetically with respect to their symmetries. If $\mathcal{C}_{world}$ is defined to be the coordinate system of the estimated single cameras, it follows immediately that λ_v has to be set to 1 since $\mathcal{C}_{rig}$ already has the correct scale.

To improve precision the estimate of the configuration is iteratively refined: For each new pose of the system the pose of each single camera is revised with respect to the points seen by that camera. Afterwards the configuration of the refined cameras is computed and averaged with the previously estimated configurations. Since the combined camera system pose estimation is somewhat sensitive to noise in the configuration parameters, this is more robust.

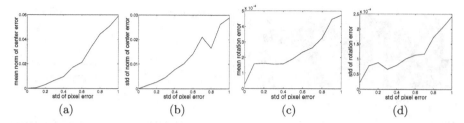

Fig. 1. Dependency of the standard deviation of the feature position noise in pixel (a) the mean of the norm of camera center error, (b) the standard deviation of the latter error, (c) the absolute value of the angular error of the cameras orientation, (d) the standard deviation of the latter error.

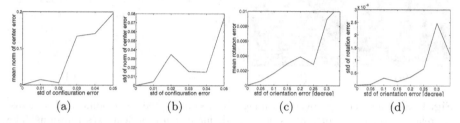

Fig. 2. Dependency of the standard deviation of the noise in the MCS configuration (a) the mean of the norm of the camera center error, (b) the standard deviation of the norm camera center error, (c) the absolute value of the angular error of the cameras orientation, (d) the standard deviation of the angular error of the cameras orientation.

5   Experiments

In this section the introduced estimation techniques for the pose of a MCS are evaluated. First we measure the robustness of the technique with synthetic data. Afterwards we use image sequences generated by a simulator and compare our results with the given ground truth data. Finally we also present experimental results for a real image sequence. To measure the noise robustness of our novel pose estimation technique we use synthetic data. The MCS is placed in front of a scene consisting of 3D-points with given 2D image points in the cameras of the MCS. At first we disturb the 2D correspondences with zero-mean Gaussian noise for each image. Afterwards we use our approach to estimate the pose of the virtual camera, with a least squares solution based on all observed image points. The norm of the position error and the angle error of the estimated orientation can be seen in figure (1). It can be seen that the proposed pose estimation is robust with respect to the pixel location error of up to 1 pixel noise.

In a second test we disturb the configuration of the MCS with a zero-mean Gaussian translation error (with sigma of up to 5% of the camera's original displacement) and a Gaussian rotation error of up to 0.35 degrees in each axis. It can be seen that the proposed pose estimation technique is robust against these disturbances but the configuration errors cause higher errors in the estimated pose than the noise in the feature positions does.

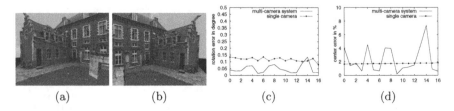

Fig. 3. (a),(b): Non-overlapping simulator images of MCS (c),(d): error of relative translation and rotation since previous estimate w.r.t. to ground truth (17 image pairs) for standard structure from motion and MCS structure from motion.

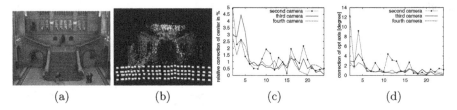

Fig. 4. Museum scene: (a) overview image, (b) reconstructed scene points and cameras, (c) relative corrections of centers in C_{rig}, (d) incremental optical axes rotations. The sequence starts in front of the arc to the left, moves parallel to some wide stairs and finishes in front of the other arc to the right. 25 times 4 images have been taken.

In order to measure the pose estimation errors of the proposed approach in a structure-from-motion framework, we use a sequence of rendered images (see fig. 3) with ground truth pose data. In this sequence a MCS with two fixed cameras with non-overlapping views is moved and rotated in front of a synthetic scene. We implemented a pose estimation algorithm with the following steps: Given a set of Harris corners and corresponding 3d points in an initial image 1.) in each image a Harris corner detector is used to get feature positions, 2.) from the corners a set of correspondences is estimated using normalized cross correlation and epipolar geometry, 3.) using these correspondences (and the referring 3d points) the pose is estimated with RANSAC using eq. (8) and (9), 4.) afterwards a nonlinear optimization is used to finally determine the pose of the MCS. The measured position and orientation errors are shown and compared to a single camera pose estimation in fig. 3. It can be seen that using the MCS pose estimation the rotation is estimated with a smaller error than in the single camera case, but the translation estimatates for a single camera is slightly better for this data.

Now we show that the pose estimation also works well on real images. The images used have been taken at the National History Museum in London using a MCS with four cameras mounted on a pole. The configuration has been computed from the image data as described in the previous section. Using standard single-camera structure-from-motion approaches, the pose estimation breaks down in front of the stairs. Due to the missing horizontal structure at the stairs there are nearly no good features. However, incorporating all cameras in our approach makes the pose estimation robust exactly in those situations, where some of the cameras can still see some features.

Using our approach to compute the MCS configuration the initial estimates for the centers are refined by about five to eight percent in C_{rig} compared to the finally stable values. After about the seventh pose estimate the center change rate reaches one percent. It is interesting that although the parameters for the second camera are not estimated very well, the system does work robustly as a whole.

6   Conclusions

We introduced a novel approach for pose estimation of a multi-camera system even in the case of non-overlapping views of the cameras. Furthermore we introduced a technique to estimate all parameters of the system directly from the image sequence itself. The new approach was tested under noisy conditions and it has been seen that it is robust. Finally we have shown results for real and synthetic image sequences.

Acknowledgement. This work has been partially funded by the European Union (Project MATRIS, IST-002013).

References

1. R. Hartley and A. Zisserman, "Multiple View Geometry in Computer Vision" *Cambridge university press, Cambrige, 2000*
2. S.J. Maybank and O. Faugeras, "A therory of self-calibration of a moving camera," *International Journal of Computer Vision*, 1992.
3. M. Pollefeys, R. Koch and L. Van Gool, "Selfcalibration and metric reconstruction in spite of varying and unknown internal camera parameters", *ICCV*, 1998.
4. Cornelia Fermüller and Yiannis Aloimonos "Observability of 3d motion" *International Journal of Computer Vision*, 37(1):43-62, June 2000
5. P. Baker, C. Fermüller, Y. Aloimonos and R. Pless, "A Spherical Eye from Multiple Cameras (Makes Better Models of the World)" *CVPR'01*, Volume 1, 2001
6. P. A. Beardsley, A. Zisserman and D. W. Murray "Sequential Updating of Projective and Affine Structure from Motion" *IJCV*, Volume 23 , Issue 3, 1997
7. Jan Neumann, Cornelia Fermüller, and Yiannis Aloimonos "Polydioptric Camera Design and 3D Motion Estimation" *IEEE Computer Society Conference on Computer Vision and Pattern Recognition*, Volume 2, pages 294-301, 2003
8. J. Neumann, C. Fermüller, and Y. Aloimonos "Eye Design in the Plenoptic Space of Light Rays" *9th IEEE Int. Conference on Computer Vision*, 2003.
9. Jan-M. Frahm and Reinhard Koch, "Camera Calibration with Known Rotation" *Ninth IEEE International Conference on Computer Vision*, Vol. 2, October 2003.
10. A. Zomet et al., "Omni-rig: Linear Self-recalibration of a Rig with Varying Internal and External Parameters", *8th Int. Conf. on Computer Vision*, 2001

Silhouette Based Human Motion Estimation

Bodo Rosenhahn[1], Reinhard Klette[1], and Gerald Sommer[2]

[1] University of Auckland (CITR)
Computer Science Department
Private Bag 92019 Auckland, New Zealand
{bros028, r.klette}@cs.auckland.ac.nz
[2] Institut für Informatik und Praktische Mathematik
Christian-Albrechts-Universität zu Kiel
Olshausenstr. 40, 24098 Kiel, Germany
gs@ks.informatik.uni-kiel.de

Abstract. In this contribution we present an algorithm for 2D-3D pose estimation of human beings. A human torso is modeled in terms of free-form surface patches which are extended with joints inside the surface. We determine the 3D pose and the angles of the arm joints from image silhouettes of the torso. This silhouette based approach towards human motion estimation is illustrated by experimental results for monocular or stereo image sequences.

1 Introduction

Modeling and tracking of human motion from video sequences is an increasingly important field of research with applications in sports sciences, medicine, animation (avatars) or surveillance. E. Muybridge is known as the pioneer in human motion capturing with his famous experiments in 1887 called *Animal Locomotion*. In recent years, many techniques for human motion tracking have been proposed which are fairly effective [2,5], but they often use simplified models of the human body by applying ellipsoidal, cylindrical or skeleton models and do not use a realistic surface model. The reader is referred to [4] for a recent survey on marker-less human motion tracking.

In this work we present and discuss a human motion capturing system which estimates the pose and angle configuration of a human body captured in image sequences. Contrary to other works we apply a 2-parametric surface representation [3], allow full perspective camera models, and use the extracted silhouette of the body as the only image information. Our algorithms are fast (400ms per frame), and we present experiments on monocular and stereo image sequences. The scenario is visualized in the left of figure 1. As it can be seen, we use a model of the human torso with its arms, and model it by using two free-form surface patches. The first patch (modeling the torso) contains 57×21 nodes and the second (modeling the arms) contains 81×21 nodes. Each arm contains 4 joints, so that we have to deal with 8 joint angles and 6 unknowns for the rigid motion resulting in 14 unknowns. The right of figure 1 gives the names of the used joints for the diagrams in the experiments.

C.E. Rasmussen et al. (Eds.): DAGM 2004, LNCS 3175, pp. 294–301, 2004.

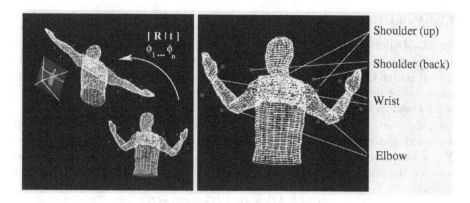

Fig. 1. Left: The pose scenario: the aim is to estimate the pose R, t and the joint angles ϕ_i. Right: The names of the used joints.

This contribution continues work reported in [7,8] on point-based, contour- and surface-based pose estimation. But whereas in these works only rigid objects are discussed or only a point-based representation scheme for modeling kinematic chains is used, in this work we want to overcome these previous limitations by introducing an approach for pose estimation of free-form surfaces, coupled with kinematic chains. It is applied to marker-less human motion tracking. We start with recalling foundations and introduce twists which are used to model rigid motions and joints. Then we continue with free-form contours and surfaces, and define a basic approach for pose estimation, followed by extensions and experiments. We conclude with a brief discussion.

2 Foundations

Clifford or geometric algebras [9] can be used to deal with geometric aspects of the pose problem. We only list a few properties which are important for our studies. The elements in geometric algebras are called multivectors which can be multiplied by using a geometric product. It allows a coordinate-free and dense symbolic representation. For modeling the pose problem, we use the conformal geometric algebra (CGA). The CGA is build up on a conformal model which is coupled with a homogeneous model to deal with kinematics and projective geometry simultaneously. In conclusion, we deal with the Euclidean, kinematic and projective space in a uniform framework and can therefore cope with the pose problem in an efficient manner. In the equations we will use the inner product, $\cdot$, the outer product, $\wedge$, the commutator, $\underline{\times}$, and anticommutator, $\overline{\times}$, product, which can be derived from the geometric product. Though we will also present equations formulated in conformal geometric algebra, we only explain these symbolically and want to refer to [7] for more detailed information.

2.1   Point Based Pose Estimation

For 2D-3D point based pose estimation we use constraint equations which compare 2D image points with 3D object points. Assume an image point $\boldsymbol{x}$ and the optical center $\boldsymbol{O}$. These define a 3D projection ray, $\underline{\boldsymbol{L}}_x = \mathbf{e} \wedge (\boldsymbol{O} \wedge \boldsymbol{x})$, as Plücker line [6]. The motor $\boldsymbol{M}$ is defined as exponential of a twist Ψ, $\boldsymbol{M} = \exp(-\frac{\theta}{2}\Psi)$, and formalizes the unknown rigid motion as a screw motion [6]. The motor $\boldsymbol{M}$ is applied on an object point $\underline{\boldsymbol{X}}$ as versor product, $\underline{\boldsymbol{X}}' = \boldsymbol{M}\underline{\boldsymbol{X}}\widetilde{\boldsymbol{M}}$, where $\widetilde{\boldsymbol{M}}$ represents the so-called reverse of $\boldsymbol{M}$. Then the rigidly transformed object point, $\underline{\boldsymbol{X}}'$, is compared with the reconstructed line, $\underline{\boldsymbol{L}}_x$, by minimizing the error vector between the point and the line. This specifies a constraint equation in geometric algebra:

$$(\boldsymbol{M}\underline{\boldsymbol{X}}\widetilde{\boldsymbol{M}}) \underline{\times} (\mathbf{e} \wedge (\boldsymbol{O} \wedge \boldsymbol{x})) = 0.$$

Note, that we deal with a 3D formalization of the pose problem. The constraint equations can be solved by linearization (i.e. solving the equations for the twist-parameters which generate the screw motion) and by applying the Rodrigues formula for a reconstruction of the group action [6]. Iteration leads to a gradient descent method in 3D space. This is presented in [7] in more detail, where similar equations have been introduced to compare 3D points with 2D lines (3D planes) and 3D lines with 2D lines (3D planes). Pose estimation can be performed in real-time and we need 2ms on a Linux 2GHz machine to estimate a pose based on 100 point correspondences.

Joints along the kinematic chain can be modeled as special screws with no pitch. In [7] we have shown, that the twist then corresponds to a scaled Plücker line, $\Psi = \theta\underline{\boldsymbol{L}}$ in 3D space, which gives the location of the general rotation. Because of this relation it is simple to move joints in space and they can be transformed by a motor $\boldsymbol{M}$ in a similar way such as plain points, $\Psi' = \boldsymbol{M}\Psi\widetilde{\boldsymbol{M}}$.

2.2   Contour-Based Pose Estimation

We now model free-form contours and their embedding into the pose problem. As it turned out, Fourier descriptors are very useful, since they are a special case of so-called *twist-generated* curves which we used to model cycloidal curves (cardioids, nephroids and so forth) within the pose problem [7]. The later introduced pose estimation algorithm for surface models goes back onto a contour based method. Therefore, a brief recapitulation of our former works on contour based pose estimation is of importance. The main idea is to interpret a 1-parametric 3D closed curve as three separate 1D signals which represent the projections of the curve along the x, y and z axis, respectively. Since the curve is assumed to be closed, the signals are periodic and can be analyzed by applying a 1D discrete Fourier transform (1D-DFT). The inverse discrete Fourier transform (1D-IDFT) enables us to reconstruct low-pass approximations of each signal. Subject to the sampling theorem, this leads to the representation of the 1-parametric 3D curve $C(\phi)$ as

$$C(\phi) = \sum_{m=1}^{3} \sum_{k=-N}^{N} \boldsymbol{p}_k^m \exp\left(\frac{2\pi k\phi}{2N+1}l_m\right).$$

The parameter m represents each dimension and the vectors $\boldsymbol{p}_k^m$ are phase vectors obtained from the 1D-DFT acting on dimension m. In this equation we have replaced the imaginary unit $i = \sqrt{-1}$ by three different rotation planes, represented by the bivectors $\boldsymbol{l}_i$, with $\boldsymbol{l}_i^2 = -1$. Using only a low-index subset of the Fourier coefficients results in a low-pass approximation of the object model which can be used to regularize the pose estimation algorithm. For pose estimation this model is then combined with a version of an ICP-algorithm [10].

2.3   Silhouette-Based Pose Estimation of Free-Form Surfaces

To model surfaces, we assume a two-parametric surface [3] of the form

$$F(\phi_1, \phi_2) = \sum_{i=1}^{3} f^i(\phi_1, \phi_2)\mathbf{e}_i,$$

with three 2D functions $f^i(\phi_1, \phi_2) : \mathbb{R}^2 \to \mathbb{R}$ acting on the different Euclidean base vectors $\mathbf{e}_i$ ($i = 1, \ldots, 3$). The idea behind a two-parametric surface is to assume two independent parameters ϕ_1 and ϕ_2 to sample a 2D surface in 3D space. For a discrete number of sampled points, $f^i_{n_1, n_2}$, ($n_1 \in [-N_1, N_1]; n_2 \in [-N_2, N_2]; N_1, N_2 \in \mathbb{N}, i = 1, \ldots, 3$) on the surface, we can now interpolate the surface by using a 2D discrete Fourier transform (2D-DFT) and then apply an inverse 2D discrete Fourier transform (2D-IDFT) for each base vector separately. Subject to the sampling theorem, the surface can be written as a Fourier representation,

$$F(\phi_1, \phi_2) = \sum_{i=1}^{3} \sum_{k_1=-N_1}^{N_1} \sum_{k_2=-N_2}^{N_2} \boldsymbol{p}^i_{k_1, k_2} \exp\left(\frac{2\pi k_1 \phi_1}{2N_1 + 1}\, l_i\right) \exp\left(\frac{2\pi k_2 \phi_2}{2N_2 + 1}\, l_i\right).$$

The complex Fourier coefficients are contained in the vectors $\boldsymbol{p}^i_{k_1, k_2}$ that lie in the plane spanned by $\boldsymbol{l}_i$. We will again call them phase vectors. These vectors can be obtained by a 2D-DFT of the sample points $f^i_{n_1, n_2}$ on the surface. We now continue with the algorithm for silhouette-based pose estimation of surface models.

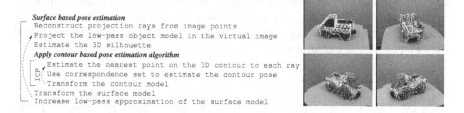

Fig. 2. Left: The algorithm for pose estimation of surface models. Right: A few example images of a tracked car model on a turn-table.

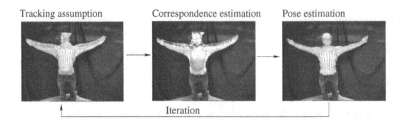

Tracking assumption   Correspondence estimation   Pose estimation

Iteration

Fig. 3. The basic algorithm: Iterative correspondence and pose estimation.

We assume a properly extracted silhouette (i.e., in a frame of the sequence) of our object (i.e., the human body). To compare points on the image silhouette we consider rim points on the surface model (i.e., which are on an occluding boundary of the object). This means we work with the 3D silhouette of the surface model with respect to the camera. To obtain this, we project the 3D surface on a virtual image. Then the contour is calculated and from the image contour the 3D silhouette of the surface model is reconstructed. The contour model is then applied within the contour-based pose estimation algorithm. Since aspects of the surface model are changing during ICP-cycles, a new silhouette will be estimated after each cycle to deal with occlusions within the surface model. The algorithm for pose estimation of surface models is summarized in figure 2 and it is discussed in [8] in more detail.

3   Human Motion Estimation

We now introduce how to couple kinematic chains within the surface model and present a pose estimation algorithm which estimates the pose and angle configurations simultaneously.

A surface is given in terms of three 2-parametric functions with respect to the parameters ϕ_1 and ϕ_2. Furthermore, we assume a set of joints J_i. By using an extra function $\mathcal{J}(\phi_1, \phi_2) \to [J_i|J_i : i\text{th. joint}]$, we are able to give every node a joint list along the kinematic chain. Note, that we use $[,]$ and not $\{,\}$, since the joints are given ordered along the kinematic chain. Since the arms contain two kinematic chains (for the left and right arm separately), we introduce a further index to separate the joints on the left arm from the ones on the right arm. The joints themselves are represented as objects in an extra field (a look-up table) and their parameters can be accessed immediately from the joint index numbers. Furthermore, it is possible to transform the location of the joints in space (as clarified in section 2). For pose estimation of a point $\underline{\boldsymbol{X}}_{n,i_n}$ attached to the nth joint, we generate constraint equations of the form

$$(\boldsymbol{M}(\boldsymbol{M}_1 \ldots \boldsymbol{M}_n \underline{\boldsymbol{X}}_{n,i_n} \widetilde{\boldsymbol{M}_n} \ldots \widetilde{\boldsymbol{M}_1})\widetilde{\boldsymbol{M}}) \underline{\times} \mathbf{e} \wedge (\boldsymbol{O} \wedge \boldsymbol{x}_{n,i_n}) = 0.$$

To solve a set of such constraint equations we linearize the motor $\boldsymbol{M}$ with respect to the unknown twist $\boldsymbol{\Psi}$ and the motors $\boldsymbol{M}_i$ with respect to the unknown angles θ_i. The twists $\boldsymbol{\Psi}_i$ are known a priori.

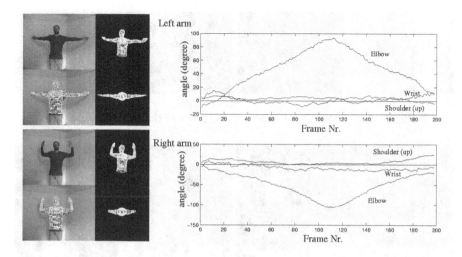

Fig. 4. Left: First pose results with a 6 DOF kinematic chain. Right: Angles of the left and right arm during the tracked image sequence.

Fig. 5. First pose results with a 8 DOF kinematic chain.

The basic pose estimation algorithm is visualized in figure 3: We start with simple image processing steps to gain the silhouette information of the person by using a color threshold and a Laplace operator. Then we project the surface mesh in a virtual image and estimate its 3D contour. Each point on the 3D contour carries a given joint index. Then we estimate the correspondences by using an ICP-algorithm, generate the system of equations, solve them, transform the object and its joints and iterate this procedure. During iteration we start with a low-pass object representation and refine it by using higher frequencies. This helps to avoid local minima during iteration.

First results of the algorithm are shown on the left of figure 4: The figure contains two pose results; it shows on each quadrant the original image and overlaid the projected 3D pose. The other two images show the estimated joint angles in a virtual environment to visualize the error between the ground truth and the estimated pose. The tracked image sequence contains 200 images. In this sequence we use just three joints on each arm and neglect the shoulder

Fig. 6. The silhouette for different arm poses of the kinematic chain.

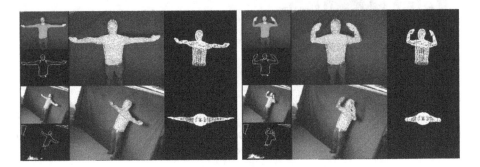

Fig. 7. Example images of a first stereo experiment.

(back) joint. The right diagram of figure 4 shows the estimated angles of the joints during the image sequence. The angles can easily be identified with the sequence. Since the movement of the body is continuous, the estimated curves are also relatively smooth.

Then we extend the model to a 8DOF kinematic chain and add a joint on the shoulder which allows the arms to move backwards and forwards. Results of the same sequence are shown in figure 5. As it can be seen, the observation of the pose overlaid with the image data appear to be good, but in a simulation environment it can be seen, that estimated joints are quite noisy. The reason for the depth sensitivity lies in the used image information: Figure 6 shows two images of a human with different arm positions. It can be seen, that the estimated silhouettes look quite similar. This means, that the used image features are under-determined in their interpretation as 3D pose configuration. This problem can not be solved in an algorithmic way and is of geometric nature. To overcome this problem we decided to continue with a stereo setup. The basic idea is, that the geometric non-uniquenesses can be avoided by using several cameras observing the scene from different perspectives. Since we reconstruct rays from image points, we have to calibrate the cameras with respect to one fixed world coordinate system. Then it is unimportant for which camera a ray is reconstructed and we are able to combine the equations from both cameras into one system of equations and estimate the pose and arm angles simultaneously. Figure 7 shows example images of our stereo implementation. In each segment, the left images show the original and filtered image of each camera. The middle images show pose results in both cameras and the right images show the pose results in a virtual environment. It can be seen that the results improved.

4   Discussion

This contribution presents an approach for silhouette-based pose estimation of free-form surfaces coupled with kinematic chains. We use our previous work, dealing with 2D-3D pose estimation of points, free-form contours and free-form surfaces and describe how to extend the approach to kinematic chains. In the experiments it turns out that pure silhouette information is not sufficient for accurate pose estimation since the extracted silhouette and its interpretation as 3D pose is under-determined. Therefore, we move on to a multi-view scenario and illustrate that the pose results can be improved remarkably in a stereo setup. Experiments have been done with image sequences between 100 and 500 frames. Further work will continue with an extension of the multi-camera set-up.

Acknowledgments. This work has been supported by the EC Grant IST-2001-3422 (VISATEC) and by the DFG grant RO 2497/1-1.

References

1. Arbter K. and Burkhardt H. Ein Fourier-Verfahren zur Bestimmung von Merkmalen und Schätzung der Lageparameter ebener Raumkurven. *Informationstechnik*, Vol. 33, No. 1, pp. 19-26, 1991.
2. Bregler C. and Malik J. Tracking people with twists and exponential maps. *IEEE Computer Society Conference on Computer Vision and Pattern Recognition*, Santa Barbara, California, pp. 8-15, 1998.
3. Campbell R.J. and Flynn P.J. A survey of free-form object representation and recognition techniques. *Computer Vision and Image Understanding (CVIU)*, Vol. 81, pp. 166-210, 2001.
4. Gavrilla D.M. The visual analysis of human movement: A survey *Computer Vision and Image Understanding*, Vol. 73 No. 1, pp. 82-92, 1999.
5. Mikic I., Trivedi M, Hunter E, and Cosman P. Human body model acquisition and tracking using voxel data *International Journal of Computer Vision (IJCV)*, Vol. 53, Nr. 3, pp. 199–223, 2003.
6. Murray R.M., Li Z. and Sastry S.S. A Mathematical Introduction to Robotic Manipulation. *CRC Press*, 1994.
7. Rosenhahn B. Pose Estimation Revisited. (PhD-Thesis) *Technical Report 0308, Christian-Albrechts-Universität zu Kiel, Institut für Informatik und Praktische Mathematik*, 2003. Available at www.ks.informatik.uni-kiel.de
8. Rosenhahn B., Perwass C. and Sommer G. Pose estimation of free-form surface models. In *Pattern Recognition, 25th DAGM Symposium*, B. Michaelis and G. Krell (Eds.), Springer-Verlag, Berling, LNCS 2781, pp. 574-581.
9. Sommer G., editor. Geometric Computing with Clifford Algebra. *Springer Verlag*, Berlin, 2001.
10. Zang Z. Iterative point matching for registration of free-form curves and surfaces. *International Journal of Computer Vision*, Vol. 13, No. 2, pp. 119-152, 1999.

Cooperative Optimization
for Energy Minimization in Computer Vision:
A Case Study of Stereo Matching

Xiaofei Huang

CallVista, Inc., Foster City, CA 94404, U.S.A.
huangxiaofei@ieee.org

Abstract. This paper presents a cooperative optimization algorithm for energy minimization in a general form. Its operations are based on parallel, local iterative interactions. This algorithm has many important computational properties absent in existing optimization methods. Given an optimization problem instance, the computation always has a unique equilibrium and converges to it with an exponential rate regardless of initial conditions. There are sufficient conditions for identifying global optima and necessary conditions for trimming search spaces. To demonstrate its power, a case study of stereo matching from computer vision is provided. The proposed algorithm does not have the restrictions on energy functions imposed by graph cuts [1,2], a powerful specialized optimization technique, yet its performance was comparable with graph cuts in solving stereo matching using the common evaluation framework [3].

1 Introduction

Stereo matching is one of the most active research areas in computer vision [3, 1,4,5]. The goal of stereo matching is to recover the depth image of a scene from a pair of 2-D images of the same scene taken from two different locations. Like many other problems from computer vision, it can be formulated as the global optimization of multivariate energy functions, which is NP-hard [6] in computational complexity.

The general methods [7] for combinatorial optimization are 1) local search [7], 2) Simulated Annealing [8], 3) genetic algorithms [9], 4) tabu search, 5) Branch-and-Bound [10,11] and 6) and Dynamic Programming [11]. The first four methods are classified as local optimization, thus having the local optimum problem. The remaining two methods do not scale well when they come to dealing with thousands to millions of variables in most vision problems.

On the specialized optimization algorithm side, if the energy function is in some special form, such as having binary variables and binary smoothness constraints [1,2], the energy minimization can be converted into the problem of finding the minimum cut in a graph which has known polynomial algorithms to solve it. Those algorithms have also been generalized [1,2] as approximate algorithms for energy functions with multi-valued variables and regular constraints [2]. They

C.E. Rasmussen et al. (Eds.): DAGM 2004, LNCS 3175, pp. 302–309, 2004.

are called the graph cut algorithms in [1,3,2], a powerful specialized optimization technique popular in computer vision. They have the best known results in energy minimization in the two recent evaluations of stereo algorithms [3, 12]. However, their convergence properties, such as the convergence rate and uniqueness of solutions, of those algorithms are not established.

The cooperative algorithm presented in this paper is a general optimization technique. It does not share the restrictions on energy functions as imposed by graph cuts. It also does not have the local minimum problem and can handle problems with ten thousands or hundred thousands of variables in practice. The proposed algorithm has a clearly defined energy function in a general form. Its operations are based on parallel, local iterative interactions. Hence, it can be implemented using one-layered recurrent neural network.

Unlike many existing optimization techniques, our algorithm has a solid theoretical foundation, including convergence property. With the new set of difference equations, it guarantees both the existence and the uniqueness of solutions as well as an exponential convergence rate. It knows if the solution is the global optimum or not, and the quality of solutions. It has been generalized using the lattice concept from abstract algebra to be more powerful and complete [13]. It has also been generalized to cover the classic local search as its special case by extending its cooperation schemes [14]. To demonstrate its power, we will show in this paper that the proposed algorithm has a performance comparable with graph cuts in handling regular binary constraints using the common evaluation framework for stereo matching [3].

2   The Cooperative Optimization Algorithm

To solve a hard combinatorial optimization problem, we follow the divide-and-conquer principle. We first break up the problem into a number of sub-problems of manageable sizes and complexities. Following that, we solve them together in a cooperative way so that the original energy function is minimized. The cooperation is achieved by asking each sub-problem solver, termed agent, to compromise its solution with the solutions of other sub-problem solvers. Hence, the algorithm uses a system of multi-agents working together cooperatively to solve an optimization problem.

To be more specific, let $E(x_1, x_2, \ldots, x_n)$ be a multivariate energy function, or simply denoted as $E(x)$, where each variable x_i has a finite domain D_i of size m_i ($m_i = |D_i|$). We break the function into n sub-energy functions E_i ($i = 1, 2, \ldots, n$), such that E_i contains at least variable x_i for each i, the minimization of each energy function E_i (the sub-problem) is computational manageable in sizes and complexities, and $\sum_i E_i = E(x)$.

For example, the binary constraint-based function

$$E(x_1, x_2, \ldots, x_n) = \sum_i C_i(x_i) + \sum_{i,j, i \neq j} C_{ij}(x_i, x_j) , \qquad (1)$$

is a very popular energy function used in computer vision, where C_i is a unary constraint on variable x_i and C_{ij} is a binary constraint on variable x_i and x_j. A straight-forward decomposition of this energy function is:

$$E_i = C_i(x_i) + \sum_{j,\ j \neq i} C_{ij}(x_i, x_j) \quad \text{for } i = 1, 2, \ldots, n \ . \tag{2}$$

The n sub-problems can be described as:

$$\min_{x_j \in X_i} E_i, \quad \text{for } i = 1, 2, \ldots, n \ , \tag{3}$$

where X_i is the set of variables that sub-energy function E_i contains.

Because of the interdependence of the sub-energy functions, as in the case of the binary constraint-based function (see Eq. (1)), minimizing those sub-energy functions in such an independent way can hardly yield a consensus in variable assignments. For example, the assignment for x_i that minimizes E_i can hardly be the same as the assignment for the same variable that minimizes E_j if E_j contains x_i. We need to solve those sub-problems in a cooperative way so that we can reach a consensus in variable assignments.

To do that, we can break the minimization of each sub-energy function (see (3)) into two steps,

$$\min_{x_i} \min_{x_j \in X_i \setminus x_i} E_i, \quad \text{for } i = 1, 2, \ldots, n \ ,$$

where $X_i \setminus x_i$ denotes the set X_i minuses $\{x_i\}$.

That is, first we optimize E_i with respect to all variables that E_i contains except x_i. This gives us the intermediate solution in optimizing E_i, denoted as $c_i(x_i)$,

$$c_i(x_i) = \min_{x_j \in X_i \setminus x_i} E_i \quad \text{for } i = 1, 2, \ldots, n \ . \tag{4}$$

Second, we optimize $c_i(x_i)$ with respect to x_i,

$$\min_{x_i} c_i(x_i) \ , \tag{5}$$

The intermediate solutions of the optimization, $c_i(x_i)$, is an unary constraint introduced by the algorithm on the variable x_i, called the assignment constraint on variable x_i. Given a value of x_i, $c_i(x_i)$ is the minimal value of E_i. To minimize E_i, those values of x_i which have smaller assignment constraint values $c_i(x_i)$ are preferred more than those which have higher ones.

To introduce cooperation in solving the sub-problems, we add the unary constraints $c_j(x_j)$, weighted by a real value λ, back to the right side of (4) and modify the functions (4) to be iterative ones:

$$c_i^{(k)}(x_i) = \min_{x_j \in X_i \setminus x_i} \left((1 - \lambda_k) E_i + \lambda_k \sum_j w_{ij} c_j^{(k-1)}(x_j) \right) \quad \text{for } i = 1, 2, \ldots, n \ , \tag{6}$$

where k is the iteration step, w_{ij} are non-negative weight values satisfying $\sum_i w_{ij} = 1$. It has been found [13] that such a choice of w_{ij} makes sure the iterative update functions converge. The energy function at the right side of the equation is called the modified sub-energy function, denoted as $\tilde{E}_i$.

By adding back $c_j(x_j)$ to E_i, we ask the optimization of E_i to compromise its solution with the solutions of the other sub-problems. As a consequence, the cooperation in the optimization of all the sub-energy functions (E_is) is achieved. This optimization process defined in (6) is called the cooperative optimization of the sub-problems.

Parameter λ_k in (6) controls the level of the cooperation at step k and is called the cooperation strength, satisfying $0 \le \lambda_k < 1$. A higher value for λ_k in (6) will weigh the solutions of the other sub-problems $c_j(x_j)$ more than the one of the current sub-problem E_i. In other words, the solution of each sub-problem will compromise more with the solutions of other sub-problems. As a consequence, a higher level of cooperation in the optimization is reached in this case.

The update functions (6) are a set of difference equations of the assignment constraints $c_i(x_i)$. Unlike conventional difference equations used by probabilistic relaxation algorithms [15], cooperative computations [5], and Hopfield Networks [16], this set of difference equations always has one and only one equilibrium given λ and w_{ij}. The computation converges to the equilibrium with an exponential rate, λ, regardless of initial conditions of $c_i^{(0)}(x_i)$. Those computational properties will be shown in theorems in the next section and their proofs are provided in [14].

By minimizing the linear combination of E_i and $c_j(x_j)$, which are the intermediate solutions for other sub-problems, we can reasonably expect that a consensus in variable assignments can be reached. When the cooperation is strong enough, i.e., $\lambda_k \to 1$, the difference equations (6) are dominated by the assignment constraints $c_j(x_j)$, it appears to us that the only choice for x_j to minimize the right side of (6) is the one that has the minimal value of the assignment constraint $c_j(x_j)$ for any E_i that contains x_j. That is a consensus in variable assignments.

Theory only guarantees the convergence of the computation to the unique equilibrium of the difference equations. If it converges to a consensus equilibrium, the solution, which is consisted of the consensus assignments for variables, must be the global optimum of the energy function $E(x)$, guaranteed by theory (detail in the next section). However, theory doesn't guarantee the equilibrium to be a consensus, even by increasing the cooperation strength λ. Otherwise, NP=P.

In addition to the cooperation scheme for reaching a consensus in variable assignments, we introduce another important operation of the algorithm at each iteration, called variable value discarding. A certain value for a variable, say x_i, can be discarded if it has a assignment constraint value, $c_i(x_i)$ that is higher than a certain threshold, $c_i(x_i) > t_i$, because they are less preferable in minimizing E_i as explained before. There do exist thresholds from theory for doing that [13]. Those discarded values are those that can not be in any global optimal solution. By discarding values, we can trim the search space. If only one value is left for each variable after a certain number of iterations using the thresholds provided theory, they constitute the global optimal solution, guaranteed by theory [13]. However, theory does not guarantee that one value is left for each variable in all cases. Otherwise, NP=P.

By discarding values, we increase the chance of reaching a consensus equilibrium for the computation. In practice, we progressively tighten the thresholds to discard more and more values as the iteration proceeds to increase the chance of reaching a consensus equilibrium. In the end, we leave only one value for each variable. Then, the final solution is a consensus equilibrium.

However, by doing that, such a final solution is not guaranteed to be the global optimum. Nevertheless, in our experiments in solving large scale combinatorial optimization problems, we found that the solution quality of this algorithm is still satisfactory, much better than that of other conventional optimization methods, such as simulated annealing and local search [13].

3   Experiments and Results

The proposed cooperative algorithm serves as a general problem solver in a unified computational model for understanding and solving all kinds of vision tasks. In general, it can find correct solutions for any vision task. It was found that any vision task (object recognition, shape from x, image segmentation, and more), can be represented as a mapping from an input space to an output space (e.g., from stimulus to interpretation). If there is no ambiguity in the mapping, or in other words there is a unique interpretation given an input set, it is guaranteed by theory the existence of a constraint model defining the mapping. The constraint calculus, offering a powerful knowledge representation framework for defining the constraint model, is a general extension of the tuple relational calculus, where the Boolean computing is extended to soft computing. The tuple relational calculus together with functions has the same expressive power as the Turing machine. Furthermore, the cooperative algorithm guarantees to find the correct solutions in theory when the noise level introduced at the input is limited (detail to be presented at Operations Research 2004). In this paper, we offer the case study of stereo matching.

For detail about the energy function definitions used for stereo matching in the framework, please see [3]. Basically, a unary constraint $C_i(x_i)$ in (1) measures the difference of the intensities between site i from one image and its corresponding site in another image given the depth of the site. A binary constraint $C_{ij}(x_i, x_j)$ measures the difference of the depths between site i and site j. This type of constraints is also referred as the smoothness constraint in literatures. It is also widely used in solving image segmentation and other vision tasks.

From information-theoretical point of view, a binary constraint contain less information than a high-arity constraint for solving vision problems. Hence, high arity constraints lead to better quality of solutions. Most literatures deal with only the binary smoothness constraint because of the limitations of many conventional optimization techniques. The algorithm proposed in this paper doesn't have such a restriction. It was found that replacing the smoothness constraint by a 9-ary constraints, the algorithm considerably outperforms graph cuts in solving image segmentation. It was ten times fast and the error rate was reduced by two to three factors.

Using the constraint model, the only difference between image segmentation and stereo vision are the contents of the unary constraints. Although we only present the experiment results using the smoothness constraint in this paper. The very promising results of applying high arity constraints in image segmentation encourage to use them for stereo matching as the future work.

To choose the propagation matrix, we can have all the options as long as the matrix is square, irreducible, and with non-negative elements as defined in Definition [13]. Since each site i in an image has four neighbors and is associated with one agent, we set w_{ij} be nonzero $(= 0.25)$ if and only if site j is the neighbor of site i.

It was found in the experiments that difference choices of the propagation matrix has much less effect on the quality of solutions than on the convergence rate. It is reasonable because the propagation process, defined in the algorithm by using the propagation matrix (6), guarantees to spread local information E_i uniformly across all agents with any choice of the matrix. Because of this uniform spreading of local information, each agent can make better decisions in solving sub-problems cooperatively. Such a propagation process makes the algorithm different from the conventional optimization methods. This is another explanation for why the algorithm has the capability of finding global optima.

In the iterative function (6), the parameter λ_k is updated as

$$\lambda_k = (k-1)/k, \quad \text{where } k \geq 1.$$

Hence, the cooperation becomes stronger as the iteration proceeds.

In the experiments, we discard variable values using thresholds. That is, for a value x_i, if

$$c_i^{(k)}(x_i) > \min_{x_i} c_i^{(k)}(x_i) + t^{(k)} ,$$

where $t^{(0)} = 100$, and $t^{(k)} = 0.92 * t^{(k-1)}$ if there are less than 0.1% values are discarded at the current iteration. Otherwise, $t(k)$ remains unchanged. Therefore, those thresholds become tighter and tighter as the iteration proceeds, and more and more values are discarded for each variable. Eventually, there should be only one value left for each one. However, by using those simple thresholds, the final solution is not guaranteed to be the global optimum because those thresholds are not those suggested by theory.

It was found through theoretical investigations that the tightening rate of the thresholds depends on how deep the valley containing the global optimum in the search space is. If it is very close to other valleys, we need a slow tightening rate. Otherwise, a fast tightening rate is required.

Using the four test image pairs from the framework, the cooperative optimization is marginally better (1.85%) than graph cut in overall disparity error. For the Tsukuba image pair, which are close to real images from stereo matching, the cooperative optimization is 5.93% better than the graph cut (see Fig. 1).

Excluding occluded areas, which are not handled by both algorithms, the cooperative one are also the best for all other types of areas. An occluded area is one that is visible in one image, but not the other.

Fig. 1. The depth images recovered by our algorithm (left) and graph cuts (right).

The following four tables show the performance of the cooperative algorithm (upper rows in a table) and the graph cut algorithm (lower rows in a table) over the four test image sets. The performance is measured on all areas, non-occluded areas, occluded areas, textured areas, texture-less areas, and discontinued areas such as object boundaries. Also, the runtimes of each algorithm (ca = cooperative algorithm, gc = graph cuts) are listed.

image = Map (runtime: $ca = 82s$ / $gc = 337s$)

	ALL	NON OCCL	OCCL	TEXTRD	TEXTRLS	D_DISCNT
Error	4.08	1.12	16.08	1.13	0.47	3.69
Bad Pixels	5.91%	0.53%	90.76%	0.52%	0.95%	5.15%
Error	3.91	1.07	15.45	1.07	0.38	3.65
Bad Pixels	5.63%	0.36%	88.76%	0.36%	0.00%	4.52%

image = Sawtooth (runtime: $ca = 288s$ / $gc = 673s$)

	ALL	NON OCCL	OCCL	TEXTRD	TEXTRLS	D_DISCNT
Error	1.40	0.68	7.31	0.71	0.42	1.62
Bad Pixels	4.41%	1.86%	92.39%	1.95%	0.99%	6.56%
Error	1.49	0.70	7.88	0.73	0.40	1.60
Bad Pixels	3.99%	1.38%	94.02%	1.49%	0.31%	6.39%

image = Tsukuba (runtime: $ca = 174s$ / $gc = 476s$)

	ALL	NON OCCL	OCCL	TEXTRD	TEXTRLS	D_DISCNT
Error	1.18	0.81	5.43	0.95	0.55	1.67
Bad Pixels	4.03%	1.75%	90.21%	2.54%	0.68%	8.11%
Error	1.25	0.92	5.35	1.04	0.73	2.02
Bad Pixels	4.24%	2.04%	87.60%	2.77%	1.05%	10.00%

image = Venus (runtime: $ca = 465s$ / $gc = 573s$)

	ALL	NON OCCL	OCCL	TEXTRD	TEXTRLS	D_DISCNT
Error	1.48	1.02	7.92	0.88	1.25	1.42
Bad Pixels	4.40%	2.77%	91.40%	2.38%	3.57%	9.68%
Error	1.47	0.95	8.33	0.81	1.18	1.31
Bad Pixels	3.58%	1.93%	91.55%	1.56%	2.68%	6.84%

4   Conclusions

A formal description of a cooperative optimization algorithm has been presented. It is based on a system of multi-agents working together with a novel cooperation scheme to optimize the global objective function of the system. A number of important computational properties of the algorithm have also been presented in this paper. To demonstrate its power, a case study of stereo matching from computer vision has been provided. Using a common evaluation framework provided by Middlebury College, the system has shown a performance comparable with the graph cut algorithm.

References

1. Boykov, Y., Veksler, O., Zabih, R.: Fast approximate energy minimization via graph cut. IEEE TPAMI **23** (2001) 1222–1239
2. Kolmogorov, V., Zabih, R.: What energy functions can be minimized via graph cuts? IEEE TPAMI **26** (2004) 147–159
3. Scharstein, D., Szeliski, R.: A taxonomy and evaluation of dense two-frame stereo correspondence algorithms. IJCV **47** (2002) 7–42
4. Zitnick, C.L., Kanade, T.: A cooperative algorithm for stereo matching and occlusion detection. IEEE TPAMI 2 (2000)
5. Marr, D., Poggio, T.: Cooperative computation of stereo disparity. Science **194** (1976) 209–236
6. Atkinson, K.: Computers and Intractability. Kluwer Academic Publishers, San Francisco, U.S.A. (1989)
7. Michalewicz, Z., Fogel, D.: How to Solve It: Modern Heuristics. Springer-Verlag, New York (2002)
8. Kirkpatrick, Gelatt, C., Vecchi, M.: Optimization by simulated annealing. Science **220** (1983) 671–680
9. Hinton, G., Sejnowski, T., Ackley, D.: Genetic algorithms. Cognitive Science (1992) 66–72
10. Lawler, E.L., Wood, D.E.: Brand-and-bound methods: A survey. OR **14** (1966) 699–719
11. Jr., E.G.C., ed.: Computer and Job-Shop Scheduling. Wiley-Interscience, New York (1976)
12. Szeliski, R., Zabih, R.: An experimental comparison of stereo algorithms. In Triggs, B., Zisserman, A., Szeliski, R., eds.: Vision Algorithms: Theory and Practice. Number 1883 in LNCS, Corfu, Greece, Springer-Verlag (1999) 1–19
13. Huang, X.: A general framework for constructing cooperative global optimization algorithms. 4th International Conference on Frontiers in Global Optimization (2003)
14. Huang, X.: Cooperative optimization for solving large scale combinatorial problems. In Grundel, D., Murphey, R., Pardalos, P., eds.: 4th International Conference on Cooperative Control and Optimization, Destin, Florida, U.S.A. (2003)
15. Rosenfeld, A., Hummel, R., Zucker, S.: Scene labelling by relaxation operations. IEEE Transactions on System, Man, and Cybernetics **SMC-6** (1976) 420
16. Hopfield, J.: Neural networks and physical systems with emergent collective computational abilities. Proceedings of the National Academy of Sciences **79** (1982) 2554–2558

Building a Motion Resolution Pyramid by Combining Velocity Distributions

Julian Eggert[1], Volker Willert[2], and Edgar Körner[1]

[1] HRI Honda Research Institute GmbH,
Carl-Legien-Straße 30, 63073 Offenbach/Main
{Julian.Eggert, Edgar.Koerner}@honda-ri.de
[2] TU Darmstadt, Institut für Automatisierungstechnik
Fachgebiet Regelungstheorie & Robotik,
Landgraf-Georg-Str.04, 64283 Darmstadt
volker@rtr.tu-darmstadt.de

Abstract. Velocity distributions are an enhanced representation of image velocity implying more velocity information than velocity vectors. Velocity distributions allow the representation of ambiguous motion information caused by the aperture problem or multiple motions at a given image region. Starting from a contrast- and brightness-invariant generative model for image formation a likelihood measure for local image velocities is proposed. These local velocities are combined into a coarse-to-fine-strategy using a pyramidal image velocity representation. On each pyramid level, the strategy calculates predictions for image formation and combines velocity distributions over scales to get a hierarchically arranged motion information with different resolution levels in velocity space. The strategy helps to overcome ambiguous motion information present at fine scales by integrating information from coarser scales. In addition, it is able to combine motion information over scales to get velocity estimates with high resolution.

1 Introduction

Traditionally, motion estimates in an image sequence are represented using vector fields consisting of velocity vectors each describing the motion at a particular image region or pixel. Yet in most cases single velocity vectors at each image location are a very impoverished representation, which may introduce great errors in subsequent motion estimations. This may, e.g., be because the motion measurement process is ambiguous and disturbed by noise. The main problems which cause these errors are the aperture problem, the lack of contrast within image regions, occlusions at motion boundaries and multiple motions at local image regions caused by large image regions or transparent motion.

To circumvent these problems, the velocity of an image patch at each location is understood as a statistical signal. This implies working with probabilities for the existence of image features like pixel gray values and velocities. The expectation is that probability density functions are finally able to tackle the addressed

C.E. Rasmussen et al. (Eds.): DAGM 2004, LNCS 3175, pp. 310–317, 2004.
© Springer-Verlag Berlin Heidelberg 2004

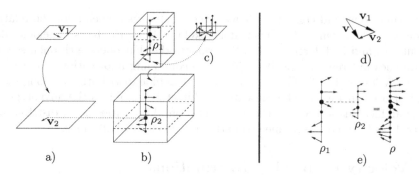

Fig. 1. Comparison of multiscale image motion representation: a) velocity vectors $\mathbf{v}_1, \mathbf{v}_2$ as standard representation and b) velocity distributions ρ_1, ρ_2 as enhanced representation. The single column with arrows in b) represents a velocity distribution at one location; it is shown in c) as the corresponding 2-dimensional graph. In d) and e) the velocity decomposition principle is shown schematically. In d), we assume that the true velocity $\mathbf{v}$ is decomposed into velocity vectors (e.g. $\mathbf{v}_1$ and $\mathbf{v}_2$ in the figure) at different scales. In e), we do the analog procedure for velocity distributions: We combine $\rho_1(\mathbf{v}_1)$ and $\rho_2(\mathbf{v}_2)$ in such a way that we get a total $\rho(\mathbf{v})$ with $\mathbf{v} = \mathbf{v}_1 + \mathbf{v}_2$.

problems related to motion processing, like ambiguous motion, occlusion and transparency, since some specific information about them can in principle be extracted from the probability functions [3]. During the last ten years velocity distributions have been motivated by several authors [3], [4], [5] mainly using two approaches: the gradient based *brightness change constraint equation* and the correlation-based *patch matching* technique.

A problem when dealing with velocity distributions is how to represent them in a multiscale pyramid. Such a pyramid is desirable e.g. for being able to represent both high and low velocities at good resolutions with a reasonable effort. This is usually done in such a way that the highest *velocities* (connected with the coarsest spatial resolution) are calculated first, then a shifted [1] version of the image is calculated using the velocities, and afterwards the velocities of the next pyramid level are calculated. These then correspond to *relative* velocities because they have been calculated in a frame that is moving along with the velocities from the coarse resolution. But still, single velocities are used for the shifted version of the image, so that the information available in the *distribution* is neglected.

In this work, we first introduce a *linear generative model* of image patch formation over time. Here, the changes in two consecutive images depend on the displacements as well as brightness and contrast variations (see Eq.2) of localized image patches. The result are contrast and brightness invariant velocity distributions based on a correlation measure comparing windowed image patches of consecutive images. Afterwards, we set up a hierarchical chain of velocity distributions from coarse to fine spatial scale and from large to smaller (relative) velocities. At each stage of the pyramid, the distributions for the overall velocities are improved using the distributions from the coarser spatial scale as a starting point and combining it with the local measurements for the relative velocity at the given scale. This is done exclusively on the basis of velocity distributions, and is different from other frameworks that operate through several hierarchies but rely on velocity fields when combining information from several hierarchy levels [1], [2]. The idea on how to combine distributions among scales is illustrated in Fig. 1. The presented architecture combines the advantages of a hierarchical structure and the representation of velocities using distributions and allows for a coarse-to-fine estimation of velocity distributions.

2   Velocity Probability Distributions

In an image sequence[1], every image $\mathbf{I}^t$ at time t consists of pixels at locations $\mathbf{x}$. Each pixel is associated with properties like its gray value $G^t_\mathbf{x}$ (scalar) and its velocity vector $\mathbf{v}^t_\mathbf{x}$, whereas $\mathbf{G}^t$ denotes the matrix of all gray values of image $\mathbf{I}^t$. The *motion field* is the set of all physical velocities at the corresponding pixel locations at a time t. The *optical flow* is an estimate for the real image motion field at a particular time t. It is usually gained by comparing localized patches of two consecutive images $\mathbf{I}^t$ and $\mathbf{I}^{t+\Delta t}$ with each other. To do this, we define $\mathbf{W} \odot \mathbf{G}^{t,\mathbf{x}}$ as the patch of gray values taken from an image $\mathbf{I}^t$, whereas $\mathbf{G}^{t,\mathbf{x}} := \mathcal{T}^{\{\mathbf{x}\}} \mathbf{G}^t$ are all gray values of image $\mathbf{I}^t$ shifted to $\mathbf{x}$. The shift-operator is defined as follows: $\mathcal{T}^{\{\Delta\mathbf{x}\}} G^t_\mathbf{x} := G^t_{\mathbf{x}-\Delta\mathbf{x}}$. The $\mathbf{W}$ defines a window (e.g. a 2-dimensional Gaussian window) that restricts the size of the patch. One possibility to calculate an estimate for the image velocities is now to assume that all gray values inside of a patch around $\mathbf{x}$ move with a certain common velocity $\mathbf{v}_\mathbf{x}$ for some time Δt, resulting in a displacement of the patch. This basically amounts to a search for correspondences of weighted patches of gray values (displaced to each other) $\mathbf{W} \odot \mathbf{G}^{t+\Delta t, \mathbf{x}+\Delta\mathbf{x}}$ and $\mathbf{W} \odot \mathbf{G}^{t,\mathbf{x}}$ taken from the two images $\mathbf{I}^{t+\Delta t}$ and $\mathbf{I}^t$.

To formulate the calculation of the motion estimate more precisely, we recur to a generative model. Our Ansatz is that an image $\mathbf{I}^{t+\Delta t}$ is causally linked with its preceding image $\mathbf{I}^t$ in the following way: We assume that an image $\mathbf{I}^t$ patch $\mathbf{W} \odot \mathbf{G}^{t,\mathbf{x}}$ with an associated velocity $\mathbf{v}^t_\mathbf{x} = \Delta\mathbf{x}/\Delta t$ is displaced by $\Delta\mathbf{x}$ during time Δt to reappear in image $\mathbf{I}^{t+\Delta t}$ at location $\mathbf{x} + \Delta\mathbf{x}$, so that for this particular patch it is

$$\mathbf{W} \odot \mathbf{G}^{t+\Delta t, \mathbf{x}+\Delta\mathbf{x}} = \mathbf{W} \odot \mathbf{G}^{t,\mathbf{x}}. \tag{1}$$

In addition, we assume that during this process the gray levels are jittered by noise η, and that brightness and contrast variations may occur over time. The brightness and contrast changes are accounted for by a scaling parameter λ and a bias κ (both considered to be constant within a patch) so that we arrive at

$$\left[\mathbf{W} \odot \mathbf{G}^{t+\Delta t, \mathbf{x}+\Delta\mathbf{x}} \right] = \lambda \left[\mathbf{W} \odot \mathbf{G}^{t,\mathbf{x}} \right] + \kappa \mathbf{W} + \eta \mathbf{1}. \tag{2}$$

---

[1] Notation: We use simple font for scalars (a, A), bold for vectors and matrices $(\mathbf{a}, \mathbf{A})$, and calligrafic font for functions and operators $(\mathcal{A})$. $\mathbf{1}, \mathbf{1}$ are vector of ones and matrix of ones, $\mathbf{A} \odot \mathbf{B}$ denotes a componentwise multiplication of two vectors or matrices and $\mathbf{A}^{@}$ a componentwise exponentiation by α of a vector or matrix.

Assuming that the image noise is zero mean gaussian with variance σ_η, the likelihood that $\mathbf{G}^{t,\mathbf{x}}$ is a match for $\mathbf{G}^{t+\Delta t,\mathbf{x}+\Delta\mathbf{x}}$, given a velocity $\mathbf{v}_{\mathbf{x}}^t$, the window function $\mathbf{W}$ and the parameters λ, κ and σ_η, can be written down as[2]:

$$\rho_{\lambda,\kappa,\sigma_\eta}(\mathbf{G}^{t+\Delta t,\mathbf{x}+\Delta\mathbf{x}}|\mathbf{v}_{\mathbf{x}}^t,\mathbf{W},\mathbf{G}^{t,\mathbf{x}}) \sim e^{-\frac{1}{2\sigma_\eta^2}\|\mathbf{W}\odot(\lambda\,\mathbf{G}^{t,\mathbf{x}}+\kappa\,\mathbf{1}-\mathbf{G}^{t+\Delta t,\mathbf{x}+\Delta\mathbf{x}})\|^2} \tag{3}$$

We now proceed to make it less influencial of λ and κ, that means a match of the patches will be almost contrast and brightness invariant. For this purpose, we maximize the likelihood Eq. 3 with respect to the scaling and shift parameters. This amounts to minimizing the exponent, so that we want to find

$$\{\lambda^*,\kappa^*\} := \mathrm{argmin}_{\lambda,\kappa}\left\|\mathbf{W}\odot\left(\lambda\,\mathbf{G}^{t,\mathbf{x}}+\kappa\,\mathbf{1}-\mathbf{G}^{t+\Delta t,\mathbf{x}+\Delta\mathbf{x}}\right)\right\|^2. \tag{4}$$

The final result of this minimization process is formulated in Eq. 7. Consider

$$\{\lambda^*,\kappa^*\} := \mathrm{argmin}_{\lambda,\kappa}\left\|\mathbf{W}\odot\left(\lambda\,\mathbf{A}+\kappa\,\mathbf{1}-\mathbf{B}\right)\right\|^2. \tag{5}$$

This leads to $\lambda^* = \dfrac{\varrho_{\mathbf{A},\mathbf{B}}\cdot\sigma_{\mathbf{B}}}{\sigma_{\mathbf{A}}}$ and $\kappa^* = \mu_{\mathbf{B}} - \lambda^*\cdot\mu_{\mathbf{A}}$.[3] $\tag{6}$

Inserting Eq. 6 into Eq. 3, so that $\lambda \to \lambda^*$ and $\kappa \to \kappa^*$, leads to the following likelihood formulation

$$\rho^t(\mathbf{x}|\mathbf{v}) := \rho_{\lambda^*,\kappa^*,\sigma_\eta}(\mathbf{G}^{t+\Delta t,\mathbf{x}+\Delta\mathbf{x}}|\mathbf{v}_{\mathbf{x}}^t,\mathbf{W},\mathbf{G}^{t,\mathbf{x}}) \sim e^{-\frac{1}{2}\cdot\left(\frac{\sigma_{\mathbf{G}^{t,\mathbf{x}}}}{\sigma_\eta}\right)^2\left(1-\varrho_{\mathbf{G}^{t,\mathbf{x}},\mathbf{G}^{t+\Delta t,\mathbf{x}+\Delta\mathbf{x}}}^2\right)}. \tag{7}$$

The weighted empirical correlation coefficient $\varrho_{\mathbf{A},\mathbf{B}}$ is well known in statistics as an effective template matching measurement. Eq. 7 shows some additional properties according to comparable likelihood measures [4], [3], [5]. The measure $\varrho_{\mathbf{G}^{t,\mathbf{x}},\mathbf{G}^{t+\Delta t,\mathbf{x}+\Delta\mathbf{x}}}^2$ ensures that the match is less affected by local changes in contrast and brightness. Local changes in illumination due to movement of an object when there is a fixed light-source or changes in illumination because of movement of the light-source itself does less reduce the accuracy of the measurement of the likelihood.

Another property of Eq. 7 is given by the ratio of variance of the patch at location $\mathbf{x}$ to the variance of the gaussian distributed noise $\sigma_{\mathbf{G}^{t,\mathbf{x}}}/\sigma_\eta$. The higher this ratio the smaller the overall variance $\sigma = \sigma_\eta/\sigma_{\mathbf{G}^{t,\mathbf{x}}}$. That means, if $\sigma_{\mathbf{G}^{t,\mathbf{x}}}$ is high, then σ is low and mainly the good patch matches contribute to the distribution and it will be clearly peaked. When there is a patch with low variance the distribution will be broader. For higher/lower noise level σ_η, more/less high contrast patches are needed to get a significantly peaked distribution, so that for low σ_η the more also poorly matching results contribute to the likelihood distribution. Therefore σ_η can act as a parameter to control the influence of the variance $\sigma_{\mathbf{G}^{t,\mathbf{x}}}$ of the patch on the confidence of the distribution.

---

[2] The symbol $\sim$ indicates that a proportional factor normalizing the sum over all distribution elements to 1 has to be considered.

3 Coarse-to-Fine Strategy

Now we regard a coarse-to-fine hierarchy of velocity detectors. A single level of the hierarchy is determined by (i) the resolution of the images that are compared (ii) the range of velocities that are scanned and (iii) the window $\mathbf{W}$ of the patches that are compared. Coarser spatial resolutions correlate with higher velocities and larger patch windows. The strategy proceeds from coarse to fine; i.e., first the larger velocities are calculated, then smaller relative velocities, then even smaller ones, etc.

For a single level of resolution, we use the local velocity estimation

$$\rho^t(\mathbf{v}|\mathbf{x}) \sim \rho^t(\mathbf{x}|\mathbf{v})\rho(\mathbf{v}) \tag{8}$$

with a common prior velocity distribution $\rho(\mathbf{v})$ for all positions $\mathbf{x}$. The prior $\rho(\mathbf{v})$ may be used to indicate preference of velocities, e.g. peaked around zero.

In the resolution pyramid, at each level k we have a different velocity estimation $\rho_k^t(\mathbf{v}|\mathbf{x})$ for the same physical velocity $\mathbf{v}$ at its corresponding physical location $\mathbf{x}$. Velocity estimations at higher levels of the pyramid (i.e., using lower spatial resolutions) are calculated using larger windows $\mathbf{W}$, therefore showing a tendency towards less aperture depending problems but more estimation errors. To the contrary, velocity estimations at lower levels of the pyramid (higher resolutions) tend to be more accurate but also more prone to aperture problems.

Nevertheless, the estimations at the different levels of the pyramid are not independent of each other. The goal of the pyramid is therefore to couple the different levels in order to (i) gain a coarse-to-fine description of velocity estimations (ii) take advantage of more global estimations to reduce the aperture problem and (iii) use the more local estimations to gain a highly resolved velocity signal. The goal is to be able to simultaneously estimate high velocities yet retain fine velocity discrimination abilities.

In order to achieve this, we do the following: The highest level of the pyramid estimates global velocities of the image. These velocities are used to impose a moving reference frame for the next lower pyramid level to estimate better resolved, more local velocities. That is, we decompose the velocity distributions in a coarse-to-fine manner, estimating at each level the relative velocity distributions needed for an accurate total velocity distribution estimation.

The advantages of such a procedure are manifold. If we want to get good estimates for both large and highly resolved velocities/distributions without a pyramidal structure, we would have to perform calculations for each possible velocity, which is computationally prohibitive. In a pyramidal structure, we get increasingly refined estimations for the velocities starting from inexpensive, but coarse initial approximations and refining further at every level.

At each level of the pyramid, we do the following steps:

1. Start with inputs

$$\mathbf{G}_k^{t+\Delta t} , \ \tilde{\mathbf{G}}_k^t . \tag{9}$$

$\tilde{\mathbf{G}}_k^t$ is the level k prediction of all gray values of image $\mathbf{I}_k^{t+\Delta t}$, using the information available at t. E.g., for the highest level with $k = 0$, $\tilde{\mathbf{G}}_0^t = \mathbf{G}_0^{t+\Delta t}$, since there are no further assumptions about velocities $\mathbf{v}$ (i.e. $\mathbf{v} = \mathbf{0}$).

2. Calculate the local likelihood for the k-th level velocity

$$\tilde{\rho}_k^t(\mathbf{x}|\mathbf{v}_k) \sim e^{-\frac{1}{2} \cdot \left(\frac{\sigma_{\tilde{\mathbf{G}}_k^{t,\mathbf{x}}}}{\sigma_\eta}\right)^2 \left(1 - \varrho^2_{\tilde{\mathbf{G}}_k^{t,\mathbf{x}}, \mathbf{G}_k^{t+\Delta t, \mathbf{x}+\Delta\mathbf{x}}}\right)} \tag{10}$$

as formulated in Eq. 7. Note that at the highest level, $\mathbf{v}_0$ is equal to the physical velocity $\mathbf{v}$ from $\rho_k^t(\mathbf{x}|\mathbf{v})$, whereas at lower levels, $\mathbf{v}_k$ is a *differential* velocity related with the likelihood estimation $\tilde{\rho}_k^t(\mathbf{x}|\mathbf{v}_k)$. Note also that ρ_k^t correlates $\tilde{\mathbf{G}}_k^{t,\mathbf{x}}$ (and not $\mathbf{G}_k^{t,\mathbf{x}}$) with $\mathbf{G}_k^{t+\Delta t, \mathbf{x}+\Delta\mathbf{x}}$.

3. Calculate the local likelihood for the *physical* velocity $\mathbf{v}$ by combining the estimation for the physical velocity from the higher stage $k - 1$ with the likelihood estimations from stage k,

$$\rho_k^t(\mathbf{x}|\mathbf{v} = \mathbf{v}_{k-1} + \mathbf{v}_k) :\sim \sum_{\mathbf{v}_k, \mathbf{v}_{k-1}} \tilde{\rho}_k^t(\mathbf{x} + \mathbf{v}_{k-1}\Delta t|\mathbf{v}_k)\, \rho_{k-1}^t(\mathbf{v}_{k-1}|\mathbf{x}) \;. \tag{11}$$

At the highest level there will be no combination because no velocity distributions from a coarser level are available and therefore $\rho_0^t(\mathbf{x}|\mathbf{v}) := \tilde{\rho}_0^t(\mathbf{x}|\mathbf{v})$.

4. Combine the likelihood with the prior $\rho_k(\mathbf{v}_k)$ to get the local a-posteriory probability for the *physical* velocity $\mathbf{v}$ according to

$$\rho_k^t(\mathbf{v}|\mathbf{x}) \sim \rho_k^t(\mathbf{x}|\mathbf{v})\, \rho_k(\mathbf{v}) \;. \tag{12}$$

5. Use the gained a-posteriory probability for the prediction of the image at time $t + \Delta t$ at the next level $k + 1$ according to

$$\tilde{\mathbf{G}}_{k+1}^t := \sum_{\mathbf{v}, \mathbf{x}} \rho_k^t(\mathbf{v}|\mathbf{x}) \mathbf{W}^{\mathbf{x} - \mathbf{v}\Delta t} \odot \mathbf{G}_{k+1}^t \;. \tag{13}$$

This is the best estimate according to level k and the constraints given by the generative model. $\mathbf{W}^{\mathbf{x} - \mathbf{v}\Delta t}$ is the window shifted by $\mathbf{x} - \mathbf{v}\Delta t$ and takes into account the correct window weightings.

6. Increase the pyramid level k and return to point 1.

4   Results

The results of the hierarchical procedure in Fig. 3 show that a combination of velocity distributions is possible within a velocity resolution pyramid and that the process combines advantages of the different levels of resolution. The coarser levels of the pyramid analyze larger patches and provide estimations for larger velocities. Nevertheless, the estimations are often inaccurate, dependent on the shape of the velocity distributions. In contrast, the finer levels of the pyramid operate more locally and analyze smaller velocities. This leads in some cases to peaked velocity distributions, but in other cases (e.g., when there is not sufficient

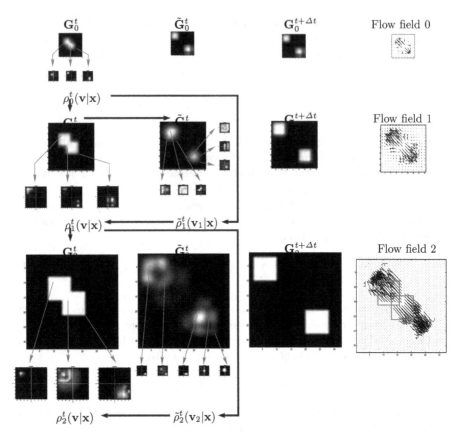

Fig. 2. The results of the hierarchical velocity distribution calculations using the resolution pyramid. The right column shows flow fields (extracted for evaluation purposes). The left three columns show the original images at time t (first column) and $t + \Delta t$ (third column), as well as the reconstructed image $\tilde{\mathbf{G}}_k^t$ (second column), which is the *prediction* of image at time $t + \Delta t$ (third column) using the available velocity distributions at time t. At each resolution level, a number of representative 2D velocity distributions $\rho_k^t(\mathbf{v}|\mathbf{x})$ (absolute velocities $\mathbf{v}$) and $\rho_k^t(\mathbf{v}_k|\mathbf{x})$ (relative velocities $\mathbf{v}_k$) are shown, with gray arrows indicating their positions in the image. For the distributions, white lines indicate the velocity coordinate system, with black/white representing low/high probabilities for the corresponding velocity. Black arrows indicate the order of the computations within the pyramid. The coarse-to-fine calculation allows the system to use the coarse velocity information for regions which at higher levels of resolution have flat distributions or ambiguous motion signals, and to refine the coarse information with additional information from the finer levels of velocity resolution. This can be seen at the flow field at the highest level of resolution ("Flow field 2"). In "Flow field 2" only the velocity vectors with high probabilities are shown.

structure) to broad distributions because of unavailable motion information. The combination of coarse and fine levels using the velocity distribution representation allows to incorporate more global velocity estimations if local information is

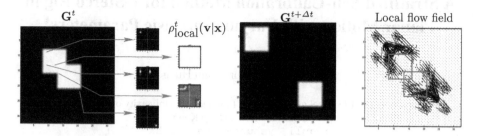

Fig. 3. For comparison, here we show the velocity distributions and the flow field calculated over the entire velocity range using fine velocity discretization and fine resolution window. In the flow field we see that the velocity signals are only unambiguous at the corners of the squares, whereas the central parts convey no motion information and the edges suffer the classical aperture problem. Using the squared magnitude of the difference between the correct and estimated flow the pyramidal approach produces 54,4% less error than this one.

missing, and to refine global velocity estimations if local information is present. An advantage of a pyramidal structure for velocity computation is that we gain the coarse estimations very fast, and can then refine the results step by step. The strategy is comparable to detecting global motions first, and then to use this information in a moving coordinate frame, in order to detect the finer relative motions still available within this frame.

References

1. *Handbook of Computer Vision and Applications*, chapter Bayesian Multi-Scale Differential Optical Flow. Academic Press, 1999.
2. J. Bergen, P. Anandan, K. Hanna, and R. Hingorani. Hierarchical model-based motion estimation. In *Proc. 2nd Europ Conf Comput Vis*, 1992.
3. E. Simoncelli, E.H. Adelson, and D.J. Heeger. Probability distributions of optical flow. In *Proc Conf Comput Vis and Pat Recogn*. IEEE Computer Society, 1991.
4. Y. Weiss and D.J. Fleet. Velocity likelihoods in biological and machine vision. In *Probabilistic Models of the Brain: Perception and Neural Function*. MIT Press, 2002.
5. Qing X. Wu. A correlation-relaxation-labeling framework for computing optical flow - template matching from a new perspective. *IEEE Transactions on Pattern Analysis and Machine Intelligence*, 17, 1995.

A Stratified Self-Calibration Method for a Stereo Rig in Planar Motion with Varying Intrinsic Parameters*

Yan Li and Yeung Sam Hung

Department of Electrical and Electronic Engineering, University of Hong Kong
Pokfulam Road, Hong Kong
{yanli, yshung}@eee.hku.hk

Abstract. Self-calibration for imaging sensors is essential to many computer vision applications. In this paper, a new stratified self-calibration method is proposed for a stereo rig undergoing planar motion with varying intrinsic parameters. We show that the plane at infinity in a projective frame can be identified by (i) a constraint developed from the properties of planar motion for a stereo rig and (ii) a zero-skew assumption of the camera. Once the plane at infinity is identified, the calibration matrices of the cameras and the upgrade to a metric reconstruction can be readily obtained. The proposed method is more flexible than most existing self-calibration methods in that it allows all intrinsic parameters to vary. Experimental results for both synthetic data and real images are provided to show the performance of the proposed method.

1 Introduction

Self-calibration methods for imaging sensors have been an active research subject in recent years. Based on the rigidity of the scene and the constancy of the internal camera parameters, many results have been obtained [1-6, 11-15]. Many existing self-calibration methods try to solve for the intrinsic parameters immediately after the projective reconstruction, which has the drawback of having to determine many parameters simultaneously from nonlinear equations. This prompts the development of stratified approaches for calibrating cameras [12, 13] and stereo rigs [2, 3, 4, 5].

'Stratified' means converting a projective calibration first to an affine calibration and then to the Euclidean calibration. Along this line, M. Pollefeys and L. Van proposed a stratified self-calibration method [13]. The method uses the modulus constraint to identify the plane at infinity in projective frame so as to upgrade the projective reconstruction to affine and then Euclidean reconstruction. But the method does not uniquely identify the plane at infinity. R.I. Hartley proposed a method to search the plane at infinity in a limited 3-dimensional cubic region in the parameter space [12]. Although the method can uniquely identify the plane at infinity, the precision of the solution is constrained by the quantization of the searching space. A Ruf et al. proposed a stratified self-calibration method for a stereo rig [3] which identifies the plane at infinity much more effectively through decomposing the

---

* The work described in this paper is partially supported by a grant from the Research Grant Council of the Hong Kong Special Administrative Region, China (Project No. HKU 7058/02E) and partially supported by CRCG of The University of Hong Kong

C.E. Rasmussen et al. (Eds.): DAGM 2004, LNCS 3175, pp. 318–325, 2004.

projective translation. The drawback of the method is that the motion of the stereo rig is restricted to pure translation. A. Zisserman et. al. proposed a calibration method for stereo rig undergoing general motion [4]. Subsequently, using different projective reconstructions that are associated with each stereo pair, R. Horaud and G. Csurka [5] proposed a stratified self-calibration method for a stereo rig in general motion. Although these stratified self-calibration methods for stereo rig can determine the plane at infinity more effectively, they all assume that the cameras of the stereo rig have constant intrinsic parameters and the stereo correspondences are known.

In this paper we shall present a new stratified self-calibration method for a stereo rig that has varying intrinsic parameters while undergoing planar motion. To identify the plane at infinity, our method does not require any information of ideal points or points in the 3D scene. The only assumption used is that the cameras are of zero skew. Simulations on synthetic data and experimental results using real image sequences show that the proposed method deals with the cases of varying intrinsic parameters effectively and is robust to noise.

2 A New Stratified Self-Calibration Method

Consider an uncalibrated binocular stereo rig undergoing planar motion, with varying intrinsic parameters. It is assumed the stereo rig is set up such that the base line of the two cameras of the stereo rig is not parallel to the motion plane. For the purpose of reference, the two cameras will be referred to as upper and the lower cameras depending on their physical position. Suppose sequences of images are captured by both cameras of the stereo pair. By matching image points across all the images, we can obtain a projective reconstruction using the method described in [7]. It is assumed that such a projective reconstruction has been performed and this will be taken as the starting point in our self-calibration method.

First, we select one image, denoted I_o, from the sequence of the lower camera as the reference image. The projection matrix for the reference image I_o can be taken as $\mathbf{P}_0 = [\mathbf{I}|\mathbf{0}]$. Let the other images taken by the stereo rig be I_i ($i=1,...,n$), with projection matrices given by $\mathbf{P}_i = [\mathbf{M}_i | \mathbf{m}_i]$, ($i=1,...,n$).

Suppose the plane at infinity π_∞ is given in the projective frame by $[\mathbf{v}^T, 1]^T$, where $\mathbf{v} = [v_1 \ \ v_2 \ \ v_3]^T$. Then, the infinite homography between images I_i and I_o can be written as:

$$\mathbf{H}_{\infty i0} = \mathbf{M}_i - \mathbf{m}_i \mathbf{v}^\mathbf{T} \ . \tag{1}$$

To upgrade the projective reconstruction to an affine one, the plane at infinity π_∞ in the projective frame must be identified. This is the most difficult step in the stratified self-calibration procedure. We will next propose a method for identifying π_∞ using the properties of planar motion.

Figure 1 shows the geometry of a camera in planar motion, where all the camera centers O_1, O_2 ... O_i lie on a plane called the camera motion plane, denoted π. Let e_{1i}

($i=2,\ldots,n$) be the epipole of image $\mathcal{I}_i$ on $\mathcal{I}_1$. The intersection lines of the plane π and the image planes are the vanishing lines of the camera motion plane in the images. Obviously, the epipoles e_{1i} ($i=2,\ldots,n$) of all the other images on $\mathcal{I}_1$ lie on the vanishing line of the camera motion plane on $\mathcal{I}_1$. So the vanishing line can be obtained by fitting a straight line to the epipoles. A similar argument can be applied to obtain the vanishing line of the plane π on any image $\mathcal{I}_i$ of the sequence.

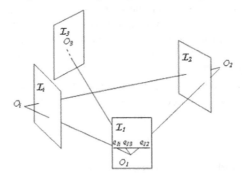

Fig. 1. Geometry of a camera making planar motion

Since the motion of the stereo rig is rigid, the motion planes of the two cameras are parallel to each other and have the same vanishing line in each image.

Select one image, denoted I_1, from the sequence of the upper camera. Using the above method, the vanishing lines of the (upper or lower) camera motion plane in the images I_o and I_1 can be identified, which will be denoted $\mathbf{l}_0$ and $\mathbf{l}_1$ respectively. Under the rule of transforming lines under infinite homography, we have

$$\mathbf{l}_0 \propto \mathbf{H}^T_{\infty 10}\mathbf{l}_1 . \tag{2}$$

where the symbol $\propto$ means equal up to an unknown scaling factor. To eliminate the unknown scalar, we write the equation (2) in the form of a cross product:

$$\left[\mathbf{l}_0\right]_\times \mathbf{H}^T_{\infty 10}\mathbf{l}_1 = \left[\mathbf{l}_0\right]_\times (\mathbf{M}_1^T - \mathbf{vm}_1^T)\mathbf{l}_1 = 0 . \tag{3}$$

where $\left[\mathbf{l}_0\right]_\times$ is the 3 by 3 skew-symmetric matrix associated with cross product. Since there are only two independent entries in a 3-vector which represents a line in homogeneous coordinate, equation (3) provides two independent equations for the three unknowns in $\mathbf{v}=[\,v_1\,,\,v_2,\,v_3]^T$. Under the assumption that the upper and the lower cameras do not lie on the same motion plane, we can make use of (3) to solve v_1 and v_2 in terms of v_3. Substituting the v_1 and v_2 back into (1), we get the infinite homographies between images I_i and I_o with one unknown variable v_3.

To determine v_3, we need another constraint on the infinite homographies. Let the image of the absolute conic (IAC) on I_o and I_i be ω_0 and ω_i, respectively. Under the rule for transforming conics by a homography, ω_0 and ω_i satisfy:

$$\omega_i \propto \mathbf{H}^{-T}_{\infty i0}\omega_0\mathbf{H}^{-1}_{\infty i0} . \tag{4}$$

The IAC ω_i on image I_i is related to the calibration matrix $K_i = \begin{bmatrix} \alpha_{xi} & s_i & x_{0i} \\ 0 & \alpha_{yi} & y_{0i} \\ 0 & 0 & 1 \end{bmatrix}$ of its

camera as:

$$
(5)
$$

$$
\omega_i = K_i^{-T} K_i^{-1} = \begin{bmatrix} \alpha_{yi}^2 & -s_i\alpha_{yi} & -x_{0i}\alpha_{yi}^2 + y_{0i}s_i\alpha_{yi} \\ -s_i\alpha_{yi} & \alpha_{xi}^2 + s_i^2 & \alpha_{yi}s_i x_{0i} - \alpha_{xi}^2 y_{0i} - s_i^2 y_{0i} \\ -x_{0i}\alpha_{yi}^2 + y_{0i}s_i\alpha_{yi} & \alpha_{yi}s_i x_{0i} - \alpha_{xi}^2 y_{0i} - s_i^2 y_{0i} & \alpha_{xi}^2\alpha_{yi}^2 + \alpha_{xi}^2 y_{0i}^2 + (\alpha_{yi}x_{0i} - s_i y_{0i})^2 \end{bmatrix}
$$

It is reasonable to assume that all cameras have zero-skew, that is $s_i=0$. In this case, we have $(\omega_i)_{12}=0$. Imposing this constraint on (4), we get one linear equation in the entries of ω_0:

$$
(H_{\infty i0}^{-T}\omega_0 H_{\infty i0}^{-1})_{12} = 0 . \tag{6}
$$

Where $(X)_{ij}$ represents the (i,j)th element of the matrix X. With five image pairs (I_o, I_i) $(i=1,2,...,5)$, five such equations can be obtained, which can be written as:

$$
AW_0 = 0 . \tag{7}
$$

where W_0 is a 5-vector made up of the distinct entries of the symmetric matrix ω_0, and A is a 5×5 square matrix parameterized by the variable v_3. Since the entries of W_0 cannot be all zero, the square matrix A must be singular, that is, A satisfies det(A)=0. This is a polynomial equation in v_3 which in general admits 8 solutions. By checking the feasibility of the solutions (i.e. v_3 must be real and the IAC must be a positive definite matrix), the variable v_3 can be uniquely determined.

In practice, with existence of noise det(A) may deviate from zero. A more robust solution for v_3 can be obtained by the following algorithm:

With n image pairs (I_o, I_i) $(i=1,...,n)$, where $n>5$, a n×5 matrix A is formed as in (7).
1. Select 5 rows form the matrix A randomly to get a 5×5 square matrix A'. Solving det(A')=0, we get eight solutions of v_3. By substituting v_3 back into the matrix A' and checking weather the IAC is positive definite, we can determine a unique solution for v_3.
2. Substituting the value of v_3 back into the matrix A, calculate the least singular value of the matrix A. Save the value of v_3 and the least singular value.
3. Repeat Steps 2 and 3 a number of (say, ten) times.
4. Compare all the least singular values obtained in Step 3 and choose as the true value of v_3 the one for which the least singular value of A is smallest.

After solving for v_3 and substituting it back into (7) and (1), ω_0 and all the infinite homographies between images I_i and I_o can be solved. With (4) the IAC's ω_i $(i=1,\ldots,n)$ can be determined. By a Cholesky factorization of ω_i, we can solve for the calibration matrices K_i for each image.

3   Experimental Results

3.1   Simulations with Synthetic Data

Simulations are carried out on image sequences of a synthetic scene. The scene consists of 50 points uniformly distributed within the unit sphere centered at the origin of the world coordinate. The synthetic stereo rig moves on the x-y plane along a circular path of 3 meter radius. The directions of the two cameras of the stereo rig are different. The intrinsic parameters are different for different views and are determined as follows: f_x and f_y are chosen randomly from the range [980, 1200] and [960, 1000] respectively, x_0 and y_0 chosen randomly from the range [498, 502] and [398, 402] respectively, and the skew is zero. The image size is 1300×1000 pixels.

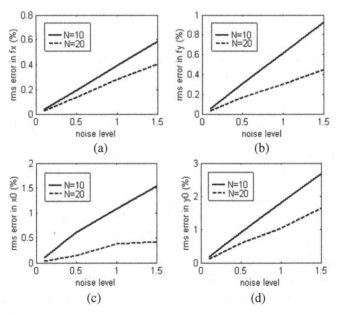

Fig. 2. Relative RMS errors on estimated camera intrinsic parameters for the image I_0 with different noise level. (a) relative RMS error of f_x [pixel] (b) relative RMS error of f_y [pixel] (c) relative RMS error x_0 (d) relative RMS error of y_0

In the simulation, N images are captured by each of the upper and lower cameras. Gaussian white noise with standard deviations of 0.1, 0.5, 1 and 1.5 pixels are added to the synthetic image points. For each noise level, the self-calibration method is run

10 times and the relative RMS errors on the estimated camera intrinsic parameters for the reference image I_0 are calculated. The simulation results of the method for $N=10$ and 20 are shown in Figure 2.

3.2 Real Sequence1

The first experiment is designed to evaluate the proposed method when each of the two cameras of the stereo rig has fixed intrinsic parameters. In the experiment, the intrinsic parameters of the upper and lower cameras are different, but the parameters of each camera are kept constant during motion. Seven images are taken by each of the upper and lower camera, two of which are shown in fig.3. The resolution of the images is 3000×2000 pixels.

Fig. 3. Pair of images used in experiment 1

Table 1. Calibration results in experiment 1

	f_x (pixel)	f_y (pixel)	x_0 (pixel)	y_0 (pixel)
upper camera	10243	10245	1598	815
	10370	10373	1546	814
	10311	10313	1583	815
lower camera	9925	9937	1577	968
	9876	9888	1578	964
	9972	9985	1561	966

In the experiment, the vanishing lines for two images I_o and I_1 are determined using all 7 images of the lower and the upper sequence respectively. Then, all the 14 images are used to form a 13×5 matrix **A**.

Three images are selected from each of the lower and upper sequences and the proposed method is used to find the intrinsic parameters for these images. The experimental results are shown in table 1, where the first three rows are for the three images taken by the upper camera, and the last three rows are for the three images taken by the lower one. Since the intrinsic parameters calculated for different images taken by the same camera are nearly constant, the calibration results are quite reasonable.

3.3 Real Sequence2

Experiment 2 is designed to evaluate the proposed method when the cameras of the stereo rig have varying intrinsic parameters. Ten images are taken by each camera of the stereo rig, three pairs of which are shown in fig.4. The CCD cameras of the stereo rig are zoomed during motion so that the focal length is different for different views. The resolution of the images is 3000×2000 pixels.

Fig. 4. Three pairs of images taken by zooming camera used in experiment 2

Table 2. Calibration results of zooming cameras

	f_x (pixel)	f_y (pixel)	x_0 (pixel)	y_0 (pixel)
upper camera	9251	9260	1500	731
	12084	12104	1242	686
	10404	10397	1263	828
lower camera	8178	8192	1555	938
	10115	10135	1486	957
	10158	10156	1579	836

Experimental results for the six images shown in Fig.4 are listed in table 2. By comparing Fig.4 and Table 2, we see that the camera's zooming positions are consistent with (the focal length of) the calibration results.

4 Conclusions

This paper describes a new method for self-calibration of a stereo rig in planar motion with varying intrinsic parameters. In previous research, calibration models used are either too restrictive (constant parameters) or not general enough (e.g. only the focal length can be varied). In practice, changes in focal length are usually accompanied by changes of the principle points. The method presented in this paper is more flexible than existing results in that it allows all intrinsic parameters to vary.

We have shown in this paper how to identify the infinite plane in a projective frame from rigid planar motion of a stereo rig. The projective calibration is upgraded to metric calibration under the assumption that the cameras are of zero skew. The simulation results show that the method is robust to the influence of noise. The two experiments with real images provide further justification for the self-calibration method.

References

1. F. Dornaika. Self-calibration of a Stereo Rig using Monocular Epipolar Geometry. ICCV01. IEEE Top Reference, 0106 BibRef (2001) 467-472
2. J. Knight and I. Reid. Active visual alignment of a mobile stereo camera platform. In Proc. International Conference of Robotics and Automation, San Francisco (2000)
3. A. Ruf, G. Csurka, and R. Horaud. Projective Translations and Affine Stereo Calibration. In Proceedings IEEE Conference on Computer Vision and Pattern Recognition, Santa Barbara, CA (1998) 475--481
4. A. Zisserman, P. A. Beardsley, and I. D. Reid. Metric Calibration of a stereo rig. In proc. IEEE Workshop on Representations of Visual Scenes, Boston. IEEE Computer Society Press (1995) 93-100
5. R. Horaud and G. Caurka. Self-calibration and Euclidean reconstruction using motions of a stereo rig. In Proc. Of ICCV (1998) 96-103
6. J. Knight and I. Reid. Self-calibration of a stereo rig in a planar scene by data combination. ICPR Barcelona, Spain (2000) 1411-1414
7. W. K. Tang and Y. S. Hung, A Factorization-based method for Projective Reconstruction with minimization of 2-D reprojection errors, In Proceedings of DAGM 2002, Zurich (2002) 387-394
8. Strum, P. Camera Self-Calibration: A Case Against Kruppa's Equations, ICIP, Chicago (1998)
9. Andrew Zisserman et al. Resolving Ambiguities in Auto-Calibration, Royal Society Typescript (1998)
10. Andrew W. Fitzgibbon et al.,Automatic 3D Model Construction for Turn-Table Sequences, SMILE '98, LNCS 1506 (1998) 155-170
11. Y. Seo and K.S.Hong. Theory and Practice on the Self-calibration of a Rotating and Zooming Camera from Two Views. VISP(148), No. 3 (2001) 166-172
12. R.I.Hartley, E. Hayman, L. de Agapito and I. Reid. Camera Calibration and the Search for Infinity. International Conference on Computer Vision, Volume 1 (1999) 510-516
13. M. Pollefeys and L. V. Gool. Stratified self-Calibration with modulus constraint. IEEE Transactions on Pattern Analysis and Machine Intelligence, Vol. 21, No.8, (1999) 707-724
14. S. Dai and Q. Ji. A New Technique for Camera Self-Calibration. International Conference on Robotics & Automation. Seoul, Korea (2001) 2165-2170
15. R. Hartley and A. Zisserman. Multiple View Geometry in Computer Vision. Cambridge University Press, UK (2000)

Efficient Feature Tracking for Long Video Sequences

Timo Zinßer*, Christoph Gräßl*, and Heinrich Niemann

Chair for Pattern Recognition, University of Erlangen-Nuremberg
Martensstraße 3, 91058 Erlangen, Germany
zinsser@informatik.uni-erlangen.de

Abstract. This work is concerned with real-time feature tracking for long video sequences. In order to achieve efficient and robust tracking, we propose two interrelated enhancements to the well-known Shi-Tomasi-Kanade tracker. Our first contribution is the integration of a linear illumination compensation method into the inverse compositional approach for affine motion estimation. The resulting algorithm combines the strengths of both components and achieves strong robustness and high efficiency at the same time. Our second enhancement copes with the feature drift problem, which is of special concern in long video sequences. Refining the initial frame-to-frame estimate of the feature position, our approach relies on the ability to robustly estimate the affine motion of every feature in every frame in real-time. We demonstrate the performance of our enhancements with experiments on real video sequences.

1 Introduction

Feature tracking provides essential input data for a wide range of computer vision algorithms, including most structure-from-motion algorithms [1]. Other important applications that depend on successful feature tracking are, for example, camera self-calibration [2] and pose estimation for augmented reality [3].

The well-known Shi-Tomasi-Kanade tracker has a long history of evolutionary development. Its basic tracking principle was first proposed by Lucas and Kanade in [4]. For tracking a feature from one frame to the next, the sum of squared differences of the feature intensities is iteratively minimized with a gradient descent method. The important aspect of automatic feature detection was added by Tomasi and Kanade in [5].

Shi and Tomasi introduced feature monitoring for detecting occlusions and false correspondences [6]. They measure the feature dissimilarity between the first and the current frame, after estimating an affine transformation to correct distortions. If the dissimilarity exceeds a fixed threshold, the feature is discarded. This method was further refined in [7], where the X84 rejection rule is used to automatically determine a suitable threshold.

---

* This work was partially funded by the European Commission's 5th IST Programme under grant IST-2001-34401 (project VAMPIRE). Only the authors are responsible for the content.

C.E. Rasmussen et al. (Eds.): DAGM 2004, LNCS 3175, pp. 326–333, 2004.

Baker and Matthews propose a comprehensive framework for template alignment using gradient descent [8], as employed by the Shi-Tomasi-Kanade tracker. In contrast to the algorithm of Lucas and Kanade, they suggest estimating the inverse motion parameters and updating them with incremental warps. Their *inverse compositional approach* facilitates the precomputing of essential operations, considerably increasing the speed of the algorithm.

As its motion estimation is completely intensity-based, the feature tracker is very sensitive to illumination changes. Jin *et al.* developed a method for simultaneous estimation of affine motion and linear illumination compensation [9]. Our first contribution is the combination of Jin's method with Baker's inverse compositional approach. We evaluate our new algorithm by comparing it with the intensity distribution normalization approach suggested in [7].

Due to small parameter estimation errors, features tracked from frame to frame will slowly drift away from their correct position. We propose to solve the *feature drift problem* by incorporating the results of the affine motion estimation. Another solution with respect to the tracking of larger templates is put forward by Matthews *et al.* in [10].

After a short overview of our tracking system in the next section, we present the combined motion estimation and illumination compensation algorithm in Sect. 3. Our approach for solving the feature drift problem is detailed in Sect. 4. Finally, we demonstrate experimental results in Sect. 5.

2   Tracking System Overview

Our goal of real-time feature tracking for long video sequences not only led to the enhancement of key components of the Shi-Tomasi-Kanade tracker, but also required a careful arrangement of the remaining components. In this section, we will shortly explain these additional design considerations.

We employ the feature detector derived in [5]. It was designed to find optimal features for the translation estimation algorithm of the tracker. Tomasi and Kanade also discovered that detected corners are often positioned at the edge of the feature window [5]. As this phenomenon can lead to suboptimal tracking performance, we use smaller windows for feature detection than for feature tracking. Consequently, even if a corner lies at the edge of the detection window, it is well inside the actual tracking window. Another possibility is to emphasize the inner pixels of the detection window by applying Gaussian weights. Unfortunately, this method did not further improve the tracking in our experiments.

When feature tracking is performed on long video sequences, losing features is inevitable. As we want to keep the number of features approximately constant, lost features have to be replaced regularly. In order to retain the desired real-time performance, we devised a hierarchical algorithm which successively selects the best features according to the ranking provided by the interest image. After the selection of one feature, only a local update of the algorithm's data structure is required. Additionally, the algorithm is able to enforce a mini-

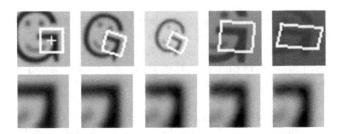

Fig. 1. In the top row, five instances of a feature that was tracked with the proposed algorithm are shown. The respective reconstructions in the bottom row illustrate the performance of the affine motion estimation and the linear illumination compensation.

mum distance between each new feature and all other features, which prevents wasting computational resources on tracking highly overlapping features.

The main task of feature tracking is to estimate the translation of a feature from one frame to the next. Lucas and Kanade observed that the basin of convergence of their gradient descent algorithm can be increased by suppressing high spatial frequencies [4]. The amount of smoothing is bounded by the size of the feature windows, because at least some structure has to remain visible for a meaningful registration. In order to increase the maximum displacement that can be tolerated by the tracker, we employ a Gaussian image pyramid coupled with a coarse-to-fine strategy for translation estimation. Usually working with three levels of downsampled images, we can considerably extend the basin of convergence. Another important addition is the linear motion prediction, which is especially beneficial when a feature moves with approximately constant velocity.

After the affine motion estimation, which is discussed in the next section, outliers have to be detected and rejected. Although the dynamic threshold computation in [7] is promising, we rely on a fixed threshold for the maximum SSD error. In our experience, the gap between correctly tracked features and outliers is sufficiently large when illumination compensation is performed. Jin *et al.* discard features whose area falls below a given threshold [9]. We extend this method by observing the singular values of the affine transformation matrix, which represent the scale of the feature window along the principal axes of the affine transformation. This way, we can also reject features that are extremely distorted, but have approximately retained their original area.

3   Efficient Feature Tracking

After estimating the translation of a feature from one frame to the next, we compute its affine motion and the illumination compensation parameters with respect to the frame of its first appearance. By continually updating these parameters in every frame, we are able to successfully track features undergoing strong distortions and intensity changes, as illustrated in Fig. 1. In addition, this approach allows us to discard erroneous features as early as possible.

In order to achieve real-time performance, we adopt the inverse compositional approach for motion estimation proposed in [8]. The traditional error function is

$$\sum_x \left(f(\boldsymbol{x}) - f_t(\boldsymbol{g}(\boldsymbol{x}, \boldsymbol{p} + \Delta \boldsymbol{p})) \right)^2 , \tag{1}$$

where $f(\boldsymbol{x})$ and $f_t(\boldsymbol{x})$ denote the intensity values of the first frame and the current frame, respectively. In our case, the parameterized warp function $\boldsymbol{g}$ is the affine warp

$$\boldsymbol{g}(\boldsymbol{x}, \boldsymbol{p}) = \begin{pmatrix} 1 + p_1 & p_2 \\ p_3 & 1 + p_4 \end{pmatrix} \boldsymbol{x} + \begin{pmatrix} p_5 \\ p_6 \end{pmatrix} , \tag{2}$$

where $\boldsymbol{x}$ represents 2-D image coordinates and $\boldsymbol{p}$ contains the six affine motion parameters. By swapping the role of the frames, we get the new error function of the inverse compositional algorithm

$$\sum_x \left(f(\boldsymbol{g}(\boldsymbol{x}, \Delta \boldsymbol{p})) - f_t(\boldsymbol{g}(\boldsymbol{x}, \boldsymbol{p})) \right)^2 . \tag{3}$$

Solving for $\Delta \boldsymbol{p}$ after a first-order Taylor expansion yields

$$\Delta \boldsymbol{p} = \boldsymbol{H}^{-1} \sum_x \left(\nabla f(\boldsymbol{x}) \frac{\delta \boldsymbol{g}}{\delta \boldsymbol{p}} \right)^T \left(f_t(\boldsymbol{g}(\boldsymbol{x}, \boldsymbol{p})) - f(\boldsymbol{x}) \right) \tag{4}$$

$$\text{with} \quad \boldsymbol{H} = \sum_x \left(\nabla f(\boldsymbol{x}) \frac{\delta \boldsymbol{g}}{\delta \boldsymbol{p}} \right)^T \left(\nabla f(\boldsymbol{x}) \frac{\delta \boldsymbol{g}}{\delta \boldsymbol{p}} \right) .$$

The increased efficiency of the inverse compositional approach is due to the fact that matrix $\boldsymbol{H}^{-1}$ can be precomputed, as it does not depend on the current frame or the current motion parameters. The new rule for updating the motion parameters is

$$\boldsymbol{g}(\boldsymbol{x}, \boldsymbol{p}_{\text{new}}) = \boldsymbol{g}(\boldsymbol{g}(\boldsymbol{x}, \Delta \boldsymbol{p})^{-1}, \boldsymbol{p}) . \tag{5}$$

We combine the efficient inverse compositional approach with the illumination compensation algorithm presented in [9], in order to cope with intensity changes, which are common in video sequences of real scenes. They can be caused by automatic exposure correction of the camera, changing illumination conditions, and even movements of the captured objects.

The linear model $\alpha f(\boldsymbol{x}) + \beta$, where α adjusts contrast and β adjusts brightness, has proven to be sufficient for our application (compare Fig. 1). With this illumination compensation model, our cost function becomes

$$\sum_x \left(\alpha f(\boldsymbol{g}(\boldsymbol{x}, \Delta \boldsymbol{p})) + \beta - f_t(\boldsymbol{g}(\boldsymbol{x}, \boldsymbol{p})) \right)^2 . \tag{6}$$

Computing the first-order Taylor expansion around the identity warp $\boldsymbol{g}(\boldsymbol{x}, 0)$ gives us

$$\sum_x \left(\alpha f(\boldsymbol{x}) + \alpha \nabla f(\boldsymbol{x}) \frac{\delta \boldsymbol{g}}{\delta \boldsymbol{p}} \Delta \boldsymbol{p} + \beta - f_t(\boldsymbol{g}(\boldsymbol{x}, \boldsymbol{p})) \right)^2 . \tag{7}$$

With the introduction of the new vectors

$$q = (\alpha \Delta p_1 \ \ \alpha \Delta p_2 \ \ \alpha \Delta p_3 \ \ \alpha \Delta p_4 \ \ \alpha \Delta p_5 \ \ \alpha \Delta p_6 \ \ \alpha \ \ \beta)^T, \tag{8}$$

$$h(x) = (\ xf_x(x) \ \ yf_x(x) \ \ xf_y(x) \ \ yf_y(x) \ \ f_x(x) \ \ f_y(x) \ \ f(x) \ \ 1\ )^T, \tag{9}$$

we can rewrite Equation (7) as

$$\sum_x \left(h(x)^T q - f_t(g(x, p)) \right)^2. \tag{10}$$

Solving this least-squares problem finally results in

$$q = \left(\sum_x h(x) h(x)^T \right)^{-1} \left(\sum_x h(x) f_t(g(x, p)) \right). \tag{11}$$

As can easily be seen, the 8×8 matrix composed of dyadic products of vector $h(x)$ is still independent of the current frame and the current motion parameters. Therefore, it only has to be computed and inverted once for each feature, which saves a considerable amount of computation time. Additionally, the simultaneous estimation of motion and illumination parameters promises faster convergence.

4   Feature Drift Prevention

There are several reasons why the feature windows in two frames will never be identical in video sequences of real scenes:

- image noise,
- geometric distortions (rotation, scaling, non-rigid deformation),
- intensity changes (illumination changes, camera exposure correction),
- sampling artefacts of the image sensor.

Although these effects are usually very small in consecutive frames, it is obvious that frame-to-frame translation estimation can never be absolutely accurate. Consequently, using only translation estimation will invariably cause the feature window to drift from its true position when the estimation errors accumulate.

As the feature drift problem only becomes an issue in long video sequences, it was not considered in early work on feature tracking [4,5]. Feature monitoring and outlier rejection as described in [6,7] can only detect this problem. Once the feature has drifted too far from its initial position, the affine motion estimation fails to converge and the feature is discarded. If subsequent algorithms require highly accurate feature positions, this shortcoming can be problematic. Jin *et al.* use affine motion estimation exclusively, thus giving up the much larger basin of convergence of pure translation estimation [9].

We propose to solve the feature drift problem with a two-stage approach. First, pure translation estimation is performed from the last frame to the current frame. Then, the affine motion between the first frame and the current frame

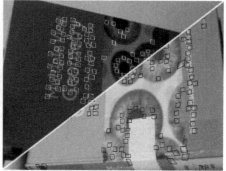

Fig. 2. Illumination compensation test sequence with 100 frames and 200 features. Left image: frame 0. Right image: frame 50 (lower right) / 99 (upper left).

is estimated. Hereby, the newly computed translation parameters and the four affine distortion parameters of the preceding frame are used as initialization. The translation parameters of the new affine motion parameters constitute the final feature position for the current frame. Our solution requires affine motion estimation, preferably with illumination compensation, in every frame. This can now be done in real-time thanks to the efficient algorithm put forward in Sect. 3. Because the coordinate system for estimating the affine motion is always centered on the original feature, small errors in the computation of the affine distortion matrix will not negatively affect the translation parameters in our approach.

5   Experimental Evaluation

All experiments in this section were performed on a personal computer with a Pentium IV 2.4 GHz cpu and 1 GB main memory. The video images were captured with a digital firewire camera at a resolution of 640×480. The feature detector, the translation estimation, and the affine motion estimation worked with window sizes of 5×5, 7×7, and 13×13, respectively.

We compared our new affine motion and linear illumination compensation algorithm of Sect. 3 with the photometric normalization approach suggested by Fusiello *et al.* [7]. They normalize the intensity distribution of the feature windows with respect to the mean and the standard deviation of the intensities. Their approach is limited to alternating estimation of motion and illumination.

The test sequence illustrated in Fig. 2 contains 100 frames and exhibits strong intensity changes created by small movements of the test object. 200 features had to be tracked without replacing lost features. The number of successfully tracked features is 162 for our algorithm and 156 for the distribution normalization algorithm. Most of the lost features were close to the edge of the object and left the field of view during the sequence. As confirmed by this experiment, in general the robustness of both approaches is very similar. The great advantage of our algorithm is the lower average number of required iterations, which is

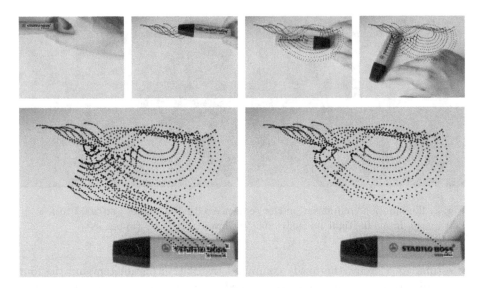

Fig. 3. Feature drift prevention test sequence with 220 frames and 10 features. The upper row shows frames 0, 60, 120, and 150 with feature drift prevention. The lower row shows frame 219 with (left) and without (right) feature drift prevention.

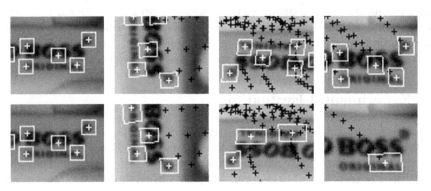

Fig. 4. Close-up views of feature tracking with (upper row) and without (lower row) feature drift prevention are shown for frames 0, 80, 120, and 219 of the test sequence.

2.21 iterations compared to 3.58 iterations for the distribution normalization algorithm. Consequently, with 20.9 ms against 23.9 ms overall computation time per frame, our tracking algorithm has a notable speed advantage.

The feature drift prevention experiments illustrated in Fig. 3 and Fig. 4 were performed on a test sequence with 220 frames. 10 features were chosen automatically with the standard feature detector described in Sect. 2. The standard approach only tracked one feature over the whole sequence, whereas the proposed feature drift prevention enabled the tracker to successfully track all 10 features. The close-up views of selected frames shown in Fig. 4 confirm the explanations given in Sect. 4. The small errors of the frame-to-frame translation estimation accumulate over time, finally preventing the affine motion estimation used for feature rejection from converging. On the other hand, using the translation parameters of the affine motion estimation as final feature positions yields very accurate and stable results.

6 Conclusion

We proposed and evaluated two enhancements for efficient feature tracking in long video sequences. First, we integrated a linear illumination compensation method into the inverse compositional approach for affine motion estimation. The resulting algorithm proved to be robust to illumination changes and outperformed existing algorithms in our experiments. Furthermore, we overcame the feature drift problem of frame-to-frame translation tracking by determining the final feature position from the translation parameters of the affine motion estimation. We demonstrated the increased accuracy and robustness of this approach in our experiments. With the described enhancements, our tracking system can robustly track 250 features at a rate of 30 frames per second while replacing lost features every five frames on a standard personal computer.

References

1. Oliensis, J.: A Critique of Structure-from-Motion Algorithms. Computer Vision and Image Understanding **84** (2001) 407–408
2. Koch, R., Heigl, B., Pollefeys, M., Gool, L.V., Niemann, H.: Calibration of Hand-held Camera Sequences for Plenoptic Modeling. In: Proceedings of the International Conference on Computer Vision, Corfu, Greece (1999) 585–591
3. Ribo, M., Ganster, H., Brandner, M., Lang, P., Stock, C., Pinz, A.: Hybrid Tracking for Outdoor AR Applications. IEEE Computer Graphics and Applications Magazine **22** (2002) 54–63
4. Lucas, B.D., Kanade, T.: An Iterative Image Registration Technique with an Application to Stereo Vision. In: Proceedings of the 7th International Joint Conference on Artificial Intelligence. (1981) 674–679
5. Tomasi, C., Kanade, T.: Detection and Tracking of Point Features. Technical Report CMU-CS-91-132, Carnegie Mellon University (1991)
6. Shi, J., Tomasi, C.: Good Features to Track. In: Proceedings of the IEEE Conference on Computer Vision and Pattern Recognition, Seattle, USA (1994) 593–600
7. Fusiello, A., Trucco, E., Tommasini, T., Roberto, V.: Improving Feature Tracking with Robust Statistics. Pattern Analysis and Applications **2** (1999) 312–320
8. Baker, S., Matthews, I.: Equivalence and Efficiency of Image Alignment Algorithms. In: Proceedings of the IEEE Conference on Computer Vision and Pattern Recognition, Kauai, USA (2001) 1090–1097
9. Jin, H., Favaro, P., Soatto, S.: Real-Time Feature Tracking and Outlier Rejection with Changes in Illumination. In: Proceedings of the International Conference on Computer Vision, Vancouver, Canada (2001) 684–689
10. Matthews, I., Ishikawa, T., Baker, S.: The Template Update Problem. In: Proceedings of the British Machine Vision Conference. (2003)

Recognition of Deictic Gestures with Context*

Nils Hofemann, Jannik Fritsch, and Gerhard Sagerer

Applied Computer Science
Faculty of Technology, Bielefeld University
33615 Bielefeld, Germany
{nhofeman, jannik, sagerer}@techfak.uni-bielefeld.de

Abstract. Pointing at objects is a natural form of interaction between humans that is of particular importance in human-machine interfaces. Our goal is the recognition of such deictic gestures on our mobile robot in order to enable a natural way of interaction. The approach proposed analyzes image data from the robot's camera to detect the gesturing hand. We perform deictic gesture recognition through extending a trajectory recognition algorithm based on particle filtering with symbolic information from the objects in the vicinity of the acting hand. This vicinity is specified by a *context area*. By propagating the samples depending on a successful matching between expected and observed objects the samples that lack a corresponding context object are propagated less often. The results obtained demonstrate the robustness of the proposed system integrating trajectory data with symbolic information for deictic gesture recognition.

1 Introduction

In various human-machine interfaces more human-like forms of interaction are developed. Especially for robots inhabiting human environments, a multi-modal and human friendly interaction is necessary for the acceptance of such robots. Apart from the intensively researched areas of speech processing that are necessary for dialog interaction, the video-based recognition of hand gestures is a very important and challenging topic for enabling multi-modal human-machine interfaces that incorporate gestural expressions of the human.

In every-day communication deictic gestures play an important role as it is intuitive and common for humans to reference objects by pointing at them. In contrast to other types of gestural communication, for example sign language [10], deictic gestures are not performed independently of the environment but stand in a context to the referenced object. We concentrate on pointing gestures for identifying medium sized objects in an office environment. Recognizing deictic gestures, therefore, means not only to classify the hand motion as *pointing* but also to determine the referenced object. Here we do not consider referencing object details. We will focus on the incorporation of the gesture

---

* The work described in this paper was partially conducted within the EU Integrated Project COGNIRON ("The Cognitive Companion") funded by the European Commission Division FP6-IST Future and Emerging Technologies under Contract FP6-002020 and supported by the German Research Foundation within the Graduate Program 'Task Oriented Communication'.

C.E. Rasmussen et al. (Eds.): DAGM 2004, LNCS 3175, pp. 334–341, 2004.
© Springer-Verlag Berlin Heidelberg 2004

context, i.e., the referenced object, into a motion-based gesture recognition algorithm resulting in a more robust gesture recognition.

According to Bobick [3], human motion can be categorized into three classes: *movement*, *activity*, and *action*. Each category represents a different level of recognition complexity: A *movement* has little variation in its different instances and is generally only subject to linear scalings, e.g., it is performed at different speeds. An *activity* is described by a sequence of movements but can contain more complex temporal variations. Both, *movement* and *activity* do not refer to elements external to the human performing the motion. Interesting for our view on deictic gestures is the class *action* that is defined by an activity and an associated symbolic information (e.g., a referenced object). Obviously, a deictic gesture 'pointing at object X' can be described with this motion schema. Here, the low level movements are accelerating and decelerating of the pointing hand and the activity is a complete *approach* motion. Combining this activity of the pointing hand with the symbolic data denoting the referenced object X results in recognizing the action 'pointing at object X'. Due to the characteristics of pointing gestures we employ a 2D representation for the hand trajectory based on the velocity and the change of direction of the acting hand in the image.

An important topic for deictic gesture recognition is binding the motion to a symbolic object: During a pointing gesture the hand approaches an object. Using the direction information from the moving hand, an object can be searched in an appropriate search region. If an object is found, a binding of the object to the hand motion can be established. We will show how this binding can be performed **during** processing of the trajectory data resulting in an integrated approach combining sensory trajectory data and the symbolic object data for recognizing deictic gestures with context. We intend to use this recognition system for the multi-modal human-machine interface on-board a mobile robot allowing humans to reference objects by speech and pointing [8].

In this paper we will first discuss related work on gesture recognition in Section 2. Subsequently, we give in Section 3 an overview of the presented system and the used modules. The Particle Filtering algorithm applied for activity recognition is described in Section 4. In Section 5 we show how this algorithm is combined with symbolic object data for recognition of deictic gestures. In Section 6 results of the system acquired in a demonstration scenario are presented, we conclude the paper with a short summary in Section 7.

2 Related Work

Although there is a large amount of literature dealing with gesture recognition, only very few approaches have actually attacked the problem of incorporating symbolic context into the recognition task. One of the first approaches exploiting hand motions and objects in parallel is the work of Kuniyoshi [7] on qualitative recognition of assembly actions in a blocks world domain. This approach features an action model capturing the hand motion as well as an environment model representing the object context. The two models are related to each other by a hierarchical parallel automata that performs the action recognition.

An approach dealing with the recognition of actions in an office environment is the work by Ayers and Shah [1]. Here a person is tracked based on detecting the face and/or neck with a simple skin color model. The way in which a person interacts with an object is defined in terms of intensity changes within the object's image area. By relating the tracked person to detected intensity changes in its vicinity and using a finite state model defining possible action sequences, the action recognition is performed. Similar to Kuniyoshi's approach, no explicit motion models are used.

An approach that actually combines both types of information, sensory trajectory data and symbolic object data, in a structured framework is the work by Moore et al. [9]. Different image processing steps are carried out to obtain *image-based*, *object-based*, and *action-based* evidences for objects and actions. Moore et al. analyze the trajectory of a tracked hand with Hidden-Markov-Models trained offline on different activities related to the known objects to obtain the *action-based* evidence.

Only the approach by Moore et al. incorporates the hand motion, while the approaches by Kuniyoshi and Ayers and Shah rely only on the hand position. However, in the approach of Moore et al. the sensory trajectory information is used primarily as an additional cue for object recognition. We present in the following an approach for reaching the oppositional goal of recognizing gestures with the help of symbolic information.

3   System Overview

Due to the requirements of a fluent conversation between a human and a machine, the system for recognizing deictic gestures has to work in real-time. The overall deictic gesture recognition system is depicted in Fig. 1. The first two modules depicted at the left are designed for operating directly on the image data. The module on the top extracts the trajectory of the acting hand from the video data by detecting skin-colored regions and tracking these region over time (for details see [4], chapter 4). The resulting regions are tracked over time using a Kalman filter with a constant acceleration model. The module at the bottom performs object recognition in order to extract symbolic information about the objects situated in the scene. This module is based on an algorithm proposed by Viola and Jones [11]. In this paper we focus on the action recognition module which contains an activity recognition algorithm that is extended to incorporate symbolic data from the object recognition. In this way, a recognition of deictic gestures with incorporation of their context is realized. The recognition results of the system can facilitate a multi-modal human-machine-interface.

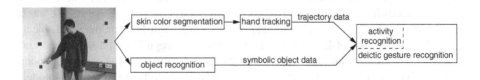

Fig. 1. Architecture of the deictic gesture recognition system.

4 Activity Recognition

Based on the trajectory generated by the acting hand of the human we can classify this trajectory. Since the start and end points of gestures are not explicitly given it is advantageous if the classification algorithm implicitly selects the relevant parts of a trajectory for classification. Additionally, as the same gestures are usually not identically executed the classification algorithm should be able to deal with a certain variability of the trajectory. The algorithm selected for segmentation and recognition of activities is based on the *Conditional Density Propagation* (CONDENSATION) algorithm which is a particle filtering algorithm introduced by Isard and Blake to track objects in noisy image sequences [5]. In [6] they extended the procedure to automatically switch between several activity models to allow a classification of the activities. Black and Jepson adapted the CONDENSATION algorithm in order to classify the trajectories of commands drawn at a blackboard [2].

Our approach is based on the work of Black and Jepson. Activities are represented by parameterized models which are matched with the input data. In contrast to the approach presented by Black and Jepson where motions are represented in an image coordinate system $(\Delta x, \Delta y)$, we have chosen a trajectory representation that consists of the velocity Δr and the change of direction $\Delta \gamma$. In this way we abstract from the absolute direction of the gesture and can represent a wide range of deictic gestures with one generic model. As the user typically orients himself towards the dialog partner the used representation can be considered view-independent in our scenario.

Each gesture model m consists of a 2-dimensional trajectory, which describes the motion of the hand during execution of the activity.

$$\mathbf{m}^{(\mu)} = \{\mathbf{x}_0, \mathbf{x}_1, \ldots, \mathbf{x}_T\}, \quad \mathbf{x}_t = (\Delta r_t, \Delta \gamma_t) \tag{1}$$

For comparison of a model $\mathbf{m}^{(\mu)}$ with the observed data $\mathbf{z}_t = (\Delta r_t, \Delta \gamma_t)$ the parameter vector $\mathbf{s}_t$ is used. This vector defines the sample of the activity model μ where the time index ϕ indicates the current position within the model trajectory at time t. The parameter α is used for amplitude scaling while ρ defines the scaling in time dimension.

$$\mathbf{s}_t = (\mu_t, \phi_t, \alpha_t, \rho_t) \tag{2}$$

The goal of the CONDENSATION algorithm is to determine the parameter vector $\mathbf{s}_t$ so that the fit of the model trajectory with the observed data $\mathbf{z}_t$ is maximized. This is achieved by temporal propagation of N weighted samples

$$\left\{ (\mathbf{s}_t^{(1)}, \pi_t^{(1)}), \ldots, (\mathbf{s}_t^{(N)}, \pi_t^{(N)}) \right\} \tag{3}$$

which represent the a posteriori probability $p(\mathbf{s}_t|\mathbf{z}_t)$ at time t. The weight $\pi_t^{(n)}$ of the sample $\mathbf{s}_t^{(n)}$ is the normalized probability $p(\mathbf{z}_t|\mathbf{s}_t^n)$. This is calculated by comparing each scaled component of the model trajectory in the last w time steps with the observed data. For calculating the difference between model and observed data a Gaussian density is assumed for each point of the model trajectory.

The propagation of the weighted samples over time consists of three steps and is based on the results of the previous time step:

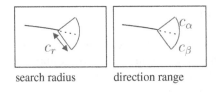

search radius   direction range

Fig. 2. The definition of the context area.

Select: Selection of N samples $s_{t-1}^{(n)}$ according to their respective weight $\pi_{t-1}^{(n)}$ from the sample pool at time $t - 1$. This selection scheme implies a preference for samples with high probability, i.e., they are selected more often.

Predict: The parameters of each sample $s_t^{(n)}$ are predicted by adding Gaussian noise to α_{t-i} and ρ_{t-1} as well as to the position ϕ_{t-1} that is increased in each time step by ρ_t. If ϕ_t is larger than the model length ϕ_{max} a new sample $s_t^{(n)}$ is initialized.

Update: Determination of the weights $\pi_t^{(n)}$ based on $p(\mathbf{z}_t | s_t^{(n)})$.

Using the weighted samples obtained by these steps the classification of activities can be achieved. The probability that a certain model μ_i is completed at time t is given by its so-called end-probability $p_{end}(\mu_i)$. This end probability is the sum of all weights of a specific activity model with $\phi_t > 0.9\phi_{max}$.

For the overall recognition system the repertoire of activities consists of *approach* and *rest*. The model *rest* is used to model the time periods where the hand is not moving at all. With these models the trajectory-based recognition of deictic gestures can be performed.

5   Recognition of Pointing Actions

As mentioned in the introduction a deictic gesture is always performed to reference an object more or less in the vicinity of the hand. To extract this fundamental information from the gesture, both the movement of the hand represented by the trajectory and symbolic data describing the object have to be combined. This combination is necessary if several objects are present in the scene as only using the distance between the hand and an object is not sufficient for detecting a pointing gesture. The hand may be in the vicinity of several objects but the object referenced by the pointing gesture depends on the direction of the hand motion. This area where an object can be expected in the spatial context of an action is called *context area*.

In order to have a variable context area we extend the model vector $\mathbf{x}_t$ (Eq. 1) by adding parameters for this area. It is defined as a circle segment with a search radius c_r and a direction range, limited by a start and end angle (c_α, c_β). These parameters are visualized in Fig. 2. The angles are interpreted relative to the direction of the tracked hand. The *approach* model consists of some time steps with increasing velocity but without a context area in the beginning later in the model a context area is defined with a shrinking distance c_r and the hand slows down.

To search objects in a context area relative to the hand position the absolute position (P_x, P_y) of the hand is required. According to this demand the complete input data consists of the observed motion data $\mathbf{z}_t$ and the coordinates P_x, P_y.

The spatial context defined in the models is incorporated in the CONDENSATION algorithm as follows. In each time-step the trajectory and context data is sequentially processed for every sample. At first the values of the sample are predicted based on the activity of the hand, afterwards the symbolic object data in relation to the hand is considered:

If there are objects in the context area of the sample at the current time index ϕ_t one object is selected randomly. For adding this symbolic data to the samples of the CONDENSATION we extend the sample vector s_t (Eq. 2) by a parameter ID_t denoting a binding with a specific object:

$$s_t = (\mu_t, \phi_t, \alpha_t, \rho_t, \mathrm{ID}_t) \tag{4}$$

This binding is performed in the *Update* step of the CONDENSATION algorithm. An object found in the context area is bound to the sample if no binding has occurred previously. Once the the sample s_t contains an object ID it will be propagated with the sample using $\mathrm{ID}_t^{(n)} = \mathrm{ID}_{t-1}^{(n)}$.

Additional we extend the calculation of the sample weight with a multiplicative *context factor* P_{symb} representing how good the bound object fits the expected spatial context of the model.

$$\pi_t^{*(i)} \propto p(\mathbf{z}_t|\mathbf{s}_t^{(i)}) \, P_{symb}(\mathrm{ID}_t|\mathbf{s}_t^{(i)}) \tag{5}$$

For evaluating pointing gestures we use a constant factor for P_{symb}. The value of this factor depends on whether a previously bound object (i.e., with the correct ID) is present in the context area or not. We use $P_{symb} = 1.0$ if the expected object is present and a smaller value $P_{symb} = P_{missing}$ if the context area does not contain the previously bound object. This leads to smaller weights $\pi_t^{*(i)}$ of samples with a missing context so that these samples are selected and propagated less often.

When the threshold for the end probability $p_{end}^{(i)}$ for one model is reached the parameter ID is used for evaluating the object the human pointed at. One approach is to count the number of samples bound with an object. But this is an inaccurate indicator as all samples influence the result with the same weight. Assuming a large number of samples is bound with one object but the weight of these samples is small this will lead to a misinterpretation of the bound object. A better method is to select an object bound to samples with a high weight, as the weight of a sample describes how good it matches the trajectory in the last steps. Consequently, we calculate for each object O_j the sum p_{O_j} of the weights of all samples belonging to the recognized model μ_i that were bound to this object.

$$p_{O_j}(\mu_i) = \sum_{n=1}^{N} \begin{cases} \pi_t^{*(n)} & \text{, if } \mu_i \in \mathbf{s}_t^{(n)} \wedge (\phi_t > 0.9\phi_{max}) \wedge \mathrm{ID}_t = O_j \\ 0 & \text{, else} \end{cases} \tag{6}$$

If the highest value $p_{O_j}(\mu_i)$ for the model is larger than a defined percentage ($T_O = 30\%$) of the model end probability $p_{end}(\mu_i)$ the object O_j is selected as being the object that was pointed at by the 'pointing' gesture. If the model has an optional spatial context and for all objects the end probability $p_{O_j}(\mu_i)$ is lower than required the model is recognized without an object binding.

The benefit of the described approach is a robust recognition of deictic gestures combined with information about the referenced object. The system is able to detect not only deictic gestures performed in different directions but also provides the object the human pointed at.

6   Results

We evaluated the presented system in an experimental setup using 14 sequences of deictic gestures executed by five test subjects resulting in 84 pointing gestures. An observed person stands in front of a camera at a distance of approximately 2m so that the upper part of the body and the acting hand are in the field of view of the camera. The person points with the right hand at six objects (see Fig. 1), two on his right, three on his left side, and one object in front of the person. We assumed perfect object recognition results for the evaluation. For this evaluation only the localization of objects was needed, as *pointing* is independent of a specific object type. The images of size 320x240 pixels are recorded with a frame-rate of 15 images per second. In our experiments real-time recognition was achieved using a standard PC (Intel, 2.4GHz) running with Linux. The models were built by averaging over several example gestures.

In the evaluation (see Tab. 1) we compare the results for different parameterizations of the gesture recognition algorithm. For evaluation we use not only the recognition rate but also the word error rate (WER) which is defined by WER $^{1} = \frac{\#I + \#D + \#S}{\#E}$. As parameters for the CONDENSATION we use N=1000 samples, the scaling factors α and ρ are between 0.65 and 1.35 with variance $\sigma = 0.15$.

Table 1. Recognition of deictic gestures

	Context								
	none	distance	directed	weighted					
$P_{missing}$	-	1.0	1.0	0.8	0.6	0.4	0.2	0.1	0.0
Correct	83	69	74	72	75	77	76	78	82
Insertion	81	9	5	5	5	5	6	5	18
Deletion	1	10	10	12	9	7	6	6	2
Substitution	0	5	0	0	0	0	0	0	0
Word error rate	97.6	28.6	17.8	20.2	16.7	14.3	14.3	13,3	23.8
Recognition rate	98.8	82.2	88.1	85.7	89.3	91.7	90.4	92.8	97.6

The second column (*'none'*) shows the results with the standard trajectory-based approach of Black et al. [2]. Without incorporation of the symbolic context no separation between departing and approaching activities is possible, every straight motion is interpreted as *pointing*. Therefore, this approach gives the highest recognition rate but it also results in the highest WER due to a huge number of insertions. Note that there is also no information about which object is referenced by the pointing gesture.

---

^{1} using I:Insertion, D:Deletion, S:Substitution, E:Expected

By using the distance (column *'distance'*) between the approaching hand and the surrounding objects mainly gestures approaching an object are recognized. But still a high rate of insertions and even substitutions (i.e., a wrong object binding) is observed. The substitutions show the disadvantage of a simple distance criterion that does not incorporate the direction of the hand motion.

Using a directed context area (column *'directed'*) we achieve a better recognition rate and a lower WER. By introducing a weighting (columns *'weighted'*) for samples not matching the expected context, the recognition rates can be further increased while reducing the WER. If samples not matching the context are deleted ($P_{missing} = 0$) the recognition rate is further increased but now also the WER is increased. This is due to the fact that all samples with a missing context area are deleted and indirectly those samples not matching the trajectory but with a bound object are propagated.

7 Summary

In this paper we presented an integrated approach to deictic gesture recognition that combines sensory trajectory data with the symbolic information of objects in the vicinity of the gesturing hand. Through the combined analysis of both types of data our approach reaches an increased robustness within real time. The recognition result provides not only the information that a deictic gesture has been performed, but also the object that has been pointed at.

References

1. D. Ayers and M. Shah. Monitoring human behavior in an office environment. In *IEEE Workshop on Interpretation of Visual Motion, CVPR-98*, Santa Barbara, CA, June 1998.
2. M. J. Black and A. D. Jepson. A probabilistic framework for matching temporal trajectories: CONDENSATION-based recognition of gestures and expressions. *Lecture Notes in Computer Science*, 1406:909–924, 1998.
3. A. Bobick and Y. Ivanov. Action recognition using probabilistic parsing. In *Proc. of CVPR*, pages 196–202, Santa Barbara, California, 1998.
4. Jannik Fritsch. *Vision-based Recognition of Gestures with Context*. Dissertation, Universität Bielefeld, Technische Fakultät, 2003.
5. M. Isard and A. Blake. Contour tracking by stochastic propagation of conditional density. *Lecture Notes in Computer Science*, 1064:343–356, 1996.
6. M. Isard and A. Blake. A mixed-state condensation tracker with automatic model-switching. In *ICCV'98*, pages 107–112, Mumbai, India, 1998.
7. Y. Kuniyoshi and H. Inoue. Qualitative recognition of ongoing human action sequences. In *Proc. International Joint Conference on Artificial Intelligence*, pages 1600–1609, 1993.
8. Frank Lömker and Gerhard Sagerer. A multimodal system for object learning. In Luc Van Gool, editor, *Pattern Recognition, 24th DAGM Symposium, Zurich, Switzerland*, Lecture Notes in Computer Science 2449, pages 490–497, Berlin, September 2002. Springer.
9. D. Moore, I. Essa, and M. Hayes. Exploiting human actions and object context for recognition tasks. In *Proceedings of IEEE Int. Conf. on Computer Vision*, Corfu, Greece, 1999.
10. T. Starner and A. Pentland. Visual recognition of american sign language using hidden markov models. In *Int. Workshop on Automatic Face and Gesture Recognition*, 1995.
11. P. Viola and M. Jones. Robust real-time object detection. In *Proc. IEEE Int. Workshop on Statistical and Computational Theories of Vision*, Vancouver, Canada, 2001.

Mosaics from Arbitrary Stereo Video Sequences

Nicolas Gorges[1], Marc Hanheide[1], William Christmas[2], Christian Bauckhage[1],
Gerhard Sagerer[1], and Joseph Kittler[2]

[1] Bielefeld University, P.O. Box 100131, 33501 Bielefeld, Germany
{ngorges, mhanheid, cbauckha, sagerer}@techfak.uni-bielefeld.de
[2] University of Surrey, Guildford GU2 7XH, UK
{W.Christmas, J.Kittler}@eim.surrey.ac.uk

Abstract. Although mosaics are well established as a compact and non-redundant representation of image sequences, their application still suffers from restrictions of the camera motion or has to deal with parallax errors. We present an approach that allows construction of mosaics from arbitrary motion of a head-mounted camera pair. As there are no parallax errors when creating mosaics from planar objects, our approach first decomposes the scene into planar sub-scenes from stereo vision and creates a mosaic for each plane individually. The power of the presented mosaicing technique is evaluated in an office scenario, including the analysis of the parallax error.

1 Introduction and Motivation

Mosaicing techniques are recently used in various different applications, even though the common basis is always to represent a sequence of images of a given scene in one image. Thus, mosaicing provides a compact, non-redundant representation of visual information. Besides the compression benefits from avoiding redundancy in mosaics, the larger field of view of the integrated mosaic image serves as a better representation of the scene than the single image data, for instance for object recognition or scene interpretation. But recent mosaicing techniques have restrictions. The main problem for building a mosaic of a non-planar scene is the occurrence of parallax effects as soon as the camera is moving arbitrarily. Parallax describes the relative displacement of an object as seen from different point of views. Each plane of the scene will move in a different relative speed in respect to each other and cause overlaps as soon as the camera center is moved. Therefore, the construction of only a single mosaic of the scene will not succeed. An avenue to deal with this problem is to control the motion of the camera and restrict it to rotation and zooming or compute mosaics on the basis of adaptive manifolds. Another possibility is to apply the mosaicing on (approximately) planar sub-scenes, which is the central assumption for the technique presented in this paper.

The mosaicing system provides visual information in terms of a *pictorial memory* as part of a cognitive vision system (CVS) which is applied in an office scenario[2]. This memory contains a compact visual representation of the scene.

C.E. Rasmussen et al. (Eds.): DAGM 2004, LNCS 3175, pp. 342–349, 2004.

The CVS uses two head-mounted cameras to access the visual outcome of the scene and a stereo video display for augmented reality[13], depicted in Fig. 1.

As the stereo camera-pair is located at the user's head, there is no control on the motion of the cameras. Thus, due to the parallax problem, it is not possible to create just one mosaic of the whole scene, but on almost planar parts. This restriction appears acceptable in an office environment since most of the objects (e.g. tables, walls,...) appear to have a rather planar nature. Therefore, we propose to decompose the scene into planes and than built a mosaic for each plane individually. The resulting set of mosaics provides the needed compact representation of the office scene.

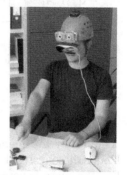

Fig. 1. The setup

This motivation leads to the two central aspects of our mosaicing system. First, a decomposition of the scene into planar sub-scenes has to be computed from stereo information, as explained in detail in Sec. 3.1. Second, the planes have to be tracked during the sequence and for each of the detected planes separate mosaics are created by registering them to a reference frame. How this is done is described in Sec. 3.2. Results from image sequences obtained in the office scenario are discussed in Sec. 4.

2   Related Work

A lot of research has been done on applications of Mosaicing [9,6] and improving their performance [14,11,10]. These approaches mainly focused on the conventional mosaicing method rather than on the restrictions. Most of these are linked with the occurrence of parallax effects. Approaches to make mosaicing invariant to any restrictions attempt to avoid parallax or use parallax explicitly. In order to overcome the restrictions for mosaicing, mosaics with parallax and layers with parallax [7] were introduced. In this case, additional information about the 3D structure is stored to take account of parallax and to make the construction of mosaic images more robust. Another approach [12] tries to present mosaicing as a progress of collecting strips to overcome most restrictions. The strip collection copes with the effects of parallax by generating dense intermediate views, but is still restricted to controlled translational parts in the motion of the camera.

Baker et al.[1] describe an approach to represent a scene as a collection of planar layers calculated from depth maps. But in contrast to our algorithm, the focus is mainly on approximating the 3D structure of the scene than on mosaics.

3   Mosaics of Planar Sub-scenes

Constructing mosaics from image sequences consists of computing a transformation from the coordinates of the current image to a reference system, warping the current image to the reference frame and integrating new pixel data into the mosaic. The warping function can easily be computed if the images were

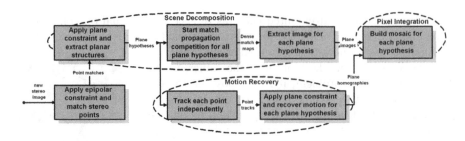

Fig. 2. System overview

acquired by a camera rotating about its fixed center or if the scene is planar. Under these restrictions, however, mosaicing is not suitable for all applications. For the more general case where the scene is not completely planar and the camera center is moving, a single transformation will not exist. But if the scene is partial planar, there will be several warping functions each of them relating different views of corresponding planar regions. This motivates to build not one but several mosaics: one for each planar sub-scene. Given stereo image data, mosaicing then becomes a three step procedure:

1. **Scene Decomposition:** Segment the current stereo image pair into pixel regions depicting coplanar areas of the scene.
2. **Plane Motion Recovery:** Recover motion of planar regions in order to calculate warping functions.
3. **Planar Mosaic Construction:** Expand mosaics and integrate warped planar regions.

Fig. 2 gives an overview of this concept and the computational modules of the framework introduced here. Next, this framework shall be presented in detail.

3.1 Scene Decomposition

Since stereo data is available due to the design of the used AR gear, identifying planes in a scene is accomplished by means of the following four steps:

1. **Local Coplanar Grouping:** Starting with extracted key points from a pair of images (e.g. by using the Harris detector [4]) and computing their correspondences using epipolar geometry, a plane hypothesis is represented by a *local* group of point matches forming a planar patch.
2. **Coplanar Grouping - Extension of local patch:** Point matches outside the local patch are added to the plane if they satisfy the plane model.
3. **Constrained Plane Propagation:** From a set of point matches, the plane is now extended to pixel regions which satisfy the plane model. The result is a dense match map of a plane which displays textured regions of the plane.
4. **Second plane propagation - A map of the plane:** Finally regions with less texture are assigned to the next neighboring textured region. The result is a boolean map which tells whether a pixel is part of the plane or not. Conjuncting this map with the current image of the scene, yields a pixel representation of the plane which is suitable for mosaicing.

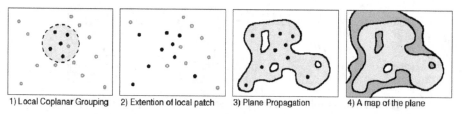

1) Local Coplanar Grouping   2) Extention of local patch   3) Plane Propagation   4) A map of the plane

Fig. 3. Identification of pixels belonging to a plane using matched stereo-key-points.

Fig. 3 illustrates this method. It shows the evolution of a single plane given a set of key points. In the first and second step, the plane is represented by a set of point matches. Black points indicate inlier points while pale points represent outliers. Note that the first two steps make use of a feature-based representation while the final steps result in an image-based representation of a plane.

The feature-based steps of this method were introduced for the following reason: It is known that two images embedded in the same plane π are related by a 2D projective transformation (homography) H and that a homography is uniquely defined by four point matches (cf. [5]). However, after extracting key points from stereo images, any four matched points will define a plane. An important issue is thus to distinguish *virtual planes* from physical ones, which is done as follows:

A *plane hypothesis* is defined as a pair (M_i, H_i) where M_i is a set of point matches and H_i a corresponding homography representing the plane model. The set of all point matches is denoted as M. The *dominant plane* $\pi_{dominant}$ of a scene is defined as the plane hypothesis which incorporates the largest amount of point correspondences, i.e.

$$\pi_{dominant} = \underset{\pi_i}{\operatorname{argmax}} ||M_i||.$$

Plane candidates π_i are found by coplanar grouping of point matches using RANSAC [3]. By choosing the actually dominant plane hypothesis $\pi_{dominant}$ and removing its point matches from M, we try to find the next dominant plane of the scene similarly until no new planes can be found or the maximum number of planes is reached. The result is a rough scene decomposition represented by a set of plane hypotheses.

In order to avoid the extraction of virtual planes, we apply a *local planarity constraint*. By restricting the choice of the four points to random local image areas and fitting plane hypotheses to this patches, it is granted that extracted planes are at least locally planar. Then, local plane hypotheses are evaluated with respect to the total number of key points. The hypothesis that accords with most global matches is chosen for further processings. Fitting planes to local patches also allows to measure the *planarity* of planes: if the relation of outlier to inlier points is below a certain threshold hypotheses are rejected.

Since planar surfaces in a scene may contain holes and as there might be regions in the scene for which we do not have enough information to assign them to a plane, we apply a pixel-based plane growing method to embed local dis-

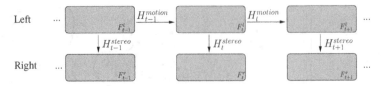

Fig. 4. Homographies between the stereo frame sequence of a plane

continuities. Based on the algorithm described in [8], we suggest an image-based propagation process which densifies the plane hypotheses. This resembles classical region growing methods for image segmentation. Instead of a homogeneity criterion, normalized cross correlation between point matches is used for region expansion. Starting from a set of matches with high textureness, the algorithm densifies the matches to regions with less textureness. Expansion stops in regions which diverge from the reference homography or have no texture. This restricts the propagation to regions which can be approximated by the plane hypothesis.

So far, only the propagation of a single plane has been considered. Given a set of plane hypotheses, the idea is to start a competition between these planes. Therefore, each plane hypothesis is also associated with the best correlation score among all its point matches. Then, only the plane π_i with the best point match $p_{best}(a, b)$ is allowed to start a single propagation step. Therefore, the neighborhood $N(a, b)$ of point match p_{best} is densified. The chosen plane provides its next best point match and the next iteration begins. The propagation stops if none of the planes has a point match left to be processed.

3.2   Plane Motion Recovery and Planar Mosaic Construction

For the construction of a planar mosaic the homographies H^{motion} between the different frames has to be computed to recover the motion of the camera. The motion of the feature points, that have been established in the decomposition stage, are also used to compute these homographies. Thus, the motion recovery performed for each plane can be divided into two steps:

1. **Tracking of plane points:** Given a set of points on a plane, each point is tracked independently. Assuming that a point is moving with constant velocity, a linear first order prediction of a point is used.
2. **Recovering plane motion:** The resulting point tracks $T_t = (p_{t-1}^i, p_t^i)$ are supposed to lie on the same plane. For two views of a plane, there exists a homography H_{t-1}^{motion} (see Fig. 4) which relates p_{t-1}^i to p_t^i. Again, RANSAC is used for a robust estimation of this homography.

Furthermore, the tracked plane has to be updated in terms of integrating new points and removing the ones gone out of sight. Therefore the homography H_t^{stereo} is recomputed and new points are added if they fulfill the planarity constraint.

Based on the interframe homographies H_t^{motion} all plane images are warped to the reference frame F_1^l of the mosaic. The integration computes the median of the warped frames to determine the value of the resulting mosaic pixel.

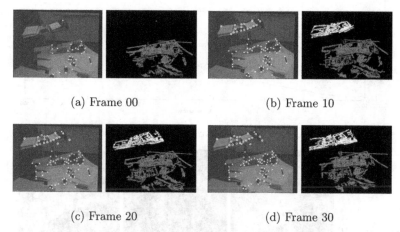

(a) Frame 00   (b) Frame 10

(c) Frame 20   (d) Frame 30

Fig. 5. Decomposition of the scene in two planes: Each left images displays the tracked feature points. Respectively, on the right, the textured regions of the planes are shown.

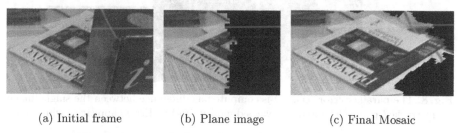

(a) Initial frame   (b) Plane image   (c) Final Mosaic

Fig. 6. An example for occlusion elimination (detail view)

4 Results

The focus of the evaluation is on the quality and the consistency of the mosaics as they are the final result of the presented procedure. The integration of new pixel data into the mosaic strongly depends on the preprocessing steps, namely *Scene Decomposition*, and *Plane Tracking*. Especially the scene decomposition plays an important role as plane tracking is based on its results. Errors occurring in this processing step are spread to all the following stages and result in erroneous mosaics. Fig. 5 presents the result of the scene decomposition of a sequence in the office. The decomposition has been limited to two dominant planes to ease the evaluation. The desk has two planes which both are detected correctly. The tracked feature points are highlighted in each frame (left images) and the propagated planes are shown in different gray shadings (right images). Note, that in frame 00 only one plane is detected, but ten frames later further points and another plane is added and tracked from now on. Another positive effect of only integrating image parts that belong to the same plane into the mosaics is depicted in Fig. 6. Because the parcel in the foreground of the scene does not belong to the same plane as the table with the journal, it is omitted from the mosaic and the occlusion is eliminated. This allows to create complete views of partially occluded objects in the scene.

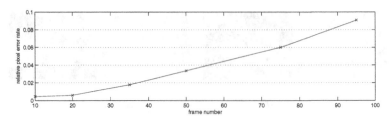

Fig. 7. Evolution of the relative parallax error over a sequence

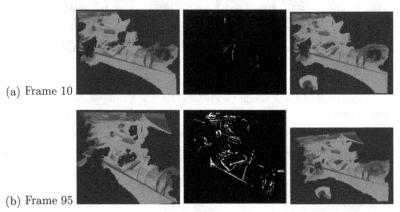

(a) Frame 10

(b) Frame 95

Fig. 8. The parallax error (center) is computed as difference between the single image of the tracked plane (left) and the warped mosaic (right). Errors appear as white dots.

If the decomposition of the scene into planes would be perfect, one would expect no parallax error in the mosaic. But due to the just approximately planar nature of extracted sub-scenes, errors will occur, especially at the borders of flat objects (e.g. a flat book lying on the table) as well as at the edges of extracted planes. We calculated the *relative parallax error* $\epsilon = \delta/s$ to evaluate these effects, which is defined as the amount of pixel differences δ the tracked plane of the frame and the so far integrated mosaic, normalized by the size s of the plane measured in pixels. For calculating that difference the mosaic is warped into the actual frame. In Fig. 7 the evolution of this error measure is plotted over the whole sequence which is partially shown in Fig. 8. As expected, the parallax error rate increased while the mosaic is growing, but even in the last frame 95, errors only occur at the edges of the objects, as can be seen in the center image of Fig. 8(b). The computation of the mosaics (tracking, and updating the homographies) can be performed in real-time after the initialization or the update respectively of the planes is done.

5   Conclusion

We presented an unique approach to create mosaics for arbitrarily moving head-mounted cameras. The three stage architecture first decomposes the scene into approximated planes using stereo information, which afterwards can be tracked and integrated to mosaics individually. This avoids the problem of parallax errors usually occurring from arbitrary motion and provides a compact and non-redundant representation of the scene. Furthermore, creating mosaics of the plane allows to eliminate occlusion, since objects blocking the sight on a plane are not integrated. This can for instance help object recognition systems and further scene interpretation in the Cognitive Vision System, this approach is part of. The proposed robust decomposition and tracking algorithms allow to apply the system in real office scene with common cameras.

Acknowledgements. This work was partly funded by VAMPIRE (IST-2001-34401) and ECVision.

References

1. S. Baker, R. Szeliski, and P. Anandan. A layered approach to stereo reconstruction. In *Proc. CVPR*, pages 434–441, 1998.
2. C. Bauckhage, M. Hanheide, S. Wrede, and G. Sagerer. A Cognitive Vision System for Action Recognition in Office Environments. In *Proc. CVPR*, 2004. to appear.
3. M.A. Fischler and R.C. Bolles. Random sample consensus: A paradigm for model fitting with applications to image analysis and automated cartography. *Communications of the ACM*, 24(6):381–395, 1981.
4. C. Harris and M. Stephens. A combined corner and edge detector. In *Proc. Alvey Vision Conference*, pages 147–151, 1988.
5. R. Hartley and A. Zisserman. *Multiple View Geometry in Computer Vision*. Cambridge University Press, 2001.
6. B. Hu and C. Brown. Interactive indoor scene reconstruction from image mosaics using cuboid structure. In *Proc. Motion & Video Computing*, pages 208–213, 2002.
7. R. Kumar, P. Anandan, M. Irani, J. Bergen, and K. Hanna. Representation of scenes from collections of images. In *Proc. IEEE Workshop on Representations of Visual Scenes*, pages 10–17, 1995.
8. M. Lhuillier and L. Quan. Robust dense matching using local and global geometric constraints. In *Proc. ICPR*, pages 968–972, 2000.
9. P. Anandan M. Irani and S. Hsu. Mosaic based representations of video sequences and their applications. In *Proc. ICCV*, 1995.
10. B. Möller, D. Williams, and S. Posch. Robust image sequence mosaicing. In *Proc. of 25th DAGM Symposium*, LNCS 2781, pages 386–293, 2003.
11. S. Peleg and J. Herman. Panoramic mosaics by manifold projection. In *Proc. ICPR*, pages 338–343, 1997.
12. S. Peleg, B. Rousso, A. Rav-Acha, and A. Zomet. Mosaicing on adaptive manifolds. *IEEE PAMI*, 22:1144–1154, 2000.
13. H. Siegl, M. Brandner, H. Ganster, P. Lang, A. Pinz, M. Ribo, and C. Stock. A mobile augmented reality system. In *Exhibition Abstracts of Int. Conf. Computer Vision Ssytems*, pages 13–14, 2003.
14. I. Zoghlami, O. Faugeras, and R. Deriche. Using geometric corners to build a 2d mosaic from a set of images. In *Proc. CVPR*, pages 420–425, 1997.

Accurate and Efficient Approximation of the Continuous Gaussian Scale-Space

Ullrich Köthe

Cognitive Systems Group, University of Hamburg, Germany
`koethe@informatik.uni-hamburg.de`

Abstract. The Gaussian scale-space is a standard tool in image analysis. While continuous in theory, it is generally realized with fixed regular grids in practice. This prevents the use of algorithms which require continuous and differentiable data and adaptive step size control, such as numerical path following. We propose an efficient continuous approximation of the Gaussian scale-space that removes this restriction and opens up new ways to subpixel feature detection and scale adaptation.

1 Introduction

Smoothing with Gaussian functions and the Gaussian scale-space have become standard tools in low-level image analysis. They are routinely used for preprocessing, estimation of derivatives, and feature extraction. With few exceptions, theories about scale-space and scale-based feature detection are derived for continuous, differentiable functions, but are then realized on discrete grids, e.g. by sampling the Gaussian kernel or replacing it with a discrete approximation (e.g. binomial filters, Lindeberg's discrete analog [7], or recursive filters [4]). To save memory and time, images are often subsampled after a certain amount of smoothing as in a Gaussian pyramid [2] or hybrid pyramid [8]. These approaches always use grids whose sampling density is at most that of the original image. However, in [6] it was shown that a higher sampling density can be necessary in order to prevent information loss during image processing. Empirical evidence for improved feature detection on oversampled data was also reported by [10,9].

In this paper, we approach the sampling issue in a radical way: instead of working on a discrete representation, we propose an abstract data type that represents the Gaussian scale-space as a function over the reals, i.e. as a continuous, differentiable mapping from $\mathbb{R}^2 \times \mathbb{R}^+ \to \mathbb{R}$, with given precision ε. Algorithms can access this data structure at arbitrary coordinates, and the requested function values or derivatives are computed *on demand*. Even for very irregular access patterns efficiency remains reasonable, as all calculations are based on splines and thus require only simple operations in relatively small neighborhoods.

By using a continuous approach, many difficult problems may find natural solutions. Consider, for example, edge following and linking: powerful path following algorithms exist in the field of numerical analysis, but they require continuously differentiable functions. Convergence statements come in the form of assymptotic theorems $(f - \hat{f})^2 = \mathcal{O}(h^n)$, where $\hat{f}$ is the approximation of f

C.E. Rasmussen et al. (Eds.): DAGM 2004, LNCS 3175, pp. 350–358, 2004.

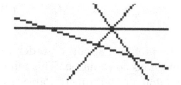

Fig. 1. Line junctions drawn on a grid usually occupy more than a single pixel and have rather unpredictable shapes. This can only be prevented with a real-valued (vector) representation.

and h the sampling step. Thus, to guarantee a given accuracy, one must be able to *adapt the sampling step locally*. We have found indications that this may also be true in image analysis: in continuous image reconstructions single pixels are often intersected by more than one edge and may contain more than one critical point. In fact, some configurations, in particular junctions, are not in general correctly representable by any grid (fig. 1). The same applies to bifurcations of critical point trajectories encountered in scale selection [7] or edge focusing [1].

Up to now, attempts to access images in real-valued coordinate systems have been based on simple interpolation schemes such as linear interpolation, low order polynomial fits, or the facet model [5,8,3]. However, these methods lead to discontinuities of the function values or the first derivatives at pixel borders, and algorithms requiring differentiability are not applicable. In contrast, we are defining a reconstruction that is everywhere differentiable (up to some order) in both the spatial and the scale directions.

2   Continuity in the Spatial Coordinates

For an observed discrete 1D signal $\hat{f}_i$, the continuous Gaussian scale-space is defined as a family of continuous functions $f_\sigma(x)$ obtained by:

$$f_\sigma(x) = g_\sigma \circledast \hat{f} = \sum_{i=-\infty}^{\infty} g_\sigma(x-i)\hat{f}_i \quad \text{with} \quad g_\sigma(x) = \frac{1}{\sqrt{2\pi\sigma^2}} e^{-\frac{x^2}{2\sigma^2}} \quad (1)$$

Unfortunately, this expression cannot directly be used on computers because Gaussian kernels have infinite support and must be clipped to a finite window. No matter how large a window is chosen, a *discontinuity* is introduced at the window borders, and this causes severe errors in the derivatives [12]. [12] recommends to remove the discontinuity of the windowed sampled Gaussian by interpolation with a spline. This is a special case of a more general strategy: first compute an intermediate discrete scale-space representation by means of some discrete prefilter, and then reconstruct a continuous scale-space from it by means of a spline. Splines are a natural choice for this task because they are easy to compute, achieve the highest order of differentiability for a given polynomial order, and have small support. The prefilter will be defined so that the net-result of the prefilter/spline combination approximates the true Gaussian as closely as possible. Ideally, we might require preservation of image structure (e.g. number and location of extrema), but this is very difficult to formalize. Instead we minimize the squared error between the approximation and the desired function:

$$E[\tilde{f}_\sigma] = \int_{-\infty}^{\infty} (f_\sigma - \tilde{f}_\sigma)^2 dx = \int_{-\infty}^{\infty} (g_\sigma \circledast \hat{f} - s_n \circledast (\hat{p}_\sigma * \hat{f}))^2 dx \qquad (2)$$

where $\tilde{f}_\sigma$ is the approximation for scale σ, $\hat{p}_\sigma$ the prefilter, s_n an nth-order B-spline, and $*$ vs. $\circledast$ distinguish discrete from continuous convolution. This minimization problem is still intractable in the spatial domain, but due to Parseval's theorem it can also be formulated and solved (with minor simplifications) in the Fourier domain:

$$E[\tilde{f}_\sigma] = \int_{-\infty}^{\infty} (G_\sigma - S_n \hat{P}_\sigma)^2 \hat{F}^2 du \qquad (3)$$

where $G_\sigma = e^{-u^2 \sigma^2/2}$, $S_n = \left(\frac{\sin(u/2)}{u/2}\right)^{n+1}$ and $\hat{P}_\sigma$ are the Fourier transforms of the Gaussian, the spline, and the prefilter. The spectrum $\hat{F}$ of the original image is of course unknown. We use the common choice $\hat{F} = 1$, i.e. a white noise spectrum, where no frequency is preferred. While other possibilities exist (e.g. natural image statistics), this doesn't significantly alter the optimal filter choice.

We have compared many different prefilters and report some of them below. To realize the suggestion of [12] the prefilter $\hat{P}_\sigma$ must be the combination of a sampled windowed Gaussian and the direct spline transform [11] which ensures that the subsequent continuous convolution with the B-spline S_n (indirect spline transform) indeed interpolates the Gaussian's sample values:

$$\hat{P}_\sigma^{(1)} = \frac{\hat{G}_\sigma}{\hat{S}_n} \quad \text{with} \quad \hat{S}_3 = \frac{4 + 2\cos(u)}{6}, \quad \hat{S}_5 = \frac{66 + 52\cos(u) + 2\cos(2u)}{120} \qquad (4)$$

$\hat{G}_\sigma$ (the transfer function of a sampled and windowed Gaussian) can be derived by using well-known properties of the Fourier transform: Windowing with a box function of radius w in the spatial domain corresponds to convolution with a scaled sinc-function in the Fourier domain. Spatial sampling with step size $h = 1$ then leads to spectrum repetition at all multiples of 2π. Unfortunately, the resulting infinite sum is intractable. However, in the product $S_n \hat{P}_\sigma$ the B-spline transfer function effectively supresses the spectrum of the prefilter for $u > 2\pi$, so that only the first spectrum repetition at $\pm 2\pi$ needs to be considered, and the effect of windowing can be neglected if $w \geq 3\sigma$. Thus,

$$\hat{G}_\sigma \simeq e^{-(u+2\pi)^2 \sigma^2/2} + e^{-u^2 \sigma^2/2} + e^{-(u-2\pi)^2 \sigma^2/2} \qquad (5)$$

A simpler prefilter $\hat{P}_\sigma^{(2)}$ is obtained by noticing that $1/\hat{S}_n$ acts as a sharpening filter that exactly counters the smoothing effect of the indirect spline transform S_n at the sampling points. When we apply the sampled Gaussian $\hat{G}_\sigma$ at a smaller scale $\sigma' < \sigma$, we can drop this sharpening, i.e. $\hat{P}_\sigma^{(2)} = \hat{G}_{\sigma'}$. Further we replaced $\hat{G}_\sigma$ with approximate Gaussians: binomial filters, Deriche's recursive filters [4], Lindeberg's discrete analogue of the Gaussian [7], and the smoothing spline filter from [11]. Space doesn't allow to give all transfer functions here. An even simpler idea is to drop the prefilter altogether, and stretch the B-spline instead so that its

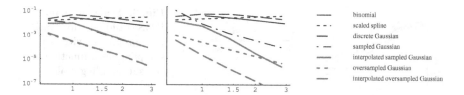

Fig. 2. Scale normalized RMS residuals for Gaussian scale-space approximation with 3rd-order (left) and 5th-order (right) splines for various prefilters and scales.

variance matches that of the desired Gaussian: $S_{n,\sigma'}(u) = S_n(\sigma'u)$, $\hat{P}_\sigma^{(3)} = 1$. All possibilities mentioned so far perform poorly at small scales ($\sigma < 1$), so we also tested oversampled Gaussians as prefilters, i.e. sampled Gaussians with sampling step $h = 1/2$ whose transfer functions are (the up-arrow denotes oversampling):

$$\hat{P}_{\sigma'\uparrow}^{(1)}(u) = \hat{P}_\sigma^{(1)}(u/2) \qquad \hat{P}_{\sigma'\uparrow}^{(2)}(u) = \hat{P}_\sigma^{(2)}(u/2) \qquad (6)$$

and the B-spline transfer function must be accordingly stretched to $S_n(u/2)$.

Figure 2 presents the scale normalized root mean square residuals $\sigma\sqrt{E}$ of the minimization problem for our prefilter variants at variuous scales. The RMS directly corresponds to the expected error in the spatial domain, and scale normalization is applied in order to make residuals comparable over scales. It can be seen that oversampled Gaussians give the best results, and interpolation (use of $\hat{P}_\sigma^{(1)}$ instead of $\hat{P}_{\sigma'}^{(2)}$) only improves 5th-order spline results. At scales $\sigma > \sqrt{2}$, non-oversampling Gaussians also achieve errors below $\simeq 10^{-3}$, which can be considered as good enough for practical applications (it roughly equals the quantization noise for 256 gray levels). We also repeated this analysis with the first and second derivatives of the Gaussian, with essentially the same results.

3   Continuity in Space with Subsampling

So far the resolution of the intermediate images was fixed. Considering that neighboring sampling points become more and more redundant as scale increases, this is rather inefficient, especially for higher dimensional data. We now replace the intermediate representation with a pyramid and analyse the residuals as a function of the scale where subsampling is performed. Usually, subsampling in a pyramid scheme is done by simply dropping every other sampling point. However, in the context of splines we can do better: Since the function space of possible splines with a given sample distance is a strict superset of the function space at half that distance, one can define an orthogonal projection from one space to the other. This projection can be realized by applying a projection filter before dropping samples [11]. The projection filter can be derived analytically,

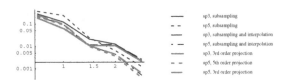

Fig. 3. Scale normalized RMS residuals for various prefilters with subsampling, as a function of the subsampling scale.

and its transfer function for 3rd-order splines is

$$\Pi_3(u) = \tag{7}$$
$$\frac{12132 + 18482\cos(u) + 7904\cos(2u) + 1677\cos(3u) + 124\cos(4u) + \cos(5u)}{16(1208 + 1191\cos(2u) + 120\cos(4u) + \cos(6u))}$$

i.e. a combination of a 5th-order FIR and a 3rd-order IIR filter. It is important to note that this filter preserves the average gray value ($\Pi_3(0) = 1$), and fulfills the equal contribution condition, i.e. the even and odd samples have equal total weights ($\Pi_3(\pi) = 0$). If used alone, the projection approximates the ideal lowpass filter (the Fourier transform of the sinc interpolator) but this causes severe ringing artifacts in the reduced images. This is avoided when the projection filter is combined with one of the smoothing prefilters $\hat{P}_\sigma$. To derive their combined transfer functions, recall that 2−fold subsampling in space corresponds to a spectrum repetition at π in the Fourier domain. The projection filter is optionally applied before subsampling. The subsampled prefilter transfer function is multiplied with the transfer function of a scaled B-spline $S_n(2u)$ (below, $\downarrow k$ means that the approximation resulted from 2^k-fold subsampling):

$$\hat{P}^{(i)}_{\sigma'\downarrow 1}(u) = \hat{P}^{(i)}_{\sigma'\downarrow 0}(u) + \hat{P}^{(i)}_{\sigma'\downarrow 0}(u - \pi) \qquad \text{(without projection)} \tag{8}$$

$$\hat{P}^{(i)+}_{\sigma'\downarrow 1}(u) = \Pi_n(u)\hat{P}^{(i)}_{\sigma'\downarrow 0}(u) + \Pi_n(u - \pi)\hat{P}^{(i)}_{\sigma'\downarrow 0}(u - \pi) \quad \text{(with proj.)} \tag{9}$$

$$\tilde{G}_{\sigma\downarrow 1}(u) = S_n(2u)\hat{P}^{(i)}_{\sigma'\downarrow 1}(u) \qquad \text{or} \qquad \tilde{G}_{\sigma\downarrow 1}(u) = S_n(2u)\hat{P}^{(i)+}_{\sigma'\downarrow 1}(u) \tag{10}$$

For higher levels k of the pyramid, this process is repeated recursively, with spectrum repetitions at $\pi/2^{k-1}$, and splines scaled to $S_n(2^k u)$. Figure 3 depicts the scale normalized RMS errors for a single downsampling step as a function of the scale where the downsampling occurs, for various prefilters (with optimized σ' and with or without the projection filter). It can be seen that an error of 0.01 is achieved for the 3rd-order spline without projection at $\sigma \simeq 2$, and an error of 0.001 for the 5th-order spline with projection at $\sigma \simeq 2.4$. Instead of the rather expensive 5th-order projection filter, 3rd-order projection has been used for 5th-order splines as well, with only a marginal increase in error. Further analysis showed that roughly the same accuracy levels are maintained if subsampling is repeated in the same manner at octave intervals.

4   Continuity in the Scale Direction

If one wants to improve feature detection by means of scale selection or coarse-to-fine tracking, function values or derivatives at arbitrary scales rather than

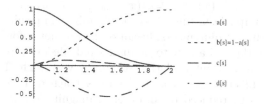

Fig. 4.   The   blending functions for scale interpolation.

at precomputed ones are often needed. If one uses simple interpolation schemes such as rounding to the nearest scale, linear interpolation or parabola fitting, the true Gaussian scale-space is not approximated very well, and the resulting representation is not differentiable with respect to scale. A much better interpolation scheme can be derived by looking at the diffusion equation whose solution for a given initial image is precisely the Gaussian scale-space

$$\frac{\partial f}{\partial \tau} = \frac{1}{2}\frac{\partial^2 f}{\partial x^2}, \qquad (\tau = \sigma^2) \qquad (11)$$

According to this equation the smoothed image at some scale $\tau + \epsilon$ can be calculated from the image at scale τ and the corrsponding second derivative by $f_{\tau+\epsilon}(x) = f_\tau(x) + \epsilon f_\tau''(x)$ if ϵ is small. This suggests that a better interpolation scheme can be defined by a linear combination of smoothed images *and* *second derivatives* (Laplacians in higher dimensions) at two neighboring scales. In particular this means that a Gaussian at scale σ can be interpolated by:

$$\tilde{g}_\sigma(x) \simeq a(\sigma)g_{\sigma_1}(x) + b(\sigma)g_{\sigma_2}(x) + c(\sigma)\frac{\partial^2}{\partial x^2}g_{\sigma_1}(x) + d(\sigma)\frac{\partial^2}{\partial x^2}g_{\sigma_2}(x) \qquad (12)$$

with $\sigma_1 \leq \sigma \leq \sigma_2$. In order for the interpolation to preserve the average gray value, we must require $b(\sigma) = 1 - a(\sigma)$. Since the same relationship holds in the Fourier domain, we can again formulate a least squares minimization problem

$$E[a, c, d] = \int_0^{2\pi}\int_{-\infty}^{\infty} (G_\sigma(u) - \tilde{G}_\sigma(u))^2 \, u \, du \, d\varphi \qquad (13)$$

Note that we defined the residual in 2D polar coordinates because this lead to a simpler functional form than the 1D formulation and to higher accuracy in 2D. Setting the derivatives with respect to a, c and d to zero leads to a linear system for the interpolation coefficients. If $\sigma_2 = 2\sigma_1$, the solution to this system is

$$\chi_1 = \sigma^2/\sigma_1^2, \qquad \chi_2 = \frac{1}{(1+\chi_1)(4+\chi_1)},$$

$$a = (62 + \chi_2(-10560 + \chi_2(32000 + 72800\chi_1)))/54 \qquad (14)$$

$$c = \sigma_1^2(15 + \chi_2(-2700 + \chi_2(6000 + 19500\chi_1)))/54 \qquad (15)$$

$$d = \sigma_1^2(240 + \chi_2(-28800 + \chi_2(96000 + 168000\chi_1)))/54 \qquad (16)$$

This is indeed a continuous, differentiable interpolation scheme, as the original Gaussians are recovered at the interpolation borders, and the diffusion equation is fulfilled there, i.e $\tilde{g}_\sigma(x)|_{\sigma=\sigma_{1,2}} = g_{\sigma_{1,2}}(x)$ and $\partial_\tau \tilde{g}_\sigma(x)|_{\sigma=\sigma_{1,2}} = \partial_{xx} g_{\sigma_{1,2}}(x)/2$. It is somewhat surprising that simple least squares error minimization results in blending formulas which fulfill these requirements, because this was not enforced during the derivation. Probably there is a (yet to be discovered) deeper reason behind this. The accuracy of the scale interpolation scheme is very high. The maximum scale normalized RMS error is 4.5×10^{-3} and is reached at $\sigma = 1.398\sigma_1$. If desired, the error can be reduced by an order of magnitude if $\sigma_2 = \sqrt{2}\sigma_1$ is chosen. Figure 4 depicts the blending functions a, b, c and d. Derivatives are interpolated likewise by replacing $g_{\sigma_{1,2}}$ with the derivative and using its Laplacian. Derivative interpolation thus requires splines of at least order 5.

5   Results and Conclusions

Our analysis suggests that an accurate continuous scale-space approximation can be obtained in two phases: First, an intermediate pyramid representation is computed by means of some optimized discrete filter. Second, function values and derivatives at arbitrary real-valued coordinates and scales are calculated on demand, using spline reconstruction and scale interpolation. These procedures can be encapsulated in an abstract data type, so that algorithms never see the complications behind the calculations. The scale-space starts at base scale σ_{base} which should be at least 0.5. The Gaussian should be windowed at $w \geq 3\sigma$.

Phase 1: Intermediate Pyramid Representation

1. Pyramid level "-1" (scale σ_{base}): Convolve original image with oversampled Gaussian $\hat{g}_{\sigma_{-1}\uparrow}$. Optionally apply the direct spline transform (interpolation prefilter).
2. Level "0" (scale $2\sigma_{\text{base}}$): Convolve original image with sampled Gaussian $\hat{g}_{\sigma_0}$. Optionally apply the direct spline transform.
3. Level "1" (scale $4\sigma_{\text{base}}$): Convolve original image with sampled Gaussian $\hat{g}_{\sigma_1}$. Optionally apply the projection filter. Drop odd samples.
4. Level "k" ($k > 1$): Convolve the intermediate image at level $k-1$ with sampled Gaussian $\hat{g}_{\sigma_2}$. Optionally apply the projection filter. Drop odd samples.

The optimal values for $\sigma_{-1}, ..., \sigma_2$ depend on the order of the spline used, on the value of σ_{base} and on whether or not the interpolation/projection prefilters are applied. Table 1 gives the values for some useful choices. They were calculated by minimizing the scale normalized RMS error between the approximation and the true Gaussian. It can be seen (last column) that these errors decrease for higher order splines, larger σ_{base} and use of interpolation/projection.

Phase 2: On-demand Calculation of Function Values or Derivatives at (x, y, σ)

1. If $\sigma = 2^{k+1}\sigma_{\text{base}}$ ($k \geq -1$): Work on level k of the intermediate representation. Calculate spline coefficients for $(\delta x, \delta y) = (x/2^k, y/2^k) - (\lfloor x/2^k \rfloor, \lfloor y/2^k \rfloor)$ and convolve with the appropriate image window around $(\lfloor x/2^k \rfloor, \lfloor y/2^k \rfloor)$.
2. If $2^{k+1}\sigma_{\text{base}} < \sigma < 2^{k+2}\sigma_{\text{base}}$ ($k \geq -1$): Use the algorithm from Phase 2.1 to calculate function values and corresponding Laplacians at levels k and $k+1$. Use the scale interpolation formula to interpolate to scale σ.

Table 1. Optimal scales for sampled Gaussian prefilters for various algorithm variants. "Optional interpolation" refers to levels -1 and 0, "optional projection" (always with 3rd-order projection filter) to levels 1 and higher.

algorithm variant	σ_{base}	σ_{-1}	σ_0	σ_1	σ_2	max. resid.
3rd-order spline without	1/2	0.4076	0.8152	1.6304	1.4121	0.018
interpolation/projection	0.6	0.5249	1.0498	2.0995	1.8183	0.0070
	$\sqrt{2}/2$	0.6448	1.2896	2.5793	2.2337	0.0031
5th-order spline without	1/2	0.3531	0.7062	1.4124	1.0586	0.017
interpolation/projection	0.6	0.4829	0.9658	1.9316	1.6728	0.0035
	$\sqrt{2}/2$	0.6113	1.2226	2.4451	2.1175	0.0018
5th-order spline with	1/2	0.4994	0.9987	1.7265	1.5771	0.0062
interpolation/projection	0.6	0.5998	1.1996	2.1790	1.9525	0.0025
	$\sqrt{2}/2$	0.7070	1.4141	2.6442	2.3441	0.0009

The computation time for a single point during phase 2 is independent of the image size. It involves only additions and multiplications (in roughly equal proportions). If σ coincides with one of the precalculated levels, we need 44 multiplications per point for a 3rd-order spline and 102 for a 5th-order one. When an intermediate scale must be interpolated, the numbers are 154 and 342 respectively. Derivative calculations are cheaper as the polynomial order of the splines reduces. When the data are accessed in a fixed order rather than randomly, the effort significantly decreases because intermediate results can be reused. On a modern machine (2.5 GHz Pentium), our implementation provides about a million random point accesses per second for the 5th-order spline. While this is not suitable for real time processing, it is fast enough for practical applications.

In the future, we will apply the new method to design high-quality subpixel feature detectors. Preliminary results (which we cannot report here due to space) are very encouraging. We also believe that a continuous scale-space representation will open up new roads to scale selection and scale adaptation. For example, variable resolution as in the human eye can be achieved by simply using a position dependent scale instead of an irregular (e.g. log-polar) sampling grid.

Acknowledgement. This work was done during a visit at KTH Stockholm. I'd like to thank Tony Lindeberg for many helpful discussions and comments.

References

1. F. Bergholm: *Edge Focusing*, IEEE Trans. Pattern Analysis and Machine Intelligence, 9(6), pp. 726-741, 1987
2. P. Burt: *The Pyramid as a Structure for Efficient Computation*, in: A. Rosenfeld (Ed.): Multiresolution Image Processing and Analysis, pp. 6-35, Springer, 1984
3. J. Crowley, O. Riff: *Fast Computation of Scale Normalized Gaussian Receptive Fields*, in: L. Griffin, M. Lillholm (Eds.): Scale-Space Methods in Computer Vision, Proc. ScaleSpace '03, Springer LNCS 2695, pp. 584-598, 2003
4. R. Deriche: *Fast algorithms for low-level vision*, IEEE Trans. Pattern Analysis and Machine Intelligence, 1(12), pp. 78-88, 1990

5. R. Haralick, L. Shapiro: *Computer and Robot Vision*, vol. 1, Addison Wesley, 1992
6. U. Köthe: *Edge and Junction Detection with an Improved Structure Tensor*, in: B. Michaelis, G. Krell (Eds.): Pattern Recognition, Proc. 25th DAGM Symposium, Springer LNCS 2781, pp. 25-32, 2003
7. T. Lindeberg: *Scale-Space Theory in Computer Vision*, Kluwer, 1994
8. T. Lindeberg, L. Bretzner: *Real-time scale selection in hybrid multi-scale representations*, in: L. Griffin, M. Lillholm (Eds.): Scale-Space Methods in Computer Vision, Proc. ScaleSpace '03, Springer LNCS 2695, pp. 148-163, 2003
9. D. Lowe: *Object recognition from local scale-invariant features*, In: Proc. 7th Intl. Conf. on Computer Vision, pp. 1150-1157, 1999
10. I. Overington: *Computer Vision*, Elsevier, 1992
11. M. Unser, A. Aldroubi, M. Eden: *B-Spline Signal Processing*, IEEE Trans. Signal Processing, 41(2), pp. 821-833 (part I), 834-848 (part II), 1993
12. I. Weiss: *High-Order Differentiation Filters That Work*, IEEE Trans. Pattern Analysis and Machine Intelligence, 16(7), pp. 734-739, 1994

Multi-step Entropy Based Sensor Control for Visual Object Tracking

Benjamin Deutsch[1*], Matthias Zobel[1*], Joachim Denzler[2], and
Heinrich Niemann[1]

[1] Lehrstuhl für Mustererkennung, Universität Erlangen-Nürnberg
91058 Erlangen, Germany
{deutsch, zobel, niemann}@informatik.uni-erlangen.de
[2] Arbeitsgruppe Rechnersehen, Universität Passau
94030 Passau, Germany
denzler@fmi.uni-passau.de

Abstract. We describe a method for selecting optimal actions affecting
the sensors in a probabilistic state estimation framework, with an application in selecting optimal zoom levels for a motor-controlled camera
in an object tracking task. The action is selected to minimize the expected entropy of the state estimate. The contribution of this paper is
the ability to incorporate varying costs into the action selection process
by looking multiple steps into the future. The optimal action sequence
then minimizes both the expected entropy and the costs it incurs. This
method is then tested with an object tracking simulation, showing the
benefits of multi-step versus single-step action selection in cases where
the cameras' zoom control motor is insufficiently fast.

1 Introduction

This paper describes a method for selecting *optimal actions* which affect the
sensors in a probabilistic state estimation framework. The contribution of this
paper is the ability to incorporate *varying costs* into the action selection process
by looking *multiple steps* into the future.

Probabilistic state estimation systems continuously estimate the current state
of a dynamic system based on observations they receive, and maintain this estimate in the form of a probability density function. Given the possibility to affect
the observation process with certain *actions*, what are the optimal actions, in an
information theoretic sense, that the estimation system should choose to influence the resulting probability density?

One sample application is the selection of optimal camera actions in motor-
operated cameras for an active object tracking task, such as pan and tilt operations or zooming. We examine focal length selection as our sample application,
using an extended Kalman filter for state estimation.

---

* This work was partly funded by the German Research Foundation (DFG) under
grant SFB 603/TP B2. Only the authors are responsible for the content.

C.E. Rasmussen et al. (Eds.): DAGM 2004, LNCS 3175, pp. 359–366, 2004.

Previous work in the areas of object recognition [10,4,3] have shown that an active viewpoint selection process can reduce uncertainty. For object tracking, active focal length selection is used to keep the target's scale constant [6,11]. Yet the focus of these works is not to find the optimal zoom level.

The information theoretic solution described in [5], which this work is based on, uses the *entropy* of the estimated state distribution. This system calculates the *expected entropy* for each action, and then chooses the action where the expected entropy is lowest.

However, this approach only works if all actions are considered equal. If the actions incur costs which may depend on the last action, examining the expected benefit of just a single action is no longer sufficient. In the example of focal length selection, the zoom lens motor has only a finite speed. A too high zoom level can cause the object to be lost when it approaches the edges of the camera image faster than the zoom motor can follow.

The solution is to obtain the best *sequence* of future actions, and to calculate the costs and benefits of the sequence as a whole. In our case of a motorized zoom lens, the tracker is able to reduce the focal length in advance, in order for the low focal length to actually be available in the time frame where it is needed.

In simulated experiments with slow zoom motors, up to 82% less object loss was experienced, as compared to the original single-step method. This reduced the overall state estimation error by up to 56%.

The next section contains a short review of the Kalman filter and the notation used in this paper. Section 3 simultaneously reviews the single-step method from [5] and shows how to extend it to multiple steps, the main contribution of this paper. The method is evaluated in section 4, and section 5 concludes the paper and gives an outlook for future work.

2   Review: Kalman Filter

As in [5], we operate on the following discrete-time dynamic system: At time t, the state of the system is described in the state vector $x_t \in \mathbb{R}^n$, which generates an observation $o_t \in \mathbb{R}^m$. The state change and observation equations are

$$x_{t+1} = f(x_t, t) + w \quad , \quad o_t = h(x_t, a_t) + r \tag{1}$$

where $f(\cdot, \cdot) \in \mathbb{R}^n$ is the state transition function and $h(\cdot, \cdot) \in \mathbb{R}^m$ the observation function. w and r are normal zero-mean error processes with covariance matrices W and R.

The parameter $a_t \in \mathbb{R}^l$ is called the *action* at time t. It summarizes all the parameters which affect the observation process. For object tracking, a_t might include the pan, tilt and the focal length of each camera. The action is performed *before* the observation is made.

The task of the state estimator is to continuously calculate the distribution $p(x_t | \langle o \rangle_t, \langle a \rangle_t)$ over the state, given the sequence $\langle o \rangle_t$ of all observations and the sequence $\langle a \rangle_t$ of all actions taken up to, and including, time t.

Assuming the action is (for now) known and constant, the Kalman filter [8], a standard algorithm, can be used for state estimation. Since the observation function is based on the non-linear perspective projection model, an *extended Kalman filter* [1] is necessary. A full description of the extended Kalman filter is beyond the scope of this paper. We use the following notation for the filter: $\widehat{x}_t^-$ and $\widehat{x}_t^+$ are the *a priori* and *a posteriori* state estimate means at time t. P_t^- and P_t^+ are the covariance matrices for the a priori and a posteriori state estimates. The extended Kalman filter performs the following steps for each time-step t:

1. State mean and covariance prediction:

$$\widehat{x}_t^- = f(\widehat{x}_{t-1}, t-1) \quad , \quad P_t^- = f_t^x P_{t-1} f_t^{xT} + W \quad . \tag{2}$$

2. Computation of the filter gain:

$$K_t = P_t^- h_t^{xT}(a_t) \left(h_t^x(a_t) P_t^- h_t^{xT}(a_t) + R \right) \quad . \tag{3}$$

3. State mean and covariance update by incorporating the observation

$$\widehat{x}_t^+ = \widehat{x}_t^- + K_t \left(o_t - h(\widehat{x}_t^-, a_t) \right) \quad , \quad P_t^+(a_t) = (I - K_t h_t^x(a_t)) P_t^- \quad . \tag{4}$$

f_t^x and $h_t^x(a_t)$ denote the Jacobians of the state transition and observation functions. Since the observation Jacobian $h_t^x(a_t)$ depends on the selected action a_t, the a posteriori state covariance does, too. In cases where no observation is made in a time step, the a posteriori state estimate is equal to the a priori one.

3   Multi-step Optimal Actions

The method described in [5] uses the entropy of the state distribution to select the next action for a single step in the future. The single-step approach works well if the optimal action can be performed at each time-step. Often, however, there will be real-world constraints on which actions are possible; for example, cameras with a motorized zoom lens can only change their focal lengths at a finite maximal speed. In general, we say that an action, or a sequence of actions, incurs a *cost*. This cost must be subtracted from the expected benefits of the actions to find the truly optimal actions.

In the case of focal length selection, the single-step method will often select a large focal length when the object is in the center of the camera image. Once the object moves towards the edge, a lower focal length is needed in order not to lose the object; this focal length may be to far for the zoom motors. The multi-step method, evaluating a sequence of actions, will detect the need for a low focal length sooner, and will start reducing the focal length ahead of time.

To evaluate an action, we use the *entropy* [2] of the state distribution as a measure of uncertainty. This measure was used in [5] to select a single action. We will show how this method can be expanded to a sequence of actions.

To evaluate a sequence of actions, we measure the entropy of the state distribution at the *horizon*. The horizon k is the number of steps to be looked ahead, starting at time step t. For the single-step variant, $k = 1$. We denote the sequences of *future* actions and observations, occurring between time steps $t + 1$ and $t + k$, as $\langle a \rangle^k$ and $\langle o \rangle^k$, respectively.

The entropy of the a posteriori state belief $p(\widehat{x}_{t+k} | \langle o \rangle_{t+k}, \langle a \rangle_{t+k})$ is

$$H(x_{t+k}^+) = -\int p(x_{t+k} | \langle o \rangle_{t+k}, \langle a \rangle_{t+k}) \log(p(x_{t+k} | \langle o \rangle_{t+k}, \langle a \rangle_{t+k})) dx_{t+k} . \quad (5)$$

This gives us information about the final a posteriori uncertainty, provided actions $\langle a \rangle^k$ were taken and observations $\langle o \rangle^k$ were observed.

However, to determine the optimal actions *before* the observations are made, this measure cannot be used directly. Instead, we determine the *expected entropy*, given actions $\langle a \rangle^k$, by averaging over all observation sequences:

$$H(x_{t+k} | \langle o \rangle^k, \langle a \rangle^k) = \int p(\langle o \rangle^k | \langle a \rangle^k) H(x_{t+k}^+) \, d \langle o \rangle^k . \quad (6)$$

This value is called the *conditional entropy* [2]. The notation $H(x_t | o_t, a_t)$ is misleading, but conforms to that used in information theory textbooks. The only free parameter is the action sequence $\langle a \rangle^k$. The optimal action sequence can then be found by minimizing the conditional entropy.

In the case of a Gaussian distibution, as is used throughout the Kalman filter, the entropy takes the following closed form:

$$H(x_{t+k} | \langle o \rangle^k, \langle a \rangle^k) = \int p(\langle o \rangle^k | \langle a \rangle^k) \left(\frac{n}{2} + \frac{1}{2} \log \left((2\pi)^n | P_{t+k}^+ (\langle a \rangle^k) | \right) \right) d \langle o \rangle^k. \quad (7)$$

We note that only $p(\langle o \rangle^k | \langle a \rangle^k)$ depends on the integrand $\langle o \rangle^k$, the covariance $P_{t+k}^+(\langle a \rangle^k)$ does not. This allows us to place everything else outside the integration, which then intergrates over a probability density function and is therefore always 1. Therefore, we only need to obtain the a posteriori covariance matrix P_{t+k}^+ to evaluate an action sequence, which means stepping through the Kalman filter equations k times. Since we do not have any future observations o, the state estimate mean $\widehat{x}^-$ can only be updated with the expected observation $h(\widehat{x}^-, a)$, which reduces equation (4) to $\widehat{x}^+ = \widehat{x}^- + 0$. The state estimate mean allows us to calculate all used Jacobians for equations (2) and (3), which give us all covariance matrices P^- and P^+ for any future time step.

In cases where an observation is not guaranteed, the final entropy is based on either the a posteriori or the a priori covariance matrix. The conditional entropy must take this into account. We define an observation to be either *visible* or *non-visible*. For example, in the case of object tracking, an observation is visible if it falls on the image plane of both cameras, and non-visible otherwise. It is important to note that a non-visible observation is still an element of the set of all observations. For a single step, splitting the observations into visible and non-visible ones results in the following entropy:

$$H(x_t | o_t, a_t) = \int\limits_{\{o_t \text{ visible}\}} p(o_t | a_t) H_v(x_t^+) do_t + \int\limits_{\{o_t \text{ ¬visible}\}} p(o_t | a_t) H_{\neg v}(x_t^-) do_t \quad (8)$$

In the Kalman filter case, where $H_v(\hat{x}_t^+)$ and $H_{\neg v}(\hat{x}_t^-)$ do *not* depend on o_t, they can again be moved outside the integration. The remaining integrations now reflect the probability of a visible (w_1) or non-visible (w_2) observation:

$$H(x_t|o_t, a_t) = w_1 \cdot H_v(x_t^+) + w_2 \cdot H_{\neg v}(x_t^-) \tag{9}$$

w_1 and w_2 can be solved efficiently using the Gaussian error function [5].

In the multi-step case with a horizon of k, there are 2^k different cases of visibility, since an observation may be visible or not at each time step, and hence 2^k different possible entropies must be combined. If we can calculate the probability and the a posteriori entropy at step $t + k$ for each case, we can again obtain the conditional entropy by a weighted sum:

$$H(x_t|o_t, a_t) = w_{vv...v}H_{vv...v}(x_t) + w_{vv...n}H_{vv...n}(x_t)$$
$$+ \ldots + w_{nn...n}H_{nn...n}(x_t) \tag{10}$$

where $vv \ldots v$ denotes the case where every time step yields a visible observation, $vv \ldots n$ denotes all visible except for the last, and so on. For such a sequence of visibilities, the probabilities and covariance matrices can be calculated by using the a priori or a posteriori covariance from the previous step as the starting point, and proceeding as in the single-step case.

This can be summarized in a recursive algorithm: For time step l, starting at $l = 1$, the Kalman filter equations use the current action a_{t+l} to produce the correct state mean ($\hat{x}_{t+l}^+$) and covariance (P_{t+l}^+, P_{t+l}^-) predictions for both cases of visibility, as well as the probabilities w_1 and w_2 for each case. If $l = k$, the conditional entropy is calculated as in equation (9), using entropies obtained from both covariance matrices through equation (7). Otherwise, this procedure is repeated twice for time $l + 1$: once using P_{t+1}^+ as its basis for the visible case, and once using P_{t+1}^-. Both repetitions (eventually) return a conditional entropy for all steps beyond l, and these are combined according to w_1 and w_2 into the conditional entropy for time step l to be returned.

4   Experiments

This algorithm was evaluated in a simulated object tracking system. Current computational restrictions make a meaningful evaluation in a real-world environment impossible, since the insufficient speed of the zoom motors, a key aspect of the problem, is no longer present.

The following simulated setup, as shown in figure 1, was used: The target object follows a circular pathway. The sensors are two cameras with parallel lines of sight and a variable focal length. The cameras are 200 units apart. The center of the object's path is centered between the two cameras, at a distance of 1500 units, its radius is 200 units.

Simulations were performed with horizons of 1, 2, 3 and 4, and with zoom motor speeds 3, 4 and 5 motor steps per time step, for a total of 12 different experiments. Each experiment tracked the object for 10 full rotations in 720

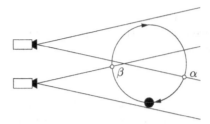

Fig. 1. Simulation setup. The object moves on a circular path. At points α and β, object loss may occur due to limited zoom motor speed.

time steps. For comparison, one experiment was also conducted with fixed focal lengths, and one with unlimited motor speed. In our implementation, a Pentium processor at 2.8 GHz takes less than two minutes for a horizon length of 1 (including output). An experiment with horizon length 4 takes about 6 hours. This implementation interates over the entire action space, without concern for efficiency. Section 5 lists several enhancements with the potential for drastic speed increases to possibly real-time levels.

Figure 2 (left) shows the number of time steps with visible observations, out of a total of 720, for each experiment. The lower the value, the longer the object was lost. The object was typically lost near points α or β in figure 1, at which the object approaches the border of a camera's image plane faster than the zoom motor can reduce the focal length.

Figure 2 (right) shows the actual focal lengths selected by the lower camera in figure 1. Two cycles from the middle of the experiments are shown. The experiments being compared both use a motor zoom speed of 3, and a horizon length of 1 and 4. Additionally, the focal lengths which occur when the zoom motor speed is unlimited are shown. One can see that a larger horizon produces similar focal lengths to a single-step system, but it can react sooner. This is visible between time steps 190 and 210, where the four-step lookahead system starts reducing the focal length ahead of the single-step variant. This results in reduced object loss. The plateaus at time steps 170 and 240 result from the object being lost in the other camera, increasing the state uncertainty.

Table 1, lastly, shows the mean state estimation error, as compared to the ground truth state. The advantage of a multi-step system is greatest in the case of a slow zoom motor (top row), where the increased probability of a valid observation more than makes up for the slight increase in information which the single-step system obtains with its larger focal lengths. This advantage diminishes once the zoom motors are fast enough to keep up with the object. The second-to-last row shows the mean error for a horizon of 1 and an unlimited motor speed. This is the smallest error achievable by using variable focal lengths. The last row contains the mean error for the largest fixed focal length which suffered no object loss. An active zoom can reduce this error by up to 45%, but only if the zoom motor is fast enough to avoid most object loss.

Table 1. Mean error, in world units, for each of the 12 experiments. The last two rows show the results for an unlimited zoom motor speed, and a fixed focal length. A variable focal length approach is always superior to a fixed one, except for the special case of slow zoom motors. These cases can be caught by a multi-step lookahead.

Zoom motor speed	horizon 1	horizon 2	horizon 3	horizon 4
3 steps	52.5	33.7	30.3	23.3
4 steps	21.2	20.4	17.1	16.1
5 steps	16.9	16.9	15.9	16.1
unlimited	15.1			
fixed	27.7			

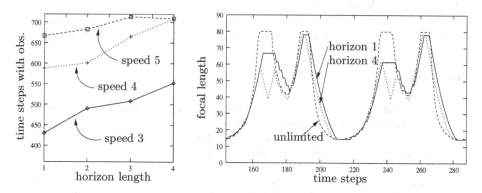

Fig. 2. *Left:* Number of time steps with observations, from a total of 720, for each experiment. Lower values mean greater object loss. *Right:* Focal lengths for two object cycles at a zoom motor speed of 3 and horizons of 1 and 4. The focal lengths from an unlimited motor speed are also shown.

5   Conclusion and Outlook

The methods presented in this paper implement a new and fundamental method for selecting information theoretically optimal sensor actions, with respect to a varying cost model, by predicting the benefit of a given sequence of actions several steps into the future. For the example of focal length selection, we have shown that, given a small action range, this multi-step approach can alleviate the problems that the single-step method faces. In our experiments, we were able to reduce the fraction of time steps with no usable observation by over 80%, which in turn reduced the mean state estimation error by up to 56%.

Future work will focus on reducing the computation time, to enable meaning-ful real-time experiments, and finally real-time applications, of multi-step action selection. For example, the results from common subexpressions, i.e. the first calculations for two action sequences with a common start, can be cached.

Another optimization is to test only a subset of all possible action sequences, with optimization methods which only rely on point evaluation. Application dependent analysis of the topology of the optimization criterion, such as axis independence and local minimality, may allow more specialized optimization methods. The efficiency may also be improved by intelligently pruning the evaluation tree, for example using methods from artificial intelligence research, such as alpha-beta pruning [9], or research in multi-hypothesis Kalman filters [1].

Though this paper only outlined the procedure for use with a Kalman filter, the method should be general enough to apply to other estimation systems, for example particle filters [7]. This is non-trivial, since this work makes use of the fact that the entropies do not depend on the actual value of the observations. This is no longer the case with more general state estimators.

Multiple camera actions have also been studied in object recognition [3] using reinforcement learning. The parallels between the reinforcement learning methods and this work will be investigated.

Lastly, these methods need to be evaluated for more general cost models, based on the "size" or "distance" of an action and not just on its feasibility.

References

1. Y. Bar-Shalom and T.E. Fortmann. *Tracking and Data Association*. Academic Press, Boston, San Diego, New York, 1988.
2. T.M. Cover and J.A. Thomas. *Elements of Information Theory*. Wiley Series in Telecommunications. John Wiley and Sons, New York, 1991.
3. F. Deinzer, J. Denzler, and H. Niemann. Viewpoint Selection – Planning Optimal Sequences of Views for Object Recognition. In *Computer Analysis of Images and Patterns – CAIP 2003*, LNCS 2756, pages 65–73, Heidelberg, August 2003.
4. J. Denzler, C.M. Brown, and H. Niemann. Optimal Camera Parameter Selection for State Estimation with Applica tions in Object Recognition. In *Mustererkennung 2001*, pages 305–312, Heidelberg, 2001.
5. J. Denzler, M. Zobel, and H. Niemann. Information Theoretic Focal Length Selection for Real-Time Active 3-D Object Tracking. In *International Conference on Computer Vision*, pages 400–407, Nice, France, 2003.
6. J. Fayman, O. Sudarsky, E. Rivlin, and M. Rudzsky. Zoom tracking and its applications. *Machine Vision and Applications*, 13(1):25–37.
7. M. Isard and A. Blake. Condensation — conditional density propagation for visual tracking. 29(1):5–28, 1998.
8. R.E. Kalman. A new approach to linear filtering and prediction problems. *Journal of Basic Engineering*, pages 35–44, 1960.
9. D.E. Knuth and R.W Moore. An analysis of alpha-beta pruning. *Artificial Intelligence*, 6(4):293–326, 1975.
10. Lucas Paletta and Axel Pinz. Active object recognition by view integration and reinforcement learnin g. *Robotics and Autonomous Systems*, 31, Issues 1-2:71–86, April 2000.
11. B. Tordoff and D.W. Murray. Reactive zoom control while tracking using an affine camera. In *Proc 12th British Machine Vision Conference, September 2001*, volume 1, pages 53–62, 2001.

Spatio–temporal Segmentation Using Laserscanner and Video Sequences

Nico Kaempchen, Markus Zocholl, and Klaus C.J. Dietmayer

Department of Measurement, Control and Microtechnology
University of Ulm, D–89081 Ulm, Germany
nico.kaempchen@e-technik.uni-ulm.de

Abstract. Reliable object detection and segmentation is crucial for active safety driver assistance applications. In urban areas where the object density is high, a segmentation based on a spatial criterion often fails due to small object distances. Therefore, optical flow estimates are combined with distance measurements of a Laserscanner in order to separate objects with different motions even if their distance is vanishing. Results are presented on real measurements taken in potentially harmful traffic scenarios.

1 Introduction

The ARGOS project at the University of Ulm aims at a consistent dynamic description of the vehicles environment for future advanced safety applications such as automatic emergency braking, PreCrash and pedestrian safety. A Laserscanner and a video camera mounted on the test vehicle retrieve the necessary measurements of the vehicles environment [1].

The Laserscanner acquires a distance profile of the vehicles environment. Each measurement represents an object detection in 3d space. Because of the high reliability of object detection and the accurate distance measurements at a high angular resolution, the Laserscanner is well suited for object detection, tracking and classification [2]. However there are scenarios, especially in dense urban traffic where the algorithms fail. The Laserscanner tracking and classification algorithms are based on a segmentation of the measurements. The measurements are clustered with respect to their distance. Objects which are close together are therefore wrongly recognised as a single segment. Thus, object tracking and classification are bound to be incorrect.

A similar problem arises in stereo vision. In [3] stereo vision is combined with optical flow estimates in order to detect moving objects even if they are close to other stationary objects. However, the approach can not differentiate between two dissimilarly moving objects. Dang et al. developed an elegant Kalman Filter implementation for object tracking using stereo vision and optical flow [4]. This algorithm uses a feature tracking approach and can be used for image segmentation based on the object dynamics.

Our approach aims at a correct Laserscanner based segmentation of objects even they are close together by analysing their motion pattern in the video image

C.E. Rasmussen et al. (Eds.): DAGM 2004, LNCS 3175, pp. 367–374, 2004.

domain. The segmentation criterion is therefore based on the distance between Laserscanner measurements and additionally the difference of the associated optical flow estimates in the video images.

2   Sensors

A Laserscanner and a monocular camera are combined in order to enable a reliable environment recognition in distances of up to 80 m. The multi–layer Laserscanner ALASCA (Automotive LAserSCAnner) of the company IBEO Automobile Sensor GmbH (Fig. 1) acquires distance profiles of the vehicles environment of up to 270° horizontal field of view at a variable scan frequency of $10 - 40$ Hz. At 10 Hz the angular resolution is 0.25° with a single shot measurement standard deviation of $\sigma = 3$ cm, thus enabling a precise distance profile of the vehicles environment. It uses four scan planes in order to compensate for the pitch angle of the ego vehicle. The Laserscanner ALASCA has been optimised for automotive application and performs robustly even in adverse weather conditions. The multi–layer Laserscanner is mounted at the front bumper of the test vehicle which reduces the horizontal field of view to 180°.

Fig. 1. The multi–layer Laserscanner ALASCA (Automotive LAserSCAnner) of the company IBEO Automobile Sensor GmbH.

The monocular camera is mounted behind the windscreen beside the inner rear mirror. The camera is equipped with a 1/2" CCD chip which has a standard VGA resolution of 640x480 pixel. With a 8 mm lens a horizontal view of 44° is realised at an average angular resolution of 0.07° per pixel.

In order to synchronise the sensors, the camera is triggered, when the rotating Laserscanner head is aligned with the direction of the optical axis of the camera. The sensors are calibrated in order to enable not only a temporal alignment given by the synchronisation but also a spatial alignment. By means of an accurate synchronisation and calibration, image regions can be associated directly with Laserscanner measurements. Therefore it is possible to assign certain image parts a distance, which is a major advantage of this fusion approach.

3   Laserscanner Based Segmentation

In order to reduce the amount of data which has to be processed, the Laserscanner measurements are combined to segments. The aim of the segmentation is to generate clusters which each represent an object in reality. Optimally there is exactly one segment per object and only one object per segment. This is, however, not always possible to realise.

The segments are created based on a distance criterion. Measurements with a small distance to neighbouring measurements are included in the same segment. Both the x and y components of the distance d_x and d_y have to be below a certain threshold θ_0. For urban scenarios a sensible choice is $\theta_0 = 0.7$ m. Especially in urban areas where the object density is high, two objects might be so close together that all measurements on these objects are combined to a single segment. This is critical for object tracking and classification algorithms which are based on the segmentation. If the measurements of two objects are combined to one single segment the object tracking can not estimate the true velocity of the two objects which is especially severe if the objects exhibit different velocities (Fig. 2). Additionally a classification of the object type (car, truck, pedestrian, small stationary objects and large stationary object) based on the segment dimensions is bound to be incorrect.

However, reducing the threshold θ_0 results in an increase of objects which are represented by several segments. This object disintegration is difficult to handle using only Laserscanner measurements. To the authors knowledge there has not yet been suggested any real time Laserscanner object tracking algorithm which is robust against a strong object disintegration in urban scenarios.

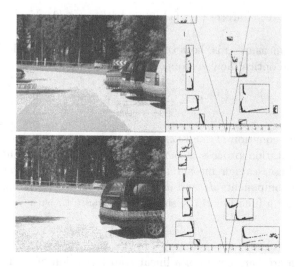

Fig. 2. Laserscanner based segmentation of a parking scenario at two time instances.

4   Spatio–temporal Segmentation Using Optical Flow

In order to improve the Laserscanner based segmentation which uses a distance criterion, an additional criterion is introduced. Considering two consecutive images the optical flow can be calculated for image regions which are associated with Laserscanner measurements. Using the optical flow as an additional segmentation criterion enables the differentiation between objects of diverging lateral motions even if they are close together.

The optical flow $\mathbf{f} = (f_u \; f_v)'$ is calculated with a gradient based method [5,6, 7]. In automotive applications, the ego motion component of the optical flow can be high even when using short measurement intervals. Therefore, a pyramidal optical flow estimation is applied in order to account for large displacements [8].

Two spatio–temporal segmentation algorithms have been developed — the constructive and destructive segmentation.

4.1   Constructive Segmentation

The constructive approach changes the segmentation distance threshold θ_0 depending on the similarity of the assigned optical flow. Extending the optical flow vector without loss of generality with the time dimension

$$\hat{\mathbf{f}} = \frac{1}{\sqrt{f_u^2 + f_v^2 + 1}} \begin{pmatrix} f_u \\ f_v \\ 1 \end{pmatrix} , \tag{1}$$

the similarity of two optical flow vectors $\hat{\mathbf{f}}_1$ and $\hat{\mathbf{f}}_2$ is given by the angle ψ between the vectors [5]

$$\psi = |\arccos\left(\hat{\mathbf{f}}_1 \cdot \hat{\mathbf{f}}_2\right)|, \qquad \text{with} \quad \psi \in [0, \pi]. \tag{2}$$

This similarity measure ψ is, however, biased towards large optical flow vectors $\mathbf{f}$. Therefore the optical flow vectors are normalised, with

$$\mathbf{f}^* = \frac{2}{\|\mathbf{f}_1\| + \|\mathbf{f}_2\|}\mathbf{f}, \tag{3}$$

before applying equation (1) and (2).

The segmentation process is performed as in the Laserscanner based approach. Two Laserscanner measurements are assigned to the same segment if their distance components d_x and d_y are below the threshold θ_0. However the threshold is now a function of the similarity measure ψ, with

$$\theta(\psi) = \theta_0(a\psi + b), \tag{4}$$

where a and b are parameters of a linear transformation of ψ. The parameters a and b are chosen so that $\theta(\psi)$ is increased for similar optical flow vectors and decreased for dissimilar vectors. If there is no optical flow assigned to the Laserscanner measurement a threshold of $\theta(\psi) = \theta_0$ is chosen.

This segmentation approach performs well if the optical flow vectors can be determined precisely even at the object boundaries where occlusions occur. As this could not be achieved with the chosen optical flow approach a second segmentation was developed which is more robust against inaccurate optical flow estimates.

4.2   Destructive Segmentation

The destructive approach is based on the segmentation of Laserscanner measurements described in section 3. The threshold θ_0 is chosen so that the object disintegration is low. Therefore, measurements on objects which are close together, are often assigned to the same segment. In this approach the video images are used to perform a segmentation based on optical flow estimates. The Laserscanner and video based segmentation are performed individually. If the optical flow segmentation indicates the existence of several objects within the image region

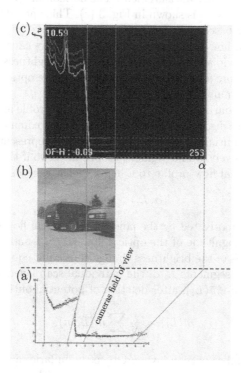

Fig. 3. Optical flow profile assigned to a Laserscanner segment. (a) shows Laserscanner measurements which are associated to the same Laserscanner segment, (b) the respective image region, (c) the horizontal optical flow component f_u for the four scan layers as a function of the viewing angle α. The dotted horizontal lines indicate the α–axis for the individual scan layers.

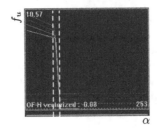

Fig. 4. Approximation of the optical flow profile by a set of linear functions. The detected object boundary is indicated with the vertical dashed lines.

of an associated Laserscanner segment, the Laserscanner segment is separated according to the optical flow segments.

Fig. 3 shows a Laserscanner segment and the associated image region of a parking situation. The distant car backs out of a parking space. The optical flow estimation is attention driven and only calculated at image regions which are assigned to a Laserscanner measurement. The horizontal optical flow component f_u for the four scan layers is shown in Fig. 3 (c). This optical flow profile is used for the optical flow based segmentation.

The raw optical flow profile is corrupted by outliers caused by reflections or other effects which violate the assumptions of the brightness change constraint equation [7]. Therefore a median filter is applied to the optical flow estimates in order to reduce the number of outliers.

The object boundaries appear in the optical flow profile as discontinuities. In order to detect these discontinuities, the profile is approximated by a set of linear functions (Fig. 4). Initially, the optical flow profile is represented by a single line segment L_i. Recursively, a line segment is split into two if the maximal distance $d(\alpha, L_i)$ of the optical flow profile to a line segment exceeds a threshold κ,

$$d(\alpha, L_i) > \kappa(\|\mathbf{f}\|). \tag{5}$$

The threshold κ is motivated by the noise in the optical flow estimates which is a function of the magnitude of the optical flow vector $\mathbf{f}$ and the expected errors caused by violations of the brightness change constraint equation. The gradients $m(L_i, n)$ of the line segments L_i of the individual scan layers n are combined to an averaged estimate $\overline{m}(L_i)$, after deletion of potential outliers

$$\overline{m}(L_i) = \frac{1}{N} \sum_n m(L_i, n), \tag{6}$$

where N is the number of scan layers. Object boundaries are classified based on the averaged gradient of the line segments $\overline{m}(L_i)$, with

$$\overline{m}(L_i) > m_{max}, \tag{7}$$

where m_{max} is the maximal allowable steepness for a line segment of a single rigid object.

The destructive segmentation assumes objects to be rigid and that object boundaries are mainly vertical in the image domain. In the parking scenarios chosen for evaluation purposes these assumptions are perfectly met.

5 Results

The presented segmentation algorithms were evaluated on parking scenarios. In all scenarios a car backs out of a parking lot. The speed of the ego–vehicle varies across the scenarios, which introduces an additional optical flow component with increasing magnitude towards the image borders. Twelve scenarios were investigated with both segmentation approaches and compared to the Laserscanner segmentation. The focus was on the car which backs out and its neighbouring car. The time stamp and the position of the moving car were recorded when the two objects were first continuously separated by the Laserscanner approach. Then, the time stamps and positions for the two other approaches were noted. The average of the differences between time and position of the optical flow based approaches with respect to the Laserscanner segmentation are concluded in Table 1.

Table 1. Gained time and the respective covered distance of the car backing out of the parking lot.

Constructive		Destructive	
Time [sec]	Distance [m]	Time [sec]	Distance [m]
2.2	1.5	2.3	1.6

In average the optical flow based segmentations detect the moving car as an individual object 2.2 sec (2.3 sec) earlier than the Laserscanner segmentation. This gained time corresponds to a covered distance of the car backing out of the parking lot of 1.5 m (1.6 m).

The two spatio–temporal segmentations perform similar in terms of an early separation of the two objects of different lateral speeds. However, the more general constructive approach exhibits a higher degree of object disintegrations. The two objects are often represented by more than two segments. This is due to inaccuracies in the optical flow estimation especially at object borders.

The destructive approach is less general, as is takes only the horizontal optical flow component into account. This is, however, the main motion component of cars moving lateral to the sensors viewing direction and therefore sufficient to consider with respect to the application. The filtering and region based linear approximation of optical flow estimates enables the algorithm to be more robust against inaccuracies in the optical flow estimation. The result is a very low degree of object disintegration.

Further examination of the results exhibited that the performance depends on two main factors independently of the chosen algorithm. First, the performance decreases with increasing velocity of the ego–vehicle as the optical flow artefacts and the noise raises and therefore the SNR decreases. Second, the performance depends on the velocity difference tangential to the viewing direction between the close objects. The higher the velocity difference the better the performance. In the scenario of a car backing out of a parking lot, the performance depends directly on its velocity which varies in the experiments between 1 and 9 km/h.

6   Conclusion

Two spatio–temporal segmentation approaches have been presented. Based on Laserscanner measurements and optical flow estimates of associated image regions a robust segmentation of objects is enabled even if objects are close together. In potentially harmful situations the correct segmentation allows a precise tracking of moving objects. The accurate segmentation and therefore tracking is an essential prerequisite for a reliable prediction of objects in dynamic scenarios for active safety systems in future cars such as automatic emergency braking.

References

1. N. Kaempchen, K. Fuerstenberg, A. Skibicki, and K. Dietmayer, "Sensor fusion for multiple automotive active safety and comfort applications," in *8th International Forum on Advanced Microsystems for Automotive Applications*, Berlin, Germany, March 2004, pp. 137–163.
2. Kay Ch. Fuerstenberg and Klaus C.J. Dietmayer, "Object tracking and classification for multiple active safety and comfort applications using multilayer laserscanners," in *Proceedings of IV 2004, IEEE Intelligent Vehicles Symposium*, Parma, Italy, June 2004, accepted.
3. Stefan Heinrich, "Real time fusion of motion and stereo using flow/depth constraint for fast obstacle detection," in *Pattern Recognition, 24th DAGM Symposium*, Luc J. Van Gool, Ed., Zurich, Switzerland, September 2002, number 2449 in Lecture Notes in Computer Science, pp. 75–82, Springer 2002, ISBN 3-540-44209-X.
4. T. Dang, C. Hoffmann, and C. Stiller, "Fusing optical flow and stereo disparity for object tracking," in *IEEE 5th International Conference on Intelligent Transportation Systems*, Singapore, September 2002, pp. 112–117.
5. J.L. Barron, D.J. Fleet, S.S. Beauchemin, and T.A. Burkitt, "Performance of optical flow techniques," in *Proc. of the IEEE Conf. on Computer Vision and Pattern Recognition*, 1992, pp. 236–242.
6. Jianbo Shi and Carlo Tomasi, "Good features to track," in *IEEE Conference on Computer Vision and Pattern Recognition*, 1994, pp. 593–600.
7. Bernd Jähne, Horst Haußecker, and Peter Geißler, Eds., *Handbook of Computer Vision and Applications*, Academic Press, ISBN 0123797705, May 1999.
8. Jean-Yves Bouguet, "Pyramidal implementation of the lucas kanade feature tracker," Tech. Rep., Intel Corporation, Microprocessor Research Labs, 2000.

Fast Statistically Geometric Reasoning About Uncertain Line Segments in 2D- and 3D-Space

Christian Beder

Institute of Photogrammetry, University of Bonn, Germany

Abstract. This work addresses the two major drawbacks of current statistical uncertain geometric reasoning approaches. In the first part a framework is presented, that allows to represent uncertain line segments in 2D- and 3D-space and perform statistical test with these practically very important types of entities. The second part addresses the issue of performance of geometric reasoning. A data structure is introduced, that allows the efficient processing of large amounts of statistical tests involving geometric entities. The running times of this approach are finally evaluated experimentally.

1 Introduction

In [5] the uncertain geometric entities point, line and plane in 2D- and 3D-space, represented using Grassmann-Cayley algebra, were used to perform statistical tests such as incidence, equality, parallelism or orthogonality between a pair of two entities. This is a very useful tool in many computer vision and perceptual grouping tasks, as both often deal with measurements of geometric entities and rely on the relational properties of the measured entities between each other (cf. [11], [8], [9]).

However, there are two major drawbacks in this approach: first the Grassmann-Caley algebra does not allow to represent localized objects, such as line segments in 2D- and 3D-space, in a straightforward manner and second there are no considerations about performing a huge amount of relational tests in an efficient manner.

Both of these drawbacks are addressed in this work. The first issue is addressed by using compound entities, i.e. to construct new geometric entities from the existing base entity classes, on the one hand and moving from the projective framework of [5] and [7] to an oriented projective framework (cf. [13]) on the other hand. The second issue is addressed by proposing a data structure for storing the entities and gaining efficiency in testing geometric relations over a large amount of data. The proposed data structure will resolve the shortcomings of the classical multi-dimensional data structures R-Tree, R*-Tree and Quadtree (cf. [6], [12],[4], [10]), that are unable to store uncertain line segments for the efficient use in statistical testing tasks.

The speed gained by using the proposed index structure for geometric reasoning, instead of simply computing all relational properties pairwise in a sequential manner, will be evaluated experimentally.

C.E. Rasmussen et al. (Eds.): DAGM 2004, LNCS 3175, pp. 375–382, 2004.

2 Compound Geometric Entities and Their Relations

2.1 Base Entities in Oriented Projective Space

The line segments will be constructed from uncertain geometric base entities in oriented projected space. For this base entities first consider the 2D-case: a point and a line may be represented by homogeneous 3-vectors $\mathbf{x}$ and $\mathbf{l}$. In oriented projective space the sign of the scalar product $\mathbf{l}^T \mathbf{x}$ can be used to indicate, if the point lies on the right hand side or on the left hand side of the line. This can be used to define the notion of direction for lines and orientation for points. Note, that points with negative orientation do not correspond to Euclidean points. If one represents the uncertainty of the entities with their covariance matrices $\boldsymbol{\Sigma}_{\mathbf{ll}}$ and $\boldsymbol{\Sigma}_{\mathbf{xx}}$ and chooses a threshold T_α according to the χ^2-distribution as proposed in [5], the statistical incidence test can be extended in the following way:

- if

$$\frac{\mathbf{l}^T \mathbf{x}}{\mathbf{l}^T \boldsymbol{\Sigma}_{\mathbf{xx}} \mathbf{l} + \mathbf{x}^T \boldsymbol{\Sigma}_{\mathbf{ll}} \mathbf{x}} < \sqrt{T_\alpha} \tag{1}$$

holds, there is no reason to reject the hypothesis, that the point lies on the left hand side of the line. This will be denoted by $\mathbf{x} \in^- \mathbf{l}$.
- if

$$-\sqrt{T_\alpha} < \frac{\mathbf{l}^T \mathbf{x}}{\mathbf{l}^T \boldsymbol{\Sigma}_{\mathbf{xx}} \mathbf{l} + \mathbf{x}^T \boldsymbol{\Sigma}_{\mathbf{ll}} \mathbf{x}} \tag{2}$$

holds, there is no reason to reject the hypothesis, that the point lies on right hand side of the line. This will be denoted by $\mathbf{x} \in^+ \mathbf{l}$.

Notice, that the two cases are not mutually exclusive, but the combination of both conditions yields the classical incidence relation, that is proposed in [5]. This will be denoted by $\mathbf{x} \in \mathbf{l}$.

In 3D-space the situation for points and planes is just the same, since every test comprising of a scalar product can be extended this way. In addition to the incidence relation the notation for the relations parallelism ($\|$, $\|^-$ and $\|^+$) and orthogonality ($\perp$, $\perp^-$ and $\perp^+$) are introduced as well in the case of scalar valued test statistics. If the test statistic instead is vector valued and bilinear, the situation is a little more involved. Let us first consider the case of a point $\mathbf{X}$ and a line $\mathbf{L}$ in 3D-space. According to [5], there is no reason to reject the hypothesis $\mathbf{X} \in \mathbf{L}$ if

$$\mathbf{d}^T \boldsymbol{\Sigma}_{\mathbf{dd}}^+ \mathbf{d} < T_\alpha \tag{3}$$

with

$$\mathbf{d} = \overline{\boldsymbol{\Gamma}}^T(\mathbf{L})\mathbf{X} \quad \text{and} \quad \boldsymbol{\Sigma}_{\mathbf{dd}} = \overline{\boldsymbol{\Pi}}^T(\mathbf{X})\boldsymbol{\Sigma}_{\mathbf{LL}}\overline{\boldsymbol{\Pi}}(\mathbf{X}) + \overline{\boldsymbol{\Gamma}}^T(\mathbf{L})\boldsymbol{\Sigma}_{\mathbf{XX}}\overline{\boldsymbol{\Gamma}}(\mathbf{L})$$

and T_α chosen according to the χ_2^2-distribution (see [5] for the definition of the matrices $\boldsymbol{\Pi}$ and $\boldsymbol{\Gamma}$). Since $\mathbf{d}$ is a vector, the notion of a single sign is not applicable here. However a test can be formulated, whether two points $\mathbf{X}$ and $\mathbf{Y}$ lie on opposite sides of $\mathbf{L}$, by requiring, that $\mathbf{X}$ and $\mathbf{Y}$ lie on opposite sides of each of the four planes defined by the rows of $\overline{\boldsymbol{\Gamma}}^T(\mathbf{L})$, that is, if $\overline{\boldsymbol{\Gamma}}^T(\mathbf{L})\mathbf{X} = -\overline{\boldsymbol{\Gamma}}^T(\mathbf{L})\mathbf{Y}$. Thus one obtains the following statistical test: if for all $i = 1..4$ the condition $\left(\frac{d_i^x}{\sigma_{d_i^x}} < T_\alpha \wedge \frac{d_i^y}{\sigma_{d_i^y}} > -T_\alpha\right) \vee \left(\frac{d_i^y}{\sigma_{d_i^y}} < T_\alpha \wedge \frac{d_i^x}{\sigma_{d_i^x}} > -T_\alpha\right)$ with

$$d_i^x = \overline{\boldsymbol{\Gamma}}_i^T(\mathbf{L})\mathbf{X} \qquad \sigma_{d_i^x}^2 = \overline{\boldsymbol{\Pi}}_i^T(\mathbf{X})\boldsymbol{\Sigma}_{\mathbf{LL}}\overline{\boldsymbol{\Pi}}_i(\mathbf{X}) + \overline{\boldsymbol{\Gamma}}_i^T(\mathbf{L})\boldsymbol{\Sigma}_{\mathbf{XX}}\overline{\boldsymbol{\Gamma}}_i(\mathbf{L})$$

$$d_i^y = \overline{\boldsymbol{\Gamma}}_i^T(\mathbf{L})\mathbf{Y} \qquad \sigma_{d_i^y}^2 = \overline{\boldsymbol{\Pi}}_i^T(\mathbf{Y})\boldsymbol{\Sigma}_{\mathbf{LL}}\overline{\boldsymbol{\Pi}}_i(\mathbf{Y}) + \overline{\boldsymbol{\Gamma}}_i^T(\mathbf{L})\boldsymbol{\Sigma}_{\mathbf{YY}}\overline{\boldsymbol{\Gamma}}_i(\mathbf{L})$$

and T_α chosen according to the χ^2-distribution holds, then there is no reason to reject the hypothesis, that $\mathbf{X}$ and $\mathbf{Y}$ lie on opposite sides of $\mathbf{L}$. This will be denoted by $(\mathbf{X}, \mathbf{Y}) \in^\otimes \mathbf{L}$. Every bilinear test statistic can be used this way, although the interpretations of the test are not as clear as in the case of point-line incidence.

2.2 Representing Line Segments and Their Tests

First consider the 2D-case again: A line segment can be represented by its two end-points $\mathbf{x}$ and $\mathbf{y}$, the line $\mathbf{l}$ connecting those two end-points and the two lines $\mathbf{m}$ and $\mathbf{n}$, orthogonally intersecting $\mathbf{l}$ in $\mathbf{x}$ and $\mathbf{y}$ and directed, such that their normals point away from the line segment. More details about the construction of such line segments can be found in [2].

Again the construction generalizes to 3D line segments in a straightforward manner, by using the end-points $\mathbf{X}$ and $\mathbf{Y}$, the connecting line $\mathbf{L}$ and the planes $\mathbf{A}$ and $\mathbf{B}$ orthogonally intersecting $\mathbf{L}$ in the points $\mathbf{X}$ and $\mathbf{Y}$, directed, such that their normals point away from the line segment.

It is now possible to perform a sequence of statistical tests on the base elements to obtain a result for the compound entity. For example the incidence of a 2D point $\mathbf{z}$ with the 2D line segment $(\mathbf{x}, \mathbf{y}, \mathbf{l}, \mathbf{m}, \mathbf{n})$ can be defined as either $\mathbf{z}$ being incident to one of the endpoints $\mathbf{x}$ or $\mathbf{y}$, or $\mathbf{z}$ being incident to the connecting line $\mathbf{l}$ and lying between the two directed lines $\mathbf{m}$ and $\mathbf{n}$. In the previous notation with logical *and* denoted by $\wedge$ and logical *or* denoted by $\vee$ this then looks like: $\mathbf{z} \equiv \mathbf{x} \vee \mathbf{z} \equiv \mathbf{y} \vee (\mathbf{z} \in \mathbf{l} \wedge \mathbf{z} \in^- \mathbf{m} \wedge \mathbf{z} \in^- \mathbf{n})$. Other statistical tests including incidence, equality, orthogonality and parallelity with 2D line segments are derived easily in a similar manner (cf. [2] for details). In case of 3D line segments some useful relations are summarized in table 1. It can be seen, that a lot of useful statistical tests can be performed very easily with the proposed representation for line segments.

3 Storing Uncertain Geometric Entities

3.1 Necessary Conditions

Now a data structure will be developed, that allows to efficiently find all uncertain entities, that match a given bilinear relation with a given uncertain entity,

Table 1. Relations with the 3D line segment $(\mathbf{X}_1, \mathbf{Y}_1, \mathbf{L}_1, \mathbf{A}_1, \mathbf{B}_1)$

Entity	Relation	Tests
point $\mathbf{Z}$	incident	$(\mathbf{Z} \equiv \mathbf{X}_1) \vee (\mathbf{Z} \equiv \mathbf{Y}_1) \vee ((\mathbf{Z} \in \mathbf{L}_1) \wedge (\mathbf{Z} \in^- \mathbf{A}_1) \wedge (\mathbf{Z} \in^- \mathbf{B}_1))$
line $\mathbf{M}$	intersect	$\mathbf{L}_1 \in \mathbf{M} \wedge (\mathbf{X}_1, \mathbf{Y}_1) \in^\otimes \mathbf{M}$
	orthogonal	$\mathbf{L}_1 \in \mathbf{M} \wedge (\mathbf{X}_1, \mathbf{Y}_1) \in^\otimes \mathbf{M} \wedge \mathbf{L}_1 \perp \mathbf{M}$
	parallel	$\mathbf{L}_1 \| \mathbf{M}$
	incident	$\mathbf{L}_1 \equiv \mathbf{M}$
plane $\mathbf{C}$	intersect	$(\mathbf{X}_1, \mathbf{Y}_1) \in^\otimes \mathbf{C}$
	incident	$\mathbf{L}_1 \in \mathbf{C}$
	orthogonal	$(\mathbf{X}_1, \mathbf{Y}_1) \in^\otimes \mathbf{C} \wedge \mathbf{L}_1 \perp \mathbf{C}$
	parallel	$\mathbf{L}_1 \| \mathbf{C}$
line segment $(\mathbf{X}_2, \mathbf{Y}_2, \mathbf{L}_2, \mathbf{A}_2, \mathbf{B}_2)$	intersect	$\mathbf{L}_1 \in \mathbf{L}_2 \wedge (\mathbf{X}_1, \mathbf{Y}_1) \in^\otimes \mathbf{L}_2 \wedge (\mathbf{X}_2, \mathbf{Y}_2) \in^\otimes \mathbf{L}_1$
	orthogonal	$\mathbf{L}_1 \in \mathbf{L}_2 \wedge (\mathbf{X}_1, \mathbf{Y}_1) \in^\otimes \mathbf{L}_2 \wedge (\mathbf{X}_2, \mathbf{Y}_2) \in^\otimes \mathbf{L}_1 \wedge \mathbf{L}_1 \perp \mathbf{L}_2$
	parallel	$((\mathbf{X}_1 \in^- \mathbf{A}_2 \wedge \mathbf{Y}_1 \in^- \mathbf{B}_2) \vee (\mathbf{X}_1 \in^- \mathbf{B}_2 \wedge \mathbf{Y}_1 \in^- \mathbf{A}_2)) \wedge \mathbf{L}_1 \| \mathbf{L}_2$
	incident	$((\mathbf{X}_1 \in^- \mathbf{A}_2 \wedge \mathbf{Y}_1 \in^- \mathbf{B}_2) \vee (\mathbf{X}_1 \in^- \mathbf{B}_2 \wedge \mathbf{Y}_1 \in^- \mathbf{A}_2)) \wedge \mathbf{L}_1 \equiv \mathbf{L}_2$
	equal	$(\mathbf{X}_1 \equiv \mathbf{X}_2 \wedge \mathbf{Y}_1 \equiv \mathbf{Y}_2) \vee (\mathbf{X}_1 \equiv \mathbf{Y}_2 \wedge \mathbf{Y}_1 \equiv \mathbf{X}_2)$

e.g. given a line segment, one is able to find all those line segments, that orthogonally intersect the given one, out of a large set of stored line segments. Therefore a necessary condition for bilinear tests like eq. (3) is derived first. The generic bilinear test has the form

$$\mathbf{d}^T \Sigma_{\mathbf{dd}}^{-1} \mathbf{d} < T_{\alpha, n} \tag{4}$$

with

$$\mathbf{d} = \mathsf{A}(\mathbf{x})\mathbf{y} \quad \text{and} \quad \Sigma_{\mathbf{dd}} = \mathsf{A}(\mathbf{x})\Sigma_{\mathbf{yy}}\mathsf{A}(\mathbf{x})^T + \mathsf{B}(\mathbf{y})\Sigma_{\mathbf{xx}}\mathsf{B}(\mathbf{y})^T$$

With σ_x^2 denoting the largest eigenvalue of $\Sigma_{\mathbf{xx}}$, σ_y^2 denoting the largest eigenvalue of $\Sigma_{\mathbf{yy}}$ and the rows of A and B denoted by $\mathbf{a}_i$ and $\mathbf{b}_i$, a necessary condition for eq. (4) is given by

$$\frac{(\mathbf{a}_1^T \mathbf{y})^2}{\sigma_y^2 \mathbf{a}_1^T \mathbf{a}_1 + \sigma_x^2 \mathbf{b}_1^T \mathbf{b}_1} + \cdots + \frac{(\mathbf{a}_n^T \mathbf{y})^2}{\sigma_y^2 \mathbf{a}_n^T \mathbf{a}_n + \sigma_x^2 \mathbf{b}_n^T \mathbf{b}_n} < T_{\alpha, n}$$

Since all terms are positive, this can only hold, if

$$\forall i \quad \frac{(\mathbf{a}_i^T \mathbf{y})^2}{\sigma_y^2 \mathbf{a}_i^T \mathbf{a}_i + \sigma_x^2 \mathbf{b}_i^T \mathbf{b}_i} < T_{\alpha, n}$$

$$\Leftrightarrow \forall i \quad \frac{|\mathbf{a}_i^T \mathbf{y}|}{|\mathbf{a}_i||\mathbf{y}|} < \sqrt{T_{\alpha, n} \left(\frac{\sigma_y^2}{\mathbf{y}^T \mathbf{y}} + \frac{\sigma_x^2}{\mathbf{a}_i^T \mathbf{a}_i} \frac{\mathbf{b}_i^T \mathbf{b}_i}{\mathbf{y}^T \mathbf{y}} \right)} \overset{(1)}{<} \sqrt{T_{\alpha, n}} \frac{\sigma_y}{|\mathbf{y}|} + \sqrt{T_{\alpha, n}} \frac{\sigma_x}{|\mathbf{a}_i|}$$

where the inequality (1) holds, because the $\mathbf{b}_i$ are projections of $\mathbf{y}$ onto some subspace for every relation considered (cf. [5]). One can also assume, that all $\boldsymbol{a}_i$ and $\boldsymbol{y}$ are spherically normalized, because the entities in oriented projective space are represented by homogeneous vectors. If one substitutes $\delta_x = \frac{2\sqrt{3}}{3}\sqrt{T_{\alpha, n}}\sigma_x$ and $\delta_y = \frac{2\sqrt{3}}{3}\sqrt{T_{\alpha, n}}\sigma_y$ a necessary condition for eq. (4) (cf. [2] for a proof) is given by

$$|\mathbf{a}_i^T \mathbf{y}| \leq \begin{cases} \cos\left(\frac{\pi}{2} - \arccos\delta_x - \arccos\delta_y\right) & \text{if } \delta_x + \delta_y \leq 1 \\ 1 & \text{otherwise} \end{cases} \tag{5}$$

This equation has a simple geometric interpretation: The hypothesis test of eq. (4) can only result in not rejecting the hypothesis, if there is a vector a' within the cone with axis a_i and opening angle $\arccos \delta_x$ and another vector y' within the cone with axis y and opening angle $\arccos \delta_y$, so that the vectors a' and y' are perpendicular.

Notice, that reasoning along the same lines yields necessary conditions for the positive and negative orientation test (cf. eq. (2) and eq. (1)):

$$\pm a_i^T y \leq \begin{cases} \cos\left(\frac{\pi}{2} - \arccos \delta_x - \arccos \delta_y\right) & \text{if } \delta_x + \delta_y \leq 1 \\ 1 & \text{otherwise} \end{cases} \tag{6}$$

Thus, associating a key (y, δ_y) with each base entity (y, Σ_{yy}), one is able to check only using this key together with eq. (5) or (6), if a statistical hypothesis test with the associated entity might result in not rejecting the hypothesis.

3.2 Combination of Keys

The next step is to combine two keys (y_1, δ_{y_1}) and (y_2, δ_{y_2}) into a new superkey $(y', \delta_{y'})$, such that the superkey yields a necessary condition for both of the keys. Since all keys represent hypercones, one looks for the enclosing hypercone to calculate the superkey. Note first, that the axis of the superkey's hypercone must lie in the hyperplane spanned by the two axes y_1 and y_2, thus one can first calculate the intersection of the hypercone (y_1, δ_{y_1}) with this hyperplane. Because it lies in the hyperplane, it can be parametrized by $y'_1 = (1 - \lambda)y_1 + \lambda y_2$ and inserting into the hypercone condition results in $\left(\frac{y'^T_1 y_1}{|y'_1|}\right)^2 = 1 - \delta^2_{y_1}$. Solving this quadratic equation for λ yields two solutions and thus two vectors y'_{11} and y'_{12}. Doing the same for the hypercone (y_2, δ_{y_2}) yields two more solutions y'_{21} and y'_{22}. Two of those four lines must lie on the surface of the enclosing cone, namely those two with the greatest enclosing angle. To find those, one must first orient the lines to point into the same direction as the corresponding hypercone axis. This can simply be achieved by checking signs of scalar products. Together with a spherical normalization one obtains $y^*_{ij} = \text{sign}\left(y^T_{ij} y_i\right) \frac{y_{ij}}{|y_{ij}|}$. Since the surface of the enclosing hypercone must lie on both sides of the axis y_2 in relation to y_1, one now determines, which lines lie on which side:

$$y^N_i = \begin{cases} y^*_{i1} & \text{if } y_{3-i}^T y^*_{i1} > y_{3-i}^T y^*_{i2} \\ y^*_{i2} & \text{otherwise} \end{cases} \qquad y^F_i = \begin{cases} y^*_{i1} & \text{if } y_{3-i}^T y^*_{i1} < y_{3-i}^T y^*_{i2} \\ y^*_{i2} & \text{otherwise} \end{cases}$$

Finally one is able to select those two oriented lines, that include both hypercones, again by simply checking scalar products:

$$m = \begin{cases} y^F_1 & \text{if } y_2^T y^F_1 < y_2^T y^N_2 \\ y^N_2 & \text{otherwise} \end{cases} \qquad n = \begin{cases} y^F_2 & \text{if } y_1^T y^F_2 < y_1^T y^N_1 \\ y^N_1 & \text{otherwise} \end{cases}$$

Thus the superkey is now given by:

$$y' = \frac{m + n}{|m + n|}$$

$$\delta_{y'} = \begin{cases} \sqrt{1 - (m^T y')^2} & \text{if } y'^T y_1^* > 0 \wedge y'^T y_2^* > 0 \\ 1 & \text{otherwise} \end{cases}$$

By definition it has the property, that whenever eq. (5), or (6) holds for any of (y_1, δ_{y_1}) or (y_2, δ_{y_2}), it must hold for $(y', \delta_{y'})$. Also notice, that it can easily be generalized to more than two keys just by sequentially enlarging the hypercone.

3.3   The Data Structure

Having defined those keys, one is now able to define an R-Tree like data structure (cf. [6]), that allows to store compound uncertain geometric entities of a single type, as follows:

- every node of the tree contains at most $2M$ and at least M elements, unless it is the root
- the elements of the leaf nodes are the compound uncertain geometric entities $((\mathbf{y}_1, \Sigma_{\mathbf{y}_1\mathbf{y}_1}), ..., (\mathbf{y}_n, \Sigma_{\mathbf{y}_n\mathbf{y}_n}))$ together with a key $((\mathbf{y}_1, \delta_{y_1}), ..., (\mathbf{y}_n, \delta_{y_n}))$ as defined in section 3.1
- every inner node's link is associated with a key $((\mathbf{y}_1', \delta_{y_1'}), ..., (\mathbf{y}_n', \delta_{y_n'}))$ constructed from the subnode's keys as described in section 3.2

Two facts follow immediately from the definition of the tree: first its height is bounded by $O(\log N)$ (cf. [1]) and second a statistical test with an entity stored in a leaf node can only result in not rejecting the hypothesis, if for all keys along the path to the root, the eq. 5 or 6 (depending on the test) holds. The second property is used to define the query algorithm for the data structure, by only descending into a subtree if the necessary condition with the key holds. Thus, the more complex the query, the better is the performance of the algorithm, since more subtrees can be truncated at an earlier point in time.

To insert an element into the tree and maintain the first property, a strategy similar to the construction of an R-Tree is used. On every level the algorithm computes for every subtree the enlargement of the opening angles of the keys hypercones and inserts the entity into the subtree, where the enlargements are minimal. If a node has more than $2M$ elements, the node is split into two subsets of size M and $M + 1$, such that the opening angles of the superkeys hypercones of the elements of each subset are minimal. To find those subsets, the quadratic split heuristic proposed in [6] is used. As shown in [1], the running time of this algorithm is bounded by $O(logN)$.

A more detailed description together with some implementation details can be found in [2]. Note also, that the data structure is not limited to line segments, but can store and perform any kind of statistical test on data, that is constructed from multiple (or single) uncertain base entities of the Grassmann-Cayley algebra. For points it is similar to the classical R-Tree, thus a similar performance can be expected in this case.

4   Experimental Evaluation

The running times of the data structure proposed in the previous section were evaluated on artificial line segment data in 3D-space. A set of N line segments inside the cube of volume 1 centered at the origin were generated randomly. The line segments were of random length between 0.05 and 0.1 and random orientation with the standard deviation of the endpoints being 0.001. All N line segments were inserted into the proposed

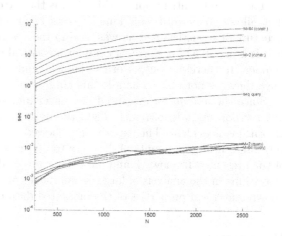

Fig. 1. Running times for construction and intersection queries of 3D line segments

data structure and another random line segment was used to retrieve all line segments from the data structure, that intersect the given one. Intersection was chosen, because it has the broadest field of application, though the other relations behave very similar. An application example for this kind of query that benefits from the proposed data structure can be found in [3]. The running times on a current standard desktop computer for different values of the nodes half size M are depicted at the bottom of figure 1.

Since classical multi-dimensional data structures do not support statistical geometric tests as query, the running time for sequentially comparing all N line segments with the given one is shown in the middle of figure 1. It can be seen, that the improvement is up to a factor of 50, depending on the number of line segments stored in the data structure.

The drawback of using an index structure is, that the construction requires time. The construction times for different values of M are depicted on top of figure 1. It can be seen, that the choice of $M = 2$ is best, since the construction time heavily depends on M and the query times do not depend on M so strongly. Certainly a large amount of queries, for example required by a spatial join algorithm, to a fairly large and static set of line segments is required to exploit the benefits of the proposed data structure.

5   Conclusion

In this work a framework was presented, that allows to perform statistical tests on uncertain geometric entities constructed from tuples of uncertain base entities in oriented projective space. It was shown, that uncertain line segments in 2D-

and 3D-space are constructible in such a way, that statistical reasoning about this practically very important geometric entities is possible in this framework. The second contribution of this work is the introduction of a data structure, that allows to perform this kind of tests in an efficient manner. The special structure of statistical testing was used in the design of the data structure, such that it is capable of performing complex statistical reasoning tasks in an efficient manner. It therefore outperforms classical multi-dimensional data structures, since they are not able to handle this kind of queries.

Since the amount of measured, i.e. uncertain, geometric data in many computer vision tasks is extremely high, the need for efficient geometric reasoning algorithms is evident. The experiments showed, that the gain in performance is very high, if large amounts of data are to be processed, so that the application of the presented framework and data structure could lead to new, more feasible algorithms in the analysis of large aerial images or large image sequences, where known statistical properties of the measured data can be used.

References

1. R. Bayer and E. McCreight. Organization and maintenance of large ordered indexes. *Acta Informatica*, 1:173–189, 1972.
2. C. Beder. Joinalgorithmus für Mengen unsicherer geometrischer Elemente. Technical report, Institut für Photogrammetrie, 2003.
3. C. Beder. A unified framework for the automatic matching of points and lines in multiple oriented images. In *Proc. 20th ISPRS Congress, Istanbul, Turkey*, 2004.
4. R. Finkel and J. Bentley. Quad trees: A data structure for retrieval on composite keys. *Acta Informatica*, 4:1–9, 1974.
5. Brunn. A. Förstner, W. and S. Heuel. Statistically testing uncertain geometric relations. In *Proc. DAGM 2000, Kiel, Germany*, pages 17–26, 2000.
6. A. Guttman. R-trees: A dynamic index structure for spatial searching. In *Proc. ACM SIGMOD Int. Conf. on Management of Data*, pages 47–57, 1984.
7. S. Heuel. Points, lines and planes and their optimal estimation. In *Pattern Recognition, 23rd DAGM Symposium*, number 2191 in LNCS, pages 92–99. Springer, September 2001.
8. S. Heuel and W. Förstner. Matching, reconstructing and grouping 3d lines from multiple views using uncertain projective geometry. In *CVPR '01*. IEEE, 2001.
9. F. Jung and N. Paparoditis. Extracting 3d free-form surface boundaries of man-made objects from multiple calibrated images: A robust, accurate and high resolving power edgel matching and chaining approach. In *Proc. of the ISPRS Conf. Photogrammetric Image Analysis*, pages 39–44, 2003.
10. D. E. Knuth. *Sorting and Searching*, volume 3 of *The Art of Computer Programming*. Addison-Wesley, 1998.
11. David G. Lowe. *Perceptual Organization and Visual Recognition*. Kluwer Academic Publishers, 1985.
12. R. Schneider R. Seeger N. Beckmann, H. Kriegel. The R*-tree: An efficient and robust access method for points and rectangles. In *Proc. ACM SIGMOD Symposium on Principles of Database Systems*, pages 322–331, 1990.
13. J. Stolfi. *Oriented Projective Geometry*. Academic Press, 1991.

A Statistical Measure for Evaluating Regions-of-Interest Based Attention Algorithms

Martin Clauss, Pierre Bayerl, and Heiko Neumann

University of Ulm, Dept. of Neural Information Processing, 89081 Ulm, Germany,
{mc,pierre,hneumann}@neuro.informatik.uni-ulm.de

Abstract. We present a new measure for evaluation of algorithms for the detection of regions of interest (ROI) in, e.g., attention mechanisms. In contrast to existing measures, the present approach handles situations of order uncertainties, where the order for some ROIs is crucial, while for others it is not. We compare the results of several measures in some theoretical cases as well as some real applications. We further demonstrate how our measure can be used to evaluate algorithms for ROI detection, particularly the model of Itti and Koch for bottom-up data-driven attention.

1 Introduction

During the last decade, several studies were conducted concerning the mechanism of attention in human and animal vision. It has been observed, that biological vision is based on the dynamic selection of regions of interest (ROI) through the guidance of the gaze towards selected scenic regions. In other words, regions in the current field of view were selected to focus high-resolution processing-ressources at locations that are likely to contain important information for the task currently performed. Multiple ROIs are then scanned in a serial manner by fixating the high-resolution fovea of the eye on these suspicious locations using saccadic movements.

Following these studies on biological vision, several computational models for adapting this principle of "regions of interest" have been proposed [3][5][9][2]. Although their internal working schemes often differ significantly, they all result in a set of locations for different regions of interest. Key mechanisms: select image locations of high information content, often measured in terms of feature contrast.

Stark and Choi [8] investigated the sequence of selected fixations. They found that the path of scanned locations repeats itself after several fixations. The authors coined the underlying mechanism of the mind's eye, the "scanpath theory" of attentive vision. However, the authors also showed, that there isn't such a thing as a global scanpath, that is, that everybody looked at the same spots in the same order. Even the scanpath of the same observer for the same stimulus isn't unique. Thus it is not possible to directly compare the results of different models, because even if both models predict the same ROIs, their order is very likely to differ. Similar problems arise when trying to evaluate a single model under various conditions, like different noise or illumination.

Existing measures for the evaluation of ROI-based attention algorithms have difficulties representing these variations in the order of regions of interest. We present a new

C.E. Rasmussen et al. (Eds.): DAGM 2004, LNCS 3175, pp. 383–390, 2004.

measure which is capable of handling such uncertainties. This enables us to evaluate these algorithms and to compare them against human or animal observer. Using this measure we will evaluate the attention model of Itti and Koch [3]. For that reason we give a short review of the model in section 2. The measure itself will be developed in section 3 and its results are then shown in section 4.

2   Review of Itti and Koch's Approach for Attention

Itti, Koch and Niebur [3] presented a popular model for computing regions of interest using a saliency map which is obtained from a pyramidal multi-resolution representation of the input data. The computation is purely data driven, as it does not incorporate any feedback or knowledge-based mechanisms.

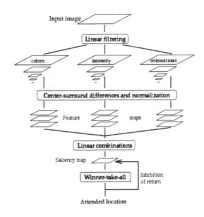

First a gaussian pyramid is built from the input stimulus. This pyramid of different scales of the image is then split into several channels selective to different features like color, intensity or orientation. Following this step, a center-surround operation is performed on each of these multi-scale representations. All these maps are then combined into a single saliency map. Different strategies of combin-

Fig. 1. Attention model of Itti and Koch [3]

ing these maps have been discussed and analysed in [4]. The simplest method is just summing up all the maps. In order to achieve this, the maps have to be scaled to the same spatial size prior to summation. More advanced methods we applied perform iterative center-surround inhibition to sharpen the data and extract local maxima [4].

On the resulting saliency map, a winner-take-all algorithm is applied which determines the most salient location which has to be attended next. In order to avoid, that this location is also attended in the next steps, the currently attended location is inhibited within the saliency map, so the selected locations are inhibited for a certain number of iterations (inhibition of return). From a biological view, it is not yet entirely clear if such a global saliency map really exists in the human brain. Recent experimental findings suggest that cortical area V4 might be a candidate [6].

3   Methods of Evaluation

In this section we will present two simple measures for evaluating models that select regions of interest. We will further explain how our new measure is calculated.

3.1   Order-Independent Measure

The measure presented in this section is the simplest method to evaluate a ROI-model. Assume that we have a ground truth consisting of n ROIs. It is then checked how many of these ROIs of the ground truth are found again within the first n results during the test-run of the model. Example: If the ground truth has 5 ROIs and 3 of them are also found during the test run, the result is simply 0.6 or 60%. This measure can be easily implemented and also be calculated very quickly. Its major limitation is that it does not at all take care of the order in which the ROIs were chosen.

3.2 Order-Dependent Measure (String Edit Distance)

Another measure to evaluate models is the "string edit distance" [1]. Each ROI from ground truth is labelled with a separate letter and these letters are concatenated in the order of appearance of the corresponding ROI to form a "ground-truth-string". After running the algorithm that is evaluated a second string is built from the ROIs selected by the algorithm.

The two strings obtained so far are furthermore compared in a way that it is calculated how "costly" one string can be transformed to the other. Costs are defined for insertion, deletion and substitution of letters. The minimum costs of this transformation are usually computed using dynamic programming.

One limitation arising with this measure is, that it is not possible to define two regions of interest of equal importance, instead one ROI has always to be preferred over another when setting up the ground truth and its labelling order.

3.3 Hybrid Measure

In order to circumvent the limitations of the two measures presented above, we develop a new measure which considers the order of the regions of interest and also accounts for systematic variations.

One calculation run of our proposed measure consists of several steps.

1. First the ROIs need to be determined. This may be done by any kind of source: Human/animal observers, by a person, or by a computational model.
2. Just like for the calculation of the minimum string edit distance, the ROIs need to be assigned numbers.
3. The relative order of the ROIs is then stored in a matrix for further processing as shown in Fig. 2.
4. All the previous steps are performed multiple times, and the resulting matrices are summed up.
5. Finally the resulting matrix is normalized by dividing it through the number of iterations the previous steps were done.
6. The obtained matrix encodes the probabilities for all (a,b), i.e. denoting that ROI a preceeds ROI b.

First, the calculation presented above has to be done once for a ground-truth-run, resulting in a matrix A. This matrix describes the relative order of ROIs for the ground truth. After that, the calculation is performed for one or more test-runs and a corresponding matrix B is returned. The two matrices are then compared by calculating the normalized crosscorrelation of the two matrices: $c = |A||B|/\sqrt{|A||B|}$

The measure presented in this section is capable of handling both strict as well as loose order of the ROIs.

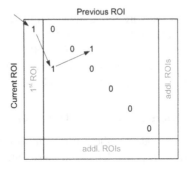

Fig. 2. The matrix created from the relative order of ROIs. The ordinate of the matrix denotes the label of the current ROI, the abscissa denotes the label of the ROI that preceeded the current one. As the very first ROI detected doesn't have any predecessor, an additional row on the abscissa is needed. Each value in this "pre-occurence matrix" represents the probability that ROI a preceeds ROI b. It can be observed that the sum of each column and row respectively has to be one. When a strict order of ROIs can be defined, the matrix obtained simply consists of all ones on the second diagonal. If there are several ROIs that should have the same importance probabilities are simply spread over several possible predecessors. In the example, the order of the ROIs is $(0 \rightarrow)1 \rightarrow 3 \rightarrow 2$. In order to account for regions of interest that were not present in the ground truth, an extra row and column exist, which sum up those additional regions of interest. For the ground truth those cells are simply all zero.

4   Results

In this section we evaluate our measure by analysing its behaviour in some theoretical scenarios. Afterwards we will compare our measure against string edit distance regarding the impact of noise on the model of Itti and Koch [3]. In order to be able to do this we need to normalize all three measures to the range [0,1]. This is done in the following way:

- order-independent measure: The values returned by this measure are within the range [0,1]
- string edit distance: $m = 1 - \frac{distance}{n}$, with n denoting the number of ROIs in the ground truth.
- hybrid measure: as all elements of the histogram matrices are positive, the results already lie within the range [0,1].

Furthermore, we will also evaluate two of the feature combination strategies presented by Itti and Koch [4] using our newly presented measure.

4.1   Theoretical Cases

First, we compare the three measures presented so far in two theoretical scenarios.

Scenario A: Suppose we have three regions of interest, labeled 1 to 3 and their correct order be $1 \rightarrow 2 \rightarrow 3$. We now assume the ROI-algorithm detects them in the order $1 \rightarrow 3 \rightarrow 2$.

For a suitable measure it is expected that the value falls below 1, as the order of detection is incorrect. The results of the three measures presented in section 3 are shown in table 1. As we can see, the order-independent measure does not account for the wrong order of detection. Both, string editing distance as well as our statistical measure correctly decrease to a lower value.

Scenario B: We assume three ROIs as before, but the ones, labeled 2 and 3 are equally important. This means, in 50% of the cases the detected order is $1 \rightarrow 2 \rightarrow 3$ and $1 \rightarrow 3 \rightarrow 2$ otherwise. As the order of ROI 2 and 3 should not matter, the measure should not decrease but stay on the maximum value of 1. Again, the results of the three measures are shown in table 1. Since the order-independent measure does not care about ROI sequence, its result still is 1, which is correct in this case. Also, our hybrid measure correctly returns 1, as the order of ROI 2 and 3 should not matter. String edit distance however cannot cope with such a situation and falls to $\frac{2}{3}$.

Table 1. Results obtained from the three measures for our theoretical scenarios.

scenario	expected	order-independent	order-dependent	hybrid
A	< 1	1	0.33	0.33
B	1	1	0.67	1

This demonstrates that our new hybrid measure can deal with both theoretical situations, strict order as well as partially ambiguous order.

4.2 Evaluation of the Model of Itti and Koch

We now take a look at how the new proposed measure performs on real applications. We will therefore evaluate the impact of noise on the model of Itti and Koch using two different feature combination strategies: Simple summation versus iterative local inhibition [4]. The input stimulus shown in Figure 3 has been motivated by recent findings about saliency and pop-out effects [7]. The evidence suggests that feature contrasts, rather than absolute values, were relevant measures that lead to target selection and boundary detection. Here the stimulus is composed of equal size disks and a smaller one thus leading to a contrast in circle diameter. As the image is symmetric, all five big circles should result in the same conspicuity. That is, their order of detection should not matter. In contrast, the small sixth circle should results in a higher saliency as it generates a strong contrast against the other disks. It is the only peak present in the corresponding spatial scale, so it ought to be the first ROI detected by the algorithm. In our test scenario we have applied white gaussian noise to the input stimulus ranging from $sigma = 0$ up to $sigma = 2$ in steps of $\delta = 0.2$. We then applied our implementation of the model of Itti and Koch on these input stimuli. We did so using two feature combination strategies, simple summation as well as iterative local inhibition. In [4] it was shown that iterative local inhibition performs better than simple summation, it is therefore expected that the proposed statistical measure quantifies this result. Figure 3 shows the corresponding results. We obtained the expected result, showing that local iterative inhibition outperforms simple summation.

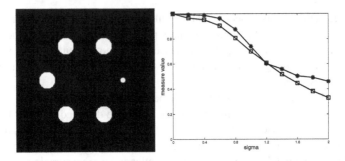

Fig. 3. Left: Input stimulus. Six radially aligned discs with equal intensity. Five of them have the same diameter, the sixth one is significantly smaller. Right: Simple summation (squares) versus local iterative inhibition (stars). It can be seen that the latter performs better than simple summation under the influence of noise. On the abscissa, sigma denotes the amount of noise applied to the input stimulus. "Measure value" on the ordinate denotes the value returned by our proposed measure.

We will now compare our statistical measure against string edit distance and the simple measure.The feature combination strategy used for the model of Itti and Koch is the local iterative inhibition. First, we select a scenario which all of the measures should be able to handle. The corresponding input stimulus is shown in Figure 4. It consists of six radially aligned circles with decreasing intensity and equal diameter. As the brightness of the circles has an order, their respective saliency is ordered as well. Therefore, there is a strict order of preference of the regions of interest. In addition, when the noise level is increased, the number of disks that can be detected decreases monotonically. Accordingly, the simple measure should also decrease.

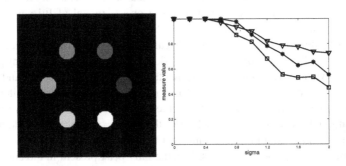

Fig. 4. Left: Input stimulus. Right: Performance of the three measures presented in section 3, string edit distance (squares), simple measure (triangles) and our proposed measure (stars). All measures remain almost constant up to around $sigma = 0.8$, from where on they fall linearly to a value of about 0.5 for $sigma = 2$. The simple measure rates the algorithm slightly better, as it only reacts on lost ROIs in contrast to the other two measures. Again, sigma denotes the amount of noise applied to the input stimulus. The "measure value" on the ordinate denotes the values returned by the three different measures.

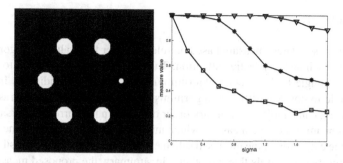

Fig. 5. Left: Input stimulus. Right: As string edit distance (squares) cannot cope with equiimportant ROIs its value drops too fast already for small values of sigma. In contrast, the simple measure (triangles) overestimates performance of the algorithm, as most of the ROIs can be detected even under strong noise, but in the wrong order. Like for figure 4 "sigma" denotes the amount of noise applied, "measure value" denotes the values returned by the three different measures.

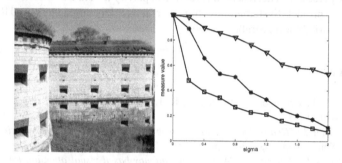

Fig. 6. Left: Input stimulus, a real scene. Right: Sigma on the abscissa denotes the amount of noise added to the image. String edit distance (squares) decreases very fast, the simple measure (triangles) falls very slowly. Our proposed measure lies between them.

We can see in Figure 4 that the expected results are returned. All measures behave similar as there is an unambigous order of ROIs and weak stimuli get lost with an increasing amount of noise.

In the next step we calculate all three measures for our first input stimulus shown in Figure 3. The results are shown in Figure 5. Again, we perform local iterative inhibition prior to feature map combination. We expect, that the string edit distance measure is not able to interpret the output of the algorithm correctly and therefore degrades too fast. In contrast, the simple measure is supposed to degrade too slow, as all features have a high intensity contrast and therefore can be detected even in noisy situations.

As expected string edit distance rates the performance of the algorithm worse and drops quickly. In contrast, the simple measure which does not handle variations in the order of ROIs decreases only very slowly. The result of our proposed measure lies between these two other measures.

Finally we evaluate the model of Itti and Koch on a real life image shown in Figure 6. As most of the windows on the fort are simlar, we expect that there are several ROIs of ambiguous order. For this reason string edit distance decays too fast.

5   Discussion

We have proposed a new measure based on relative order for evaluating algorithms that detect ROIs such as for selective attention. This new measure has shown to be able to evaluate one single ROI-detection algorithm under alternating conditions. In addition, it is also able to compare different algorithms against each other. In contrast to string edit distance it can handle any arbitrary order of ROIs. In the current proposal, all ROIs have the same impact on the measure, which might not be sufficient for some situations. One possible extension of the proposed scheme, therefore, could be the possibility to put more weight on some ROIs than on others. In summary, the proposed measure is able to rate performance of algorithms where the order of the ROIs may be ambiguous. This is necessary when trying to compare a computational model with biological studies on human or animal observers.

Acknowledgements. This research is funded in part by the state of Baden-Württemberg as a part of the project "Systemarchitekturen zur Gewährleistung sicherer und Ressourcen schonender Mobilität im Straßenverkehr".

References

1. Corman, T. H., Leiserson, C. E., Rivest, R. L.: *"Introduction to Algorithms"*, New York: McGraw-Hill, 1997
2. Deco, G., Zihl, J.: *"Neurodynamical Mechanism of Binding and Selective Attention for Visual Search"*, Neurocomputing, 32-33, pp. 693-699, 2000.
3. Itti, L., Koch, C., Niebur, E.: *"A model of saliency-based visual attention for rapid scene analysis."*, IEEE Transactions on pattern analysis and machine intelligence, Vol. 20, No 11, pp. 1254-1259, November 1998
4. Itti, L., and Koch, C.: *"A Comparison of Feature Combination Strategies for Saliency-Based Visual Attention Systems."*, SPIE human vision and electronic imaging IV(HVEI'99), San Jose, CA, pp. 473-482.
5. Kohonen, T.: *"Modeling of automatic capture and focusing of visual attention."*, Proceedings of the National Academy of Sciences of the USA, Vol. 99, No. 15, pp. 9813-9818, July 2002
6. Mazer, J. A. & Gallant, J. L.: *"Goal-Related Activity in V4 during Free Viewing Visual Search: Evidence for a Ventral Stream Visual Salience Map"*, Neuron, Vol. 40, pp. 1241-1250, December 2003
7. Nothdurft, H.C.: *"Texture segmentation and pop-out from orientation contrast."*, Vision Research 31, pp. 1073-1078, 1991
8. Stark, L. W., Choi, Y. S.: *"Experimental Metaphysics: The scanpath as an epistemological mechanism."*, W. H. Zangemeister, H. S. Stiehl, & C. Freska (Eds.), Visual attention and cognition, pp. 3-69. Amsterdam: Elsevier Science B.V.
9. Tsotsos, J. K., Culhane, S. M., Wai, W. Y. K., Lai, Y. H., Davis, N., Nuflo, F.: *"Modeling visual attention via selective tuning."*, Artificial Intelligence, Vol 78, No 1-2, pp. 507-545, October 1995

Modelling Spikes with Mixtures of Factor Analysers

Dilan Görür, Carl Edward Rasmussen, Andreas S. Tolias, Fabian Sinz, and
Nikos K. Logothetis

Max Planck Institute for Biological Cybernetics
72076 Tübingen, Germany
{first.last}@tuebingen.mpg.de

Abstract. Identifying the action potentials of individual neurons from
extracellular recordings, known as spike sorting, is a challenging problem.
We consider the spike sorting problem using a generative model, *mixtures
of factor analysers*, which concurrently performs clustering and feature
extraction. The most important advantage of this method is that it quantifies the certainty with which the spikes are classified. This can be used
as a means for evaluating the quality of clustering and therefore spike
isolation. Using this method, nearly simultaneously occurring spikes can
also be modelled which is a hard task for many of the spike sorting methods. Furthermore, modelling the data with a generative model allows us
to generate simulated data.

1 Introduction

Recording the spiking activity from well isolated single neurons is important for
studying the physiological functions of the brain. Although intracellular electrodes provide good quality signals from a single neuron, recording with an
intracellular electrode in awake behaving animals is extremely difficult. Extracellular electrodes introduced into the brain isolating a single neuron have been
successfully used for years. Recently, there has been excitement about recording
simultaneously from multiple neurons in order to study their interactions. Electrodes placed in the extracellular medium can record the activity of multiple
nearby neurons but this leads us to the question of distinguishing between the
activity of individual neurons known as spike sorting. Under the assumption that
the extracellular space is electrically homogeneous, four-tip electrodes (tetrodes)
provide the minimal number necessary to identify the spatial position of a source
based on the relative spike amplitudes on different electrodes. Recording with
multi-tip electrodes improves the identification of individual neurons compared
to standard single-tip electrodes ([3]).

Spike sorting is usually done in three steps, namely spike detection, feature
extraction and clustering. Determination of the occurrence of spikes, which is
usually achieved by high-pass filtering followed by thresholding is known as the
spike detection step. In the feature extraction stage, a feature vector for each
spike is calculated and clustering is done on this low dimensional feature space.

C.E. Rasmussen et al. (Eds.): DAGM 2004, LNCS 3175, pp. 391–398, 2004.
© Springer-Verlag Berlin Heidelberg 2004

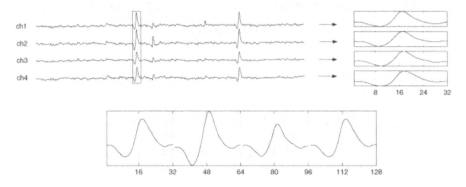

Fig. 1. Data recording and representation: Extracellular waveforms are recorded with a tetrode. Every time the signal exceeded the threshold in one of the channels, a window of 1ms around this event was extracted from the recordings of each channel and joined to form the data vectors

In most laboratories the clustering is done manually, usually using only the peak-to-peak amplitude data as features in order to make visualisation possible. There are also automatic spike sorting techniques that have been proposed which use different methods for feature extraction and clustering (see [5] for a review). A common problem of the spike sorting techniques is that the true labels for the recorded data cannot be known without the verification of intracellular recordings, which makes it very hard to evaluate the results obtained by clustering techniques.

Here, we present an automated way of spike sorting based on mixtures of factor analysers (MFA) using data collected with tetrodes. MFA is a statistical method that concurrently performs clustering and feature extraction. It models the spike waveforms and therefore overcomes the major cause of separation error, overlapping clusters in the low dimensional feature space. MFA can also model the nearly simultaneously occurring spikes which is a hard task for many spike sorting methods. It assigns responsibility degrees to each cluster for each spike and the entropy of these responsibilities can be used as a means for clustering evaluation. In addition, modelling the data with a generative model allows us to generate simulated data. The next section describes the data used in this study. In section 3, the clustering method is explained and in section 4 we demonstrate the method with real data collected with tetrodes.

2   Data Collection

We used data recorded with tetrodes from awake behaving macaque monkeys. The data were collected using a multi-channel data acquisition system (Cheetah Inc.). The signal was band-pass filtered between 600-6000Hz and digitised at 32kHz. The neuronal spikes were acquired via an interrupt-driven, spike voltage threshold-triggered data acquisition system. That is, when a signal above threshold was detected in one of the channels, the occurrence of a spike was assumed and therefore the signal in all channels was stored within a window length of 1 ms around the triggering event with a corresponding time stamp. The 32-dimensional signals of all four channels were joined to form the 128-dimensional data vectors for the MFA model (see figure 1).

3   Methods

In unsupervised learning, dimensionality reduction and clustering are usually two steps that come sequentially. In dimensionality reduction, the features that are highly correlated are compressed, whereas in clustering, the data with similar features are grouped. MFA combines a well known dimensionality reduction technique, factor analysis, with a widely used clustering technique, mixture of Gaussians.

3.1   Factor Analysis

Factor analysis (FA) is a latent variable model in which a p-dimensional real-valued data vector $\mathbf{y}$ is modelled using a k-dimensional vector of factors where $k << p$. Dimensionality reduction is achieved by finding a low dimensional projection of the high dimensional data that captures most of the correlation structure of the data. The generative model is given by:

$$\mathbf{y} = \Lambda \mathbf{x} + \mu + \varepsilon \tag{1}$$

where Λ is called the *factor loading matrix*. The factors $\mathbf{x}$ and the noise are assumed to be normally distributed, $\mathbf{x} \sim \mathcal{N}(0, \mathbf{I})$ and $\varepsilon \sim \mathcal{N}(0, \Psi)$, where Ψ is a diagonal matrix. Therefore, $\mathbf{y}$ is also normally distributed with mean μ and covariance $\Lambda\Lambda^T + \Psi$. If Ψ is constrained to be $\delta\mathbf{I}$, then in the limit $\delta \to 0$, the FA becomes a PCA. In FA, the scaling of the coordinates is not important, but the axis rotation in which the original data arrived is important since noise is independent along the axes the input data are represented [7].

3.2   Mixtures of Factor Analysers

By using a mixture of factor analysers, dimensionality reduction and clustering can be achieved simultaneously. If we consider a mixture of M factor analysers, the distribution of the data becomes:

$$P(\mathbf{y}) = \sum_{i=1}^{M} \pi_i \mathcal{N}(\mu_i, \Lambda_i\Lambda_i^T + \Psi) \tag{2}$$

where π_i denote the mixing proportions.

Given a set of observations $\mathbf{Y} = \{\mathbf{y}_1, \ldots, \mathbf{y}_N\}$, we can describe the joint distribution of the data and the hidden factors using binary indicator variables $z_i, i = 1, \ldots, M$ as

$$P(\mathbf{Y}, \mathbf{x}, z) = \prod_{j=1}^{N} \sum_{i=1}^{M} P(z_i) P(\mathbf{x}|z_i) P(\mathbf{y}_j|\mathbf{x}, z_i) \tag{3}$$

where $z_i = 1$ indicates that the example was generated by the ith mixture. The unknown parameters Λ_i, μ_i, π_i and Ψ that best model the covariance structure of the data can be found by maximum likelihood estimation using the EM algorithm, described below.

In the following, $\mathbf{Y}$ is the observation matrix and $\mathbf{H}$ are the unobserved (missing) quantities, in our case the latent variables of the factor analysis model ($\mathbf{x}$) and the identity of the mixture component which generated the observation (z_i). For *any* distribution Q over the latent variables, the log likelihood ($\mathcal{L} \equiv \ln P(\mathbf{Y}|\theta)$) can be lower bounded using Jensen's inequality:

$$\mathcal{L} = \ln \int d\mathbf{H} P(\mathbf{H}, \mathbf{Y}|\theta) \geq \int d\mathbf{H} Q(\mathbf{H}) \ln \frac{P(\mathbf{H}, \mathbf{Y}|\theta)}{Q(\mathbf{H})} \equiv \mathcal{F}(Q, \theta), \qquad (4)$$

defining the $\mathcal{F}(Q, \theta)$ functional. Alternately optimising $\mathcal{F}$ with respect to the distribution of the hidden variables $Q(\mathbf{H})$, and the parameters θ is guaranteed not to decrease $\mathcal{L}$.

In the E step, we specify the distribution of the hidden variables that maximises $\mathcal{F}^1$ and calculate the expectation of the log likelihood with respect to this distribution. In the M step, we maximise the expected log likelihood, $\log P(\mathbf{H}, \mathbf{Y}|\theta)$, with respect to the parameters, keeping the Q distribution constant.

There are two sets of conditionally independent hidden variables, thus the Q distribution is of the form $Q(\mathbf{x}, z_i) = Q(\mathbf{x}|z_i)Q(z_i)$. Therefore, in the E step we compute the distributions of the hidden factors given the indicator variables $Q(\mathbf{x}|z_i)$, the distribution of the indicator variables $Q(z_i)$ and the expected log likelihood with respect to the Q distribution (for details see [2]).

In the M step, the update rule for the parameters is obtained simply by setting the derivative of the expected log likelihood with respect to the parameters to zero and solving for the parameters[2]:

$$\tilde{\Lambda}_i = [\Lambda_i \, \mu_i] = (\sum_j \mathbf{y}_j \langle z_i \mathbf{x}|\mathbf{y}_j \rangle^T)(\sum_j \tilde{\Lambda}_i \langle z_i \mathbf{x}\mathbf{x}^T|\mathbf{y}_j \rangle)^{-1} \qquad (5)$$

$$\Psi = \frac{1}{N} \operatorname{diag}(\sum_{ij} \langle z_i|\mathbf{y}_j \rangle \mathbf{y}_j \mathbf{y}_j^T - \sum_{ij} \Lambda_i \langle z_i \mathbf{x}|\mathbf{y}_j \rangle \mathbf{y}_j^T) \qquad (6)$$

$$\pi_i = \frac{1}{N} \sum_j \langle z_i|\mathbf{y}_j \rangle \qquad (7)$$

3.3   Split and Merge EM

The EM algorithm is a hill climbing approach, thus local maxima is a serious problem of EM. When there are many components in one part of the space, and too few in another, it might not be possible to move a component from the overpopulated region to the underpopulated region without passing through

---

[1] This is equivalent to minimising the KL-divergence between $Q(\mathbf{H})$ and $P(\mathbf{H}, \mathbf{Y}|\theta)$.
[2] $\langle . \rangle$ denotes expectation wrt. Q

positions that has lower likelihood. To overcome this problem we used split and merge EM (SMEM) algorithm of Ueda et al. [8].

In the SMEM algorithm, when the model converges using the EM steps described above, two components are merged into one, and one component is split into two. Then, only the parameters of these three components are updated until convergence (referred to as the *partial EM procedure*). If this helps to increase the likelihood, the new parameters are accepted, otherwise another set of candidates are selected for splitting and merging and the partial EM procedure is repeated. The ordering of the split and merge candidates is important for the speed of the SMEM algorithm. We have used the criteria given in [8] to sort the candidates which suggests that the components that share the responsibilities[3] of many examples are good candidates for merging:

$$\mathcal{J}_{\text{merge}}(i, j; \theta) = \frac{\mathbf{R}_i(\theta)^T \mathbf{R}_j(\theta)}{\|\mathbf{R}_i(\theta)\| \, \|\mathbf{R}_j(\theta)\|} \tag{8}$$

where $\mathbf{R}_i(\theta)$ is the N-dimensional vector consisting of the responsibilities of the ith model for each of the examples. The split criterion uses the *local KL divergence* between the local density $f_k(\mathbf{y})$ around the kth model and the density of the kth model specified by the current parameters θ:

$$\mathcal{J}_{\text{split}}(k; \theta) = \int f_k(\mathbf{y}; \theta) \log \frac{f_k(\mathbf{y}; \theta)}{P(\mathbf{y}|z_k, \theta_k)} d\mathbf{y} \tag{9}$$

where z_k denotes the indicator variables of the kth model. The local density is defined as:

$$f_k(\mathbf{y}; \theta) = \frac{\sum_{n=1}^{N} \delta(\mathbf{y} - \mathbf{y}_n) P(z_k|\mathbf{y}_n; \theta)}{\sum_{n=1}^{N} P(z_k|\mathbf{y}_n; \theta)} \tag{10}$$

3.4   Model Selection

An important issue in using MFA is choosing the number of factors (k) and the number of mixtures (M) to be used. The likelihood of the fit of the model to data is used to assess the goodness of fit in the maximum likelihood models. Factor analysis is a constrained Gaussian model, therefore, the best likelihood one can achieve using a FA is that of the full Gaussian model and the likelihood gets closer to this limit as the number of factors is increased. Thus, a k value can be chosen depending on the closeness of the likelihood of different models to the full Gaussian model. Cross-validation can be used for determining the number of mixtures, in which several values of M are fit to the data and the log likelihood on a validation set is used to select the the final value. Alternatively, a Bayesian analysis in which these parameters are determined automatically may also be used [1,6].

---

[3] $r_{ij} = \langle z_i | \mathbf{y}_j \rangle$

4   Results

We first trained FA models with varying number of factors to decide how much dimensionality reduction we could have while keeping a good representation of the data. The results obtained by modelling the raw data was not very promising since only the likelihood of the models with large number of factors were close to the limiting likelihood value mentioned in section 3.4. As mentioned in section 3.1, the FA is sensitive to the orientation of the input axis. Therefore we tried to find a representation of the data that would allow good dimensionality reduction. Using the Fourier transform coefficients of the data helped to have high likelihood with lower number of factors (see figure 2 for a comparison). As seen in the figure, both raw data and Fourier transformed data likelihood converges to the full Gaussian model likelihood. The Fourier transformed data gets closer to this value with fewer factors (32 in this case). Therefore, we used the Fourier transformed data to train the MFA models that had 32 factors per mixture. It should be emphasised that we have used all coefficients of the Fourier transform obtained by a linear transform of the data, thus kept all information about the waveforms.

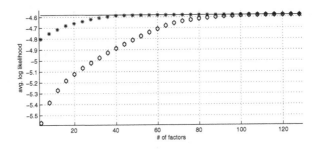

Fig. 2. Log likelihood for the FA models with only single mixture components trained with raw data (o) and with Fourier transformed data (*). The solid line shows the full Gaussian model likelihood, which is the limiting value. Note that using MFA, this limit can be exceeded, therefore this approach gives only an approximation of the necessary number of factors

After determining the number of components used in each mixture, the next step was to find an optimal number of mixtures M in terms of the data likelihood and neuron isolation. We used a cross-validation scheme of MFA models trained on the whole waveform to determine M. We evaluated the resulting model by looking at the value of the entropies, observing the waveforms assigned to different clusters and comparing with manual clustering. In manual clustering the amplitude of one channel versus another is plotted in 2-D graphs in every possible combination of the channels, and the human operator manually draws boundaries around regions of high spike density. Therefore, we plotted the same kind of amplitude plots for comparison.

We trained the MFA models using SMEM algorithm to avoid local maxima. The cross-validation scheme determined $M = 9$ to be the optimal number of

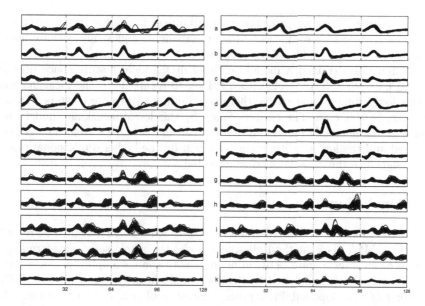

Fig. 3. Recorded samples assigned to different clusters by the model (left) and samples generated by the model (right). Waveforms produced by (a-f) different neurons, (g-j) nearly simultaneously firing neurons, (k) noise

clusters. Unfortunately the average entropy of the responsibilities over all test samples was not as small as expected. In addition, we observed that the spikes assigned to some of the clusters seemed to be generated from different neurons, because their waveforms showed large deviations. As a consequence of this, those clusters were composed of multiple disjoint regions in the the amplitude plots and therefore did not match with the manual clustering. Thus we concluded that the clustering was not successful in terms of finding meaningful clusters. This inability to isolate the spikes with different characteristics is probably due to the fact that the model gets caught in local maxima where it cannot escape even with the help of the SMEM. To overcome this problem, we trained a model that had many more mixtures than the assumed number of neurons and merged some of the clusters after training, using the merge criteria of the SMEM algorithm.

Training a model with 30 mixtures and merging these clusters after training resulted in clusters that were similar to those of manual clustering. Specifically for the data set used in this study, the MFA model found all clusters that were found in manual clustering with similar boundaries, except for one cluster which it clustered as a part of noise. On the other hand, the model found some tiny clusters that had double spike waveforms, which correspond to nearly synchronously firing neurons. Also, the model identified another big cluster as a neuron, which was assigned to be noise in manual clustering due to its low amplitude. Figure 3 shows the examples that are assigned to different clusters. The trained model was also used to generate simulated data. As can be seen in figure 3, the simulated signals are very realistic in the sense that they resemble the recorded waveforms while showing some deviations.

Furthermore, the entropy of the responsibilities of both the training and test examples is close to zero, meaning that the model is almost always sure about to which cluster it should assign an example.

We have also trained a model on the 4 dimensional feature space used in manual clustering. SMEM algorithm helped to escape from the local maxima in this lower dimensional space, therefore training with more clusters was not necessary in this case. The clusters found by this low dimensional model were similar to the manually found clusters, but the double spike waveforms were not detected and the low amplitude cluster found by the higher dimensional model was assigned to the noise cluster, as expected.

5   Conclusion

We have demonstrated a successful approach to spike sorting of tetrode recordings using MFA. This method allows to model the whole spike waveforms and therefore can discriminate between neurons with similar amplitude characteristics across channels and also detect nearly simultaneously occurring spikes. The entropies of the responsibilities gives a measure of quality of clustering. The trained model can also be used to synthesise realistic data sets with labels that can be used to compare different spike sorting methods. A drawback of this method is that it is not fully unsupervised. The spike waveforms assigned to the resulting clusters should be assessed by an expert.

Acknowledgements. CER was supported by the German Research Council (DFG) through grant RA 1030/1.

References

1. Ghahramani Z., Beal M.J.: Variational inference for Bayesian mixtures of factor analysers. In Adv. Neur. Inf. Proc. Sys. 12, MIT Press, 2000
2. Ghahramani Z., Hinton G.E.: The EM algorithm for mixtures of factor analysers. Technical Report CRG-TR-96-1, Dept. of Comp. Sci., Univ. of Toronto, 1996
3. Gray CM, Maldonado PE, Wilson M, McNaughton B.: Tetrodes markedly improve the reliability and yield of multiple single-unit isolation from multi-unit recordings in cat striate cortex. J Neurosci Methods. 1995 Dec;63(1-2):43-54
4. Harris K.D., Henze D.A., Csicsvari J., Hirase H., Buzsáki G.: Accuracy of tetrode spike separation as determined by simultaneous intracellular and extracellular measurements
5. Lewicki M.S.: A review of methods for spike sorting: the detection and classification of neural action potentials. Network 9 R53-R78, 1998
6. Rasmussen C.E.: The infinite Gaussian mixture model, In Adv. Neur. Inf. Proc. Sys. 12, MIT Press, 2000
7. Roweis S.T., Ghahramani Z.: A unifying review of linear Gaussian models. Neural Computation 11(2):305-345, 1999
8. Ueda N., Nakano R., Ghahramani Z., Hinton G.E.: SMEM algorithm for mixture models. In Adv. Neur. Inf. Proc. Sys. 11, MIT Press, 1999

An Algorithm for Fast Pattern Recognition with Random Spikes

Udo A. Ernst, David Rotermund, and Klaus R. Pawelzik

Inst. for Theoretical Neurophysics, University Bremen, D-28359 Bremen, Germany
{udo,davrot,pawelzik}@neuro.uni-bremen.de

Abstract. The human brain classifies natural scenes and recognizes objects in complex visual patterns with a high precision in a minimum amount of processing time. Only few action potentials (spikes) per neuron and per processing stage are sufficient to achieve this astonishingly high performance, despite the random nature of the incoming spike trains. In this contribution, we present a novel algorithm which updates the internal representation of patterns in a generative model with each incoming spike. We first demonstrate that our algorithm is capable of learning a suitable representation of pattern ensembles from stochastically generated spike trains. This representation is then used for classifying test patterns, requiring less than one spike per input node to achieve a performance comparable to standard algorithms in pattern recognition.

1 Introduction

Recently, experimental work has shown that humans can categorize natural scenes within 150 ms after onset of the presentation [8]. At least ten different, hierarchically ordered processing stages (brain areas) are involved in this task. With typical firing frequencies of about 50 Hz, this leaves only time for less than one spike per neuron for a successful processing of the stimuli. Making things even worse, spikes in the cortex are elicited randomly, their statistics resembling a Poissonian process.

These observations pose a challenge for pattern recognition algorithms which are required to achieve a high performance under restrictive boundary conditions. In our case we have three main constraints: the recognition process should rely on single spikes, it should be robust against a high degree of noise, and it should require only about one spike per input node until the scene or pattern is recognized. To explain the brain's performance, one has to propose a suitable neuronal algorithm which fulfills all three of these requirements, while taking advantage of the parallel processing properties of neuronal populations.

Previous work has shown that analog values can be transmitted faithfully with single spikes in a population code [2,1]. However, this approach requires the allocation of several channels for only one analog value. In a different paradigm devised by Thorpe et al. [9], this excessive usage of resources is overcome by employing a rank order code for spike emission. Images to be represented are decomposed into their principal components, and spikes are transmitted in an

C.E. Rasmussen et al. (Eds.): DAGM 2004, LNCS 3175, pp. 399–406, 2004.
© Springer-Verlag Berlin Heidelberg 2004

order determined by the strength of the component's coefficients. However, this rank order code can be sensitive to noise, and the decomposition process requires extensive pre-processing of the images which can take a lot of extra time in the brain.

In this article, we present a different approach by modifying a generative model [4] to work with single, random spikes. The model has originally been used in the context of non-negative matrix factorization. A generative model can be described as a network consisting of input nodes connected to hidden nodes (Fig.1, left). The connections are interpreted as conditional probabilities to observe an activation in one of the input nodes, given an activation in one of the hidden nodes. The dynamics in a generative model updates the internal representation in the hidden nodes (reconstruction/estimation) and/or the conditional probabilities (learning). The goal of this update is to accurately predict the input from the hidden representation. In terms of neuronal information processing, a successful prediction can be interpreted as a correctly perceived stimulus. While in a probabilistic framework, connections are *interpreted* in a top-down manner, the flow of information in a generative model (i.e., the spikes) proceeds bottom-up like in a feed-forward neural network.

In the next sections, we will first present algorithms for batch learning, on-line learning and reconstruction. Then the algorithms will be applied to a standard benchmark of handwritten digit recognition (USPS). Finally, the results will be shown and discussed in the contexts of machine learning and neuronal networks.

2   Generative Model

The generative model (Fig.1, left) consists of $s = 1, \ldots, M$ input nodes, $i = 1, \ldots, H$ hidden nodes, and conditional probabilities $p(s|i)$. The K input patterns $v_k(u) \in [-\infty, +\infty], k = 1, \ldots, K$ are converted to firing rates $r_k(s) \geq 0$, from which spike trains are drawn for all input nodes s. Accordingly, the probabilities for observing a spike in node s are given by $p_k(s) = r_k(s)/\sum_{m=1}^{M} r_k(m)$. In this way the sequence of active input nodes is generated from a Bernoulli process given by the probabilities $p_k(s)$. Real time is then re-parameterized by the number of spike events which we here denote by t for simplicity. Note, however, that this spike-by-spike clocking implies that real time is proportional to the average of $t/\sum_i r_i$, i.e. it is scaled by the total rate of the population. Each time t a spike is observed at node s^t, the hidden representation $h(i)$ and/or the $p(s|i)$ are updated. One presentation of a pattern k extends over T input spikes. The input is then fully specified by the sequence vector of temporally ordered indices $s^T = \{s^1, \ldots, s^t, \ldots, s^T\}$ of the nodes at which those spikes were observed. During update, the goal is to maximize the likelihood $P\left(s^T | h(i), p(s|i)\right)$ of observing s^T over the model parameter space $h(i)$ and $p(s|i)$. With $\hat{p}(s) = 1/T \sum_{t=1}^{T} \delta_{s,s^t}$ counting the relative number of spikes at node s in the observation sequence over the time window T, the likelihood is given by

$$P\left(s^T | \{h(i), p(s|i)\}_{i=(1,\ldots,H),s=(1,\ldots,M)}\right) = D\Pi_{s=1}^{M} p(s)^{T\hat{p}(s)} \tag{1}$$

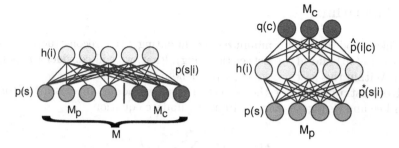

Fig. 1. Spike-by-Spike network comprised of M input and N hidden nodes connected by the conditional probabilities or weights $p(s|i)$ (left). During training of the network, the pattern and its correct classification are presented together to the first M_p, and the remaining M_c input nodes, respectively. Modified Spike-by-Spike network for reconstruction and classification (right). The M_c weight vectors used for training have been transposed and normalized to form the new weight vectors $\hat{p}(i|c)$ which are used to classify the test patterns.

with $p(s) = \sum_{j=1}^{H} p(s|j)h(j)$ and the combinatorial factor D. For practical reasons, we minimize the negative logarithm of the likelihood,

$$- \log(P/T) = - \log(D/T) - \sum_{s=1}^{M} \hat{p}(s) \log p(s) . \tag{2}$$

This minimization problem is penalized by the non-negativity constraints $p(s|i) \geq 0$ and $h(i) \geq 0$ and the normalization constraints $\sum_{s=1}^{M} p(s|i) = 1$ and $\sum_{i=1}^{H} h(i) = 1$, respectively.

To avoid situations in which an input pattern of negative values leads to problems in the spike generation process in the input nodes, the original patterns $v_k(u)$ are pre-processed yielding the input rates $r_k(s)$: in a first step, patterns $v_k(u)$ (with $L = M/2$ components) are corrected by subtracting the individual mean for each pattern $< v_k(u) >^L = 2/M \sum_{u=1}^{L} v_k(u)$,

$$\tilde{v}_k(u) := v_k(u) - < v_k(u) >^L . \tag{3}$$

Each of the L components is duplicated and distributed over the even and uneven input node pairs, yielding M non-negative rate components $r_k(s)$ according to the expressions

$$r_k(2u - 1) = \begin{cases} +\tilde{v}_k(u) & \text{for } \tilde{v}_k(u) > 0 \\ 0 & \text{otherwise} \end{cases} \tag{4}$$

$$r_k(2u) = \begin{cases} 0 & \text{for } \tilde{v}_k(u) > 0 \\ -\tilde{v}_k(u) & \text{otherwise} \end{cases} . \tag{5}$$

This pre-processing is motivated by the nature of our brain: the splitting into negative and positive values closely resembles the analysis of visual stimuli by on- and off-cells in the lateral geniculate nucleus (LGN).

3   Algorithms

The likelihood P can be minimized by updating $h(i)$ (reconstruction), or by updating $p(s|i)$ and $h(i)$ together (learning). First, we will consider the $p(s|i)$ as fixed. Within this section, superscripts denote time indices.

Reconstruction. For the reconstruction, we adopt an existing algorithm from Lee and Seung [4] starting from the update equation

$$h^{t+1}(i) = h^t(i) \sum_{s=1}^{M} p(s|i) \frac{\hat{p}(s)}{p^t(s)} \ . \tag{6}$$

In our case, we observe only one spike per time step in input node s^t, and not the whole pattern $\hat{p}(s)$. Thus, we require the algorithm to predict the next spike by first substituting $\hat{p}(s)$ by δ_{s,s^t} in Eq.(6). Because the next spike is almost always not representative for the whole input pattern $\hat{p}(s)$, we apply an additional low-pass filter with time constant ϵ leading to the reconstruction algorithm

$$h^{t+1}(i) = h^t(i) \left[(1 - \epsilon) + \epsilon \frac{p(s^t|i)}{p^t(s^t)} \right] \ . \tag{7}$$

Batch Learning. In general, our brain acquires its knowledge and experience over long time scales ranging from hours to years, while the fast spiking dynamics takes place on a time scale of milliseconds. Therefore, it is reasonable to separate the update time scales of $h(i)$ and $p(s|i)$. While $h(i)$ is changed every time a spike occurs, $p(s|i)$ will be changed only after the presentation of K patterns with T spikes each. For such a batch learning rule, we can apply the corresponding formula of Lee and Seung [4]

$$\tilde{p}^z(s|i) = p^z(s|i) \sum_{k=1}^{K} < h_k(i) >^\Delta \hat{p}_k(s) \Big/ \sum_{j=1}^{H} p^z(s|j) < h_k(j) >^\Delta \tag{8}$$

$$p^{z+1}(s|i) = \tilde{p}^z(s|i) \Big/ \sum_{u=1}^{M} \tilde{p}^z(u|i) \ , \tag{9}$$

with $< h_k(i) >^\Delta = 1/\Delta \sum_{t=T-\Delta}^{T} h_k^t(i)$. Each time a new pattern is presented, the hidden nodes are initialized with $h_k^0(i) = 1/H$.

Online Learning. Eq.(8) has a slight disadvantage, because it requires to remember the final average mean internal states $< h_k(i) >^\Delta$ of K pattern presentations for one update step. While a computer has no problems in fulfilling this requirement, the brain could lack the possibility to temporarily store all $< h_k(i) >^\Delta$'s. This limitation can be overcome by deriving an on-line learning rule from scratch, which uses only one pattern at once and takes the form

$$p^{t+1}(s|i) = p^t(s|i) \left\{ 1 + \frac{\gamma h(i)}{1 + \gamma h(i) \frac{p^t(s^t|i)}{p^t(s^t)}} \left[\frac{\delta_{s,s^t}}{p^t(s)} - \frac{p^t(s^t|i)}{p^t(s^t)} \right] \right\} \ . \tag{10}$$

γ is an update constant which is in general much smaller than ϵ. The derivation of Eq.(10) is based on optimization under Karush-Kuhn-Tucker conditions with positivity constrains, following the procedure described on pages 1400–1402 in [3] and substituting $\hat{p}(s)$ by δ_{s,s^t} like in Eq.(6).

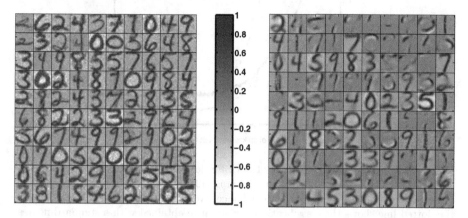

Fig. 2. Conditional probabilities or weight vectors $p^*(s|i)$ for the online learning (left), and for the batch learning algorithm for $H = 100$ hidden nodes (right). Each vector is displayed in a quadratic raster of 16×16 pixels. The individual vectors i for even and odd input nodes are combined and normalized to a grey value g_u between 1 and -1 by means of the transformation $\tilde{g}_u = p^*(2u - 1|i) - p^*(2u|i)$, $g_u = \tilde{g}_u/\max\{|\tilde{g}_u|\}$. Parameters for on-line learning were $w = 0.9$, $\epsilon = 0.9375$, $\gamma = 0.0005$, and $T = 2000$. Parameters for batch learning were $w = 0.5$, $\epsilon = 0.1$, $\Delta = 500$ and $T = 5620$. During on-line learning, all training patterns were presented only once. In contrast, training patterns were presented repeatedly during 20 learning steps in the batch procedure.

4 Simulations

Learning and classification. For the learning, M input nodes are divided into M_p pattern nodes and M_c classification nodes. K_{tr} training patterns v_k^{tr} together with their correct classification c_k^{tr} (coded in the firing probabilities in the M_c input nodes; see Fig.1, left) are presented successively to the network, while $p(s|i)$ and $h(i)$ are updated according to Eqs.(7), (8), (9), and (10).

For the classification run, the network uses only the first M_p input nodes for pattern input. The first part of the weight vectors $p(s|i)$ are re-normalized yielding the new weights $p^*(s|i) = p(s|i)/\sum_{u=1}^{M_p} p(u|i)$. The remaining M_c weight vectors are transposed and normalized yielding the classification weights $\hat{p}(i|c) := p(c + M_p|i)/\sum_{l=1}^{M_c} p(l + M_p|i)$ for $c = 1, \dots, M_c$. From $h(i)$ and $\hat{p}(i|c)$, the probabilities $q_k(c) = \sum_{i=1}^{H} \hat{p}(i|c)h_k(i)$ for each of the K_{ts} test patterns v_k^{ts} to belong to the class c are computed, leading to the predicted classification $\hat{c}_k = \text{argmax}_c\ q_k(c)$ The mean classification error e over all patterns is then computed by $e = 1/K_{ts} \sum_{k=1}^{K_{ts}} \delta_{c_k^{ts}, \hat{c}_k}$.

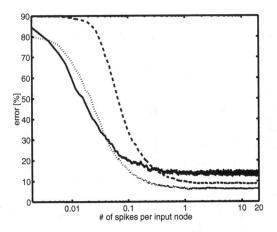

Fig. 3. Mean classification error e for the USPS database shown for the batch learning rule (dashed line) and for the on-line learning rule (solid line), in dependence of the mean number of spikes per input node. Chance level is at 90 percent. For a comparison, the dotted line shows the classification performance obtained with a standard nearest neighbor algorithm, for which the $\hat{p}(s)$ for different spike vector lengths T were used. Parameters for on-line and batch learning were chosen as in Fig.2.

Data Base. We subjected our algorithms to the problem of recognizing handwritten digits. The data base from the United States Postal Service (USPS) consists of $K_{tr} = 7291$ training patterns v_k^{tr} and $K_{ts} = 2007$ test patterns v_k^{ts}. Each pattern comprises $M_p/2 = 16 \times 16$ grey scale values (pixels) ranging from -1 (white) to 1 (black). During the test run, the patterns v_k^{ts} were applied according to Eq.(5), leading to input rates r_k^{ts}. During the training run, however, the patterns v_k^{tr} are first normalized and duplicated according to Eq.(5). Together with the correct assignment $c_k^{tr} \in \{0, \ldots, 9\}$ to one digit class, the input rates to all $M = M_p + 10$ nodes s are defined as

$$r_k(s) = w\, r_k^{tr}(s) \left/ \sum_{u=1}^{M_p} r_k^{tr}(u) \right. \quad \text{for } s \in [1, M_p] \tag{11}$$

$$\text{and} \quad r_k(s) = (1-w)\delta_{s+M_p, c_k^{tr}} \quad \text{otherwise.} \tag{12}$$

The weighting parameter w controls the balance between the pattern and classification inputs.

5 Results

We applied the learning and reconstruction algorithms to the USPS database, varying the parameters ϵ, γ, and w to achieve the best possible performance. In Fig.2, the comparison between the weights shows that the on-line learning rule leads to the formation of digit templates, whereas the batch learning rule in addition extracts typical features common to more than one digit. Consequently, batch learning is slower during the first 0.3 spikes per input node, but achieves a lower classification error in the long run (Fig.3). The minimum error of 8.9% shows that the algorithm performs suitably well, but does not reach entirely the performances of other classifiers around $4 - 5\%$ (for an overview, see [7]). We also subjected our algorithms to different types of noises in order to test for robustness of learning and classification: first, a varying number of rows or columns in the digit image has been occluded by setting the corresponding pixels to a value of 0. Up to a number of about 6 rows or columns, the classification error nevertheless remains below 20 percent (Fig.4, left). With increasing coverage, vertical occlusion has a stronger impact on recognition because the digit patterns normally occupy an area whose height is larger than its width. Second, we superimposed each digit pattern $v_k(u)$ with an image entirely consisting of random pixel values $v_k^{rnd}(u)$ uniformly distributed between -1 and 1. The noise level was varied by means of a parameter $\eta \in [0,1]$ by combining the original pattern and noise as $(1-\eta)v_k(u) + \eta v_k^{rnd}(u)$. Fig.4 (right) shows that it requires a fair amount of noise of $\eta \approx 0.35$ to increase the error rate to values above 20 percent.

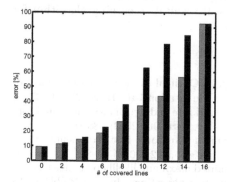 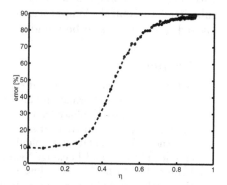

Fig. 4. Minimum classification error in dependence on the number of horizontally (light bars) or vertically occluded (dark bars) lines in the digit images (left), and in dependence on the amount of noise η on the digit pixels (right). Parameters for the learning were chosen as in Fig.2.

6   Summary and Discussion

In this contribution, we have developed a framework which can explain the tremendous speed of our brain in processing and categorizing natural stimuli, provided that the neural hardware can realize such a generative model. Our 'Spike-by-Spike'-network is able to classify patterns with less than one spike from each input node, despite the randomness in the information transmission. In addition, we presented two algorithms for on-line and batch learning being capable of finding suitable representations for arbitrary pattern ensembles. In general, the update of the hidden nodes occurs in real time more frequently when the number of input nodes increases. This implies that the required number of mathematical operations per unit time increases, too. However, this potential problem for a machine can be solved by parallel processing in the brain.

Further development of our algorithms will focus on classifying mixtures of patterns and on non-stationary pattern presentations. Preliminary studies indicate that the Spike-by-Spike algorithm can, under special circumstances, extract the different sources which were superimposed on one input pattern (blind source separation). As an example for non-stationary stimuli, it is possible to learn and to estimate the intended arm movement of a neural prosthesis from the spike data recorded in the motor system of primates [5].

A similar approach for classifying *temporal* patterns from one input channel has been investigated by Wiener and Richmond [10]. They use an iterative Bayesian scheme to successfully re-estimate the presence of a specific time-varying stimulus with each incoming spike.

While the brain is highly modular, our Spike-by-Spike network is only a two-layered system with no hierarchy. Therefore, it remains to show that these networks can be used like logical modules in a computer, grouping arbitrary functional units together in order to realize more complex computations. First results with hand-coded weights are very promising (Ernst, Rotermund, and Pawelzik; submitted to Neural Computation), but still a suitable learning algorithm for layered networks has to be found.

References

1. Bethge, M., Rotermund, D. and Pawelzik, K. Optimal short-term population coding: When Fisher information fails. Neural Computation **14(10)** (2002) 2317–2351; and: A second order phase transition in neural rate coding: Binary encoding is optimal for rapid signal transmission. Phys. Rev. Lett. **90** (2003) 088104.
2. Gerstner, W. Population Dynamics of Spiking Neurons: Fast Transients, Asynchronous States, and Locking. Neural Computation **12** (2000) 43–89.
3. Lanteri, H., Roche, M., and Aime, C.: Penalized maximum likelihood image restoration with positivity constraints: multiplicative algorithms. Inverse Problems **18** (2002) 1397–1419.
4. Lee, D.D., Seung, S.H.: Learning the parts of objects by non-negative matrix factorization. Nature **401** (1999) 788–791.
5. Pawelzik, K.R., Rotermund, D., and Ernst, U.A.: Building representations spike by spike. In: Elsner, N., Zimmermann, H. (eds.): Proceedings of the 29th Göttingen Neurobiology Conference, Georg Thieme Verlag, Stuttgart, (2003) 1041.
6. Pawelzik, K.R., Ernst, U.A., Trenner, D., and Rotermund, D. Building representations spike by spike. In: Proceedings of the Society of Neuroscience Conference 2002, Orlando, (2002) 557.12.
7. Schölkopf, B. Support Vector Learning, R. Oldenbourg Verlag, München, 1997 (http://www.kernel-machines.org/papers/book_ref.ps.gz).
8. Thorpe, S., Fize, D., and Marlot, C. Speed of processing in the human visual system. Nature **381** (1996) 520–522.
9. Thorpe, S., Delorme, A., van Rullen, R. Spike-based strategies for rapid processing. Neural Networks **14** (2001) 521–525.
10. Wiener, M., and Richmond, B.J.: Decoding spike trains instant by instant using order statistics and the mixture-of-Poissons model. J. Neurosci. **23** (2003) 2394–2406.

The Perceptual Influence of Spatiotemporal Noise on the Reconstruction of Shape from Dynamic Occlusion

Theresa Cooke, Douglas W. Cunningham, and Heinrich H. Bülthoff

Max Planck Institute for Biological Cybernetics, Spemannstrasse 38,
72076 Tübingen, Germany
{firstname.lastname}@tuebingen.mpg.de
http://www.kyb.mpg.de/

Abstract. When an object moves, it covers and uncovers texture in the background. This pattern of change is sufficient to define the object's shape, velocity, relative depth, and degree of transparency, a process called Spatiotemporal Boundary Formation (SBF). We recently proposed a mathematical framework for SBF, where texture transformations are used to recover local edge segments, estimate the figure's velocity and then reconstruct its shape. The model predicts that SBF should be sensitive to spatiotemporal noise, since the spurious transformations will lead to the recovery of incorrect edge orientations. Here we tested this prediction by adding a patch of dynamic noise (either directly over the figure or a fixed distance away from it). Shape recognition performance in humans decreased to chance levels when noise was placed over the figure but was not affected by noise far away. These results confirm the model's prediction and also imply that SBF is a local process.

1 Introduction

The Peacock Flounder can change its coloration such that there are no easily detectable differences in luminance, color, or texture patterns between itself and its surroundings, rendering it almost invisible. When the flounder moves, however, it is immediately and easily visible. This and similar observations suggest that patterns of change over time may be sufficient to visually perceive an object.

This observation was formalized by Gibson [1], who claimed that the pattern of texture appearances and disappearances at the edges of a moving object (i.e., dynamic occlusion) should be sufficient to define that object's shape. Several researchers have shown that this pattern is indeed sufficient for humans to properly perceive not only an object's shape, but also its velocity, relative depth, and degree of transparency [2]. The process of using this dynamic pattern to perceive the shape of an object is referred to as Spatiotemporal Boundary Formation (SBF). The types of transformation that lead to SBF extend well beyond simple texture appearances and disappearances, however, and include changes in the color, orientation, shape, and location of texture elements [3–5]. The use of dynamic information to define a surface avoids many of the problems inherent in static approaches to object perception, and offers a robust way of determining most of the properties of an object from very sparse information while making few assumptions. Machine vision implementations of SBF could be a welcome addition to current object perception techniques.

C.E. Rasmussen et al. (Eds.): DAGM 2004, LNCS 3175, pp. 407–414, 2004.
© Springer-Verlag Berlin Heidelberg 2004

In a first step towards such an implementation, Shipley and Kellman [5] provided a mathematical proof showing that the orientation of a small section of a moving object (a "local edge segment", or LES) could be recovered from as few as three element transformations. Briefly, each pair of element transformations is encoded as a local motion vector. The vector subtraction of two local motion vectors yields the orientation of the edge. This model predicts that LES recovery, and thus all of SBF, will fail if the elements are spatially collinear, a phenomenon which Shipley and Kellman subsequently psychophysically demonstrated [5]. Likewise, the model suggests that the recovery of the orientation of an LES is sensitive to the spatiotemporal precision of the individual transformations. That is, the more error there is in knowing where and when the elements changed, the more error there will be in the recovered orientation. This implies that SBF should be very sensitive to the presence of dynamic noise (element transformations not caused by dynamic occlusion). Finally, Shipley and Kellman's proof also showed that one should be able to substitute the object's global velocity vector for one of the local motion vectors (which we will refer to as velocity vector substitution), in which case only two element transformations are needed to recover an LES.

Cunningham, Graf and Bülthoff [6–8] revised this proof and embedded it in a complete mathematical framework for SBF. With this framework, the complete global form and velocity of a surface moving at a locally constant velocity can be recovered. The framework consists of three stages. The first stage is similar to Shipley and Kellman's: The orientations of the figure's edges (the LES's) are recovered by integrating element transformations from a local neighborhood in space-time. The elements' locations and the times when they were transformed are encoded relative to each other (i.e., the framework is agnostic on the actual representational format of the changes; it does require them to be encoded as motion vectors). In the second phase, the orientations of the LES's are used in conjunction with the relative spatiotemporal locations of the element transformations to recover the global velocity of the figure. This process, which requires at least two LES's of differing orientations, is mathematically very similar to that used to recover an LES's orientation. If all of the orientations are the same, one can only recover that portion of the global velocity that is perpendicular to the LES's (this is the well-known motion aperture effect). Finally, the global motion of the figure, the orientations of the LES's, and the locations of the element transformations, are used to determine the minimum length of each LES necessary to cause those transformations, as well as the relative locations of the LES's. To complete the process, the LES's may be joined to form a closed contour using a process similar to illusory contour perception (for example, see [9–11]).

Cunningham et al. [12] explicitly tested whether humans can take advantage of the velocity vector substitution process predicted by the model. To do this, they added a set of additional texture elements that had the exact same velocity as the moving shapes. The same set of additional elements was used for all shapes, so they did not provide additional static shape information. Cunningham et al. found that the extra motion information did indeed improve shape identification performance, but only if the new elements were seen as being on the surface of the figure. That is, velocity vector substitution is possible, but only when the extra element motion is seen as belonging to the figure.

So far, all of the model's predictions reflect human performance: Collinearity of the transformations prevents SBF [5], identical orientations of the LES's hinders proper velocity recovery [13], and velocity vector substitution can improve the quality of the recovered shape [12]. What about the prediction that SBF should be strongly affected by dynamic noise (i.e., the presence of transformations that are not caused by dynamic occlusion)? In an inconclusive test of this prediction, Shipley and Kellman [5] performed an experiment that included a condition with a large second element field that jumped around the screen randomly. The presence of this second field impaired SBF (strongly at low element field densities, less so at higher densities). This field may be described as a set of individual elements that flicker on and off, creating appearances and disappearances similar to those produced by dynamic occlusion (in which case the impairment in shape perception demonstrates SBF's sensitivity to dynamic noise). It may also, however, be described as a single element field with a rapidly changing (i.e., Brownian) velocity, and thus the impairment could be accounted for by substituting the Brownian global velocity vector into the LES recovery stage. This latter explanation also accounts for the results in their other experimental conditions, and is consistent with Cunningham et al.'s [12] work on velocity vector substitution, and thus is the most parsimonious explanation.

Both Shipley and Kellman's proof, and Cunningham et al.'s mathematical framework predict, however, that the flickering elements should impair SBF. Here, we explicitly test this prediction by adding a flickering surface texture (i.e., a patch of dynamic noise) to the moving object. Since we can detect the global velocity of dynamic noise fields, and since additional, consistent global velocity information improves SBF, the motion of a flickering surface texture should provide valid global motion information, which should improve SBF. On the other hand, the presence of spurious appearances and disappearances (i.e., flickering elements) near the edges of the object should impair SBF. As a control condition, we examined the effect of a flickering texture that is far away from the moving figure. Since the global motion of a distant texture field does not affect SBF [12], the flickering elements should only affect SBF in the control condition if the spatial integration window for SBF is rather large (i.e., if SBF is more of a "global" than a "local" process).

2   Methods

Ten people were paid 8 Euro per hour to participate in the experiment, which lasted about 30 min. Displays were presented on a 17" CRT monitor. Participants were positioned approximately 50 cm from the screen.

The displays consisted of a 14.6 x 14.6 cm field (visual angle of about 16.3°) of single-pixel, white dots distributed randomly on a black background. One of ten radially monotonic shapes, shown in Figure 1, moved over the random dot field along a circular trajectory of radius 5.72°. The shape completed a single circuit of the trajectory in six seconds. The shapes were identical to those used by Shipley and colleagues in their experiments. This set of shapes has been shown to provide a reliable means of determining which variables affect SBF [2].

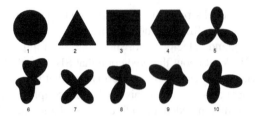

Fig. 1. The ten shapes used in the experiment.

This experiment only used the "unidirectional" type of displays: Whenever the leading edge of the form moved over a white dot, the dot was transformed to black and "disappeared" from the display. When the trailing edge of the form reached the dot, the dot was changed back to white, thus "reappearing" in the display. A second type of display that is typically used, called a "bidirectional" display, is identical to a unidirectional display, with the sole exception that elements may either appear or disappear along any edge (i.e., half of the elements are only visible outside of the figure, as in the unidirectional displays, and half are only visible inside the figure). Well-defined shapes are seen in the bidirectional displays, despite the absence of any form of shape information except dynamic occlusion [5]. Bidirectional displays were not used in the current experiment for theoretical reasons (i.e., there are some concerns about surface formation, the direction of surface binding, and the role of velocity vector substitution in bidirectional displays, see Cunningham et al. [12] for more on this topic). The number of dots was systematically varied: The background had 100, 200, or 400 elements.

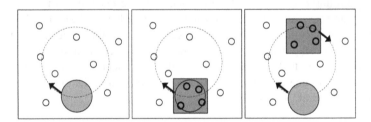

Fig. 2. Sketch of the three experimental conditions: a) "noise-free": the occluder moves through the random dot field along a circular path; b) "noise near": the noise pattern, represented by dark black dots inside a square, is superimposed on the moving figure; c) "noise far": the moving figure and noise pattern are separated by 180°.

Three noise conditions were used: a condition without noise, a condition where dynamic (i.e., spatiotemporal) noise was placed near the object, and a condition where dynamic noise was placed far from the object (see Figure 2). The dynamic noise pattern was a set of white dots which appeared at random locations inside a virtual box of fixed size. The size of the box was chosen such that it circumscribed the largest object. In this way, the object could not be identified using the size or the shape of the noise pattern. The number of dots placed inside the box was 15% of the number of dots in the background. The noise dots had a limited lifetime – the location of the noise dots was changed every four frames. Note that the noise dots themselves never moved. The new location of each dot was chosen to be within the virtual box. In the "noise-near" condition, the box containing the noise dots was superimposed on the moving figure. In the "noise-far" condition, the noise pattern was placed 180° away from the figure along the circular trajectory.

The experiment consisted of a single block of 90 randomized trials (10 figures x 3 densities x 3 noise conditions). Participants were asked to identify the shape moving in each display using a ten-alternative forced-choice task. Static images of the ten possible choices were shown at all times on the left side of the monitor. Each shape moved around its circular trajectory until the participant responded or until the shape completed two cycles through the trajectory, whichever came first. If the participant did not respond before the end of the second cycle, the display was cleared (except for the 10 reference shapes on the side of the screen), and remained blank until the participant responded.

3   Results

3.1   Effect of Density

In both the "noise-free" and "noise far" conditions, there was a significant effect of density, consistent with previous work on SBF. All tests were performed using a two-tailed t-test for independent samples with equal variances; all conditions for using these tests were met. Average performance was significantly higher at density 200 than at density 100 (all t's$(18) > 4.1$, all p's< 0.001), and significantly higher at density 400 than at density 200 (all t's$(18) > 2.1$, all p's< 0.05). There was no effect of density for the noise-near condition – performance was at chance (the performance level expected from blind guessing) at all density levels. This is almost certainly due to a floor effect, meaning that improvements in performance would probably have been observed had the task been easier or the number of choices greater.

3.2   Effect of Noise

At no density level was mean performance in the "noise near" condition significantly different from chance (all t's$(9) <= 1.8$, all p's> 0.1). Moreover, mean performance in the "noise near" condition differed significantly from mean performance in the "noise-free" condition at all density levels (all t's$(18) >= 2.60$, all p's< 0.05). At the two higher density levels, mean performance in the "noise near" condition also differed significantly from mean performance in the "noise far" condition ($t(18) = 7.19$, $p < 0.001$ at density 200; $t(18) = 12.38$, $p < 0.001$ at density 400). At a density of 100, the difference was not significant ($t(18) = 1.80$, $p > 0.05$ (n.s.)), but performance in the "noise far" condition did vary significantly from chance at this density level ($t(9) = 2.75$, $p > 0.01$).

The mean accuracies in the "noise-free" and "noise far" conditions were not significantly different at any density level (all t's$(18) <= 0.7$, all p's> 0.2).

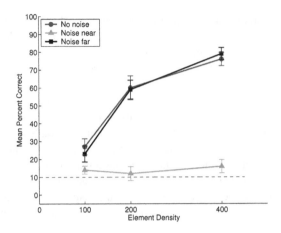

Fig. 3. Shape identification accuracy plotted as a function of element density for the three conditions. Error bars represent the standard error. The dotted line represents chance performance.

4   Conclusions and Discussion

At all density levels, shape identification performance was reduced to chance when spatiotemporal noise was placed near the figure, whereas it was unaffected by noise placed far away. The fact that the dynamic noise in the "noise-near" condition prevented accurate shape recognition suggests that the spurious appearances and disappearances were being treated as dynamic occlusion signals. This would, according to the model, impair LES recovery and prevent shape perception. Since shape recognition performance was at chance level in the present experiment, it is possible that the presence of dynamic noise prevented SBF from occurring at all. That is, the low signal-to-noise ratio may be a signal that the entire SBF process should not be performed. In Shipley and Kellman's [5] experiment with dynamic noise, however, the noise merely reduced recognition accuracy. Since the same shapes, task, density levels, and shape velocity were used in both experiments, the differences in shape recognition performance are probably due to the differences in the dynamic noise. The dynamic noise patch was much denser in the present experiment, and was focused around the shape itself. Thus, it seems that the individual noise signals are being integrated with the dynamic occlusion transformations, which produces LES's that are incompatible with the true shape of the moving figure, which in turn leads to failures in the subsequent global form reconstruction. This suggests that one might use dynamic noise to carefully probe the exact characteristics of LES recovery. For example, one might vary the location, density, or distribution of noise to precisely determine the spatial and/or temporal integration windows, element grouping processes, or global form reconstruction mechanism of SBF.

It should be possible to implement an iterative consistency filter to remove at least some of the inconsistent LES's, reducing the sensitivity of SBF to dynamic noise. Although the human visual system does not seem to employ such a filter, machine vision implementations of SBF (such as that by Cunningham et al. [7, 8]) might benefit from such a filter.

The insensitivity of SBF to the velocity of the dynamic noise patch in the noise-far condition confirms Cunningham et al.'s [12] claim that only global motion seen as coming from a surface's texture affects SBF. The insensitivity of SBF to the spurious transformations produced by distant dynamic noise patch provides evidence that SBF is a strictly local process. This finding places convenient restrictions on the LES's recovery stage, and eases the computational overhead that would be involved in an iterative filter to remove inconsistent LES's.

Perceptually, it was clear in these displays that the dynamic noise patch was moving coherently *as a whole*, yet this global motion information did not seem to help SBF. It is possible that the global motion pattern did help, but that this positive contribution was outweighed by the detrimental effect of the spurious flickering of the noise patch. Another interesting possibility is that the improvement in SBF produced by adding a coherent surface texture found by Cunningham et al. [12] was not due to the motion of the surface *texture*, but to the motion of the surface *texture elements*. Since the individual elements in the noise patches did not move, there was no motion to disturb SBF (static element fields imposed on dynamically defined figures do not affect SBF very strongly [14]).

The results presented here confirm some previously untested predictions of Cunningham et al.'s model of SBF and provide additional constraints on potential computational implementations of SBF. It seems that SBF is a robust method for extracting most properties of a moving object from very sparse information while making few assumptions about the structure of the world.

References

1. J. J. Gibson, G. A. Kaplan, H. N. Reynolds, Jr., and K. Wheeler. The change from visible to invisible: A study of optical transitions. *Perception & Psychophysics*, 5:113 – 116, 1969.
2. T. F. Shipley and D. W. Cunningham. Perception of occluding and occluded objects over time: Spatiotemporal segmentation and unit formation. In T. F. Shipley and P. J. Kellman, editors, *From fragments to objects: Segmentation and grouping in vision*, pages 557 – 585. Elsevier Science, Oxford, 2001.
3. T. F. Shipley and P. J. Kellman. Optical tearing in spatiotemporal boundary formation: When do local element motions produce boundaries, form, and global motion? *Spatial Vision: Special Issue: In honor of Bela Julesz*, 7:323 – 339, 1993.
4. T. F. Shipley and P. J. Kellman. Spatiotemporal boundary formation: Boundary, form, and motion perception from transformations of surface elements. *Journal of Experimental Psychology: General*, 123:3 – 20, 1994.
5. T. F. Shipley and P. J. Kellman. Spatiotemporal boundary formation: The role of local motion signals in boundary perception. *Vision Research*, 37:1281 – 1293, 1997.
6. D.W. Cunningham, A.B.A. Graf, and H.H. Bülthoff. A relative encoding approach to modelling spatiotemporal boundary formation. *Journal of Vision, VSS Abstract*, page 120, 2002.
7. D.W. Cunningham, A.B.A. Graf, T. Cooke, C. Wallraven, and H.H. Bülthoff. The perception of objects from dynamic occlusion: A relative encoding implementation. under review, 2004.
8. T. Cooke, D. W. Cunningham, and C. Wallraven:. Local processing in spatiotemporal boundary formation. *Proceedings of the 7th Tübingen Perception Conference*, page 65, 2004.

9. S. Grossberg and E. Mingolla. Neural dynamics of form perception: Boundary completion, illusory figures, and neon color spreading. *Psychological Review*, 92:173–211, 1985.
10. T. F. Shipley and P. J. Kellman. Boundary completion in illusory contours: Interpolation or extrapolation? *Perception*, 32:985–999, 2003.
11. Lance R. Williams and David W. Jacobs. Stochastic completion fields: A neural model of illusory contour shape and salience. *Neural Computation*, 9(4):837–858, 1997.
12. D. W. Cunningham, T. F. Shipley, and P. J. Kellman. Interactions between spatial and spatiotemporal information in spatiotemporal boundary formation. *Perception & Psychophysics*, 60:839 – 851, 1998.
13. H. Wallach. Über visuell warhgenomme bewegungsrichtung. *Psychologische Forshcung*, 20:325 – 380, 1935.
14. D. W. Cunningham, T. F. Shipley, and P. J. Kellman. The dynamic specification of surfaces and boundaries. *Perception*, 27:403 – 416, 1998.

Level Set Based Image Segmentation with Multiple Regions*

Thomas Brox and Joachim Weickert

Mathematical Image Analysis Group, Faculty of Mathematics and Computer Science,
Saarland University, Building 27, 66041 Saarbrücken, Germany
{brox,weickert}@mia.uni-saarland.de
www.mia.uni-saarland.de

Abstract. We address the difficulty of image segmentation methods based on the popular level set framework to handle an arbitrary number of regions. While in the literature some level set techniques are available that can at least deal with a fixed amount of regions greater than two, there is very few work on how to optimise the segmentation also with regard to the number of regions. Based on a variational model, we propose a minimisation strategy that robustly optimises the energy in a level set framework, including the number of regions. Our evaluation shows that very good segmentations are found even in difficult situations.

1 Introduction

Image segmentation has a long tradition as one of the fundamental problems in computer vision. Relatively early, the problem has been formalised by Mumford and Shah as the minimisation of an energy functional that penalises deviations from smoothness within regions and the length of their boundaries [13]. Later, Zhu and Yuille found out that this formulation is closely related to the *minimum description length* criterion and the *maximum a-posteriori* criterion [22]. They presented a new energy functional that unified many of the existing approaches on image segmentation. It can be interpreted as the joint minimisation of the boundary length (as in the Mumford-Shah functional) and the Bayes error in the regions' interior. This is based on the fact that segmentation is actually a clustering problem with a neighbourhood constraint. Since penalising the Bayes error is optimal from the statistical point of view, the variational formulation of Zhu-Yuille describes the segmentation problem very accurately.

However, a tricky issue on image segmentation is the representation of regions and their boundaries. Although there exist neat energy functionals like the one of Mumford-Shah or that of Zhu-Yuille, it is not easy to minimise them in practice. A very nice tool to deal with this problem appeared with the introduction of level sets [8,14]. One application to image segmentation has been the active contour model [3,4,10], which is completely edge based, and therefore a rather local approach to image segmentation. Level set based segmentation that takes the region information into account has been proposed later in [15] and [5]. Using level sets for image segmentation has many advantages. First of all, level sets yield a nice representation of regions and their boundaries on the pixel grid

---

* We gratefully acknowledge partial funding by the *Deutsche Forschungsgemeinschaft (DFG)* and many interesting discussions with Mikaël Rousson from INRIA Sophia-Antipolis.

C.E. Rasmussen et al. (Eds.): DAGM 2004, LNCS 3175, pp. 415–423, 2004.

without the need of complex data structures. This considerably simplifies optimisation, as variational methods and standard numerics can be employed. Furthermore, level sets can describe topological changes in the segmentation, i.e. parts of a region can split and merge. Finally, the possibility to describe the image segmentation problem with a variational model increases the flexibility of the model and allows to employ, for instance, additional features [1], shape knowledge [11,7], or joint motion estimation and segmentation [6].

The main problem of the level set representation lies in the fact that a level set function is restricted to the separation of two regions. As soon as more than two regions are considered, the level set idea looses parts of its attractiveness. This is why only a few papers focus on level set based segmentation in the case of more than two regions. In [21], a level set function is assigned to each region. This framework has been adapted to classification in [18]. In another approach, the bi-modal case is extended to tri-modal segmentation [20]. Both techniques, however, assume an initially fixed number of regions. This assumption is omitted in [16] where the number of regions is estimated in a preliminary stage by means of a Gaussian mixture estimate of the image histogram. This way, the number of mixture coefficients determines the number of regions. However, this kind of estimation is only loosely connected to the energy functional that is minimised. A considerably different approach is proposed in [19]. Here, the level set functions are used in such a way that N regions are represented by only $\log_2 N$ level set functions. Unfortunately, this will result in empty regions, if less than N regions are present in the image. These empty regions have undefined statistics, though the statistics still appear in the evolution equations.

Altogether, the prominence of level set based segmentation is yet lost as soon as more than two regions come into play, and other segmentation methods based for instance on algebraic multigrid [9] often perform better. The purpose of this paper is to solve the remaining problem of the level set framework while saving its advantages.

We show a way how to minimise the energy of Zhu-Yuille by means of level sets. This includes also the minimisation with regard to the number of regions. As the objective function can be assumed to have plenty of local minima, we employ multi-scale ideas and a divide-and-conquer strategy. The most precarious part of the segmentation, namely the determination of the number of regions as well as the initialisation of the level set functions, is based on the very robust two-region segmentation which splits a domain into two parts in a way that is optimal according to the energy (Section 2). The multi-phase level set evolution has then just to adapt the regions in the global scope with more than two regions present (Section 3). With this minimisation strategy the level set framework can be fully exploited, what leads to excellent segmentation results. This will be demonstrated in some experiments in Section 4.

2   Two-Region Segmentation

Contrary to the general segmentation problem, two-region segmentation by means of a level set framework is well understood. Consider the Bayes error, i.e. the probability of misclassified pixels

$$L = 1 - \int_{\Omega_1} p_1 P_1 \, dx - \int_{\Omega_2} p_2 P_2 \, dx \qquad (1)$$

with the probability densities $p_1 = p(x|\Omega_1)$ and $p_2 = p(x|\Omega_2)$ of the regions Ω_1 and Ω_2, and under the side conditions $\Omega = \Omega_1 \cup \Omega_2$ and $\Omega_1 \cap \Omega_2 = \emptyset$, i.e. the regions cover the whole image domain Ω and do not overlap. The a-priori probabilities of both regions are equal, so $P_1 = P_2 = 0.5$. Moreover, instead of minimising the Bayes error directly, it is beneficial from the numerical point of view to work on the logarithms. Together with a penalty on the length of the boundary Γ, weighted by the parameter ν, this leads to the energy functional

$$E(\Omega_1, \Omega_2, p_1, p_2) = -\int_{\Omega_1} \log p_1 \, dx - \int_{\Omega_2} \log p_2 \, dx + \nu \int_{\Gamma} ds. \qquad (2)$$

For minimising this energy, now a level set function is introduced. Let $\Phi : \Omega \to \mathbb{R}$ be the level set function with $\Phi(x) > 0$ if $x \in \Omega_1$ and $\Phi(x) < 0$ if $x \in \Omega_2$. The zero-level line of Φ is the searched boundary between the two regions. We also introduce the regularised Heaviside function $H(s)$ with $\lim_{s \to -\infty} H(s) = 0$, $\lim_{s \to \infty} H(s) = 1$, and $H(0) = 0.5$. This allows to rewrite Eq. 2 as

$$E(\Phi, p_1, p_2) = -\int_{\Omega} H(\Phi) \log p_1 + (1 - H(\Phi)) \log p_2 - \nu |\nabla H(\Phi)| \, dx. \qquad (3)$$

The minimisation with respect to the regions can now be performed according to the gradient descent equation

$$\partial_t \Phi = H'(\Phi) \left(\log \frac{p_1}{p_2} + \nu \operatorname{div} \left(\frac{\nabla \Phi}{|\nabla \Phi|} \right) \right) \qquad (4)$$

where $H'(s)$ is the derivative of $H(s)$ with respect to its argument. Note that the side conditions are automatically satisfied due to the level set representation.

However, the probability densities p_1 and p_2 still have to be estimated. This is done according to the *expectation-maximisation principle*. Having the level set function initialised with some partitioning, the probability densities can be computed by a nonparametric Parzen density estimate using the smoothed histogram of the regions. Then the new densities are used for the level set evolution, leading to a further update of the probability densities, and so on. This iterative process converges to the next local minimum, so the initialisation matters.

In order to attenuate this dependency on the initialisation, two measures are recommendable. Firstly, the initialisation should be far from a possible segmentation of the image, as this enforces the search for a minimum in a more global scope. We always use an initialisation with many small rectangles scattered across the image domain.

The second measure is the application of a coarse-to-fine strategy. Starting with a down-sampled image, there are less local minima, so the segmentation is more robust. The resulting segmentation can then be used as initialisation for a finer scale, until the original optimisation problem is solved.

Under the assumption of exactly two regions in the image, this framework works very well. For some nice results obtained with this method we refer to [17,1]. The only remaining problem is the fact, that the assumption of exactly two regions in an image is mostly not true.

3   Multiple Region Segmentation

For the before-mentioned reasons, the generalised version of the segmentation problem with an arbitrary number of regions N will now be considered. The general model is described by the energy of Zhu-Yuille [22]

$$E(\Omega_i, p_i, N) = \sum_{i=1}^{N} \left(- \int_{\Omega_i} \log p_i \, dx + \frac{\nu}{2} \int_{\Gamma_i} ds + \lambda \right). \tag{5}$$

The additional term of this energy functional penalises the number of regions with the parameter λ. Now also the number of regions is a free variable that has to be optimised. Moreover, this variable is discrete and the increased number of regions is very sensitive to different initialisations. Furthermore, the nice splitting into two regions by a single level set function as described in the last section is not applicable anymore.

Reduced problem with N regions. In order to cope with all these additional difficulties, the complexity of the problem is first reduced by setting N fixed and assuming that a reasonable initialisation of the regions is available. In this case it is possible to introduce again a level set based energy functional with a set of level set functions Φ_i, each representing one region as $\Phi_i(x) > 0$ if and only if $x \in \Omega_i$.

$$E(\Phi_i, p_i) = \sum_{i=1}^{N} \left(- \int_{\Omega} H(\Phi_i) \log p_i - \frac{\nu}{2} |\nabla H(\Phi_i)| \, dx \right) \tag{6}$$

Note that, in contrast to the two-region case, this formulation does not implicitly respect the side condition of disjoint regions anymore. Minimising the energy according to the expectation-maximisation principle and the following evolution equations

$$\partial_t \Phi_i = H'(\Phi_i) \left(\log p_i - \max_{j \neq i, H(\Phi_j) > 0} \left(\log p_j \right) + \frac{\nu}{2} \, \mathrm{div} \left(\frac{\nabla \Phi_i}{|\nabla \Phi_i|} \right) \right). \tag{7}$$

ensures the adherence to the side conditions at least for the statistical part, since the maximum a-posteriori criterion ensures that a pixel is assigned uniquely to the region with the maximum a-posteriori probability. The smoothness assumption, however, can result in slight overlapping of regions close to their boundaries, like in all existing level set based methods dealing with an arbitrary number of regions, beside [19]. If this is not wanted in the final result, the pixels of such overlapping areas can be assigned to the region, where the level set function attains its maximum value.

So up to this point we can handle the following two cases:

- A domain of the image can be split into two parts by the two-region segmentation framework.
- A set of regions can evolve, minimising the energy in Eq. 5, if the number of regions is fixed and reasonable initialisations for the regions are available.

Solving the general problem. By means of these two special cases, also the general problem according to the model in Eq. 5 can be solved. Starting with the whole image domain Ω being a single region, the two-region segmentation can be applied in order

Fig. 1. Segmentation of two artificial texture images: In both cases 4 regions were detected.

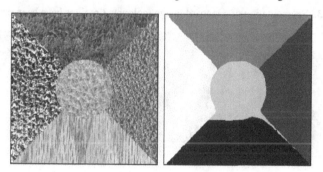

Fig. 2. Segmentation of a texture image: 5 regions have been detected.

to find the best splitting of the domain. If the energy decreases by the splitting, this results in two regions. On these regions, again the two-region splitting can be applied, and so on, until the energy does not decrease by further splits anymore. With this proceeding, not only the optimum number of regions is determined, but also suitable initialisations for the regions. Of course, the resulting partitioning is not optimal yet, as for the two-region splitting, possibilities of a region to evolve have been ignored. However, as the region number and the initialisation are known, the energy can now be minimised in the global scope by applying the evolution of Eq. 7, adapting the regions to the new situation where they have more competitors.

This procedure is applied in a multi-scale setting. Starting the procedure as described on the coarsest scale, with every refinement step on the next finer scale, it is checked whether any further splitting or merging decreases the energy before the evolution according to Eq. 7 is applied. So for each scale the optimum N is updated, as well as the region boundaries and the region statistics.

Though a global optimum still cannot be guaranteed[1], this kind of minimisation avoids quite reliably to be trapped by far-away local minima, as it applies both a coarse-to-fine strategy and the divide-and-conquer principle. The two-region splitting completely ignores the cluttering rest of the image. This consistently addresses the problems of optimising the discrete variable N and of not knowing good initialisations for the regions.

---

[1] This will only be the case, if the simplified objective function at the coarsest scale is unimodal and the global optimum of each next finer scale is the optimum closest to the global optimum at the respective coarser scale.

Fig. 3. Segmentation of a leopard image (colour): 3 regions have been detected.

Fig. 4. Segmentation of a penguin image (colour): 3 regions have been detected.

4   Results

We evaluated this scheme with a couple of artificial and real-world images. In order to handle texture and colour images, the features were computed and incorporated as described in [1]. We also used the local scale measure proposed in [2] as additional texture feature.

As Fig. 1 reveals, the method works fine for the artificial texture images. The optimum number of regions has been detected. The same holds for the test image depicted in Fig. 2, which is often used in the literature, e.g. in [9]. Often much more difficult, are real world images. Comparing, however, the segmentation result of the penguin image in Fig. 4 to the result in [12] shows that our method is competitive to other well-known methods. While in [12] 6 regions have been detected, the 3 regions found by our method are more reasonable. Our level set framework also compares favourably to the algebraic multigrid method in [9], as can be observed by means of the difficult squirrel image in Fig. 5a. Also Fig. 5b and Fig. 6 show an almost perfect segmentation.

It should be noted that all parameters that appear in the method have been set to fixed values, so all results shown here have been achieved with the *same* parameters. This is important, as of course it is much easier to obtain good segmentation results, if the parameters are tuned for each specific image. However, we think that this contradicts somehow the task of *unsupervised* segmentation.

The algorithm is reasonably fast. The 169×250 koala image took 22.5 seconds on an Athlon XP 1800+ including feature computation.

Fig. 5. LEFT: (a) Segmentation of a squirrel image: 2 regions have been detected. RIGHT: (b) Segmentation of a koala image (colour): 4 regions have been detected.

Fig. 6. Segmentation of a castle image (colour): 3 regions have been detected.

5   Summary

In this paper we proposed a level set based minimisation scheme for the variational segmentation model of Zhu-Yuille. While the popular level set framework has so far only been used for two-region segmentation or segmentation with a fixed number of regions, we described a way how to optimise the result also regarding the number of regions. Moreover, the divide-and-conquer principle provides good initialisations, so the method is less sensitive to local minima than comparable methods. All advantages of the level set framework are preserved, while its main problem has been solved. The performance of the variational model and its minimisation strategy has been demonstrated in several experiments. It compares favourably to existing approaches from the literature.

References

1. T. Brox, M. Rousson, R. Deriche, and J. Weickert. Unsupervised segmentation incorporating colour, texture, and motion. In N. Petkov and M. A. Westenberg, editors, *Computer Analysis of Images and Patterns*, volume 2756 of *Lecture Notes in Computer Science*, pages 353–360. Springer, Berlin, 2003.
2. T. Brox and J. Weickert. A TV flow based local scale measure for texture discrimination. In T. Pajdla and J. Matas, editors, *Proc. 8th European Conference on Computer Vision*, Lecture Notes in Computer Science. Springer, Berlin, May 2004. To appear.

3. V. Caselles, F. Catté, T. Coll, and F. Dibos. A geometric model for active contours in image processing. *Numerische Mathematik*, 66:1–31, 1993.
4. V. Caselles, R. Kimmel, and G. Sapiro. Geodesic active contours. In *Proc. Fifth International Conference on Computer Vision*, pages 694–699, Cambridge, MA, June 1995. IEEE Computer Society Press.
5. T. Chan and L. Vese. An active contour model without edges. In M. Nielsen, P. Johansen, O. F. Olsen, and J. Weickert, editors, *Scale-Space Theories in Computer Vision*, volume 1682 of *Lecture Notes in Computer Science*, pages 141–151. Springer, 1999.
6. D. Cremers. A multiphase levelset framework for variational motion segmentation. In L. D. Griffin and M. Lillholm, editors, *Scale Space Methods in Computer Vision*, volume 2695 of *Lecture Notes in Computer Science*, pages 599–614. Springer, Berlin, June 2003.
7. D. Cremers, N. Sochen, and C. Schnörr. Towards recognition-based variational segmentation using shape priors and dynamic labeling. In L. D. Griffin and M. Lillholm, editors, *Scale Space Methods in Computer Vision*, volume 2695 of *Lecture Notes in Computer Science*, pages 388–400. Springer, Berlin, June 2003.
8. A. Dervieux and F. Thomasset. A finite element method for the simulation of Rayleigh–Taylor instability. In R. Rautman, editor, *Approximation Methods for Navier–Stokes Problems*, volume 771 of *Lecture Notes in Mathematics*, pages 145–158. Springer, Berlin, 1979.
9. M. Galun, E. Sharon, R. Basri, and A. Brandt. Texture segmentation by multiscale aggregation of filter responses and shape elements. In *Proc. IEEE International Conference on Computer Vision*, pages 716–723, Nice, France, Oct. 2003.
10. S. Kichenassamy, A. Kumar, P. Olver, A. Tannenbaum, and A. Yezzi. Gradient flows and geometric active contour models. In *Proc. Fifth International Conference on Computer Vision*, pages 810–815, Cambridge, MA, June 1995. IEEE Computer Society Press.
11. M. E. Leventon, W. E. L. Grimson, and O. Faugeras. Statistical shape infuence in geodesic active contours. In *Proc. 2000 IEEE Computer Society Conference on Computer Vision and Pattern Recognition*, volume 1, pages 316–323, Hilton Head, SC, June 2000. IEEE Computer Society Press.
12. J. Malik, S. Belongie, J. Shi, and T. K. Leung. Textons, contours and regions: cue integration in image segmentation. In *Proc. IEEE International Conference on Computer Vision*, pages 918–925. Corfu, Greece, Sept. 1999.
13. D. Mumford and J. Shah. Boundary detection by minimizing functionals, I. In *Proc. IEEE Computer Society Conference on Computer Vision and Pattern Recognition*, pages 22–26, San Francisco, CA, June 1985. IEEE Computer Society Press.
14. S. Osher and J. A. Sethian. Fronts propagating with curvature-dependent speed: Algorithms based on Hamilton–Jacobi formulations. *Journal of Computational Physics*, 79:12–49, 1988.
15. N. Paragios and R. Deriche. A PDE-based level-set approach for detection and tracking of moving objects. In *Proc. Sixth International Conference on Computer Vision*, pages 1139–1145, Bombay, India, Jan. 1998.
16. N. Paragios and R. Deriche. Coupled geodesic active regions for image segmentation: A level set approach. In *Proc. Sixth European Conference on Computer Vision*, number 2, pages 224–240, Dublin, Ireland, 2000.
17. M. Rousson, T. Brox, and R. Deriche. Active unsupervised texture segmentation on a diffusion based feature space. In *Proc. 2003 IEEE Computer Society Conf. on Computer Vision and Pattern Recognition*, volume 2, pages 699–704, Madison, WI, June 2003.
18. C. Samson, L. Blanc-Féraud, G. Aubert, and J. Zerubia. A level set model for image classification. *International Journal of Computer Vision*, 40(3):187–197, 2000.
19. L. Vese and T. Chan. A multiphase level set framework for image segmentation using the Mumford and Shah model. *International Journal of Computer Vision*, 50(3):271–293, Dec. 2002.

20. A. Yezzi, A. Tsai, and A. Willsky. A statistical approach to snakes for bimodal and trimodal imagery. In *Proc. 7th International Conference on Computer Vision*, volume 2, pages 898–903, Kerkyra, Greece, Sept. 1999.

21. H. Zhao, T. Chan, B. Merriman, and S. Osher. A variational level set approach to multiphase motion. *Journal of Computational Physics*, 127:179–195, 1996.

22. S. Zhu and A. Yuille. Region competition: unifying snakes, region growing, and Bayes/MDL for multiband image segmentation. *IEEE Transactions on Pattern Analysis and Machine Intelligence*, 18(9):884–900, Sept. 1996.

CVPIC Colour/Shape Histograms for Compressed Domain Image Retrieval

Gerald Schaefer

School of Computing and Technology
The Nottingham Trent University
Nottingham, United Kingdom
gerald.schaefer@ntu.ac.uk

Abstract. Compressed domain image retrieval allows image indexing to be performed directly on the compressed data without the need of decoding. This approach hence provides a significant gain in terms of speed and also eliminates the need to store feature indices. In this paper we introduce a compressed domain image retrieval technique based on the Colour Visual Pattern Image Coding (CVPIC) compression algorithm. CVPIC represents an image coding technique where the compressed form is directly meaningful. Data that is readily available includes information on colour and edge (shape) descriptors of image subblocks. It is this information that is utilised by calculating a combined colour and shape histogram. Experimental results on the UCID dataset show this novel approach to be both efficient and effective, outperforming methods such as colour histograms, colour coherence vectors, and colour correlograms.

Keywords: Image retrieval, compressed domain image retrieval, midstream content access, CVPIC

1 Introduction

With the recent explosion in availability of digital imagery the need for content-based image retrieval (CBIR) is ever increasing. While many methods have been suggested in the literature only few take into account the fact that - due to limited resources such as disk space and bandwidth - virtually all images are stored in compressed form. In order to process them for CBIR they first need to be uncompressed and the features calculated in the pixel domain. Often these features are stored alongside the images which seems counterintuitive to the original need for compression. The desire for techniques that operate directly in the compressed domain providing, so-called midstream content access, seems therefore evident [9].

Colour Visual Pattern Image Coding (CVPIC) is one of the first so-called 4-th criterion image compression algorithms [12,11]. A 4-th criterion algorithm allows - in addition to the classic three image coding criteria of image quality, efficiency, and bitrate - the image data to be queried and processed directly in its compressed form; in other words the image data is directly meaningful

C.E. Rasmussen et al. (Eds.): DAGM 2004, LNCS 3175, pp. 424–431, 2004.

without the requirement of a decoding step. The data that is readily available in CVPIC compressed images is the colour information of each of the 4×4 blocks the image has been divided into, and information on the spatial characteristics of each block, including whether a given block is identified as a uniform block (a block with no or little variation) or a pattern block (a block where an edge or gradient has been detected).

In this paper we make direct use of this information and propose an image retrieval algorithm that allows for image retrieval directly in the compressed domain of CVPIC. Since both colour and shape (edge) information is precalculated and readily available in the CVPIC domain, a simple combined histogram of these can be obtained very efficiently. Exploiting these histograms allows for image retrieval based on both colour and shape contents. Experimental results obtained from querying the UCID [14] dataset show that this approach not only allows retrieval directly in the compressed domain but also clearly outperforms popular techniques such as colour histograms, colour coherence vectors, and colour correlograms.

The rest of this paper is organised as follows: in Section 2 the CVPIC compression algorithm used in this paper is reviewed. Section 3 describes our novel method of image retrieval in the CVPIC domain while Section 4 presents experimental results. Section 5 concludes the paper.

2   Colour Visual Pattern Image Coding

The Colour Visual Pattern Image Coding (CVPIC) image compression algorithm introduced by Schaefer et al. [12] is an extension of the work by Chen and Bovic [2]. The underlying idea is that within a 4×4 image block only one discontinuity is visually perceptible.

CVPIC first performs a conversion to the CIEL*a*b* colour space [3] as a more appropriate image representation. As many other colour spaces, CIEL*a*b* comprises one luminance and two chrominance channels; CIEL*a*b* however, was designed to be a uniform representation, meaning that equal differences in the colour space correspond to equal perceptual differences. A quantitative measurement of these colour differences was defined using the Euclidean distance in the L*a*b* space and is given in ΔE units.

A set of 14 patterns of 4×4 pixels has been defined in [2]. All these patterns contain one edge at various orientations (vertical, horizontal, plus and minus $45°$) as can be seen in Figure 1 where + and - represent different intensities. In addition a uniform pattern where all intensities are equal is being used.

Fig. 1. The 14 edge patterns used in CVPIC

The image is divided into 4x4 pixel blocks. Determining which visual pattern represents each block most accurately then follows. For each of the visual patterns the average L*a*b* values μ_+ and μ_- for the regions marked by + and - respectively (i.e. the mean values for the regions on each side of the pattern) are calculated according to

$$\mu_+ = \frac{\sum_{i\in+} p_i}{\sum_{i\in+} 1} \text{ and } \mu_- = \frac{\sum_{j\in-} p_j}{\sum_{j\in-} 1} \tag{1}$$

where p_i and p_j represent the pixel vectors in L*a*b* colour space.

The colour difference of each actual pixel and the corresponding mean value is obtained and averaged over the block according to

$$\epsilon = \frac{\sum_{i\in+} \|p_i - \mu_+\| + \sum_{j\in-} \|p_j - \mu_-\|}{16} \tag{2}$$

The visual pattern leading to the lowest ϵ value (given in CIEL*a*b* ΔE units) is then chosen. In order to allow for the encoding of uniform blocks the average colour difference to the mean colour of the block is also determined according to

$$\sigma = \frac{\sum_{\forall i} \|p_i - \mu\|}{16} \text{ where } \mu = \frac{\sum_{\forall i} p_i}{16} \tag{3}$$

A block is coded as uniform if either its variance in colour is very low, or if the resulting image quality will not suffer severely when coded as a uniform rather than as an edge block. To meet this requirement two thresholds are defined. The first threshold describes the upper bound for variations within a block, i.e. the average colour difference to the mean colour of the block. Every block with a variance below this value will be encoded as uniform. The second threshold is related to the difference between the average colour variation within a block and the average colour difference that would result if the block were coded as a pattern block (i.e. the lowest variance possible for an edge block) which is calculated by

$$\delta = \sigma - min_{\forall patterns}(\epsilon) \tag{4}$$

If this difference is very low (or if the variance for a uniform pattern is below those of all edge patterns in which case σ is negative) coding the block as uniform will not introduce distortions much more perceptible than if the block is coded as a pattern block. Hence, a block is coded as a uniform block if at least one of the following criteria is met:

(i) $\sigma < 1.75$
(ii) $\delta < 1.25$

We adopted the values of 1.75 ΔE and 1.25 ΔE for the two thresholds from [12].

For each block, one bit is stored which states whether the block is uniform or a pattern block. In addition, for edge blocks an index identifying the visual pattern needs to be stored. Following this procedure results in a representation of each block as 5 bits (1 + 4 as we use 14 patterns) for an edge block and 1 bit for a uniform block describing the spatial component, and the full colour information for one or two colours (for uniform and pattern blocks respectively).

In contrast to [12] where each image is colour quantised individually, the colour components are quantised to 64 universally pre-defined colours (we adopted those of [10]). Each colour can hence be encoded using 6 bits. Therefore, in total a uniform block takes $7 (= 1 + 6)$ bits, whereas a pattern block is stored in $17 (=5+2*6)$ bits. We found that this yielded an average compression ratio of about 1:30. We note, that the information could be further encoded to achieve lower bitrates. Both the pattern and the colour information could be entropy coded. In this paper however, we refrain from this step as we are primarily interested in a synthesis of coding and retrieval.

3 CVPIC Image Retrieval by Colour and Shape

We note from above that for each image block in CVPIC both colour and edge information is readily available in the compressed form: each block contains either one or two colours and belongs to one of 15 edge classes. We propose to make direct use of this information for the purpose of image retrieval. In a sense our approach is similar to the work by Jain and Vailaya [6] where image retrieval is performed based on colour and shape (edge) information. However, our method differs in two important aspect. In stark contrast to their work, our method runs directly in the compressed domain without any further need for calculating these descriptors. Furthermore due to the low dimensionality of our features we are able to build a combined colour and shape histogram rather than two separate descriptors that need to be re-integrated in the retrieval process.

It is well known that colour is an important cue for image retrieval. In fact, simple descriptors such as histograms of the colour contents of images [16] have been shown to work well and have hence been used in many CBIR systems such as QBIC [7] or Virage [1]. A colour histogram is built by (uniformly) quantising the colour space into a number of bins (often $8 \times 8 \times 8$) and counting how many pixels of the image fall into each bin. From the description of the CVPIC algorithm it can be easily deduced how a colour histogram can be efficiently calculated there. First, CVPIC colour histograms need only 64 entries since there are only 64 colours in the palette used during the encoding. This in turn means that the dimensionality is much lower compared to traditional colour histograms which again implies that the comparison of these histograms requires fewer computations. Since each block contains one or two colour indices and an edge index an exact colour histogram can be calculated by weighing the respective two colours by the number of pixels they occupy. While this method requires fewer computations than are needed for obtaining histograms in the pixel domain we propose a yet more efficient approach. Instead of applying weights according to the layout of each pattern we simply increment the relevant histogram bins for each block[1].

---

[1] We note, that by doing so we put more emphasis on the colour content of edge blocks compared to uniform blocks.

While image retrieval based on colour usually produces useful results, integration of this information with another paradigm such as texture or shape will result in an improved retrieval performance. Shape descriptors are often calculated as statistical summaries of local edge information such as in [6] where the edge orientation and magnitude is determined at each pixel location and an edge histogram calculated. Exploiting the CVPIC image structure an effective shape descriptor can be determined very efficiently. Since each (pattern) block contains exactly one (precalculated) edge and there are 15 different patterns a simple histogram of the edge indices could be built. However, since both colour and shape features are of low dimensionality we propose to integrate them into a combined colour/shape histogram rather than building two separate descriptors as in [6]. We further reduce the dimensionality by considering only 5 edge classes: horizontal and vertical edges, edges at plus and minus 45°, and no edge (uniform blocks). Thus, we end up with a 64×5 colour/shape histogram $H_{cs}(I)$ for an image I:

$$
\begin{aligned}
H_{cs}(I)(i,1) &= \Pr((c_1 = i \vee c_2 = i) \wedge p \in \{1,2,3\}) & \text{horizontal} \\
H_{cs}(I)(i,2) &= \Pr((c_1 = i \vee c_2 = i) \wedge p \in \{4,5,6\}) & \text{vertical} \\
H_{cs}(I)(i,3) &= \Pr((c_1 = i \vee c_2 = i) \wedge p \in \{7,8,9,10\}) & -45° \\
H_{cs}(I)(i,4) &= \Pr((c_1 = i \vee c_2 = i) \wedge p \in \{11,12,13,14\}) & +45° \\
H_{cs}(I)(i,5) &= \Pr((c_1 = i \wedge p = 15)) & \text{uniform} \quad (5)
\end{aligned}
$$

where c_1, c_2, and p are the colour and pattern indices (the patterns are numbered according to Figure 1, going from left to right, top to bottom) of a block.

It should be pointed out that these CVPIC colour/shape histograms $H_{cs}(I)$ can be created extremely efficiently. In essence, per 4×4 image block only 1 addition is needed (to increment the relevant histogram bin). This makes it unnecessary to store any information alongside the image as the indices can be created online with hardly any overhead to reading the image file. As thus it automatically lends itself to online retrieval e.g. of the web which - due to the dynamic structure of the Internet - is impossible to achieve with traditional index based approaches.

Two CVPIC colour/shape histograms $H_{cs}(I_1)$ and $H_{cs}(I_2)$ obtained from images I_1 and I_2 are compared using the histogram intersection measure introduced in [16]

$$
s_{cs}(I_1, I_2) = \sum_{i=1}^{64} \sum_{j=1}^{5} \min(H_{cs}(I_1)(i,j), H_{cs}(I_2)(i,j)) \quad (6)
$$

which provides a similarity score between 0 and 1 (for normalised histograms).

4 Experimental Results

We evaluated our method using the recently released UCID dataset [14]. UCID[2], an Uncompressed Colour Image Database, consists of 1338 colour images all pre-

---

[2] The UCID dataset is available from `http://vision.doc.ntu.ac.uk/`.

served in their uncompressed form which makes it ideal for the testing of compressed domain techniques. UCID also provides a ground truth of 262 assigned query images each with a number of predefined corresponding matches that an ideal image retrieval system would return.

We compressed the database using the CVPIC coding technique and performed image retrieval using the algorithm detailed in Section 3 based on the queries defined in the UCID set. As performance measure we use the modified average match percentile (AMP) from [14] and the retrieval effectiveness from [4]. The modified AMP is defined as

$$MP_Q = \frac{100}{S_Q} \sum_{i=1}^{S_Q} \frac{N - R_i}{N - i} \tag{7}$$

with $R_i < R_{i+1}$ and

$$AMP = \frac{1}{Q} \sum MP_Q \tag{8}$$

where R_i is the rank the i-th match to query image Q was returned, S_Q is the number of corresponding matches for Q, and N is the total number of images in the database. A perfect retrieval system would achieve an AMP of 100 whereas an AMP of 50 would mean the system performs as well as one that returns the images in a random order. The retrieval effectiveness is given by

$$RE_Q = \frac{\sum_{i=1}^{S_Q} R_i}{\sum_{i=1}^{S_Q} I_i} \tag{9}$$

where R_i is the rank of the i-th matching image and I_i is the ideal rank of the i-th match (i.e. $I = \{1, 2, ..., S_Q\}$). The average retrieval effectiveness ARE is then taken as the mean of RE over all query images. An ideal CBIR algorithm would return an ARE of 1, the closer the ARE to that value (i.e. the lower the ARE) the better the algorithm.

Table 1. Results obtained on the UCID dataset.

	AMP	ARE
Colour histograms	90.47	90.83
Colour coherence vectors	91.03	85.88
Border/interior pixel histograms	91.27	82.49
Colour correlograms	89.96	95.61
CVPIC colour & shape	**93.70**	**57.82**

In order to relate the results obtained we also implemented colour histogram based image retrieval (uniformly quantised $8 \times 8 \times 8$ RGB histograms with histogram intersection) according to [16], colour coherence vectors [8], border/interior pixel histograms [15] and colour (auto) correlograms [5]. Results for all methods are given in Table 1. From there we see that our novel approach is not only capable of achieving good retrieval performance, but that it clearly outperforms all other methods. While the border/interior pixel approach achieves an AMP of 91.27 and all other methods perform worse, CVPIC colour/shape histograms provide an average match percentile of 93.70, that is more than 2.50

Fig. 2. Sample query together with 5 top ranked images returned by (from left to right, top to bottom) colour histograms, colour coherence vectors, border/interior pixel histograms, colour correlograms, CVPIC retrieval.

higher than the best of the other methods. This is indeed a significant difference as a drop in match percentile of 2.5 will mean that 2.5% more of the whole image database need to be returned in order to find the images that are relevant; as typical image database nowadays can contain tens of thousands to hundreds of thousands images this would literally mean additionally thousands of images. The superiority of the CVPIC approach is especially remarkable so as it is based on images compressed to a medium compression ratio, i.e. images with a significantly lower image quality compared to uncompressed images whereas for all other methods the original uncompressed versions of the images were used[3]. Furthermore, methods such as colour histograms, colour coherence vectors and colour correlograms are known to work fairly well for image retrieval and are hence among those techniques that are widely used in this field. An example of the difference in retrieval performance is illustrated in Figure 2 which shows one of the query images of the UCID database together with the five top ranked images returned by all methods. Only the CVPIC techniques manages to retrieve four correct model images in the top five while colour correlograms retrieve three and all other methods only two.

5   Conclusions

In this paper we present a novel image retrieval technique that operates directly in the compressed domain of CVPIC compressed images. By utilising the fact that CVPIC encodes both colour and edge information these features can be directly exploited for image retrieval by building a combined colour/shape histogram. Experimental results on a medium-sized colour image database show that the suggested method performs well, outperforming techniques such as colour histograms, colour coherence vectors, and colour correlograms.

---

[3] Compressing the images to a size similar to the CVPIC images using a standard coding technique such as JPEG will result in a further performance drop as has been shown in [13], hence the results presented here are indeed based on a best case scenario.

Acknowledgements. The author would like to thank the Nuffield foundation for supporting this work under grant number NAL/00703/G.

References

1. J. Bach, C. Fuller, A. Gupta, A. Hampapur, B. Horowitz, R. Humphrey, and R. Jain. The Virage image search engine: An open framework for image management. In *Storage and Retrieval for Image and Video Databases*, volume 2670 of *Proceedings of SPIE*, pages 76–87, 1996.
2. D. Chen and A. Bovik. Visual pattern image coding. *IEEE Trans. Communications*, 38:2137–2146, 1990.
3. CIE. *Colorimetry*. CIE Publications 15.2, Commission International de L'Eclairage, 2nd edition, 1986.
4. C. Faloutsos, W. Equitz, M. Flickner, W. Niblack, D. Petkovic, and R. Barber. Efficient and effective querying by image content. *Journal of Intelligent Information Retrieval*, 3(3/4):231–262, 1994.
5. J. Huang, S.R. Kumar, M. Mitra, W-J. Zhu, and R. Zabih. Image indexing using color correlograms. In *IEEE Int. Conference Computer Vision and Pattern Recognition*, pages 762–768, 1997.
6. A.K. Jain and A. Vailaya. Image retrieval using color and shape. *Pattern Recognition*, 29(8):1233–1244, 1996.
7. W. Niblack, R. Barber, W. Equitz, M.D. Flickner, D. Glasman, D. Petkovic, and P. Yanker. The QBIC project: Querying images by content using color, texture and shape. In *Conf. on Storage and Retrieval for Image and Video Databases*, volume 1908 of *Proceedings of SPIE*, pages 173–187, 1993.
8. G. Pass and R. Zabih. Histogram refinement for content-based image retrieval. In *3rd IEEE Workshop on Applications of Computer Vision*, pages 96–102, 1996.
9. R.W. Picard. Content access for image/video coding: The fourth criterion. Technical Report 195, MIT Media Lab, 1994.
10. G. Qiu. Colour image indexing using BTC. *IEEE Trans. Image Processing*, 12(1):93–101, 2003.
11. G. Schaefer and G. Qiu. Midstream content access based on colour visual pattern coding. In *Storage and Retrieval for Image and Video Databases VIII*, volume 3972 of *Proceedings of SPIE*, pages 284–292, 2000.
12. G. Schaefer, G. Qiu, and M.R. Luo. Visual pattern based colour image compression. In *Visual Communication and Image Processing 1999*, volume 3653 of *Proceedings of SPIE*, pages 989–997, 1999.
13. G. Schaefer and M. Stich. On the influence of image compression on the performance of content based image retrieval. In *6th Int. Conference on VISual Information Systems*, pages 426–431, 2003.
14. G. Schaefer and M. Stich. UCID - An Uncompressed Colour Image Database. In *Storage and Retrieval Methods and Applications for Multimedia 2004*, volume 5307 of *Proceedings of SPIE*, pages 472–480, 2004.
15. R.O. Stehling, M.A. Nascimento, and A.X. Falcao. A compact and efficient image retrieval approach based on border/interior pixel classification. In *Proc. 11th Int. Conf. on Information and Knowledge Management*, pages 102–109, 2002.
16. M.J. Swain and D.H. Ballard. Color indexing. *Int. Journal Computer Vision*, 7(11):11–32, 1991.

The Redundancy Pyramid and Its Application to Segmentation on an Image Sequence*

Jocelyn Marchadier, Walter G. Kropatsch, and Allan Hanbury

Pattern Recognition and Image Processing Group (PRIP),
Vienna University of Technology
Favoritenstraße 9/1832, A-1040 Vienna, Austria
jm@prip.tuwien.ac.at

Abstract. Irregular pyramids organize a sequence of partitions of images in such a way that each partition is deduced from the preceding one by union of some of its regions. In this paper, we show how a single pyramid can be used to encode redundant subparts of different partitions. We obtain a pyramid that accounts for the redundancy of the partitions. This structure, naturally called the redundancy pyramid, can be used for many purposes. We also demonstrate and discuss some applications for studying image sequences.

1 Introduction

Image segmentation is an important component of many machine vision applications such as object recognition and matching for stereo reconstruction. In general, segmentation techniques aim to partition an image into connected regions having homogeneous properties.

A major issue with segmentation algorithms is their stability. The partitions produced by different segmentation algorithms will be to some extent different. The same is true when a single segmentation algorithm is applied on an image sequence of a static scene under varying illumination. Comparing and merging several partitions seems an obvious way to partially solve the problem of stability.

Several techniques in computer vision and pattern recognition handle several partitions of images. A combination of different segmentations to obtain the best segmentation of an image has been suggested by Cho and Meer [2] based on the cooccurrence probabilities of points in partitions. However, they make use of small differences resulting from random processes in the construction of a Region Adjacency Graph (RAG) pyramid to generate their segmentations. Matching segmentations of different images is usually addressed as a pairwise problem, without exploiting the redundancy inherent to highly redundant images. Recently, Keselman and Dickinson [4] have proposed a method for computing common substructures of RAGs, called the lowest common abstraction. They try to find isomorphic graphs obtained from different RAGs by fusing adjacent

---

* This work was supported by the Austrian Science Foundation (FWF) under grants P14445-MAT, P14662-INF and S91 03-N04.

C.E. Rasmussen et al. (Eds.): DAGM 2004, LNCS 3175, pp. 432–439, 2004.

regions. While their approach is attractive, it suffers from a certain number of drawbacks. When handling real world segmentations, noise can split or merge arbitrary regions and the lowest common abstraction can not cope with these processes.

Basically these approaches try to exploit the redundancy of observations, which is widely used in robust estimation, and more generally, but implicitly, in robust computer vision techniques. In (robust) estimation, redundancy is defined as the difference between the number of parameters of a functional model, and its number of equations [3]. When the redundancy increases, the computed model is not only more precise but also more reliable [3].

Our approach is based on basic topology. We exploit the redundant structures of topological partitions. The use of this formalism guarantees that the proposed theoretical results are independent of the dimension of the space being partitioned. In section 2, we propose a set of definitions. After having recalled standard definitions in topology, we introduce new basic tools for comparing several partitions, the greatest common multiple and the lowest common divisor of partitions, whose definitions and properties are analogous to classical definitions on the set of integers. We then propose the definition of a pyramid in this framework. In section 3 we propose a fundamental theorem which enables the definition, based on these concepts, of a structure that plays a key role in the comparison of several partitions. We also propose an efficient method for constructing an approximation of the redundancy pyramid on a digital image of dimension 2. In section 4, we propose a proof of concept. The analysis of the redundancy of the structure of a segmentation of images in a sequence of moving objects in a static background leads to interesting results discussed in this section. Very redundant parts are part of a good segmentation of the background. Moderately redundant parts are moving objects, with a certain tolerance to pauses during the object's displacement. This lead to a very reliable process of background segmentation on image sequences with drastically varying illumination.

2   Basic Definitions

We recall here basic definitions from topology and propose new definitions that will help to define partitions, pyramid of partitions and the redundancy pyramid.

2.1   Topology

A topology on a set E is a family $\mathcal{T}$ of subsets of E (the "open" subsets of E) such that a union of elements of $\mathcal{T}$ is an element of $\mathcal{T}$, a finite intersection of elements of $\mathcal{T}$ is an element of $\mathcal{T}$, and $\emptyset$ and E are elements of $\mathcal{T}$. E equipped with a topology $\mathcal{T}$ is called a topological space.

A topological space is connected if it cannot be partitioned into two disjoint, nonempty open sets. A (topological) subspace G of a topological space E is a subset G of E such that the open sets in G are the intersection of the open sets of E with G. The complement of $F \in \mathcal{T}$ is the set $\overline{F} = E/F$. The sets $\overline{F}$ are called closed sets.

The interior $int(e)$ of a subset e of E is the largest open set contained in e. The closure $cl(e)$ of a subset e of E is the smallest closed set containing e. The boundary of a subset e of E is the intersection of its closure and the closure of its complement.

We call region a closed connected subset r of E such that $int(r) \neq \emptyset$. We define the following relations for regions. If $r \cap r' \neq \emptyset$ and $int(r \cap r') = \emptyset$ and $int(r \cup r')$ is connected, we say that regions r and r' are adjacent. r and r' are overlapping if $int(r \cap r') \neq \emptyset$. If r and r' are neither adjacent nor overlapping, we say that they are disjoint. These definitions are illustrated in Figure 1. In the example 1.c, the interesection of the two regions is composed of a single point which is on the boundary of the union. Thus the interior of their union is composed of two connected components, and we say that the regions are disjoint.

a) Adjacent regions b) Disjoint regions c) Disjoint regions d) Overlapping regions

Fig. 1. Relations between regions

2.2 Regional Covers, Divisors, Multiples, and Pyramids

We define a regional cover of a region I (e.g. the support of an image) as a set P_i of regions $r_j \in P_i$ such that two different regions from P_i are either disjoint or adjacent and $I = \cup_{P_i} r_j$. A regional cover of I is a "partition" of I into regions whose overlapping parts are thin.

We will now introduce new concepts that can be interesting when comparing several regional covers. Let P_i and P_i' be two regional covers of I. We say that P_i divides P_i' if and only if each region of P_i' has a regional cover in P_i (i.e. each region of P_i' is equal to the union of adjacent regions of P_i). We note, for convenience, $P_i | P_i'$. P_i is called a divisor of P_i', and P_i' is a multiple of P_i. A divisor of a regional cover can be obtained by splitting its regions whereas a multiple can be obtained by merging its regions.

The least common multiple of n regional covers $P_{i,1 \leq i \leq n}$ of a region I is the multiple P of $P_{i,1 \leq i \leq n}$ such that any regional cover P_i' with $P_i | P_i' | P$ is not a multiple of one or more covers $P_{j,j \neq i}$. The greatest common divisor of n regional covers $P_{i,1 \leq i \leq n}$ of a region I is the regional cover P of $P_{i,1 \leq i \leq n}$ such that any regional cover P_i' of I with $P | P_i' | P_i$ is not a multiple of one or more regional cover $P_{j,j \neq i}$. The least common multiple (resp. the greatest common divisor) of a set of regional covers can be seen as the regional cover obtained by intersecting (resp. merging) two by two the boundaries of the initial regional covers. These definitions are illustrated in Figure 2.

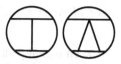

a) Two regional covers b) Greatest Common Divisor c) Least Common Multiple

Fig. 2. The least common multiple and the greatest common divisor of two regional covers.

Irregular pyramids are well studied data structures in computer vision [5, 1]. They enable the representation of hierarchies of partitions of images. Our definition of a pyramid differs slightly from the existing ones in that we use regional covers instead of cellular partitions or graphs. This definition, although based on the same structure, leads to a simple and elegant formulation, which is expressed in a topological framework rather than in a graph framework.

We define for our purpose a pyramid $\mathcal{P}$ as a set of n regional covers $\mathcal{P} = \{L_1, ..., L_n\}$ satisfying $L_1|L_2|...|L_n$. The regional covers L_i are the levels of the pyramid, L_1 is its base level and L_n its top level. An example of a pyramid with three levels is depicted in Figure 3.

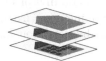

Fig. 3. A pyramid of regional covers.

3 The Redundancy Pyramid

Segmentation processes are noisy processes which can remove arbitrary regions or boundaries. The smallest common multiple of a set of covers obtained by segmentation is not stable. However, a more reliable manner to analyze common substructures of m "noisy" regional covers is to compute all the smallest common multiples of certain number i of regional covers. The smallest common multiples depend on the covers used to compute them. It then makes sense to compute their greatest common divisor L_i, which can be seen as the union of their boundary points. In this section, we will show that the L_i form a pyramid. We will give an efficient way to compute this pyramid using digital 2D images.

3.1 Definition

The following lemma simply results from the definitions. It enables one to understand how the structure of the redundancy pyramid is built.

Lemma 1. *Let $\mathcal{F}$ be a set of regional covers $P^1_{i,1\leq i\leq m_1}$. Let L_1 be their greatest common divisor. Let $P^2_{i,1\leq i\leq C^2_{m_1}}$ be all the possible smallest common multiples*

of two regional covers, and L_2 be the greatest common divisor of the covers P_i^2. Then we have $L_1|L_2$.

The idea of the proof is that any intersection or difference between regions taken from different regional covers can be obtained by the union of regions from L_1. Thus regions of L_2 are equal to nonempty unions of regions of L_1 and $L_1|L_2$.

The following theorem is fundamental as it shows that the structure of the redundancy pyramid is a pyramid.

Theorem 1. *Let $\mathcal{F}$ be a set of regional covers $P_{i,1\leq i\leq m_1}^1$, and let*

- *L_1 be the greatest common divisor of $P_{i,1\leq i\leq m_1}^1$,*
- *L_i with $1 < i$ is the greatest common divisor of all the least common multiples of i regional covers of $P_{i,1\leq i\leq m_1}^1$.*

Then the set $\mathcal{P} = \{L_1, ..., L_n\}$ is a pyramid. It is called the redundancy pyramid of $P_{i,1\leq i\leq m_1}^1$.

Let us note P_j^i all the smallest common multiples of i regional covers taken from the original set, and L_i their greatest common divisor. Let $P_j^{\prime i+1}$ be all possible least common multiples of two regional covers taken from P_j^i. We remark that L_{i+1} is equal to the greatest common divisor of the $P_j^{\prime i+1}$. Then we can apply the lemma 1 in order to prove the inference $L_j|L_{j+1}$. As it is true for L_1 and L_2, we have $L_1|L_2|...|L_m$. Note that by definition L_n the least common multiple of $P_{i,1\leq i\leq m_1}^1$.

3.2   Construction with Morphological Operators

The algorithm presented in this section is based on a boundary representation of each regional cover of digital images. The idea is that the set of boundary points of the level L_i of the redundancy pyramid is composed of points which are boundary points of i regional covers. Accumulating directly boundary points will not lead directly to the construction of the pyramid, as some combinations of boundary points can lead to pendant edges or isolated points. A first filtering is therefore done to remove them. On certain configurations, applying only this algorithm is not enough to filter out all undesired edges, but it produces satisfying results in most real world situations. A simple example is depicted in Figure 4. This figure shows the initial regional covers ("partitions") of three different projected cubes, similar to the example studied by Keselman et al. [4]. The redundancy pyramid can be seen on the fourth figure, where edges have been colored according to their redundancy. The dark edges are of higher redundancy (i.e. 3), and are the common boundaries of the regions of the last level of the redundancy pyramid. The other edges have redundancies of 1, as they appear in a single image.

Although the redundancy pyramid can be built using any kind of partitions, the implementation of the preceding algorithm is straightforward when dealing with digital 2D images. The initial partitions $P_{i,1\leq i\leq n}$ are described by binary

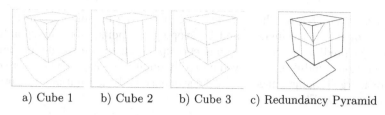

a) Cube 1   b) Cube 2   b) Cube 3   c) Redundancy Pyramid

Fig. 4. Redundancy pyramid of images.

images (referred to as contour map in the following text) indicating the presence of contours at each point, i.e. $P_i(x,y) = 1$ if the point of integer coordinates (x,y) is a contour point for partition i and $P_i(x,y) = 0$ otherwise. Examples of contour maps are drawn in Figure 5. Typically, such images can be obtained by watershed transforms [6] or by marking contour points of labeled image partitions.

The construction of the boundary redundancy pyramid is based on an accumulation process of the contour maps. The main steps of the pyramid construction are:

- Each contour point of each contour map is accumulated in an image R of natural numbers.
- A hierarchical watershed of R is computed. We use the leveling transform of [6]. The advantage of this watershed algorithm is that ones obtain a well nested crest network and thus the pyramid in a digital form without using extra operations.

The result of this algorithm is an integer image describing the hierarchical watershed. By applying a threshold i to this image, we obtain the contours describing the ith level of the redundancy pyramid. This algorithm is not only simple but also very efficient.

4   Application to Motion Analysis and Background Segmentation on an Image Sequence

The initial data of this application is an image sequence obtained by a static camera. The captured scene can be subject to drastic illumination changes, and moving objects can occlude some parts of the static scene. A good background segmentation cannot be obtained from a single image. The main idea here is to construct initial segmentations of a certain number of images in the sequence, and to compute the redundancy pyramid of these segmentations. The low level of the pyramid will give information on the moving object, while the higher level of the pyramid will tend to segment the static scene using information merged from the sequence.

The experiment was done on a sequence where illumination varied in a way that certain images are saturated, while others are dark. On the sequence, a person is moving in front of a static background. The initial regional covers were obtained by computing the watershed of [6] on the modulus of the Deriche's gradient of the initial images, and by keeping the points not corresponding to basins. As predicted, certain regions corresponding to the sought background segmentation couldn't be retrieved correctly on all the images. They were either split or merged. Some images from the sequence and their initial segmentations are presented in Figure 5.

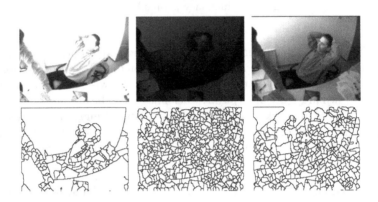

Fig. 5. Images from the sequence and their partitions (Image sequence provided by Advanced Computer Vision (ACV), Vienna).

The redundancy pyramid of the computed regional covers was computed. It is shown in Figure 6. Each image was treated in less than 2s on a laptop computer with an AMD Athlon processor at 1.8GHz. The program used was not subject to any optimization and can easily be implemented on dedicated hardware in real time.

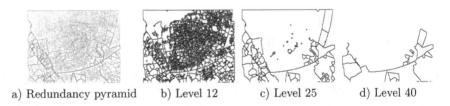

a) Redundancy pyramid   b) Level 12   c) Level 25   d) Level 40

Fig. 6. Redundancy pyramid of the image sequence

The best segmentation was obtained at an intermediate level of the pyramid. This can be explained by the fact that the contours of the background are not detected correctly on all the images. The lower levels are very noisy, which is due to the over-segmentation of the initial images. However, the trajectory of the movement can clearly be seen. The quality of the segmentations obtained at intermediate levels is outstanding, considering the initial over-segmentations used. Remark that no parameter was employed for producing the segmentations and the pyramid. The only parameter of this method is the Deriche's α which was equal to 1.5. In conditions not so extreme, the direct application of the previous method should result in stable higher levels of the pyramid. A single calibration step expressed in a number of frames would then be required in order to obtain a segmentation of a static scene of the quality as image c of Figure 6.

5   Conclusion

We have proposed new structure, the redundancy pyramid, expressed in a topological framework. We proposed an efficient algorithm in order to compute this structure on 2D digital images of partitions. It can be used in a wide number of applications ranging from segmentation fusion to generic object recognition, motion analysis and background subtraction over a sequence of images under drastically varying illumination. Some results of the last application were proposed. This validated the approach in a very complicated case. Future work include a statistical evaluation of the approach, the generalization of the algorithm to higher dimensions, to continuous images, and to images that cannot be directly superimposed on one another.

References

1. L. Brun and W. G. Kropatsch. Construction of combinatorial pyramids. In *Proceedings of the 4th IAPR-TC15 Workshop on Graph-based Representations in Pattern Recognition*, pages 1–12, 2003.
2. K. Cho and P. Meer. Image segmentation from consensus information. *Computer Vision and Image Understanding*, 68(1):72–89, 1997.
3. W. Förstner. Generic estimation procedures for orientation with minimum redundant information. 2nd Course on Digital Photogrammetry, 1999.
4. Y. Keselman and S. Dickinson. Generic model abstraction from examples. In *Proc. IEEE Conference CVPR*, volume 1, pages 856–863, December 2001.
5. W. G. Kropatsch. Abstraction Pyramids on Discrete Representations. In the proc. of DGCI2002, pages 1–21, Bordeaux, France, 2002.
6. J. Marchadier, S. Michelin, D. Arquès, Thinning Grayscale Well-Composed Images. Pattern Recognition Letters 25, pages 581–590, 2004.

A Higher Order MRF-Model for Stereo-Reconstruction

Dmitrij Schlesinger[1], Boris Flach[1], and Alexander Shekhovtsov[2]

[1] Dresden University of Technology
[2] IRTC ITS Kiev

Abstract. We consider the task of stereo-reconstruction under the following fairly broad assumptions. A single and continuously shaped object is captured by two uncalibrated cameras. It is assumed, that almost all surface points are binocular visible. We propose a statistical model which represents the surface as a triangular (hexagonal) mesh of pairs of corresponding points. We introduce an iterative scheme, which simultaneously finds an optimal mesh (with respect to a certain Bayes task) and a corresponding optimal fundamental matrix (in a maximum likelihood sense). Thus the surface is reconstructed up to a projective transform.

1   Introduction

Even though stereo-reconstruction is a thoroughly investigated problem of image processing, which had attracted attention for decades, we should admit, that at least a handful crucial open problems remain on the agenda. These are mainly modeling problems, e.g. modeling stereo reconstruction for complex scenes (many objects, occlusions and self occlusions, depth discontinuities etc.) [1,4,5,6]. On the other hand, it is noteworthy, that even under much simpler conditions there are still some open questions.

The aim of our paper is to show, how at least two of them can be solved under not too restrictive assumptions. The first one deals with the interplay of surface reconstruction and camera calibration. Usually, most approaches for surface reconstruction require either rectified images or equivalently, calibrated cameras. On the other hand there are many methods to estimate the epipolar geometry, given corresponding image points. That is, corresponding image points should meet a certain epipolar geometry and on the other hand, to determine a latter one, corresponding image points are needed.

The second problem arises in most approaches, which try to estimate dense disparity (or depth) fields: in order to calculate local qualities for possible matches, they usually utilize fix-sized windows. This becomes inaccurate if the surface is not ortho-frontal. To improve this, it is necessary to know the local projective transformation (let's say from the left to the right image). But, again, this transformation is determined by the unknown surface.

To overcome these problems we propose a biologically inspired model consisting in the following. A surface is described by a field of abstract (binocular) units. The state (label) of each unit is a pair of corresponding image points. These units are arranged in an abstract regular hexagonal lattice. This allows to incorporate a-priori assumptions for the expected surfaces like binocular visibility or continuity/smoothness by either hard or statistical restrictions. For instance, to avoid reconstructions with self occlusions, we require coherent orientations for the states of elementary triangles of the lattice: the states of a triangle of vertices define triangles in the left and right image – which should

C.E. Rasmussen et al. (Eds.): DAGM 2004, LNCS 3175, pp. 440–446, 2004.

be coherently oriented. Image similarity as well as consistency with epipolar geometry are modeled in a statistical way. For the first one we calculate image similarities for the corresponding image triangles – this allows to account (automatically) for local projective transforms. Given an epipolar geometry, the consistency of a pair of corresponding image points is measured in terms of their distances from corresponding epipolar lines. Consequently, we obtain a statistical model for the state field of our units and the images parametrized by unknown epipolar geometry (denoted by the fundamental matrix). This allows to pose the surface reconstruction as a Bayes task and to estimate the epipolar geometry in a maximum-likelihood sense. Some of the internal parameters of the model are automatically estimated in a similar way.

2 The Model

Let V be a finite set of abstract vertices arranged in a planar and regular hexagonal lattice. The edges of this lattice are denoted by $e \in E$ and the elementary triangles are denoted by $t \in T$. Each vertex $v \in V$ has a four dimensional integer-valued state vector $x(v) \in \mathbb{Z}^4$, which represents a pair of image positions $x(v) = (x_L(v), x_R(v))$ in the left and right image. A complete state field (or labeling) is a mapping $x: V \to \mathbb{Z}^4$ and defines corresponding triangular image meshes. We denote the images by I_L and I_R respectively, e.g. $I_L(x_L)$ being the intensity or color value of the pixel x_L of the left image (see Fig. 1). The epipolar geometry is represented in terms of a fundamental matrix F.

Assuming surface continuity and binocular visibility, we consider the following statistical model

$$p(x, I_L, I_R; F) = p(x; F) \cdot p(I_L, I_R \mid x) =$$
$$\frac{1}{Z} \exp\Big[-E_a(x) - E_g(x, F) - E_d(x, I_L, I_R) \Big], \qquad (1)$$

where as usual Z denotes a (unknown) normalizing constant. The terms in the exponent – usually called energy terms – are described below.

Let us begin by explaining the a-priori energy $E_a(x)$. It expresses our a-priory assumptions and is local additive in the triangles and edges of the hexagonal lattice:

$$E_a(x) = \sum_{t \in T} \chi\big(x(t)\big) + \sum_{e \in E} \delta\big(x(e)\big).$$

The first sum is over all elementary triangles and the function χ is zero if the abstract triangle t and both image triangles $x_L(t)$ and $x_R(t)$ are all coherently oriented. It is infinity otherwise – zeroing the probability of a state field in such case. The second sum is over all edges of the abstract lattice and the function δ is zero if the disparities in the vertices connected by the edge e differ not more than a predefined value. It is infinity otherwise – again zeroing the probability of a state field in such case. Hence, the second sum can be seen as a kind of continuity term.

The second energy term $E_g(x, F)$ in (1) penalizes state fields x, which strongly deviate from the epipolar geometry F:

$$E_g(x, F) = \frac{1}{\sigma_g} \sum_{v \in V} D\big(x(v), F\big).$$

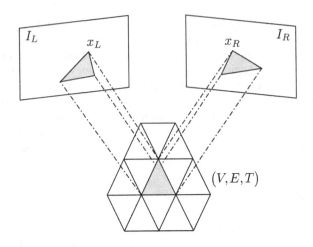

Fig. 1. The model

It is a sum over all vertices $v \in V$ of our lattice and the function D is simply the symmetrized distance between the image positions $x_L(v)$, $x_R(v)$ and the corresponding epipolar lines:

$$D\big(x(v), F\big) = D^2\big(x_L(v), F \cdot x_R(v)\big) + D^2\big(x_L(v) \cdot F, x_R(v)\big),$$

where $D^2(x, l)$ is the squared distance of a point x from the line l.

The third and last energy term $E_d(x, I_L, I_R)$ in (1) is the data energy

$$E_d(x, I_L, I_R) = \frac{1}{\sigma_d} \sum_{t \in T} q\big(x(t), I_L, I_R\big).$$

It is a sum over all elementary triangles of the lattice where the function q is a similarity measure for corresponding pairs of image triangles. In the simplest case it is the sum of squared differences of intensities/colors in the image triangles $x_L(t)$ and $x_R(t)$. To calculate it, the triangles are coherently subsampled and the color values for noninteger image positions are obtained e.g. by bilinear interpolation. If non-lambertian reflexion is assumed, a more sophisticated similarity measure can be used instead.

Summarized, we obtain a Gibbs probability distribution of order three: the highest order contributions (χ and q) are defined on (elementary) triangles. According to the well known theorem of Hammersley and Clifford this p.d. is Markovian with respect to the hexagonal lattice.

3   Task Formulation and Solution

Assuming for a moment that the epipolar geometry is known, we formulate the surface reconstruction problem as Bayes decision with respect to the following loss function

$$C(x, x') = \sum_{v \in V} \|x(v) - x'(v)\|^2,$$

which is local additive. Each local addend measures the squared deviation of the esti-mated correspondence pair $x(v)$ from the (unknown) true correspondence pair $x'(v)$. Minimizing the average loss (i.e. the risk) gives the following Bayes decision [8]

$$x^*(v) = \sum_{s \in \mathbb{Z}^4} s \cdot p_v\big(x(v){=}s \mid I_L, I_R; F\big),$$

where $p_v\big(x(v){=}s \mid I_L, I_R; F\big)$ denotes the marginal a-posteriori probability for the cor-respondence pair $x(v) = s$ in the vertex v, given the images and the epipolar geometry:

$$p_v\big(x(v){=}s \mid I_L, I_R; F\big) = \sum_{x:\, x(v)=s} p\big(x \mid I_L, I_R; F\big). \tag{2}$$

Hence, we need these probabilities for the Bayes decision. It is noteworthy, that the latter gives non-integer decisions, though the states are considered as integer valued vectors.

Let us return to the general case of unknown epipolar geometry. In order to estimate the fundamental matrix in a maximum likelihood sense, we have to solve the task

$$F^* = \arg\max_F \sum_x p(x \mid I_L, I_R; F). \tag{3}$$

Because we don't know, how to perform the above sum over all state fields explicitly (in polynomial time), we propose to use the EM-algorithm in order to solve the problem iteratively. The standard approach gives the following task, which should be solved in each iteration:

$$F^{new} = \arg\max_F \sum_x p(x \mid I_L, I_R; F^{old}) \cdot \ln p(x, I_L, I_R; F).$$

Substituting our model (1) in the ln and omitting all terms which do not depend on F, we obtain

$$F^{new} = \arg\max_F \frac{1}{\sigma_g} \sum_x p(x \mid I_L, I_R; F^{old}) \sum_v D\big(x_L(v), x_R(v), F\big).$$

It is important to notice, that this step is possible, because the unknown normalizing constant Z in (1) does not depend on F. Exchanging the summations we finally obtain the task

$$F^{new} = \arg\max_F \sum_v \sum_{s \in \mathbb{Z}^4} D\big(s, F\big) \cdot p_v\big(x(v){=}s \mid I_L, I_R; F^{old}\big), \tag{4}$$

where again $p_v\big(x(v){=}s \mid I_L, I_R; F^{old}\big)$ denotes the marginal a-posteriori probability for the correspondence pair $x(v) = s$ in the vertex v given the images and the epipolar ge-ometry F^{old}. For a crisp set of correspondences the fundamental matrix can be estimated by standard techniques (see e.g. [3]). Such techniques can be easily extended for our case (4): we consider all possible correspondences, each one weighted by its marginal a-posteriori probability. It should be remarked, that the model parameters σ_g and σ_d of the model can be learned in a similar way [7].

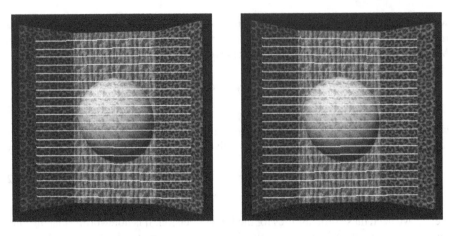

Fig. 2. An artificial stereo pair and the estimated epipolar geometry

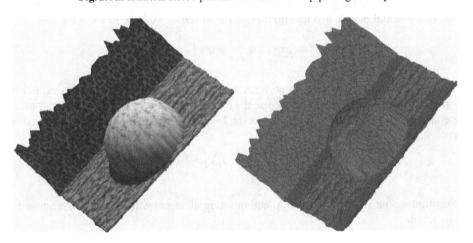

Fig. 3. Views of the reconstructed surface

Summarizing, we see, that both, the Bayes decision for the state field and the maximum likelihood estimation of the fundamental matrix can be performed, provided that the marginal a-posteriori probabilities for the states i.e. positions of corresponding points are known. We don't know how to perform the summation in (2) effectively. Nevertheless it is possible to estimate the needed probabilities using a Gibbs sampler [2]. In our particular case we iteratively choose a vertex v, fix the states in all six neighboring vertices (denoted by $\mathcal{N}(v)$) and randomly generate a new state in v according to its a-posteriori conditional probability, given fixed states in neighboring vertices

$$
p_v\big(x(v) \mid x(\mathcal{N}(v)), I_L, I_R; F\big) \sim
$$
$$
\exp\Big[\sum_{t:v\in t} \chi\big(x(t)\big) + \sum_{e:v\in e} \delta\big(x(e)\big) + \frac{1}{\sigma_g} D\big(x(v), F\big) + \frac{1}{\sigma_d} \sum_{t:v\in t} q\big(x(t), I_L, I_R\big)\Big].
$$

Fig. 4. A real stereo pair of a church fragment and the estimated epipolar geometry

Fig. 5. Views of the reconstructed surface

According to [2], the relative state frequences, observed during this sampling process, converge to the needed marginal probablities.

4   Experiments

To compare the surface reconstruction and the estimated epipolar geometry with ground truth, we used a stereo pair generated artificially by a ray-tracer (image size 350×350, disparity range 18 pixels, pan $\pm 6°$). The input images with overlaid estimated epipolar geometry are shown in Fig. 2. To check the correctness of the reconstruction results, we compared the obtained disparities with ground truth for a set of points. The maximal disparity deviation was 4.3 pixels, whereas the mean squared difference for all points was 0.2 pixels. Two views of the reconstructed surface are shown in Fig. 3.

The next example shows results obtained for a real stereo pair of a church fragment (Fig. 4). The obtained surface is shown both as a rotated view and as the obtained triangular mesh (Fig. 5). To give a better impression, we virtually cut out the deepest part of the mesh by an ortho-frontal plane.

5   Open Questions

Although our first results obtained with the proposed approach seem to be promising, there are at least three open questions. Our approach requires a good initialization for both, the initial fundamental matrix and the initial state field. So far we use standard methods – like e.g. the maximum a-posteriori decision in a simplified model for the mesh.

The second question regards the maximum likelihood estimation of the fundamental matrix. It may be preferable to consider it as a stochastic variable (instead of an unknown parameter) and to use sampling for solving a suitable posed Bayes task.

It might be preferable to use a smoothness energy term instead of the hard continuity constraint. Obviously, it is possible to express the deviation from coplanarity for pairs of neighboring triangles in terms of their states and the fundamental matrix.

References

1. Luis Alvarez, Rachid Deriche, Javier Sanchez, and Joachim Weickert. Dense disparity map estimation respecting image discontinuities: A pde and scale-space based approach. Rapport de recherche 3874, INRIA, January 2000.
2. Stuart Geman and Donald Geman. Stochastic relaxation, Gibbs distributions and the bayesian restoration of images. *IEEE Transactions on Pattern Analysis and Machine Intelligence*, 6(6):721–741, 1984.
3. R. I. Hartley and A. Zisserman. *Multiple View Geometry in Computer Vision*. Cambridge University Press, 2000.
4. Vladimir Kolmogorov and Ramin Zabih. Computing visual correspondence with occlusions via graph cuts. In *International Conference on Computer Vision*, pages 508–515, 2001.
5. Vladimir Kolmogorov and Ramin Zabih. What energy functions can be minimized via graph cuts? In A. Heyden et al., editor, *ECCV 2002*, number 2352 in LNCS, pages 65–81, Berlin Heidelberg, 2002. Springer-Verlag.
6. R. Sara. The class of stable matchings for computational stereo. Technical Report CTU-CMP-1999-22, Czech Technical University, 1999.
7. D. Schlesinger. Gibbs probability distributions for stereo reconstruction. In Gerald Krell Bernd Michaelis, editor, *Pattern Recognition*, volume 2781 of *LNCS*, pages 394–401. Springer Verlag, 2003.
8. Michail I. Schlesinger and Vaclav Hlaváč. *Ten Lectures on Statistical and Structural Pattern Recognition*, volume 24 of *Computational Imaging and Vision*. Kluwer Academic Press, 2002.

Adaptive Computer Vision:
Online Learning for Object Recognition

Holger Bekel, Ingo Bax, Gunther Heidemann, and Helge Ritter

AG Neuroinformatics, Bielefeld University
P.O. Box 10 01 31, D-33501 Bielefeld, Germany
{hbekel, ibax, gheidema, helge}@techfak.uni-bielefeld.de

Abstract. The "life" of most neural vision systems splits into a one-time training phase and an application phase during which knowledge is no longer acquired. This is both technically inflexible and cognitively unsatisfying. Here we propose an appearance based vision system for object recognition which can be adapted online, both to acquire visual knowledge about new objects and to correct erroneous classification. The system works in an office scenario, acquisition of object knowledge is triggered by hand gestures. The neural classifier offers two ways of training: Firstly, the new samples can be added immediately to the classifier to obtain a running system at once, though at the cost of reduced classification performance. Secondly, a parallel processing branch adapts the classification system thoroughly to the enlarged image domain and loads the new classifier to the running system when ready.

1 Introduction

The introduction of neural networks to the field of computer vision has brought about a change of paradigms: No longer hard-wired knowledge is used to solve recognition tasks, instead, domain specific knowledge is acquired from examples, in a way both technically easier and cognitively more adequate. However, most neural recognition systems are still a half-hearted realization of this idea, because knowledge acquisition ends after an initial training phase. To accomplish online-learning, three basic requirements have to be fulfilled: (*i*) Flexibility of the neural system to allow the fast incorporation of new knowledge without performing an entire training cycle; (*ii*) close to real-time processing within the entire system; and (*iii*) a subsystem for human-machine interaction that allows to present new object knowledge in a natural manner of communication.

The system proposed in this paper is part an office task assistance system. To fulfill the aforesaid requirements, a neural three-stage system is applied that combines feature extraction with classification. When trained online, the last and most easy to train stage can be quickly adapted to provide a provisional solution. While the system is running continuously, in a parallel thread a new version of the neural system is trained from scratch and loaded to the running system when ready to improve performance.

C.E. Rasmussen et al. (Eds.): DAGM 2004, LNCS 3175, pp. 447–454, 2004.

To cope with the requirements of processing speed and human-machine inter-action, an attentional subsystem allows the fast localization of regions of interest for object classification, and the simultaneous evaluation of pointing gestures to establish a common focus of attention (FOA) of human and machine.

While view-based systems often require large training sets [9,8] to cover the variety of possible views, the system proposed here needs only a few frames of an object to facilitate interactive online training. This is achieved by artificially multiplying the available images to obtain new object views.

While solutions to several of the subtasks outlined above have been investi-gated, integration to larger vision systems is still rarely to be found. The *Perseus* system is able to reference objects a user is pointing at [3]. Ref. [10] proposes a communication model between image processing and the adjacent data interpre-tation for object recognition. A system for hand tracking and object reference that also allows the integration of modalities other than vision was proposed for the Cora robot system [13]. The approach presented here goes beyond these systems in three aspects: (*i*) Several vision capabilities are integrated in a com-mon framework, (*ii*) using the neural approach, a single type of system deals with two sub-tasks in a unified way, and (*iii*) online learning is realized in a human-machine interaction loop.

 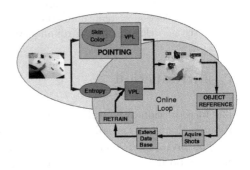

Fig. 1. Left: Office scenario, the user is pointing at objects. Right: Processing flow, starting with an image of the desk (left). In parallel, the scene is scanned (a) for pointing gestures (upper branch) using skin color segmentation and one instance of the VPL-classifier, and (b) for known objects (lower branch). If an object is pointed at, the "online loop" (right ellipse) is started. Once the referenced object location is identified, images are acquired. The database is extended by artificially distorted views (scale/shear transformation, translatory offset), then the VPL-classifier employed for object recognition is retrained (section 3.2). Note the two instances of the VPL are independent from each other.

The experimental setup is part of the VAMPIRE project (Visual Active Mem-ory Processes and Interactive REtrieval). The work is aimed at the development of an active memory and retrieval system in the context of an augmented reality scenario. An important subtask is the recognition of objects and simple actions

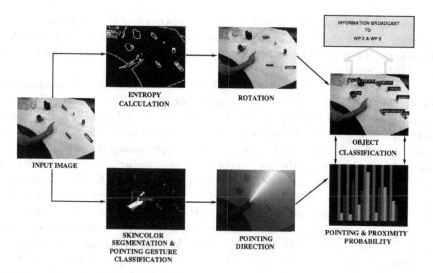

Fig. 2. Intermediate processing results. In the upper branch, the input image is processed for object classification, in the lower branch, hand gestures are detected. Objects are located by saliency maps, the example shows an entropy map. Hands can be detected by skin color. Located objects are virtually rotated to a normalized position to facilitate recognition. Recognized pointing gestures are "translated" into an attention map which shows a "beam" of activation in the pointing direction. The attentional subsystem described in [1] establishes the correspondence between pointing direction and one of the objects. In the right column, labeled objects and, below, probabilities for objects being pointed at are shown.

in an office environment. Here, a user sits in front of a desk, two cameras observe the scene, which permanently classify objects on the desk and interpret pointing gestures (Fig. 1 left). If either a completely unknown object is presented or if the system does not recognize an already trained object correctly, the user leads the system by gestures to train or retrain the object classifier. We will first describe the standard data flow of the object recognition (section 2), then in section 3 the online training triggered by hand gestures.

2   Object Recognition System

Fig. 1 depicts the processing flow of the trained recognition system in the left ellipse, Fig. 2 shows some intermediate processing results. For object localization, saliency maps are computed using different mechanisms as described in [1]. Fig. 2 depicts only the "entropy map" as an example, which derives "conspicuity" of regions from their information content after the algorithm of [4]. The method relies on the assumption that semantically meaningful areas have also a high information content in the sense of information theory. Several saliency maps are integrated in the attentional subsystem to a joint saliency map. Parameterization of this module allows the selection of the scale on which structures are evaluated (here: scale of office objects). Maxima of the joint saliency map indicate candidate regions for object classification. The representation of object locations by attention maps facilitates the integration of pointing directions to establish object reference (Fig. 2, for details see [1]).

Subsequently, the neural net based VPL-classifier classifies the candidate regions. The result is either a class number for an already trained object, or a reserved class label for "unknown". The VPL is a neural classification architecture which is particularly well suited for a fast, online training and retraining from a small data base. "VPL" stands for three processing stages, which combine feature extraction from the pixel level with classification: **V**ector quantization, **P**CA and **L**LM-networks (see [1] and references therein). The VPL-classifier extracts features from the input by local PCA, which are subsequently classified by a bank of LLM-networks. An overview of the processing flow is given in Fig. 3.

The VPL is trained as follows: The first level ("V") uses vector quantization (VQ) to partition the input space. For VQ, the algorithm proposed in [2] is employed. In the second level ("P"), for the training data assembled in the Voronoi tessellation cells of each of the resulting reference vectors, the principal components (PCs) are computed by the neural algorithm proposed in [12] to reduce dimensionality. I.e., to each reference vector a single layer feed forward network is attached for the successive calculation of the local PCs. In combination, the first two processing stages perform local PCA, which can be viewed as a nonlinear extension of simple, global PCA [14].

On the third processing level, to each PCA-net one "expert" neural classifier of the Local Linear Map – type (LLM network) is attached. The LLM network is related to the self-organizing map [5], see e.g. [11] for details. After the unsupervised training of the first and second level, the LLM-nets are now trained supervised.

The trained VPL-classifier is applied to classify in succession each of the candidate regions. Input are the raw pixel data of windows of pre-defined size located at the maxima of the saliency map. To each input vector, the best match reference vector is selected. Features are then extracted by projection of the input onto the local PCs. The overlap with the PCs is the input to the attached LLM-net, which yields the final classification.

3   Online Learning

If object classification is erroneous or new objects are to be added to the set, the user can activate the teaching mode. The teaching mode is realized as a finite state machine. It is activated by keyboard input, then the new or wrongly classified object on the desk must be indicated by a pointing gesture. The system memorizes the position of the object to be learned and starts to acquire shots of the object. After a sample image of the object has been taken, the system waits for the users hand to reappear and move the object to a different pose. When the hand is out of sight again, the system takes the next image automatically, and so on. The user decides when all relevant poses have been captured and finally

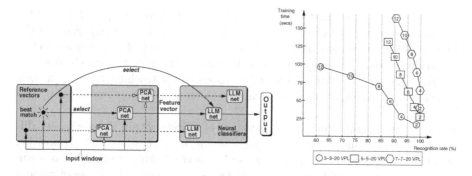

Fig. 3. Left: VPL-classifier. Features are extracted by local PCA and classified subsequently by neural classifiers. Right: Classification rates and training times for different size parameters of the VPL-classifier with respect to the number of objects learned (denoted within the symbols) using the *full training mode*.

ends the procedure by declaring the object either as "new" by giving it a new label, or as "improved" by using an old label (again using the keyboard).

After image acquisition, the system trains the currently used VPL-classifier in *fast training mode* and resumes classification. In parallel, a new VPL-classifier is trained in *full training mode*. In the following, the components of the online training are described.

3.1 Pointing Gesture Recognition

For pointing gesture recognition, a system proposed in [1] is applied, which can be described only in short. It is based on an adaptive skin color segmentation motivated by [7]. If a skin colored blob is found, the corresponding image region is classified by another instance of the VPL-classifier ("VPL-HAND"), which is not connected to the module employed for object recognition. VPL-HAND yields two pieces of information: (a) whether the skin-colored blob is a pointing hand at all, and, if so, (b) the pointing direction. The attention module then establishes the correspondence of the pointing direction and the referenced object, as described in [1].

3.2 Retraining the Classifier

The *full training mode* of the VPL-classifier comprises the three steps described in section 2: VQ, local PCA, and training of the LLM-networks. The novel, labeled object views are added to the existing set of training views, then a VPL-classifier is trained from scratch. Training time depends approximately linearly on the number of objects, most time consuming is the training of the PCA-nets. Therefore, the *fast training mode* leaves the V- and P-level unchanged and retrains only the LLM-nets. The method relies on the assumption that the existing feature extraction by local PCA is able to capture also the novel object.

So, for the newly captured views only feature vectors are computed and added to the existing set of feature vectors (which must be memorized). Each of the LLM-nets is then trained anew for the best match samples of its reference vector. Naturally, recognition rates are not as high as for the fully trained classifier.

To minimize the effort the user has to spend on teaching the system new objects, the set of online-captured training views is artificially expanded by two methods:

Scale/shear expansion: The appearance of objects within the workspace differs in scale and shear due to varying camera distance. Since the 3D-position of a newly acquired object is known, scaling and shearing transformations can be used to generate additional artificial views which cover the range of camera distances.

Translatory offset: The attentional subsystem is not always able to locate the reference frame — from which features are extracted — exactly at the object center. Therefore, object views with minor translatory offsets are added to the training set to improve classification robustness.

4   Evaluation

The VPL-classifier was tested for two aspects of online learning:

- How do different size parameters for the VPL-classifier affect training times and classification rates with respect to the number of objects?
- How do classification rates and training times differ for the *full training mode* and the *fast training mode* ?

For systematic evaluation, for each of 12 typical office objects (e.g. stapler, sharpener, highlighter) a set of 60 images was recorded in the following way: On the desk, six fixed positions were marked and the objects were placed at each of these positions. Then, 10 arbitrary poses of each object were recorded. The resulting set of images contains 720 samples of size 61×61 pixels. The 120 images recorded at a fixed reference position were used for training, the remaining 600 for testing.

The size parameters of the VPL are the number of reference vectors N_V, the number of local principal components N_P, and the number of LLM-nodes, N_L. So, VPL-size is given in the form N_V-N_P-N_L. Fig. 3, right, shows the results using the size parameters 3-3-20, 5-5-20 and 7-7-20 for the *full training mode*. The 3-3-20 classifier can be trained quite fast, but the recognition rate drops significantly as the number of objects to be learned is increased. The 5-5-20 and the 7-7-20 classifiers have better capabilities to learn more objects at high recognition rates, but the computational time needed for training increases.

Fig. 4 shows recognition rates for classifiers that were first trained in *full training mode* to recognize 2, 4, ... 10 objects and subsequently extended to recognize additional objects using the *fast training mode*. As expected, in all cases the recognition rate for a fixed total number of objects is better if all of them were trained in *full training mode*, as compared to some being learned in *fast training mode*. The recognition rate drops when more objects are trained in *fast training mode*. However, this decay is much smaller if the classifier initially holds more objects (acquired in *full training mode*), because in this case the feature extraction covers a larger variety of appearances. While for two initial objects (recognized by 100%) performance drops dramatically, for eight objects the still good initial performance of 90% only reduces to 82%. In all cases, however, the drop in recognition rate after adding just *one* new object is tolerable.

Fig. 4 shows the average training times comparing fast and fully trained classifiers with respect to different numbers of objects. Training times for *fast training mode* clearly remain below the *full training mode*.

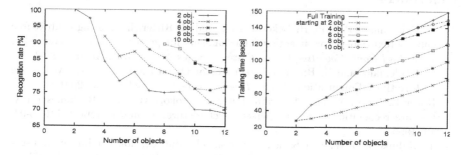

Fig. 4. Left: Classification rates for the *fast training mode*: Each curve visualizes the drop of the classification rate starting with classifiers that were fully trained on 2, 4, 6, 8 and 10 objects, respectively, and extended using the *fast training mode*. Size parameters were 3-8-20. Right: Training times for the *fast training mode* compared to full training mode. The main curve represents the training times for the *full training mode* and the forked curves represent training times for the *fast training mode* starting off with classifiers trained on 2, 4, 6, 8 and 10 objects, respectively.

5   Conclusion

We have presented a computer vision system for interactive online object learning guided by pointing gestures. The learning mechanism allows both to acquire new object knowledge and to improve classifications of already known objects. The system relies on a neural classifier, which builds a view based object representation. The system can be adapted fast to obtain a provisional version, while a full training is performed in the background. The performance of the provisional, fast training improves the more objects the system already knows — a property which is plausible also from a cognitive point of view.

An important goal of future research is a "self-diagnosis" of the system, which can give confidence values for the systems ability to classify objects correctly. By this means, an estimate for the necessary object views could be given during online training, depending on the object's complexity. Moreover, the system could ask for more training views of objects where classification appears unreliable. The self-diagnosis should also be able to judge whether the existing feature extraction is sufficient for a newly acquired object. Thus, it would be possible to decide in which cases *fast training mode* makes sense. Another goal is accelerating the offline feature adaptation, a promising approach is e.g. proposed in [6].

Acknowledgment. This work was supported within the project VAMPIRE, which is part of the IST programme (IST-2001-34401).

References

1. G. Heidemann, R. Rae, H. Bekel, I. Bax, and H. Ritter. Integrating context-free and context-dependent attentional mechanisms for gestural object reference. In *Proc. Int'l Conf. Cognitive Vision Systems*, pages 22–33, Graz, Austria, 2003.
2. G. Heidemann and H. Ritter. Efficient Vector Quantization Using the WTA-rule with Activity Equalization. *Neural Processing Letters*, 13(1):17–30, 2001.
3. Roger E. Kahn, Michael J. Swain, Peter N. Prokopowicz, and R. James Firby. Gesture recognition using the perseus architecture. Technical Report TR-96-04, 19, 1996.
4. T. Kalinke and W. von Seelen. Entropie als Maß des lokalen Informationsgehalts in Bildern zur Realisierung einer Aufmerksamkeitssteuerung. In B. Jähne, P. Geißler, H. Haußecker, and F. Hering, editors, *Mustererkennung 1996*, pages 627–634. Springer Verlag Heidelberg, 1996.
5. T. Kohonen. *Self-Organizing Maps*. Springer Verlag, 1995.
6. A. Leonardis, H. Bischof, and J. Maver. Multiple eigenspaces. *Pattern Recognition*, 35(11):2613–2627, 2002.
7. H. J. Andersen, M. Stoerring and E. Granum. Physics-based modelling of human Skin colour under mixed illuminants. *Robotics and Autonomous Systems*, 35(3–4):131–142, 2001.
8. B. W. Mel. SEEMORE: Combining color, shape, and texture histogramming in a neurally-inspired approach to visual object recognition. *Neural Computation*, 9:777–804, 1997.
9. H. Murase and S. K. Nayar. Visual Learning and Recognition of 3-D Objects from Appearance. *Int'l J. of Computer Vision*, 14:5–24, 1995.
10. J. C. Ossola, F. Bremond, and M. Thonnat. A communication level in a distributed architecture for object recognition. In *8th International Conference on Systems Research Informatics and Cybernetics*, Aug 1996.
11. H. J. Ritter, T. M. Martinetz, and K. J. Schulten. *Neuronale Netze*. Addison-Wesley, München, 1992.
12. T. D. Sanger. Optimal Unsupervised Learning in a Single-Layer Linear Feedforward Neural Network. *Neural Networks*, 2:459–473, 1989.
13. C. Theis, I. Iossifidis, and A. Steinhage. Image Processing Methods for Interactive Robot Control. In *Proc. IEEE Roman International Workshop on Robot-Human Interactive Communication*, Bordeaux and Paris, France, 2001.
14. M. E. Tipping and C. M. Bishop. Mixtures of probabilistic principal component analyzers. *Neural Computation*, 11(2):443–482, 1999.

Robust Pose Estimation for Arbitrary Objects in Complex Scenes

Peter Dörfler and Clemens Schnurr

Chair of Technical Computer Science,
University of Aachen, Germany,
doerfler@techinfo.rwth-aachen.de,
http://www.techinfo.rwth-aachen.de

Abstract. Viewer-centered estimation of the pose of a three dimensional object has two main advantages: No explicit models are needed and error-prone corner detection is not necessary. Eigenspace methods have been successful in pose estimation especially for faces. However, most eigenspace-based algorithms fail if the images are corrupted, e. g. if the object is occluded, the background differs from the training images or the image is geometrically transformed. EigenTracking by Black and Jepson uses robust estimation to find the correct pose. We show that performance degrades for objects whose silhouette changes greatly with 3D rotation. To solve this problem we introduce masks that adapt to the estimated object pose. To this end we used hierarchical eigenspaces containing both the appearance and mask descriptions. We illustrate the improvement in pose estimation precision for some typical objects.

1 Introduction

The pose of a known object is needed in many applications, most notably when the object is to be manipulated by a robot. In a real world situation the object will be part of a complex scene, i. e. the background is cluttered and the object may be partially occluded. Further, the location of the object in the scene is only vaguely known and the camera could be rotated by a small angle.

Viewer-centered approaches are often preferred to object-centered approaches due to their robustness and straightforwardness. Especially, algorithms using the eigenspace method (also PCA or Karhunen-Loeve transform) are popular since they have low complexity. However, PCA is highly sensitive to structured noise which can originate from occlusion, different background or geometric transformation of the object.

Several researches use template matching in eigenspace to solve the problem of translation. Pentland et al. use modular eigenspaces of nose, mouth and eyes for face recognition [1]. While making their approach robust to local distortions of the image, such predefined regions of interest are not available for general objects. Yoshimura and Kanade [2] efficiently find the rotation of a 2D template in the image plane through multi-resolutional eigenimages. This approach is not tolerant to occlusions and is not easily generalized to 3D objects. Chang

C.E. Rasmussen et al. (Eds.): DAGM 2004, LNCS 3175, pp. 455–462, 2004.

```
for sigma=sigma_max .. sigma_min
  for layer=highest .. lowest
    estimate coefficients c
    estimate similarity transform a
    project a and c to next layer
  endfor
endfor
```

Fig. 1. Pseudo code of the principle of EigenTracking

et al. [3] use the energy of each region in eigenspace and its second derivative to find the best match. Rotated or scaled versions of the trained objects are not found by this approach. Chang et al. also introduce a quadtree-like partition technique to achieve robustness against occlusion. There must be some partitions without occlusions for this method to work. Ohba and Ikeuchi [4] also partition the image into smaller regions centered around corners. Thus, shift invariance is given but rotation and scale of the object are not detected. Leonardis and Bischof [5] extract several models based on sets of pixels to achieve robustness against partial occlusion. The number of models needed depends on the amount and structure of the occlusion as well as on the density of pose-relevant pixels and can be very high. In a recent work they adapt their algorithm to scaled and translated objects [6]. Rotations are not detected.

Black and Jepson [7] introduce an algorithm for tracking 3D objects by their appearance. It simultaneously finds an optimal match for the appearance of the object with an eigenspace approach and estimates an affine transform for the image. While their EigenTracking algorithm works well for several situations we show its limitations for pose estimation of objects whose silhouette varies with 3D rotation in a complex scene. To overcome this problem we introduce three strategies to introduce masks to EigenTracking. They are based on an hierarchical eigenspace approach.

The remainder of this paper is organized as follows: The second section gives a brief overview of the EigenTracking algorithm. Extentions of this algorithm are introduced in section three. Section four gives illustrative examples of the improvement through masks in Eigentracking. The fifth section contains concluding remarks.

2   Using EigenTracking for Pose Estimation

Eigentracking is based on a generalization of the optical flow method. It alternates between the optimization of eigenspace coefficients and geometric (here similarity) transform. To achieve robustness against outliers an error function which gives less emphasis to large values than the square error is chosen. The amount of error tolerated is controlled by a parameter σ which decreases iteratively. Due to the confinedness of optical flow to small deviations a coarse-to-fine scheme is used as well. Figure 1 shows pseudo-code for the algorithm. We assume the reader is familiar with the concept of coarse-to-fine optimization. Thus, we will only quickly review the estimation steps from [7].

2.1   Robust Estimation of Coefficients and Affine Transform

Instead of the square error usually minimized by PCA Black and Jepson [7] use an error function $\rho(x, \sigma)$:

$$E(c) = \sum_{x} \rho\left(r(x) - [Uc](x), \sigma\right) \tag{1}$$

with the test image r, its reconstruction Uc and image index x. The column vectors of U are the eigenimages and c is a coefficient vector. The error function $\rho(x, \sigma)$ and its derivative $\psi(x, \sigma)$ are defined as.

$$\rho(x, \sigma) = \frac{x^2}{\sigma^2 + x^2} \qquad\qquad \psi(x, \sigma) = \frac{2x\sigma^2}{(\sigma^2 + x^2)^2} \ . \tag{2}$$

To compensate geometric transformations of the test image with respect to the training images, the test image is warped by a similarity transform $s(x, a)$, with a a four dimensional parameter vector. Further, image regions can be excluded from the optimization by a mask m. Including this information into (1) we obtain the error function:

$$E(c, a) = \sum_{x} m(x) \cdot \rho\left(r(x + s(x, a)) - [Uc](x), \sigma\right) \tag{3}$$

which depends on the eigenspace coefficients c and the similarity transform a. A Gauss-Newton optimization is used to minimize the error by keeping one parameter constant while optimizing the other. The mask m can contain the outliers found in a previous run of the algorithm or can depend on another source of information. We will use the latter in the following section.

3   Masks in EigenTracking

The training images used for the pose estimation each contain a single view of the object before a uniform background (cf. Fig. 2). Pixels that belong to the background in all views have zero variance and thus the corresponding element of all eigenimages is zero. Thus, areas which belong to the background in every training image are disregarded automatically.

EigenTracking is proven to work well for rotationally symmetric objects like object062. Black and Jepson also showed experiments for hand form tracking in front of a uniform background. We found, however, that the pose of objects with varying silhouette such as object001 from the COIL database, cannot be robustly determined by EigenTracking in complex scenes.

The authors suggested using masks to overcome these limitations but have not introduced an algorithm for this. In the following we employ hierarchical eigenspaces to estimate a mask for the observed view.

Fig. 2. Two objects taken from the COIL-100 database [8]. While the shape of object001 changes greatly with 3D rotation the shape of object062 is close to constant.

3.1 Hierarchical Eigenspaces

The concept of hierarchical eigenspaces is well known from Active Appearance Models [9]. First we build two separate eigenspaces: The image eigenspace with transform U_I as before and a second eigenspace for masks with transform U_M. The coefficients c_I and c_M of each view are concatenated to a combined data vector $r_C = [\, c_I \; c_M \,]$ (Weighting mask coefficients has not improved results). The corresponding transform is $\hat{r}_C = U_C c_C$ using a reduced number of dimensions. Due to the linearity of the transform U_C can be split into two parts $U_{C,I}$ and $U_{C,M}$ for images and masks. We can thus reconstruct image and mask with

$$\hat{r}_I = U_I U_{C,I} c_C \; , \qquad \hat{r}_M = U_M U_{C,M} c_C \; . \tag{4}$$

To retrieve a mask for a test image we first calculate c_I with the robust PCA estimation. Since c_M is unknown, $r_C = [\, c_I \; 0 \,]$ is used to find c_C via the robust PCA estimation, marking the c_M as outliers. The mask is reconstructed with (4).

The reconstructed mask is thresholded to receive a boolean mask which marks all pixels that are not likely to belong to the object as outliers. The threshold is decreased iteratively during optimization. For the initial guess of the coefficients, the mean mask is used. Figure 3 shows an example.

3.2 Integration into EigenTracking

There are several possibilities to integrate the mask approach into the Eigentracking algorithm (cf. Fig. 1):

- *Static Mask.* Straightforward integration of masks into Eigentracking leads to reconstruction of a mask before the optimization of the eigenspace coefficients.
- *Concurrent Masking.* The mask is updated for every step of the robust PCA coefficient estimation.
- *Combined Optimization.* Instead of optimizing the coefficients of the image eigenspace the coefficients of the combined eigenspace are optimized by robust PCA.

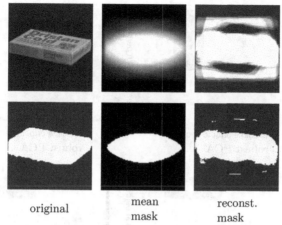

| original | mean
mask | reconst.
mask |

Fig. 3. First row: view of `object001`, mean of all masks of that object, reconstruction of mask for view. Second row: training mask of view, thresholded mean mask and thresholded reconstruction.

| occlusion & background change | occlusion, background change &
geometric transform |

Fig. 4. Typical test images of the two objects under consideration. Left: complex background and occlusion, right: additionally similarity transform applied.

4 Results

Due to the limited space available we show illustrative results for the two objects seen in Fig. 2. Performance for other objects is similar, corresponding to the amount of variation in the silhouette. We examine two scenarios: For the first experiment the background of the images is exchanged with an irregular pattern and the objects are occluded with another COIL object which covers approx. $1/8^{th}$ of the image at a random position. The second scenario involves geometric transformation of the images as well. Translations of ±10 pixels, rotation of $\pm10°$ and scale from 0.9 to 1.1 were randomly applied. Figure 4 shows some examples.

As expected the robust estimation of the eigenspace coefficients used in EigenTracking works well for objects with constant silhouette and fails when the shape of the object varies greatly (e. g. `object001`). The first row of Fig. 5 shows results for test images with occlusion and background variation. The improvement achieved with the hierarchical approach can be seen in the second row. Both mask estimation methods show similar results with Combined Optimization being slightly better. We show only those results in the following.

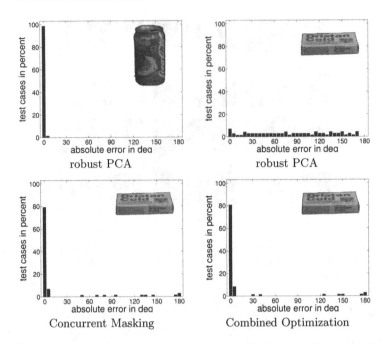

Fig. 5. Absolute error in degrees for pose estimation. First row: performance of original robust PCA. Second row: results for two novel methods.

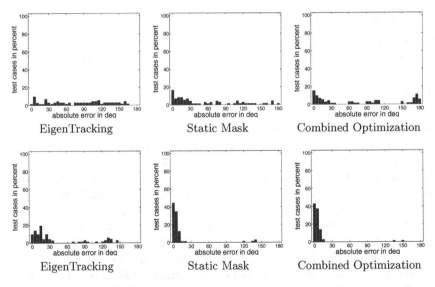

Fig. 6. Accuracy of the pose estimation without geometric transform for the robust estimation technique by Black and Jepson and for two enhancements using masks.

The second scenario was used to examine the original EigenTracking algorithm and two approaches with masks: Static Mask and Combined Optimization. Figure 6 shows results for object001 in the first row and for object062 in the second. The higher error as compared to scenario one can be explained through the similarity of neighboring views under geometric transformation.

The execution times of the algorithms vary depending on the number of iterations needed for convergence. All experiments were made on an Intel P4 2.4 GHz machine. The original EigenTracking algorithm takes 3.1 to 4.4 s, the Static Mask version 4.5 to 5.2 s, Concurrent Masking 4.7 to 6.1 s and the Combined Optimization approach approx. 10 s.

5   Concluding Remarks

We have shown that the EigenTracking algorithm by Black and Jepson is useful for pose estimation of 3D objects in cluttered scenes and under geometric transformation. However, the approach works well in complex scenes only for objects whose silhouette does not vary much depending on the view. We introduced three different methods to include masks for the object shape into EigenTracking. They improve the accuracy of the pose estimation significantly, especially when no geometric transform of the object is present. Considering the algorithmic complexity, concurrent estimation of an appropriate mask during the robust estimation of eigenspace coefficients is recommended. In the future we aim to replace the geometric transform estimation with a more robust approach than Optical Flow.

References

1. Pentland, A., Moghaddam, B., Starner, T.: View-based and modular eigenspaces for face recognition. In: IEEE Conference on Computer Vision and Pattern Recognition (CVPR'94). Volume 1., Seattle, USA (1994) 84–91
2. Yoshimura, S., Kanade, T.: Fast template matching based on the normalized correlation by using multiresolution eigenimages. In: IEEE/RSJ/GI International Conference on Intelligent Robots and Systems, Advanced Robotic Systems and the Real World. Volume 3., New York, USA (1994) 2086–2093
3. Chang, C.Y., Maciejewski, A.A., Balakrishnan, V., Roberts, R.G.: Eigendecomposition-based pose detection in the presence of occlusion. In: IEEE/RSJ International Conference on Intelligent Robots and Systems (IROS), Maui, HI (2001) 569–576
4. Ohba, K., Ikeuchi, K.: Detectability, uniqueness and reliability of eigen windows for stable verifikation of partially occluded objects. IEEE Transactions on Pattern Analysis and Machine Intelligence 19 (1997) 1043–1048
5. Leonardis, A., Bischof, H.: Robust recognition using eigenimages. Computer Vision and Image Understanding: CVIU 78 (2000) 99–118
6. Wildenauer, H., Bischof, H., Leonardis, A.: Eigenspace pyramids for robust and efficient recognition of scaled eigenimages. In: Proc. Computer Vision Winter Workshop (CVWW), Valtice, Czech Republic (2003) 115–120

7. Black, M.J., Jepson, A.D.: EigenTracking: Robust matching and tracking of articulated objects using a view-based representation. International Journal of Computer Vision **26** (1998) 63–84
8. Nene, S.A., Nayar, S.K., Murase, H.: Columbia object image library (COIL-100). Technical Report CUCS-006-96, Columbia University (1996)
9. Cootes, T.F., Edwards, G.J., Taylor, C.J.: Active appearance models. In Burkhardt, H., Neumann, B., eds.: Proc. European Conference on Computer Vision. Volume 2., Springer (1998) 484–498

Vectorization-Free Reconstruction of 3D CAD Models from Paper Drawings

Frank Ditrich, Herbert Suesse, and Klaus Voss

Friedrich-Schiller-University Jena, Department of Computer Science
Ernst-Abbe-Platz 1-4
D-07743 Jena, Germany
ditrich@minet.uni-jena.de, {nbs,nkv}@uni-jena.de
http://pandora.inf.uni-jena.de

Abstract. We propose a new approach for the reconstruction of 3D CAD models from paper drawings. Our method uses a combination of the well-known fleshing-out-projections method and accumulation techniques from image processing to reconstruct part models. It should provide a comfortable method to handle inaccuracies and missing elements unavoidable in scanned paper drawings while giving the user the chance to observe and interactively control the reconstruction process.

1 Introduction

In the past a lot of research and development work was done to find solutions for the challenging task of reconstructing 3D CAD models from 2D drawings given either on paper or in a machine-readable format like DXF.

Two main techniques can be found in the literature: The first is the fleshing-out-projections principle published by Wesley and Markovsky [6] which delivers surface models. The second are algorithms which focus on the extraction of manufacturing features[1] directly from the 2D input data (e. g. [1,3,5]).

Both require high-quality complete vector data. Therefore vectorization techniques are used to convert bitmap data into vector data, but this is a very complicated process which requires a great amount of user interaction and parameter adjustment to get satisfying results. Nevertheless it is practically impossible to extract exact data from paper drawings since the drawings themselves are imperfect. The complete description of a part can only be obtained by interpreting the geometric sketches together with the textual information like measures or symbols.

Another group of methods wich are of interest in this context perform the extraction of manufacturing features directly from 3D boundary-representation models (for example from IGES or STEP files) [2,4].

---

[1] The term "feature" is well-known in the context of image processing and pattern recognition. However, it is also used in computer-aided design and manufacturing to denote basic construction or manufacturing elements like solids made by sweeping a profile along a line or around an axis or shapes resulting from milling or drilling.

C.E. Rasmussen et al. (Eds.): DAGM 2004, LNCS 3175, pp. 463–470, 2004.

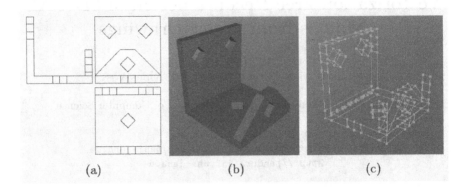

Fig. 1. A sample part with three projections and its pseudo-wireframe.

Our solution tries to overcome the difficulties associated with the vectorization by directly combining the 2D bitmap data in 3D space and extracting manufacturing features from this generated data.

2   Basic Idea

In Fig. 1a,b a sample 3D part with three projections (left, top, front) is shown. In these projections all edges are drawn as solid lines regardless of visibility. The first stage of the fleshing-out-projections algorithm [6] is applied to these projections to construct a so-called pseudo-wireframe also shown in Fig. 1c. This pseudo-wireframe is different from the wireframe of the original part because it contains some additional vertices and edges, which are discarded in later stages of the algorithm. But to the human observer there is a great amount of similarity between the part and the pseudo-wireframe. The basic structure and shape of the part is clearly visible.

The basic idea behind the creation of the pseudo-wireframe is to combine the projections in 3D space to get candidates for vertices and edges. A somewhat similar technique can be applied also to the bitmap data instead of the vector data: Fig. 2a shows scanned pencil drawings of the three projections with some perturbations and changes in the quality of lines as they usually appear in CAD drawings. Now the following is done: The projections are mapped to the XY, XZ and YZ planes of a coordinate system in a 3D lattice so that every projection is properly aligned with each other. That means that for example the X coordinates of the XY and XZ qprojections of a 3D point are the same. Now we create a 3D voxel structure from these projections by adding the intensities of corresponding projection image pixels (and normalizing the resulting intensity range to $[0.0, 1.0]$ through division by the maximum value afterwards).

Fig. 2c shows the resulting histogram of voxel intensities for our sample part (scaled in y-direction by factor 50). We distinguish four ranges: 0 to 0.5, 0.5 to 0.7, 0.7 to 0.9 and 0.9 to 1. They can be interpreted as containing different elements of the voxel model: Suppose our images would only contain black lines

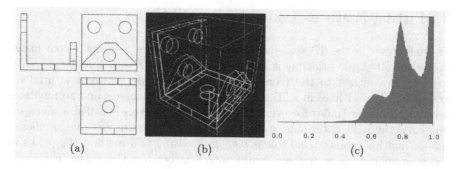

(a)   (b)   (c)

Fig. 2. Three projections of a sample part scanned from paper, the resulting voxel model (intensities from 0.0 to 0.45) and its histogram, scaled by factor 50 in y-direction.

(intensity 0) on a white background (intensity 1). By adding the pixel intensities and performing a normalization as described above we would get four different voxel intensities: 0, $\frac{1}{3}$, $\frac{2}{3}$ and 1. Obviously we would have a small number of voxels with intensity 0 and a very large number with intensity 1 (for this reason the histogram has to be scaled to make the ranges visible). If we take the voxels from the first range, we get the structure shown in Fig. 2b. To get a better quality for later recognition tasks, here we took the range 0 to 0.45. Such a correction could easily be done manually by the user according to his visual impression.

Obviously there is a remarkable similarity between the pseudo-wireframe constructed above and the resulting voxel structure. Indeed the following can be shown: If we have projections of a part, then two voxel sets can be obtained: The first by creating the pseudo-wireframe and rastering its edges into a 3D voxel space (intensities 0 and 1, painting a voxel black if it is intersected by a line), the second by rasterizing the projections into 2D bitmaps and creating a 3D voxel model as described above. If we extract the sets of black voxels V_1 and V_2 from both models, then V_1 is a subset of V_2.

By using this method it should be possible to get 3D data to which real 3D features can be fitted without an intermediary vectorization which can introduce an additional loss of information. Besides this, the voxel model could give a person whose task is to make a 3D part from a drawing a first impression of the structure of the part and could be used as a component of a comfortable user interface to a feature recognition system working on this data. The user gets the ability to interact with and guide the system supporting his work. This is useful because it seems quite sure that a fully automatic recognition/reconstruction system cannot be built due to the great variety of paper drawings and the problems concerning the quality of drawings.

One practical problem should be mentioned here: For processing larger scanned drawings a great amount of memory would be necessary if we would store the voxels in a three-dimensional array. But this can be overcome by first determining the interesting range from the histogram (which can be calculated without storing all voxels) and afterwards storing only those voxels which lie in this range in an appropriate data structure.

3   Fitting Features Using Accumulation

To fit features in the 3D space we use an accumulation technique from image processing. Its basic principle is known as *randomized Hough transform* (*RHT*, see [7]). In contrast to the (conventional) Hough transform as it is used for example to dectect lines in a 2D set of points, which calculates and accumulates several parameter tuples for every single point (in [7] this is called a *diverging mapping*) the RHT determines and accumulates one parameter tuple for chosen sets of multiple points (*converging mapping*). Using this method the peaks in the accumulator space become significantly sharper (for the above mentioned case of detecting lines the RHT accumulator contains the squared values of the Hough accumulator). Furthermore, in [7] it is shown that it is not necessary to accumulate over all possible point subsets, even the accumulation over an adequate number of randomly chosen subsets gives sharp peaks, which decreases the running time.

The RHT method can be generalized to other objects which can be described by a set of parameters. The drawback is that if we have some more parameters we also need a larger accumulation space in which only small regions are really used. One possible solution to overcome this problem is doing the accumulation not in the accumulation space itself but in lower-dimensional projections of it.

The drawback of this variant is the loss of information caused by the projection process to lower-dimensional parameter spaces. It can be very hard resp. impossible to find the right peaks in these projections since there can be pseudo-peaks which arise simply through adding all hits along a projection line instead of being produced by existing objects.

Another solution to the above mentioned problem is a clustering technique: Instead of using an accumulator array we maintain a list of clusters. Our algorithm for this accumulation process (using the random selection of points) is given in the following. It is controlled by three functions and three values (we denote with $\mathbf{p}$ a parameter tuple $(p_1, \ldots, p_k)$):

- A test function $t(\mathbf{p})$ with the return values "valid" and "invalid", which checks if a tuple $\mathbf{p}$ is a valid parameter tuple for an object we search for,
- a quality function $\mu(\mathbf{p})$ which determines a properly defined quality measure for the object determined by $\mathbf{p}$,
- a distance function $d(\mathbf{p}, \mathbf{q})$ which determines the distance of two parameter tuples,
- a number $step_{max}$ which gives the maximum number of point tuples to be chosen,
- a minimum quality measure μ_{min} which gives a minimum quality for an object to be accumulated,
- a minimum distance d_{min} to consider two parameter tuples to be different.

The algorithm gets a set of points as input and delivers a list of accumulated parameter tuples (together with a weight and quality for each). Especially the quality function μ is of great importance, since it constrains the number of clusters being created during the accumulation process. Since for every parameter tuple created for a randomly selected point set the difference to every existing cluster has to be calculated, the running time of the algorithm would make it unsuitable for practical application if there were no criterion to eliminate unusable clusters. In the above example for accumulating lines such a quality function could count the number of points near the line described by two parameters.

1. Set $step = 0$.
2. Increment $step$ by 1. If $step > step_{max}$ the algorithm is completed.
3. Otherwise choose a tuple of n points randomly and calculate the parameter tuple $\mathbf{p}$.
4. If the test function $t(\mathbf{p})$ yields "invalid" go to 2.
5. If the quality function $\mu(\mathbf{p})$ yields a value lower than a minimum quality μ_{min} then go to 2.
6. If the list of accumulation clusters is empty then initialize the list with $\mathbf{p}$ as the first element (with weight 1) and go to 2.
7. Search the accumulation list for a tuple $\mathbf{q}$ with a distance $d(\mathbf{p}, \mathbf{q}) < d_{min}$. If there are several such tuples, choose one with a minimum value $d(\mathbf{p}, \mathbf{q})$.
8. If such a tuple $\mathbf{q}$ is found (we denote its weight with $w_{\mathbf{q}}$) then replace it by $\mathbf{q}' = (w_{\mathbf{q}}\mathbf{q} + \mathbf{p})/(w_{\mathbf{q}} + 1)$ with the new weight $w_{\mathbf{q}'} = w_{\mathbf{q}} + 1$ and go to 2.
9. If no such tuple is found then add $\mathbf{p}$ with the weight 1 as a new tuple to the accumulation list and continue with 2.

3.1   Boxes

With our accumulation method not only geometric primitives but also complex shapes can be found, for example axis-parallel rectangular boxes described by six parameters $\mathbf{p} = (x_{min}, x_{max}, y_{min}, y_{max}, z_{min}, z_{max})$. We search for boxes the edges of which are contained in our voxel data. To achieve this we define the quality function in an appropriate manner: If we have a box described by the six parameters we divide every edge in a number of cells and check how many percent of these cells contain data points (here we use 10 cells per edge). As a distance between two tuples we simply use the maximum distance between corresponding parameters:

$$d(\mathbf{p}, \mathbf{q}) = \max_{i=1,\ldots,6} |p_i - q_i| .$$

To get the six parameters we simply choose n points and determine their bounding box. The choice of the number n influences the recognition quality and should depend on the kind of data we have: If there is a point set which consists only of one box (and our task is only to determine its parameters) we should choose a higher number of points to increase the chance to hit the whole box after a few iterations. But if there is additional noise in the data (a lot of separate points not being part of the box) we should choose a smaller n since the greater n is, the greater is the chance to choose some of the wrong points, so there will be a smaller chance to get the correct box.

We carried out some experiments and found out that 4, 5, and 6 are suitable values for n for our purposes. In the following we used $n = 6$.

Besides the presence of noise, another problem is the correct recognition of several objects. If we have a scene with k boxes the probability of choosing n points belonging to the same box is $\left(\frac{1}{k}\right)^{n-1}$ (if chosing the same point multiple times is allowed), which significantly decreases with increasing k. Nevertheless it makes sense to apply our method to the voxel data: We do not try to find all boxes contained in the data automatically but give the user the chance to direct the recognition process. In our software prototype it is possible to select a region of voxels to be used for recognition. Here we use the fact that a user is able to get a principal impression of the model structure and can select interesting regions containing boxes. After the accumulation process is done the found boxes are presented to the user and he can iterate through them (they can be sorted by their qualities or the weights of their clusters) and choose the right ones. A sample is shown in Fig. 3a.

3.2   Cylinders

Another class of objects which can be found using the accumulation method are axis-parallel cylinders. They appear in the voxel structure as two circles on parallel planes (assumed the planar faces of the part are also axis-parallel). To describe them we use six parameters: The coordinate direction which is parallel to the axis of the cylinder (p_1), two coordinates to describe the position of the axis in a plane perpendicular to the axis direction (p_2, p_3), the radius (p_4) and two values for the coordinate range the cylinder covers along the axis direction (p_5, p_6). Of course we have to slightly modify our list accumulation algorithm to handle the first parameter correctly: It is a flag describing one of three directions, so the new cluster cannot be calculated as described above, instead our distance function must guarantee that tuples with different directions are never collected in the same cluster. Here the distance between two parameter tuples $\mathbf{p} = (p_1, \ldots, p_6)$ and $\mathbf{q} = (q_1, \ldots, q_6)$ is defined as

$$d(\mathbf{p}, \mathbf{q}) = \begin{cases} \infty & \text{if } p_1 \neq q_1 \\ \max_{i=2,\ldots,6} |p_i - q_i| & \text{otherwise} \end{cases} .$$

For the calculation of parameter tuples we choose three points and calculate one possible tuple for any of the three possible axis directions. Suppose the axis direction is given it is easy to determine the position of the axis and the radius. As the covered range we use the appropriate minimum and maximum coordinate values of the three points.

To determine the quality of a parameter tuple we also divide the two circles into cells and count how many percent of them contain points (in our prototype we use 20 cells for each).

3.3   Extrusions

The accumulation cannot only be used to detect shapes but also to find transformations between point sets. This can be used for example to find features

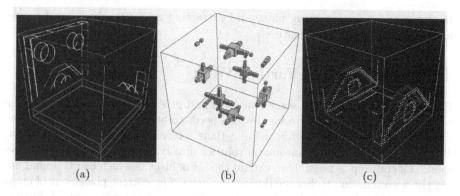

Fig. 3. A recognized box in a selected subset of the voxels from Fig. 2b (see Section 3.1), the accumulator content after accumulating translations for an axis-parallel box and a recognized translation (see Section 3.3).

which are created by a translational sweep of a profile (usually called *extrusion* or *extrusion feature*). To find the corresponding translations we use a three-dimensional accumulator and accumulate for every pair of distinct points the translation which maps one point onto the other (we do not choose the point pairs randomly). If the voxel structure contains profiles which are "connected" through a translation we should get corresponding peaks in the accumulator.

But there is one problem: The edges contained in the voxel structure would also produce peaks since there are a lot of pairs with points lying on the same edge with the same distance. To solve this problem we should check if there are a lot of points near the line connecting the two points. An appropriate data structure can easily be built from the voxel set in a preprocessing step.

The list accumulation described above is not so well-suited for this purpose since a large number of clusters will be generated which increases the running time of the algorithm.

Fig. 3b shows the content of an accumulator for an axis-parallel box, the size of the cubes illustrates the number of hits in the cells. As expected there are prominent peaks for the six translations connecting the three pairs of rectangles forming the boundary of the box. In Fig. 3c the sample part with a detected translation is shown. Since arbitrary translations are allowed there are a lot of translations besides the six most prominent which have also a significant number of hits in the accumulator.

Of course we can limit to searching for axis-parallel translations, which could be found using three one-dimensional accumulators and would restrict the set of pairs which need to be checked.

The computational effort raised through the checking of all pairs can also be decreased by equally thinning the voxel set, if the resulting accuracy is sufficient.

If some translations are detected for every translation the two sets of points which are mapped onto the other by this translation can be built and visualized in the user interface (see Fig. 3c). The sets can be further processed for example by determining a supporting plane and extracting contours which can be used as a base for an extrusion feature.

4   Conclusions and Further Work

Finally we like to mention some problems and give some prospects on further work. One very important problem which needs to be solved is the correct alignment of the three views before adding their intensities to get the voxel data. Perhaps here also a semi-automatic solution involving user interaction can be found. Of course it is possible to extend the set of objects which can be found using the accumulation technique described above. The correct placement of cross sections within the voxel data is another extension to our paradigm. A further important task is the automatic selection of interesting voxel subsets on which the accumulation procedure will be applied. Currently this has to be done by the user. A first simple solution could be the search for connected components in the voxel data, since holes appear in most cases separated from the other edges of the part. Ideally the system would be able to find those regions automatically and to extract the contained features. Then all possible combinations of the found features using boolean operations could be built to create the possible parts. Perhaps this set could be constrained using geometric properties like for example the fact that an isolated cylinder must always be a hole. From each of these generated parts the 2D views could be derived and compared to the original ones using an appropriate similarity measure.

The relationship and degree of similarity between the voxel model and the pseudo-wireframe resp. between the sets V_1 and V_2 from Section 2 is also an interesting subject to further theoretical investigations.

References

1. Ganesan, R.; Devarajan, V.: *Intersecting features extraction from 2D orthographic projections*. Computer-Aided Design 30(11), pp. 863-873, 1998.
2. Mäntylä, M.; Nau, D.; Shah, J.: *Challenges in Feature-Based Manufacturing Research*. Communications of the ACM, 39(2), pp. 77-85, 1996.
3. Meeran, S.; Taib, J.M.: *A Generic Approach to Recognising Isolated, Nested, and Interacting Features from 2D Drawings*. Computer Aided Design 31(14), pp. 891-910, 1999.
4. Requicha, A.A.G.: *Geometric Reasoning for Intelligent Manufacturing*. Communications of the ACM, 39(2), pp. 71-76, 1996.
5. Shum, S. S. P.; Lau, W. S.; Yuen, M. M. F.; Yu, K. M.: *Solid reconstruction from orthographic views using 2-stage extrusion*. Computer-Aided Design 33(1), pp. 91-102, 2001.
6. Wesley, M. A.; Markowsky, G.: *Fleshing out projections*. IBM Journal of Research and Development, 25(6), pp. 934-954, November 1981.
7. Xu, L.; Oja, E.: *Randomized Hough Transform (RHT): Basic Mechanisms, Algorithms, and Computational Complexities*. CVGIP: Image Understanding, 57(2), pp. 131-154, March 1993.

Globally Consistent 3-D Reconstruction by Utilizing Loops in Camera Movement

Ingo Scholz* and Heinrich Niemann

Lehrstuhl für Mustererkennung, Universität Erlangen-Nürnberg,
Martensstr. 3, 91058 Erlangen, Germany
{scholz,niemann}@informatik.uni-erlangen.de

Abstract. A common approach to 3-D reconstruction from image sequences is to track point features through the images, followed by an estimation of camera parameters and scene geometry. For long sequences, the latter is done by applying a factorization method followed by an image-by-image calibration. In this contribution we propose to integrate the tracking and calibration steps and to feed back already known camera parameters to both tracking and calibration. For loop-like camera motion, reconstruction can thus be optimized by using loop-closing algorithms known from robot navigation.

1 Introduction

Reconstructing 3-D scene geometry and camera parameters from a sequence of images is a common problem in many computer vision applications. One of these applications, for which the approach described in the following was developed, is the computation of light fields [5]. The light field is an image-based scene model where a set of original images is used to render new views of a scene from arbitrary camera positions. Beside image data and geometry information light fields require very accurately determined camera parameters for good rendering results.

If no information is available about the camera pose and internal parameters they are estimated by so-called structure-from-motion approaches [7]. Using feature detection and tracking algorithms point correspondences are established between the images of a sequence. These are used by a factorization algorithm to simultaneously determine the scene geometry (structure) and camera poses (motion) of multiple images. Usually there are not enough point correspondences to process the whole image sequence at once using one factorization, therefore the camera parameters of the rest of the sequence are computed image by image using camera calibration methods. This approach is described in detail in [3].

The main problem arising during this extension process is that, though errors may be small from one image to the next, they accumulate over a large number of images leading to inconsistencies in the geometry reconstruction. In the following

---

* This work was funded by the German Research Foundation (DFG) under grant SFB 603/TP C2. Only the authors are responsible for the content.

C.E. Rasmussen et al. (Eds.): DAGM 2004, LNCS 3175, pp. 471–479, 2004.

we will consider the case that a hand-held camera is moved in loops around a scene, e. g. to view an object from every direction or to get a dense sampling. The approach we will introduce was inspired by solutions in the field of simultaneous localization and mapping (SLAM) for robot navigation. Here, the goal is to generate a globally consistent map of the surroundings of a robot [6], while the data from the robot's sensors, e. g. odometry and a camera, are unreliable. Consistency of the map can be established when the robot returns to a previous position and recognizes landmarks it has seen before. The accumulated error can then be determined and the rest of the map corrected accordingly. For the case of 3-D reconstruction we will now use the occurrence of a loop in camera movement to update the pose of all previous cameras in the loop. The error introduced by this process is reduced by bundle adjustment.

The idea of using topology information to improve reconstruction was implemented before in [4], where a zigzag motion of the camera was utilized to track a feature in an increased number of images. In [1] the accumulated reconstruction error of a turntable image sequence is distributed to all camera position estimates by aligning several sub-sequences. A similar distribution of errors is done in [9] for image mosaics, although in this case the camera motion is constrained to rotations only.

A description of the linear, integrated structure-from-motion approach of tracking, factorization and frame-wise extension will be given in Section 2. The closing of loops by information feedback and optimization is the topic of Section 3, and its experimental evaluation is described in Section 4. A summary and outlook to the future are given in the conclusion.

2   Linear Calibration Process

The usual processing chain for a 3-D reconstruction of a scene is to first generate the required point correspondences for all images followed by the respective algorithms for structure-from-motion. In the work at hand we want to demonstrate the usefulness of feeding back information from the calibration step to the tracking and subsequent calibration. Therefore, tracking and calibration are first integrated into a linear processing chain as shown in Figure 1.

First, feature tracking is done until the number of tracked points reaches a lower bound and a factorization is performed for the images so far. In the second loop the features are tracked to the subsequent images and a camera calibration is applied for each. Thus the camera movement and 3-D points are recovered image by image. Last, the reconstruction is optimized by bundle adjustment on all camera positions and points.

The individual steps of this linear processing chain will be described in more detail in the following, whereas the extension to an iterative process, including information feedback, will be introduced in Section 3.

2.1   Feature Detection and Tracking

In order to get accurate point correspondences over a large number of images feature detection and tracking are performed using the gradient-based algorithm

Initialize frame number: $i := 0$	
	Track point features to frame i and detect new ones
	$i := i + 1$
UNTIL min. number of features visible in all frames reached or $i = N - 1$	
Apply factorization method to first i frames	
WHILE $i < N$	
	Track point features to frame i and detect new ones
	Triangulate 3-D points and calibrate frame i
	$i := i + 1$
Apply bundle adjustment to all frames and 3-D points	

Fig. 1. Linear tracking and calibration over N images in two steps: factorization of initial subsequence and calibration of subsequent images

by Tomasi and Kanade [11] and the extension by Shi [8]. In the latter robustness is increased by considering affine transformations for each feature window.

This procedure has been further augmented by a hierarchical approach which computes a Gaussian resolution pyramid for each image, thus increasing the maximum disparity allowed between two images. A final improvement incorporates illumination compensation which solves for many problems occurring in environments which are not particularly lighted [14].

2.2 Factorization and Calibration Extension

For the images in the first block of Figure 1 structure and motion in the sequence are recovered using a factorization method assuming weak-perspective projection [7]. It yields the camera pose parameters for a set of images and the 3-D position of each feature visible in every image. In order to gain a perspective reconstruction of the camera poses perspective projection matrices are constructed from the result of the preceding factorization. Since the intrinsic parameters are unknown the principal point is assumed to be in the image center. For the focal length a rough approximation of the correct one is chosen as described in [3]. Camera parameters and 3-D points are then optimized using the Levenberg-Marquardt algorithm minimizing the back-projection error. Intrinsic parameters are assumed to be constant which results in a small but acceptable error due to the wrongly estimated focal length.

Once this initial reconstruction of the first subsequence is available, it can be used as a calibration pattern for calibrating the subsequent images. Features which are visible in the next image to be calibrated but whose 3-D positions are not yet available are triangulated using their projections in the already calibrated images. With these correspondences the camera position can be estimated using common calibration algorithms [12], and the result is optimized again by minimizing the back-projection error. In fact this optimization is accurate enough so that for small camera movements it can be initialized with the position of the last camera and the calibration step can be omitted entirely.

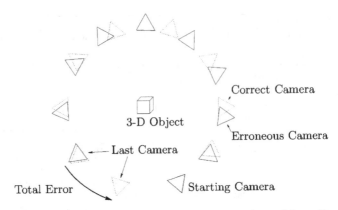

Fig. 2. Example reconstruction of a camera path around an object. Correct camera positions are denoted by dotted triangles, erroneous ones by solid triangles.

2.3 Bundle Adjustment

The optimization of the camera parameters and 3-D points in the steps before was always done for one camera after another and in turn with the point positions. In contrast to that the idea of bundle adjustment is to optimize all these parameters at once to reduce the back-projection error globally. This straightforward approach, as used in [2] for scene reconstruction, has the disadvantage of a very large parameter space to be optimized. Therefore the less complex interleaved bundle adjustment [10] is used in the following.

Bundle adjustment is usually applied to an image sequence as a whole. For long sequences with more than 100 images it is very time consuming, especially if it is repeated every m images as explained later in Section 3.3. Therefore the method was adapted to support the optimization of only a few cameras at a time. The camera positions in such a subsequence are optimized jointly but without considering the rest of the sequence, while the 3-D points are optimized considering all cameras. Thus, back-projection error is only slightly increased for cameras outside the subsequence, while it is improved for those inside.

3 Feedback Loop

The main problem of the linear calibration process described in Section 2 is that small errors from one frame to the next accumulate over time and may thus lead to serious displacements of the camera positions. This is demonstrated in Figure 2, where a camera moves in a circle around an object taking 10 images in the process. The correct camera positions are equally spaced around the object, but an error of only about four degrees from each camera to the next adds up to more than 35 degrees. In order to get a correct reconstruction the circle must be closed again by removing this inconsistency. This situation is equivalent to a robot moving in a loop through some complex environment, and the approach introduced in the following is used similarly for mapping the robot's environment.

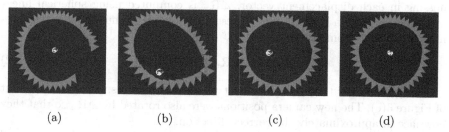

(a)   (b)   (c)   (d)

Fig. 3. (a) Linear, erroneous reconstruction. (b) Loop closed without considering rotation. (c) Loop closed considering rotation. (d) Final, optimized reconstruction.

3.1   Closing Loops

Although in case of a hand-held camera it may be moved back to any earlier position, we assume here that N camera positions form a loop and that camera 0 follows again on camera $N-1$. In contrast to the linear calibration process used before features are now tracked from image $N-1$ to image 0, thus establishing a relationship between the two images. By applying the extension step of Section 2.2 the displacement between the last and the first camera position, $\Delta \mathbf{t}_{N-1}$, is calculated with a much higher accuracy than before when the accumulated error was included. Going back to the image of a robot this is the equivalent of recognizing a formerly seen landmark.

Using this new information the task of closing the loop is again formulated as an optimization process. For now, only the translation vector of each camera, $\mathbf{t}_n$, is considered. The displacement vector between two cameras is denoted by $\Delta \mathbf{t}_n = \Delta \tilde{\mathbf{t}}_n = \mathbf{t}_{n+1} - \mathbf{t}_n$ for $0 \leq n < N-1$. Additionally, $\Delta \tilde{\mathbf{t}}_{N-1}$ constitutes the current displacement vector between last and first camera while $\Delta \mathbf{t}_{N-1}$ is the corresponding target displacement calculated above. Thus, for $0 \leq n < N$ the $\Delta \mathbf{t}_n$ form the desired set of displacements while the $\Delta \tilde{\mathbf{t}}_n$ are the displacements to be optimized. The residual vector is defined as

$$\epsilon = \left((\Delta \mathbf{t}_0 - \Delta \tilde{\mathbf{t}}_0)^T, (\Delta \mathbf{t}_1 - \Delta \tilde{\mathbf{t}}_1)^T, \ldots, (\Delta \mathbf{t}_n - \Delta \tilde{\mathbf{t}}_n)^T \right)^T \qquad (1)$$

and using the Levenberg-Marquardt algorithm the camera positions $\mathbf{t}_n, n > 0$ are optimized by minimizing the residual $\epsilon^T \epsilon$. The first camera position $\mathbf{t}_0$ is kept unchanged.

The result of an erroneous, linear reconstruction of an example sequence is shown in Figure 3(a). Here, an object was placed on a turntable and rotated in 40 steps with one image taken for each. Applying the optimization above for closing this circle yields the reconstruction of Figure 3(b), which is obviously not satisfactory. The rotations between the displacement vectors $\Delta \mathbf{t}_n$ do not sum up to a full circle, therefore the optimization does not yield a circle either.

The solution is to incorporate the missing rotation to a full circle into the computation of the residual vector. This rotation is calculated as the rotation difference between the last and the first camera pose, $\Delta \mathbf{R} = \mathbf{R}_0 \mathbf{R}_{N-1}^T$. Lacking any other knowledge we assume that the $\frac{n}{N}$th part of this rotation, $\Delta \mathbf{R}_n$, is missing in each displacement vector. $\Delta\mathbf{R}_n$ is computed using spherical linear interpolation [13] on a quaternion representation of $\Delta\mathbf{R}$. Thus the new displacement vectors are computed as

$$\Delta\hat{\mathbf{t}}_n = \Delta\mathbf{R}_n\mathbf{R}_n(\mathbf{t}_{n+1} - \mathbf{t}_n). \tag{2}$$

Using these new target displacement vectors $\Delta\hat{\mathbf{t}}_n$ the result improves to that of Figure 3(c). The new camera positions were also rotated by $\Delta\mathbf{R}_n$ so that they now face in approximately the correct direction.

Usually an image sequence does not consist of exactly one revolution around an object. More circular camera movements may follow the first one, and in such cases it is not desired to change the camera positions in a loop already closed before. From there on, the position of a camera once adjusted is kept untouched, and the algorithm above is only applied to later cameras.

3.2   Optimizing Reconstruction

Changing the camera positions renders the 3-D point positions invalid, as seen in Figures 3(b) and 3(c), and they have to be recalculated. This is done by again minimizing the back-projection error during an optimization of the 3-D points.

Finally the result is again optimized globally using bundle adjustment as described in Section 2.3. The intrinsic parameters are assumed to be correct and bundle adjustment is only applied for the extrinsic parameters. The final result of such an optimization is shown in Figure 3(d). If only some cameras of a loop were adjusted in the closing step before, only those are optimized now, too.

3.3   Finding Loops

In a common application such as scene reconstruction from the images of a hand-held camera it is not known when a camera loop has been completed and the closing algorithm should be applied. The example of Figure 3 of an object on a turntable thus constitutes a special case since the end of the circle is known beforehand. For the general case a simple comparison scheme is used. A camera position is a neighbour of the current camera if its distance is smaller than k times the average distance between two consecutive camera positions and is not one of the m last positions. k and m are user-defined values. In order to assure that the corresponding images show approximately the same part of the scene a maximum viewing direction difference can be defined additionally.

An unsolved problem using this method is that large displacements, as in the example above, are not detected, while the closing algorithm makes the more sense the larger the accumulated error. This contradiction will be exemplified in the experiments in Section 4.

4   Experiments

Measuring the accuracy of a structure-from-motion reconstruction is a difficult problem especially for real scenes. The back-projection error is often used as

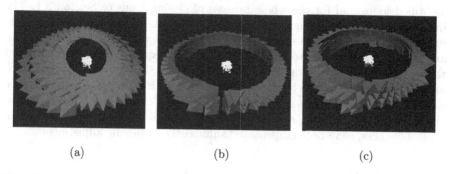

(a)   (b)   (c)

Fig. 4. Reconstruction of the Santa Claus image sequence: (a) linear reconstruction, (b) only bundle adjustment on loops, (c) loops closed and bundle adjustment.

Table 1. Back-projection errors and camera position differences for the two example image sequences

	back-projection error [pixel]			position difference		
	linear rec	only bundle	close+bundle	linear rec	only bundle	close+bundle
Sequence 1	1.28	1.75	2.06	11.7	11.5	5.18
Sequence 2	1.15	2.96	3.61	13.5	7.49	8.34

a measure, but it depends highly on the quality of feature points, and a low back-projection error may still not give a satisfactory result.

Given ground-truth data for the camera positions a direct comparison to the reconstruction is possible and more meaningful. Therefore, two example sequences were chosen of an object being placed on a turntable and with a camera mounted on a robot arm above the table. Sequence 1 was already shown in Figure 3. It consists of 40 images of a coke can, taken during one revolution of the turntable. Sequence 2 was taken from a Santa Claus figure with five revolutions of the turntable and 40 images each, where the robot arm was moved upward on a circle by 3 degrees after each revolution. The result of only a linear calibration is shown in Figure 4(a). For the improved calibration loops were detected automatically every tenth image after reconstruction of the first revolution, yielding the much improved results of Figures 4(b) and 4(c).

For comparison, the ideal camera positions were calculated from the turntable and robot arm positions. The reconstruction differs from the ideal one by a rotation, translation and scale factor. Using axis-angle notation for the rotation the 7 parameters of this transformation are estimated using (again) Levenberg-Marquardt to optimally register the two reconstructions with each other. The error value for the camera positions is calculated as the average distance of two corresponding cameras.

As mentioned before in Section 3.3 the closing of loops makes the more sense the larger the accumulated error. This issue is reflected in the experimental results of Table 1. Both the average back-projection errors and camera position differences are given for the reconstruction using only bundle adjustment on identified loops and for the whole process of closing loops of Section 3.1. The linear reconstruction of sequence 1 has a large accumulated error therefore closing loops has a great effect on the position difference while just applying bundle adjustment is insufficient to reduce this error. For sequence 2 on the other hand the accumulated error is rather low (the gap visible in Figure 4(b)) and thus, although this gap is closed for the reconstruction with closing in Figure 4(c), the camera position difference is still lower without the closing step. The inaccuracies introduced by closing, represented by the increased back-projection error in both sequences, were not compensated sufficiently by bundle adjustment.

5   Conclusion

In this contribution we proposed a method for creating a globally consistent scene reconstruction from an image sequence of a hand-held camera. Loops in the movement of the camera are detected and the accumulated error due to the linear calibration process is compensated by closing this loop. This approach is used similarly in robot navigation for simultaneous localization and mapping (SLAM). The results of each loop are optimized by bundle adjustment.

Since the closing introduces some error on each camera position it works well for the compensation of large errors, but for small displacements using only bundle adjustment may yield better results. Thus the main issues for future work are the identification of loops despite large errors and the reduction of errors introduced during the closing process.

References

1. A. W. Fitzgibbon and A. Zisserman. Automatic camera recovery for closed or open image sequences. In *European Conference on Computer Vision (ECCV)*, volume 1, pages 311–326, 1998.
2. R. Hartley. Euclidean reconstruction from uncalibrated views. In *Lecture Notes in Computer Science*, pages 237–256. Springer-Verlag, 1994.
3. B. Heigl. *Plenoptic Scene Modeling from Uncalibrated Image Sequences*. ibidem-Verlag Stuttgart, January 2004.
4. R. Koch, M. Pollefeys, B. Heigl, L. van Gool, and H. Niemann. Calibration of hand-held camera sequences for plenoptic modeling. In *International Conference on Computer Vision (ICCV)*, volume 1, pages 585–591, September 1999.
5. M. Levoy and P. Hanrahan. Light field rendering. In *Proceedings SIGGRAPH '96*, pages 31–42, New Orleans, August 1996. ACM Press.
6. F. Lu and E. Milios. Globally consistent range scan alignment for environmental mapping. *Autonomous Robots*, 4:333–349, October 1997.
7. C. J. Poelman and T. Kanade. A paraperspective factorization method for shape and motion recovery. *IEEE Transactions on Pattern Analysis and Machine Intelligence*, 19(3):206–218, March 1997.
8. J. Shi and C. Tomasi. Good features to track. In *IEEE Conference on Computer Vision and Pattern Recognition (CVPR)*, pages 593–600, Seattle, Washington, 1994. IEEE Computer Society.

9. H.-Y. Shum and R. Szeliski. Construction and refinement of panoramic mosaics with global and local alignment. In *Sixth International Conference on Computer Vision (ICCV'98)*, pages 953–958, Bombay, January 1998.

10. R. Szeliski and P. Torr. Geometrically constrained structure from motion: Points on planes. In *European Workshop on 3D Structure from Multiple Images of Large-Scale Environments (SMILE)*, pages 171–186, Freiburg, Germany, June 1998.

11. C. Tomasi and T. Kanade. Detection and tracking of point features. Technical report, Carnegie Mellon University, April 1991.

12. E. Trucco and A. Verri. *Introductory Techniques for 3-D Computer Vision.* Addison–Wesley, Massachusets, 1998.

13. A. Watt and M. Watt. *Advanced Animation and Rendering Techniques.* Addison–Wesley, 1992.

14. T. Zinßer, C. Gräßl, and H. Niemann. Efficient feature tracking for long video sequences. In *DAGM '04: 26th Pattern Recognition Symposium*, August 2004. To appear.

A Probabilistic Framework for Robust and Accurate Matching of Point Clouds

Peter Biber, Sven Fleck, and Wolfgang Strasser

WSI/GRIS, University of Tübingen

Abstract. We present a probabilistic framework for matching of point clouds. Variants of the ICP algorithm typically pair points to points or points to lines. Instead, we pair data points to probability functions that are thought of having generated the data points. Then an energy function is derived from a maximum likelihood formulation. Each such distribution is a mixture of a bivariate Normal Distribution to capture the local structure of points and an explicit outlier term to achieve robustness. We apply our approach to the SLAM problem in robotics using a 2D laser range scanner.

1   Introduction

Matching point clouds is an important problem in computer vision and robotics. For example 3D range scans taken from di.erent positions have to be integrated to build 3D models. In this case a six-vector of parameters has to be estimated. The case of 2D point clouds with three parameters to be estimated (a 2Dtranslation and a rotation) is significant for the simultaneous localization and mapping (SLAM) problem in robotics when using a 2D laser range scanner as sensor. Such a device measures range values of a 2D slice of the environment and is a common input sensor for mobile platforms. Scenarios in large buildings, where long cycles have to be closed, require both accurate scan matching results and good estimates of uncertainty to distribute accumulated errors accordingly. At the same time the scan matcher should be robust, because real environments tend to be non-static: People are moving, doors are opening and closing and so on. Such events give raise to outliers and the better the scan matcher tolerates this the better it can be used for mapping and localization.

This paper focuses on 2D point clouds with an Euclidian 2D transformation to be estimated. Nevertheless, we claim that our view of the problem is also relevant for other cases, for example for the full 3D case. The emphasis is on the probabilistic framework that is used to derive our scan matching algorithm. In previous work we have shown experimentally the capability of our algorithm to build accurate maps in realtime using range scan matching [2]. Here we give both a theoretical justification and improvements.

2   Previous Work

The standard approach to the rigid registration problem is the *Iterated Closest Point (ICP)* algorithm or variants thereof. The name ICP was introduced in the

C.E. Rasmussen et al. (Eds.): DAGM 2004, LNCS 3175, pp. 480–487, 2004.
© Springer-Verlag Berlin Heidelberg 2004

seminal paper by Besl and McKay [1], but similar ideas were developed independently at the same time by Zhang [21] and Chen and Medioni [5]. We will now repeat this algorithm brie.y and thereby introduce the notation utilized in the rest of the paper. Although the role of the two point clouds to be matched is exchangeable we speak of data points which are to be registered with a model or model points. Let $\mathbf{x}_i$ be a data point and assume that an initial estimate of the parameters is given. Then map each $\mathbf{x}_i$ according to these parameters into the coordinate frame of the model. Without explicitly noting, the $\mathbf{x}_i$ are alwaysthought of as being mapped by the current parameter estimation in the rest of the paper, that is $\mathbf{x}_i$ is in effect a function of the transformation parameters. The ICP algorithm now iterates two subsequent steps:

1. Correspondence: For each $\mathbf{x}_i$, find the closest point $\mathbf{m}_i$ of the model.
2. Estimate new parameters, such that the sum of squared distances between each $\mathbf{x}_i$ and $\mathbf{m}_i$ pair is minimized. Update the $\mathbf{x}_i$ according to the new parameters.

There is a closed form solution for the second step. Several researchers noted that the convergence properties of this point-to-point approach is poor and that point-to-plane correspondences (as used by Chen [5]) perform much better (e.g. [17]). In the field of mobile robotics Lu and Milios estimated normals from the scan [13] and this way incorporated kind of a point-to-line metric. Robust methods typically consist of leaving out points that have too large residuals.

Fitzgibbon [9] proposed to replace the closed-form solution by a non-linear energy function and to use the Levenberg-Marquard (LM) algorithm to minimize it. This allowed him to incorporate a robust kernel, as it is used in M-Estimators [16, 19]. The immediate problem here is the calculation of first derivatives that are needed by the LM algorithm. His solution is to *calculate* distances to closest points on a regular grid (instead of the closest points themselves). This way, the spatial derivatives can be calculated numerically at each grid point and interpolated in between. Interestingly, a similar approach using even an octree (but without using robust kernels) was already proposed 1992 [4]. Our solution is similar in that we use a regular spatial grid. But the information at each grid point is much more sophisticated in that it contains also a model of the local environment going beyond simple interpolation. For optimization we use Newton's algorithm instead of LM. This algorithm has better convergence properties at the cost of requiring "real" second derivatives (compared to the Gauss-Newton approximation of the Hessian used in LM). One benefit of our method is that these can be calculated analytically.

3   A Probabilistic Approach

This section presents a probabilistic interpretation of the ICP algorithm, constituting the base for the design of a robust energy function that captures the local structure of points. As mentioned earlier, the correspondence step pairs each point $\mathbf{x}_i$ to a model point $\mathbf{m}_i$. Assuming that the location of points which correspond to m_i were generated by a normal distributed random process with parameters $\mathbf{m_i}$ and σ_i, the likelihood of having measured $\mathbf{x_i}$ is:

$$p(\mathbf{x_i}) \equiv \exp. - \frac{d_i^2}{2\sigma_i^2}, \tag{1}$$

with $d_i = |\mathbf{x_i} - \mathbf{m_i}|$. So the Normal Distribution $N(\mathbf{m_i}, \sigma_i)$ can be interpreted as a *generative process* for $\mathbf{x_i}$: It is assumed that the location of $\mathbf{x}_i$ has been generated by drawing from this distribution.

Now the problem of estimating the transformation parameters can be formulated as a Maximum Likelihood problem: The parameters are optimal if the resulting transformed data points $\mathbf{x}_i$ maximize the following likelihood function:

$$\Psi = \sum_i \exp. - \frac{d_i^2}{2\sigma_i^2}, \tag{2}$$

Equivalently the negative log-likelihood of Ψ can be minimized:

$$-\log \Psi = \sum_i \frac{d_i^2}{2\sigma_i^2}, \tag{3}$$

If the variances are equal for each i this is the energy function that is minimized by ICP. In a similar manner a point-to-line measure can be formulated. Then d_i denotes the distance to the line. Solely the domain has to be limited to a finite range. Otherwise the integral over the probability function is unlimited and cannot be normalized.

Fig. 1(a) and (b) show the underlying probability density functions (*pdf* s). Both can be generalized by a bivariate Normal Distribution:

$$p(x) \equiv \exp. - \frac{1}{2}(\mathbf{x_i} - \mathbf{m})^t \mathbf{C}^{-1}(\mathbf{x_i} - \mathbf{m}) \tag{4}$$

where $\mathbf{C}$ is a symmetric 2×2 matrix. If $\mathbf{C}^{-1}$ has two equal eigenvalues, it becomes the Point-to-Point measure. If one eigenvalue is near zero, the pdf becomes the Point-To-Line measure. Figure 1(d) illustrates such a distribution and how it can be understood as a product of two univariate Normal Distributions.

Our view is now as follows: In the correspondence step each data point is assigned a generative process in the form of a pdf that is considered to have generated its coordinates. This probability function is not necessarily restricted to be a Normal Distribution, any pdf that captures the structure of points locally well is a candidate pdf.

Now we deal with how to choose a good probability density function: The pdf should be able to approximate common structures (like lines) well and should at the same time be robust against outliers. This paper proposes to use a mixture of a bivariate Normal Distribution and an uniform distribution. That mixture reads:

$$p(\mathbf{x}) = \xi_1 \exp. \frac{1}{2}(\mathbf{x} - \mathbf{m})^t \mathbf{C}^{-1}(\mathbf{x} - \mathbf{m}) + \xi_2 p_{\text{outlier}}, \tag{5}$$

where p_{outlier} is the expected ratio of outliers.

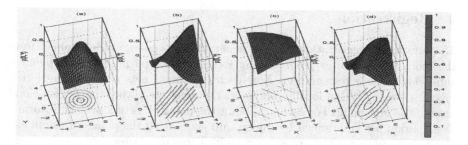

Fig. 1. Some probability density functions which are interpreted as generative processes for the points of the point cloud. (a) Point-To-Point (b) Point-To-Line (c) Point-To-Line, orthogonal to the line of (b) with larger variance (d) Product of (b) and (c): A bivariate Normal Distribution that is determined by a point and a covariance matrix.

The constants ξ_1 and ξ_2 can be determined by requiring that the probability mass of p must equal one in a finite region (for example one by one meter). As shown above, the use of a bivariate Normal Distribution allows the modelling of points, lines and anything in-between with inclusion of expected variances. The influence of data points is therefore weighted in a sound way. On the other hand, the log-likelihood of this mixture probability ful.lls the requirements for robust functions used in M-estimators: It grows subquadratically and the influence of outliers vanishes at some point. Figure 2 illustrate these claims. Together, this mixture leads to an accurate and robust energy function.

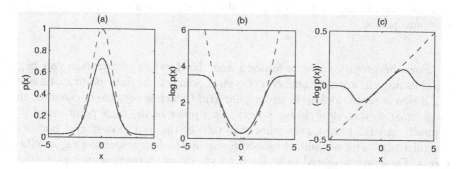

Fig. 2. Comparison between Gaussian generative process (red dashed) and a mixture process with outlier model (blue solid). Likelihood (a), negative log-likelihood (b) and influence function (c) which is the derivative of (b). For parameter estimation the negative log-likelihood of the generative process is used to build the function that is to be minimized. The influence function characterizes the bias that a particular measurement has on the solution [3]. For the Gaussian the influence of outliers grows without bounds.

4   Registration

To perform the registration, at first generative processes are determined from the model's points in a preprocessing step. For this purpose the 2D plane is subdivided into a regular grid. Now each grid point gets a pdf assigned (the mixture, see eq. 5) that locally represents the structure of the model point cloud around the grid point. For each grid point the parameters of a bivariate Normal Distribution are determined by taking into account all the points of the model cloud that are in a certain range around it. These parameters are simply determined by the mean and the covariance matrix of all these points. The expected outlier ratio is set to a constant (we use 0.3). If a density function around a grid point should not be approximated well, it will become rather uniform (large variances in both principal directions). If it can be approximated well it will provide strong constraints by small variance in at least one principal direction. At the same time it will still be robust through the outlier term. Figure 3 shows some examples.

Fig. 3. Bivariate Normal Distributions calculated around several example grid points in real laser range scans. The cells shown here have a dimension of one by one meter. One such distribution is determined by the covariance matrix and the mean of the contained points.

Now the preprocessing is finished and the iterative registration can begin. Establishing the correspondence between a point of the data point cloud and a pdf is now a simple lookup in the regular grid (which is possible in constant time in contrast to finding a closest point). As a point of the data point cloud does typically not fall onto a grid point, the pdfs of the four closest grid points are assigned to it. This is handled by adding up all the four respective log-likelihood terms. These are weighted bi-linearly, which assures a continuous log-likelihood function. Summing up all the data point's log-likelihood terms results in an energy function which is to be optimized with respect to the transformation's parameters.

5   A Computational Advantageous Approximation for Optimization

The summands of the energy function to be optimized consist of terms that have the form $log(c_1 exp - \frac{1}{2}(x - m)^t C(x - m) + c_2$. These have no simple first and second derivatives. This section presents an approximation that allows a cheap analytical computation of gradient and Hessian (needed by Newton's algorithm). A look at fig. 2(b) suggest, that a robust log-likelihood function of the form $p(x) = -\log(c_1 e^{-\frac{x^2}{\sigma^2}} + c_2)$ could be approximated by a Gaussian: $\tilde{p}(x) = d_1 e^{-\frac{d_2 x^2}{\sigma^2}} + d_3$. Parameters d_i are fitted by requiring that $\tilde{p}(x)$ should behave like $p(x)$ for $x = 0$ and $x \to \infty$, and additionally $p(\sigma) = \tilde{p}(\sigma)$ (in the bivariate case the function's values are required to be equal at the one sigma contour). The derivatives of this approximation do now have an extremely simple form and can be calculated cheaply. Main computational effort is the evaluation of only one exponential function per data point to calculate both gradient and Hessian.

6   Some Experimental Results

First we present some examples. Fig. 4 shows the log-likelihood functions generated by several typical laser range scans with bright values meaning high probabilities, approximated by the method of the last section. Here, black values do not stand for zero probability but for the logarithm of the expected outlier probability! The typical scan match time (including calculation of the log-likelihood functions' parameters) is under 10 ms if the initial guess by odometry is taken into account. The initial error is then only around a few centimeters and some degrees in rotation. Newton's algorithm converges in the majority of cases in two to five iterations. The distance between grid points is 50 cm and an environment of one by one meter is used to calculate means and covariance matrices.

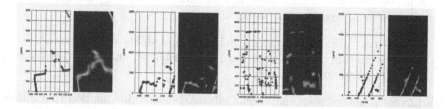

Fig. 4. Some example log-likelihood functions around grid points.

We use the scan matcher as the basis for building maps using a mobile robot equipped with a laser scanner as data acquisition platform. Our approach here belongs to a family of techniques where the environment is represented by a graph of spatial relations obtained by scan matching [14, 11, 10]. A spatial relation consists of the parameters estimated by our technique and a measure of uncertainty. This measure is provided by the Hessian of the energy function at the optimum and is used to distribute errors accordingly through the graph. Details and more experimental results can be found in [2]. Figure 5 gives an impression of the accuracy of our method. The data set there consist of 600 scans taken in a large (around 50 by 60 meters) environment with two long loops to be closed.

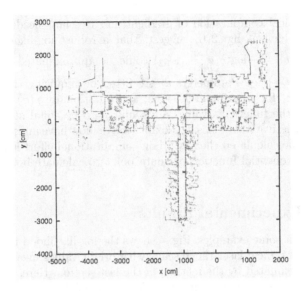

Fig. 5. A map built using our registration technique with data acquired from a 2D laser range scanner, visually demonstrating the accuracy of our results. Range scan data courtesy of T. Duckett, University of Örebro.

7   Conclusion

This paper presented a probabilistic framework for the registration of point clouds. The main contributions were:

1. The concept of explicitly pairing points to probability distributions.
2. Using a mixture of a bivariate Normal Distribution and an outlier term to model local structure of points.

We further proposed a computational advantageous approximation that allows simple calculation of gradient and Hessian. In our approach, each "magic" number has a clear defined meaning thanks to the probabilistic framework.

We applied our technique to the SLAM problem in robotics with excellent experimental results on various data sets. Some of the data sets consisted of several tens of thousand scans and we take the succesful processing of these sets as an experimental proof for the claimed robustness.

Future work will focus on techniques for robust estimation of the probability functions in the regular grid and on higher order models to derive probability functions from. Another challenge is the design of mixtures with components that adapt over time like it has been done in computer vision applications for tracking [12], perhaps also integrating the simultaneous tracking of moving objects.

Acknowledgements. Peter Biber gratefully acknowledges his funding by a DFG grant (STR 465/11-1).

References

1. P.J. Besl and N.D. McKay. A method for registration of 3d shapes. *IEEE Transactions on Pattern Analysis and Machine Intelligence*, 14(2):239–256, 1992.
2. P. Biber and W. Straßer. The normal distributions transform: A new approach to laser scan matching. In *International Conference on Intelligent Robots and Systems (IROS)*, 2003.
3. M. Black and A. Rangarajan. On the unification of line processes, outlier rejection, and robust statistics with applications in early vision. *IJCV*, 19(1):57–92, July 1996.
4. Guillaume Champleboux, Stephane Lavallee, Richard Szeliski, and Lionel Brunie. From accurate range imaging sensor calibration to accurate model-based 3-d object localization. In *CVPR'92*, pages 83–89, 1992.
5. Y. Chen and G.G. Medioni. Object modeling by registration of multiple range images. *Image and Vision Computing*, 10(3):145–155, 1992.
6. I.J. Cox. Blanche: An experiment in guidance and navigation of an autonomous robot vehicle. *IEEE Transactions on Robotics and Automation*, 7(2):193–204, 1991.
7. J.E. Dennis and R. B. Schnabel. Numerical Methods for Unconstrained Optimization and Nonlinear Equations. *SIAM Classics in Applied Mathematics*, 1996.
8. Chitra Dorai, Juyang Weng, and Anil K. Jain. Optimal registration of object views using range data. *IEEE TPAMI*, 19(10):1131–1138, 1997.
9. Andrew Fitzgibbon. Robust registration of 2d and 3d point sets. In *Proceedings of the British Machine Vision Conference*, pages 662–670, 2001.
10. Udo Frese and Tom Duckett. A multigrid approach for accelerating relaxationbased slam. In *Proc. IJCAI Workshop on Reasoning with Uncertainty in Robotics (RUR 2003)*, 2003.
11. Jens-Steffen Gutmann and Kurt Konolige. Incremental mapping of large cyclic environments. In *Proceedings of the 1999 IEEE International Symposium on Computational Intelligence in Robotics and Automation*.
12. Allan D. Jepson, David J. Fleet, and Tomas F. El-Maraghi. Robust online appearance models for visual tracking. *IEEE Transactions on Pattern Analysis and Machine Learning*, 25(10), October 2003.
13. F. Lu and E. Milios. Robot pose estimation in unknown environments by matching 2d range scans. In *CVPR94*, pages 935–938, 1994.
14. F. Lu and E.E. Milios. Globally consistent range scan alignment for environment mapping. *Autonomous Robots*, 4:333–349, 1997.
15. Takeshi Masuda and Naokazu Yokoya. A robust method for registration and segmentation of multiple range images. *CVIU*, 61(3):295–307, 1995.
16. Peter Meer, Doron Mintz, Azriel Rosenfeld, and Dong Yoon Kim. Robust regression methods for computer vision: A review. *IJCV*, 6(1):59–70, 1991.
17. K. Pulli. Multiview registration for large data sets. In *Int. Conf. on 3D-DIM*, 1999.
18. Szymon Rusinkiewicz and Marc Levoy. Efficient variants of the ICP algorithm. In *Proc. of the Third Intl. Conf. on 3D-Dim*, pages 145–152, 2001.
19. Charles Stewart. Robust parameter estimation in computer vision. *SIAM Review*, 41(3):512–537, 1999.
20. Bill Triggs, Philip McLauchlan, Richard Hartley, and Andrew Fitzgibbon. Bundle adjustment – A modern synthesis. In W. Triggs, A. Zisserman, and R. Szeliski, editors, *Vision Algorithms: Theory and Practice*, LNCS, pages 298–375. Springer Verlag, 2000.
21. Z. Zhang. Iterative point matching for registration of free-from curves and surfaces. *International Journal of Computer Vision*, 13(2):119–152, 1994.

Large Vocabulary Audio-Visual Speech Recognition Using the Janus Speech Recognition Toolkit

Jan Kratt, Florian Metze, Rainer Stiefelhagen, and Alex Waibel

Interactive Systems Laboratories
University of Karlsruhe (Germany)
{kratt, metze, stiefel, waibel}@ira.uka.de

Abstract. This paper describes audio-visual speech recognition experiments on a multi-speaker, large vocabulary corpus using the Janus speech recognition toolkit. We describe a complete audio-visual speech recognition system and present experiments on this corpus. By using visual cues as additional input to the speech recognizer, we observed good improvements, both on clean and noisy speech in our experiments.

1 Introduction

Visual information is complementary to acoustic information in human speech perception, especially in noisy environments. Humans can disambiguate an acoustically confusable phoneme using visual information because many phonemes which are close to each other acoustically are very different from each other visually. The connection between visual and acoustic information in speech perception is demonstrated by the so-called McGurk Effect [1]. Visual information such as gestures, expressions, head-position, eyebrows, eyes, ears, mouth, teeth, tongue, cheeks, jaw, neck, and hair, could improve the performance of machine speech recognition [2,3]. Much research has been directed towards developing systems that combine the acoustic and visual information to improve accuracy of speech recognition [4,5,6,7]. Many of the presented audio-visual speech recognition systems work on a very limited domain, i.e. either only spelled digits [8,9,10] or letters [11,12,13] are recognized, or only a small vocabulary is addressed [14]. For large vocabulary audio-visual speech recognition, the work by Potamiamos, Neti et al. [15,16,17] has been presented. Their AVSR system is probably the most sophisticated system today.

In this work we also targeting the task of large vocabulary audio-visual speech recognition. Our approach is to use the Janus speech recognition toolkit [18,19], which was developed in our lab and to integrate visual speech recognition into this system. For our experiments we use the data that was used during the workshop on audio-visual speech recognition held at John-Hopkins University in 2000 [15]. In the experiments we observed improvements, both on clean and noisy speech, by using visual cues as additional input to the speech recognizer and hope to further improvements by an enhanced preprocessing and normalization of the data.

C.E. Rasmussen et al. (Eds.): DAGM 2004, LNCS 3175, pp. 488–495, 2004.

Fig. 1. Some pictures of the recorded faces taken from the videos.

2   Databasis

The data provided for our experiments consists of nearly 90 GB of video footage with an overall duration of about 40 hours. During recording of the videos, the speakers were placed in front of a light-colored wall and looked right into the camera. All videos have a resolution of 704 x 480 pixels and a frequence of 30Hz. Figure 1 depicts some sample pictures from the videodata.

Audio data was recorded at a sampling rate of 16kHz in a relatively clean audio environment. The utterances were made in a quiet office with only the noise of some computers in the background.

The utterances are composed of a vocabulary of about 10500 words. For the training we got about 17000 utterances from 261 speakers with a total length of about 35 hours. The testset is made of 26 speakers with about 1900 utterances. These utterances have a total length of four and a half hours. The exact numbers are given in table 1.

Table 1. Available audio visual stored utterances for training and test.

Set	Utter.	Duration	Spk.
Training	17111	34.9 h	261
Test	1893	4.6 h	26

In this work, not all speakers could be used for visual recognition, because the extraction of visual cues failed for some speakers. The biggest set we used consisted of 120 speakers for training a stream-recognizer (see section 4.3). For this system, 17 speakers were used for testing.

The speakers, for which the detection of the region of interest is most robust are selected by an automatic process which considers the variation in the position of the mouth, the variation in the width of the mouth and the number of frames, where the facial features could not be detected at all. Only those speakers were selected, where the respective values are below a certain thresholds.

3   Visual Preprocessing

In order to use the video images of a user's lips for speech recognition, the lips first have to be found and tracked in the video images. We use the program described in [20] to find eyes, nostrils and the lip corners in the pictures. The found lip corners are used to detect the mouth region for the visual training/recognition. For this purpose, a square around the corners is taken with them at the left and right border at about half of the height.

To compensate different illumination conditions and different skin tone of the subjects in the video images, we normalize the extracted mouth regions for brightness. A sample image is depicted in Figure 2.

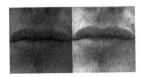

Fig. 2. The effects of the normalization of the brightness.

As the audio processing works with 100 timeslices every second it would be best to have a video stream with 100 frames per second, but the videos are recorded at a rate of 30Hz. To achieve a signal with 100Hz the existing frames are repeated three times and every third frame four times.

Once having a video stream with a frequency of 100Hz, the pictures are cosine transformed and the 64 coefficients with the highest summation over all training frames are searched as the best coefficients. During selection of the best 64 coefficients the first row and column is ignored because they consist of constant informations which gives no information for the shape of the mouth. Only the 64 best coefficients are used for training and recognition, they keep nearly all information about the video signal. The results are the same when taking all 4096 elements but the training and recognition takes much longer.

As a next step the video signal is delayed by 60ms to achieve better synchronization of acoustic and visual cues. This step is performed because the movements of the lips usually start some time before a sound is produced [12, 21].

4   Experiments

This section describes the audio-visual speech recognition experiments we performed. The first step in building the audio-visual speech recognizer was to train an audio-only recognition system. This was done by using an existing speech recognizer to label the transcriptions of the audio-visual data with exact timestamps. Once this was done, a new speech recognizer was trained on all 261 speakers in the audio-visual data set to get an audio-only reference system.

For the training of the visual recognizer, we use only up to 120 speakers. This was done because the visual lip-tracking module did not provide useful results for all of the video sequences and because training of the visual recognizer was quite time-consuming.

For the visual recognizer, we used a set of 13 visemes, as proposed by [15]. Twelve of these visemes were modeled with three states (begin, middle, end), resulting in 37 viseme states.

In the remainder of this section, we describe the different experiments that we performed. We then present and discuss the obtained results in Section 5.

4.1   Concatenation of Feature Vectors

As a first experiment, we simply concatenated the acoustic and visual input features and trained a speech recognizer on the combined feature vector. The acoustic part of the input vector consists of 13 cepstral coefficients per frame; as visual features, 64 DCT-coefficients are used. In order to provide context to the recognizer, five frames before and after the actual one are connected to the feature vector, which results in a feature vector with 847 elements. To reduce the dimensionality of the feature vector, a linear discriminant analysis (LDA) is calculated. The resulting 42 most significant coefficients are then used as input feature vector for the recognizer.

By concatenating the visual and acoustic input features, an acoustic speech recognition system can easily be adapted to perform audio-visual recognition with little changes. This approach, however, has several drawbacks: First, since the feature vector becomes large, training of the system becomes computationally expensive. A more severe disadvantage is that the importance or contribution of audio- and videodata to the recognition process gets unbalanced, since more features are used for the visual input than for acoustic input. Thus, important information in the audiodata might get lost by performing LDA.

4.2   Reducing the Feature Space

As the first case is not very flexible in changing the given weights for the video- and audio data a more flexible approach is needed to combine acoustic and visual cues. In [15] a hierarchical LDA approach (HiLDA) to reduce the audio-visual feature space was suggested. In this approach, LDA is performed on the visual and acoustic input vector separately. The resulting reduced vectors are then combined and again LDA on the combined audio-visual feature vector is performed.

This procedure has two advantages: First, the computational load is reduced. Now three matrix multiplications are needed for calculating the LDA transformation instead of one before, but the matrices are much smaller. As the needed operations for a matrix multiplication grow by $O(n^3)$ the overall needed number decreases. Second, this approach allows for better adjusting of the weights of the different modalities. We obtained good results when first reducing the visual feature vector to only 10 coefficients and the acoustic vector to 90 coefficients. During the second LDA step a reduction to 42 coefficients is performed.

4.3   Stream Recognizer

While the hierarchical LDA approach gives much more flexibility than a simple concatenation, it still has some disadvantages that could be solved by a stream recognizer which processes acoustic and visual features independently. For building such a system, a separate classifier is trained to compute likelihoods for each of the input streams separately. Results are then combined at a later stage. This system has proven to give the best results. For the combination the possible hypotheses are scored for each stream and then combined by the given stream weights. For our system best results were achieved if the audiodata gets weighted by 70%.

As the weights for audio- and videodata are not combined before the recognition process it is not necessary to train a stream recognizer again because of changing the weights. This behavior can save a lot of time while testing different scenarios because only the test must be computed for each one. In the two cases described before the training must be computed again for each test.

Another advantage of this additional flexibility is the possibility to automatically adapting the recognizer to a given environment, e.g. by measuring the signal-to-noise ratio of the audio-signal.

5   Results

Now the results of the different audio visual speech recognizers are presented. As the stream recognizer provides the best results the most detailed results are available for this system. Tests on small subsets show the advantage of the HiLDA and stream recognizer to the simple feature concatenation attempt. First we trained three audio-visual recognition systems and an audio only system with 14 speakers. Testing was done on five separate speakers. As can be seen in table 2 the audio only system performs best in this case, followed by the stream recognizer and the HiLDA approach. The concatenation is the worst of the tested scenarios.

The poor audio-visual recognition results in this case are likely due to the little amount of training data. As there is a high variability in the video, more training data is needed.

In our second experiment, we therefore trained the systems with 30 speakers (see Table 2). As you can see, now audio-visual recognition outperforms pure acoustic recognition, even on clean audio data. Testing was again done on five subjects.

In our last experiment we trained an audio-visual stream recognition system with a much bigger training set. Since the acoustic and visual parts of the stream recognizer can be trained independently, different amount of training data can be used for each modality. To train the acoustic part of the recognizer, we used

Table 2. Audio visual word error rates for a System trained on clean audiodata, five speakers are used for the test set.

	14 speakers	30 speakers
audio	48.28%	39.29%
concat	51.36%	40.11%
HiLDA	49.16%	38.48%
stream	49.28%	38.24%

Table 3. Audio visual word error rates for a System trained on 120 speakers for the video part and all 261 speakers for the audio case.

stream weights audio:video	clean audio	noisy audio
100:0 (audio-only)	**25.26%**	**53.94%**
90:10	24.78%	51.19%
80:20	24.30%	48.53%
70:30	**24.10%**	**47.37%**
60:40	24.29%	48.05%
50:50	25.52%	52.72%

all 261 speakers. For the visual part, we used only those 120 speakers, were the automatic tracking of the lips performed the best. Testing was done on 17 subjects.

Table 3 depicts the recognition results depending on the stream weights. It can be seen that weighting the acoustic stream by 70% led to the best recognition results, both on clean and on noisy audio. On clean speech, WER of the audio-visual system is 1% lower than the audio only system (5% relative improvement). In the case of noisy audio, the relative WER decreases by 12.5%: word error rate is dropped from 53.94% absolute to 47.37% absolute.

The noise level was selected to get a similar dimension of WER as in [15]. Figure 3 shows the progression of recognition rates for different SNR values. For rising noise levels higher improvements of the audio visual against the audio only recognition rates are achieved.

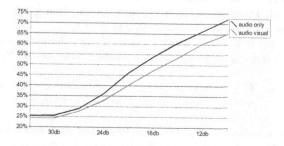

Fig. 3. Plot of word error rates for different SNR values.

6   Conclusion and Future Results

In this paper we have described how audio-visual speech recognition can be done with the Janus speech recognition toolkit, a HMM-based state of the art speech recognizer. Experiments were performed on a large vocabulary speaker independent continuous speech recognition task. We obtained good experimental results by training a stream recognizer, which first computes log likelihoods for each of the input modalities and then combines these hypotheses using the stream weights. With this approach, relative improvements on both clean and noisy speech were obtained. The achieved amount of improvements in relative WER is by now about half of the improvements reported in [15]. We think that this is mainly due to the fact that we could only use a fraction of the data used in [15].

The presented system provides a good basis for further audio-visual speech recognition research. We are now working on the improvement of the facial feature tracking approach in order to being able to use more speakers from the database. In fact, we are now already able to use 200 speakers instead of 120 used for the presented experiments.

Among the first things that we plan to improve is the visual preprocessing of the data. So far, only histogram normalization is done. Since we observed that some subjects tilted their heads quite significantly, we hope to improve the recognition results by appropriate rotation of the input images in the future. Adaptive adjustment of the combination weights for the input modalities should also improve the recognition results in the future.

Acknowledgments. This research has been funded by the European Communities project CHIL, Contract Number IST-506909.

References

1. H. McGurk and J. MacDonald. Hearing lips and seeing voices. Nature, 1976
2. G. Potamianos, C. Neti, S. Deligne. Joint Audio-Visual Speech Processing for Recognition and Enhancement. Proceedings of AVSP 2003, 2003
3. R. Goecke, G. Potamianos, C. Neti. Noisy Audio Feature Enhancement using Audio-Visual Speech Data. ICASSP 02, 2002
4. M.E. Hennecke, K.V. Prasad, D.G. Stork. Using deformable templates to infer visual speech dynamics. 28th Annual Asimolar conference on Signal speech and Computers.
5. A.J. Goldschen, O.N. Gracia, E. Petajan. Continuous optical automatic speech recognition by lipreading. 28th Annual Asimolar conference on Signal speech and Computers.
6. J.R. Movellan. Visual speech recognition with stochastic networks. NIPS 94, 1994
7. P. Duchnowski, U. Meier, A. Waibel. See me, hear me: Integrating automatic speech recognition and lip-reading. Internation Conference on Spoken Language Processing, ICSLP, pages 547-550, 1994

8. S. Deligne, G. Potamianos, C. Neti. Audio-Visual speech enhancement with avcdcn (Audio-Visual Codebook Dependent Cepstral Normalization), IEEE workshop on Sensor Array and Multichannel Signal Processing in August 2002, Washington DC and ICSLP 2002

9. S. Dupont and J. Luettin. Audio-visual speech modeling for continuous speech recognition. IEEE Trans. Multimedia, vol. 2, pp. 141-151, 2000

10. J. Huang, G. Potamianos, C. Neti. Improving Audio-Visual Speech Recognition with an Infrared Headset. Proceedings of AVSP 2003, 2003

11. Uwe Meier, Rainer Stiefelhagen, Jie Yang, Alex Waibel. Towards Unrestricted Lipreading. International Journal of pattern Recognition and Artificial Intelligence, Vol. 14, No. 5, pp. 571-785, 2000, Second International Conference on Multimodal Interfaces (ICMI99), 1999.

12. C. Bregler and Y. Konig. Eigenlips for robust speech recognition. Proc. IEEE Intl. Conf. Acous. Speech Sig. Process, pp. 669-672, 1994

13. I. Matthews, J.A. Bangham, S. Cox. Audiovisual speech recognition using multi-scale nonlinear image decomposition. Proc. 4th ICSLP, vol. 1 pp. 38-41, 1996

14. A. Ogihara, S. Asao. An isolated word speech recognition based on fusion of visual and auditory information using 30-frames/s and 24-bit color image. IEICE Trans. Fund. Electron., Commun. Comput. Sci., vol. E80A, no 8, pp. 1417-1422, 1997

15. C. Neti, G. Potamianos et al. Audio-Visual Speech Recognition - Workshop 2000 Final Report. Center for Language and Speech Processing, The Johns Hopkins University, Baltimore, 2000

16. G. Potamianos, C. Neti, G. Iyengar, Eric Helmuth. Large-Vocabulary Audio-Visual Speech Recognition by Machines and Humans, Proc. Eurospeech, 2001

17. G. Potamianos, A. Verma, C. Neti, G. Iyengar, S. Basu. A Cascade Image Transformation For Speaker Independent Automatic Speechreading. Proceedings of the IEEE International Conference on Multimedia and Expo, pp. 1097-1100, 2000

18. M. Finke, P. Geutner, H. Hild, T. Kemp, K. Ries, M. Westphal "The Karlsruhe-VERBMOBIL Speech Recognition Engine", in Proceedings of ICASSP, Munich, Germany, 1997.

19. H. Soltau, F. Metze, C. Fügen, A. Waibel, "A One Pass-Decoder Based on Poly-morphic Linguistic Context Assignment", in Proc. of ASRU, Trento, Italy, 2001.

20. Rainer Stiefelhagen and Jie Yang. Gaze Tracking for Multimodal Human-Computer Interaction. Proc. of the International Conference on Acoustics, Speech and Signal Processing: ICASSP'97, Munich, Germany, April 1997.

21. G. Gravier, G. Potamianos and C. Neti. Asynchrony modeling for audio-visual speech recognition. Proc. Human Language Technology Conference, 2002

Lesion Preserving Image Registration with Applications to Human Brains

Stefan Henn[1], Lars Hömke[2], and Kristian Witsch[1]

[1] Mathematisches Institut, Heinrich-Heine Universität Düsseldorf,
Universitätsstraße 1, D-40225 Düsseldorf, Germany.
{henn,witsch}@am.uni-duesseldorf.de
http://www.am.uni-duesseldorf.de/~{henn,witsch}
[2] Institut für Medizin, Forschungszentrum Jülich GmbH,
D-52425 Jülich, Germany.
l.hoemke@fz-juelich.de

Abstract. The goal of image registration is to find a transformation that aligns one image to another. In this paper we present a novel automatically image registration approach for images with structural distortions (e.g. a lesion within a human brain). The main idea is to define a suitable matching energy, which effectively measures the similarity between the images. The minimization of the matching energy is an ill-posed problem. Hence, we add a regularity energy borrowed from linear elasticity theory, which incorporates smoothness constraints into the displacement. The resulting energy functional is minimized by a Levenberg-Marquardt iteration-scheme. Finally, we give a two-dimensional example of these applications.

1 Introduction

An important problem in two- and three-dimensional medical image analysis is to match two similar images, resulting from the same or from different imaging modalities. Especially in brain research the development of fast deformable image registration algorithms has been an active topic of research in recent years. Here, a typical approach is the minimization of a suitable distance functional. Minimization strategies currently used deal with Navier-Stokes equilibrium equations for linear elasticity given by a partial differential equation (PDE). Here, the external forces, given by the derivatives of the distance functional, are applied to the template-image. The template-image is deformed until an equilibrium state (described by the PDE) between the external forces and internal forces resisting the deformation is achieved. The resulting displacement field u satisfies the PDE with external forces f, see, e.g. [1,2,6,10,16].

Driven by ever more powerful computers, these algorithms have become important tools, e.g. in guidance of surgery, diagnostics, quantitative analysis of brain structures (interhemispheric, interareal and interindividual), ontogenetic differences between cortical areas, and interindividual brain studies. Although these techniques have been applied very successfully for both the uni- and the

C.E. Rasmussen et al. (Eds.): DAGM 2004, LNCS 3175, pp. 496–503, 2004.

multimodal case (e.g. see [1,2,6,7,8,9,10,12,16,17,20]) these techniques may be less appropriate for studies using brain-damaged subjects, since there is no compensation for the structural distortion introduced by a lesion (e.g. a tumor, ventricular enlargement, large regions of a typical pixel intensity values, etc.).

Generally the computed solution cannot be trusted in the area of a lesion. The magnitude of the effect on the solution depends on the character of the registration scheme employed. It is not only that these effects are undesirable, but also that in some cases one is especially interested in where the lesion would be in the other image. If, for instance, we want to know which function of the brain is usually performed by the damaged area, we could register the lesioned brain to an atlas and map the lesion to functional data within the reference space.

In more general terms the problem can be phrased as follows. Given are a deformable template image T and a reference image R as well as a domain G including a segmentation of the lesions. The aim of the proposed image registration algorithm is to find a "smooth" displacement-field u, which:

Minimizes a given similarity functional between T and R under the condition that:

The lesion G is conserved in the transformed template image T.

The main idea is to define a suitable distance functional, which effectively measures the similarity between the images. The presented approach can be seen as the well known "image inpainting approach" (e.g. see [3,4,5]) for the unknown displacement-field u, see [13]. The minimization of the presented matching energy is an ill-posed problem (see [16]). Hence, we investigate a Levenberg-Marquardt scheme for minimization of the novel distance functional. Here, we first linearize the least squares functional. The linearized functional is minimized within a so-called trust region around the actual solution. The trust region is quantified by a metric, which measures the elastic energy of the displacement.

2   A Lesion Preserving Image Registration Algorithm

2.1   A Lesion Preserving Similarity Functional

In the situation that the intensities of the given images are comparable, a proper choice of for a distance functional is the so-called sum of squared differences between the images

$$D(u) = \frac{1}{2} \int_{\Omega} \Big(T\big(x_1 - u_1(x), \cdots, x_d - u_d(x)\big) - R\big(x_1, \cdots, x_d\big) \Big)^2 dx.$$

This is a common criterion. It is used, for example, in the case that the images are recorded with the same imaging machinery, the so-called mono-modal image registration. Due to the absence of information in the domain G, we define a lesion-mask by

$$\lambda_G(x) = \begin{cases} 1 \text{ if } x \in \Omega \setminus G, \\ 0 \text{ if } x \in G \end{cases}$$

and consider the following similarity functional

$$D_\epsilon(u) = \frac{1}{2} \int_{\Omega \setminus G} \Big(T\big(x_1 - u_1(x), \cdots, x_d - u_d(x)\big) - R\big(x_1, \cdots, x_d\big) \Big)^2 dx$$

$$= \frac{1}{2} \int_\Omega \lambda_G(x) \Big(T\big(x_1 - u_1(x), \cdots, x_d - u_d(x)\big) - R\big(x_1, \cdots, x_d\big) \Big)^2 dx.$$

2.2 A Levenberg-Marquardt Iteration for Minimizing the Similarity Functional

In order to minimize the functional $D_\epsilon(u)$ we use the Levenberg-Marquardt iteration scheme. The Levenberg-Marquardt method is a variant of the Gauß-Newton iteration for the minimization of D_ϵ. Here, for a current approximation $u^{(k)}(x)$ the nonlinear image difference $h(u) = T\big(x - u(x)\big) - R\big(x\big)$ is replaced by its linearization around $u^{(k)}(x)$ within a ball of radius $||u||_E^2 \leq \eta$ where the energy norm $|| \cdot ||_E$ is defined by

$$||v||_E = \sqrt{\langle v, v \rangle_E} \quad \text{with inner product} \quad \langle v, w \rangle_E = \int_\Omega w^t(x) L v(x) dx$$

and a symmetric positive definite operator L. For our specific application we use the following operator

$$Lu(x) := -\mu \Delta u(x) - (\mu + \lambda) \nabla(\nabla u(x))$$

with the so-called Lamé constants λ and μ. Using the method of Lagrange multipliers, this is easy seen to be equivalent to minimize the quadratic functional

$$Q(u) = \int_\Omega \frac{\lambda_k(x)}{2} \big(h_k + J_k u(x) \big)^2 dx + \alpha \langle Lu, u \rangle, \tag{1}$$

where $h_k := h(u^{(k)}(x)) = T\big(x - u^{(k)}(x)\big) - R\big(x\big)$,

$$J_k := J_h(u^{(k)}(x)) = \frac{\partial h}{\partial u}(u^{(k)}(x)) = \left(\frac{\partial h}{\partial u_1}(u^{(k)}(x)), \cdots, \frac{\partial h}{\partial u_d}(u^{(k)}(x)) \right)$$

and the mask

$$\lambda_k(x) = \begin{cases} 1 \text{ if } x \in \Omega \setminus G_k, \\ 0 \text{ if } x \in G_k \end{cases}$$

for the transformed subdomain $G_k = \{ y \mid y = x - u^{(k)}(x) \quad \forall x \in G \}$.

2.3 The Model of a Clamped Elastic Membrane

The second term in equation (1) can be regarded as a penalty for "elastic stresses" resulting from the displacements of the images. This is a suitable model in many medical applications, for example, when pressure or movement is applied to a patient. By using Dirichlet boundary conditions the resulting displacements may be interpreted physically as the displacement of a clamped elastic membrane. For each iteration step we have the following result.

Theorem 1. *Using Dirichlet boundary conditions for the operator L at $\partial\Omega$, the unique minimizer $u^*(x) \in \left(H_0^1(\Omega)\right)^d$ of (1) is characterized by the following variational equation*

$$\int_\Omega \varphi^t(x)(\frac{\lambda_k(x)}{2}J_k^t J_k + \alpha L)u(x)dx = -\int_\Omega \lambda_k(x)J_k^t h_k \varphi(x)dx \quad \forall \varphi \in \left(H_0^1(\Omega)\right)^d.$$

(2)

Proof. Noting that

$$\int_\Omega \frac{\lambda_k(x)}{2}\left(h_k + J_k u(x)\right)^2 dx + \alpha \int_\Omega u^t(x)Lu(x)dx = \int_\Omega \lambda_k(x)(2J_k^t h_k u(x) + h_k^2)dx$$

$$+ \int_\Omega u^t(x)(\lambda_k(x)J_k^t J_k + \alpha L)u(x)dx.$$

Since the operator L is symmetric positive definite by using Dirichlet boundary conditions and $J_k^t J_k$ is symmetric positive semidefinite, it follows that the bilinear form

$$B[u, v] := \int_\Omega u^t(x)(\lambda_k(x)J_k^t J_k + \alpha L)v(x)dx$$

is symmetric and positive definite. Consequently, the weak solution of (1) is unique and given by the solution of (2). $\qquad\square$

Note that by the definition of $\lambda_k(x)$ the classical solution of (2) is given by the boundary value problem

$$(\alpha L + J_k^t J_k)u(x) = -J_k^t h_k \quad \text{for} \quad x \in \Omega \setminus G_k,$$ (3)

$$\alpha L\, u(x) = \quad 0 \quad \text{for} \quad x \in G_k,$$ (4)

$$u(x) = \quad 0 \quad \text{for} \quad x \in \partial\Omega.$$ (5)

2.4   A Parameter Choice Rule

An important problem is the proper choice of the parameter α in practical applications. A small α leads to strong artifacts due to the influence of high-frequency structures in the image data (e.g. the noise). Increasing α removes the artifacts and allows only smoother transformations. The result becomes worse if the parameter increases further.

The optimal balance between the two extremes is a tough issue. In practice the costs of tuning the parameter are high and for most methods only "trial and error" approaches are available. In our implementation we determine α using a trust-region approach as presented in [12].

2.5   Discretization and Approximation of the Boundary Value Problem

In order to discretize the operator J_k in equation (3), we have to fix an overlap between the subdomains G_k and $\Omega \setminus G_k$. Therefore we enlarge G_k by one point

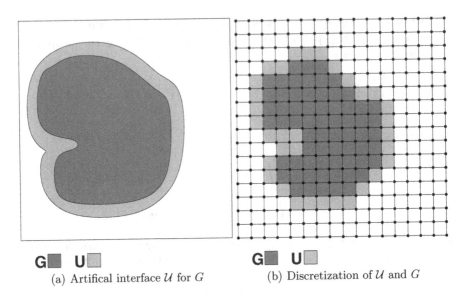

G▪ **U**▫
(a) Artifical interface $\mathcal{U}$ for G

G▪ **U**▫
(b) Discretization of $\mathcal{U}$ and G

Fig. 1. The image information is missing on the domain G.

parallel to the boundary of G_k, see figure 1. The extended domain is named by $\mathcal{U}$. The operator J_k is approximated by using central differences for all points $x \in \Omega \setminus (G_k \cup \mathcal{U})$. For instance for the three-dimensional case, we have

$$J_k = \frac{1}{2} \left(T^k_{i+1,j,l} - T^k_{i-1,j,l}, \; T^k_{i,j+1,l} - T^k_{i,j-1,l}, \; T^k_{i,j,l+1} - T^k_{i,j,l-1} \right)^t, \qquad (6)$$

where

$$T^k_{i,j,l} = T\left(x_i - u^{(k)}_1(x_i, x_j, x_l), x_j - u^{(k)}_2(x_i, x_j, x_l), x_l - u^{(k)}_3(x_i, x_j, x_l)\right)$$

the template image deformed by $u^{(k)}$. In order to discretize the elliptic operator L, we use a finite difference approach and we approximate the partial derivatives by second order approximations, for details see [11].

2.6   Fast Solution Methods

In practice, the solution of the linear system (3)–(5) is the time consuming part of the Levenberg-Marquardt iteration. For the resulting discrete system a multigrid Correction Scheme (CS) was used (with optimal multigrid complexity $\mathcal{O}(N)$ for N picture elements) as a solver, for details see e.g. [11,15]. Since the resulting system is symmetric and positive definite other solvers like Krylov subspace methods [21], can be used. Note, that the underlying operator is anisotrop and consequently fast Fourier transformation (FFT) (see [22]) based solver cannot be used.

In order to speed up the minimization process, we have implemented the Levenberg-Marquardt iteration within a scale-space framework as presented in [14].

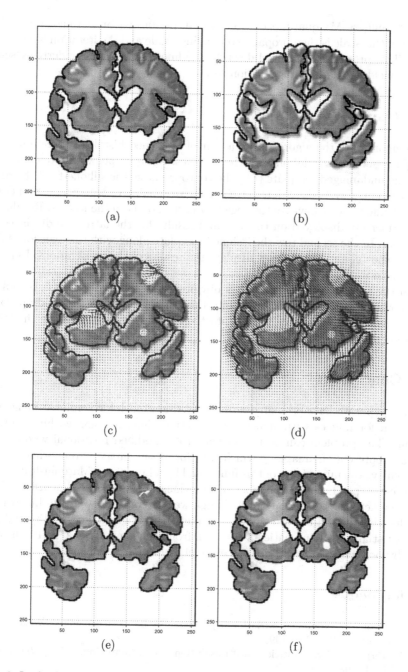

Fig. 2. In the first row the reference (a), template (b) are shown. Registrations without and with the definition of a region G have been performed. In the second column the lesioned template and the transformation fields for the former (c) and the latter (d) are displayed. The corresponding results can be found in the last row. The contour around the sections corresponds to the silhouette of the reference.

The Levenberg-Marquardt iteration is first performed on a rough scale. The result of this scale is then propagated to a finer scale and the iteration is restarted here. This process is continued down to the finest scale of the underlying scale-space, yielding the final registration result.

3   Results

We demonstrate the algorithm on a pair of deformed histological sections. The template section was lesioned in three places. Figure 2 shows the reference (a) and the undamaged template (b). The contour marks the silhouette of the reference section. Two registrations have been performed. One where no region G has been defined and one where the region G corresponds to the lesions. Results for the former are displayed on the left, and results for the latter are displayed on the right. In the second row the lesioned template along with the transformation field is shown, and the last row displays the results of the registrations. Here the we used $\mu = \lambda = 1$.

From the transformation fields it is obvious that when no region G is defined the surrounding tissue is "pulled" into the lesion. With the proposed approach the transformation is interpolated into the regions defined by G and the lesion is preserved.

4   Conclusion

In this paper we have presented a pixel-based approach for nonlinear image registration for images with structural distortions (e.g. a lesion within a human brain). The problem can be traced back to a modified functional whose minimizers represent the mapping which transforms one image into another.

We achieve the minimizing of this functional by a Levenberg-Marquardt iteration in a few steps. The small number of iterations and the finite dimension of the problem act as a regularization. Although we have only showed two-dimensional results, the method has already been applied in artificial 3D cases [13], and in a patient study involving patients suffering from ischaemic lesions [18,19], using a Landweber scheme instead of the Levenberg-Marquardt scheme.

References

1. Y. Amit. A nonlinear variational problem for image matching. *SIAM J. Sci. Comput.*, 15:207–224, 1994.
2. R. Bajcsy and S. Kovacic. Multiresolution elastic matching. *Computer Vision*, 46:1–21, 1989.
3. M. Bertalmio, G. Sapiro, V. Caselles, and C. Ballester. Image inpainting. In K. Akeley, editor, *Siggraph 2000, Computer Graphics Proceedings*, pages 417–424. ACM Press / ACM SIGGRAPH / Addison Wesley Longman, 2000.
4. T. Chan, S. Kang, and J. Shen. Euler's elastica and curvature based inpaintings. *J. Appl. Math.*, 63(2):564–592, 2002.

5. T. Chan and J. Shen. Mathematical models for local nontexture inpaintings. *SIAM Journal on Applied Mathematics*, 62(3):1019–1043, 2002.
6. G. Christensen, M. Miller, M. Vannier, and U. Grenander. Individualizing neuroanatomical atlases using a massively parallel computer. *IEEE Computer*, 29(1):32–38, 1996.
7. U. Clarenz, S. Henn, M. Rumpf, and K. Witsch. Relations between optimization and gradient flow methods with application to image registration. *Proceedings of the 18th GAMM-Seminar Leipzig*, 2002.
8. M. Davis, A. Khotanzad, D. Flaming, and S. Harms. A physics based coordinate transformation for 3d medical images. *IEEE Trans. on medical imaging*, 16(3):317–328, 1997.
9. M. Droske and M. Rumpf. A variational approach to non-rigid morphological registration. *SIAM Appl. Math.*, 64(2):668–687, 2004.
10. B. Fischer and J. Modersitzki. Curvature based image registration. *JMIV*, 18:81–85, 2003.
11. S. Henn. *Numerische Lösung und Modellierung eines inversen Problems zur Assimilation digitaler Bilddaten, Phd thesis Heinrich-Heine-Universität Düsseldorf.* Logos-Verlag Berlin, Berlin, 2001.
12. S. Henn. A levenberg-marquardt scheme for nonlinear image registration. *BIT Numerical Mathematics*, 43(4):743–759, 2003.
13. S. Henn, L. Hömke, and K. Witsch. *A generalized image registration framework using incomplete image information – with applications to lesion mapping. Springer Series in Mathematics in Industry.* Springer-Verlag, Berlin Heidelberg New York, 2004.
14. S. Henn, T. Schormann, K. Engler, K. Zilles, and K. Witsch. *Elastische Anpassung in der digitalen Bildverarbeitung auf mehreren Auflösungsstufen mit Hilfe von Mehrgitterverfahren.* Informatik aktuell Mustererkennung Springer-Verlag: 392–399, 1997.
15. S. Henn and K. Witsch. A multigrid-approach for minimizing a nonlinear functional for digital image matching. *Computing*, 64(4):339–348, 1999.
16. S. Henn and K. Witsch. Iterative multigrid regularization techniques for image matching. *SIAM J. Sci. Comput. (SISC)*, 23(4):1077–1093, 2001.
17. S. Henn and K. Witsch. Multi-modal image registration using a variational approach. *SIAM J. Sci. Comput. (SISC)*, 25(4):1429–1447, 2004.
18. L. Hömke, B. Weder, F. Binkofski and K. Amunts. Lesion mapping in MRI data - an application of cytoarchitectonic probabilistic maps. *WWW: http://www.am.uni-duesseldorf.de/~hoemke/posters/lesionmapping.pdf.* Second Vogt-Brodmann Symposium, Jülich 2004.
19. B. Weder, K. Amunts, L. Hömke, H. Mohlberg, L. Bönig, C. Fretz and F. Binkofski Lesion analysis in high-resolution MR-images of patients with unilateral tactile agnosia using cytoarchitectonic mapping Presented at the *10th Annual metting of the Organization for Human Brain Mapping*, June 13-17, 2004, Budapest.
20. S. Keeling and W. Ring. Medical image registration and interpolation by optical flow with maximal rigidity. *Journal of Mathematical Imaging and Vision JMIV (to appear).*
21. Y. Saad. *Iterative methods for sparse linear systems.* 2000.
22. C. F. Van Loan. *Computational Frameworks for the Fourier Transform*, volume 10 of *Frontiers in Applied Mathematics.* SIAM, Philadelphia, 1992.

Snake-Aided Automatic Organ Delineation

Weibing Xu[1], Saad A. Amin[1], Olivier C.L. Haas[2], Keith J. Burnham[3], and
John A. Mills[4]

[1] BIOCORE, School of Mathematical and Information Sciences
[2] Biomedical Engineering Research Group
[3] Control Theory and Applications Centre
Coventry University, Priory Street, Coventry CV1 5FB, UK.
{w.xu@, s.amin, o.haas}@coventry.ac.uk
[4] Radiotherapy Physics, University Hospitals Coventry and Warwickshire N.H.S. Trust,
Coventry, UK

Abstract. This paper presents a knowledge-based image segmentation tool for organ delineation in CT (Computed Tomography) images. The noise and low contrast make the detection difficult. Therefore in this method, radial search, noise reduction method and post-processing algorithm have been implemented to improve the quality of contour detection. Three edge detection algorithms have been used and after detection several optimization methods have been employed to get the accurate contour from three detected contours. Finally to achieve higher accuracy of detection, active contour model (ACM), snake, has been used after the contour detected by previous methods.

1 Introduction

Radiotherapy is one of the most common cancer treatment techniques. It makes use of radiation beams to eradicate cancerous tissues. To plan radiotherapy treatment [1, 2], the location and the shape of region of interests (ROI) need to be identified. In many hospitals in the U.K., the delineation or outlining process is performed manually on a number of CT (Computed Tomography) images. Such process is prone to a high probability of interpersonal errors and lacks consistency [3]. To improve the consistency of the delineation process, semi-automatic delineation tools with computer-aided processing have been developed, see [2 - 4]. Computers can provide more consistency and repeatability.

The aim of this work is to develop an accurate and efficient delineation tool for contour detection in CT images. Due to the low contrast between tissues and organs, and noise in CT images [3, 5], automatic outlining is still difficult. To overcome these difficulties, knowledge has been imported and more than one algorithm have been used to improve the accuracy of the delineation.

The noise and contrast problems restrict the performance of edge detection algorithms, so noise reduction methods have been used to improve the quality of the image [6]. Edge detection algorithms are based on different principles. Hence, each algorithm may give a different contour for the same region in the same image. This has been presented in Vickers's work [5]. Once the edge pixels have been found by

C.E. Rasmussen et al. (Eds.): DAGM 2004, LNCS 3175, pp. 504–511, 2004.
© Springer-Verlag Berlin Heidelberg 2004

those algorithms, the decision needs to be made select the most appropriate contour. Genetic algorithms and dynamic programming [7, 8] have been used in image processing, they are however time consuming [9]. In this work, the level-2 refinement method has been applied to reduce the processing time.

Finally active contour model has been used for the higher accuracy of contour detection in this work. The Active Contour Model (ACM) firstly presented by Kass *et al.* [10] has been widely used for medical image segmentation recently. It differs from traditional low-level edge detection methods. High-level knowledge has been involved to find the appropriate local minimum. This deformable method developed by Kass is also known as 'Snake'. It is energy minimizing based. Snake minimizes the energy function and moves the contour dynamically to the true border of ROI.

Traditional snake needs the initial position of the snake as close as possible to the proper edge of the object, otherwise it will get lost during the convergence. This problem has been pointed out and solved by Cohen [11], who developed balloon force for snake convergence. Still the snake has the problem of detecting the concave object, so Xu *et al.* developed GVF snake [12] to solve this problem.

Snake is a time-consuming method for contour delineation. Cohen increased the capture range of the snake, but when the initial snake is far away from the true border of ROI the processing time becomes another bottleneck of radiotherapy treatment planning. In this paper, the initial position of the snake provided by radial search method is close enough to the true contour, so the initial position of the traditional snake has been solved and also the processing time of detection is reduced.

This paper describes the delineation tools developed to outline automatically ROI in the pelvic area. Section 2 presents the image processing strategy developed, which combines radial search with pre- and post-processing, and then the contour pixels analysis is explained, which focuses on edge pixel selection and contour refinement. Section 3 describes the implementation of active contour model in this application. Section 4 presents results of experiments. Section 5 draws a conclusion of this work.

2 Automatic Delineation

The radial search method (RSM) is widely used in contour detection because of its simplicity and scalability. Han [13] uses radial search method combined with thresholding, and Ruiz [14] uses radial search method with LoG. To improve the quality of processing, they use pre-processing to suppress the noise in images. Because each edge detection method has its own limitation, only one edge detection method used in their application can lead to misdetection. LoG is sensitive to noise pixels and threshold acts badly in low contrast images. To avoid the limitation of different methods, in this work more than one edge detection method is applied. This delineation tool combines pre-processing, three edge detection methods, and post-processing. Radial search methods have a number of limitations and fail to outline some concave objects. In this work however, attention is focused on outlining the bladder, which is mostly convex. To improve the accuracy of the detection techniques presented in [15], a number of modifications have been made and are described in thereafter.

2.1 Structure of Radial Searching Method

The main structure of this delineation tool is:
- Pre-processing for noise reduction;
- Three edge detection algorithms with Bresenham line drawing algorithm to find edge pixels in ROI;
- Post-processing for contour refinement;

The pre-processing is using median filter for noise reduction. In [15], three pre-processing techniques were investigated, namely median filtering, mean filtering and limit filtering, and it was found that median filter gives the best performance when associated with the edge detection algorithms used. Three edge detection algorithms are: Thresholding, Mean value ± 3 standard deviation, and Mean value ± 3 standard deviation within a fixed window size W, which are named as C1, C2, and C3. The detail of radial searching has been discussed in [15].

2.2 Level 1 Post-processing

Global noise reduction has been done by median filter, which removes some noise pixels in the CT image. After edge detection, there are still some noise pixels on the contour, which have big difference in location with its neighbor pixels and make the contour of ROI discontinuous. According to local features of edge pixels, noise pixels on the contour will be adjusted by considering features of neighbor pixels.

To avoid the misdetection on the radius:
- Once a potential edge pixel x_k has been detected, the following N pixels: from x_{k+1} to x_{k+N}, are checked as shown in Figure 1.
- If $M\%$ (M defined by user, 60% is used in this work.) of them has same properties as x_k, x_k is an edge pixel; if not, use to find another potential edge pixel on the radius and repeat these processes.
-

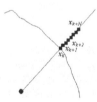

Fig. 1. Judge the edge pixel on the radius

In pre-processing the global noise reduction has been employed. Since it cannot remove all noise pixels on the contour, median filter again has been used for smoothing. Instead of removing the noise on radius based on the gray level of pixels, it works based on the length of radii to adjust the pixels location on the contour. During the processing, some radii with significant length difference are replaced by the medium value of neighboring radii.

2.3   Level 2 Post-processing: Contour Pixels Analysis

In this work, three different algorithms have been used for edge detection. Each of them works independently, so after detection three different sets of contour pixels are presented. It is necessary to select the precise contour points from three sets of pixels.

2.3.1   Edge Pixel Selection

To choose the 'best' edge pixel on the radius, two methods have been investigated.
Selection 1: medium value selection
The decision of choosing the edge pixel has been made according to the length of the radii created by three potential edge pixels. In this selection, the pixel with radius, which is the medium value of three radii, is considered as the best choice for edge pixel on the contour.

- At θ, three edge pixels, which are detected on a ray, have radii known as $R1$, $R2$, and $R3$; (Here $R1$ is the radius from C1, $R2$ is from C2, and $R3$ is from C3.)
- Sort $(R1, R2, R3)$ to get the medium value R of them;
- According to R, the best edge pixel in three can be found;

Selection 2: voting and mean value
This selection is based on voting. It assumes that the edge pixel should appear at the most likely place. It means the edge pixel should be close to two of three detected pixels, which are closer to each other. For example, at θ three edge pixels are detected on a ray, have radii known as R1, R2, and R3. The selection will be made as following,

Case 1: If $|R1\text{-}R2|<|R1\text{-}R3|$ and $|R1\text{-}R2|<|R2\text{-}R3|$, $R_v=(R1+R2)/2$;
Case 2: If $|R1\text{-}R3|<|R1\text{-}R2|$ and $|R1\text{-}R3|<|R2\text{-}R3|$, $R_v=(R1+R3)/2$;
Case 3: If $|R3\text{-}R2|<|R3\text{-}R1|$ and $|R3\text{-}R2|<|R2\text{-}R1|$, $R_v=(R3+R2)/2$;
Here R_v is the average value of radius.

2.3.2   Contour Refinement

Due to the low contrast and noise in CT images, the edge detection algorithm cannot find the edge, which is heavily blurred or with large number of noise pixels. The result of detection will be some gaps on the contour or spikes on the contour. This causes the biggest error of contour detection. To avoid or reduce this error, further refinements are necessary. Here two methods are investigated for contour refinement.
Refinement 1: discontinuity removing
It is a method to detect the discontinuity on the contour.

1. Set up a threshold T_R for the difference of neighbor radii.
2. If $|R(i+1)\text{-}R(i)|>T_R$, then record i;
3. If $|R(j+1)\text{-}R(j)|>T_R$, then record j;
4. If $R(j)$ and $R(i)$ are neighbors, i.e. $j\text{-}i=1$, just pull the pixel back, $R(j)=R(i)$;
5. If $R(j)$ and $R(i)$ are not neighbors, then the value between $R(j)$ and $R(i)$ will be calculated by linear interpolation to fill the gap.

This operation starts from first pixel on the contour and also need to compare the last pixel with the first one and then the gap or spike on the contour will be removed. The threshold T_R is obtained from the manually outlined contour by comparing the difference of neighbor pixels' radii. The largest difference is selected as the threshold.
Refinement 2: median smooth

The median filter here is used on the radii, which are based on the edge pixels selected. Median filter will work on smoothing the spike on the contour. Here this refinement method is similar as the one mentioned in section 2.2.

3 Active Contour Model

Active contour model is a deformable model, which is based on the energy minimization of the snake. The two types of energy, internal and external energy, create internal and external force to pull the snake to the border of the ROI. In this work, the initial position is provided by RSM and snake is a refinement method to improve the accuracy of delineation.

3.1 Theory of Active Contour Model

In Kass's work, the contour of the object is defined as an energy function, which can be written as following expression,

$$E_{total} = \int_0^1 E_{snake}(v)dv = \int_0^1 [E_{int}(v) + E_{ext}(v)]dv \tag{1}$$

The snake consists of internal energy E_{int} and external energy E_{ext}:

$$E_{int}(v) = \frac{1}{2}[\alpha |x'(v)|^2 + \beta |x''(v)|^2] \tag{2}$$

$$E_{ext}(v) = -|\nabla[G_\sigma * I]|^2 \tag{3}$$

α and β are weighting parameters that control the internal force to make the snake continuous and smooth. The external energy is based on the information of image, like border information, region information and so on. This force attracts the snake moving to the desired edge of the object. To minimize the energy E_{total}, (4) must satisfy the Euler-Lagrange equation.

$$\alpha * x'' - \beta * x'''' - \nabla E_{ext} = 0 \tag{4}$$

3.2 Snake-Aided Radial Search

The traditional snake has the limited capture range. This means the initial contour must be close to the true boundary; otherwise it will be lost. Cohen solved this problem by using the inflation force. Unfortunately this increases the processing time, when initial snake is far away from true border of ROI. In this work, those two problems have been solved by RSM. RSM provides the initial contour close enough to the true border. Since the initial contour is close to the true boundary, the snake does not need to move faraway to the boundary. This reduces iterations of the snake and shortens the whole processing time. Traditional snake cannot converge to concave shapes, because of lack of capture range [12]. The initial position of the snake given by radial search is close to the true border, so the concave shape can be outlined.

Active Contour Model in this work becomes a procedure of coarse-to-fine scheme. It is used to improve the accuracy of contour delineation. The strategy of this work can be presented as following,

♦ Use RSM to detect the contour of ROI;

♦ Use the contour detected by RSM as the initial position of the snake;

♦ Use snake to refine the contour detected;

Finally to reduce the discontinuity, the neighbor pixels have been checked again by comparing the length of the radiuses. This method is similar as the one mentioned in section 2.3.2, the discontinuity removing.

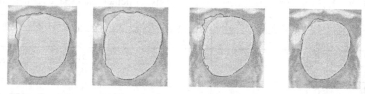

Fig. 2. Contour detection and refinements. From left to right: RSM, RSM + level-2 refinement, snake-applied RSM, and refined-snake application.

Fig. 3. Contour detection and refinements. From left to right: initial snake by RSM, snake in process, result after 50 iterations, and result of snake and manual outlining.

4   Experiment Results

The initial seed point needs to be within ROI for radial search method, so it is extracted from the average position of the center of the bladder in 30 CT images. By investigation, the range of center of bladder in 30 CT images is within the square (245, 159) and (272, 204). The given point used in this work is (260, 178). It is not compulsory to have a center of the bladder as the given pixel, because the algorithm can work as long as the given pixel within ROI.

The results of contour delineation tool at different stages can be presented in Figure 2.

From the figure above, the accuracy of detection has been improved. RSM provides the initial position of the snake quite close to the true border, so only after few iterations snake can be attracted to the contour of ROI. Figure 3 shows the efficiency of the whole processing.

To measure the performance of contour detection, relative error is measured by comparing with manual outlining, which can be expressed by following equation:

$$E_{rel}\% = \frac{K}{360}\sum_i | R_{com}(i) - R_{man}(i)| / R_{man} \times 100 \tag{5}$$

Here R_{com} is the computer-processed radius and R_{man} is manual outline. The improvements by snake can be expressed by following equation,

$$R_{imp}(\%) = 100x(R_{refine} - R_{snake})/R_{refine} \tag{6}$$

Here R_{imp} stands for the ratio of improvements and R_{refine} stands for the error by level-2 refinement and R_{snake} stands for the error by snake. The snake has been tested on a series of images. The improvement can be seen from following table,

Table 1. Error comparison between two levels refinement and snake refinement

Images	Level-2 refine (%)	snake refined (%)	Improvements (%)
V1	4.25	3.42	19.5
V2	3.1	0.13	95.8
V3	1.53	1.06	30.7
V4	6.73	2.45	63.6
V5	2.24	0.61	72.8
V6	7.68	6.28	18.2
V7	6.52	3.45	47.1
V8	1.74	1.69	2.9
V9	4.93	1.25	74.6
V10	1.47	1.24	15.6
Average	3.99	2.16	45.9

The largest improvement by snake can be up to 95.8% and the average improvement is 45.9%. These data show the snake provides the good contour delineation in medical image processing. Those images are selected randomly. Generally snake can improve the accuracy of detection. From the data above, the snake still has the problem if the image is suffered with noise and low contrast, like image V6. The result of snake has 6.28% error because the noise attracts the snake to wrong local minima; therefore some other methods need to be developed to overcome it.

5   Conclusions and Further Work

This work presents successful edge detection in medical image application. Due to low contrast of some medical images, single edge detection algorithm might fail to find the edge pixels. Therefore for more accurate contour of ROI, more than one algorithm have been implemented to have more choices for edge pixel on the contour. To improve the accuracy, the pre- and post-processing have been used. These methods improve the individual algorithm's performance. For the contour detected it is the combination of the results of those algorithms. The final edge analysis is made by contour pixel selection and refinement methods.

This method of edge detection can be scalable. More edge detection algorithms can be added for precise edge detection. More algorithms provide more options for edge pixels. This will improve the accuracy of voting edge pixel selection and avoid misdetection. Active contour model shows its affectivity for adjusting the contour detected by RSM. Even if there are the 2-level refinement methods applied after the RSM, to process some low contrast images this method is still not very successful. As it is displayed in previous section, snake can be used for further refinement. Snake finally pulls the contour as close as possible to the true border of ROI.

References

1. Haas O.C.L., Radiotherapy Treatment Planning: New System Approaches, Springer Verlag London, Advances in Industrial Control Monograph, ISBN 1-85233-063-5, 220, 1999
2. Meinzer, H.P., Thorn, M., Vetter, M., Hassenpflug, P., and Wolf, I., Medical imaging: examples of clinical applications, ISPRS Journal of Photogrammetry & Remote Sensing 56, pp. 311-325, 2002.
3. Bueno, M.G., Computer Aided Segmentation of Anatomical Structures in Computed Tomography Images, PhD thesis, Coventry University, 1998.
4. Van den Berge, D.L., Ridder, M.D., and Storme, G.A., Imaging in radiotherapy, European Journal of Radiology 34 pp.41 – 48, 2000.
5. Vickers, J.P., Burnham, K.J., Dil, A., Haas, O.C.L., Mills, J.A., Knowledge-Based Organ Segmentation in Low Contrast Medical Computed Tomography Images, Proc 14th Int. Conf. On Systems Science, Vol. 3, Ed. Zdzislaw Bubnicki & Adam Grzech, Wroclaw (Pol), pp. 381-388, 2001.
6. Gonzalez, R.C., and Woods, R.C., Digital Image Processing, Addison-Wesley Publishing Company, Inc., 1992.
7. Milios, E. and Petrakis, E., Shape Retrieval Based on Dynamic Programming, IEEE transactions on Image Processing, Special Issue on Image and Video Processing for Digital Libraries, Vol.9 (1), pp. 141-147, 2000.
8. Amini, A., Weymouth, T.E., and Jain, R.C., Using Dynamic Programming for Solving Variational Problems in Vision, IEEE transactions Pattern Analysis and Machine Intelligence, Vol.12 (9), 1990.
9. Kang, D.J., Kim, C.Y., and Seo, Y.S., A Fast and Stable Method for Detecting and Tracking Medical Organs in MRI Sequences, IEICE Trans. Inf. & Syst., Vol.E82-D, No.2, pp. 497-499, 1999.
10. Kass, M., Witkin, A., and Terzopoulos, D., Snake: Active Contour Models, International Journal of Computer Vision, pp. 321-331, 1988.
11. Cohen, L.D., On Active Contour Models and Balloons, CVGIP: Image Understanding, vol. 53 (2), pp. 211-218, 1991.
12. Xu, C. and Prince, J.L., Snakes, Shapes, and Gradient Vector Flow, IEEE transactions on Image Processing, pp. 359-369, 1998.
13. Han, C.Y., Lin, K.N. and Wee, W.G., Knowledge-Based Image Analysis for Automated Boundary Extraction of Transesophageal Echocardiographic Left-Ventricular Images, IEEE transactions on Medical Imaging, vol. 10 (4), pp. 602-610, 1991.
14. Ruiz, E.E.S. and Fairhurst, M.C., Improved approach to boundary location in two-dimentional echocardiographic images, IEE Proc.-Vis. Image Signal Process, vol. 142 (3), pp. 121-127, 1995
15. Xu, W., Amin, S.A., Haas, O.C.L., Burnham, K.J., Mills, J.A., Contour detection by using radial searching for CT images, Proc of the 4th Annual IEEE Conf on Information Technology Applications in Biomedicine, UK pp.346-349, 2003

Practical Gaze Point Detecting System

Kang Ryoung Park, Juno Chang, Min Cheol Whang, Joa Sang Lim,
Dae-Woong Rhee, Hung Kook Park, and Yongjoo Cho

Division of Media Tech., SangMyung Univ., 7 Hongji-Dong, JongRo-Gu, Seoul,
Republic of Korea

Abstract. In this paper, we propose the new gaze detection system
with dual cameras (a wide and a narrow view camera). In order to
locate the user's eye position accurately, the narrow-view camera
has the functionalities of auto focusing/panning/tilting based on the
detected 3D eye positions from the wide view camera. In addition, we
use the IR-LED illuminators for wide and narrow view camera, which
can ease the detecting of facial features, pupil and iris position. To
overcome the problem of specular reflection on glasses by illuminator,
we use dual IR-LED illuminators for wide and narrow view camera.
Experimental results show that the gaze detection error between the
computed positions and the real ones is about 2.89 cm of RMS error.

Keywords: Gaze Detection, Dual Cameras, Dual IR-LED Illuminators

1 Introduction

Gaze detection system is important in many applications such as virtual reality and video conferencing. In addition, they can help the handicapped to use
computers and are also useful for those whose hands are busy controlling other
menus on the monitor[18]. Most Previous studies were focused on 2D/3D head ro-
tation/translation estimation[2][14], the facial gaze detection[3-9][15][16][18][21]
and the eye gaze detection[10-13][17][22-25]. Recently, the gaze detection considering both head and eye movement has been researched. Ohmura and Ballard
et al.[5][6]'s methods have the disadvantages that user's Z distance should be
measured manually and take much time (over 1 minute) to compute the gaze
position. Gee et al.[7] and Heinzmann et al.[8]'s methods only compute gaze
direction vector and do not obtain the gaze position on a monitor. In addition,
if 3D rotation and translation of the head happen simultaneously, they cannot
estimate the accurate 3D motion. Rikert et al.[9]'s method has the constraints
that user's Z distance must be maintained unchanged during training and testing procedures, which can give much inconvenience to user. In the methods of
[11-13][15][16], a pair of glasses having marking points is required to detect facial
features, which can be also inconvenient to a user. The researches of [3][4][19]
show the gaze detection methods only considering head movements and have
the limits that the gaze errors are increased in case that the eye movements
happen. To overcome such problems, the research of [20] shows the gaze detection considering both head and eye movements, but uses only one wide view

C.E. Rasmussen et al. (Eds.): DAGM 2004, LNCS 3175, pp. 512–519, 2004.
© Springer-Verlag Berlin Heidelberg 2004

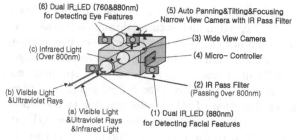

Fig. 1. The gaze detecting system

camera, which can capture the whole face of user. In such case, the eye image resolution is too low and the fine movements of user's eye cannot be exactly detected. Wang et al.[1]'s method provides the advanced approaches that combines head pose determination with eye gaze estimation by a wide view camera and a panning/tilting narrow camera. However, their method supposes that they know the 3D distance between two eyes and that between both lip corners. and there is no individual variation for the 3D distances. In addition, they suppose that they know the 3D diameter of eye ball and there is no individual variation for that. Based on the assumptions, they compute the gaze position on a monitor. However, our preliminary experiments show that there are much individual variations for the 3D distances/3D diameter and such cases can increase much gaze errors. To overcome above problems, we propose the new method and system for detecting gaze position.

2   Localization of Facial Features in Wide View Image

In order to detect gaze position on a monitor, we first locate facial features (both eye centers, eye corners, nostrils) in wide view images. To detect facial features robustly in any environment, we use the method of detecting specular reflection on the eyes. For that, we implement the gaze detection system as shown in Fig. 1. As shown in Fig. 1, the IR-LED(1) is used to make the specular reflections on eyes. The IR pass filter(2) in front of camera lens can only pass the infrared light (over 800 nm) and the brightness of input image is only affected by the IR-LED(1) excluding external illumination. The reason of using IR-LED(1) of 880nm is that human eye can only perceive the visible and the near infrared light (below about 880nm) and our illuminators do not make dazzling to user's eye, consequently. When a user starts our gaze detection system, the micro-controller(4) turns on the illuminator(1) synchronized with the even field of CCD signal and turns off it synchronized with the next odd field of CCD signal, successively[20]. From that, we can get a difference image between the even and the odd image and the specular reflection points on both eyes can be easily detected because their image gray level are higher than other regions[20]. In addition, we use the Red-Eye effect and the method of changing Frame Grabber decoder value in order to detect more accurate eye position[20]. In general, the NTSC signal from camera has high resolution ($0 \sim 2^{10}-1$), but the range of A/D conversion by conventional decoder of the Frame Grabber is low resolution ($0 \sim 2^8 - 1$). So, the NTSC signal in high saturated range is represented as 255 ($2^8 - 1$) gray level of image and both the specular reflection on eye (cornea) and the some reflection region on facial skin can be represented as same image level ($2^8 - 1$), which makes it difficult to discriminate the corneal specular reflection only by image processing algorithm. However, the NTSC signal level of corneal specular reflection is higher than that of other reflection due to the reflectance rate. So, if we make the decoder brightness value lower, then the A/D conversion range of decoder can be shifted to the upper direction. In such case, there is no high saturated range and the corneal specular reflection and the other reflection can be discriminated, easily. Around the detected corneal specular reflection points, we determine the eye candidate region of 30*30 pixels and locate the accurate eye (iris) center by the circular edge detection method. Because the eye localization is performed in the restricted region, it can be done in real-time (below 3 ms in Pentium-III 866MHz). After locating the eye center, we detect the eye corner by using eye corner shape template and SVM (Support Vector Machine)[20]. We get 2000 successive image frames for SVM training and additional 1000 images are used for testing. Experimental results show the classification error for training data is 0.11% and that for testing data is 0.2%. The classification time of SVM is so small as like 8 ms in Pentium-III 866MHz. After locating eye centers and eye corners, the positions of nostrils can be detected by anthropometric constraints in a face and SVM. In order to reduce the effect by the facial expression change, we do not use the lip corners for gaze detection. Experimental results show that RMS error between the detected feature positions and the actual positions (manually detected positions) are 1 pixel (of both eye centers), 2 pixels (of both eye corners) and 4 pixels (of both nostrils) in 640×480 pixels image. From them, we use 5 feature points (left/right eye corners of left eye, left/right eye corners of right eye, nostril center) in order to detect facial gaze position.

3 4 Steps for Computing Facial Gaze Position

After feature detection, we take 4 steps in order to compute a gaze position on a monitor[3][4][20]. At the 1st step, when a user gazes at 5 known positions on a monitor ((1),(6),(12),(18),(23) of Fig. 3), the 3D positions (X, Y, Z) of initial 5 feature points (detected in the section 2) are computed automatically[3][4]. At the 2nd step and 3rd step, when the user rotates/translates his head in order to gaze at one position on a monitor, the new (changed) 3D positions of those 5 features can be computed from 3D motion estimation. Considering many limitations of previous motion estimation researches, we use the EKF (Extended Kalman Filtering)[2] for 3D motion estimation and the new 3D positions of those features can be computed by the EKF and affine transform[3][20]. At the 4th step, one facial plane is determined from the new (changed) 3D positions of the 5 features and the normal vector (whose origin exists in the middle of the forehead) of the plane shows a gaze vector by head (facial) movements. The gaze position on a monitor is the intersection position between a monitor and the gaze vector[3][4][20].

4   Auto Panning/Tilting/Focusing of Narrow View Camera

Based on the new (changed) 3D positions of the 5 feature points (which are computed at the 2nd and 3rd step as mentioned in section 3), we can pan and tilt the narrow view camera in order to capture the eye image. For that, we also perform the coordinate conversion between monitor and narrow view camera using the internal/external camera parameters, which are obtained at initial calibration stage. Such calibration method is same to that between the wide view camera and the monitor. Detail accounts can be referred in [3]. When the user rotates his head severely, one of his eyes may disappear in camera view. So, we track only one visible eye with auto panning/tilting narrow view camera. Conventional narrow view camera has small DOF (Depth of Field) and there is the limitation of increasing the DOF with the fixed focal camera. So, we use the auto focusing narrow view camera in order to capture clear eye image. For auto focusing, the Z distance between the eye and the camera is required and we can obtain the Z distance at the 2nd and 3rd step (as mentioned in section 3). In order to compensate the focusing error due to the inaccurate Z distance measure, we use an additional focus quality checking algorithm for the input eye image. If the focus quality does not meet our threshold (70 of the range ($0 \sim 100$)), then we perform additional focusing process by sending the moving command of focus lens to camera micro-controller. In this stage, we should consider the specular reflection on glasses. The surface of glasses can make the specular reflection, which can cover the whole eye image. In such case, the eye region is not detected and we cannot compute the eye gaze position. So, we use dual IR-LED illuminators like Fig. 1(6). When the large specular reflection happens from one illuminator (right or left illuminator), then it can be detected from image. As mentioned in section 2, the NTSC analog level of specular reflection region is higher than any other region and they can be detected by changing decoder brightness setting. When the large specular region proves to exist with the changed decoder brightness value, then our gaze detection system change the illuminator (from left to right or right to left) and the specular reflection on glasses does not happen, consequently.

5   Localization of Eye Features in Narrow View Image

After we get the focused eye image, we perform the localization of eye features as shown in Fig. 2. We detect $P_1 \sim P_4'$ in right eye image as shown in Fig. 2 and also detect $P_5 \sim P_8'$ in left eye image for computing eye gaze detection. Here, the P_1 and P_1' show the pupil center and the P_2 and P_2' does the iris center. J. Wang et al.[1] uses the method that detects the iris outer boundary by vertical edge operator, morphological "open" operation and elliptical fitting. However, the upper and lower region of iris outer boundary tend to be covered by eyelid and inaccurate iris elliptical fitting happens due to the lack of iris boundary pixels. In addition, their method computes eye gaze position by checking the shape change of iris when a user gazes at monitor positions. However, our experimental results

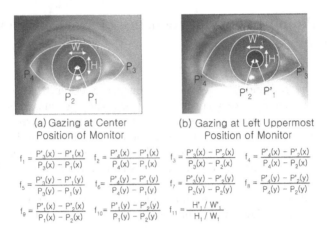

(a) Gazing at Center
Position of Monitor

(b) Gazing at Left Uppermost
Position of Monitor

$$f_1 = \frac{P'_3(x) - P'_1(x)}{P_3(x) - P_1(x)} \quad f_2 = \frac{P'_4(x) - P'_1(x)}{P_4(x) - P_1(x)} \quad f_3 = \frac{P'_3(x) - P'_2(x)}{P_3(x) - P_2(x)} \quad f_4 = \frac{P'_4(x) - P'_2(x)}{P_4(x) - P_2(x)}$$

$$f_5 = \frac{P'_3(y) - P'_1(y)}{P_3(y) - P_1(y)} \quad f_6 = \frac{P'_4(y) - P'_1(y)}{P_4(y) - P_1(y)} \quad f_7 = \frac{P'_3(y) - P'_2(y)}{P_3(y) - P_2(y)} \quad f_8 = \frac{P'_4(y) - P'_2(y)}{P_4(y) - P_2(y)}$$

$$f_9 = \frac{P'_1(x) - P'_2(x)}{P_1(x) - P_2(x)} \quad f_{10} = \frac{P'_1(y) - P'_2(y)}{P_1(y) - P_2(y)} \quad f_{11} = \frac{H'_1 / W'_1}{H_1 / W_1}$$

Fig. 2. The features for eye gaze detection from right eye

show that the shape change amount of iris is very small and it is difficult to detect the accurate eye gaze position only by that information. So, we use the positional information of both pupil and iris. Also, we use the information of shape change of pupil, which does not tend to be covered by eyelid. In general, the IR-LED of short wavelength (700nm $\sim$ 800nm) makes the high contrast between iris and sclera. On the other hand, that of long wavelength (800nm $\sim$ 900nm) makes the high contrast between pupil and iris. Based on that, we use the IR-LED illuminator of multi-wavelength (760nm and 880nm) as shown in Fig. 1(6). As shown in Fig. 2(b), the shapes of iris and pupil are almost ellipse, when the user gazes at a side position of monitor. So, the method of circular edge detection cannot be used. Instead, we use the canny edge operator to extract edge components and a 2D edge-based elliptical Hough transform. From that, we can get the center positions and the major/minor axes of iris/pupil ellipses. In order to detect the eye corner position, we detect the eyelid as shown in Fig. 2. That is because the upper and lower eyelids meet on two eye corner positions. To extract the eyelid region, we use the region-based eyelid template deformation and masking method. In detail, we make the eyelid edge image with canny edge operator and apply the deformable template as the eyelid mask. Here, we use 2 deformable templates (parabolic shape) for upper and lower eyelid detection, respectively. From that, we can detect the accurate eye corners as shown in Fig. 2. Experimental results show that RMS errors between the detected eye feature positions and the actual ones (manually detected) are 2 pixels (of iris center), 1 pixel (of pupil center), 4 pixels (of left eye corner) and 4 pixels (of right eye corner). Based on the detected eye features, we select the 22 feature values ($f_1 \sim f_{11}$ are used in case that right eye image can be captured by narrow view camera as shown in Fig. 2 and $f_{12} \sim f_{22}$ are used in case that left eye image can be captured). With those feature values, we can compute eye gaze position on a monitor. Detail accounts are shown in section 6.

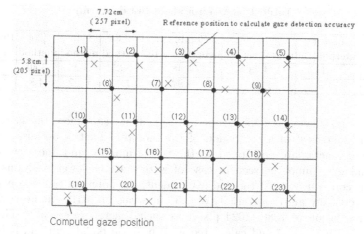

Fig. 3. An example of gaze detection errors on a 19" monitor

6 Detecting the Gaze Position on a Monitor

In section 3, we explain the gaze detection method only considering head movement. As mentioned before, when a user gazes at a monitor position, both the head and eyes tend to be moved simultaneously. So, we compute the additional eye gaze position with the detected 22 feature values (as mentioned in section 5) and a neural network (multi-layered perceptron). Here, the input values for neural network are normalized by the distance between the iris/pupil center and the eye corner, which are obtained in case of gazing at monitor center. That is because we do not use a zoom lens in our camera. That is, the more the user approaches the monitor (camera), the larger the eye size becomes and the farther the distance between the pupil/iris and the eye corner becomes, consequently. After detecting eye gaze position based on the neural network, we can determine a final gaze position on a monitor by head and eye movements based on the vector summation of each gaze position (face and eye gaze) [20].

7 Performance Evaluations

The gaze detection error of the proposed method is compared to that of our previous methods[3][4][18][20] as shown in Table 1. The test data are acquired when 95 users gaze at 23 gaze positions on a 19" monitor as shown in Fig. 3. Here, the gaze error is the RMS error between the actual gaze positions and the computed ones. Shown in Table 1, the gaze errors are calculated in two cases. The case I shows that gaze error about test data including only head movements and the case II does that the gaze error including head and eye movements. Shown in Table 1, the gaze error of the proposed method is the smallest in any case.

Fig. 3 shows an example of the gaze detection errors on a 19" monitor. The reference positions are marked as "black circle" and the computed gaze

Table 1. Gaze error about test data (cm)

Method	Linear interpol.[18]	Single neural net[18]	Combined neural nets[18]	[3] method	[4] method	[20] method	Proposed method
case I	5.1	4.23	4.48	5.35	5.21	3.40	2.24
case II	11.8	11.32	8.87	7.45	6.29	4.8	2.89

positions are shown as "X". From the Fig. 3, we can know the gaze errors are more increased in lower region of the monitor. That is because our gaze detecting cameras are positioned on the top of monitor and fine movement of head and eye cannot be seen in case of gazing at the lower positions of the monitor, consequently. At the 2nd experiment, the points of radius 5 pixels are spaced vertically and horizontally at 1.5" intervals on a 19" monitor with the screen resolution of 1280×1024 pixels as such Rikert's research[9]. The RMS error between the real and calculated gaze position is 2.85 cm and it is much superior to Rikert's method (almost 5.08 cm). Our gaze error is correspondent to the angular error of 2.29 degrees on X axis and 2.31 degrees on Y axis. In addition, we tested the gaze errors according to the Z distance (55, 60, 65cm). The RMS errors are 2.81cm at 55cm, 2.85cm at 60cm, 2.92cm at 65cm. It shows that the performance of our method is not affected by the user's Z position. Last experiment for processing time shows that our gaze detection process takes about 500ms in Pentium-III 866MHz and it is much smaller than Rikert's method (1 minute in alphastation 333MHz). The research[1] shows the smaller angular error of below 1 degree, but their method supposes that they know the 3D distance between two eyes and both lip corners and there is no individual variation for the 3D distances and the 3D diameter of eye ball. However, our preliminary experiments show that there are much individual variations and such cases can increase much gaze errors (the angular error of more than 5 degree).

8   Conclusions

This paper describes a new gaze detecting method. In future works, we have plans to research the method of capturing higher resolution eye image with zoom lens and it will increase the accuracy of final gaze detection.

References

1. J. Wang and E. Sung, 2002. Study on Eye Gaze Estimation, IEEE Trans. on SMC, Vol. 32, No. 3, pp.332-350
2. A. Azarbayejani., 1993, Visually Controlled Graphics. IEEE Trans. PAMI, Vol. 15, No. 6, pp. 602-605
3. K. R. Park et al., Apr 2000, Gaze Point Detection by Computing the 3D Positions and 3D Motions of Face, IEICE Trans. Inf.&Syst.,Vol. E.83-D, No.4, pp.884-894
4. K. R. Park et al., Oct 1999, Gaze Detection by Estimating the Depth and 3D Motions of Facial Features in Monocular Images, IEICE Trans. Fundamentals, Vol. E.82-A, No. 10, pp. 2274-2284

5. K. OHMURA et al., 1989. Pointing Operation Using Detection of Face Direction from a Single View. IEICE Trans. Inf.&Syst., Vol. J72-D-II, No.9, pp. 1441-1447
6. P. Ballard et al., 1995. Controlling a Computer via Facial Aspect. IEEE Trans. on SMC, Vol. 25, No. 4, pp. 669-677
7. A. Gee et al., 1996. Fast visual tracking by temporal consensus, Image and Vision Computing. Vol. 14, pp. 105-114
8. J. Heinzmann et al., 1998. 3D Facial Pose and Gaze Point Estimation using a Robust Real-Time Tracking Paradigm. Proceedings of ICAFGR, pp. 142-147
9. T. Rikert, 1998. Gaze Estimation using Morphable Models. ICAFGR, pp.436-441
10. A.Ali-A-L et al., 1997, Man-machine Interface through Eyeball Direction of Gaze. Proc. of the Southeastern Symposium on System Theory, pp. 478-82
11. A. TOMONO et al., 1994. Eye Tracking Method Using an Image Pickup Apparatus. European Patent Specification-94101635
12. Porrill-J et al., Jan 1999, Robust and Optimal Use of Information in Stereo Vision. Nature. vol.397, no.6714, pp.63-6
13. Varchmin-AC et al., 1998, Image based Recognition of Gaze Direction Using Adaptive Methods. Gesture and Sign Language in Human-Computer Interaction. Int. Gesture Workshop Proc. Berlin, Germany, pp. 245-57.
14. J. Heinzmann et al., 1997. Robust Real-time Face Tracking and Gesture Recognition. Proc. of the IJCAI, Vol. 2, pp. 1525-1530
15. Matsumoto-Y, et al., 2000, An Algorithm for Real-time Stereo Vision Implementation of Head Pose and Gaze Direction Measurement. Proc. the ICAFGR. pp. 499-504
16. Newman-R et al., 2000, Real-time Stereo Tracking for Head Pose and Gaze Estimation. Proceedings the 4th ICAFGR 2000. pp. 122-8
17. Betke-M et al., 1999, Gaze Detection via Self-organizing Gray-scale Units. Proc. Int. Workshop on Recog., Analy., and Tracking of Faces and Gestures in Real-Time System. pp. 70-6
18. K. R. Park et al., 2000. Intelligent Process Control via Gaze Detection Technology. EAAI, Vol. 13, No. 5, pp. 577-587
19. K. R. Park et al., 2002. Gaze Position Detection by Computing the 3 Dimensional Facial Positions and Motions. Pattern Recognition, Vol. 35, No.11, pp. 2559-2569
20. K. R. Park et al., 2002, Facial and Eye Gaze detection. LNCS, Vol.2525, pp. 368-376
21. Y. Matsumoto, 2000. An Algorithm for Real-time Stereo Vision Implementation of Head Pose and Gaze Direction Measurement, ICFGR, pp.499-505
22. B Wolfe, D. Eichmann, 1997. A Neural Network Approach to Tracking Eye Position, International Journal Human Computer Interaction, Vol. 9, No.1, pp. 59-79
23. David Beymer and Myron Flickner, 2003. Eye Gaze Tracking Using an Active Stereo Head, IEEE Computer Vision and Pattern Recognition
24. J. Zhu et al., 2002. Subpixel Eye Gaze Tracking, International Conference on Face and Gesture Recognition
25. R. Stiefelhagen, J. Yang, and A. Waibel, 1997. Tracking Eyes and Monitoring Eye Gaze, Proceedings of Workshop on Perceptual User Interfaces, pp. 98-100

Using Pattern Recognition for Self-Localization in Semiconductor Manufacturing Systems

Michael Lifshits, Roman Goldenberg, Ehud Rivlin, and Michael Rudzsky

Technion, Computer Science Department, Haifa, Israel.
{protezhe,romang,ehudr,rudzsky}@cs.technion.ac.il

Abstract. In this paper we present a new method for self-localization on wafers using geometric hashing. The proposed technique is robust to image changes induced by process variations, as opposed to the traditional, correlation based methods. Moreover, it eliminates the need in training on reference patterns. Two enhancements are introduced to the basic geometric hashing scheme improving its performance and reliability: using quadtree for efficient data access and optimal rehashing for Bayesian voting. The approach proved to be highly reliable when tested on real wafer images.

1 Introduction

As computational power has increased over the past decade, machine vision systems have become far more capable than before. In semiconductor industry, where highest levels of precision and robustness are required, they evolved to become a mainstream automation tool enabling computers to replace human vision and guide robotic handling, assembly, and inspection processes. Various semiconductor manufacturing equipment require precise self-localization, so that operations such as lithography, cutting and inspection can be performed to extremely tight tolerances. That is why self-localization on wafers has emerged as a very important task.

There is a demand from machine vision tools to become more adaptive to in-process variations and allow location of reference patterns despite changes in visual appearance occurring during the manufacturing process. Such changes may include non-linear contrast variation, color inversion, re-scaling, rotations and partial pattern obliteration [7].

Traditional tools, found in most commercial packages today, adopt normalized grayscale correlation (NGC) which is adequate for locating patterns under ideal conditions, but cannot cope with pattern appearance changes at run-time. Correlation scores are sensitive to degraded images and exhibit low tolerance to image changes in scale, angle, obliteration and contrast variation. Some vendors are recently proposing different techniques for self-localization to counteract such negative effects. For example, PatMax software from Cognex applies geometric feature analysis to find patterns on the wafer. Individual key features are first found, so that attributes such as shape, angles, arcs and shading can

C.E. Rasmussen et al. (Eds.): DAGM 2004, LNCS 3175, pp. 520–527, 2004.

be used to achieve invariant matching. Stemmer Imaging utilizes different tools, such as Support Vector Machines (SVM), neural networks, and optimized Hough transform, besides NGC, to accomplish invariant pattern recognition. All these approaches somewhat limited, as they build upon training on particular, predefined feature (known as an "acquisition target") printed at certain position on a wafer. During online self-localization this feature must appear in the field of view of the tool (it might be transformed though). Straightforward comparing current query image with all feasible features is unrealistic.

In this paper we propose a method for self-localization on wafers. It establishes a correspondence between the pattern currently observed in the field of view of the imaging tool and the previously constructed wafer map. It is fast enough for inline microscopy, robust to process variations and does not require training on the acquisition targets. The method is based on geometric hashing [2,4,5,6], a well known pattern recognition algorithm. Tests performed on real wafer images demonstrate the high reliability of the suggested approach.

2   Self-Localization as Pattern Recognition Task

Pattern recognition is a process of identifying objects from perceptual data. Recognition is achieved by finding the correspondence between a given pattern and a set of predefined patterns. In the model-based PR approach, the predefined patterns are described in terms of various properties, such as shape, color, etc. These descriptions are referred to as "models". A query pattern is then matched to one of those models.

Localization on the wafer is defined in the following manner: given an "eye point" (e.g. partial image of the wafer) estimate its exact position on the wafer map. Therefore, map-based self-localization can be interpreted as model-based pattern recognition as follows. First the wafer map is constructed from partial images captured by a microscope imaging system moving over the wafer surface. A possible alternative is to use wafer layout file specifying its geometric structure. Wafer map can be divided into many adjacent parts to be identified during localization. These parts correspond to models in pattern recognition framework, whereas the eye-point plays a role of a query pattern. Matching the current eye-point to one of the previously prepared parts of the wafer map during localization is essentially the same, as associating a query pattern to one of the predefined models in pattern recognition. An example of the wafer eye-point and the corresponding part of the wafer map is shown in Figure 1.

To cope with the enormous amount of geometric structures contained in wafer images, we choose to address the problem of self-localization using geometric hashing. Matching between query eye-point and wafer map is achieved by spatial correspondence of geometric features extracted from the images. These features are used to compose invariant model representations, stored in a database during the offline preprocessing stage of the algorithm. When analyzing the eye-point during localization, the same invariant representation is used as an indexing key to access the hash table and vote for the possible model matches. The model

Part of wafer "map"   eye-point

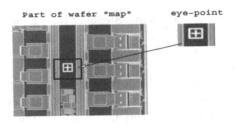

Fig. 1. Example of the eye-point within a wafer map

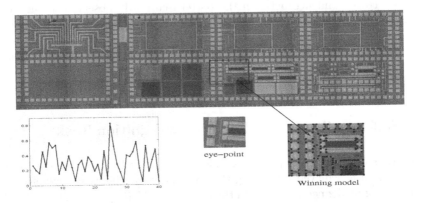

Fig. 2. Outline of the localization process. A wafer map that is constructed from 40 model images is shown on the top. Voting results for the eye-point shown in the middle are plotted on the left. The enlarged image of the winning model (25) with its feature points marked with black dots is presented on the right.

accumulating a significant number of votes indicates the correspondence of current eye-point with that model. An example of a typical localization process is presented in Fig. 2. This scheme provides low online complexity which determines the actual localization time. It linearly depends on the number of features contained in the eye-point and independent of the number of models stored in the system. This allows to perform a fast localization even on very large scale maps.

The localization algorithm is completed by verification. Given a set of candidate models that accumulated the highest number of votes, one has to determine which is the best match to the query eye-point. The eye-point is characterized in terms of a feature points set $\{\mathbf{x}_i'\}$ in $\mathbb{P}^2$, and each of the candidate matching models likewise described by its feature points $\{\mathbf{x}_i\}$. First, it is essential to find all $\mathbf{x}_i \leftrightarrow \mathbf{x}_i'$ point correspondences to compute a similarity transformation H which transforms a model to the eye-point: $\mathrm{H}\mathbf{x}_i = \mathbf{x}_i'$ for each i. Two correspondences are enough to compute H, however, since the points in the query eye-point are measured inexactly (due to noise), all of the correspondences should be used to determine the "best" transformation given the data. Every true correspondence gives rise to two independent equations in the entries of H, while the outliers are

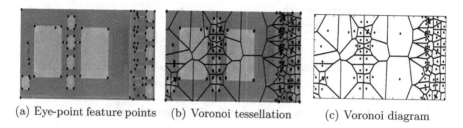

(a) Eye-point feature points   (b) Voronoi tessellation   (c) Voronoi diagram

Fig. 3. The process of constructing the Voronoi tessellation of the eye-point for verification acceleration.

robustly eliminated by the RANSAC algorithm. Then H is calculated by finding the least-squares solution of the over-determined linear system.

An important issue is how to efficiently find all of the correspondences. The voting stage of the algorithm provides one corresponding basis (two point-to-point correspondences) between the candidate model and the eye-point. This allows us to approximate the desired transformation H_S by $\widehat{H_S}$ and then, after applying $\widehat{H_S}$ on the candidate model, every model point $\widehat{H_S}\mathbf{x}_i$ will correspond to the closest eye-point feature $\mathbf{x}'_i$.

Thus, to compute all of the point correspondences it is possible to check the distance of each point $\mathbf{x}'_i$ to every transformed model point $\widehat{H}\mathbf{x}_i$. If the model contains m points and the eye-point contains n points, those inter-set distances are computed in $O(m\,n)$ time. This computation can be accelerated by employing a *Voronoi tessellation* [3] for segmentation of the eye-point image. Voronoi tessellation is partitioning of a plane with n points into n convex polygons such that each polygon contains exactly one point and every point in a given polygon is closer to its central point than to any other. We start the verification by constructing the Voronoi tessellation from the points in the query eye-point, which is done in $O(n \log(n))$ time [3] (see Fig. 3). This allows us to find the corresponding point of $\mathbf{x}_i$ in $O(log(n))$ by checking what polygon within the Voronoi tessellation contains the transformed point $\widehat{H}\mathbf{x}_i$ and choosing its center point. It follows that the time needed for point correspondences calculation is reduced from $O(m\,n)$ to $O(m\,log(n))$.

3 Algorithm Performance Enhancements

In this section we suggest two enhancements to the basic method improving its performance and reliability. They address the most problematic issues of the proposed localization method (as well as the general geometric hashing technique), which are the performance degradation in presence of noise and non-uniform occupancy of hash bins.

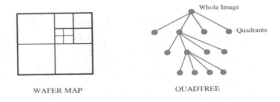

WAFER MAP   QUADTREE

Fig. 4. Decomposition of the wafer map with quadtree.

3.1   Quadtree

Unlike the absolute localization on the wafer, in the incremental localization discussed here, the initial position is assumed to be known approximately at the beginning of the localization session. The goal is then to refine the eye-point position estimation. Thus, it is possible to search for the eye-point only in relatively small "expectation region" on the wafer map, based on the known initial location. One can observe that in the case of localization on the wafer the set of models is actually formed from the neighboring wafer image tiles. This allows us to refine the basic algorithm using the *quadtree* - a technique for encoding an image as a tree structure (Figure 4).

The root node represents the entire image; its children represent the four quadrants of the entire image; their children represent the sixteen sub-quadrants, and so on.

Basic algorithm uses 2D hash table, while its bins are accessed according to the computed invariant coordinates. Multiple entries within single bin are organized in a linked list and retrieved altogether when the corresponding bin is accessed. The proposed enhancement replaces the linked list with a quadtree at each bin in the hash table. These trees correspond to the space partitioning of the global wafer map. This way it is possible to access only the relevant part of each tree during voting and thus, exclusively count for models from the "expectation region". To put it differently, the quadtree allows to select any partial wafer area to be searched for the query eye-point. Practically, the quadtree approach reduces the number of irrelevant entries accessed in a hash table, without actually removing any contained data.

3.2   Rehashing for Bayesian Voting

Ideally, for every feature point of the query eye-point image there is a single model point in the corresponding hash table bin. In practice, features generated by other models can fall into the same bin or even coincide. To deal with this problem one may suggest to reduce the bin size. Unfortunately, the feature points are non-uniformly distributed over the hash table. Therefore, for any bin size there will be either overpopulated or empty bins. It is generally proposed to use rehashing to deal with the problem of non-uniform occupancy of hash bins [8].

Another problem is that the uncertainty in feature point position caused by image noise, shifts it away from the corresponding model feature. This can be

Fig. 5. Examples of the real wafer images used as models in the algorithm.

solved by looking for the matching model feature in a certain, error dependent, neighborhood of the eye-point feature - voting region (see for example Bayesian approach in [9]).

To combine and take the best from both approaches we propose to use a scheme that equalizes voting regions rather then feature density, as suggested before. This is achieved by re-mapping the hash entries using the mapping T : $(u,v) \rightarrow (u',v')$, such that

$$
\begin{cases}
u' = \frac{\pi^2}{\sqrt{r+e^2}}ln(1+r) \\
v' = \arctan(\frac{v}{u})
\end{cases},
$$

where $r = \sqrt{u^2 + v^2}$. The detailed derivation and the theoretical basis of the scheme is reported elsewhere [1]. This allows to improve localization (as well as general geometric hashing) computational performance by minimizing the hash table size and the number of bins accessed, while maintaining optimal recognition rate. Alternatively, the proposed scheme can be used in classical single bin voting to improve recognition rate.

4   Experimental Results

In this section we demonstrate the capabilities of the proposed localization algorithm and provide a systematic evaluation of its performance and effectiveness. We performed tests on real wafer images obtained on KLA-Tencor 5200XP overlay metrology tool using 750 micron field of view. These images were used to construct a map covering an area of 2.25x12.75 millimeters on the wafer surface. Examples with enlarged partial images after preprocessing and corner detection are shown in Figure 5. There are two sequential stages involved in the localization algorithm: indexing based voting and candidates verification. During voting, eye-point invariant description is calculated and used to index into the hash table and vote for all the accessed entries. This description is based on a pair of features, a basis, see [6]. In many practical situations, there is a good chance that one of the points used to form a basis was reported by mistake and does not match any model point. Therefore, one should make multiple attempts using different bases (e.g. different descriptions), to ensure with sufficiently high probability that at least one of them is free of outliers. We evaluate the localization algorithm performance by varying the number of different eye-point feature bases being used in voting.

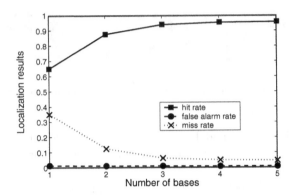

Fig. 6. System behavior with different number of bases being used in voting.

We tested the algorithm on a total of 10^4 different localization tasks to obtain a statistically meaningful measure of its performance. Each time we select a random eye-point and then, if correct location on the wafer "map" is reported by the algorithm (ground truth was available due to the nature of data set formation), the result is considered to be true positive (TP). In case of incorrect or no location (simply because none of the database models got enough votes), the result is regarded as a false positive (FP) or miss accordingly.

The summary of the obtained results is presented in Figure 6. Hit rate $HR = \frac{\#TP}{\#Tests}$ reaches 95% with 4% false alarm rate and 1% miss rate when 4 bases are being used. The inaccuracy of the localization result may be formulated as follows. Assuming the eye-point features are measured with Gaussian error of standard deviation σ, it can be shown that the RMS distance of the estimated point location from its true value is $\sigma(d/2n)^{1/2}$, where n is number of correspondences used and d is the number of transformation parameters. Thus substituting $d = 4$ for similarity, and taking 50 sample points, results in the estimation error of 0.2 pixels. If the eye-point image of size 200x200 pixels is taken at resolution of 50 micron we come up with the localization accuracy of 50 nanometer.

HR of 100% is not achieved as the constructed map contains areas difficult for localization: having no distinguishable features or filled with repetitive geometric structures. Note that even a human would have serious difficulties in solving the task of self-localization for "degenerate" eye-points selected from these unfavorable areas. Generally, we found that the algorithm performed well for eye-points from most of the wafer areas.

5   Summary

We presented a new method for self-localization on wafers, based on the geometric hashing technique. The method is invariant to changes in visual appearance, such as non-linear contrast variation, scale, rotation and partial obliteration.

Two enhancements were proposed to the basic geometric hashing algorithm, improving its computational performance by optimally distributing the entries over the hash table and allowing an efficient access to the table entries. We showed how a verification can be significantly accelerated by applying a voronoi tessellation of the eye-point. Extensive experimental analysis demonstrate the high reliability of the proposed method.

Acknowledgement. This work was conducted as part of the Wafer Fab Cluster Management (WFCM) Consortium supported by the "MAGNET" program of the Chief Scientist Office at the Israeli Ministry of Industry and Trade.

References

1. I. Blayvas, R. Goldenberg, M. Lifshits, E. Rivlin, and M. Rudzsky, Geometric hashing: Rehashing for bayesian voting, Accepted to *International Conference of Pattern Recognition*, 2004.
2. A. Kalvin, E. Schonberg, J. T. Schwartz, M. Sharir, Two-dimensional, model-based, boundary matching using footprints, *International Journal of Robotics Research*, vol. 5, no. 4, pp. 38–55, 1986.
3. M. V. Kreveld, M. Overmars, O. Schwarzkopf, and M. V. K. Mark de Berg, *Computational Geometry*, 2nd ed. Berlin: Springer Verlag, 2000, ch. Voronoi Diagrams: The Post Office Problem, pp. 147–163.
4. Y. Lamdan, J. T. Schwartz, and H. J. Wolfson, Object recognition by affine invariant matching, Proc. *IEEE Conference on Computer Vision and Pattern Recognition*, USA, pp. 335–44, June 1988.
5. Y. Lamdan, J. T. Schwartz, and H. J. Wolfson, Affine invariant model-based object recognition, *IEEE Transactions on Robotics and Automation*, vol. 6, no. 5, pp. 578–589, 1990.
6. Y. Lamdan, and H. J. Wolfson, Geometric hashing: A general and efficient model-based recognition scheme, Proc. *2nd International Conference on Computer Vision*, USA, pp. 238–49, June 1988.
7. S. Melikian, Geometric searching improves machine vision, *Lasers and Optronics*, vol. 18, no. 7, pp. 13, 1999.
8. I. Rigoutsos, and R. Hummel, Several results on affine invariant geometric hashing, Proc. *8th Israeli Conference on Artificial Intelligence and Computer Vision*, Israel, December 1991.
9. I. Rigoutsos, and R. Hummel, A bayesian approach to model matching with geometric hashing, *Computer Vision and Image Understanding*, vol. 62, no. 1, pp. 11–26, 1995.

Feature and Viewpoint Selection for Industrial Car Assembly

Dirk Stößel[1], Marc Hanheide[1], Gerhard Sagerer[1], Lars Krüger[2], and
Marc Ellenrieder[2]

[1] Faculty of Technology, Bielefeld University
P.O. Box 100131, 33501 Bielefeld, Germany
{dstoesse, mhanheid, sagerer}@techfak.uni-bielefeld.de
[2] Research and Technology, DaimlerChrysler AG
Wilhelm-Runge-Str. 11, D-89081 Ulm, Germany
{lars.krueger, marc.ellenrieder}@daimlerchrysler.com

Abstract. Quality assurance programs of today's car manufacturers
show increasing demand for automated visual inspection tasks. A typical example is just-in-time checking of assemblies along production lines.
Since high throughput must be achieved, object recognition and pose
estimation heavily rely on offline preprocessing stages of available CAD
data. In this paper, we propose a complete, universal framework for CAD
model feature extraction and entropy index based viewpoint selection
that is developed in cooperation with a major german car manufacturer.

1 Introduction

Quality assurance and final inspection are fundamental steps in production work
flow. Automated visual inspection of assemblies is therefore in the focus of recent
research (cf. [8], [6], [9] and [5]). Because CAD data of the assembled parts must
be available for construction processes, model-based object recognition and pose
estimation are eligible methods to allow automated visual inspection. Real-time
production processes dictate the need for fast and accurate online algorithms.
The framework we propose hence transfers as much of the algorithmic effort
as possible to an *offline* preprocessing stage, yielding very fast and accurate
online visual inspection. Our framework is based on a new generalized definition
of features that supports the incorporation of different feature types under a
common layer of abstraction.

Besides the efficient online application, the selection of appropriate camera viewpoints is fundamental to robust visual inspection of assemblies. Our
framework therefore also predicts viewpoints which optimally separate different
expected assembly configurations of valid and invalid mounting scenarios.

The article is structured as follows: In Section 2, we propose a generalized
definition of features for model-based object recognition and pose estimation. It
will be shown how the framework models rigid objects and flexible collections
of objects. In Section 3, we will discuss how to accurately predict occlusions
by applying a mixture of rule-based lookups and bounding volumes intersection

C.E. Rasmussen et al. (Eds.): DAGM 2004, LNCS 3175, pp. 528–535, 2004.

tests. Section 4 then addresses the calculation of optimal camera viewpoints using 3D to 2D projection pursuit with collective entropy index. Finally, Section 5 details the framework's performance in feature extraction, occlusion prediction and object recognition.

2 Characteristic Localized Features

The framework proposed in this paper is a preprocessing stage suited for model-driven 3D/2D object recognition and pose estimation algorithms like the ones introduced by Lowe [7] and Araújo et al. [1]. In general, they use an initial object pose estimate to project features of a given 3D model on the camera view plane. Afterwards, they iteratively obtain improved estimates by matching the projected features with features extracted from real world images. Object recognition algorithms generally require features that are highly *characteristic*. For pose estimation, features have to be *localized* (must have a spatial position) in the model and image domain. Thus, our framework must automatically extract *Characteristic Localized Features (CLFs)*. In order to be suitable for any 3D/2D object recognition scheme, each CLF must at least meet the following set of requirements:

1. **Projection:** CLFs are spatially represented in 3D. To allow for 2D comparison, CLFs must be projected on a camera view plane, given a camera model and an estimated pose. An appropriate projection prescript has to be defined for every type of CLF.
2. **Visibility determination:** Since CLFs can become occluded under 2D projections, their visibility has to be determinable for any given view. CLFs that are visible are called *active*.
3. **Visual Appearance:** Projected CLFs are compared to image features. Therefore, 2D projection must imply some visual outcome recognizable in real world images. E.g., in case of edges, the visual appearance would typically be a strong local image gradient perpendicular to the edge direction.

These requirements form a unique layer of abstraction that enables the proposed framework to perform all tasks without incorporating any further knowledge about feature types.

Good CLFs are reliably trackable features in image sequences, as presented by Shi and Tomasi [11] or Schmid et al. [10]. Since they have been empirically shown to be appropriate, edges are commonly used (cf. [6]). We chose *contour edges*, i.e. edges that potentially form the object's outline, to explain our approach in the following. Additionally, the framework incorporates functionality to deal with localized color and texture features.

Edges which possibly form the contour of an object are interesting CLF candidates because the object's silhouette is always formed by a subset of contour edges. The silhouette will usually appear in real world images as intensity gradients. What is more, Kettner and Welzl [4] provided empirical evidence that the number of contour edges in a 3D model is usually much smaller than the total

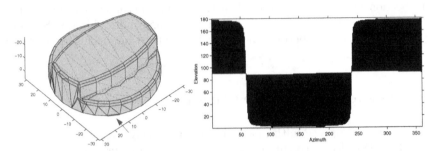

Fig. 1. *Left*: Automatically extracted CLFs (axis units in mm). Model edges are displayed as thin dashed lines, extracted CLFs as thick black ones. *Right*: Visibility map of the CLF highlighted on the left side. Black denotes view angles under which the CLF is active. Axis units denote the view angle measured in degrees.

number of edges. The framework determines the set E_c of a model's potential contour edges by analyzing the angle between all its adjacent triangles:

$$E_c = \left\{ E | isconvex(E) \wedge \alpha_E = \sphericalangle(\boldsymbol{N}_E^1, \boldsymbol{N}_E^2) > 0 \right\} \tag{1}$$

where $\boldsymbol{N}_E^1, \boldsymbol{N}_E^2$ represent the normals of two adjacent triangles and E the edge shared by the triangles. The angle α_E allows to assign a score to each element of E_c, because a more acute angle yields a more frequent appearance of the edge under different projections.

All elements of E_c with a certain minimum score are new contour edge CLFs. To meet requirement 2., the visibility of the edge elements is pre-calculated relative to all possible discrete view-angles and stored in separate run-length-encoded *visibility maps*. An example of automatically generated contour edge CLFs and a particular visibility map is displayed in Fig. 1.

Based on the specification of CLFs, a *(basic) model* can be defined as a set of CLFs referring to the same rigid object and object coordinate system. Furthermore, an *aggregation* can be described as a tree in which the root node represents the aggregation's pose with respect to the world coordinate system. Each sub-node represents a basic model and the model's *pose* (6DOF) relative to the parent node.

3   Occlusion Prediction

Inferring aggregation poses from real world images by means of 3D/2D object recognition schemes always involves the projection of the aggregation features on 2D camera planes. Regarding our framework, the projection of CLFs belonging to an aggregation might result in inactive (occluded) CLFs. Fig. 2 shows that any CLF might either become occluded by parts of the basic model it is attached to or by other basic models of the aggregation. The former occlusion type will be termed *intramodel occlusion*, the latter *intermodel occlusion*. Automated inspection in car industry requires fast online occlusion prediction. Intermodel

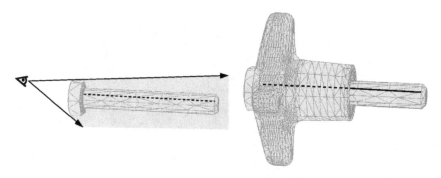

Fig. 2. The two occlusion types occurring with aggregations. *Left*: Intramodel occlusion. A contour edge CLF along the bolt's thread (dashed black line) is hidden behind the same bolt's head. *Right*: Intermodel occlusion. The same contour edge CLF, partly occluded (dashed black line) by a knob.

occlusions are correctly predicted by lookup operations in the visibility maps. In the worst case, these maps consume space in the order of $O(c{\cdot}v)$, with c denoting the number of CLFs and v referring to the number of scanned view angles during map calculation. The lookup operation has efficient constant time complexity per call.

Extending the lookup strategy to aggregations would require to pre-calculate the visibility maps for all CLFs attached to every possible aggregation configuration. This would lead to combinatorial explosion of storage space consumption. Therefore, intermodel occlusion prediction is based on tightly wrapping each aggregated model in a small number of simple geometric bounding volumes such as boxes or spheres. Our framework performs this task offline during aggregation creation. The online part of occlusion prediction first checks the pre-calculated visibility maps. For each visible candidate, view-rays between a virtual camera and points on the candidate CLF are tested for intersection with each bounding volume, thus ruling out features that are (partially) hidden behind parts of the aggregation. The intersection tests have a reasonable worst case time complexity of $O(c_v{\cdot}b)$, with b denoting the number of bounding volumes and c_v the number of CLFs passing the visibility map test.

4   Viewpoint Selection

In order to support robust recognition, a further task of the framework is to determine those viewpoints from which an assembly might be inspected best. In this context, Vázquez et al. [13] proposed the information theoretic measure *viewpoint entropy*. It expresses the amount of information conveyed in a certain scene that is being watched from a given point. Measures like viewpoint entropy are often based on the *visual appearance* of a *specific* feature. Though we use an entropy measure, too, the CLF abstraction enables us to estimate the underlying probability distributions from the *location* of a *variety* of features. The entropy measure employed here was recently introduced as a class separability index [12]

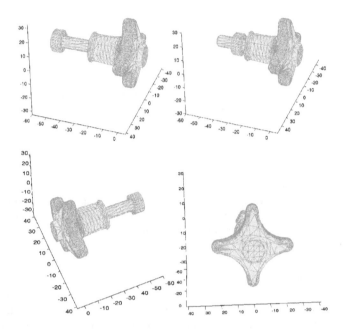

Fig. 3. *Top*: A knob, screw and nut aggregation in configurations typical for invalid (left) and valid (right) mounting. *Bottom*: The good quality view (left) allows good distinction between different nut positions. In the bad quality view (right), the nut position is hard to infer as large parts of it are hidden behind the knob.

and is called *collective entropy*. It estimates the quality of a view by measuring how *distinguishable* aggregation configurations will be under projection onto a given camera plane. An example with two configurations is shown in Fig. 3.

Generally, collective entropy describes how well measurements in Cartesian space, each belonging to a distinct class, might be separable from each other with respect to the class labels. It is calculated by partitioning the N measurements m_i into d-dimensional cells with hyper-cuboid topology:

$$m_i = (m_{i_1}, \cdots, m_{i_d}) \in \mathbb{R}^d, \ i = 1, \ldots, N \tag{2}$$
$$R_j = \left[\min m_{i_j}, \max m_{i_j} \right], \ 1 \leq j \leq d, \ i = 1, \ldots, N. \tag{3}$$

The faces of the hyper-cuboid cells are constructed by dividing each range of values R_j into B parts of equal length. An initial cell resolution is chosen and the m_i are partitioned accordingly. Afterwards, one obtains the conditional entropy which Cover and Thomas [2] define as

$$H(X|Z) = - \sum_{z \in Z} p(z) \cdot \sum_{x \in X} p(x|z) \cdot \log_2 p(x|z). \tag{4}$$

where each $z \in Z$ is a non empty hyper-cuboid cell and $x \in X$ is the set of measurement class labels. Thus, $H(X|Z)$ indicates how uniformly distributed the

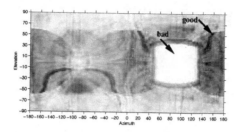

Fig. 4. Complete map of collective entropy indices. Dark areas denote high quality view angles, light areas indicate bad quality (all axis units in degrees). The arrows point to the map positions corresponding to the bottom two views in Fig. 3.

measurements are, given a certain partitioning resolution. However, $H(X|Z)$ is not robust against the shifting of cell borders. Singh [12] therefore repeatedly lowers the cell resolution and recalculates the conditional entropy until a minimum resolution is reached. Collective entropy is then taken as the area under the curve of the conditional entropy values with respect to cell resolution.

Viewpoint selection iteratively places a virtual camera at discrete view angles in an orbit around an aggregation. For each iteration and for each expected configuration, the positions of visible CLFs are projected to the camera plane. Afterwards, the probability distributions in (4) are obtained by Monte Carlo sampling from the CLF location domain. The complete scheme can be regarded as 3D to 2D projection pursuit with collective entropy as projection pursuit index (cf. [3]). To our knowledge, it has not been tried before. The process yields a map that indexes the degree to which any discrete view angle conveys separable information about the observed scene. Some results are shown in Fig. 3.

5   Performance

During object recognition, the step inducing the highest computational load is the 3D to 2D projection of features because it involves online occlusion prediction. Therefore, we evaluated the performance of our online algorithm in the following way: First, we chose an evaluation candidate out of a set of aggregations with varying complexity. Single basic models with a total number of less than 1000 CLFs were considered to be of low complexity. In contrast to this, aggregations of more than two basic models with a total number of more than 2000 CLFs were considered to be of high complexity. Each candidate was randomly rotated in 3D and online occlusion prediction carried out in 1000 runs. We then calculated the average execution times which are visualized in Fig. 5). It shows that even for the most complex aggregation the algorithm executes in less than 12ms. The execution time scales in average approximately linear to the total number of CLFs. To ensure that the results of our automated feature selection are suited for model-based object recognition, we first determined the average amount of active CLFs similar to the above evaluation scheme. The results are listed in Table 1. The average amount of active CLFs is well balanced for the

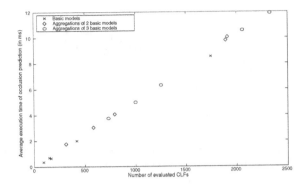

Fig. 5. Performance of occlusion prediction on a Pentium 4 PC (2GHz, 512MByte).

Table 1. Average number of active CLFs compared to their total number.

object	total no. CLFs		avg. act. CLFs	
nut	92	(100%)	13.6	(14.8%)
bolt	148	(100%)	28.0	(18.9%)
flat washer	164	(100%)	37.2	(22.7%)
oil lid	418	(100%)	32.7	(7.8%)
knob	1747	(100%)	74.0	(4.2%)
assembly	2059	(100%)	112.4	(5.5%)

Table 2. Average and standard deviation of relative and absolute pose estimation accuracy.

DOF	$\mu_{relative}$	$\sigma_{relative}$	$\mu_{absolute}$	$\sigma_{absolute}$
x [mm]	-0.15	0.53	-0.31	0.53
y [mm]	-0.002	0.4	-0.81	0.73
z [mm]	-0.007	4.76	-2.6	3.9
roll [°]	0.006	1.27	0.578	1.4
pitch [°]	0.097	0.9	-0.513	1.57
yaw [°]	0.068	0.84	-0.45	1.8

first three objects in Table 1 and rather low for the "oil lid", "knob" and the assembly of "knob", "bolt" and "flat washer", indicating that their CLF sets should be compressed.

Object recognition and pose estimation performance was evaluated with an industrial system (cf. [6]). A standard camera with 320x240 resolution was moved around a mounted oil lid at constant speed and a distance of approx. 70mm, recording 420 images. The object pose was calculated for each image. The average and standard deviation of relative (i.e. image-to-image) and absolute accuracy are given in Table 2. Note that the average error of parameter estimation relative to the distance of the camera is always smaller than 1%. Thus, model-based pose estimation meets the strong accuracy requirements of car industry.

6   Conclusion

We presented a complete, universal framework for automated selection of features and viewpoints for model-based visual inspection that was developed in co-operation with the DaimlerChrysler AG. Given CAD data of real world objects, the framework extracts characteristic features and prepares them for fast and robust occlusion prediction. It further determines high quality viewpoints to inspect an assembly from. Our feature extraction approach has been demonstrated for contour edge features. Performance results for the offline model preparation were given accordingly. For online occlusion prediction, execution time in the average case scaled approximately linear to the amount of processed features. The tests have been carried out on CAD models of car production assemblies and standard industrial fixation elements.

The underlying concepts for occlusion prediction and viewpoint selection are not restricted to contour edges, but can also be used for a wide selection of other kinds of 3D localized features which meet the CLF requirements. The proposed framework is thus based on a novel layer of abstraction for features in general. It was successfully tested with an industrial object recognition system.

References

1. H. Araújo, H. L. Carceroni, and C. M. Brown. A fully projective formulation to improve the accuracy of Lowe's pose-estimation algorithm. *Computer Vision and Image Understanding*, 70(2):227–238, 1998.
2. T. M. Cover and J. A. Thomas. *Elements of Information Theory*. Wiley series in telecommunications. Wiley-Interscience, 1991.
3. J. H. Friedman and J. W. Tukey. A projection pursuit algorithm for exploratory data analysis. *IEEE Trans. on Computers*, C-23(9):881–889, 1974.
4. L. Kettner and E. Welzl. Contour edge analysis for polyhedron projection. In *Geometric Modelling: Theory and Practice*, pages 379–394. Springer, 1997.
5. K. Khawaja, A. Maciejewski, D. Tretter, and C. Bouman. A Multiscale Assembly Inspection Algorithm. *IEEE Robotics & Automation Magazine*, 3(2):15–22, 1996.
6. Thorsten Kölzow. *System zur Klassifikation und Lokalisation von 3D-Objekten durch Anpassung vereinheitlichter Merkmale in Bildfolgen*. PhD thesis, Bielefeld University, 2002. in german.
7. D. G. Lowe. Fitting parameterized three-dimensional models to images. *IEEE Trans. on Pattern Analysis and Machine Intelligence*, 13(5):441–450, 1991.
8. J. Miura and Katsushi Ikeuchi. Task planning of assembly of flexible objects and vision-based verification. *Robotica*, 16:297–307, 1998.
9. J. Noble. From inspection to process understanding and monitoring: a view on computer vision in manufacturing. *Image and Vision Computing*, 13(3):197–214, 1995.
10. C. Schmid, R. Mohr, and C. Bauckhage. Evaluation of interest point detectors. *International Journal of Computer Vision*, 37(2):151–172, 2000.
11. Jianbo Shi and Carlo Tomasi. Good features to track. In *Proc. IEEE Conf. Computer Vision and Pattern Recognition*, pages 593–600, 1994.
12. S. Singh. PRISM - a novel framework for pattern recognition. *Pattern Analysis and Applications*, 6(2):134–149, 2003.
13. P. P. Vázquez, M. Feixas, M. Sbert, and W. Heidrich. Viewpoint selection using viewpoint entropy. In T. Ertl, B. Girod, G. Greiner, H. Niemann, and H. P. Seidel, editors, *Vision, Modeling, and Visualization 2001*, pages 273–280, 2001.

Automating Microscope Colour Image Analysis Using the Expectation Maximisation Algorithm

Alexander Ihlow and Udo Seiffert

Leibniz Institute of Plant Genetics and
Crop Plant Research (IPK) Gatersleben
Corrensstr. 3, 06466 Gatersleben, Germany
Pattern Recognition Group
{ihlow, seiffert}@ipk-gatersleben.de
http://bic-gh.ipk-gatersleben.de/wgrp/mue

Abstract. Dyed barley cells in microscope colour images of biological experiments are analysed for the occurrence of haustoria of the powdery mildew fungus by a fully automated screening system. The region of interest in the images is found by applying Canny's edge detector to the hue channel of the HSV colour space. Potential haustoria regions are extracted in RGB colour space by an adaptive Gaussian mixture classifier based on the Expectation Maximisation (EM) algorithm. Since the classes *cell* and *haustorium* are at very close quarters, their correct separation is a crucial part and needs a constraining mechanism which ties the EM algorithm to its initialisation data to prevent a too large deviation from it.

1   Introduction

Automating the screening and the analysis of biological experiments is a challenging research area in the field of bioinformatics and engineering. This paper is related to a project where resistance mechanisms of crop plants against the powdery mildew fungus are studied from the genetical point of view. In the experiments, young barley leaves are bombarded with DNA-coated tungsten particles to "switch on or off" desired genes in cells. For analysis purposes, an additional reporter gene[1] is expressed in cells that were hit by a particle. This dyes the affected genetically transformed cells greenish blue and allows their identification by bright field microscopy [8]. The task is to evaluate the susceptibility of the genetically transformed cells to the powdery mildew fungus under the impact of different test genes. A successful penetration of the fungus into the cell is indicated by the development of a haustorium – a dark object with "fingers" that is located between the cell wall and the cell membrane and feeds the fungus by leaching the cell. These objects have to be counted in an automatic analysis procedure.

Since there are many genes to be considered for a potential resistance of the plant against pathogens, a big number of experiments has to be performed to

---

[1] β-glucuronidase (GUS) reporter gene

C.E. Rasmussen et al. (Eds.): DAGM 2004, LNCS 3175, pp. 536–543, 2004.

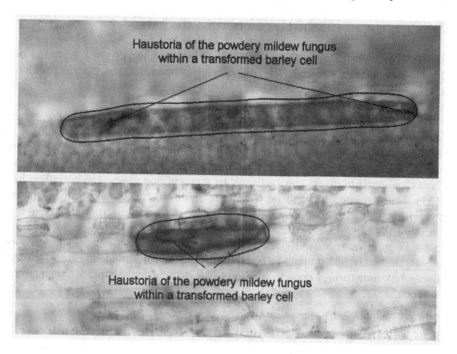

Fig. 1. Cutouts of microscope images of barley cells. The dyed cells are genetically transformed, both cells contain two haustoria of the powdery mildew fungus. At coarse scales, Canny's edge detector marks these cells by a closed boundary.
Color version available via http://bic-gh.ipk-gatersleben.de/wgrp/mue/prj03.php

attain a sufficient statistical confidence. Therefore, an automated image acquisition system and an automatic analysis procedure is needed. Manual screening is a tedious, subjective and time-consuming task that cannot be handled by laboratory assistants due to that huge amount of data. For an automatic image acquisition, the microscope slides are mounted on an x-y table which scans a number of preparations fully automatically under the control of a computer, e.g., overnight. Now, finding genetically transformed cells and therein assessing the development status of the haustoria without human interaction is the task and the challenge of the analysis procedure.

This paper describes a method to automatically identify suspicious objects, i.e., parts of genetically transformed cells that may be a haustorium. It is organised as follows: Section 2 introduces the properties of the image material and explains how the regions of interest, i.e., genetically transformed cells, are found in the images. Afterwards, Section 3 describes the identification of potential haustoria via the Expectation Maximisation (EM) algorithm, before Section 4 concludes the paper.

2   Preprocessing of the Image Material

Figure 1 shows two typical cutouts of microscope images, both containing one dyed genetically transformed cell with two haustoria of the powdery mildew fungus inside. By default, the microscope camera produces images of 2600×2060 pixel in 24-bit colour.

In [5] we have shown that the dyed genetically transformed cells can be reliably detected by applying Canny's edge detector [2] to the hue channel of the HSV colour space, rather than performing multi-dimensional edge detection in the RGB colour space or using histogram-based methods. At a coarse scale Canny's algorithm marks the dyed cells by a closed boundary. The bounding box of these closed contours will be the input of the further haustorium detection procedure. Unfortunately, the haustoria stand out scarcely from the dyed cell, and there is no such straightforward colour space transformation to separate them as good as the dyed cells from the remaining cell tissue. Therefore, we stay in the RGB colour space, which contains the entire image information, and show what haustorium detection results can be achieved by pixel classification methods.

3   Cell Image Analysis by Clustering in Colour Space

3.1   Naive Bayes Classification

Suppose a naive Bayes classifier at first. A number of N d-dimensional data vectors $\mathbf{x}_n \in \mathbb{R}^{d \times 1}$ from the entire data set $\mathbf{X} \in \mathbb{R}^{d \times N}$ has to be classified into K classes. If the prior (a priori) probabilities $P(k)$ and the probability density functions $p(\mathbf{x}|k)$ of the $k = 1 \ldots K$ classes are known, then the posterior (a posteriori) probability $P(k|\mathbf{x}_n)$ of a sample vector $\mathbf{x}_n$ to belong to class k can be calculated by Bayes' rule [1] (maximum likelihood decision) according to

$$P(k|\mathbf{x}_n) = \frac{P(k)\, p(\mathbf{x}_n|k)}{\sum_{j=1}^{K} P(j)\, p(\mathbf{x}_n|j)} \, . \tag{1}$$

Inspecting our data in the RGB colour space, we can decompose the mixture distribution of colours into three stretched ellipsoids, representing the three dominant image matters, namely *background*, *cell*, and *haustorium*. Such ellipsoidal distribution can be well modelled by the multivariate Gaussian distribution, which is described by the mean vector $\boldsymbol{\mu}$, specifying the center point of the ellipsoid, and the covariance matrix $\boldsymbol{\Sigma}$, which is responsible for the shape and the orientation of the ellipsoid.

$$p(\mathbf{x}|\boldsymbol{\mu}_k, \boldsymbol{\Sigma}_k) = \frac{1}{\sqrt{\det \boldsymbol{\Sigma}_k (2\pi)^d}} e^{-\frac{1}{2}(\mathbf{x}-\boldsymbol{\mu}_k)^T \boldsymbol{\Sigma}_k^{-1}(\mathbf{x}-\boldsymbol{\mu}_k)} \tag{2}$$

See Figure 2 for the segmentation results of this naive Bayes classification where the parameters of the classes were taken from typical samples. In the upper

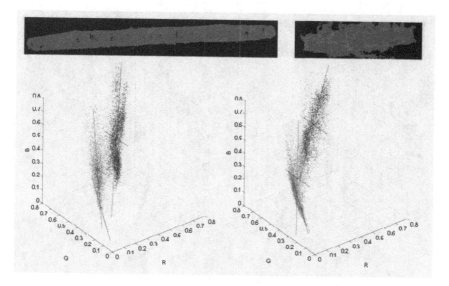

Fig. 2. Segmentation by a naive Bayes pixel-classification in RGB colour space modelling the classes by multivariate Gaussians.

images, the pixel-labels are depicted in a soft-output manner, i.e., the vector of the posterior probabilities $[P(k = 3|\mathbf{x}), P(k = 2|\mathbf{x}), P(k = 1|\mathbf{x})]^T$ is assigned to the RGB value of each pixel, making the saturation of the colour follow the reliability of the estimate. The lower figures show both the clusters in RGB colour space as well as the principal components (eigenvectors) of each cluster. As can be seen, simply assigning parameters from typical images for the three classes and performing a naive Bayes classification does not provide satisfactory results because the parameter set will never match the actual scenario sufficiently due to some inevitable variations in colour and illumination in the image data. Therefore, some "self adaptation" of the classification algorithm to the actual data is needed to improve the classification results.

3.2   EM Classification Using the Complete Data Set

The Expectation Maximisation (EM) algorithm [4,7] is known to be a powerful clustering technique for mixture distributions where the parameters of the underlying probability density functions are adapted in an iterative way, trying to yield the best recovery of the mixture components. Its clustering performance depends on two major conditions: the precision the actual data is represented by the data model, as well as the initialisation parameters, because it can converge to local extrema instead of finding the global optimum. Such clustering methods are used for many different applications in image processing, e.g., skin detection [6]. In [3] an advanced image querying system is described which applies the EM algorithm to an eight-dimensional space of colour, texture, and position features, where the number of mixture components is chosen following the Minimum Description Length (MDL) principle. Fortunately, we know the number

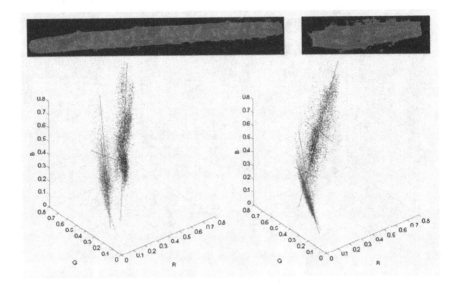

Fig. 3. Segmentation results of the EM algorithm when iterating on the entire data set of RGB colour vectors.

of mixture components in feature space very well due to the speciality of our image material. Furthermore, colour appears as the dominant feature, therefore we can ignore texture and position features and use the RGB colour information as the only feature.

We initialise the a priori probability of the classes with $P(k) = 1/K = 1/3$ (since we do not know $P(k)$ in advance) and perform a data-driven initialisation of the mean vectors and covariance matrices of the classes from exemplary, hand-segmented image parts, as already done for the naive Bayes classification. Then, the iteration of the EM algorithm is run in the following manner:

The probability (at iteration step t) of each data vector $\mathbf{x}_n$ to belong to class k is calculated (expectation step) by

$$P^t(k|\mathbf{x}_n) = \frac{P^t(k)\, p(\mathbf{x}_n|\boldsymbol{\mu}_k^t, \boldsymbol{\Sigma}_k^t)}{\sum\limits_{j=1}^{K} P^t(j)\, p(\mathbf{x}_n|\boldsymbol{\mu}_j^t, \boldsymbol{\Sigma}_j^t)} . \tag{3}$$

A new parameter set for the iteration step $t+1$ containing the prior probabilities, mean vectors and covariance matrices for each class is calculated according to (maximisation step)

$$P^{t+1}(k) = \frac{1}{N} \sum_{n=1}^{N} P^t(k|\mathbf{x}_n) \tag{4}$$

$$\boldsymbol{\mu}_k^{t+1} = \frac{1}{N P^{t+1}(k)} \sum_{n=1}^{N} P^t(k|\mathbf{x}_n)\, \mathbf{x}_n \tag{5}$$

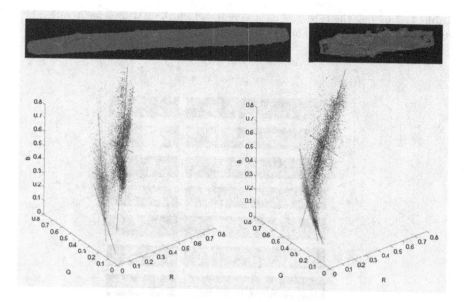

Fig. 4. Segmentation results of the EM algorithm iterating data vectors that were estimated by a reliability of at least $R_{min} = 0.65$.

$$\Sigma_k^{t+1} = \frac{1}{NP^{t+1}(k)} \sum_{n=1}^{N} P^t(k|\mathbf{x}_n) \, (\mathbf{x}_n - \boldsymbol{\mu}_k^{t+1}) \, (\mathbf{x}_n - \boldsymbol{\mu}_k^{t+1})^T. \tag{6}$$

The algorithm is terminated when the labelling in the segmented image does not change anymore.

As can be seen in Figure 3, the clustering separates the *background* and *cell* class very well but it suffers from an overestimation of the *haustorium* class. This solution is optimal from the EM point of view, but it is not our desired result for an appropriate segmentation. In spite of different initial parameters, the EM algorithm tends towards bad results of the same manner. Incrementing the model order, i.e., providing more classes generally does not yield more solid results, especially for the right hand image.

3.3 Constraining the EM by Reliability Information

A straightforward solution to achieve appropriate segmentation results is found in constraining the algorithm to the initial parameter set, which is known quite well in our particular case. Using the complete data set (all image pixels) makes a large number of *cell* labels to turn over into *haustorium* labels during the iterations. Iterating on reliably estimated data vectors only (instead on the entire data set) prevents the algorithm from deviating too much from its initial parameters. The classification reliability of each sample is given by $R = \max_k\{P^t(k|\mathbf{x}_n)\} \in [1/K \ldots 1]$ and is inherently calculated in each iteration.

Table 1. Tapering the subset of data samples which the EM uses for iteration by a stepwise variation of the reliability parameter R_{min}.

In the following, we restrict the data set, which the EM operates on, to data samples that were classified with a reliability of at least R_{min}. Note that the lower bound of this parameter depends on the number of classes and that an appropriate parameter value has to be found empirically by a visual inspection of the segmentation results. See Table 1 for a test series of our particular segmentation problem. It can be observed that there is a significant changeover between $R_{min} = 0.50 \dots 0.60$. Choosing R_{min} larger than 0.75, we observed convergence problems of the algorithm for the right hand image, where the algorithm oscillated harmonically between two states instead of terminating. This can be explained by the recurrent changing of the considered data set parts during the iterations and needs further attention.

Figure 4 shows the detailed segmentation results for $R_{min} = 0.65$. Despite some misclassified objects in the *haustorium* class it shows the haustoria quite good — with this method we are able to automatically identify suspicious objects, i.e., potential haustoria. Now, further analysis on the detected objects is needed to distinguish haustoria from discolourations or other parts inside the cell that have a similar colour, e.g., the cell nucleus. As a next step, therefore these image parts have to be further evaluated, taking form parameters of the detected objects into account, e.g., by detecting the "fingers" of the haustoria. This will be examined in the near future and is out of the scope of this paper.

This paper is accompanied by a continuative web site of the presented results. Visit http://bic-gh.ipk-gatersleben.de/wgrp/mue/prj03.php for a more detailed compilation of exemplary cell images and their clustering results.

4   Conclusions

The Expectation Maximisation (EM) algorithm is applied in the RGB colour space to perform a segmentation of microscope colour images for the identification of small objects which stand out scarcely from the region of interest. To provide satisfactory results, it is shown that this special problem needs a constraint mechanism which ties the EM algorithm to its initialisation parameters and forbids a too large deviation from it. This constraint mechanism is realised by dynamically restricting the data set the algorithm operates on to a reliably estimated part only. The mechanism is parametrised by a reliability threshold parameter which has to be determined empirically. This technique prevents a defection of the desired segmentation and provides good retrieval results of suspicious objects via an automatic analysis procedure.

Acknowledgements. We thank Patrick Schweizer and Grit Zimmermann for their support concerning the biological background. Thanks also to Christian Schulze and Tobias Czauderna for fruitful discussions. This work was supported by the German Ministry of Education and Research (BMBF) under grant 0312706A.

References

1. Thomas Bayes. An essay towards solving a problem in the doctrine of chances. *Philosophical Transactions of the Royal Society of London*, 53:370–418, 1753. (available via http://www.stat.ucla.edu/history/essay.pdf).
2. John F. Canny. A computational approach to edge detection. *IEEE Transactions on Pattern Analysis and Machine Intelligence (PAMI)*, 8(6):679–698, November 1986.
3. Chad Carson, Megan Thomas, Serge Belongie, Joseph M. Hellerstein, and Jitendra Malik. Blobworld: A system for region-based image indexing and retrieval. In *Third International Conference on Visual Information Systems*. Springer, 1999.
4. Arthur P. Dempster, Nan M. Laird, and Donald B. Rubin. Maximum likelihood from incomplete data via the EM algorithm. *Journal of the Royal Statistical Society, Series B*, 39(1):1–38, 1977.
5. Alexander Ihlow and Udo Seiffert. Microscope color image segmentation for resistance analysis of barley cells against powdery mildew. In *9. Workshop "Farbbildverarbeitung"*, ZBS Zentrum für Bild- und Signalverarbeitung e.V. Ilmenau, Report Nr. 3/2003, pages 59–66, Ostfildern-Nellingen, Germany, October 2003.
6. Michael J. Jones and James M. Rehg. Statistical color models with application to skin detection. In *IEEE Conference on Computer Vision and Pattern Recognition '99*, pages 274–280, June 1999.
7. Richard A. Redner and Homer F. Walker. Mixture densities, maximum likelihood, and the EM algorithm. *SIAM Review*, 26:195–239, 1984.
8. Patrick Schweizer, Jana Pokorny, Olaf Abderhalden, and Robert Dudler. A transient assay system for the functional assessment of defense-related genes in wheat. *Molecular Plant-Microbe Interactions*, 12(8):647–654, 1999.

Camera Orientation of Mars Express Using DTM Information

Christian Heipke[1], Heinrich Ebner[2], Ralph Schmidt[1], Michael Spiegel[2],
Rüdiger Brand[1], Albert Baumgartner[2], Gerhard Neukum, and the
HRSC Co-Investigator Team

[1] Institute of Photogrammetry and GeoInformation,
Universität Hannover, Nienburger Str. 1,
30167 Hannover, Germany
schmidt@ipi.uni-hannover.de

[2] Chair for Photogrammetry and Remote Sensing,
Technische Universität München, Arcisstr. 21,
80333 München, Germany
spiegel@bv.tum.de

Abstract. In January 2004 the High Resolution Stereo Camera (HRSC) on board the ESA mission Mars Express started imaging the surface of planet Mars in colour and stereoscopically in high resolution. The Institute of Photogrammetry and GeoInformation (IPI) of the University of Hannover and the Chair for Photogrammetry and Remote Sensing (LPF) of the Technische Universität München are jointly processing the data of the HRSC: Using automatically extracted tie points and Mars Orbiter Laser Altimeter (MOLA) data, the exterior orientation of the Mars Express spacecraft is being calculated perpetually in a combined photogrammetric bundle adjustment during the two years lasting mission. This paper describes the used approaches for tie point matching and bundle adjustment. On the basis of two selected orbits the results of the matching and the achieved accuracy of the bundle adjustment are presented and evaluated.

1 Introduction

In June 2003 the European Space Agency (ESA) launched the Mars Express spacecraft from the Baikonur launch pad in Kazakhstan. After a journey of about six months the orbiter was successfully inserted into a polar orbit around Mars. During its two years mission the High Resolution Stereo Camera (HRSC) on board of Mars Express images large parts of the Mars surface. The HRSC is a multisensor pushbroom camera consisting of nine charge coupled device (CCD) line sensors mounted in parallel for simultaneous high resolution stereo, multispectral, and multi-phase imaging [1]. At pericenter about 300 km above the surface of Mars a ground resolution of approximately 12 m is attained. The Camera Unit (CU) of the HRSC addition

C.E. Rasmussen et al. (Eds.): DAGM 2004, LNCS 3175, pp. 544–552, 2004.

ally comprises a Super Resolution Channel (SRC) which captures frame images embedded in the basic HRSC swath at a ground resolution of up to 2.5 m.

The three-dimensional position and attitude of the spacecraft is constantly determined by the European Space Agency (ESA) by combining techniques of measuring Doppler shifts, acquiring ranging data, triangulation measurements and a star tracker camera. These measurements result in a three-dimensional position and attitude of the spacecraft over time which can be considered as approximate exterior orientation in classical photogrammetry. However, these values are not consistent enough for high accuracy photogrammetric point determination. Therefore, a bundle adjustment (EO) has to be performed using these values as direct observations for the unknown EO parameters. As further input for the bundle adjustment automatically extracted tie points derived via digital image matching (DIM) are being used. Additionally, ground control points (GCPs) are necessary to transform the results into a Mars-fixed coordinate system. Because on Mars very few classical GCPs exist, a globally available digital terrain model (DTM) is applied.

In section two of this paper the approach for the determination of the EO of Mars Express is presented. In section three the results of the tie point matching and the bundle adjustment derived from two selected test orbits are shown and discussed.

2 Photogrammetric Point Determination

The processing of the HRSC data is divided into two steps. At first tie points are being extracted using software developed at IPI in Hannover. The derived tie points serve together with the observed EO and the DTM as input for the bundle adjustment developed at LPF in Munich. With the resulting adjusted EO of the Mars Express Orbiter it is possible to derive high level products such as DTMs, ortho photos and shaded reliefs from the imagery.

The principle of the transformation from object (X, Y, Z) to image coordinates (x, y) is explained in [2]. The starting point is the set of collinearity equations [4]:

$$
\begin{pmatrix} x - x_0 \\ y - y_0 \\ -c \end{pmatrix} = \lambda M^T \left(\Delta\varphi, \Delta\omega, \Delta\kappa \right) D^T \left(\varphi, \omega, \kappa \right) \left[\begin{pmatrix} X \\ Y \\ Z \end{pmatrix} - \begin{pmatrix} X_0 + \Delta X_0 \\ Y_0 + \Delta Y_0 \\ Z_0 + \Delta Z_0 \end{pmatrix} \right]
\tag{1}
$$

The EO refers to a camera coordinate system common to all CCD lines and is expressed for a given readout cycle n as X_0, Y_0, Z_0, φ, ω, κ. The interior orientation (IO) parameters x_0, y_0, c are defined in the image coordinate system, three separate values exist for each line. The transformation between the image coordinate system and the camera coordinate system is given by ΔX_0, ΔY_0, ΔZ_0, $\Delta\varphi$, $\Delta\omega$, $\Delta\kappa$, which have been determined in the geometric calibration for each line separately. M as well as D are rotation matrices, λ is a scale factor. The image coordinates are given by x and y, which are derived automatically in this case via DIM.

The IO of the HRSC has been calibrated in a laboratory at Dornier, Friedrichshafen and has been verified during the six month journey to Mars by means of star observations. So far no deviations from the calibration have been experienced so that the IO of the HRSC is considered to be stable.

2.1 Image Matching

Our matching approach follows a coarse to fine strategy which means the matching result is refined step by step through image pyramids. As input data the HRSC imagery, the observed EO and the calibration data of the IO are needed. As an optional input it is possible to use a DTM as approximate information. On Mars a high accuracy DTM derived from data of the MOLA instrument is available [10].

At first point features are extracted using the Förstner operator [6] and the images are matched pairwise in all combinations using the cross correlation coefficient as similarity measure. Each image is divided into subareas to ensure an even distribution of the tie points over the whole area. To reduce ambiguities and computing time the matching location and a search space for the corresponding feature is computed when transferring a feature from one image to the other. Since no epipolar geometry exists for linescanner imagery a feature in one image is transferred to the next image via equation (1). For the transformation from object space to image space as a function of the image line (readout cycle) n an additional condition (2) has to be applied where x points in flight direction.

$$x(n)=x\left(n, X_0(n), Y_0(n), Z_0(n), \varphi(n), \omega(n), \kappa(n)\right)=0 \tag{2}$$

This problem can be solved using the well known Newton-method for the above zero-crossing detection where the derivative $x'(n_i)$ is replaced by the pixelsize of the image.

$$n_0 = initial\ value\ for\ the\ image\ line$$
$$n_{i+1} = n_i - x\left(n_i\right)/\ pixelsize \qquad i = 0,1,... \tag{3}$$

After matching all overlapping images pairwise in all combinations an undirected graph is generated. The nodes of the graph are the point features, the edges are the matches between them. This graph is divided into connected components. The next step is the generation of the point tuples, whereas one point tuple is characterised by the property that not more than one feature per image is admissible. The complexity of this problem can grow exponentially. Instead of using tree search or binary programming techniques a RANSAC (Random Sample Consensus) procedure [5] is applied. The method relies on the fact that the likelihood of hitting a good configuration (correct tuple) by randomly choosing a set of observations (features of the subgraph) is large after a certain number of trials. The advantage of this method is the high probability of obtaining a good point. Including a geometric consistency check, the method also eliminates blunders [3].

From the start pyramid level (lowest resolution) to the so-called intermediate level (medium resolution) feature based matching is carried out using the whole images.

Going down the image pyramid the image size increases, as well as the number of extracted features. Besides the heavily increasing computational time, the matching of the complete images would result in too many tie points for the camera orientation. Therefore the matching procedure is carried out only for selected "image chips", starting below the intermediate pyramid level. This means that tie points are searched in areas only where points have been found before due to good texture [13].

To further refine the result Multi Image Least Squares Matching (MILSM) is carried out following the approach of Krupnik [9]. In this approach the tie points are matched in all images simultaneously. A detailed description of the implemented MILSM can be found in [7]. Because it is the most accurate matching technique available it is possible to further refine the result of the feature based matching. In our implementation we can decide whether to apply MILSM or not for each pyramid level. To save computing time it is advisable to carry out MILSM only on the last level, which denotes the original resolution.

Finally, model points are derived via a forward intersection of the image coordinates of the tie points. They serve as an approximation for the reduction of the search space on the next lower pyramid level instead of the MOLA points. A more detailed description of the application flow can be found in [11].

2.2 Bundle Adjustment Using Control Information

In the bundle adjustment the concept of orientation images proposed by Hofmann et al. [8] is used. This approach estimates the parameters of the EO only at a few selected image lines, at so-called orientation images [12]. The EO for all other image lines is interpolated from the values at the orientation images. The differences for each image line can be considered as correction terms that have to be added to the interpolated values. This solution keeps the number of orientation parameters small and, what is more important, allows to exploit the good relative accuracy of the observed orientation parameters. The mathematical model for photogrammetric point determination with a 3-line camera is based on the well known collinearity equations (1).

The starting point of the discussion about bundle adjustment using a DTM as control information is an approach presented in [12]. This approach uses a least squares adjustment with additional conditions to obtain a relation between a DTM and the bundle adjustment without control information. In case of Mars it is possible to use the MOLA DTM as control information. One suitable way is to use the terrain surface derived by MOLA points and fit the matched HRSC points into the MOLA DTM. This is advantageous because there are more MOLA points than HRSC points.

At locations where HRSC points are available the MOLA data can be described as a local surface. The surface is defined either by three original MOLA points or by four points of a DTM grid, which are interpolated using the original MOLA measurements. In the first case the local surface is described by three irregularly spaced MOLA points, which stem from the original MOLA measurements. This structure is based on original MOLA points and the vertical distance d of HRSC point H to the plane defined by M_1, M_2, and M_3 (Fig. 1, left). In the second case, the HRSC points have to lie on a bilinear surface defined by four neighbouring DTM points, which enclose the HRSC point and show a grid structure. The distance d is defined as vertical distance between HRSC point H to the bilinear surface defined by the four points M'_1, M'_2, M'_3, and M'_4 (Fig. 1, right). In the current implementation the approach using the MOLA DTM has been applied because the advantages of using the MOLA DTM outweigh the usage of the raw MOLA points.

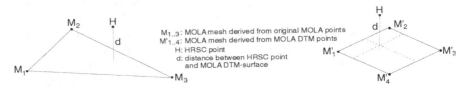

M1..3: MOLA mesh derived from original MOLA points
M'1..4: MOLA mesh derived from MOLA DTM points
H: HRSC point
d: distance between HRSC point
    and MOLA DTM-surface

Fig. 1. Left: Structure based on original MOLA points. Right: Regular DTM grid

The mathematical model of the bundle adjustment is given in equation (4):

$$v_x = f\left(X, Y, Z, x_0, y_0, c, X_0, Y_0, Z_0, \varphi, \omega, \kappa\right) - x_i$$
$$v_y = f\left(X, Y, Z, x_0, y_0, c, X_0, Y_0, Z_0, \varphi, \omega, \kappa\right) - y_i \tag{4}$$

with:
$$X_0 = \bar{X}_{B_0} + \bar{X}_0, \ Y_0 = \bar{Y}_{B_0} + \bar{Y}_0, \ Z_0 = \bar{Z}_{B_0} + \bar{Z}_0, \ \varphi = \bar{\varphi}_B + \bar{\varphi}, \ \omega = \bar{\omega}_B + \bar{\omega}, \ \kappa = \bar{\kappa}_B + \bar{\kappa}$$

whereas the EO is composed of biases $\left(\bar{X}_{B_0}, \bar{Y}_{B_0}, \bar{Z}_{B_0}, \bar{\varphi}_B, \bar{\omega}_B, \bar{\kappa}_B\right)$ valid for the entire strip and terms $\left(\bar{X}_0, \bar{Y}_0, \bar{Z}_0, \bar{\varphi}, \bar{\omega}, \bar{\kappa}\right)$ valid for a single CCD line only.

Additionally one observation equation (5) is used for each HRSC point

$$v_d + d = f(X_H, Y_H, Z_H, X_{M_i}, Y_{M_i}, Z_{M_i}) \ i = 1..4 \tag{5}$$

with three unknowns (X, Y, Z of HRSC tie point), one observation (difference d between HRSC point and MOLA surface) and twelve constants (X, Y, Z for all four MOLA DTM points) for each surface. The accuracy of the observed difference is determined by the accuracy of the MOLA points.

3 Processing of HRSC Imagery

In this section, first the used HRSC imagery will be described. In the second part the results of the matching and bundle adjustment will be presented and discussed on the basis of the orbits 18 and 68.

3.1 Data

For the evaluation of the matched tie points and the achieved accuracy of the bundle adjustment, imagery of the orbits 18 and 68 have been chosen which have been received in the early phase of the Mars Express mission. The observations of the EO and the calibration data of the IO as well as the MOLA DTM are used as input for the DIM and the bundle adjustment. The a priori accuracy has been introduced into the bundle adjustment with a value of 1000 m for the position and 28 mgon for the attitude. The trajectory of the orbiter is considered to be very stable. Additionally the HRSC imagery is used for the matching.

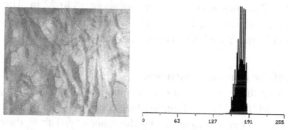

Fig. 2. Left: Part of orbit 68 with high texture. Right: Histogram of region with low contrast

The CCD arrays of the HRSC consist of 5176 active pixels each, which yields a swath width of about 65 km on the surface of Mars. The strips can have a length of up to 300.000 lines, spanning about 4.000 km on the surface. Due to a limited bandwidth between Mars and Earth only the nadir channel is able to operate at full resolution. Generally the resolution of the two stereo channels has to be reduced by a factor of 2 and the remaining channels by a factor of 4. To obtain an equivalent scale the nadir channel has to be resampled to the resolution of the stereo channels for the matching. Depending on the covered region on Mars the imagery shows areas with high texture and areas with hardly any texture and low contrast (Fig. 2).

3.2 Results

3.2.1 Results of the Matching

In a first evaluation the ray intersections of the tie points are analysed. The values of the EO from ESA have been fixed in the bundle adjustment and no DTM as control information has been introduced. This can be considered as a forward intersection. The obtained values are compared to the results calculated by the bundle adjustment improving φ and κ. This means a constant bias is estimated for both angles along the entire orbit. Biases for φ and κ were introduced, because only these two parameters can be improved using tie points.

Table 1. Theoretical standard deviations of the object coordinates

orbit	altitude [km]	σX [m]	σY [m]	σZ [m]
18	275 - 375	11.0 / 5.9	13.0 / 6.6	34.0 / 18.0
68	269 - 505	30.3 / 10.3	26.6 / 10.9	48.8 / 17.8

In Tab. 1 the accuracies of the object coordinates of the ray intersections are shown for the selected orbits. The left value is the standard deviation of the ray intersections using the EO from ESA. The right value shows the achieved theoretical standard deviation of the ray intersections after improving φ and κ. The accuracies of all computed orbits are in a range of about 6 to 11 m in X and Y, depending on different imaging altitudes. Z accuracies of all orbits are about 18 to 22 m. The standard deviations of the ray intersections are improved by a factor of 2 to 3 and a final accuracy of about 0.4 pixel in X and Y and 0.8 pixel in Z is achieved.

3.2.2 Results of the Bundle Adjustment

The second part of the results shows the evaluation after HRSC object points have been fitted to the MOLA DTM. Here, the biases of all six parameters of the EO (X_0, Y_0, Z_0, φ, ω, κ) have been improved along the trajectory. Tab. 2 shows the improved values and their standard deviations for the three orbits. In most cases the values can be determined with high significance, because the standard deviations of the bias values are lower than the bias values themselves.

The standard deviations of the object coordinates for the orbits 18 and 68 are shown in Tab. 3, which depend on two results. At first there are the accuracies of the ray intersection (Tab. 1) determining the accuracies within the orbit itself. Second, there are the accuracies of the absolute orientation between orbit and MOLA DTM (Tab. 2). Thus, the precision of the point determination is a combination of these two accuracies. The standard deviations of the object points in all three dimensions are less than 20 m (Tab. 3).

Table 2. Theoretical standard deviations of orbit determination

orbit		X_0 [m]	Y_0 [m]	Z_0 [m]	φ [mgon]	ω [mgon]	κ [mgon]
18	bias value	90.4	-64.6	-38.2	-51.1	-64.4	-6.2
	bias σ	7.3	11.0	1.6	0.3	1.5	0.1
68	bias value	-12.1	-112.3	-41.2	-24.9	-12.1	-35.9
	bias σ	10.7	16.7	6.7	0.4	1.9	0.6

Table 3. Theoretical standard deviations of HRSC points fitted to MOLA DTM

orbit	σ X [m]	σ Y [m]	σ Z [m]
18	9.1	10.6	17.0
68	14.4	16.7	17.5

Finally, the root-mean-square (RMS) Z differences between object coordinates of the HRSC tie points and the MOLA DTM were investigated. In one case the result is computed without DTM as control information and in the other case with DTM information. The RMS Z differences between DTM and HRSC object points are in the range of 200 m (orbit 18: 177 m, orbit 68: 200 m). After the bundle adjustment including DTM control information the RMS Z differences decrease by a factor of three (orbit 18: 84 m, orbit 68: 63 m). Therefore, the adaptation of HRSC data to the MOLA reference system has succeeded.

4 Conclusion

The results show the efficiency of the image matching and bundle adjustment approaches to achieve an improved exterior orientation with MOLA DTM as control information. The tie points are distributed evenly over the whole block with a good rate of 3-fold points. An accuracy of 0.4 pixel in position and 0.8 pixel in height is achieved. The significant improvement of the position of the exterior orientation increases from an a priori accuracy of 1000 m to less than 20 m in all three dimensions (Tab. 2). The accuracy of the attitude increases from 28 mgon to 1-2 mgon in all angles. The position and attitude could be improved by an average factor of 30 to 50. Thus, after the bundle adjustment the object coordinates of the tie points have a very high accuracy. Finally, there is a high consistency between HRSC points and MOLA DTM, which constitutes the valid reference system on Mars.

Acknowledgement. This work is funded by Deutsches Zentrum für Luft- und Raumfahrt e.V. (DLR) under grant no. 50 QM 0103 and 50 QM 0104. This support is gratefully acknowledged.

References

1. Albertz, J., Scholten, F., Ebner, H., Heipke, C., Neukum, G.: Two camera experiments on the Mars 94/96 missions. Geo-Informations-Systeme (6) 4 (1993) 11-16
2. Brand R., Ohlhof T., Stephani, M.: Processing of 3-line imagery on a digital photogrammetric workstation. In: McKeown, Jr., D., M., McGlone, J. C., Jamet O. (eds.): Integrating Photogrammetric Techniques with Scene Analysis and Machine Vision III, (3072), Proceedings of SPIE, Orlando, Florida (1997) 2-10
3. Brand, R., Heipke, C.: A system for automatic aerial triangulation. IntArchPhRS (32) 2 (1998) 27-32
4. Ebner, H., Kornus, W., Ohlhof, T.: A simulation study on point determination for the MOMS-02/D2 space project using an extended functional model. Geo-Informations-Systeme (7) 1 (1994) 11-16
5. Fischler, M.A., Bolles, R.C.: Random Sample Consensus: A paradigm for model fitting with applications to image analysis and automated cartography. Communications of the ACM (24) 6 (1981) 381-395

6. Förstner, W.: A feature based correspondence algorithm for image matching. IntArchPhRS (26) 3/3 (1986) 150-166
7. Heipke, C., Schmidt, R., Brand, R., Oberst, J., Neukum, G. and the HRSC Co-Investigator Team: Performance of automatic tie point extraction using HRSC imagery of the Mars Express mission. IntArchPhRS (35) (2004)
8. Hofmann, O., Navé, P., Ebner, H.: DPS – A digital photogrammetric system for producing digital elevation models and orthophotos by means of linear array scanner imagery. IntArchPhRS (24) 3 (1982) 216-227
9. Krupnik, A.: Multiple-patch matching in the object space for aerotriangulation. *Technical Report 428*, Department of Geodetic Science and Surveying, The Ohio State University, Columbus (1994)
10. Neumann, G.A., Lemoine, F.G., Smith, D.E., Zuber, M.T.: The Mars Obiter Laser Altimeter archive: Final precision experiment data record release and status of radiometry. Lunar Planet. Sci. XXXIV, Lunar and Planetary Institute, Houston (2003)
11. Schmidt, R., Brand, R.: Automatic determination of tie points for HRSC on Mars Express. ISPRS Workshop High Resolution Mapping from Space 2003, October 6-8, Hannover (2003)
12. Spiegel, M., Baumgartner, A., Ebner, H.: Orientation of Mars Express/HRSC imagery using laser altimeter data as control information. ISPRS Workshop High Resolution Mapping from Space 2003, October 6-8, 2003, Hannover (2003)
13. Tang, L., Heipke; C.: Automatic relative orientation of aerial images. PE&RS (62) 1 (1996) 47-55

Detection and Classification of Gateways for the Acquisition of Structured Robot Maps

Derik Schröter, Thomas Weber, Michael Beetz, and Bernd Radig

Munich University of Technology
Boltzmannstr. 3, 85748 Garching b. München, Germany
{schroetd, webert, beetz}@in.tum.de
http://www9.in.tum.de/people/schroetd/Research/

Abstract. The automatic acquisition of structured object maps requires sophisticated perceptual mechanisms that enable the robot to recognize the objects that are to be stored in the robot map. This paper investigates a particular object recognition problem: the automatic detection and classification of gateways in office environments based on laser range data. We will propose, discuss, and empirically evaluate a sensor model for crossing gateways and different approaches to gateway classification including simple maximum classifiers and HMM-based classification of observation sequences.

1 Introduction

So far robot maps primarily support safe and efficient navigation [2,7], see [11] for an extended overview of state-of-the-art mapping approaches. The next generation of maps will in addition provide better support for the achievement of service tasks. They will do so by explicitly representing the environment structure and by modeling relevant objects of the environment.

In our previous research, we have proposed Region & Gateway Maps (RG Maps) as resources for autonomous mobile robots acting in structured human indoor environments [4]. RG maps are tuples $\langle R, G \rangle$, where R denotes a set of regions and G is a set of gateways that represent the possible transitions between regions. A region has a compact geometric description, a bounding box, a list of adjacent gateways, and a set of models that represent the task relevant objects within the region. The second key component of RG maps are gateways, prominent and recognizable areas that connect different parts of the robot's environment. The recognition of gateways allow robots to autonomously extract the environment structure and represent it in the map [8,3,1].

In two companion papers we have detailed our mechanisms for acquiring compact geometric descriptions of regions [4] and for the acquisition of models of rectangular task relevant objects [10]. This paper addresses the problem of automatically detecting and classifying crossing gateways.

Gateways form perceptually recognizable, characteristic transitions between two or more adjacent regions. They can be traversed in any direction and are the only possibility to pass from one region into another. The partitioning of floor plans is based on gateways such as cross-ways, junctions, turns and narrow passages, see also figure 1. In our

C.E. Rasmussen et al. (Eds.): DAGM 2004, LNCS 3175, pp. 553–561, 2004.
© Springer-Verlag Berlin Heidelberg 2004

approach gateways are specified by a class label, adjacent regions, traversal directions, crossing-points and gateway-points that can be used for detecting when a gateway is entered and left. The set of discrete **gateway points** is derived from features extracted from a single laser scan (see section 2). Pairs of these gateway points form passages, the robot can pass through. Narrow passages or open-close-transitions are characterized by a single pair of gateway points, whereas multi-passage gateways like junctions for example contain several passages. It is also possible to combine multiple gateway structures as encountered in office environments (refer to Fig. 1). We will focus here on crossing gateways, i.e. gateways which connect hallway regions. The detailed concepts and properties of such gateways can be found in [4].

The computational problem of gateway recognition and classification can be formulated as follows: Given a single scan or a sequence of scans provided by a laser range finder and a set of gateway models, the robot autonomously detects and classifies crossing gateways. We will solve the gateway recognition problem in a computational process that executes a sequence of three steps: (1) Generating hypotheses for virtual line models (VLMs) (sec. 2), (2) Determining weights according to general and specific gateway models (sec. 3), (3) Using the generated observation vector for classification (sec. 5). Finally, we empirically evaluate the proposed methods (sec. 5) and conclude.

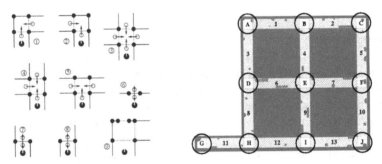

Fig. 1. Left: Classes of Gateways - Right/Left Turn (1,2), X-Crossing (3), T-Junction/Forking (4,5), Narrow Passage (6), Right/Left Opening (7,8), Combination of Gateways (9); (● gateway point, ○ crossing point, ← traversal direction, ... region border); **Right**: Example environment - letters denote gateways, numbers denote regions

2 Generating Hypotheses for Virtual Line Models (VLMs)

In order to represent gateway hypotheses we propose virtual line models (VLMs) as an appropriate feature language. VLMs are based on the assumptions that environments are rectangular and hallways have approximately the same width. The VLM consists of a left, right and front virtual line as well as a hidden virtual line (Fig. 2). To generate VLM hypotheses, we first extract low-level features, i.e. virtual lines and depth singularities from the line segment and point scan, respectively. In the next step, those virtual lines are grouped to form hypotheses with respect to the VLM in Fig. 2. In the first processing step the algorithm generates a line segment scan L_{LS} from the point scan L_P by the means of linear regression according to [6].

Virtual Lines. Line segments from L_{LS} which lie approximately on the same line are grouped and represented by that line, also referred to as virtual line (see Fig. 2).

Depth Singularities. This point feature is extracted from L_P and denotes discontinuities in the distance measurements of a laser scan, see Fig. 2. The parameter Δd_{min} indicates the minimum distance difference of two succeeding distance measurements to represent a depth singularity. $P_i \in L_P$ is the point where the distance measurement d_i ends. P^i_{ds} are the points at the depth singularities.

$$P^i_{ds} = \{P_i \ : \ (d_i < d_{i\pm1}) \ \wedge \ (|d_i - d_{i\pm1}| > \Delta d_{min})\}$$

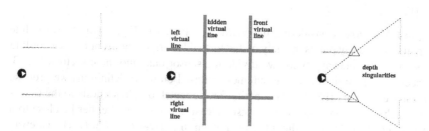

Fig. 2. Point scan of an X-Crossing (left); Virtual Line Model for Crossing Gateways, i.e. X-Crossing, L/R-Turn, T-Junction (middle); Depth singularities in a laser scan (right)

Virtual Line Grouping. Based on the virtual lines and depth singularities we generate hypotheses for VLMs, which signal that a crossing gateway of some kind may be present. To generate candidates for the virtual left and right line, we search for parallels among the virtual lines, where the robot is in between. Virtual front lines intersect a pair of parallels approximately in a right angle and in front of the robot. Finally, we estimate the virtual hidden lines. Therefore, we consider depth singularities, that are close to the virtual left or right line. The hidden line is constructed such that it is parallel to the virtual front line and intersects with the given depth singularity. To deal with situations where no valid depth singularities are present, we add hypotheses where the estimation of the hidden line is solely based on the environment assumptions. As a result we obtain a set of annotated virtual line quadruples, which represent hypotheses for VLMs. The gateway points are defined by the intersections of those virtual lines.

3   Evaluating the VLM Hypotheses

We evaluate gateway hypotheses by assessing the similarity of a perceived VLM and a specific gateway class. Therefore, we propose the following measures:

1. rectangularity and distance measure to reflect the general model quality and
2. freespace measure to account for the match with a specific gateway class.

As a result we obtain an observation vector for each VLM hypothesis. Additionally, we track VLM hypotheses over consecutive measurements while the robot is moving towards the gateway to generate observation sequences.

Distance Measure. The expected hallway width d_{hw} has been manually measured. Deviations from this value are weighted according to:

$$w_{distance}^i = 1 - \sqrt{\frac{|d_i - d_{hw}|}{d_{hw}}} \qquad W_d = \frac{\sum_{i=1}^4 w_{distance}^i}{4}$$

Whereas d_i is the Euclidian distance between two neighboring gateway points and W_d denotes the averaged distance weight.

Rectangularity Measure. The rectangularity criterion refers to the inner angles α_i ($i = 1...4$) of the convex quadrangle, given by the VLM. We define the rectangularity by the deviation of the inner angles α_i from $\frac{\pi}{2}$.

$$W_r = 1 - \frac{\sum_{i=1}^4 |\alpha_i - \frac{\pi}{2}|}{2\pi}$$

Freespace Measure. Considering the VLM as depicted in Fig. 2 (right), we define three pairs of gateway points, namely on the virtual left, right and front line. According to those pairs of gateway points, we divide the sensor data into three sectors, Fig. 3. Each sector S_i comprises N_{S_i} measurements. Based on those definitions we propose the freespace measure (FSM) as a quantity for the match of a hypothesis to the sensor data. In each of the three sectors the sensor measurements should either be close to a given line (*On Line FSM*) or should cross a given line (*Over Line FSM*). The gateway class determines which of the two FSM variants applies to a certain sector. For example, considering an *L-Turn* the measurements in the front sector are expected to match the virtual front line (*On Line FSM*). Whereas for an *X-Crossing*, measurements in the same sector are expected to cross the virtual front line (*Over Line FSM*), see Fig. 3.

On Line FSM. P_i denotes a laser measurement from the point scan L_P and $d(P_i)$ is the respective distance measurement. We compute a point P_i^{vl} on the considered virtual line and its distance to the robot $d(P_i^{vl})$, whereas P_i and P_i^{vl} lie on the same ray from the robot. Then we count all measurements for which the difference of $d(P_i)$ and $d(P_i^{vl})$ lies between a given lower and upper threshold. Finally, we normalize this on-line-count (C_{ol}) with the overall number of measurements in the sector:

$$W_{on\ line}^{S_i} = C_{ol}^{S_i}/N_{S_i}$$

Over Line FSM. This measure only applies to the front sector. We construct a line l_{par} parallel to the virtual front line and set back by a given distance. Then we count all measurements which intersect l_{par}, and normalize the resulting over-line-count. Analogous to the *On Line FSM* we get $W_{over\ line}^{S_i}$, see also Fig. 3.

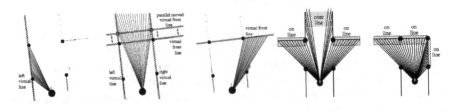

Fig. 3. From Left to Right: Freespace measure (FSM) for different cases - *On Line FSM* (1,3), *Over Line FSM* (2), (• gateway point, — laser scan measurement, - - line for free space evaluation); FSM configurations for *XCrossing* (4) and *LTurn* (5)

Generating Gateway Weights and Observation Sequences. Utilizing the proposed measurements, we define weights for each VLM hypothesis with regard to a certain gateway class GW:

$$W(GW, VLM) = \frac{f_{vlm}}{2} \cdot (W_d(VLM) + W_r(VLM)) + \frac{f_{gw}}{3} \cdot \sum_{i=1}^{3} W_{FSM}^{S_i}(GW)$$

Whereas f_{vlm} and f_{gw} denote weighting factors for the general and gateway specific measurements, respectively. As a result we obtain an observation vector for each VLM hypothesis, where the entries quantify the similarity of the hypothesis to a specific gateway class. In most practical cases the mobile platform approaches the gateway area. Thus, we observe the same VLM hypotheses from different positions, where the distance to the gateway is continuously decreasing. The VLM hypotheses tracking is based on the gateway points and Euclidian distances. If all gateway points of two VLM hypotheses have an approximate match, they are considered to be identical. Based on this tracking, we obtain sequences of observation vectors. A sequence starts when the hypothesis is first observed and the distance falls below a threshold. It is finished or corrupted when it is either lost or the robot enters the gateway.

4 Classification

We now investigate the computational task of classifying the obtained observation sequences with regard to the introduced gateway classes, by means of the following classification methods: based on the observation vector closest to the gateway, weighted average over all observation vectors in a sequence and Hidden Markov Models.

1. Single Observation and Averaged Sequence Based Classification

Observations close to a gateway imply a more complete coverage of the gateway area by the sensors, hence they are in general the most informative. The single observation classifier (SOC) considers the maximum weight to determine the gateway at hand. This approach demonstrates the discrimination power of the freespace measurements and the resulting weights. It is, however, very sensitive to sensor noise, occlusions and dynamic changes in the environment. A simple alternative is the fusion of consecutive measurements by calculating a weighted average over the observation sequence, where the weights are inversely proportional to the distance. Afterwards, SOC is used to decide which specific gateway is present. Whereas the approach considers the complete observation sequence, it does not fully exploit probabilistic properties of observations and temporal relations between them.

2. Classification Based on Hidden Markov Models (HMMs)

A more promising approach to gateway classification is the use of HMMs. They provide mechanisms to model temporal structures in sequences, by the use of probabilistic observation and state transition models. A detailed description of the theory can be found in [9]. In the next paragraphs we briefly outline the steps necessary to use HMMs in the context of gateway detection based on the introduced sensor model.

Clustering the Data and Initializing the HMM. Since our sensor model provides continuous measurements we use HMMs with continuous outputs. To deal with the implicated complexity of such HMMs we explicitly cluster the data using the k-means-algorithm [5]. The clusters are then used to built the observation model (mean and covariance matrices), and to define the structure of the HMM. Since the coverage of the gateway area by the sensor differs for different positions, we expect the data to represent clusters for different distance intervals, and we compute the start values for the k-means-algorithm accordingly. This assumption is verified by the fact that the mean values are only altered slightly by the k-means clustering. To get a further intuition we labeled each observation vector according to distance intervals: I_1, I_2, I_3. After the clustering we sorted the clusters according to the intervals, and counted how much of the prelabeled data has been assigned to which cluster. In Table 1 it can be seen that all of the clusters contain a reasonable amount of samples (over all sum), and that clusters are built according to distance intervals (max/min distance). They contain either observations from disjunctive or slightly overlapping distance intervals or represent different distributions for the same interval. Those findings are very important for the choice of the HMM structure and initialization, but they also allow for interpretation of the learned model.

Table 1. Clustering for T-Crossing data, columns refer to different cluster, rows depict cluster properties; all distance measurements in millimeter

cluster id	1	2	3	4	5	6	7	8
$I_1 = 7m...4m$	475	508	685	795	2	1	0	0
$I_2 = 4m...2m$	0	0	0	16	277	252	1143	44
$I_3 = 2m...$	0	0	0	0	0	0	32	437
over all sum	475	508	685	811	279	253	1175	481
mean distance	6112	5796.4	5770.2	4455	3796.8	3538.3	2706.2	1755.5
max distance	6872.2	6956.1	6976.3	4968.7	4009.4	4103.6	3591.7	2310.3
min distance	4854.5	4960.8	4878	3954.8	3438.6	3037.8	1775.9	1427.9

To initialize the HMM all clusters C_k that cover approximately the same distance interval are assigned to the same HMM state S_i. More precisely, the covariance matrix and the mean of each C_k add a dimension to the observation model of S_i. Considering Table 1, we obtain an HMM with five states, where $[C_1, C_2, C_3]$ present the first state, C_4 the second, $[C_5, C_6]$ the third, C_7 and C_8 the fourth and fifth, respectively. The mixture matrix M_{mix} is initialized uniformly, the dimension is given by the number of states Q and the maximum number of mixture components M. The states are arranged to form a left-right HMM, and according to the sequences, left refers to large and right to small distances. Although, in a left-right HMM consequently all entries below the diagonal of the transition matrix T are zero, we initialized the full matrix with 1/Q. Fig. 4 (left) shows a left-right model, where the arrows denote the possible transitions from state S_i to S_j with probability p_{ij}.

Learning and Evaluation of the Hidden Markov Model. We fix the observation model obtained from clustering and use expectation-maximization (EM) learning to determine appropriate values for T, M_{mix} and the state prior, according to [9]. Since the observation space given by our sensor model is filled very sparsely and the covariances of the data are all considerably small, we encountered problems of overfitting. That means, observation

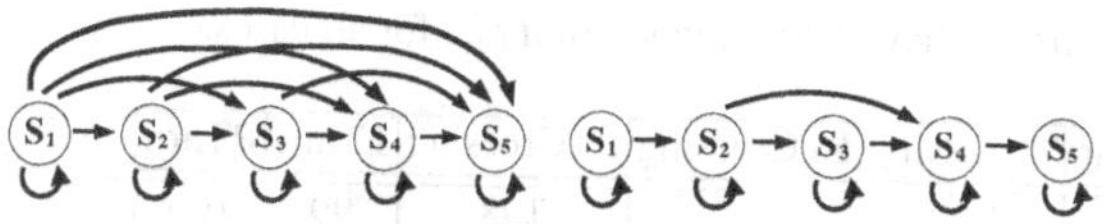

$$\begin{pmatrix} 0.8 & 0.2 & 0 & 0 & 0 \\ 0 & 0.58 & 0.417 & 0.003 & 0 \\ 0 & 0 & 0.37 & 0.63 & 0 \\ 0 & 0 & 0 & 0.68 & 0.32 \\ 0 & 0 & 0 & 0 & 1 \end{pmatrix}$$

Fig. 4. Graph of left-right HMM (left) and learned HMM for case presented in Table 1 (right); Also given is the transition matrix T, presenting the respective transition probabilities p_{ij}.

probabilities tend to zero and cause numerical instabilities. To anticipate those problems, we add noise to the clustering data, to artificially spread the distributions. The task to find the best HMM is to optimize the learning with regard to the number of clusters and the noise to be added. Too many clusters cause some clusters to not cover a sufficient number of samples, and too few reduce the discrimination power. On the other hand too much noise reduces the discrimination power but increases the generality of the model. None or little noise results in over-selective HMMs. By now we semiautomatically search for an optimal solution. Fig. 4 (right) shows the graph of the HMM and its transition matrix that were learned for the case presented in Table 1. As expected we obtained a left-right model (no backward transitions), and most states are only connected with the next state.

5 Experimental Results

In this section, we will empirically evaluate the proposed approaches. To acquire a sufficient amount of data for different hallway environments we used a simulator (RHINO Navigation Software, also applied in [2]) which provides laser measurements, based on the sensor model of the real SICK LMS200 laser range finder. Also, we annotated the maps, in order to automatically label the recorded observation sequences. As a result we obtained about 200000 observation vectors for eight different environments, which adds up to approximately 20000 observation sequences (divided in training and test data). The environments differ in the amount of clutter that is present, and the width of hallways (2, 2.5 and 3 meter). The environment depicted in Fig. 1 is referred to as *2m uncluttered*. For images of all environments refer to our homepage.

It can be seen from Tab. 2, that in some cases the recognition rate for the single observation classifier is very high, but in particular for *L/RTurn* it is rather poor. This is due to the fact, that the last observation is not necessarily the best, e.g. when the robot is cutting the edge in a left or right turn. The classifier "last but one" in Tab. 2 works like the SOC but considers the observation before the last. It improves the classification for some classes, but for others, like *TCrossing*, it slightly degrades. That means, it is difficult to determine which single observation should be used for SOC. Furthermore, the classification is slightly worse, when clutter is present, due to ambiguous measurements. For the averaged sequence classifier (ASC) the classification is strongly dependent on the weighting function, the more we rely on the closer measurements the better. Whereas the classification results are comparable to the SOC, we gain a little more robustness due to the averaging. The classification results can be improved when the weights for *Hallway/Deadend* are ignored, but this way it is difficult to evaluate ambiguous situations.

Table 2. Classification results for the SOC (last obs and last but one) and the averaged sequence classifier (ASC) (averaged seq); *DeadEnds* have 100% recognition rate for all cases.

Gateway class	XCrossing	TCrossing	LTCrossing	RTCrossing	LTurn	RTurn
2m uncluttered	581	390	200	198	99	106
averaged seq	86.8%	96.9%	98%	99.5%	14.1%	41.5%
last obs	86%	100%	95.5%	97.5%	50.5%	100%
last but one	86.8%	100%	99%	99.5%	100%	100%
2m cluttered	148	169	70	42	30	38
averaged seq	83.7%	39.6%	90%	61.9%	6.7%	2.6%
last obs	95.6%	93.5%	77.2%	57.2%	40%	94.7%
last but one	98.2%	90.5%	97.2%	59.5%	46.7%	97.4%

Table 3. HMM based classification; given data of two gateways to the two respective HMMs.

environment	2m uncluttered	2m cluttered	2.5m cluttered	3m uncluttered
lturn/rturn	100/100%	100/100%	96.3/100%	100/100%
lturn/tcrossing	100/100%	100/93.5%	98.75/93.5%	100/100%
rturn/tcrossing	100/100%	100/92.9%	100/23%	100/100%
lturn/xcrossing	100/100%	100/100%	99.4/100%	100/100%

The EM learning converged to left-right HMMs with expected apriori probabilities for all types of sequences and training data from one or more environments. When we train the HMM for a single environment only, the classification rate is 100 percent for the respective test data, which shows the validity of the HMM approach. Since it is difficult to determine the optimal HMM for a certain gateway type and data from different environments, we did not yet obtain an optimal set of HMMs to handle all classes with satisfying discrimination power in the general case. But we give examples for pairwise classification in Tab. 3. The experiments have been performed on the same test data used for the SOC/ASC evaluation. It can be seen that the hallway width does not influence the discrimination power, but as for the SOC/ASC, the recognition rate decreases in the presence of clutter. Besides the difficulty of finding the optimal HMMs, the presented approach seems to be very promising in the context of the automatic generation of structured robot maps. The advantage is, that the resulting HMM based classifier provides probabilities for observation sequences with regard to the different gateways. Thus, it is possible to globally fuse the results of different observation sequences in a very formal way by the means of a Bayes filter.

6   Conclusion

In this paper we proposed a sensor model for the detection and classification of different classes of crossing gateways. The model is based on the virtual line model (VLM) and different general and gateway specific measures, that enable us to assess the similarity of the perceived sensor data and the different gateway classes. As a result we obtained observation sequences for when the robot is approaching gateway areas. We investigated the properties of that data, and showed that it is a discriminating feature language well suited for the given task. We proposed three classifiers, based on the generated observation sequences. The simple classifiers perform well for certain classes in uncluttered and static environments, but the tuning of some parameters, like the weighting function, are neither trivial nor very general. Also, it is difficult to handle exclusion classes like *Hallway/DeadEnd* without decreasing the performance. On the other hand, we presented theory and experiments for the HMM based sequence classification. It could be seen, that the approach is very promising, with regard to global fusion of observations and reasoning under uncertainty, but learning appropriate models is a challenging task.

The next step is to learn the set of HMMs for all classes of gateways, so as to maximize the discrimination power across the set of HMMs, and also the tolerance to changes in the environment.

References

1. P. Beeson, M. MacMahon, J. Modayil, J. Provost, F. Savelli, and B. Kuipers. Exploiting local perceptual models for topological map-building. *IJCAI-2003 Workshop RUR-03*.
2. W. Burgard, A.B. Cremers, D. Fox, D. Hähnel, G. Lakemeyer, D. Schulz, W. Steiner, and S. Thrun. Experiences with an interactive museum tour-guide robot. *Artificial Intelligence*, 114(1-2), 2000.
3. Eric Chown. Gateways: An approach to parsing spatial domains. In *ICML 2000 Workshop on Machine Learning of Spatial Knowledge*, 2000.
4. J.-S. Gutmann D. Schröter, M. Beetz. RG Mapping: Learning Compact and Structured 2D Line Maps of Indoor Environments. In*Proc. of 11th IEEE ROMAN 2002*, Berlin/Germany.
5. R. O. Duda, P. E. Hart, and D. G Stork. *Pattern Classification*. New York: John Wiley & Sons, Inc., second edition., 2001.
6. J.-S. Gutmann. Robuste Navigation autonomer mobiler Systeme (in German). Akademische Verlagsgesellschaft Aka, Berlin, 2000. Doctoral Thesis *University of Freiburg*.
7. D. Haehnel, D. Fox, W. Burgard, and S. Thrun. A highly efficient FastSLAM algorithm for generating cyclic maps of large-scale environments from raw laser range measurements. In *Proc. of IEEE IROS*, Las Vegas/USA, 2003.
8. David Kortenkamp. *Cognitive Maps for mobile robots: A representation for mapping and navigation*. PhD thesis, University of Michigan, 1993.
9. L. R. Rabiner and B. H. Juang. An introduction to hidden Markov models. *IEEE ASSP Magazine*, pages 4–15, January 1986.
10. D. Schröter and M. Beetz. Acquiring Modells of Rectangular Objects for Robot Maps. In *Proc. of IEEE ICRA*, New Orleans/USA, 2004.
11. S. Thrun. Robotic mapping: A survey. In G. Lakemeyer and B. Nebel, editors, *Exploring Artificial Intelligence in the New Millenium*. Morgan Kaufmann, 2002.

Real Time High Speed Measurement of Photogrammetric Targets

Georg Wiora[1], Pavel Babrou[1], and Reinhard Männer[2]

[1] DaimlerChrysler AG, RBP/SR, Wilhelm-Runge-Str. 11,
89081 Ulm, Germany
{georg.wiora,pavel.babrou}@daimlerchrysler.com
[2] Universität Mannheim, Lehrstuhl für Informatik V, B6, 26,
68131 Mannheim, Germany
maenner@ti.uni-mannheim.de

Abstract. A pipelined parallel highspeed image processor implementation in an FPGA for applications in close range photogrammetry is described. The bottleneck of high speed photogrammetry is the accurate sub-pixel measurement of retro-reflective targets. We use an enhanced sobel edge detector and a special filling algorithm to compute the segmentation of the targets. The segmented regions are labeled and the weighted center of gravity is computed for each region.

The incoming image data is processed in realtime. To achieve a high throughput the pixel based processing is done for ten image columns simultaneously. A total throughput of over 660 million pixels per second has been demonstrated with a design clock of only 66 MHz.

An automotive application of the image processor is presented, that measures the 3-d wheel position of a driving car.

1 Introduction

Close range photogrammetry is widely used for precision measurements in static scenes. The generic case is a single camera that is used to take many pictures of the measurement object. In an offline process the target positions are extracted from the images and the 3-d co-ordinates of the targets as well as the camera locations and calibration are computed. For time resolved short-term measurements of moving objects film and video cameras with various frame rates are used. The image processing is still done off-line. The measurement time is typically limited to a few seconds due to limits in memory size or film length.

1.1 Motivation

There are many interesting motion processes that require both, a high speed image acquisition and long term measurement. High speed recording of images is technically possible but expensive. The evaluation of the recorded images is usually very time consuming. This was the reason to create a system that can extract the important information from photogrammetric images in realtime. The photogrammetric evaluation relies mainly on the coordinates of the target centers and the target size. Since this information needs less

C.E. Rasmussen et al. (Eds.): DAGM 2004, LNCS 3175, pp. 562–569, 2004.

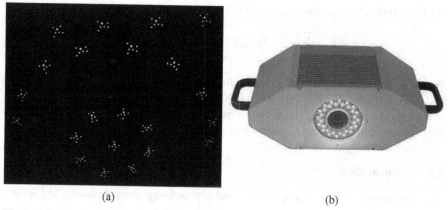

(a)   (b)

Fig. 1. a) An image of the high speed camera mounted on a car. b) The high speed photogrammetry system consisting of a camera, a high-energy LED-flash and an integrated FPGA board (not visible). The image coordinates are transfered over a TCP/IP connection. The housing has a width of approximately 35 cm.

than 150 bits per target, the data reduction factor exceeds 600. The image coordinates can be stored very compact or transfered to a computer to be processed by a photogrammetry software, that computes 3-d information in real-time.

1.2   Premises

Figure 1(a) on page 563 shows a typical image of a photogrammetric measurement. The targets have a high contrast and the background is mainly black. This is a result of using a ring light source around the objective and retro-reflective material for the targets. Because of this nicely choosen conditions a grey level threshold is often sufficient to separate the targets from the background. More robust than a grey level threshold is an edge based segmentation, that is used here.

The challenge is, to do the image measurement robust and in real time. The camera we use has a resolution of 1280×1024 pixels and a frame rate of up to 485 Hz. The resulting data rate is 660 million pixels per second. We developed a stand alone board that consists chiefly of a CameraLink interface for the connection to the camera, a Virtex-II-Pro XC2VP30 FPGA, a micro-controller and an ethernet interface for the connection to the host computer. The following sections describe the algorithm and the implementation of the image processing on this FPGA.

2   Algorithm

The computation of the image co-ordinates of photogrammetric targets is usually based on template matching or on the weighted centre of gravity (WCG) method. Template matching is slightly more precise for small targets but needs more resources [1,2]. The

WCG co-ordinates u_{wcg} and v_{wcg} of a target are given by

$$u_{\text{wcg}} = \frac{\sum b_{u,v} \cdot g_{u,v} \cdot u}{b_{u,v} \cdot g_{u,v}}, \quad v_{\text{wcg}} = \frac{\sum b_{u,v} \cdot g_{u,v} \cdot v}{b_{u,v} \cdot g_{u,v}}. \tag{1}$$

Where $g_{u,v}$ is the grey value of a pixel with the coordinates u and v. The quality of the WCG co-ordinates depends very much on the proper selection of the pixels that are included into the calculation. This is controlled by the binary function $b_{u,v}$. It determinates the pixel group that belongs to a certain target.

2.1   Segmentation

The computation of $b_{u,v}$ is designated in image processing as segmentation and is done here in three steps:

1. searching the target contour
2. filling the target contour
3. connecting the line segments of a target

The detection of a contour can be grey level based or edge based. A good example for a grey level based method is given in [3]. The edge based approach is more robust against shading variations since it does not rely on a global grey level threshold. When searching the contours not only the presence or absence of an edge at a given position is interesting but also the edge direction.

Edge Detection: A fast and noise insensitive method of finding the local edge direction is the Sobel operator $S = |S_x| + |S_x|$. Each of the partial operators is the combination of a directional smoothing kernel and a derivation that is rotated by 90° to the smoothing direction. The local edge direction $\phi_{u,v}$ is given by the application of the two parts on the grey image $g_{u,v}$ with the center position (u, v):

$$\phi_{u,v} = \tan^{-1} \frac{S_y \cdot g_{u,v}}{S_x \cdot g_{u,v}} \tag{2}$$

In [4] is shown that the error of the local direction can be reduced by a factor of 7, just by using different coefficients in the sobel kernel. We use this optimized sobel kernel:

$$S_u = \begin{bmatrix} 3 & 0 & -3 \\ 10 & 0 & -10 \\ 3 & 0 & -3 \end{bmatrix}, \quad S_v = \begin{bmatrix} 3 & 10 & 3 \\ 0 & 0 & 0 \\ -3 & -10 & -3 \end{bmatrix} \tag{3}$$

The normalization factor of $1/32$ is left out since the absolute value of the Sobel is not interesting for edge detection.

The criterion C for the existance of an edge is the sum of the absolut values of the two sobel parts or the edge strength:

$$C_{u,v} = |S_x \cdot g_{u,v}| + |S_y \cdot g_{u,v}| \tag{4}$$

The edge image $c_{u,v}$ is obtained from $C_{u,v}$ by binarizing it with a given threshold. This binary edge image is robust to noise in the grey image due to the smoothing part in the Sobel operator. To allow an inside-outside distinction while scanning the image line by line, the local edge direction is used. For a horizontal scanning it is sufficient to watch the sign s of the Sobel operator's horizontal part:

$$s = \text{sign}\left(S_x \cdot g_{u,v}\right) \tag{5}$$

For bright targets on a dark background it is negative at the left side of its border and positive for the right side.

Region Filling: The second step of the segmentation is filling. On the basis of the edge criterion c and the edge direction s the contours can be filled. The result of the filling operation is the binary function $b_{u,v}$ which defines closed regions. The whole processing can be done line by line and pixel by pixel up to this step and is thus easy to parallelize and not memory intensive.

Computation of the WCG moments: The next step of the algorithm is the intraline computation of the WCG moments. This happens separately for each line segment of each target. The following moments have to be computed and stored:

$$\sum b_{u,v} \cdot g_{u,v}, \qquad \sum b_{u,v} \cdot g_{u,v} \cdot u, \qquad \sum b_{u,v} \cdot g_{u,v} \cdot v, \qquad \sum b_{u,v} \tag{6}$$

Also the horizontal extents $u_{\min}$ and $u_{\max}$ of the target line and the vertical position v are saved. The moments are summed up when adjacent line segments are fusioned.

Connecting Line Segments: The next step of the algorithm is the connectivity analysis. For each line segment the moments and the horizontal extents are known. To find connected line segments it is sufficient to compare the horizontal extents $u_{\min}$ and $u_{\max}$ of the current target's line segment with the line segments of the previous line which are stored in a FIFO. The result of the comparison defines a status to the moment. There are three possibilities:

1. The current segment belongs to a new target.
2. The current segment belongs to the oldest target in the list.
3. The oldest target in the list is done.

In case 1 the current segment is stored in the FIFO. In case 2 the oldest target in the list and the current segment are combined and stored in the FIFO. In case 3 the oldest target in the list is moved to the output buffer.

2.2 Classification

The target area which is given by $\sum b_{u,v}$ and the minimum $(u_{\min}, v_{\min})$ and maximum extents $(u_{\max}, v_{\max})$ of the targets are used to do a pre-classification of the targets to reduce the amount of noise in the data output. Targets that are too small or too large or have a large aspect ratio are filtered.

3 Implementation

The block diagram for the implementation of the above described algorithm is shown in fig. 2. The goal was to realize a real time target measurement with minimum latency and maximum throughput. The camera delivers the pixels with a clock frequency of 66 MHz. Ten pixels with each 8 bits are transfered in one clock cycle. That means the input vector for the design is 80 bits wide.

3.1 Segmentation

Since the kernel of the Sobel filter is 3×3 pixels wide three lines of image data have to be stored in the input register wich consists of FIFOs. In practice we need two lines plus 20 pixels because of pipeline delays. The FIFO stucture allows the simultaneous access to 33 grey values from an 12×3 pixel wide area. According to (3) the grey values are multiplied by 3 and by 10 and the sums for each of the 10 center pixels are calculated.

The filling process is implemented with logical functions for 10 pixels parallel. The input information used for this is the binarized edge strength c_u and the horizontal edge direction s_u from (5). The fill status of a pixel b_{u+1} depends on the following Bool expression:

$$b_{u+1,v} = c_{u+1,v} \ \vee \tag{7}$$
$$\left[b_{u,v} \wedge b_{u+1,v-1} \wedge \overline{(c_{u,v} \wedge (s_{u,v} > 0))} \right]$$

Verbaly that means that a pixel in $b_{u+1,v}$ is filled if the pixel is an edge, or if the pixel left of it and the pixel above it is filled and the pixel left of it is not a right edge. This expression is computed for 10 pixels simultaneously.

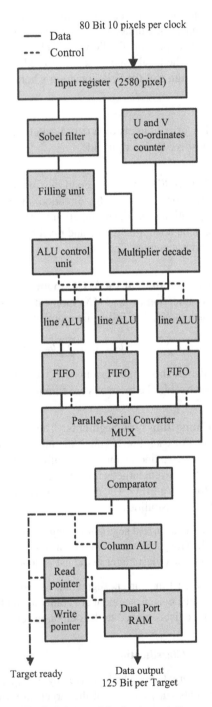

Fig. 2. Scheme of the implementation.

3.2   Intra Line Computation of the WCG

The minimum size of a target is one pixel. Since the Sobel operator finds an edge to the left and to the right of this single pixel the minimum region size of a target is three by three pixels. The minimum distance of two targets is two pixels. If there is only one pixel distance between two targets they are handled as one target. This means that the maximum number of targets in a ten pixel block is three. Therefore the intra line computation needs three identical ALUs to compute the moments for three targets simultaneously. The inputs of the ALUs are the grey values g_u, the horizontal and vertical momentums $u \cdot g_u$ and $v \cdot g_u$, the coordinates u and v and the binary segmentation function b_u. Since v is constant in a line it is left out in the indices.

The vector b_u is segmented into a maximum of three connected areas by the ALU control unit. Each area is directed to one of the three ALUs.

Since the processing of one input block with 10 pixels has to be done in parallel, all components of the ALU can handle all input data parallel. One ALU includes the following components:

- 10-input summation unit for $\sum b_u \cdot g_u$
- 10-input summation unit for $\sum b_u \cdot g_u \cdot u$
- 10-input summation unit for $\sum b_u \cdot g_u \cdot v$
- summation unit for $\sum b_{u,v}$
- recording u_{min}, u_{max} and v_{min}, v_{max} co-ordinates

The output vector of each ALU is stored in a FIFO. Up to this point the whole design is based on the pixel clock and does the processing synchronously. The delay is less than $4\mu s$ and results from the input buffer for two image lines.

After this point the processing continues in a fully serial pipeline with list based data and does not rely on the pixel clock any more. This point is well suited to be used for the clock domain change from the input pixel clock to the system clock of the FPGA. That is done by three FIFOs and a parallel to serial converter (MUX).

3.3   Connectivity Analysis

The connectivity analysis unit compares the u_{min} and u_{max} co-ordinates of the current line v moments from MUX and the oldest moments in the dual ported RAM from line $v - 1$. The result of the comparison are the control signals for the column ALU and the read and write pointers for the RAM. If the co-ordinates of the moments from MUX and RAM show overlapping regions the two segments belong to the same target and the moments can be summed. The resulting moments are written back to the RAM.

If the current target is to the left of the oldest target in the RAM ($u_{max,v} < u_{min,v-1}$) the current target is new and is written to the RAM. If the current target is to the right of the oldest target in the RAM ($u_{min,v} > u_{max,v-1}$) the target is removed from the RAM and written to the data output.

4   Experimental Results

To demonstrate the maximum data rate we acquired a sequence of a few targets on a rotating fan and about 20 static targets in the background. Figure 3(a) on page 568

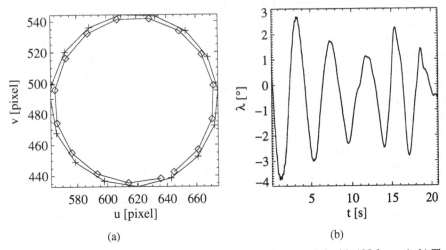

(a)   (b)

Fig. 3. a) The image space trajectory of two targets on a fan recorded with 485 frames/s. b) The steering angle λ in degrees of a slalom manoever over 21 seconds.

shows the trajectory of two targets for one revolution. The fan was rotating with about 2000 RPM. The system acquired the image coordinates with the full data rate of 485 frames per second. The time step between two positions is 2.0625 ms.

The target measurement stability was tested in the application setup that is described below. A sequence of 10000 images with stable camera and object position was acquired and evaluated. The standard deviations σ_u and σ_v of the image point coordinates were below 0.009 pixels. The maximum deviation Δ_u and Δ_v from the average coordinate was below 0.05 pixels.

A good measure for the stability and consistency of the whole system is the photogrammetric bundle adjustment that is used to calibrate the camera. A calibration with 48 images and 172 object points had a standard deviation of image point co-ordinates below 0.033 pixels.

5   Application

The image processing module was developed for the *WheelWatch* photogrammetry system that can measure the wheel position of a driving car in realtime [5,6]. The camera head with the integrated fpga module is shown in fig. 1(b).

The car body and the wheel are signalized with retroreflective targets like shown in fig. 1(a). The 3-d co-ordinates of the targets are measured with static photogrammetry before the test drive begins and are thus well known. The measurement camera is calibrated with a photogrammetric standard procedure.

In the measurement mode the relative orientation of the wheel to the car body can be computed with a variant of the photogrammetric resection. The results are the six degrees of freedom of the wheel movement relativ to the car body: The position P of the axis center and the orientation angles ω, ϕ and κ of the axis. From these values the steering angle λ and the tilt angle θ can be derived.

In fig. 3(b) on page 568 the measured steering angle λ of a 21 second test drive is shown. The results of the first test drives show, that the measurement of the wheel position with a precision better than 0.1 mm and of the wheel angles with better than $0.01°$ is possible.

6   Conclusion

6.1   Resume

It has been shown, that real time photogrammetry with very high data rates is possible. This enables the use of photogrammetry not only in short term analysis like crash test, but also for long term investigations. A further use of the system is in control loops for positioning systems or robots which is only possible due to the short latency of only 4 milliseconds.

6.2   Outlook

With the proposed system the image processing is not any more the limiting factor of photogrammetric data handling. The current implementation runs with a relatively low clock frequency of 66 MHz. If needed this can be increased easily by a factor of two or more. Since there are still 40% of free resources in the FPGA a further parallelization is also possible. The bottle neck is currently the CameraLink interface with a limit of 660 Megapixels per second. To increase this any further the FPGA needs a more direct connection to the camera chip which would reduce the modularity of the system.

References

1. Shortis, M.R., Clarke, T.A., Robson, S.: Practical Testing of Precision and Accuracy of Target Image Centring Algorithms. SPIE Proceedings **2598** (1995) 65–76
2. West, G.A.W., Clarke, T.A.: A survey and examination of subpixel measurement techniques. SPIE Proceedings Close-Range Photogrammetry Meets Machine Vision **1395** (1990) 456–463
3. Mandler, E., Oberländer, M.F.: One-pass encoding of connected components in multi-valued images. In: Proceedings of International Conference on Pattern Recognition, Los Alamitos, California. USA, IEEE Computer Society (1990) 64–69
4. Jähne, B., Scharr, H., Körkel, S.: 6. In: Principles of Filter Design. Volume 2. Academic Press, San Diego (1999) 125–152
5. Wiora, G., Babrou, P., Willbold, M., Kofler, R., Mergenthaler, E.: WheelWatch: Online-Photogrammetrie mit FPGA-Bildverarbeitung. In Luhmann, T., ed.: Tagungsband der 3. Oldenburger 3D-Tage, Heidelberg, Wichmann Verlag (2004)
6. Wiora, G., Babrou, P.: WheelWatch - Berührungslose Hochgeschwindigkeitsmessung der Radbewegung am fahrenden Fahrzeug. In Gerlach, G., ed.: GMA - Sensoren und Messsysteme 2004, VDI/VDE (2004)

A Simple New Method for Precise Lens Distortion Correction of Low Cost Camera Systems

Christian Bräuer-Burchardt

Fraunhofer IOF Jena,
Albert-Einstein-Str. 7, D-07745 Jena, Germany
braeuerc@iof.fhg.de

Abstract. A new methodology to determine and correct lens distortion typically occurring in low cost camera systems is presented. The method is easy to apply and leads to very accurate results with moderate effort. The method combines the radial lens distortion as the main part of the global distortion with the remaining weaker parts. Distortion models are presented and their validity are shown. The algorithm needs some reference points with known coordinates. Examples and accuracy results are presented and discussed.

1 Introduction

Photographs or digital images are often used in industrial applications to perform quantitative measurements. These tasks should usually be solved by use of camera systems without lens distortion. However, this is not always possible, or the costs for distortion free systems are too high. Using cameras that suffer from lens distortion, the measurements become erroneous. Here, an exact distortion correction may help to overcome the problem.

A number of methods was published which obtain the parameters of the radial distortion function and correct the images [1-5,8-14]. Usually, the determination of the distortion function is performed in the context of camera calibration. This requires considerable effort which should be sometimes avoided.

Conventionally, lens distortion is described by a distortion function including radial, decentering, and affine parameters. The main part of the distortion usually has the radial distortion. Therefore, in the majority of works no other distortion than the radial one is considered [1,2,4,5,8,9,11,12]. This may be sufficient, if the required measuring accuracy is not very high or if the actual distortion is sufficiently exactly described by the radial distortion. Some authors take into account decentering distortion [10,14]. This may improve the correction. However, some other kind of distortion may still be present.

Kruck [6] suggests an approach including some 30 parameters describing the lens distortion. However, the use of so may parameters brings some disadvantages. First, a powerful calculation system for processing the data is necessary. Second, some

C.E. Rasmussen et al. (Eds.): DAGM 2004, LNCS 3175, pp. 570–577, 2004.

of the parameters are not independent from each other. Third, the noise may influence the measurement and the reproducibility may be not sufficient.

Our proper aims of this work were to find a simple and robust methodology for the exact correction of lens distortion effects.

2 Distortion Models and Approach

In order to solve the problem it should be taken into account that the main contribution to the distortion results from the radial lens distortion. The next one is the decentering distortion, and finally, there can occur a number of small other effects which are often difficult to describe as a function of the image coordinates.

Therefore, the deviation of the actual image from the ideal one, obtained by applying the pinhole camera model should be called the global distortion. The global distortion is the sum of the radial distortion, the decentering distortion, and the remaining distortion. We assume that the radial distortion has the highest contribution to the global distortion.

2.1 Approach

The approach for the determination of the global distortion is the following. First, it is assumed that only radial distortion occurs. The radial distortion is calculated and the result, i.e. the corrected image, is compared with the ideal image obtained by estimation of the ideal pinhole mapping. This estimation is obtained by fitting a projective 2D-2D-transform to the known original point coordinates (these coordinates are actually 3D but in a common plane, thus the z-coordinate may be set to be equal to zero) to the corrected image coordinates. The remaining error can include distortion errors, too, but these are compensated by the fitted projective transform.

The difference between the corrected and the ideal coordinates is the input for further distortion determination which will be described later.

2.2 Radial Distortion Model

The description of radial lens distortion is commonly known from the literature [1-14]. The following (and even more) models can be applied:

$$r' = r(1 + a_2 r^2 + a_4 r^4 + ...)$$

$$r' = \frac{r}{1 + b_2 r^2 + b_4 r^4 + ...}$$

$$r = r'(1 + c_2 r'^2 + c_4 r'^4 + ...)$$

$$r = \frac{r'}{1 + d_2 r'^2 + d_4 r'^4 + ...} \tag{1}$$

Here, r is the undistorted and r' the distorted distance of an image point $p=(x,y)$, or $p'=(x',y')$, respectively, from the distortion centre $S=(X_S,Y_S)$. The a_i, b_i, c_i, and d_i are the distortion coefficients, respectively.

Usually, the coefficients x_6 and higher are not necessary, and will be neglected consequently. However, it is important to decide whether x_4 is used or not. This mainly depends on the quality of the lens. The decision about using one or two coefficients should be made after a first analysis (see section 4). Assume that this decision has been done. However, one of the weakly differing four models should be selected. Which is the best one? Unfortunately, this depends on the actual distortion which is to be determined.

Thus, two ways are possible to select the right model. First, all models are applied. A quality measure evaluates the results, and the model leading to the best result is selected. We however, suggest the following procedure: The model which has the best performance (best numerical behaviour and implementation) is applied. In our case, this is the model with the coefficients d_2 and d_4 (see [1,2]). Finally, it can be tested, whether a model conversion improves the result, or the remaining errors due to the model deviation are processed in the final step of distortion determination (see section 2.4).

2.3   Decentering Distortion

Decentering distortion is a result of the decentering of the lenses (see[7]) and can be described by the following approach [3]:

$$\Delta x_{dec} = b_1 \cdot (r'^2 + 2x'^2) + 2b_2 \cdot x' \cdot y'$$
$$\Delta y_{dec} = b_2 \cdot (r'^2 + 2y'^2) + 2b_1 \cdot x' \cdot y' \qquad (2)$$

where Δx_{dec} and Δy_{dec} are the pixel errors resulting from decentering distortion as a function of the distorted coordinates. Equivalently, the model

$$\Delta x_{dec} = a_1 \cdot (r^2 + 2x^2) + 2a_2 \cdot x \cdot y$$
$$\Delta y_{dec} = a_2 \cdot (r^2 + 2y^2) + 2a_1 \cdot x \cdot y \qquad (3)$$

as a function of the unstorted coordinates can be considered. The determination of the decentering distortion can be obtained within the camera calibration procedure or separately by iterative methods [10,14]. One of the iteration method will be briefly outlined in section 4.2.

2.4   Remaining Distortion

After removal of the radial and decentering distortion some camera systems are already very close to the ideal pinhole model. However, especially low cost cameras suffer from some remaining distortion which can not be described by a simple function. Our approach for the description of the remaining distortion is outlined briefly next.

The distortion is characterised by a number of vectors placed on certain points in the image. The number of these vectors depends on the local change of the remaining distortion and is set by the user. In the extreme case, every pixel in the image has its own distortion vector. For illustration see fig.3. Here the length of the distortion vectors is 100 times higher (for illustration) than the actual distortion.

2.5 Quality Criterion

In order to evaluate the quality of the distortion determination and correction, a quality measure is defined. Assuming that an ideal image is present (which is obtained by some good estimation) the quality of the correction is expressed by the averaged residual error ARE (also known as RMS) and the maximum residual error (MRE) between the corrected image and the ideal one:

$$ARE = \frac{1}{n} \sum_{i=1}^{n} \sqrt{\left(x_i - x_i^{id}\right)^2 + \left(y_i - y_i^{id}\right)^2}$$

$$MRE = \max_i \left\{ \sqrt{\left(x_i - x_i^{id}\right)^2 + \left(y_i - y_i^{id}\right)^2} \right\}$$

$$(4)$$

3 Calibration Patterns

In order to determine and correct the lens distortion of several camera systems, two calibration patterns were used. The first one was a grid pattern from a tripod table (see fig.1). Here the intersection points of the horizontal and vertical lines were used. The second one was a dot pattern (see fig.2) where the centre points of the dots were used.

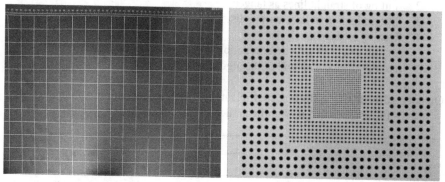

Fig. 1. Grid pattern   **Fig. 2.** Point pattern

4 Algorithms

4.1 Determination of the Radial Distortion Function

The used algorithm to obtain the radial distortion parameters X_S, Y_S, d_2, and d_4 is described in detail elsewhere [1,2] and is only briefly outlined here.

All points which are collinear in reality should be on a straight line in the undistorted image. These points are used to construct point triples. Finally, a linear optimisation task is formulated which has the distortion coefficients d_2 and d_4 as a solution with known coordinates of the distortion centre. The unknown distortion centre and the distortion coefficients are determined within an iterative process starting with the image centre as the distortion centre.

4.2 Determination of the Decentering Distortion Function

Assume that decentering distortion is present. A simple fitting of a projective transform of the real point coordinates to the image coordinates obtained by radial distortion correction is not the right way to determine the decentering distortion, because convergence is not sure. A better algorithm can be constructed using the properties of the decentering distortion. A straight line is transformed into a curve which does not intersect this straight line. Here, the approximation of the ideal image by fitting tangents to the distorted straight lines is better than fitting the points with minimal Euclidean distance (see fig.3).

The iterative algorithm to obtain decentering distortion is the following:

Input: - uncorrected distorted point coordinates assigned to straight lines,
          - radial distortion parameters

Algorithm
  1. Point correction with radial distortion parameters
  2. Fitting of straight lines as tangents
  3. Determination of decentering distortion coefficients
  4. Quality measure analysis
      improvement → new determination of radial distortion parameters, goto 1
      no improvement → end of the algorithm

Output: - decentering distortion coefficients and new radial distortion parameters or
         - information that no significant decentering distortion present

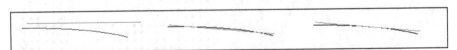

Fig. 3. Left: straight line with distorted curve (simulated with overstatement), middle: distorted curve with fittet line, right: distorted curve with tangent; the tangent is closer to the undistorted line and thus the chance to achieve convergence is higher

4.3 Analysis of Residuals

After correction of the radial and decentering distortion, the remaining errors concerning to the expected ideal coordinates of the corrected points can be considered. Figure 3 shows an example of such residual errors.

The residual errors in fig.4 seem to be systematic, but other error sources must be considered, too. One error source is the possible deviation of the original points from the expected coordinates. Second, there may be errors in the determination of the distorted point coordinates in the original image. Errors resulting from noise can be a third source.

In order to avoid these influences, a meaningful averaging of the residual error vectors should be applied. The first influence can be excluded by averaging views with rotated optical axis (covering the whole range) and views from different calibration patterns. The second one can also be reduced by averaging images with a weakly rotated optical axis (a few degree are sufficient). The errors resulting from noise are already reduced by the first two averaging procedures. Assuming that the distortion changes are locally slow, a number of pixels can be united to cells with a common distortion value. See fig.5 for an example of averaged residuals.

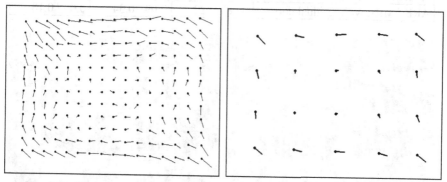

Fig. 4. Residuals from single image   **Fig. 5.** Averaged residuals

5 Experiments and Results

A number of images of the described calibration pattern were recorded using different digital cameras (Kodak DC210, Casio QV3500, Olympus C2500). To avoid the effect of changing distortion depending on the distance from the pattern to the camera, the images were taken from a constant distance. The determination of radial and decentering distortion was performed with each single image, and the resulting distortion coefficients were averaged. Note that the radial coefficients d_2 and d_4, and the decentering coefficients b_1 and b_2 were calculated by least squares techniques [2].

The corrected images were used to perform residual analysis as described. Now, every corrected image was newly corrected in such a way that every point coordinate was corrected with the mean residual vector from the corresponding cell. The quality criterion to evaluate the correction result was applied again and the ARE and MRE values are used to characterise the correction result.

All results are summarised in table 1. The distortion parameters and the ARE and MRE values are given for the uncorrected images, for the images with radial and decentering correction, and for the finally corrected images. Figure 6 shows an example of a distorted image and fig.7 shows the corresponding corrected one. In order to illustrate the distortion effect a stretched view is added in both cases.

Table 1. Results of distortion determination and correction

Camera	Kodak	Casio	Olympus
Image size	1152 x 864	1024 x 768	856 x 684
Symmetry point X,Y	578 / 381	496 / 387	427 / 367
Radial coefficients d_2	$-1.62 * 10^{-7}$	$-1.87 * 10^{-7}$	$-3.37 * 10^{-7}$
Radial coefficient d_4	$+2.36 * 10^{-13}$	$+1.81 * 10^{-13}$	$+2.75 * 10^{-13}$
Decentering coefficient b_1	$2.31 * 10^{-7}$	n.s.	n.s.
Decentering coefficient b_2	n.s.	n.s.	n.s.
ARE / MRE without correction	1.49 / 2.71	1.86 / 4.94	2.63 / 5.00
ARE / MRE after rad.+dec. corr.	0.18 / 0.45	0.17 / 0.62	0.13 / 0.53
ARE / MRE with residual corr.	0.08 / 0.22	0.09 / 0.34	0.06 / 0.18

Fig. 6. Distorted image   **Fig. 7.** Corrected view

6 Summary, Discussion, and Outlook

A simple new methodology to determine and correct lens distortion typically occurring in low cost camera systems was presented. This method considerably improves measurements obtained by such cameras and makes these systems applicable for precise measurements.

The results for the averaged residual error of less than 1/10 pixel show that almost no other error is present after final correction. It should be taken into account that in the calibration patterns there can be deviations of the dot centres or line intersection points from the ideal ones. This error, in our example given by ±0.008mm standard deviation which means about ±0.04 pixels. Another error source occurs in the determination of the dot centres or line intersection points by means of image processing. Here, an uncertainty (standard deviation) of ±0.02 up to 0.05 pixels was determined experimentally. The use of a calibration pattern improves the accuracy as compared with methods using only line segments of urban scenes (see [1,5]).

A remaining error which can not be determined by this method is reduced to a similarity transform of the image and leads to a change of the extrinsic and intrinsic camera parameters. Thus, this error can be neglected.

Future work should be concerned with a further analysis of typical distortion pattern and finding analytical descriptions. Additionally, the known dependence of the distortion on the distance between object and camera should be considered and included in the modelling.

References

1. C.Bräuer-Burchardt: Automatic Correction of Weak Radial Lens Distortion in Single Views of Urban Scenes Using Vanishing Points. Proc 9th Int. Conf. On Image Processing, vol.III, Rochester, 2002, 865-868
2. C.Bräuer-Burchardt, K.Voss: Automatic lens distortion calibration using single views. In Mustererkennung 2000 (Proc. 22. DAGM-Symposium), Kiel, Springer, 2000, 187-194
3. D.C.Brown: Close-range camera calibration. Photogram.Eng. 37(8), 1971, 855-866
4. F.Devernay, O.Faugeras: Automatic calibration and removal of distortion from scenes of structured environments. SPIE (2567), 1995, 62-72
5. F.Devernay, O.D.Faugeras: Straight lines have to be straight. Machine Vision and Applications (13), No. 1, 2001, pp. 14-24.
6. E.Kruck: Lösung großer Gleichungssysteme für photogrammetrische Blockausgleichungen mit erweitertem funktionalem Modell. Dissertation, Wiss. Arbeiten der Fachrichtung Vermessungswesen der Universität Hannover, Nr. 128, 1983
7. Th.Luhmann, *Nahbereichsphotogrammetrie*, Wichmann Verlag, 2003
8. Y.Nomura, M.Sagara, H.Naruse, A.Ide: A simple calibration algorithm for high-distortion-lens camera. IEEE Trans. PAMI(14), No 11, 1992, 1095-1099
9. B.Prescott, G.McLean: Line-based correction of radial lens distortion. GMIP(59), No.1, 1997, 39-47
10. S.Shah and J.K.Aggarwal: Intrinsic parameter calibration procedure for a (high distortion) fish-eye lens camera with distortion model and accuracy estimation. PR(29), No.11, pp. 1775-1788, 1996
11. S.Shih, Y.Hung, W.Lin: When should we consider lens distortion in camera calibration. PR(28), No 3, 1995, 447-461
12. G.P.Stein: Lens distortion calibration using point correspondences. Proc CVPR 1997, 602-608
13. R.Tsai: An efficient and accurate camera calibration technique for 3-D machine vision. IEEE Proc CCVPR, 1986, 364-74
14. J.Weng, P.Cohen, M.Herniou: Camera calibration with distortion models and accuracy evaluation. PAMI(14), No 11, 1992, pp. 965-980

Author Index

Aach, Til   163
Amin, Saad A.   504

Babrou, Pavel   562
Bahlmann, Claus   220
Bakır, Gökhan H.   54, 245, 253, 262
Barth, Erhardt   163
Bauckhage, Christian   179, 342
Baumgartner, Albert   544
Bax, Ingo   447
Bayerl, Pierre   95, 383
Beder, Christian   375
Beetz, Michael   553
Bekel, Holger   447
Biber, Peter   480
Bousquet, Olivier   270
Bräuer-Burchardt, Christian   570
Brand, Rüdiger   544
Brox, Thomas   415
Bülthoff, Heinrich H.   407
Burkhardt, Hans   137
Burnham, Keith J.   504

Chang, Juno   512
Cho, Yongjoo   512
Christmas, William   342
Clauss, Martin   383
Cooke, Theresa   407
Cremers, Daniel   36
Cunningham, Douglas W.   407

Dahlkamp, Hendrik   71
Denzler, Joachim   359
Deselaers, Thomas   154, 228
Deutsch, Benjamin   359
Dietmayer, Klaus C.J.   367
Ditrich, Frank   463
Dörfler, Peter   455

Ebner, Heinrich   544
Eggert, Julian   310
Ellenrieder, Marc   528
Ernst, Udo A.   399

Felsberg, Michael   103
Flach, Boris   440

Fleck, Sven   480
Frahm, Jan-Michael   286
Franz, Matthias O.   18, 54, 245, 262
Fritsch, Jannik   334

Görür, Dilan   391
Goldenberg, Roman   520
Gorges, Nicolas   342
Gräßl, Christoph   326
Granlund, Gösta   103
Gretton, Arthur   262
Gruendig, Martin   45

Haas, Olivier C.L.   504
Haasdonk, Bernard   220
Hanbury, Allan   432
Hanheide, Marc   342, 528
Heidemann, Gunther   447
Heiler, Matthias   120
Hein, Matthias   270
Heipke, Christian   544
Hellwich, Olaf   45
Henn, Stefan   496
Hermes, Thorsten   87
Herzog, Otthein   87
Hömke, Lars   496
Hofemann, Nils   334
Huang, Xiaofei   302
Hung, Yeung Sam   318

Ihlow, Alexander   536

Jaakkola, Tommi S.   1
Jacobs, Arne   87

Kaempchen, Nico   367
Keuchel, Jens   120
Keysers, Daniel   154, 228
Kienzle, Wolf   54
Kittler, Joseph   342
Klette, Reinhard   294
Koch, Reinhard   27, 286
Körner, Edgar   310
Köser, Kevin   286
Köthe, Ullrich   350
Kratt, Jan   488

Kropatsch, Walter G.   432
Krüger, Lars   528
Kwon, Younghee   18

Lal, Thomas Navin   270
Lange, Tilman   9
Leibe, Bastian   145
Li, Hongdong   137
Li, Yan   318
Lifshits, Michael   520
Lim, Joa Sang   512
Logothetis, Nikos K.   391

Männer, Reinhard   562
Marchadier, Jocelyn   432
Martinetz, Thomas   187
Metze, Florian   488
Mills, John A.   504
Mota, Cicero   163

Nagel, Hans-Hellmut   71
Neukum, Gerhard   544
Neumann, Heiko   95, 383
Neumann, Julia   212
Ney, Hermann   154, 228
Niemann, Heinrich   326, 359, 471

Osher, Stanley J.   36
Ottlik, Artur   71

Park, Hung Kook   512
Park, Kang Ryoung   512
Pawelzik, Klaus R.   399
Pece, Arthur E.C.   71

Quiñonero Candela, Joaquin   245

Radig, Bernd   553
Rätsch, Matthias   62
Rasmussen, Carl Edward   18, 245, 391
Reisert, Marco   137
Rhee, Dae-Woong   512
Rilk, Markus   129
Ritter, Helge   447
Rivlin, Ehud   520
Rohr, Karl   111
Romdhani, Sami   62
Rosenhahn, Bodo   294
Rotermund, David   399
Roth, Volker   9

Rudzsky, Michael   520

Sagerer, Gerhard   179, 334, 342, 528
Schaefer, Gerald   424
Schiele, Bernt   145, 195
Schlesinger, Dmitrij   440
Schmidt, Ralph   544
Schnörr, Christoph   120, 212
Schnurr, Clemens   455
Schölkopf, Bernhard   18, 54, 237, 262
Schönfelder, Christoph   129
Scholz, Ingo   471
Schröter, Derik   553
Seiffert, Udo   536
Shekhovtsov, Alexander   440
Sinz, Fabian H.   245, 391
Soatto, Stefano   36
Sommer, Gerald   171, 294
Spiegel, Michael   544
Steck, Harald   1
Steidl, Gabriele   212
Stein, Fridtjof   79
Stiefelhagen, Rainer   488
Stößel, Dirk   528
Strasser, Wolfgang   480
Stuke, Ingo   163
Suesse, Herbert   463

Thurau, Christian   179
Tolias, Andreas S.   391
Tsuda, Koji   253

Vetter, Thomas   62
Vogel, Julia   195
Voss, Klaus   463

Wahl, Friedrich M.   129
Waibel, Alex   488
Wang, Jingchun   204
Weber, Thomas   553
Weickert, Joachim   415
Whang, Min Cheol   512
Willert, Volker   310
Winkelbach, Simon   129
Wiora, Georg   562
Witsch, Kristian   496
Wöhler, Christian   278
Woelk, Felix   27
Wörz, Stefan   111

Xu, Weibing   504

Zang, Di   171
Zhang, Changshui   204
Zhou, Dengyong   237
Zhou, Yonglei   204

Zien, Alexander   253
Zinßer, Timo   326
Zobel, Matthias   359
Zocholl, Markus   367

Lecture Notes in Computer Science

For information about Vols. 1–3077

please contact your bookseller or Springer

Vol. 3220: J.C. Lester, R.M. Vicari, F. Paraguaçu (Eds.), Intelligent Tutoring Systems. XXI, 920 pages. 2004.

Vol. 3208: H.J. Ohlbach, S. Schaffert (Eds.), Principles and Practice of Semantic Web Reasoning. VII, 165 pages. 2004.

Vol. 3207: L.T. Jang, M. Guo, G.R. Gao, N.K. Jha, Embedded and Ubiquitous Computing. XX, 1116 pages. 2004.

Vol. 3205: N. Davies, E. Mynatt, I. Siio (Eds.), UbiComp 2004: Ubiquitous Computing. XVI, 452 pages. 2004.

Vol. 3198: G.-J. de Vreede, L.A. Guerrero, G. Marín Raventós (Eds.), Groupware: Design, Implementation and Use. XI, 378 pages. 2004.

Vol. 3194: R. Camacho, R. King, A. Srinivasan (Eds.), Inductive Logic Programming. XI, 361 pages. 2004. (Subseries LNAI).

Vol. 3186: Z. Bellahsène, T. Milo, M. Rys, D. Suciu, R. Unland (Eds.), Database and XML Technologies. X, 235 pages. 2004.

Vol. 3184: S. Katsikas, J. Lopez, G. Pernul (Eds.), Trust and Privacy in Digital Business. XI, 299 pages. 2004.

Vol. 3183: R. Traunmüller (Ed.), Electronic Government. XIX, 583 pages. 2004.

Vol. 3182: K. Bauknecht, M. Bichler, B. Pröll (Eds.), E-Commerce and Web Technologies. XI, 370 pages. 2004.

Vol. 3178: W. Jonker, M. Petkovic (Eds.), Secure Data Management. VIII, 219 pages. 2004.

Vol. 3177: Z.R. Yang, H. Yin, R. Everson (Eds.), Intelligent Data Engineering and Automated Learning – IDEAL 2004. XVIII, 852 pages. 2004.

Vol. 3175: C.E. Rasmussen, H.H. Bülthoff, M.A. Giese, B. Schölkopf (Eds.), Pattern Recognition. XVIII, 581 pages. 2004.

Vol. 3174: F. Yin, J. Wang, C. Guo (Eds.), Advances in Neural Networks - ISNN 2004. XXXV, 1021 pages. 2004.

Vol. 3172: M. Dorigo, M. Birattari, C. Blum, L. M.Gambardella, F. Mondada, T. Stützle (Eds.), Ant Colony, Optimization and Swarm Intelligence. XII, 434 pages. 2004.

Vol. 3166: M. Rauterberg (Ed.), Entertainment Computing – ICEC 2004. XXIII, 617 pages. 2004.

Vol. 3158: I. Nikolaidis, M. Barbeau, E. Kranakis (Eds.), Ad-Hoc, Mobile, and Wireless Networks. IX, 344 pages. 2004.

Vol. 3157: C. Zhang, H. W. Guesgen, W.K. Yeap (Eds.), PRICAI 2004: Trends in Artificial Intelligence. XX, 1023 pages. 2004. (Subseries LNAI).

Vol. 3156: M. Joye, J.-J. Quisquater (Eds.), Cryptographic Hardware and Embedded Systems - CHES 2004. XIII, 455 pages. 2004.

Vol. 3155: P. Funk, P.A. González Calero (Eds.), Advances in Case-Based Reasoning. XIII, 822 pages. 2004. (Subseries LNAI).

Vol. 3154: R.L. Nord (Ed.), Software Product Lines. XIV, 334 pages. 2004.

Vol. 3153: J. Fiala, V. Koubek, J. Kratochvíl (Eds.), Mathematical Foundations of Computer Science 2004. XIV, 902 pages. 2004.

Vol. 3152: M. Franklin (Ed.), Advances in Cryptology – CRYPTO 2004. XI, 579 pages. 2004.

Vol. 3150: G.-Z. Yang, T. Jiang (Eds.), Medical Imaging and Augmented Reality. XII, 378 pages. 2004.

Vol. 3149: M. Danelutto, M. Vanneschi, D. Laforenza (Eds.), Euro-Par 2004 Parallel Processing. XXXIV, 1081 pages. 2004.

Vol. 3148: R. Giacobazzi (Ed.), Static Analysis. XI, 393 pages. 2004.

Vol. 3146: P. Érdi, A. Esposito, M. Marinaro, S. Scarpetta (Eds.), Computational Neuroscience: Cortical Dynamics. XI, 161 pages. 2004.

Vol. 3144: M. Papatriantafilou, P. Hunel (Eds.), Principles of Distributed Systems. XI, 246 pages. 2004.

Vol. 3143: W. Liu, Y. Shi, Q. Li (Eds.), Advances in Web-Based Learning – ICWL 2004. XIV, 459 pages. 2004.

Vol. 3142: J. Diaz, J. Karhumäki, A. Lepistö, D. Sannella (Eds.), Automata, Languages and Programming. XIX, 1253 pages. 2004.

Vol. 3140: N. Koch, P. Fraternali, M. Wirsing (Eds.), Web Engineering. XXI, 623 pages. 2004.

Vol. 3139: F. Iida, R. Pfeifer, L. Steels, Y. Kuniyoshi (Eds.), Embodied Artificial Intelligence. IX, 331 pages. 2004. (Subseries LNAI).

Vol. 3138: A. Fred, T. Caelli, R.P.W. Duin, A. Campilho, D.d. Ridder (Eds.), Structural, Syntactic, and Statistical Pattern Recognition. XXII, 1168 pages. 2004.

Vol. 3137: P. De Bra, W. Nejdl (Eds.), Adaptive Hypermedia and Adaptive Web-Based Systems. XIV, 442 pages. 2004.

Vol. 3136: F. Meziane, E. Métais (Eds.), Natural Language Processing and Information Systems. XII, 436 pages. 2004.

Vol. 3134: C. Zannier, H. Erdogmus, L. Lindstrom (Eds.), Extreme Programming and Agile Methods - XP/Agile Universe 2004. XIV, 233 pages. 2004.

Vol. 3133: A.D. Pimentel, S. Vassiliadis (Eds.), Computer Systems: Architectures, Modeling, and Simulation. XIII, 562 pages. 2004.

Vol. 3132: B. Demoen, V. Lifschitz (Eds.), Logic Programming. XII, 480 pages. 2004.

Vol. 3131: V. Torra, Y. Narukawa (Eds.), Modeling Decisions for Artificial Intelligence. XI, 327 pages. 2004. (Subseries LNAI).

Vol. 3130: A. Syropoulos, K. Berry, Y. Haralambous, B. Hughes, S. Peter, J. Plaice (Eds.), TeX, XML, and Digital Typography. VIII, 265 pages. 2004.

Vol. 3129: Q. Li, G. Wang, L. Feng (Eds.), Advances in Web-Age Information Management. XVII, 753 pages. 2004.

Vol. 3128: D. Asonov (Ed.), Querying Databases Privately. IX, 115 pages. 2004.

Vol. 3127: K.E. Wolff, H.D. Pfeiffer, H.S. Delugach (Eds.), Conceptual Structures at Work. XI, 403 pages. 2004. (Subseries LNAI).

Vol. 3126: P. Dini, P. Lorenz, J.N.d. Souza (Eds.), Service Assurance with Partial and Intermittent Resources. XI, 312 pages. 2004.

Vol. 3125: D. Kozen (Ed.), Mathematics of Program Construction. X, 401 pages. 2004.

Vol. 3124: J.N. de Souza, P. Dini, P. Lorenz (Eds.), Telecommunications and Networking - ICT 2004. XXVI, 1390 pages. 2004.

Vol. 3123: A. Belz, R. Evans, P. Piwek (Eds.), Natural Language Generation. X, 219 pages. 2004. (Subseries LNAI).

Vol. 3122: K. Jansen, S. Khanna, J.D.P. Rolim, D. Ron (Eds.), Approximation, Randomization, and Combinatorial Optimization. IX, 428 pages. 2004.

Vol. 3121: S. Nikoletseas, J.D.P. Rolim (Eds.), Algorithmic Aspects of Wireless Sensor Networks. X, 201 pages. 2004.

Vol. 3120: J. Shawe-Taylor, Y. Singer (Eds.), Learning Theory. X, 648 pages. 2004. (Subseries LNAI).

Vol. 3118: K. Miesenberger, J. Klaus, W. Zagler, D. Burger (Eds.), Computer Helping People with Special Needs. XXIII, 1191 pages. 2004.

Vol. 3116: C. Rattray, S. Maharaj, C. Shankland (Eds.), Algebraic Methodology and Software Technology. XI, 569 pages. 2004.

Vol. 3114: R. Alur, D.A. Peled (Eds.), Computer Aided Verification. XII, 536 pages. 2004.

Vol. 3113: J. Karhumäki, H. Maurer, G. Paun, G. Rozenberg (Eds.), Theory Is Forever. X, 283 pages. 2004.

Vol. 3112: H. Williams, L. MacKinnon (Eds.), Key Technologies for Data Management. XII, 265 pages. 2004.

Vol. 3111: T. Hagerup, J. Katajainen (Eds.), Algorithm Theory - SWAT 2004. XI, 506 pages. 2004.

Vol. 3110: A. Juels (Ed.), Financial Cryptography. XI, 281 pages. 2004.

Vol. 3109: S.C. Sahinalp, S. Muthukrishnan, U. Dogrusoz (Eds.), Combinatorial Pattern Matching. XII, 486 pages. 2004.

Vol. 3108: H. Wang, J. Pieprzyk, V. Varadharajan (Eds.), Information Security and Privacy. XII, 494 pages. 2004.

Vol. 3107: J. Bosch, C. Krueger (Eds.), Software Reuse: Methods, Techniques and Tools. XI, 339 pages. 2004.

Vol. 3106: K.-Y. Chwa, J.I. Munro (Eds.), Computing and Combinatorics. XIII, 474 pages. 2004.

Vol. 3105: S. Göbel, U. Spierling, A. Hoffmann, I. Iurgel, O. Schneider, J. Dechau, A. Feix (Eds.), Technologies for Interactive Digital Storytelling and Entertainment. XVI, 304 pages. 2004.

Vol. 3104: R. Kralovic, O. Sykora (Eds.), Structural Information and Communication Complexity. X, 303 pages. 2004.

Vol. 3103: K. Deb, e. al. (Eds.), Genetic and Evolutionary Computation – GECCO 2004. XLIX, 1439 pages. 2004.

Vol. 3102: K. Deb, e. al. (Eds.), Genetic and Evolutionary Computation – GECCO 2004. L, 1445 pages. 2004.

Vol. 3101: M. Masoodian, S. Jones, B. Rogers (Eds.), Computer Human Interaction. XIV, 694 pages. 2004.

Vol. 3100: J.F. Peters, A. Skowron, J.W. Grzymała-Busse, B. Kostek, R.W. Świniarski, M.S. Szczuka (Eds.), Transactions on Rough Sets I. X, 405 pages. 2004.

Vol. 3099: J. Cortadella, W. Reisig (Eds.), Applications and Theory of Petri Nets 2004. XI, 505 pages. 2004.

Vol. 3098: J. Desel, W. Reisig, G. Rozenberg (Eds.), Lectures on Concurrency and Petri Nets. VIII, 849 pages. 2004.

Vol. 3097: D. Basin, M. Rusinowitch (Eds.), Automated Reasoning. XII, 493 pages. 2004. (Subseries LNAI).

Vol. 3096: G. Melnik, H. Holz (Eds.), Advances in Learning Software Organizations. X, 173 pages. 2004.

Vol. 3095: C. Bussler, D. Fensel, M.E. Orlowska, J. Yang (Eds.), Web Services, E-Business, and the Semantic Web. X, 147 pages. 2004.

Vol. 3094: A. Nürnberger, M. Detyniecki (Eds.), Adaptive Multimedia Retrieval. VIII, 229 pages. 2004.

Vol. 3093: S. Katsikas, S. Gritzalis, J. Lopez (Eds.), Public Key Infrastructure. XIII, 380 pages. 2004.

Vol. 3092: J. Eckstein, H. Baumeister (Eds.), Extreme Programming and Agile Processes in Software Engineering. XVI, 358 pages. 2004.

Vol. 3091: V. van Oostrom (Ed.), Rewriting Techniques and Applications. X, 313 pages. 2004.

Vol. 3089: M. Jakobsson, M. Yung, J. Zhou (Eds.), Applied Cryptography and Network Security. XIV, 510 pages. 2004.

Vol. 3087: D. Maltoni, A.K. Jain (Eds.), Biometric Authentication. XIII, 343 pages. 2004.

Vol. 3086: M. Odersky (Ed.), ECOOP 2004 – Object-Oriented Programming. XIII, 611 pages. 2004.

Vol. 3085: S. Berardi, M. Coppo, F. Damiani (Eds.), Types for Proofs and Programs. X, 409 pages. 2004.

Vol. 3084: A. Persson, J. Stirna (Eds.), Advanced Information Systems Engineering. XIV, 596 pages. 2004.

Vol. 3083: W. Emmerich, A.L. Wolf (Eds.), Component Deployment. X, 249 pages. 2004.

Vol. 3080: J. Desel, B. Pernici, M. Weske (Eds.), Business Process Management. X, 307 pages. 2004.

Vol. 3079: Z. Mammeri, P. Lorenz (Eds.), High Speed Networks and Multimedia Communications. XVIII, 1103 pages. 2004.

Vol. 3078: S. Cotin, D.N. Metaxas (Eds.), Medical Simulation. XVI, 296 pages. 2004.